D0759912

THE DENT MASTER MUSICIANS

ELGAR

Series edited by Stanley Sadie

The Dent Master Musicians

Titles available in paperback

Bach *Malcolm Boyd*
Bartók *Paul Griffiths*
Beethoven *Denis Matthews*
Berlioz *Hugh Macdonald*
Brahms *Malcolm MacDonald*
Britten *Michael Kennedy*
Dufay *David Fallows*
Grieg *John Horton*
Haydn *Rosemary Hughes*
Liszt *Derek Watson*
Mahler *Michael Kennedy*
Mendelssohn *Philip Radcliffe*

Monteverdi *Denis Arnold*
Rachmaninoff *Geoffrey Norris*
Rossini *Richard Osborne*
Schoenberg *Malcolm MacDonald*
Schubert *John Reed*
Schumann *Joan Chissell*
Sibelius *Robert Layton*
Richard Strauss *Michael Kennedy*
Tchaikovsky *Edward Garden*
Verdi *Julian Budden*
Vivaldi *Michael Talbot*
Wagner *Barry Millington*

Titles available in hardback

Brahms *Malcolm MacDonald*
Elgar *Robert Anderson*

Liszt *Derek Watson*
Stravinsky *Paul Griffiths*

In preparation

Handel *Donald Burrows*
Prokofiev *Christopher Palmer*

A list of all Dent books on music is obtainable from the publishers:
J.M. Dent
The Orion Publishing Group
Orion House
5 Upper St Martin's Lane
London WC2H 9EA

THE DENT MASTER MUSICIANS

ELGAR

Robert Anderson

J.M. DENT, LONDON

First published 1993
© Text, Robert Anderson 1993

Music examples set by Steven Carr

Filmset by Selwood Systems, Midsomer Norton
Printed and bound in Great Britain by
Butler & Tanner Ltd, Frome and London

for
J.M. Dent
The Orion Publishing Group
Orion House
5 Upper St Martin's Lane
London WC2H 9EA

British Library Cataloguing-in-Publication Data

A catalogue record for this book is available
from The British Library

ISBN 0 460 86054 2

For Thomas Dausgaard and
St Bartholomew's Hospital Choral Society

Contents

Illustrations

Abbreviations

A	alto	MR	*Music Review*
acc.	accompanied by/ accompaniment	MT	*Musical Times*
		ob	oboe
arr.	arrangement, arranged by/for	OM	Order of Merit
		orch	orchestra
B	bass	orchd	orchestrated
Bar	baritone	org	organ
BBC	British Broadcasting Corporation	orig.	original(ly)
		perf., perfs	performance(s)
b cl	bass clarinet	pf	piano
BL	British Library	pic	piccolo
bn	bassoon	PRMA	Proceedings of the Royal Musical Association
C	contralto		
cl	clarinet	pubd	published
cor a	cor anglais	pubn	publication
db	double bass	qnt	quintet
dbn	double bassoon	qt	quartet
ed.	editor/edited by, edition	repr.	reprinted
		rev.	revised/revision
EMI	Electrical and Musical Industries	S	soprano
		str	string(s)
ESJ	*Elgar Society Journal*	T	tenor
ESN	*Elgar Society Newsletter*	*TLS*	*Times Literary Supplement*
fl	flute		
fp	first performance(s)	timp	timpani
glock	glockenspiel	tpt	trumpet
gui	guitar	trans.	translation
hn	horn	trbn	trombone
inc.	incomplete	unacc.	unaccompanied
LSO	London Symphony Orchestra	unpubd	unpublished
		va	viola
Mez	mezzo-soprano	vc	cello
ML	*Music & Letters*	vn	violin(s)
MM	*Music & Musicians*	ww	woodwind
movt	movement		

Preface

Elgar has now taken his rightful place among the last great Romantic composers, as much an heir to the mainstream musical tradition as Mahler or Strauss. It was once customary to overemphasize his Englishness, which is as obvious as Shakespeare's and of much the same significance. It was natural enough, when at last the land without music had produced a composer who could easily stake a claim to world eminence, that local pride should claim him fiercely for its own. His fall from European favour after the First World War seemed to reinforce the point. And at a time when Europe had few courts to which a composer might attach himself, Elgar preserved some of the age-old instincts that put his art at the service of his sovereign and the realm, in readiness to commemorate high state occasions and sing the proud advantage of Britain's imperial destiny. Wilfrid Mellers put it succinctly: 'Elgar had the power to make us believe, momentarily, that the Edwardian world was as grand as his music.' Undoubtedly he was the laureate of an opulent age, genuine in the gratitude and affection he felt towards Edward VII, recipient of generous plaudits from the time of *King Olaf* and the *Imperial March* until the First Symphony and the Violin Concerto. It was a turning-point when the work dedicated to the memory of Edward VII, the Second Symphony, was received with comparative coolness. After the war he paid the price for previous adulation. Though Master of the King's Musick and hoping vainly for a peerage from the royal house, he had nothing new to say to a society that craved novelty.

Constant Lambert spoke for Elgar's musical grandchildren when finding in his work 'an almost intolerable air of smugness, self-assurance and autocratic benevolence'. But, as Lambert was ready to admit, Elgar had in the days of his greatness captured the heart of the nation; and he held it, despite the vicissitudes of critical fashion that allowed him scant virtue at the centenary of 1957 yet was ready to acknowledge his mastery by 1984 and the fiftieth anniversary of his death. Elgar's music had not changed, but the perception of it had. Music since Elgar's day had produced less of value than might have been expected and was certainly hoped for; with the general public it had made comparatively little impact. It no longer seemed to matter that certainly Lady Elgar (and probably her husband) was bored by Stravinsky and that Elgar showed not the slightest interest in the far-flung explorations of Schoenberg. While the younger man was wrestling with *Moses und Aron*, Elgar in old age was amusing himself by trying to cobble together a Ben Jonson ballad opera. The vulgarities and lapses of taste that rightly exercised Dent in the early 1920s were imperceptible to a generation inured to seeing Beethoven jostled by the Beatles in the columns of *The Times* or *The New Grove*. Above all, fresh biographical discoveries made it clear that in some respects Elgar was as wounded and bewildered as those born a hundred years after him. The magnificence of his orchestral sound again evoked wonderment in post-imperial Britain as well as nostalgia for the chevaleresque bravery that once was in the land; but it was Elgar's still small voice of contained suffering that made a new appeal.

Yet my own attitude to Elgar seems to have changed little over the fifty years I have been aware of him. He first took hold of me in my mid-teens, that most dangerous age, at a concert that included both the Brahms–Haydn Variations and the 'Enigma' set. The juxtaposition I now know was meant to demonstrate the immeasurable superiority of Brahms. For me it worked otherwise, and curiosity soon took me to enchantment with the concertos, the symphonies, the string works, *Gerontius* and *The Kingdom*. I came later to *The Apostles* and have never much admired it. Perhaps my strictures about this work and others will seem harsh. Now and again I have been unable to conceal my disappointment when Elgar is obviously below his best. Often, though, I have kept counsel, in the sure knowledge that the sheer splendour of its presentation will allow an undistinguished tune or inferior page to pass muster.

For me the core of Elgar's achievement has always been the Variations, the Introduction and Allegro, *Falstaff*, the Cello Concerto, the String Quartet, *Gerontius* and *The Kingdom*, with the Violin Concerto and Second Symphony only marginally behind. It is not a large total, but with Strauss I can do no better, and with Mahler much less well. At one time the marches were a stumbling-block to purists; I doubt whether they still are. I have always rejoiced in them, and have come more and more to appreciate the orchestral miniatures, which even the usually supercilious Beecham found 'generally fanciful and occasionally exquisite'. Elgar wrote at a time when 'lengths' in the concert room tended to be the heavenly ones of Schubert. Since then other lengths have so invaded programmes that there is scant room for the finely turned pieces that Elgar could produce with such impeccable judgment.

The partsongs seem better than ever. Jaeger was aware this was major music-making packed into small space, music that dismisses at a stroke the notion that Elgar was insensitive to words or that his strength was mainly in the grand gesture. Here the quiet heartbeat of humanity finds tenderest expression.

If I have had much pleasure from playing the major chamber works, from conducting most of the choral masterpieces, it is perhaps from editorial tasks on the Elgar Complete Edition that I have come most to admire his unerring skill. Genius cries aloud from the pages of his full scores, where the notes are so distributed as to produce an orchestration that Tovey considered 'astoundingly subtle, uncannily efficient, and utterly original'. But there is far more than that. In sketch and draft, through the pages covered with such sureness by the boldly sloping hand, up to the fine flourish of the 'Edward Elgar' that signs away the completed work, there is abundant evidence of a quicksilver creative mind at work. A silly drawing here, a word-square there, a gargling duet for him and Alice to relieve tension while working on *Gerontius*, and a series of Deadeye Dick portraits of the apostles kept his restless mind busy if music was for a moment intractable. Then there is the sheer professionalism shown at each stage of a score's production, the meticulous marking, detailed care with proofs, and an easy cameraderie with those responsible for the ultimate printing of his music.

This is the third 'Master Musicians' volume on Elgar. No one can hope to match the intimate warmth of W. H. Reed's 1939 portrait, based on long personal association, and his eager enthusiasm for the music, even when somewhat tempered by Eric Blom's cool-hearted additions to the second edition of 1943. I cannot boast the sleuthing temperament of Ian Parrott, tireless both before the 1971 book and after in probing the depths of certain Elgarian mysteries. But twenty years on, I can summon to my aid not only the searching studies of Diana McVeagh, Percy Young and Michael Kennedy, but above all the invaluable volumes of Jerrold Northrop Moore, with whose patterning of Elgar's life it is almost impossible to take issue. Having worked through the many diaries in Dr Moore's typewritten transcription, sifted the four collections of letters edited by him, browsed through the treasures of the Elgar Birthplace Museum, examined manuscript material at the British Library and in private collections, I can only admit to treading where he has trod before. Throughout a long collaboration in the editing of Elgar he has always proved the most generous of colleagues; that I can seldom disagree with him or supplement him now will not surprise him. I have also had much recourse to the letters of the Elgar–Atkins friendship, and Wulstan

Atkins has been unfailingly helpful in response to questions. My admiration for Percy Young's letter, lecture, and biographical publications on Elgar has since been increased by work on his *Spanish Lady* edition. The ready availability of so much Elgar correspondence has obviated the necessity for too many footnotes.

Other Elgar holdings I have pleasurably consulted are those of Mrs P. Hedley-Dent, Raymond Monk, Oliver Neighbour, and Richard Westwood-Brookes; their courteous assistance has been greatly appreciated. Christopher Grogan and Christopher Kent have lent me copies of their theses, from Eric Sams I have gleaned all I know about Elgar's fascination with cryptograms, and Geoffrey Hodgkins has generously helped with bibliographical matters. At Elgar's Birthplace the curator Jim Bennett and his son Christopher have kept my table loaded with Elgarian riches, locking me in till long after darkness so that there was no escape till perusal was done. With their aid bits of research have been tidied up by telephone, and it is from the Birthplace collection, by permission of the Trustees, that all the photographs have been reproduced. For all this generosity I am most grateful.

Finally I must acknowledge the support I have received from my publisher: Malcolm Gerratt first nerved me to the attempt; Julia Kellerman has calmed me along the way; Ingrid Grimes and Audrey Twine tidied innumerable inconsistencies and obscurities; and Steven Carr has watched with scrupulous care over the music examples. If I dedicate the book to the Bart's Choral Society and my successor as their conductor, it is in remembrance of glorious singing at the Albert Hall in *The Dream of Gerontius*, *The Kingdom* and *The Music Makers* and in the hope that 870 years of unbroken medical tradition may reach its millennium not without Elgar.

R.D.A.
London, 28 October 1992

Edward Elgar (1857–1934)

A boy among the reeds on Severn shore
Sound-bathing: a ghost humming his 'cello tune
Upon the Malvern hills: and in between,
Mostly enigma. Who shall read this score?

The stiff, shy, blinking man in a norfolk suit:
The martinet: the gentle-minded squire:
The piano-tuner's son from Worcestershire:
The Edwardian grandee: how did they consort

In such luxuriant themes?

C. Day-Lewis: from The Gate

1

Aspirations social and musical (1857–1889)

Kent was the ancestral home of the Elgars, and their main centre was Dover. The family tree authenticated by the College of Arms when Elgar became a baronet attests to Elgars within easy distance of Dover, in such places as Stelling Minnis, Elham and Dymchurch. Elgar claimed a Dover pilot for great-uncle, and spent some time in Winchelsea churchyard to see whether his great-grandfather, apparently hanged for sheep-stealing, had been given Christian burial. Elgar's father, William Henry (1821–1906), had studied with Mr Sutton, organist of St Mary's, Dover, himself a pupil of Beethoven's pupil, Ferdinand Ries. William Henry was apprenticed to Coventry & Hollier of London, and it was from there that Thomas Stratford of Worcester requested a piano tuner. William Henry arrived in 1841, and it became his home. His skill as piano tuner took him to great houses in the neighbourhood, of which the most important was Witley Court, bought by the first Earl of Dudley in 1835. From 1843 to 1846 his tenant was the dowager Queen Adelaide. The royal connection was useful to William Henry when advertising his business, but it was Lord Dudley who wished to further his career.

Carice Elgar Blake, the composer's daughter, kept a ledger on family matters,[1] and described the impression made by her grandfather's touch and skill at the keyboard: 'Lord Dudley wanted him to do more than be an ordinary tuner – offered to pay for a course to make him finest player in England. Refused. Too nervous.' She added also that 'greatest treats for congregation was W. H. extemporising'. This was at St George's Roman Catholic Church, Worcester, where he became organist in 1846 though not at the time a Catholic. According to the ledger, the choir 'attained under WHE to being called the finest choir out of London' within Catholic circles. Some of W. H. Elgar's music has survived at the Elgar Birthplace. One volume was given him by his teacher, H. W. Sutton. It contains Handel arrangements, Corelli sonatas adapted for the organ, and voluntaries by Eberlin, William Clark of

---

[1] In possession of Raymond Monk.

1

Edinburgh and Charles Trinks, organist of St John's, Calcutta. Another volume has choral music, many pieces by Meyer Lutz of Southwark Roman Catholic Cathedral, and much Vincent Novello. William Henry had also many friends among players who came with visiting opera companies, and was himself an accomplished violinist.

The ledger enlarges on William Henry's domestic style: 'Had to be economical & lodged in Mealcheapen St – (The Shades Tavern). Not a public house but more a refreshment place (cafe) ... Kept by man [probably from 1843] whose wife was a Miss Greening & she got her sister to help in the business.' The sister was Ann Greening (1822–1902), from a family of the 'Three Choirs' counties. Her father Joseph came from Gloucester; she was born in Hereford and W. H. Elgar married her on 19 January 1848 at St Mary's, Islington.

Ann Elgar had a strong influence on her children. A scrapbook of hers at the Elgar Birthplace contains a riddle she wrote at the age of nine:

> My head like a bulrush, it hangs very low,
> And yet it is white as the driven snow.
> My body is green as a greengage plum
> Tell me the riddle, I'll give you my thumb.

A sampler she worked in 1833, also at the Birthplace, is inscribed with a text from *Proverbs* xxx in the Anglican, King James version: 'Remove far from me vanity and lies give me neither poverty nor riches feed me with food convenient for me.' The scrapbook has evidence, too, of her wide interests. There are cuttings on the landscape painter John Crome, on Indian art, on the Great Wall of China, and the discovery of the royal mummies at Deir el-Bahari in Egypt. Many of her interests were to be those of her second son, Edward. She loved the mystification of writing her name backwards. She ranged over much literature in the scrapbook, quoting Spenser, Byron, Disraeli, and above all Longfellow, whose autobiographical novel *Hyperion* was a special favourite. Longfellow's baron was prophetic: 'We must pardon much to men of genius. A delicate organization renders them truly susceptible to pain or pleasure. And then they idealise everything.' She illustrated her teachings with an extract on 'Vulgar People': 'Being poor is not of itself a disqualification for being a gentleman. To be a gentleman is to be elevated above others in sentiment rather than situation.' In December 1897 she wrote to her granddaughter Carice: 'when I was a very little girl I used to think I should read all the books I ever met with'. She took a sidelong glance at heraldry, rejoicing that 'The seal of the Knight Templars was, two men riding on one horse'. She had above all a lively feeling for nature, pasting into her book a sentence from Charles H. Wood, 'When surrounding nature is glorious, conversation seems out of place and harmony'; and a question from Bulwer Lytton: 'What is a farm but a mute gospel?' But her essential priorities are contained in some lines from a poem, *Little Tyrant*:

> Let Mozart's music stop!
> Let Phidias' chisel drop!
> Baby sleeps.

The Elgars had seven, and possibly eight children.[2] John Henry was born in October 1848 and baptized an Anglican. He was followed by Lucy Ann in May 1852, and it was probably now that Ann Elgar became Catholic, since all further baptisms in the family are by the Roman rite. There follows a ledger entry, 'Mary died', the only reference to another Elgar daughter. Susannah Mary ('Pollie') was born in December 1854. The eldest children had been born, in Lucy's words, 'within the shadow of our dear, dear Cathedral' at 2 College Precincts.[3] Restoration on the east end of the cathedral may have been a factor in the family's move to Broadheath, some three miles outside the city, where Edward William was born on 2 June 1857. Lucy invested the day with poetry: 'The air was sweet with the perfume of flowers, bees were humming, and all the earth was lovely.'

Ann Elgar was at home in the country, and she passed on to her children its simple lessons, as Lucy remembered: 'We were always taught to adore Him in the smallest flower that ever grew, as every flower loves its life. And we were told never to *dare* destroy what we could not give – that was, the life – ever again.' Broadheath was less convenient for the father, whose business continued to thrive. Stabling was provided for 'Jim' the pony, but a visit to Stratford, for instance, involved a total journey of fifty miles. During the summer of 1859 the family returned to Worcester, with address at 1 Edgar Street. The next child, Frederick Joseph ('Jo'), was probably born there in August 1859. This was now William Henry's business headquarters, and it was from here he wrote on 11 December to ask his brother Henry to join him. He wished to advertise as 'Messrs W. H. & H. Elgar' so as to prevent those requiring tuners from 'making arrangements with foreigners'. There followed another move, to 2 College Yard, which was in fact their old home under a different name opposite the east end of the cathedral. Francis Thomas ('Frank') was born there in October 1861. In November 1863 a final move to 10 High Street was announced in the *Worcester Herald*: the 'Nobility, Clergy, and Gentry of Worcester

[2] See Kenneth E. L. and Marion Simmons, *The Elgars of Worcester*, p. 20, n. 12.
[3] Simmons, *op. cit.*, p. 5.

and Neighbourhood' were informed that pianos by 'esteemed makers, in walnut and rosewood cases in great variety' were for sale or hire; harmoniums too, and all new music would be at half price. Home and shop were now under one roof. The last of the Elgar children, Helen Agnes ('Dot') was born there on 1 January 1864. Despite a severe childhood illness, Dot survived to become a nun and eventual Superior General of five linked Dominican convents.

But Ann Elgar's vigilance could not save two of her boys. Her eldest son Harry died aged fifteen in May 1864. Lucy remembered that 'This grief nearly cost my Father his reason, but by Mother's bravery and fortitude that awful calamity was averted'. The younger boy Jo had such musical sensitivity that he was known in the family as 'Beethoven'; but his health was poor, and in September 1866 he too died. When Ann Elgar sent a photo of the five surviving children to a nephew in September 1882, she mentioned the dead boys:

> Two have been removed for safety,
> Lo, she cannot send you them.

Edward William was nine when Jo died. His birth at Broadheath marked him off from his surviving brother and sisters. It was a place he returned to for childhood holidays; he urged close friends to visit it; and later in life, the birth cottage was the only one of his homes he wished kept for posterity. Moreover, 'Humoreske a tune from Broadheath', copied into a sketchbook and dated '1867',[4] is the earliest Elgar music to have survived. Carice noted in her ledger that 'Worcs was everything to him, the very look of spring coming the cottages the gardens the fields & fruit orchards were different in his mind in Worcs from anywhere else'. Late in life, when driving along the wooded road to Drakes Broughton, Elgar said: 'I shall come back to haunt this place'.

Elgar's formal schooling involved little music. He joined his sisters Lucy and Pollie at Miss Walsh's 'Middle Class School for Girls' in Britannia Square. His next school was at Spetchley Park, home since the sixteenth century of the Catholic Berkeleys. Elgar had to walk two and a half miles to this school run by the Sisters of St Paul. In 1955 the critic Ernest Newman wrote: 'Elgar told me that as a boy he used to gaze from the school windows in rapt wonder at the great trees in the park swaying in the wind.' His last school was in another direction, across the River Severn. It was a school, Littleton House, where 'Young gentlemen are prepared for Commercial pursuits by MR REEVE. Elgar's constant companion on these school journeys, sometimes taken across

---

[4] BL, Add.MS 63154, f.57*v*.

the Severn bridge, at other times, and more excitingly, by ferry from the cathedral steps, was Hubert Leicester, his elder by two years. Elgar later recalled his mother saying 'Wherever Hubert goes or whatever he does, you may join in'. In old age Elgar remembered the way to school, quoting Henry Vaughan: 'at our backs "the unthrift sun shot vital gold", filling Payne's Meadows with glory and illuminating for two small boys a world to conquer and to love'.[5] It was to Francis Reeve, headmaster of Littleton House, that the boy first used the words 'Sir Edward Elgar'; in answering his name he had forgotten to add a respectful 'Sir'. When reprimanded he made the prophetic correction. Elgar later claimed that it was Reeve who first set his mind working on the 'Apostles' project. Certainly he remembered him with gratitude, sending him in 1903 a libretto of the completed *Apostles*, and the following year, just after receiving his knighthood, a copy of Canon Gorton's essay on the work, with an affectionate note that 'Some of your boys try to follow out your good advice & training, although I can answer for one who falls only too far short of your ideal.'[6]

Musically there was much in Worcester to stimulate the young Elgar. His father's choir at St George's was capable of tackling Masses by Haydn, Mozart and Hummel. William Done, organist at the cathedral, observed Elgar's exceptional interest. But above all it was sheet-music stored at 10 High Street (his father was supplier to the cathedral) that introduced Elgar to an absorbing range of music. A single semibreve used to spell the musical notes BACH (German B natural) shows him familiar at the age of eight with G and C clefs. His mother added the date, 'March 24th 1866'.[7] An early attempt to write music found him drawing a stave of four instead of five lines. This may have been a natural result of Gregorian music seen at the church.

In a 1904 interview for *The Strand Magazine* Elgar recalled: 'I was a very little boy indeed when I began to show some aptitude for music and used to extemporise on the piano.' His first teacher was Sarah Ricketts, 'a singer in the Catholic Church'. During a theory lesson with her, his father suggested the boy should try his hand at composition; she said he 'soon had a few lines written'. He had inherited his father's gift for improvisation, as F. V. Atwater affirmed in a *Musical Courier* article of 1896: 'Whilst still nothing more than a child, he could extemporize in such a way as to astonish those privileged to hear him.' Elgar himself wrote about his playing at Castle House in the cathedral precincts: 'Grown-up people came (I knew later it was to hear me

[5] Foreword to *Forgotten Worcester* by Hubert Leicester.
[6] Birthplace Museum.
[7] Birthplace Museum.

play): also, amongst them old gentlemen – very courtly ... the two
ladies received their friends with an old-world state that I loved to
see.' In a letter to the banker and musical connoisseur Edward
Speyer he recalled that 'My father had the complete set of Vivaldi's
concertos & from the cembalo part of this I made my first infantile
petticoated attempts to play from figured bass.' The habit of thinking
in such figures never left Elgar; sketches for his unfinished opera, *The
Spanish Lady*, started when he was over seventy, preserve the practice.

The Three Choirs festivals gave opportunity at Worcester to hear
choral and orchestral music on the grandest scale. Elgar's father played
among the second violins, his Uncle Henry among the violas. The 1866
festival was the first the young Elgar was allowed to share. Beethoven's
C major Mass was to be performed, and Carice's ledger gives Hubert
Leicester's recollection: 'H. says he can remember E. running down
the street from 10 High St to the Cathedral with a large score under
his arm. They listened to the performance, & when it was over E. said
to Hubert – "If I had that orchestra under my own control & given a
free hand I could make it play whatever I liked".'

At the 1869 festival Elgar presented himself as surreptitious composer. *Messiah* was to be performed, and the parts were to be supplied
by Elgar Bros. This gave the lad his opportunity. He had composed 'a
little tune of which I was very proud. I thought the public should hear
it'. While his father worked over the parts, Elgar took action: 'Very
laboriously I introduced my little tune into the music. The thing was
an astonishing success, and I heard that some people had never enjoyed
Handel so much before! When my father learned of it, however, he
was furious!' What enormously impressed him in *Messiah* was the
ritornello to 'O thou that tellest', with its virtuoso unison for all the
violins (an effect Mozart's arrangement, in general use at the time,
scrupulously preserved). Elgar's ambition now was to play the ritornello
himself. Borrowing a violin from the shop, he struggled until 'at the
end of a fortnight he had mastered' the instrument.

A result of Elgar's proving so natural a violinist was his father's
taking him to the monthly meetings of the Glee Club at the Crown
Hotel. He could be a useful second violin. The Club was largely social:
'Round the walls and at numerous small tables are seated perhaps a
hundred men, of all ages and conditions, from prosperous city fathers
to young clerks. Half a dozen buxom waitresses flit about with trays
of tankards and glasses and the air is heavy with smoke.' Elgar, himself
a lifelong smoker who took pride in his varied array of pipes, noted
on proofs of a *Musical Times* article of October 1900, 'And they
smoked all the time'. The article mentioned the repertoire: 'Corelli
was largely drawn upon, Handel's Overture to Saul was a favourite,

and Haydn's symphonies were often heard. The rich store of our great glee writers furnished the vocal music.' Overtures by such composers as Auber, Balfe, Bellini, Mozart, Rossini and Wallace were gradually introduced, and German partsongs found a place. Elgar became accompanist and eventually conductor; the limited group of players meant much arranging, and it was for the Glee Club that he supplied a version of the *Flying Dutchman* overture in 1876.

In *The Strand Magazine* article Elgar also talked about his self-instruction: 'it is well known that I am self-taught in the matter of harmony, counterpoint, form, and in short, the whole of the "mystery" of music, and people want to know what books I used ... In my young days they were repellent. But I read them and I still exist.' It was a lifetime's habit of Elgar's to annotate his books, often with comments pithy and caustic. One of the earliest books he worked through seems to have been Reicha's *Orchestral Primer*. Elgar possessed it before his tenth birthday, as it is inscribed with his name and dated 7 March 1867. He wrote out information on diatonic and chromatic intervals and transposing instruments. 'Cor Anglais' is dismissed as an erroneous translation of 'Basset-horn'; he writes 'bad' against a too low second oboe part, 'Melody too low' against an ineffective bassoon tune; he crosses out discussion of such irrelevant wonders as the fife, serpent and Kent bugle; and writes 'Why not' against a bolder horn part of his own. Many of the books he studied belonged to 'Novello's Library for the Diffusion of Musical Knowledge'. One mentioned in the interview was *A Treatise on Harmony* by Charles Simon Catel. Elgar wrote a wry 'Alas!' when informed that Catel was 'born at L'Aigle'; he draws a butterfly opposite a reference to 'Papillon de la Ferté'; reading that this is the book on which Catel's 'reputation will chiefly rest', Elgar jotted 'no wonder the other things failed'. According to the interview, Catel was followed by Cherubini, from whose *Counterpoint* he used the start of a theme to launch an organ fugue in G minor. He continued that 'The first real sort of friendly leading I had, however, was from *Mozart's Thorough-bass School*. There was something in that to go upon – something human.' Whatever he read, he corrected the errors. He changed a tenor clef to alto for a canon in Ernst Pauer's *Musical Forms*, altered time signatures in John Stainer's *Composition*, greeted with ribaldry a statement in *The Scientific Basis of Music* by W. H. Stone 'that E sharp is higher than F flat'. He hunted and marked consecutives in such works as the 'Jupiter' and 'Pastoral' symphonies and Mendelssohn's *St Paul*, all to be found as music examples in Stainer's *A Treatise on Harmony*; in the same book he puts a marginal '!' against a reference to Schumann's 'Symphony in C. No.4'; he queries what Stainer defines as a 'chord of the major seventh' in one of Mendelssohn's op. 59 partsongs, and hazards, 'Is not this the 3rd. inversion of the chord of the 11th. on the subdominant?'; he also works four of the exercises at the back of the book. He is incredulous about a story in Stainer and Barrett's *Dictionary of Musical Terms* which refers to a trombonist's embellishing the opening solo in Mendelssohn's *Lobgesang*; 'Impossible', he writes in the bottom margin, '3 trombones in unison'.

Despite disclaimers in later life, it is clear that Elgar built up a formidable theoretical basis to his musical knowledge. But more importantly, every branch of his knowledge was tested in practice. By his early teens he was writing tunes for a play that the younger members of the family hoped to perform at Broadheath. The play did not materialize, but the *Wand of Youth* suites incorporated some of the tunes. Of 'Moths and Butterflies' Elgar attested the youthful origin: 'I do not remember the time when it was not written in some form or other.'[8] During his last year at Littleton House School Elgar dedicated to his sister Lucy the first of his completed and dated compositions. This was a song, *The Language of Flowers*. For title page he used the inside front cover of Beethoven's Piano Sonata op. 49 no. 2; it was stamped 'Elgar Brothers, Music Sellers, Worcester'. Within two months he was playing Mass for the first time at St George's.

At the end of his schooldays it seemed Elgar might be diverted from music. On 26 June 1872 he entered the office of the solicitor, W. A. Allen, a Catholic, treasurer of St George's and long-standing friend of his father. He had also taken part in the Elgars' domestic music-making. At fifteen Elgar was treated more or less as an office boy, and a year later he determined to leave. But the experience was not without benefit. Meticulous penmanship had been encouraged, and Elgar's early manuscripts are as calligraphic as Wagner's. A natural precision of mind encouraged him to date documents, so that the chronology even of sketches is sometimes clear. He developed his quick eye for misprints, and became a proof-reader of such reliability that in later days Novello were to bypass their own readers in the knowledge that little would escape him. At some time he acquired for his library Croake James's *Curiosities of Law and Lawyers*. Perhaps it was with a certain irony that he marked a sentence about the bar, that *there* would 'resound the last cry of expiring freedom'. Characteristically he mocked legal jargon in a 'Bill of Costs' submitted to his father after a Hereford concert in April 1873. The last item, assessed at ten shillings, was set out as follows: 'Attending you to the Hereford Railway Station accompanying you to your residence in Worcester and conferring on

[8] MS in possession of Jerrold Northrop Moore

the business of the day and conferring as to the advisability of your washing yourself to renovate your spirits and to remove the depression which you stated had come over you, & advising.' This formality was at the opposite extreme from Elgar's usual mode of expression, which was immediate, direct, tuned to the emotion of the moment and made him an admirable and vivid correspondent. Carice Elgar wrote of her grandfather that 'W. H. E. always found it impossible to settle down to work on hand but could cheerfully spend hours over some perfectly unnecessary and entirely unremunerative undertaking.' The result was that the business did not continue to thrive as it should, and Elgar decided that his comparatively trained mind might be of best service in the shop.

Ann Elgar had introduced her son to much that was fine in prose and verse. Aspiration led her to those described by the baron in Longfellow's *Hyperion* as 'the high nobility of Nature – lords of the Public Domain of Thought'. His father's handyman, Ned Spiers, had worked in theatres as a carpenter. According to Hubert Leicester, he 'had seen all the great actors and quoted Shakespeare and speeches from all the repertory of the companies'. Then there was a bookseller who stored his stock in an Elgar loft. Elgar later remembered that this was how he 'made the acquaintance of Sir Philip Sydney's *Arcadia*, Baker's *Chronicles*, Drayton's *Polyolbion*, etc.' He tried but failed to interest an early girlfriend in sharing a translation of Voltaire with him. But the seeds were early laid for the voracious reader and omnivorous seeker after knowledge that Elgar became.

It was the organ and worship at St George's that provided the main stimulus to original composition. After leaving Allen's office, Elgar had hoped to study in Leipzig and started learning German. But requisite funds were not available. His first known work after giving up the law is a Credo of July 1873 based on themes from Beethoven's Fifth, Seventh and Ninth Symphonies. He announced it with a German name, as 'arranged by Bernhard Pappenheim'. The score shows that the music was performed, and Elgar went on to write settings of the *Salve Regina* and *Tantum ergo*, texts that had featured largely in his father's music collection.

Elgar's earliest violin lessons had been with Fred Spray, a leading light of the Glee Club. He is described in the ledger as 'Honest & told him he could not teach him any more & E. decided to go to Pollitzer'. At nineteen Elgar was teaching in his own right, and had already embarked on a peripatetic round that was to drain him for more than twenty years. An early pupil, K. M. Lechmere, recounted one teaching round: 'He would come once a week by train from Worcester to Upton-on-Severn, walk a mile to the vicarage of Hanley Castle, where one of his small pupils lived, walk another two miles to my father's house to give me a lesson.' His wage for this lesson was '5s and a glass of sherry'; he was remembered as 'a very unassuming, shy youth, but painstaking and kind'. He later likened his teaching to turning a millstone with a dislocated shoulder, and towards the end of his life underlined a phrase in a Charles Mackay poem: 'Oh, vile, vile catgut-scrapers'.

From this drudgery it seemed that Adolphe Pollitzer might offer an escape. Elgar's finances were meagre, and he claimed to have 'lived on two bags of nuts a day' so as to afford the journey to London and Pollitzer's fee. The violinist was distinguished as player and teacher. He had performed the Mendelssohn concerto in the composer's presence, led the most important London orchestras and taught at the London Academy of Music. Elgar's dedication impressed him. Asked to obtain a book of studies, Elgar had mastered them all by the next lesson. He devised technical studies of his own, later published as *Etudes caractéristiques* with a dedication to Pollitzer. Elgar's main failing as a violinist, a small tone, convinced Pollitzer that Elgar could never have a virtuoso career. He was impressed, though, when Elgar played a Haydn quartet part and filled the violin rests with snatches from the cello part. Pollitzer asked if he knew the whole work. 'Of course.' – 'Do you compose yourself?' – 'I try'. The result of this exchange was that Elgar was given by Pollitzer an introduction to August Manns, conductor of the Crystal Palace concerts. Manns granted Elgar a rehearsal pass, which enabled him to spend many a strenuous day, setting out at six in the morning and returning to Worcester about 10.30 p.m., in pursuit of new musical experiences.

In Worcester his activities expanded. He led the newly founded Amateur Instrumental Society and was responsible for coaching its different sections. To increase his competence with the woodwind he took up the bassoon. An offshoot was a quintet, known as 'The Brothers Wind', in which Hubert Leicester and Frank Exton were flautists, his brother Frank played oboe, William Leicester was the clarinettist, and Elgar himself provided the bassoon. For this combination Elgar arranged music but also composed much. As generic title for the larger movements he coined 'Harmony Music' from the German 'Harmoniemusik'. But first came a 'Peckham March' at the end of 1877, perhaps reminiscent of journeys to the nearby Crystal Palace. There was also an 'Evesham Andante' with variations. There followed a series of Promenades and Intermezzos with playful titles. The music, often composed during a St George's sermon, was ready for instant performance later on the Sunday. These quintets became known as 'Shed' music from their place of first rehearsal.

The first of Elgar's sketchbooks to survive is dated 21 May 1878, within a fortnight of his twenty-first birthday. Five early sketchbooks cover as many years, and here is evidence of the local activities that preoccupied him, as also of his valiant attempts to mould large forms from his ideas. It is clear that some of the wind music was originally conceived for strings, that random themes, harmonic progressions and rhythmic patterns might not find an ultimate home till years later. For sketchbook references Elgar devised a system he never changed. An indication such as '24/III' meant that the motif Elgar had in mind would be found on p. 24 of Sketchbook III.

At the Worcester Festival of 1878 Elgar was among the second violins with his father. He played in *Messiah*, the Mozart Requiem, Haydn's *Creation*, Spohr's *Last Judgment*, and Mendelssohn's *Elijah* and *Hymn of Praise*. But the work that influenced him most was Mozart's G minor Symphony K550. This was rehearsed for the Wednesday evening secular concert, and Elgar took it as blueprint for a symphonic exercise of his own. Though he did not pursue the matter far, he began filling Mozart's outline for the first movement and minuet with themes of his own.

In January 1879 Elgar became 'composer in ordinary' to the Worcester City & County Lunatic Asylum at Powick. Music played a considerable part at the hospital. The Elgars had often performed there, but the offer of an official post was attractive, with annual salary of £30 for attendance one day a week and additional fees for music composed. Polkas and quadrilles took shape in the sketchbooks with evocative titles like the 'Shed' music. One was 'La Brunette'; another, 'Die Junge Kokette' was dedicated to the asylum pianist, Miss J. H. Holloway. Elgar did not always rely on the motley array of instruments available at Powick. Members of the Glee Club, for instance, performed there in March 1880. Elgar's programme began with Gounod's *Romeo and Juliet* ballet music; then came *A Franklyn's Dogge*, a partsong by Mackenzie, an extract from Thomas's *Mignon*, and the finale from Rossini's *William Tell*. A concert of February 1884 by the Worcester Amateur Instrumental Society was reviewed in the local press: 'The band, which comprised nearly 30 instrumentalists, was under the able direction of Mr. Edward Elgar, who, it may be mentioned, conducted throughout without the score.'

By the end of 1879 Elgar was living at the home of his sister Pollie, who had married William Grafton, a fellow Catholic well known to the family. Elgar's first trip abroad was with Charles Pipe, future husband of Elgar's eldest sister, Lucy. Departure for Paris was on 17 August 1880. At the beginning of the month Elgar had bought a guide, *Paris in Four Days*, in which he ticked essential places of interest. In fact they were away a week, and Elgar kept a diary at the back of the guide. It is the first such record of his to survive and is now at the Birthplace.

Of the crossing to Dieppe Elgar wrote, 'Rough passage, Not very ill'. They stayed at the Hotel Buckingham, 'Near the Madeleine, recommended here by Beare'. This was John Beare, an instrument dealer well known to the Elgars, who was later to publish some early Elgar. Charles Pipe wrote that 'Of course with E. E.'s mind already musical, he went to hear M. Saint-Saens at the Madeleine'. At the end of the first day Elgar noted they were 'too tired to eat'. A visit to the Louvre on 19 August was followed after supper by a café 'for billiards with some English. laughed consumedly at two Frenchmen playing'. Finally they went to a 'Cafe chantant' where the programme was '*rather* leggy'. Next morning they were at Père Lachaise. In the guide Elgar marked Rossini's tomb for inspection, but also added 'Georges Bizet'. In the afternoon they visited Notre Dame; then Elgar 'went into the Morgue alone, Charlie would not'; there he indulged an always insatiable curiosity by seeing 'one male corpse', 'black from ——'. At the Théâtre du Châtelet that evening they saw *Les pilules du diable*, 'A most absurd piece, full of startling stage effects'. Elgar enlivened a visit to Versailles by drawing railway officials with their peaked caps. The musical fruit of the French excursion was a set of quadrilles for Powick entitled 'Paris'.

Elgar's gifts took him frequently into the musical households of the neighbourhood. Important among them was Severn Grange, home of E. W. Whinfield, director of an organ-building firm and acquaintance of Franz Lachner, who had known Beethoven and Schubert and was later an adversary of Wagner's in Munich. His character may have provided hints for the Mr Errinsmore who features in a strange story Elgar wrote in 1879. It strays into the supernatural, with the ghostly appearance of Lady Nordath, already eleven years dead. Elgar was often at Severn Grange, and may well have led or played the solo part in Handel's op. 4 Organ Concertos, of which Whinfield's orchestral parts are still extant. In 1886 Whinfield gave Elgar five Ruskin volumes, including *Sesame and Lilies* and *The Seven Lamps of Architecture*. When three years later Elgar planned a move to London, Whinfield wrote: 'I think I may say that a considerable part of my pleasure in Worcester will have left, when *you* go.' And eighteen months later his circle was 'musically, like Hamlet, without a Hamlet!'

Whinfield mentioned too that 'Mrs: Fitton also misses you very much – you being a congenial Schumannite, & Brahmsite, and many = other-modern = ite(!)' This was the accomplished pianist Harriet Fitton, who had had lessons from Chopin's pupil Henry Brinley Richards. She and Elgar explored the violin sonata repertoire and played trios with Edward Capel Cure (a local Anglican curate), or with Henry Bellasis from the Birmingham Oratory. Two of the Fitton daughters joined in as well, the violist Isabel (the future 'Ysobel' of the 'Enigma' Variations) and Hilda, a cellist who later married Capel Cure. In disappointment at lack of progress as a composer, Elgar asked Mrs Fitton for a testimonial at the beginning of 1890. She bade him 'make use of my name & recommendation at any time. I shall only be too happy to feel I am of any use to you.'

Elgar's local reputation did not rest only on the dance music for Powick. In June 1879 the fiftieth anniversary of St George's Church was celebrated. A *Tantum ergo* and *Domine, salvam fac* of Elgar's were performed. A Glee Club concert of March 1881 contained the partsong, *Why so Pale and Wan?* and a *Pas redoublé* march for orchestra; and in the May an *Air de ballet* was heard at the Amateur Instrumental Society. In February 1882 the Society performed the *Air de ballet* and a second *Pas redoublé* at a concert for the convention of the British Medical Association. Worcester was the venue because the Association had been founded fifty years previously by a Worcester man, Sir Charles Hastings. The *Air de ballet* was noticed as having 'so much character and sparkling life' that it could not easily be forgotten; indeed it was encored. Among the delegates was Charles William Buck, a doctor cellist from Settle in Yorkshire and friend of John Beare, whose sister was to become his first wife. On this occasion he reinforced the cello section of the orchestra. He was impressed by Elgar as player, conductor and composer, liked him personally, and invited him to his home at Giggleswick, where his mother was pianist enough for trios. The musical firstfruits that autumn was a Menuetto and Trio for violin, cello and piano. Buck also became a confidant by correspondence: Elgar's letters to him catalogue his volatile moods, his musical and emotional ambitions, successes and failures.

The earliest surviving letter sets the tone: 'It seemed awfully slow down here giving my lessons after scrambling about your Hills.' He said he was going to 'play near *London* on Saturday next. If I do *well* I will send word: If I fail I shall throw myself in the Thames!' At the end of 1882 Elgar informed Buck he had been elected conductor of the Amateur Instrumental Society and announced his plans for January 1883: 'My holiday this time will be much broken up; I am going to Leipzig for a fortnight or so.'

The visit to Leipzig was not only to fulfil a youthful ambition; it was to coincide with a year's study there by Helen Weaver, the first of the girls to whom Elgar became engaged. The family lived in Worcester High Street, and their shoe shop was within easy distance of no.10. The bassoon part in Harmony Music no.2 was headed 'Nelly Shed' after a pet name Elgar had for Helen. Three of the Powick polkas were also connected with her. The first bears her 'Nelly' name; 'La blonde' is dated October 1882, but the double bass part is inscribed '*HJW* in Leipzig gewidmet', thus recording the dedication to her while in Leipzig; a third is called 'Helcia', after another name he gave her.

Soon after his return to Worcester he moved to the house of Charles and Lucy Pipe. From there he wrote to Buck on 1 July 1883 that musically the German visit was all he hoped for: 'I got pretty well dosed with Schumann (my ideal!), Brahms, Rubinstein, & Wagner, so had no cause to complain.' He had heard Schumann's Overture, Scherzo and Finale, First Symphony and Piano Concerto; there had been Brahms songs and the op. 88 String Quintet; he had been to *Tannhäuser, Lohengrin* and heard the *Parsifal* Prelude. Later that year he made a piano arrangement of the minstrels' entry in *Tannhäuser* Act 2, and devised a modest keyboard piece from the Scherzo in Schumann's op. 52. The relationship with Helen deepened. Her Leipzig companion Edith Groveham recalled 'how much he loved Longfellow's prose ... he sent Helen the book containing Hyperion – & being all about the Heidelberg student life we loved it'. In the same letter to Buck he announced Helen's return: 'The vacation at Leipzig begins shortly; my "braut" arrives here on Thursday next.' During that Worcester summer they became engaged. From the outset the engagement was overshadowed by the illness of Helen's stepmother, to whom she was devoted. On 11 November 1883 Elgar wrote to Buck: 'Well, Helen has come back!! Mrs. Weaver is so ill, dying in fact, so the child thought it best to return & nurse her; so we are together a little now & then & consequently happy.' Two days later Mary Weaver died, and Helen decided not to continue her Leipzig studies.

Elgar had been playing in William Stockley's concerts at Birmingham, and the first of his works heard at that important Midlands centre was an *Intermezzo moresque* performed on 13 December 1883. It was well received. The *Birmingham Gazette* found Elgar emulating 'the modern French style', with 'passages in his *Intermezzo* which remind us of some things by Delibes'. The *Birmingham Post* considered that 'the principle theme is rather Slavonic than Arabic in character; but the music is melodious, graceful, and pleasing; and the scoring, more particularly for the strings, upon which the burden of the work devolves, is tasteful and musicianly'. Buck was informed of the Birmingham success, but the same letter of 14 January 1884 told of trouble in connection with his father at St George's: 'the younger generation at the Catholic Ch: have taken an objection to him & have got him turned out of the Organist's place; this he had held for 37 years!!'

Elgar himself took over the post in autumn 1885, and in January 1886 told Buck about it: 'I am a full fledged organist now & – *hate* it. I expect another three months will end it; the choir is awful & no good to be done with them.'

Elgar's engagement to Helen Weaver did not prosper. Tradition within her Protestant family had it that 'He was too serious, too much like a professor; and then there was the Catholic element'. His situation contrasted strongly with that of Buck, who was to marry during the summer, and on 21 April 1884 Elgar wrote in considerable dejection: 'My prospects are about as hopeless as ever. I am not wanting in energy I think; so, sometimes, I conclude that 'tis want of ability & get in a mouldy desponding state which is really terrible.'

He had now written the work that was to gain him a first London hearing, *Sevillana*. Pollitzer had shown it to August Manns, and it was to be performed on 12 May. Like the *Intermezzo moresque*, *Sevillana* revealed a fascination with the music of Spain, a country he never visited. The date of the première was also the day Hans Richter gave the first British performance of Brahms's Third Symphony. Elgar heard that too. Mozart's G minor Symphony and Brahms's in F were the only works to which Elgar devoted a complete lecture as Birmingham professor of music, and he relished conducting them both. At the 1884 Worcester Festival Elgar played under Dvořák in the Sixth Symphony and *Stabat Mater*. He expressed his enchantment to Buck on 28 September: 'I wish you could hear Dvořák's music. It is simply ravishing, so tuneful & clever & the orchestration is wonderful; no matter how few instruments he uses it never sounds thin.' Dvořák for his part enjoyed meeting 'all the élite of beautiful ladies'. Under the stimulus of such new impressions Elgar resigned from the Powick Asylum in October.

On the rebound from his broken engagement Elgar had met a girl with his own 'E. E.' initials during a Scottish holiday in August 1884. Again he kept a diary. One day he sailed past Fingal's Cave; in his guidebook he wrote two of the Mendelssohn themes. Another musical jotting noted the chimes at St Augustus Abbey near Inverness. It was on 15 August that he met 'E. E.' and 'went with her to Corpach'. The following day they were in Inverness together. He saw her off to Edinburgh, and then followed her there. They went to the 'Forestry exhbt (bamboo 86 *ft* Band Scots Guards'; finally it was 'Adieux! Flowers'. The acquaintance was brief, but significant enough for Elgar to write an *Idylle* for violin and piano with dedication to 'E. E., Inverness'. John Beare printed it the following year, and Buck was curious. In reply (8 March 1885) Elgar was evasive: 'Miss E. E. at Inverness is nobody – that is to say that I shall ever see again. I wrote

15

down the little air when I was there & dedicated it to her "with estimation the most profound" as a Frenchman would say, that's all.'

Elgar again visited Buck, now married, in the summer of 1885. Local tradition has it that Elgar requested the hand of Sarah-Anne Wilkinson Newholme of Hellifield Green. She was of landowning stock, and Elgar's social position and prospects made him an improbable suitor. If there was such a rebuff, it did not deflect Elgar from seeking a wife in classes considered above him. One such may have been Gertrude Walker, daughter of the rector and squire of Abbots Morton in Worcestershire. She had a trained soprano voice, having studied under Charles Santley, and was a leading light in local music-making. Elgar was on a similar circuit to hers, and perhaps the first concert they appeared in together was at the Corn Exchange, Alcester, on 1 April 1883. Gertrude sang a solo in Sterndale Bennett's *May Queen*, then Elgar played violin obbligato to her performance of Braga's *La Serenata*. This miscellaneous concert got scant approval from Elgar; 'Gott in Himmel!!!' he wrote at the bottom of his programme. Elgar's first extant letter to Gertrude dates from 21 December 1887: 'Enclosed I send the "Title-page" of my new Song which is just publishing. I write, with much diffidence, to ask if I may dedicate it to you?' The song was *As I Laye a-thynkynge*, again published by John Beare. In the end no dedication appeared. Gertrude received her copy in May 1888 'With the composer's Compliments'. Perhaps she rejected the dedication at the same time as rejecting another proposal; 1887 is the year Elgar is supposed to have suggested marriage. Gertrude also had literary interests. She was the local secretary of the British Shakespeare Society and played Hermione in *The Winter's Tale* at the Royal Court Theatre, London, in 1911. Elgar did not lose touch, and after Lady Elgar's death in 1920 he wrote that the 'blossom & the feeling of spring always remind me of the old days of Alcester & the many places where you sang'.

By the time any Gertrude Walker hopes were dashed, Elgar had already met his future wife. Like Miss Walker, she was a member of the Worcestershire Musical Union and in his 1886 diary Elgar noted, 'Miss Roberts. 1st lesson. Oct.6th'. She came to him for lessons in accompaniment. Caroline Alice Roberts was at the time a passable pianist, but the coachman who drove her to the lessons 'was heard to say that he thought "there was more in it than music"'. She was born on 9 October 1848 in the Residency at Bhooj, in what is now Gujerat, India. Her father, Henry Gee Roberts (1800–61), joined the East India Company in 1818 to launch a distinguished military career up to the rank of major-general. During the Indian Mutiny he commanded the Rajputana Field Force and captured the town of Kota in March 1858.

He was cited with others in a parliamentary motion of thanks approved in the Commons for the skill 'by which the late Insurrection has been effectively suppressed'. He was knighted and more than justified the family motto, 'fortiter et fide'. He had married in 1838 Julia Maria Raikes, who came from a family distinguished in medicine and the church. Her grandfather, a Gloucester printer, spread the idea of schools on Sunday to aid underprivileged children towards literacy. On leaving India the Roberts family resided at Hazeldine House, Redmarley d'Abitot, at the south-east corner of Worcestershire.

Alice Roberts developed wide interests. Geological studies led her to the Rev W. S. Symonds of Pendock. In 1872 he published a book on the geology, natural history and antiquities of Wales, Devon and Cornwall; in it he thanked her 'for efficient aid in carrying the MSS through the press, and for the copious Index'. She planned a work of her own, to be called 'Worlds from my Window'. She wrote about the Malvern Hills, which were 'believed to belong to the most ancient of all geological formations, the Laurentian'.

More important for her future were Alice Roberts's literary activities. A two-volume novel, *Marchcroft Manor*, was published in 1882. Perhaps its motto from Boccaccio was prophetic: 'amor può molto più che no voi ne io possiamo'. *The Academy* described it as 'an idyll of modern years: with an aesthetic barrister for one of its heroes, and an accomplished and engaging vicar to look on and play chorus'. There was also much poetry, including translations from Italian and German. Her major effort was *Isabel Trevithoe* of 1879, an extended work in blank verse with a heroine inspired to good works:

> Then Isabel,
> Fresh fired to speech, would pour forth such a strain
> Of burning words regarding women's work,
> Their duties high, how they were bound to use
> Their mighty influence to clear the world
> Of wrong and endless sin ...

A painting by Burne-Jones, 'The Golden Stairs', now in the Tate but first shown at the Royal Academy Summer Exhibition of 1880, also elicited verse:

> For nothing earthly do they care
> But ever dreaming onward fare,
> With pensive, distant air,
> Adown the golden stair.

Most of the ethereal figures carry musical instruments, and among them was said to be represented Mary Stuart Wortley, mother of an important future friend.[9]

Lady Roberts died at the end of May 1887, and her daughter was now mistress of Hazeldine. Elgar had taken tea with the mother, and gave the mourning Alice a copy of *The Dream of Gerontius* by Cardinal Newman, into which she transferred markings made by General Gordon of Khartoum that Elgar already had. Henceforth music and poetry interacted. Elgar's Suite for strings was performed under the Rev Edward Vine Hall on 7 May 1888. Its three movements were called 'Spring Song', 'Elegy', 'Finale'. Alice Roberts recalled the performance in three stanzas. The first described how the music told

> Of rivers fringed with wavering reeds,
> Of hills awaking to the Spring.
> Of all the pleasant sights fair earth may bring.

The second had a loftier strain:

> But lo! they seem
> Hushed to a finer, mystic dream.
> The weaving rhythm of the song
> Ascends and bears the soul along ...

The third told

> Of joy and love, and yearnings past:
> Of hopes divine and longings vast;
> No instrument could breathe it all
> So subtle, strange, the harmonies that fall.

Elgar gave his own description to Buck in a letter of 8 July 1888: 'I have since written, for the Society here, three movements for String Orchestra, classical Style; they were played on May 7 & took well. *I like 'em.* (The first thing I ever did). Also there's a terrific (!!!) song in this month's Maga of Music.' The string Suite does not survive as such but may have given ideas to the Serenade for Strings op. 20. The song won a prize in the *Magazine of Music*; it was *The Wind at Dawn*, the first Alice Roberts poem set by Elgar. An overt musical tribute to her was the *Liebesgruss* of July 1888, later published as *Salut d'amour*. It was dedicated 'à Carice', a word coined from conflating her two names.

Betrothal followed in the autumn, when Elgar wrote, 'September 22nd 1888. Engaged to dearest A.' There was little enthusiasm from the Roberts and Raikes families. Carice Elgar later summed up their attitude: 'They said he was an unknown musician; his family was in

[9] See *The Pre-Raphaelites* (London, 1984), pp. 235–6.

trade; and anyway he looked too delicate to live any length of time.'
Alice Roberts was unswerving, and many important decisions were
made for Elgar's future. Their home would be in London. As foretaste
they spent a week there in January 1889, seeing *The Merry Wives of
Windsor* ('good'), hearing the Beethoven C major Mass at the Farm
Street church ('awful'), and finally parting, with Elgar at least 'Miser-
imus' [*sic*]. London would imply the end of the teaching round, the
end of routine choir work at St George's, freedom from irksome school
timetables. At nearly thirty-two Elgar should finally devote himself to
composition. His hopes were high as he catalogued the 'last' occasion
for various Worcestershire activities, pleasant and unpleasant: 'Mr.
Whinfield's for last time 3 to 10': 'Ladies class *last*. Ch: rehearsal very
last'. The marriage took place at the Brompton Oratory, London, on
8 May 1889. The Graftons and Elgar's Uncle Henry were there, and
Dr Buck came; Alice's side was represented by the barrister William
A. Raikes and his wife Veronica.

The question now was what influence Alice might have on Elgar's
musical development. Spiritually he had embraced the ripest fruits of
German Romanticism. Wagner already exerted a strong attraction,
and in December 1886 he had expressed his view of Brahms in a letter
to the *Malvern Advertiser*: 'By a certain dreamy romanticism, or,
perhaps more correctly, mysticism, he suggests Schumann as his model,
but the unvarying breadth and grandeur of his ideas mark him as the
true successor of Beethoven.' A succession of violin pieces, songs, and
orchestral vignettes made up into suites suggested that Elgar was
essentially a miniaturist. Works on a larger scale had usually been
abandoned. A visit to the Lake District with Buck, and the Scottish
holiday seemed as if they would both produce an overture. A letter to
Buck of 8 March 1885 explained the situation: 'The lakes overture is
done with – I am on the Scotish (with one t) lay just now & have a
big work in tow. Of course all these things are of no account.'
Moreover, they did not materialize. Nor did the many string quartets
started and given up. His only successful efforts to bring a sonata
movement to completion were in music for the 'Brothers Wind', where
the thematic material and its working might just as well have been
anonymous.

2

Ideals pictured within (1889–1899)

The Elgars spent their honeymoon in the Isle of Wight, where the landlady was charmed by 'their simplicity and lack of ostentation or "swank"'.[1] Along the shore they visited a cave and almost got cut off by the tide. Elgar noted then and later: 'Had to wade Kissed her wet foot. She remembered this the week she died.' During the honeymoon he wrote to Buck: 'This is a time of deep peace & happiness to me after the vain imaginings of so many years & the pessimistic views so often unfolded to you on the Settle highways have vanished! God wot!' They returned to London by train, travelling third class, and made for 3 Marloes Road, Kensington, where they had rented accommodation for three months. Alice Elgar had made financial arrangements for her husband, as indicated by her banker: 'Mr Elgar may sign cheques in his own name – These cheques will be charged to your account.'[2] Elgar took full advantage of London opportunities for concerts and opera. Again he heard Brahms's Third under Richter, as also Schubert's 'Great' C major Symphony. At the Lyceum there were the first London performances of Verdi's *Otello* under Faccio, with the original Otello and Iago; the Elgars heard the first two acts. On his programme for *Carmen* at Covent Garden Elgar noted that Don José had come out as 'Jowsy – !' Above all he heard three much-cut performances of *Die Meistersinger* in Italian. As Bernard Shaw wrote in *The Star*, 'How *Johannistag* sounds as *solenne di*, and *Wahn! wahn!* as *Si, si*, may be imagined.'

A main hope from the London move was to interest publishers. International contact had been made through the London offices of Schott, who published Elgar's op. 1 *Romance*, and a violin Gavotte dedicated to Buck; Schott also accepted *Salut d'amour* and paid two guineas for its outright purchase. John Beare had produced songs and violin pieces; the Catholic firm, Alphonse Cary, had taken *Ecce sacerdos magnus*, written for the visit of a bishop to St George's. Stanley Lucas

---

[1] Communication to Carice Elgar Blake; Birthplace Museum.
[2] Birthplace Museum.

had published *Through the Long Days*, and G. Metzler a piano version of *Sevillana*. On 22 July Elgar visited Orsborn & Tuckwood, leaving songs for consideration; that same day a letter in German accompanied the violin piece *Bizarrerie* to Simrock in Berlin: it was refused, as was *Liebesahnung (Mot d'amour)*. Hawkes & Son turned down a rescored *Sevillana*.

There was little encouragement during this brief London stay. None the less, Alice Elgar made a start on the diaries that were to outline the activities of most days in the thirty-year marriage.[3] Her literary gifts found no place in them: occasionally there is a happy phrase, but for the most part characters in the Elgar story make their entrances and exits with no more than conventional praise or blame. An entry such as 'E. at Settle. unsettled weather' is about as near as she comes to the sort of jape her husband enjoyed. Elgar himself remains virtually above criticism. There was clearly no thought of publication, and probably none that the intimate and sometimes almost nonsensical baby language the Elgars shared would ever be subject to public gaze. She early put value on her husband's letters and sketches, seeking to preserve as much as possible despite his habit of scattering manuscripts among friends. If her poetry occasionally inspired him, she was pleased; if her formidable mix of tact and determination might further a masterpiece or loosen a diplomatic tangle, well and good. Her own ambitions were sunk in his.

During this first London period Elgar also made diary notes. He recorded their attendance at such local churches as Our Lady of Victories, 'pro-cathedral' until the construction of the new Westminster Cathedral; on one occasion 'Cardl. Manning preached'. Lucy and Charlie Pipe visited; Pollitzer dined with them; and Alice's uncle General Robert Napier Raikes called. Elgar made his first visit to the London Library, of which Alice was already a member. When the time came for removal at the end of July, Elgar wrote of certain suspicions to Frank Webb, a Worcester violinist: 'the man who is packing our china has on today a shirt which looks like the first cousin to the one I have on with the name picked out'.[4]

They went to Malvern, where Alice still had a lease on a house called 'Saetermo'. There was much chamber music, often at the Fittons', where 'Miss Isabel's 21st Birthday' was celebrated on 8 August with dinner and music. There were also piano trios with Basil Nevinson and Hew Steuart-Powell, the 'B.G.N.' and 'H.D.S.-P.' of the 'Enigma' Variations. For string quartets he turned to Frank Webb, writing to

[3] Hereford and Worcester Record Office.
[4] Birthplace Museum.

him on 4 September: 'I have Mozart's 10 IVtetts here – could you bring your Haydn? He also wanted to 'try the Mendelssohn in E♭ (op. 12)'. When energetic, Elgar climbed the Worcestershire Beacon; to relax he sat in the garden's large ash tree, named by him 'Ygdrasil' in homage to Wagner and the *Ring*. While at Saetermo Elgar laid plans for his first extended choral work, *The Black Knight*. Perhaps the plans were as much his wife's as his: the two double sheets outlining a scheme for the work are signed 'C. Alice & Edward Elgar Aug: 29: 1889'. The poem was from Longfellow's *Hyperion*, a book that had already played a significant part in Elgar's life. Though *The Black Knight* had to wait three years for completion, the seed of a major achievement had been sown. Nine days later copies of *Salut d'amour* arrived from Schott, and on 6 October Elgar wrote to Buck about it: 'I send you the *score* which may amuse you: they do it for *p.f. Solo – vn. & p.f. – orch.* parts & *score*!!! four editions!! gosh!!!'

The lease on Saetermo ran out at the end of September, and for the fortnight before they could move to the Norwood house offered them by William and Veronica Raikes the Elgars took an apartment at 4 The Lees, Great Malvern. While still in London, Elgar had written to Hubert Leicester, 'I may tell you I am in "rude" health a thing unknown to me before'. Leicester had always regarded him as 'a delicate boy', and he was now bothered with a recurring affliction. He wrote about it to Dr Buck: 'my eye (the one that was hurt) suddenly took cold & got inflamed & we have been stuck here, unpleasantly enough'.

The main advantage of Upper Norwood for Elgar was proximity to the Crystal Palace. On 11 October, the day after their arrival at 'Oaklands', *Salut d'amour* was performed by Manns. Sometimes there were distractions during the music, as on 28 October: 'Dogs commenced to arrive C. P. & spoilt afternoon concert howling'. Next day the Elgars went to the dog show. The Dulwich picture gallery was near, and they could indulge another major interest. Religious provision seemed less satisfactory: Mass at a Norwood convent was 'not nice at all Girls' voices only'. A grand piano from Worcester was installed at the house; then came the organ on which Elgar worked at the *Vesper Voluntaries* that largely occupied him during the rest of the year.

On 10 December the doctor came to see Mrs Elgar; she was indeed pregnant. At the same time Elgar received his first important commission, for an orchestral work as novelty at the following September's Worcester Festival. He wrote at once to Joseph Bennett, the *Daily Telegraph* critic, a Gloucestershire man. He wished to establish his local credentials:

I am afraid my name is unknown to you, but I thought you would forgive my writing (not wishing to prejudice any criticism of the committee's choice you may make) to tell you that I am a native of Worcester and have written several orchestral works (including a suite of four movements for full orchestra and a set of pieces for string orchestra) which have been produced at Mr. Stockley's Birmingham concerts and others by Mr. Manns at the daily concerts of the Crystal Palace.

A notice appeared in the *Daily Telegraph* on 12 December and Elgar was now committed to production of a major work by a fixed date.

For Christmas Elgar sent his sister Dot a card that showed four monkeys being conducted by a fifth. He inscribed it 'Worcester Cath: (olic) Choir', referring it to both the cathedral and St George's. He added the characteristic comment, 'I cannot help sending the enclosed card though. A. does not hold with it'. Alice concluded the 1889 diary thus: 'End of our first year together: happy and loving: trusting and hoping together, as one! – Deo gratias'. The Worcester commission was honorary and without his teaching Elgar had little to show financially. Orsborn & Tuckwood paid five guineas for the *Vesper Voluntaries*, but at the beginning of March Elgar had to call at Spink & Co., where he 'Sold dearest A's precious pearls'. Manns gave his Suite in D at the Crystal Palace, and Elgar made his first contact with Novello, hoping that distinguished firm would publish the partsong setting of Andrew Lang's *My Love Dwelt in a Northern Land*. The Elgars' time at Oaklands was running out and, because of Alice's condition, it was Elgar who had to house-hunt. He summed up a week's experience in the rhythm of Longfellow's *Hiawatha*:

> In the breezy heights of Hampstead,
> In the Classic Highgate's Archway,
> In the mediaeval Bromley,
> In the precincts round by Barnum,
> All the agents sang unto me
> Of the houses & the gardens
> In most melancholy suburbs,
> And the noisiest of streets.

His conclusion about the agents has echoed down the years: 'What a lying lot they are!'

The final choice was again Kensington, and 51 Avonmore Road. A fortnight after the move, the diary entry for Sunday 6 April 1890 recorded that Elgar went 'to Carmelites 11 oc. Began Overture for Worcester'. Its title was to be 'Froissart', reflecting Elgar's interest in the fourteenth-century chronicler and also the discussion of him in Scott's *Old Mortality*. In his copy of Froissart Elgar marked a passage

23

that evoked matters familiar to him: 'I am Lord of Berkeley, a very handsome castle situated on the river Severn, on the borders of Wales.' The full score quoted Keats, 'when chivalry / Lifted up her lance on high'. The creation of the overture was surrounded by visits to the opera, including Meyerbeer's *Le prophète* and two more hearings of *Die Meistersinger*. On 29 July Elgar wrote to Frank Webb: 'My Overture is finished & I do not think will be liked but that must take its chance'; he thought he would soon be watching 'the simple Vigornians execute a dance of triumph on the grave of my Overture!'

It turned out differently, and he was the one to dance. He informed his mother on 8 August that Novello had agreed to publish the string parts in time for the festival: 'A fool might have been seen dancing along Oxford St: on one leg! for an hour after the interview'. A daughter was born to the Elgars on 14 August; she was named Carice, thus perpetuating the *Salut d'amour* dedication to her mother, and Irene. *Froissart* was rehearsed at St George's Hall, London, and Elgar conducted the Worcester première on 10 September. *Froissart* ended the first half of the concert, and in the interval Elgar made the acquaintance of a staunch ally. This was Ivor Atkins, at the time assistant to George Sinclair at Hereford, but also future organist of Worcester Cathedral. For Atkins, as for many since, it was instant recognition: 'I knew that Elgar was the man for me, I knew that I completely understood his music, and that my heart and soul went with it.'

Joseph Bennett gave a judicious assessment of *Froissart*: 'The work, which properly aims at a tone of chivalry, is one of considerable interest, arising rather from promise than actual achievement. It is in parts crude, and chiefly lacks the broad outline which in music of modern character is more than ever essential.' The stimulus of having successfully produced a large orchestral work lasted till the end of the year, when Elgar was planning a violin concerto. According to the diary entry of 28 November, Elgar 'worked at Concerto'; by the side he wrote later, '(Violin – since destroyed)'.

The violin was now assuming a less pleasant position in his life. With no improvement in London prospects, he decided to resume his former teaching round. On 19 November 'E. left for Worcester'; that day he is recorded as teaching Frank Webb's two sisters. Sometimes he was away from London three nights at a stretch, returning only at midnight on the fourth day. The logical consequence was noted on 24 January 1891: 'Thinking of leaving London'. The London fogs were also a trial, as he told Frank Webb on 8 February: 'I groped my way to church this morning & returned in an hour's time a weird and blackened thing with a great & giddy headache.' The decision for

Worcestershire was taken, and the Elgars paid farewell visits to the London galleries. They also commenced a 'Chart of Painters' in which they listed favourite painters and their works.[5]

House-hunting began in Malvern on 20 May; two days later Alice Elgar and Isabel Fitton came across 'Forli', the Elgars' home for the next eight years. The name, after Melozzo da Forli, Renaissance painter of angel musicians, was auspicious. The house was semi-detached, in a quiet road of its own, with an extensive garden opposite and a fine view of the Worcestershire Beacon. They moved in on 20 June, and a week later Elgar's father came to tune the piano. Creatively there was little to show for the rest of the year apart from the violin piece, *La Capricieuse*. There was compensation for renewed teaching in the purchase of a Gagliano violin. Elgar took a rehearsal for the local Christmas Day Mass: 'dismal little scene (3 choir arrived)'. Rather than persevere to performance, the Elgars accepted an invitation from William Meath Baker of Hasfield Court ('W.M.B.' of the Variations), an old friend of the Roberts family. They stayed for 'music and Coruscations' over the New Year.

Alice had now decided to sell Hazeldine. Ann Elgar at 10 High Street was given a 'palm-leaf' table, and Elgar interested himself in a shield from Hazeldine, also taking into Worcester swords for cleaning. On 16 March 1892 Alice Elgar signed the final documents, and it was to be twenty years before she came into possession of a comparable home to display the remainder of the General's Indian legacy.

The spring brought a suggestion for Bayreuth in the summer from Minnie Baker, sister of 'W.M.B.', and renewed creativity. The Serenade for Strings was completed, and again Elgar gave credit to his wife on a page dated 13 May 1892: 'Braut helped a great deal to make these little tunes signed EE'. Hugh Blair, assistant organist to William Done at Worcester Cathedral, was a frequent visitor at Forli. On 11 June 'E. played Mr. Blair's Harvest Cantata (proofs) & Black Knight in the evening'. It may have been then that Blair promised Elgar a performance if he would finish the work. The following day came news that Novello had accepted for publication the *Spanish Serenade*, again to words of Longfellow. Elgar scored it at once, 'all in one day!' By the time of departure for Bayreuth Elgar had most of the *Black Knight* vocal score complete and left it with Novello. The firm did not finally agree to publication until November.

The Elgars joined Minnie Baker (now known as the 'Mascotte' after Audran's most successful operetta) at Margate on 22 July. They were away three weeks. They wondered at Cologne Cathedral, visited the

[5] In possession of Raymond Monk.

Beethovenhaus at Bonn, took a Rhine steamer to Mainz (and 'heard much about the Hudson'); they 'firebranded round Mainz', failed to get food at Nuremberg ('station chaotic') and 'dawdled on' to Bayreuth. There they saw *Parsifal, Tristan, Die Meistersinger*, and again *Parsifal* (with a wander 'into the Pine wood' after Act 1). They spent two nights in Nuremberg paying their respects to Hans Sachs and Albrecht Dürer. From there Elgar wrote on 2 August to his Grafton nephews and nieces describing the guard on trains: 'he does not shout out "tickets please!" but makes a bow & says "will the worshipful company be so friendly as to shew their tickets!"' Next was Munich, with the picture and sculpture galleries. The furthest point they reached was Oberstdorf, in the Bavarian mountains and almost on the Austrian border. They returned via Heidelberg, the more significant to them because of Longfellow, *Hyperion*, and Elgar's work in progress, *The Black Knight*. On 12 August Elgar wrote to his mother: 'I must send a line from *here* about which we have read & thought so much.' The previous evening, he explained, there had been 'a great procession of Students – torchlight – the three duelling guilds with a brass band & marching – all their faces wounded (silly fools) & many with bandages on – gay uniforms & no end of torches: it did remind me of Hyperion'.

Back in London, Elgar went to Breitkopf about the Serenade for Strings and to Novello about *The Black Knight*. At home both Elgars were at work, Alice writing poems and Elgar setting them. One of the poems was on the Spanish Armada, with title '1588'. It began 'Loose, loose the sails, the anchor slip'. The music does not survive unless, as in the case of other songs of the period, it was absorbed into some larger work. *The Black Knight* was finished by the end of September. Novello sent proofs and, after returning a set, Elgar mentioned on 28 December a matter concerning which he was always meticulous: 'I am sorry I forgot to add the Metronome marks to scene I.'

Elgar was now teaching at the High School for girls in Worcester. To consolidate his position as player and instructor, he gave lecture-recitals on the Beethoven violin sonatas throughout the autumn. Alice was not allowed to attend the first and went to a lecture on Virgil instead. At the second she was late, but considered herself a 'proud Braut'. The third was noticed in the *Worcester Herald* of 19 November: 'the recital is more than an enjoyment, it is an education, made more interesting by the clear explanations of Mr. Elgar as to the meaning and form of classical compositions'.

The Elgars spent Christmas at Hasfield Court again, where Elgar began to play golf. Richard Townshend ('R.B.T.' of the Variations), who later wrote a book on the game, was there to instruct, and there were theatricals as well. Golf became a major pastime with Elgar; he described his form to Robert Buckley, his earliest biographer: 'if not of the first force he was animated by the best intentions'. While orchestrating *The Black Knight*, Elgar received from Breitkopf the full score, parts, and keyboard arrangement of the Serenade for Strings. This was the first Elgar full score in print, and it was significant that it came from a German house.

To Novello he wrote about orchestral parts of *The Black Knight* on 29 January: 'as an amateur orchl. contingent forms part of the constitution of the Society I venture to ask you to make the date as early as possible'. The nature of his forces was also the reason why Elgar greatly increased the number of cue letters in the vocal score, for ease of reference and as a safety measure in case of trouble. It was the same instinct that made him insist always on as much cueing as possible in the parts.

Elgar had two premières in April 1893. The *Spanish Serenade* was performed at Hereford on 7 April. Alice wrote of 'Everyone admiring'; Rosa Burley, their headmistress friend from Malvern, observed differently: 'The two ladies behind me seemed less interested in the music than in its composer. What appeared to strike them as remarkable, however, was not that he could write music, but that he had married a member of their own social circle.' *The Black Knight* on 18 April was a notable success. Though Elgar would not call it a 'cantata', he had given Worcester the sort of choral music it could readily welcome, had provided Novello with a work that was eminently marketable, and – for better or worse – had charted his own probable course for the immediate future.

Again a Bavarian holiday with more Wagner was planned for the summer, this time with Rosa Burley. For his thirty-sixth birthday on 2 June Elgar received a vocal score of *Tristan und Isolde* (Alice noted that it arrived the previous evening). Opposite the start of the Prelude Elgar wrote an inscription: 'This Book contains the Height, – the Depth, – the Breadth, – the Sweetness, – the Sorrow, – the Best and the whole of the Best of This world and the Next.' The Elgars saw it at Covent Garden under Emil Steinbach on 28 June. Departure for Germany was on 2 August, and the month's holiday was divided mainly between Garmisch and Munich. In Garmisch they stayed at the establishment of the Slingsby Bethells. There was an expedition to Oberammergau in company of the Archbishop of Nuremberg. On another occasion Elgar took the 'Old Mule track' and reached the Benedictine monastery of Ettal. He heard the organ there and remarked on the 'Fresco in dome', with its 400 figures worshipping the Trinity. He noted also that 'Count Pappenheim lives in Ettal'; this was the name with which he had signed his 'Beethoven' Credo.

At Munich the main business was Wagner, with *Meistersinger* on the first evening. There they met Miss Burley as arranged, and she left a vivid account of the Elgars at ease. Of Elgar she said that the 'holiday had brought out the most charming side of the Genius I had ever seen ... in Munich was a new-found freedom which gave an unaccustomed zest to life'. Munich also suited Alice: 'The German culture was one with which she was clearly in deep sympathy and I suspected that she felt more at home in Munich than she would have done in many parts of England.' Miss Burley noted occasions when Elgar, with a sally of robust humour, deliberately distressed his wife. He thought that Hans Sachs, as a medieval cobbler, would probably have blown his nose through his fingers; and he reminded her that Brahms's 'favourite amusement in beer gardens was to take servant girls on his knee and tickle them'.

They saw the *Ring* (with a *Tannhäuser* parody on the day between the last two operas), *Die Feen, Tristan*, and *Tannhäuser*. Miss Burley observed Elgar's absorption in the music: 'The fact is that he had begun to understand very fully how the new music was put together and was realizing that he could convert this knowledge to his own use. Throughout the holiday he took copious notes of what he had heard and spent many hours over them at his rooms.'

There was no immediate composition back home; indeed the need for return had been dictated by the Worcester Three Choirs Festival, in which Elgar played the violin for the last time. On the festival brochure he wrote: 'I played 1st Violin for the sake of the fee as I cd. obtain no recognition as a composer.' The Wagnerian fascination continued with a scheme to arrange the *Parsifal* 'Good Friday' music for the Worcester High School forces. Schott concurred on 6 November. There was golf during the autumn, but on 11 December Elgar went for a long walk: 'E. after 2 lessons went to Worcester & after 2 lessons walked to Broadheath & back to Worcester.' Six days after the visit to the place of his birth, Elgar wrote 'the Andante religioso', eventually to be called *Sursum corda*.

On 3 January 1894 Elgar played golf with the Rev T. Littleton Wheeler, a canon of Worcester Cathedral, and valuable contact as secretary of the Worcester branch of the Three Choirs Festival. The following day Alice mentioned the writing of three songs, *The Wave*, of which there is now no trace, the *Muleteer's Song* (to text from *Don Quixote* but later absorbed into an ultimately rejected passage of *King Olaf*), and Longfellow's translation of a *Rondel* by Froissart. One day there was music at Ham Court, and she described Elgar as leading the Mozart 'Dissonance' Quartet 'like a flame of fire'. During the winter Elgar had much trouble with his throat; oysters seemed the most acceptable remedy. None the less there was some encouragement on the publishing front: Novello wrote 'that they wd. publish 'Happy Eyes' & *pay* for it'. This was the partsong *O Happy Eyes*, written at 'Oaklands' in 1889 and turned down at the time by Novello. The fee was now three guineas.

Hugh Blair had requested *Sursum corda* for a performance in the cathedral on 8 April in honour of a visit by the future George V, then Duke of York. Elgar attended the afternoon rehearsal, but the *Worcester Herald* reported that a 'doctor's veto prevented him assisting in the performance of it in the evening'. By the beginning of June the *Parsifal* arrangement was complete and in rehearsal at the High School. It was scored for three violins, cello, two pianos and organ. Equally Wagnerian, but more significant, was Alice Elgar's first mention in the diary of the future *King Olaf*, the work in which Elgar was to show his profound understanding of 'how the new music was put together'; on 15 July she noted that 'E. wrote Sagas all day'.

The summer of 1894 broke the usual pattern: the Elgars were again in Bavaria, but they did not return for the Three Choirs Festival. A joint card informed his mother that 'he bought a delightful cloak in Munich in wh. he looks like a magician'. At Garmisch the archbishop was again in residence, and the Fittons arrived on 9 August. Five days later the Elgars took their rucksacks and began walking to Mittenwald. Their wanderings took them as far as Innsbruck on what Elgar called 'A very lovely & ever to be remembered little excursion'. Near Seefeld, in Elgar's words, they had 'walked across the pastures to a curious roman-looking chapel. Christ over altar with *real* hair'. They returned to Garmisch on 19 August, were again in Oberammergau, and left for Munich on 13 September. This time they saw *Götterdämmerung* and *Die Meistersinger*.

During the autumn Elgar continued teaching, but occasionally missed a day if it was 'Too wet for E. to go'. He celebrated Advent by orchestrating a cantata of Hugh Blair's. On 14 December Elgar was at The Mount, Miss Burley's school, and 'Brought home books of Sagas'. Other schemes were also afoot at the end of the year. Minnie Baker, the 'Mascotte', had sent for consideration a libretto she had been asked to compile from St Augustine's *Civitas Dei*. Charles Swinnerton Heap, a Birmingham man who had studied in Leipzig on a Mendelssohn Scholarship, came to Forli on 21 December. He had just conducted *The Black Knight* in Walsall, admired it, and now wanted something bigger.

It was Alice who, as so often, provided immediate inspiration. She suggested his setting two of her poems from *Isabel Trevithoe*; these became partsongs, *The Snow* and *Fly, Singing Bird*, and were accepted by Novello for twelve guineas. A more important work of early 1895 was *Scenes from the Bavarian Highlands*, in which the Elgars jointly recalled experiences from the neighbourhood of Garmisch. Elgar might suggest the rhythm of music in his mind, and Alice would oblige with verse to fit it. Elgar conducted a successful performance of *The Black Knight* in Wolverhampton on 26 February, and a week later Alice had completed her fair copy of the Bavarian poems. Elgar finished the music on 9 April and submitted it to Novello, where the opinion was unfavourable: '? Saleable. No. 6 is the best. Nos. 1 & 3 next': the final decision was 'No'. In the end the 'Bavarians' were published by Joseph Williams.

The day after completing the Bavarian scenes, Elgar began systematic work on the Organ Sonata for Hugh Blair, the four movements of which were to form his grandest instrumental design to date. At the same time Alice Elgar had been requested for information about her father, Sir Henry, for a notice in the *Dictionary of National Biography*. This act of piety involved considerable research, and the diary entry of 22 June showed the household advancing on both fronts: Alice was 'writing all day, & finishing the sketch for Dic. of Nat Biography. Mr. Blair to dine & stay. Heard Organ Sonata'. The Elgars celebrated the completion of their tasks by an expedition on 13 July. They took a train part of the way, 'then walked to Broadheath & saw the house in wh. he was born'.

Elgar's close connection with Hugh Blair, from 1895 Done's successor as cathedral organist, was a factor in his hope for another Worcester Festival commission. He had contacted Edward Capel Cure, now vicar of Bradninch in Devon, for a libretto, and the choice of *Lux Christi*, to be based on Christ's healing of the blind man as told by St John, was made. Before the Bavarian holiday of 1895 there were therefore two projects under consideration, a first oratorio, and the Longfellow 'Sagas' idea.

On the last day of July the Elgars left for the Continent. They lunched at Paddington with Minnie Baker, engaged since April to Alfred Penny, rector of Wolverhampton Collegiate Church. On the way to Garmisch they went to the Valhalla near Regensburg; to Salzburg and 'the house where Mozart was born'; and from Kaprun in the Tirol they sent Elgar's mother a card on 22 August: 'our "carriage" was like a large bath-chair – a little horse harnessed with ropes. He bossed the whole show: took his own pace, chose his own road – stopped at every public house on the way & *squealed* at every horse he met.'[6] They were only a week at Garmisch, where the

---

[6] Birthplace Museum.

Slingsby Bethells accepted dedication of the 'Bavarians'. They left on 4 September, saw *Der fliegende Holländer* in Munich, and came home via Strasbourg and Paris.

By the end of the year commissions for *King Olaf* and *Lux Christi* had been confirmed. Ella Arnold, wife of Richard Arnold ('R. P. A.' of the Variations) wrote to Alice about the former on 12 October: 'Dick has just come in & told me the deeply interesting news that Mr. Elgar has been asked to write for the Staffordshire Festival ... Dick has come home perfectly *possessed* by Mr Elgar & his wonderful cleverness, (that is hardly the word) – He says Schumann was a babe compared to him.' Elgar had been playing parts of the *Olaf* music. On 18 November Littleton Wheeler of the Worcester Three Choirs Committee wrote to Elgar: 'I am glad to hear you have something which you can offer us.' *Lux Christi* was then discussed over golf.

Elgar's reputation was greatly enhanced by a performance in Birmingham of *The Black Knight* by Swinnerton Heap's choir on 5 December 1895. Elgar had a bad headache in the morning, but he and Alice went to the Oratory at Edgbaston, where Cardinal Newman had presided for so many years, where the *Dream of Gerontius* poem had been written, and where Dvořák had met the cardinal. Robert Buckley wrote warmly about the concert, pointing out that there was talent in other English composers, but 'too little genius'. The Elgars went on to Wolverhampton, where Minnie Baker was now installed as second wife to the rector of St Peter's. This was their first meeting with Dora Penny, daughter of the rector's first marriage. As 'Dorabella', she became the only member of the 'Enigma' gallery to write a book about the composer. She remembered that 'Mr. Elgar was left for me to look after. I quickly found out that music was the last thing he wanted to talk about. I think we talked about football. He wanted to know if I ever saw the Wolverhampton Wanderers.' He won her friendship (she was twenty-one at the time) by offering to mend a chair: ' "Now clearly understand," he said, "if this is a success *I* mended it; if it's a failure *you* did it." ' By the end of the year Elgar had revised the Organ Sonata for publication by Breitkopf & Härtel and dedicated it to Swinnerton Heap.

With two major works to finish for performance in the autumn of 1896, Elgar was under considerable pressure. Rosa Burley recounted Elgar's initial exhilaration over a festival commission. She went on: 'This was always followed by a period of black despair over the intractability of the material and the utter impossibility of ever getting it into a satisfactory shape.' It was then that constant encouragement was needed. She pointed out that Elgar 'did not begin at page one and write the work in the order in which it would be played'. He would put it together 'as fancy and the inspiration of this or that passage of the libretto dictated'.

The first three months of 1896 were busy and productive. Years later, in December 1922, Elgar wrote to Ivor Atkins about the genesis of *King Olaf*: 'it seems strange that the strong (it is *that*) characteristic stuff shd. have been conceived & written (by a poor wretch teaching all day) with a splitting headache after dinner & at odd, sustained moments – but the spirit and will was there'. By the end of March *King Olaf* and *Lux Christi* were virtually complete in vocal score. In both works Elgar used previously written music. 'The Death of Olaf' incorporated a *Millwheel Song* written to Alice's words in December 1892; and 'O Thou, in heaven's dome' was transcribed from an Ophelia song (*Hamlet*, Act 4, scene v). During the same period Elgar also orchestrated the 'Bavarians'.

On 31 March the Elgars were ready for an interview at Novello about publication of both the festival works. Despite a stipulation that the Elgars should provide a guarantee of £60 for the 'saga' and £40 for the oratorio, agreement was reached, and they left 'with thankful hearts'. Berthold Tours, the Novello editor, required some changes. *Olaf* was to be considerably cut; recitatives certainly went, and a portion of the finale. Rosa Burley claimed that '*King Olaf*, which he had planned as a continuous work with orchestral interludes connecting the choral passages, had been broken up into a series of disjointed sections'. This is almost certainly an exaggeration. In the case of *Lux Christi*, only one eight-part choral passage was to remain, and Elgar's Latin title was to be changed to *The Light of Life* to calm Anglican sensibilities. Ultimately it was August Jaeger, Elgar's future 'Nimrod', close associate and dear friend, who saw both works through the press.

The first performance with orchestra of *Scenes from the Bavarian Highlands* took place at a concert of the Worcester Festival Choral Society on 21 April 1896; Elgar conducted. His next task was scoring of the two festival works. This started on 15 May and was largely undertaken in a tent on the lawn opposite the front garden of Forli. Robert Buckley described how Elgar might keep intruders at bay: 'From the tent-pole a flag fluttered in the breeze, delicate hint that the composer was at work, and must not be lightly disturbed.' But the flag was often struck. The *Light of Life* full score was finished on 20 June. When Dorabella visited Forli on 17 August, Elgar's *Olaf* orchestration had already reached the Olaf–Thyri duet. The flag was presumably flying, as he greeted her with 'You can't come in here – it's private'.

In 1896 there was still a Leeds contingent to reinforce the Three Choirs Festival. On 25 August Elgar went north to rehearse it, met the influential Henry Embleton, patron and secretary of the Leeds Choral Union, and went on to Dr Buck's. The London rehearsal on 3 September impressed Sir Walter Parratt, Master of the Queen's Musick, and Charles Harford Lloyd, once Gloucester Cathedral organist and now precentor of Eton. Alberto Randegger, conductor of the Queen's Hall concerts, was reported by the *Worcestershire Echo* as saying 'it was the best English work he has heard during the last 20 years'. At the première in Worcester Cathedral on 8 September the soloists were Edward Lloyd (the Blind Man), Watkin Mills (Christ), Anna Williams (Mother of the Blind Man), and Jessie King (Narrator). There was much local enthusiasm; but the significance of the work was more widely recognized. The *Leeds Mercury* noted the influence of Wagner as well as Gounod, Dvořák and Mendelssohn, but reported 'an underlying individuality of his own that Mr. Elgar may be trusted to develop'. The *Sunday Times* commented on 'the marked superiority of his scoring as compared with his vocal writing – his choruses as compared with his solos', and looked to Elgar 'for a really fine work when he comes across a "book" which appeals in every sense'.

Certainly Elgar had not yet found such a 'book', but at this stage he was more concerned to transform the musical content of the festival commission rather than to upgrade its literary worth. Charles Stanford was in Worcester soon after the festival and played his new Requiem to the Elgars after lunch at Forli. He went with Elgar on a favourite walk to Birchwood, a place that was soon to gain Elgar's special affection. Stanford was to have called again to hear *King Olaf* but was unwell. When *Olaf* was heard publicly for the first time on 30 October it was a triumphant success. Elgar had the highest opinion of the North Staffordshire Festival Chorus, 'made up almost exclusively of working people'. The national press was enthusiastic about *King Olaf*, and its performance placed Elgar at a stroke among the leading lights of English music. The *Worcester Herald* had every reason to gloat: 'The greatest English genius since Henry Purcell,' had been the verdict of one critic; another had said 'there is a power of musical description that recalls the magic of Dvorâk'. Fault was again found with the libretto, a conflation of Longfellow and the work of a Malvern neighbour, H. A. Acworth. It was left to August Jaeger, in a letter to Hubert Parry, to sum up Elgar's latest works: 'He is not yet very *deep*, but he will grow, I feel sure. "The Light of Life" I do *not* care for, *nor does he*! He spoke of it as a "written to order effort". "Olaf" is very different stuff. Whether he will ever do anything *great*, the future will prove.'[7]

---

[7] Jeremy C. Dibble, 'Parry and Elgar: a new perspective', *MT*, cxxv (1984), pp. 639–43.

Harry Acworth made a shrewd point the day after the performance: 'In one respect I am sorry for you. You have now the obligation of living up to a great reputation, a reputation which if I read the critics aright places you at the head of living composers.' The reaction set in. After thanking Swinnerton Heap in a letter of 4 November for his encouragement, Elgar crowned his triumph with a denial of any further interest in his art: 'My work is done and I feel I have proved myself a man! but I cannot afford to write any more.' Thus began a long series of resignations from music.

Novello, however, now believed in Elgar. The firm was willing to provide a guarantee of twenty guineas for a Crystal Palace performance of *King Olaf* and commissioned two works for the 1897 celebrations of Queen Victoria's Diamond Jubilee. Elgar was at work on both *The Banner of St George* and the *Imperial March* before the end of the year. Music for the cantata was well under way before he received Shapcott Wensley's libretto. Elgar sent three trial sketches to Novello on 30 November and was anxious to receive the text: 'If I have the libretto I could finish the whole work early in January'. When the verses came, they inspired Elgar to some ribaldry. A reference to 'The aged monarch' elicited a jotted '*go it agèd*!'; and instead of Sylene in the opening line, Elgar wrote 'Within Sylence's walls no sound'. On 7 December there were tidings of the March: 'Enclosed I send as promised a first Sketch of an "Imperial March" and shall be glad to know if it meets your requirements.' Novello was not altogether satisfied: 'It seems to us however that it might be adversely criticised on account of the fact that it contains so many short phrases of two bars & even one bar.' The correspondence involved Elgar's first letter to Alfred H. Littleton, chairman of the publishing house. On 14 January 1897 he wrote about his adjustments to the work in some detail, adding: 'I hope you will like the March as a whole: of course I am *sure* of my orchl. effects but the piano is rather out of my sphere.' The full score of the March was sent to Novello on 6 February, and the vocal score of *The Banner of St George* went nine days later.

King Olaf at the Crystal Palace on 3 April was not well attended and caused Elgar financial loss despite the Novello guarantee. It was boat-race day, and there was football at Sydenham. The *Daily Telegraph* observed that 'the champions of the two Britains, North and South' were battling 'almost within earshot of strains which celebrated the achievements of one who was himself a strenuous fighter'. The critic of *The World* enlarged on the advantages of Elgar's provincial upbringing and present way of life: 'Perhaps if he had settled in London he would by now be a professor giving eighty lessons and dining out seven times a week and scribbling royalty ballads in his scanty leisure.

As it is, he has composed *King Olaf*.' It was shrewdly argued.

The Diamond Jubilee was taken very seriously at the Crystal Palace, and the commemoration was to open on 19 April with the National Anthem played by five of the Guards bands and the 'Crystal Palace Orchestral Band'. It hardly mattered that on this occasion the première of the *Imperial March* was ascribed to 'Richard' Elgar. Performances within the year at Queen's Hall, a Royal Garden Party, a State Concert, the Albert Hall, and the Three Choirs Festival went some way towards launching Elgar as a laureate of the old queen's reign. A jubilee concert in Worcester on 26 April included 'Selections from English Composers who have lived during the reign of Queen Victoria'. Elgar played for Gertrude Walker in the first performance of *Roundel*, to words by Swinburne. *The Banner of St George* had a modest première in Earl's Court, London, when the St Cuthbert's Hall Choral Society performed it on 18 May to the accompaniment of 'a few strings and a pianoforte'.

At Forli Elgar was busy with a *Te Deum and Benedictus* commissioned for the Hereford Three Choirs Festival. This was the idea of George Robertson Sinclair, cathedral organist and the future 'G.R.S.' of the Variations. When staying with Sinclair between 5 and 7 June, Elgar played the new work and entered in the visitors' book the first of the 'Moods of Dan', brief character sketches of Sinclair's bulldog, who was also to feature in the Variations.[8] The title on this occasion was 'He sleeps'. That same month another 'variationee' made an initial entry in Alice Elgar's diary when Troyte Griffith came to play bowls on 26 June. He was a frequent and welcome visitor, acquiring the nickname 'Ninepin'. Another outdoor activity of the jubilee summer was kite-flying. The diary for 16 July chronicled progress on the *Te Deum and Benedictus* and the new pastime: 'E. orchestrating   Flew kites after dinner. Mr. Griffiths came. "Isabel" kite came down on roof of Mr. Lunn's house.'

It was also a summer in which Elgar consolidated important friendships. Ivor Atkins was appointed organist of Worcester Cathedral, and it became a tradition that he should spend Fridays with the Elgars. When the *Te Deum and Benedictus* arrived at Novello, Jaeger wrote and was described by Alice as 'quite as enthusiastic as he shd. be over E's music for Hereford'. Elgar replied at once: 'You praise my new work too much – but you understand it.' Knowing he had a sympathetic audience, he wrote again on 6 August: 'Now my music, such as it is, is alive, you say it has heart – I always say to my wife (over any piece or passage of my work that pleases me): "if you cut that it would bleed!" ' Almost on the spur of the moment the Elgars again decided

[8] Hereford Cathedral Library.

on a Bavarian holiday. They embarked for Flushing on 10 August, and saw a Munich *Tristan* (conducted by Strauss) on their way to Garmisch, once more the centre for mountain jaunts. A fancy-dress ball displayed Elgar as a Japanese magnate and Alice in Bavarian costume. On the return journey Munich offered *Don Giovanni* under Strauss and *Der fliegende Holländer*.

The *Te Deum and Benedictus* was performed at the opening service of the Hereford Festival on 12 September. The *Morning Post* had a mixed impression: 'For the most part the music indeed is more suggestive of a warlike song of triumph than an expression of Christian praise and prayer'. Sinclair had considered the work daringly modern, and Elgar had ended the MS full score with the words 'Inter spem et metum' (Between hope and fear). Jaeger made a special detour from Huddersfield to hear it, and then wrote: 'I too can appreciate a good thing & see genius in musicians that are *not* yet dead.' One of the festival musicians had in fact died, and Elgar mourned him in a letter to the *Daily Telegraph*. This was a robin which had added a part to Schubert's 'Unfinished' Symphony in the opening service: 'He was captured and caged, the intention being to liberate him in the cathedral after the last performance. But he pined away, and died this morning.'

The Three Choirs meeting produced another ally in Nicholas Kilburn, a Cambridge bachelor of music who preferred to remain an amateur; from his base at Bishop Auckland he became influential among choral societies of the north-east. There was an instant meeting of minds, and in a letter of 29 September Elgar outlined a current plan: 'I am writing (perhaps a series) of illustrative movements for orchestra with "mottoes".' These were to be historical character sketches and to include St Augustine and Caractacus, but they were never written. Instead Elgar wrote a keyboard minuet for the Kilburns' son Paul, later orchestrated as op. 21.

There was another Elgar première at the Crystal Palace. The programme of 22 October 1897 announced 'Ethnological Groups' in the south transept, with Indians, Bushmen, Zulu Kaffirs, Mexican Indians, Hindoos, Tibetans, and so on; there was also 'The Royal Exhibition of Working Ants'. Elgar's contribution was *Characteristic Dances*, to be conducted by August Manns; the following day they were announced as *Three Bavarian Dances* and conducted by Elgar. The pseudonymous performance was a common Manns device for getting round lack of rehearsal time. Sir George Grove heard these dances that Elgar had extracted from the choral suite and wrote of his enjoyment on 24 October: 'I confess (though I hope I don't hurt you) I liked them better than "King Olaf" – I find it very hard to bring my mind to Siegfried and Olaf and hoc genus omne.'

The autumn of 1897 saw the foundation of the Worcestershire Philharmonic Society. During the negotiations towards setting it up, Elgar had suggested it might be called 'The County of Worcester Choral & Orchestra Association'. He thought the initials would 'pan out' well: 'C.O.W.C.O.A.' would suggest temperance. The joint secretaries were to be Martina Hyde and Winifred Norbury ('W.N.' in the Variations). Elgar wrote to Joseph Bennett about the new venture on 15 November: 'The people here are much afraid I was leaving so they have started a brand new socy "The *Worcestershire Philharmonic*" which I am to conduct – a sort of toy I suppose for a petulant child.' The society's motto 'Wach' auf!' was taken from Hans Sachs's poem in *Die Meistersinger*, and Wagner's chorale setting was sung at the beginning of each concert. Elgar's patience with amateurs was limited, and many rehearsals were both irritating to him and frustrating to the players. Rosa Burley said he found it difficult to explain exactly what effect he was after: 'Again and again he would stand shading his eyes with one hand (a very characteristic position) and would exclaim angrily "No, no, that was all wrong", until the more sensitive were nearly in tears and the more stolid were reduced to a mulish obstinacy.'

The last and most ambitious of Elgar's dramatic cantatas, *Caractacus*, was the result of a Leeds commission, for which the terms were negotiated by Henry Embleton. Elgar's mother spent part of the summer of 1897 at Colwall, at the back of the Malvern Hills and in full view of the Herefordshire Beacon, traditional site of Caractacus's camp. One evening she said to Elgar, 'Oh! Ed. Look at the lovely old Hill. Can't we write some tale about it?' Elgar urged her to try, but she said her day was done. It now seemed that the 'Caractacus' project would be a cantata rather than an orchestral sketch.

Again Elgar turned to Harry Acworth. This time the libretto was his own, based on such classical authors as Tacitus and Dio Cassius. Elgar in jubilee mood relished the splendour of the Roman triumph when Caractacus would be led captive before the Emperor Claudius and win honourable retirement. Yet Claudius's generosity must somehow provide occasion for a vision of Britain's imperial future. And here Elgar played a considerable part. As an immigrant, Jaeger felt the jingoism of the libretto was getting out of hand; he objected to such lines as

> Though round your path of Pow'r,
> The menial cohorts gather,
> And jealous tyrants low'r.

On 21 June 1898 Elgar was very little repentant: 'any nation but ours is allowed to war whoop as much as they like'. He admitted he had suggested some patriotism in the finale, 'when lo! the *worder* (that's good) instead of merely paddling his feet goes & gets naked & wallows in it'. But 'menial' was not meant for Germany; more likely 'hill tribes' of some imperial outpost.

On the last day of 1897 Jaeger too was patriotic: 'England expects every man to do his duty & no musician in your great & glorious country has a greater duty to fulfil than you.' According to Alice's diary, on 24 February 1898 Elgar was 'writing Caractacus with enthusiasm'. During March they made frequent visits to Birchwood Lodge, the tree-girt sanctum that proved a steady inspiration to Elgar over the next years; but at the end of the month Elgar wrote to Nicholas Kilburn: 'I have just arrived at hating what I have done & feeling a fool for having done it – but my wife says I always do that at certain stages.'

There was another night at George Sinclair's on 19 April after a choral performance of the 'Bavarians'. Dan was given another theme in the visitors' book: 'He muses (on the muzzling order)' later became the 'Prayer' motif in *The Dream of Gerontius*. The first Worcestershire Philharmonic Society concert took place on 7 May. The start was 'Wach' auf!' from *Die Meistersinger* (two evenings later the Elgars heard at Forli a 'wonnigliche Nachtigall'). Then came the *Egmont* overture, Gounod's *Gallia*, and the Tchaikovsky Elegy for strings. This last Elgar described in his programme note as structurally 'simplicity itself; poetically its meaning is boundless, or bounded only by the susceptibility of the listener'. The main work was Humperdinck's *Die Wallfahrt nach Kevlaar*, a setting of a Heine ballad receiving its first English performance. Elgar drew attention to its complex use of leitmotifs: 'not, be it noted, the intricacy of the mere contrapuntist, but elaboration abounding in poetic and suggestive touches'. Elgar insisted that it should be sung in German; Rosa Burley described the result: 'strange chewing noises were produced that sounded like no known European language'.

William and Ann Elgar had celebrated their Golden Jubilee in January 1898, when a local newspaper congratulated them not only on fifty years' marriage but also on the length of time 'spent in one business in one establishment' and on 'the rapid strides with which their eldest (living) son Mr. Edward Elgar, has attained the rank of one of the first composers of our time'. William still tuned pianos, including his son's; and occasionally Ann Elgar would spend a night at Forli. They rarely came together.

Elgar completed *Caractacus* in vocal score on 12 June and started the orchestration nine days later. His was a different business in a different establishment, and Elgar was now anxious to secure a dedication of *Caractacus* to Queen Victoria. Through Sir Walter Parratt permission was granted; and Elgar further agreed to set for 'a sort of Victorian Triumphs of Oriana' a poem by Frederick Myers, *To her Beneath whose Steadfast Star.* He reached the end of the MS full score, p. 435, on 21 August. He wrote at once to Nicholas Kilburn: 'I feel frightened at my score (which is big) & if I ask for justice, surely I shall hang? Anyway, I *tried*.' The first performance in Leeds Town Hall on 5 October 1898 was conducted by Elgar, with Medora Henson, Edward Lloyd, Andrew Black, John Browning, and Charles Knowles. *The Globe* considered Druids 'unmitigated bores', and regretted that Acworth had been so 'liberal in his supply of these wearisome personages'. Elgar's music was much praised, in the *Yorkshire Post* for the power and abundance of its invention, in *The Times* for its individuality, with seldom 'a momentary suggestion of any other composer's work'. Parry assessed the music in his diary as 'clear but the style rather menial and wants grip. Some very vigorous scoring.' The word 'menial' had indeed been transferred. And what of Elgar himself? Rosa Burley described him as leaving Leeds 'with the air of one who has fought, and is inclined to think he has lost, a heavy engagement'.

In a letter to Jaeger of 20 October Elgar mentioned a 'Gordon' symphony he had in mind. This was to celebrate the hero of Khartoum, murdered in January 1885, and whose latter reading had included Newman's *Dream of Gerontius.* He was proposing it for the 1899 Worcester Festival, but at the moment he could express only pessimism: 'I have to earn money somehow & its no *good* trying this sort of thing.' None the less he wrote that day a theme of magnificent potential for the symphony, easily outstripping anything in *Caractacus.* It was eventually to become the 'Committal' passage in *Gerontius.* For the moment, as he told F. G. Edwards of *The Musical Times*, he was bidding 'adieu (or a diable) to a munificent public'. Notice that the 'Gordon' project was finally abandoned was given to the Worcester committee on 18 May 1899: 'The Conductor reported that Mr. Elgar found it impossible to carry out his promise to write a new Symphony.'

During the evening of 21 October 1898, after a hard day's violin teaching, another scheme took shape. This resulted in Elgar's most ambitious orchestral work to date and the launching of his international fame. It began with a 'tune', and Elgar later described the occasion to J. A. Forsyth for publication in *The Music Student.* He was improvising after dinner, 'and suddenly my wife interrupted by saying, "Edward, that's a good tune." I awoke from the dream "Eh! tune, what tune!" and she said, "Play it again, I like that tune."' After more strumming, he found the tune again, and it was to become the theme of the Variations. He continued extemporizing on it and asked, ' "Whom does that remind you of?" – "Why," said she, quick as lightning, "that's Billy Baker going out of the room." ' And so the tune might be used to describe such friends as 'W. M. B.' Before the end of October a sketch headed 'Theme' was sent to Jaeger 'to be critikised please', and already on the 24th ideas about the future work had taken shape:

> Since I've been back I have sketched a set of Variations (orkestry) on an original theme: the Variations have amused me because I've labelled 'em with the nicknames of my particular friends – *you* are Nimrod. That is to say I've written the variations each one to represent the mood of the 'party' – I've liked to imagine the 'party' writing the var: him (or her) self and have written what I think they wd. have written – if they were asses enough to compose – it's a quaint idea & the result is amusing to those behind the scenes & won't affect the hearer who 'nose nuffin'.

The birth of the 'Theme' had been on a Friday, and Elgar had had the weekend to mature his plan. On the Sunday 'Troyte' came to lunch, and in the afternoon they walked to Birchwood, taking tea at Sherridge, the home of Winifred Norbury ('W.N.'). Elgar had spent the night of 11 October, when he had to attend a Worcestershire Philharmonic practice, at Richard Arnold's ('R.P.A.'). On 29 October he was in Hereford to celebrate George Sinclair's fiftieth organ recital. This was the occasion for writing no. 4 of 'The Moods of Dan' in the visitors' book. The music was chromatic, in 'Tempo uncertain', and depicted 'Dan uneasy', 'Fidgets', 'and ... *fffz* Barks'; it was to be repeated 'about 39 times'. Dan's falling into the Wye, as later described by Elgar, paddling upstream, and rejoicing bark on finding a landing place may well have occurred during this visit. Six other 'variationees', including the Elgars ('C.A.E.' and 'E.D.U.') had been at the *Caractacus* première, so that October overflowed with 'friends pictured within'.

Towards the end of 1898 Elgar had written to Alfred Littleton at Novello about the possibility of a commission for the 1900 Birmingham Festival; but for the moment the Variations were all-important. Rosa Burley felt it was an unusually happy time for Elgar: 'The fact is that for once he was not writing on commission but for the pleasure of doing so. I doubt if he saw at the beginning that he had begun an important work.' Elgar began orchestrating the Variations on 5 February and the task was finished thirteen days later. In the hope that Hans Richter might conduct the first performance, Elgar sent the MS full score to his concert manager, N. Vert (Narciso Vertigliano) on 21 February. Vert replied at once that he was sending the score to Richter in Vienna and explaining about Elgar's success with *Caractacus*.

With Richter the Variations were their own advocate. It was announced in the *Daily News* of 7 April that he would perform them in his forthcoming London season. It was only when the score finally reached Novello that Jaeger was instructed to add the word 'Enigma' above the theme. Remarks by Elgar quoted in C. A. Barry's programme note for the first performance on 19 June added further mysteries and were considered somewhat ill-advised. He had spoken of 'the idiosyncracies of fourteen of my friends' but said that this 'need not have been mentioned publicly'. He went on to further provocation: 'The Enigma I will not explain – its "dark saying" must be left unguessed, and I warn you that the apparent connection between the Variation and the Theme is often of the slightest texture; further, through and over the whole set another and larger theme "goes", but is not played.' Here was obfuscation enough almost to divert attention from the music. Of more significance at the time was the interest and friendship of one of the world's greatest conductors, who had launched Wagner's *Ring*, Brahms's Second and Third Symphonies, and the Dvořák Sixth Symphony. It was said that Richter found the finale of the Variations an insufficiently weighty peroration; but at supper afterwards Alexander Mackenzie noted 'the enthusiastic terms of admiration, shared by us all, which the conductor addressed to the composer'. In his diary Parry called the Variations 'first rate. Quite brilliantly clever and genuine orchestral music.' A week later he wrote to Elgar of his delight 'that Richter is going to preside over their presentation to the Viennese. It will wake them up and no mistake.' Ann Elgar understood the meaning of this new success when she wrote to Alice on 23 June: 'I feel that he is some great historic person – I cannot claim a little bit of him now he belongs to the big world.'

3

Charged with the grandeur of God (1899–1903)

Elgar's ambitions for the 1900 Birmingham commission had been outlined to Littleton: 'I want to make this my chief work & to devote myself to it with something like a free mind.' But he was still teaching and being urged by Novello to produce popular music after the manner of Edward German's *Henry VIII* dances, which he always heard with 'exquisite pleasure'. 'I can't write that sort of thing', Elgar had told Jaeger. In fact he could, most expertly, and did so throughout his career. He proved the point while still composing the Variations. Towards the end of January 1899 he reworked movements from the 1888 Suite in D to make the *Three Characteristic Pieces*. They were to be dedicated to Lady Mary Lygon ('L.M.L.' of the Variations sketches, and then '∗∗∗'), presented to her before she left for Australia with her brother Lord Beauchamp, and published as op. 10.

Alice Elgar was house-hunting from the beginning of February 1899, looking for something larger than Forli. Elgar was otherwise engaged, as he told Jaeger on 21 February, the day he despatched the Variations to Vert: 'I'm just off to the Beagles & shall be away all day – no music like the baying of hounds after all.' At the beginning of March he completed what he called the 'Partrigal' for Queen Victoria's 'Triumphs' (*To her Beneath whose Steadfast Star*), and on 6 March he sent Novello 'an easy Violin & pianoforte piece' as companion to the *Chanson de nuit* of 1897; he 'suggested calling this "cheerful" piece "Chanson de Matin"'. Alice eventually found at Malvern Wells a suitable house called Wedham Lodge. Elgar made an anagram of the family names to produce 'Craeg Lea'. A main attraction of the house was its outlook, as Elgar told Rudolph de Cordova in his 1904 interview for *The Strand Magazine*: 'I get a wonderful view of the surrounding country. I can see across Worcestershire, to Edgehill, the Cathedral of Worcester, the Abbeys of Pershore and Tewkesbury, and even the smoke from round Birmingham. It is delightfully quiet.' Elgar also enjoyed the garden as it sloped towards the Malvern Hills. Its care was the subject of a set of instructions to his daughter Carice, now in her ninth year. Her husbandry was alternately approved and disapproved: 'I hereby discharge my Man without wages'; 'I hereby engage my Man again & he can have ten tisses [kisses] for wages *now*.'

Elgar was exercised over the criticisms of the 'Enigma' finale. A letter to Jaeger of 27 June expressed caution: 'You won't frighten me into writing a logically developed movement where I don't want one'; by 12 July the new coda had been approved by Jaeger: 'I'm heartily glad you like the TAIL; *I do* now it's done.'

Elgar had again been at Sinclair's for the second weekend in July, 8–10. This time he described 'Dan triumphant (after a fight)' and wrote for him what was to become the impetuous opening of *In the South*. But that summer he had to complete the *Sea Pictures* cycle for Clara Butt to sing at the Norwich Festival, and did so on 18 August. Because of a temporary estrangement between Elgar and Novello, the songs were published by Boosey. Elgar was angered by Littleton's suggestion that Vert should not have paid the orchestra for an extra rehearsal of the Variations. Elgar explained the matter to Jaeger in a letter of 1 September: 'I confess the prospect of a rich man seriously considering the fleecing of those poor underpaid overworked devils in the orchestra *quite* prevented me from feeling Xtian.'

For the 1899 Worcester Festival two of Elgar's works had been substantially altered. On 13 September *The Light of Life*, with changes to the libretto and solo vocal parts, was performed in the cathedral, and that evening Elgar conducted the 'Enigma' Variations with extended finale for the first time. The following day Alice noted in her diary that 'E. walked with Father Bellasis'. This was Richard Bellasis, former pupil in Cardinal Newman's Oratory school at Birmingham, and now an Oratory priest. Three weeks later at Norwich Elgar conducted the *Sea Pictures* première on 5 October. His host, James Mottram, likened him as he raised the baton to 'a hawk dreaming poetry in captivity'; at his side Clara Butt had 'a wonderful dress, the material of which, it was whispered, indicated appropriately the scales of a mermaid's sinuous form'.[1]

The 'Enigma' Variations was the first major Elgar work to be printed in full score. It was a subject he had already broached with Jaeger: 'When I have met German musicians (for instance) I never talk about having written anything: cos why? Cos they ask to see a score & think nothing of you if you haven't one in print, *and they are quite right too*.' There was a further triumph when Elgar spent his first night at Windsor Castle on 18 October. He reported to his sister Dot: 'Yes it was a concert at Windsor & 3 princesses were at it – they did *ten* of

[1] R. H. Mottram, *Portrait of an Unknown Victorian* (London, 1936), p. 253.

my pieces.' He also 'sent a line to Dad as I thought it might please him'.

No decision had yet been made for the Birmingham commission. Elgar had two possibilities in mind: a setting of Cardinal Newman's *Dream of Gerontius*, with which he had certainly been familiar since early 1887; or a work on the teaching of the apostles, another project that had long been maturing. Towards the end of 1899 the 'Apostles' idea seemed uppermost. On 15 November Elgar wrote to Jaeger and enclosed a musical motif to illustrate the biblical words 'Then Jesus said unto him – That thou doest do quickly – he [Judas] went immediately out: *and it was night*'. Capel Cure, Anglican librettist of *The Light of Life* came to Craeg Lea for two nights, but Elgar was daunted at the thought of having to compile a 'book' of his own and thereupon resigned the Birmingham commission.

On the first day of 1900 doubts were finally resolved. G. H. Johnstone came to Craeg Lea on behalf of the Birmingham Festival, convinced Elgar that *The Dream of Gerontius* was a practical proposition, and undertook to negotiate terms of publication with Novello. Later in January Elgar was at the Birmingham Oratory discussing the poem with Newman's executor, Father Neville. He did not tell Jaeger of the plan till 5 February: 'I am setting Newman's "Dream of Gerontius" – awfully solemn & mystic.' At the same time the Judas motif needed a new context: 'I say that Judas theme will *have* to be used up for death & despair in this work – so don't peach.' The violin teaching continued, and Rosa Burley at The Mount observed progress on the work: 'Edward seemed to think of nothing else. Again and again manuscript fragments were brought to the Mount on the lesson day, tried over and discussed.' Elgar's habit of working on one section and then moving to another if some problem arose made the chronology of the work impossible to chart. The point was proved when the Elgars spent an evening at the Jaegers' on 25 February. Already he could play the Angel's solo 'My work is done' from near the beginning of Part II; but it was not until 2 March that he sent Jaeger the first forty-four pages of *Gerontius* vocal score, as far as 'Sanctus fortis'. Elgar apologized for some messy pages: 'To improve it my wife's Sal-volatile bottle bust a-coming home – hence the stains.' He expressed justifiable pride in his work when he wrote to Nicholas Kilburn on 11 March: 'I like what I have done – I am bold & have shirked nothing – I've made my own "atmosphere" & stuck to it.' Progress continued steadily until 20 March, when Elgar sent the end of Part I: 'the final chos. is godly effective &, I think, not quite cheap'.

After playing the proofs of Part I, Jaeger expressed his enthusiasm on 13 April: 'Since "Parsifal" nothing of this mystic, religious kind of music has appeared to my knowledge that displays the same power & beauty as yours.' Elgar was gratified but also anxious that the Birmingham chorus should start learning the work. He suggested on 29 April that printing could continue till the end of the demons' chorus. He had doubts about the notation of the Angel of the Agony section (the original Judas idea), as he wrote to Jaeger on 21 May: 'It's in D – but the enharmonic changes are so ghastful that I've written it phonetically.' The 'Praise to the Holiest' chorus (Elgar called it 'the great blaze') was despatched at the end of May, and the vocal score finished on 6 June.

As Jaeger pondered the complete work, his admiration was tempered by one criticism. Of the 'Angel's Farewell' he said he had not seen 'any such lovely writing of a quiet soothing character since Die Meistersinger'; but he felt Elgar had failed at the moment when 'the Soul goes within the presence of the Almighty'. Many letters on the subject were exchanged, with Jaeger urgent and Elgar reluctant. Jaeger persisted, and his final thrust on 30 June was cruel but effective: 'I grant you, it wanted a Wagner or R. Strauss to do that, nobody else could dare attempt it.' Elgar responded with one of the work's great moments, the eighteen bars leading up to the shattering climax at cue 120: 'Very well; here's what I thought of at *first*.' Elgar's acknowledgment was grudging but, as with the Variations, Jaeger was again largely responsible for a major feature in an Elgar masterpiece.

Elgar was conscious of his achievement and wrote movingly about it to Nicholas Kilburn on 27 June: 'I am not suggesting that I have risen to the heights of the poem for one moment – but on our hillside night after night looking across our "illimitable" horizon (pleonasm!) I've seen in thought the Soul go up & have written my own heart's blood into the score.' Much of the orchestration was done at Birchwood Lodge, where Elgar also learnt to ride a bicycle. Scoring was complete on 3 August, the day Alice Elgar wrote to Mrs Kilburn, slightly misquoting Newman's poem: 'E. loves orchestrating here in the deep quiet hearing the "sound of summer winds amidst the lofty pines".' At the head of the MS full score Elgar wrote a dedication to the greater glory of God, 'A.M.D.G.' (the Jesuit motto), and a quotation from Virgil, 'Quae lucis miseris tam dira cupido', to which he added John Florio's 1603 version of a Montaigne translation, 'Whence doth so dyre desire of light on wretches grow?' At the end he added some Ruskin words from *Sesame and Lilies*: 'This is the best of me; for the rest, I ate, and drank, and slept, loved and hated, like another; my life was as the vapour and is not; but *this* I saw and knew: this, if anything of mine, is worth your memory.'

Before the end of August Elgar heard that the Birmingham chorus was enjoying *Gerontius*. He returned to Craeg Lea and continued to cycle on a 'new Mr. Phoebus' (the bicycle was made by the Sunbeam firm). The new work had made its impression at Novello, and F. G. Edwards, editor of its house journal *The Musical Times* came to Malvern on 7 September with the view of writing a lengthy article. Elgar spoke about *Gerontius*: 'It seems absurd to say that I have written the work to order for Birmingham. The poem has been soaking in my mind for at least eight years. All that time I have been gradually assimilating the thoughts of the author into my own musical promptings.' The fact that there was only one full score of *Gerontius*, for the making of orchestral parts, proof-reading, and final checking by Elgar, meant that Richter, who was to conduct the première, had only belated opportunity for study.

Jaeger wrote to Alice Elgar that Julius Buths, 'one of the *Ultra moderns* of Germany, great propagandist for Richard Strauss' and conductor of the Lower Rhine Festival, had been sent a copy of the Variations, commented on them favourably, and was now to attend the Birmingham Festival. Alice wrote in some detail to Edwards about the forthcoming *Musical Times* article, urging that Craeg Lea should not be described as a '*villa*', that her father was a KCB, that 'Robert Raikes was my *great* grandfather, please not relegate my birth into nearly the last century!', and that above all, as '*E*. has nothing to do with the business in Worcester, would you please leave out details which do not affect him & with which he has nothing to do'. Elgar pursued the matter further: 'I only know I was kept out of everything decent, " 'cos his father keeps a shop" – I believe I'm always introduced so now, that is to say – the remark is invariably made in an undertone.'

The London rehearsal of *Gerontius* on 24 September was something of a triumph for Richter, who had seen the full score only the previous day. But F. A. Baughan sounded a note of warning in the *Morning Leader*: 'A work such as Elgar's "Dream of Gerontius" requires more orchestral rehearsal than it has been given, and more than one full rehearsal of soloists, chorus, and orchestra, which is all it will get at Birmingham.' Morale in the chorus had been sapped by the death, on 11 June, of Swinnerton Heap, their gifted trainer and a devoted Elgarian. The replacement was the seventy-year-old William Stockley, stalwart of an earlier generation who had little sympathy with the latest trends in music. Elgar, at Richter's side for much of the combined rehearsal, berated the singers for their lack of knowledge and commitment. Despite Richter's calling an extra rehearsal and beseeching the choir on behalf of an English masterpiece, the performance on 3 October was poor. Rosa Burley had no doubt about the extent of the failure: 'It was appalling – far far worse than one had thought possible.' As Dorabella was to write, 'It was all rather dreadful and I felt afterwards that I wanted to get home quickly and meet nobody'. Robert Buckley, who had always championed Elgar, told Hubert Leicester he had never been so disappointed: he thought there was nothing in the work and it would never be heard again.

Yet many critics recognized the masterpiece behind the inadequate performance, and in the *Morning Leader* of 4 October Baughan was enthusiastic: 'I can honestly and frankly say that no composition by an Englishman equals it in sheer technique, to say nothing of real poetic feeling.' More important than the British critics, Buths from Düsseldorf had acknowledged the calibre of the work. For the moment Elgar was crushed. He wrote to Jaeger on 9 October:

> I have worked hard for forty years &, at the last, Providence denies me a decent hearing of my work: so I submit – I always said God was against art & I still believe it I have allowed my heart to open once – it is now shut against every religious feeling & every soft, gentle impulse *for ever*.

In the middle of October, at the instigation of Charles Stanford, Elgar was offered a Cambridge doctorate in music. His first instinct was to refuse, on the grounds that he could not afford the robes; but under persuasion he accepted. Depression had not lifted by 26 October when he wrote to Jaeger again: 'I really wish I were dead over & over again – but I dare not, for the sake of my relatives, do the job myself.' Yet there was a dramatic change of mood by 4 November. He had been playing 'Nimrod' and thought it was a good likeness of Jaeger, 'you solemn, wholesome hearty old dear'. He had also started another orchestral piece: 'Don't say anything about the prospective overture yet – I call it "Cockayne" & it's cheerful & Londony – "stout and steaky".' Ten days later thought of the Cambridge degree made him 'feel Gibbonsy, Croftish, Byrdlich & foolish all over'; but, as he continued to Jaeger, the new overture was becoming

> A work to tweak a teetotaller's beak
> And make a methody swear.

He included in the letter a drawing of Worcestershire Philharmonic ladies making lofty steps towards the Cambridge ceremony on 22 November. The Elgars lunched at King's College, and Alice found the Senate House ceremonial made a 'Memorable & Delightful scene'. Frederick Cowen also received a degree and described the gowns: 'Elgar's did not reach much below his knees, and mine trailed upon the ground, and we presented the funniest picture imaginable.'[2] About

[2] Birthplace Museum.

47

Elgar the public orator quoted Homer: 'I am self-taught, but God has planted in my mind all manner of songs.'

Towards the end of 1900 Elgar started learning the trombone. When he wrote to Joseph Bennett about *Cockaigne*, he mentioned one of the results: 'As I play the trombone myself the parts for this family are rather more dressed than usual.' When the overture was finished on 24 March 1901, he appended a heartfelt line from Langland's *Piers Plowman*: 'Meteless & moneless on Malverne hilles'. Buths had put his conviction about the Variations to a practical test at Düsseldorf on 7 February. Jaeger was delighted: 'So there! first performance in Germany in Nimrod's native place!' Alice reported that they had celebrated in their own way: 'Der Tondichter & I have just been playing "Nimrod" as a duet for *Trombone* & piano!'

Elgar rehearsed part of *Gerontius* for a Worcestershire Philharmonic concert. Though 'nick's chorus' was omitted on 9 May, enough was heard to prove that the difficulties experienced at Birmingham were not insuperable. As Elgar explained to F. G. Edwards, 'the work is within the means of an intelligent chorus with a (fairly) intelligent Conductor'. Lady Hampton, wife of the society's vice-president, had written appreciatively and Jaeger saw her letter: 'Let us hope her dream of a performance in a Cathedral may come true some day. Perhaps when the new Roman Catholic Cathedral at Westminster is opened Cardinal Vaughan may be tempted.' That particular performance had to wait two more years.

Jaeger was already a victim of the ill health that was to kill him nine years later. Elgar was concerned and arranged for him to visit a Harley Street specialist who had seen to his own '(supposed) hopeless throat'. He paid for the consultation and declared himself ready to 'sell my last book, stick & golfball for you, if necessary'. Elgar acted generously towards another friend that summer. Herbert Brewer, organist of Gloucester Cathedral, had undertaken to complete a choral work, *Emmaus*, for the Three Choirs Festival in September. Difficulties over the libretto by Joseph Bennett had delayed matters, and Brewer felt he must withdraw. Elgar offered to orchestrate the work for him. He wrote to Jaeger hoping the suggestion would relieve Brewer's mind 'and perhaps his wife's – oh these wives of musicians – what they go through & *suffer*'. With the task complete, Elgar wrote modestly to Brewer on 7 July: 'Now: please *accept* my work on your score and never think I want any return whatever: keep a kind thought for a fellow sometime – that's all.' Brewer replied in the only terms possible: 'If there were a few more men in the world as unselfish and sympathetic as you we should all be the happier.' Rediscovery of the *Emmaus* score, lost for many years, allowed a third Gloucester Festival performance in 1992.[3]

Cockaigne was not the only virtuoso orchestral work of 1901. At the beginning of the year Jaeger was told, 'Gosh! man I've got a tune in my head'. Dorabella heard it on 10 May and described Elgar's glee: 'Child, come up here. I've got a tune that will knock 'em – knock 'em flat.' He then played *Pomp and Circumstance March* no. 1, with its trio tune that was to spread Elgar's name further than any other music of his. The first two Marches were completed during the summer, and by then *Cockaigne* had had a successful première under Elgar on 20 June at Queen's Hall, London.

On 15 August Elgar went to South Wales at Rosa Burley's invitation. She had taken a house at Llangranog and a letter from him decided her: 'I realized that he was in one of his moods of black depression. I therefore wrote by return and suggested that he should join us.' She was critical of his Malvern social life, describing it as 'the too artificial milieu which was at once his gaol and his goal'. Escape from it released 'the sunniest side of his character'. He was in Wales only four nights, but the break was musically rewarding. Themes eventually used in the 'Apostles' project and in the Introduction and Allegro op. 47 were conceived there, annotated with the name of a small island the party often visited, 'Ynys Lochtyn'. Back in Malvern he embarked on another hobby, printing some photographs for the first time. Wales, however, was very much in his mind when he wrote to Jaeger on 28 August: 'I have returned a week from *Llangringoggywoggypygwyssill*.'

The Elgars stayed at Hasfield Court with the Bakers for the Gloucester Festival, during which *Cockaigne* and the prelude to *Gerontius* were performed. Alice's diary for 9 September mentions 'E. on the moat – "Nanty Ewart" In the Fort'. The house had been bought by 'W.M.B.' in 1864 and much altered. But it was Elizabethan in origin and an ideal setting for Elgar and the three Baker boys to play historical games. They were Roundheads and Cavaliers; the eldest boy was indeed 'Prince Rupert', nephew of Charles I, and his expert cavalry commander. But Elgar was 'Nanty Ewart' from a different century, Walter Scott's drunken sea captain in *Redgauntlet*, working erratically for the Jacobean cause of the Young Pretender. So Elgar, given instructions by Prince Rupert, 'hiccougheth acknowledgement thereof'. But he also 'beseeches your Highness to relieve him from the vexation intolerable of living four lives at once in three different centuries'.

Creatively Elgar now went further into the past. He was asked to provide music for *Diarmuid and Grania*, a play by George Moore and

---

[3] Gloucester Festival programme book for 1992, pp. 138–42.

W. B. Yeats to be produced in Dublin on 21 October. The Celtic subject concerned the third-century Finn, his ill-starred attempts to gain Grania and his eventual killing of Diarmuid, the nephew who won her. Elgar wrote to Jaeger about his music on 1 October: 'there's a funeral march which you wd. like & it sounds big & weird'. A Leeds visit to conduct the Variations allowed Elgar to visit Dr Buck, have conversation with the Kilburns, and meet the Edward Speyers, whose house at Ridgehurst became a favourite Elgarian retreat. Meanwhile George Moore was most impressed with the *Grania* music and urged Elgar to develop it further: 'The sooner you begin writing the opera the better, the subject evidently suits you.'

The forthcoming coronation of Edward VII suggested other ideas. Covent Garden was planning a gala event, and Elgar wondered whether *Caractacus*, dedicated to the new king's mother and treating of, if hardly celebrating, a British worthy, might form the basis of an opera. Jaeger saw at once that 'Britons tied captive to the Conquerors' wheels!' was hardly coronation stuff. Eventually A.C. Benson's *Coronation Ode* became the vehicle for Elgar's homage, with the tune that would 'knock 'em flat'. The *Pomp and Circumstance Marches* in D and A minor were first heard in Liverpool under A. E. Rodewald on 19 October. Rodewald was in cotton, but a gifted musician who had studied conducting under Richter (his only pupil). He became a devoted Elgarian. Three days later Henry Wood gave the London première, playing the marches in reverse order. Stanford wrote that 'they both came off like blazes, & are uncommon fine stuff'. The success of the D major March had been such that Wood played it three times, 'Merely to restore order'.[4] Stanford thought it 'translated Master Kipling into Music' and managed to say ' "blooming beggar" in quite his style'; but he preferred the A minor.

The Elgars began their first stay at Ridgehurst, home of Edward and Antonia Speyer, on 1 November. The host's habit of recording in his visitors' book the statistics of his guests gave Alice a weight of nine stone six pounds; Elgar was a stone heavier and five foot nine and a half inches tall.[5] Fellow guests included the tenor, pianist and composer William Shakespeare, 'who played through Gerontius at midnight', and Donald Tovey, always ambiguous in his attitude to Elgar's music and hardly a devotee of *Gerontius*. It was a very musical household, and previous visitors had included Joachim, Paderewski, Richter, Eugenie Schumann, Richard Strauss and Felix Weingartner.

The Variations and *Cockaigne* were spreading Elgar's reputation

---

[4] Henry Wood, *My Life of Music* (London, 1938), p. 154.
[5] Private Collection.

wide. Felix Weingartner in Germany was impressed with the Elgar scores he had seen: 'Ich lese mit wachsende Freude die Partituren von Elgar, der wirklich ein interessanter, famoser Kerl ist. Die Ouverture ist ein PRACHTWERK.'[6] Elgar expressed to Jaeger his glee about the catalogue of foreign performances: 'They [the Variations] are down *zum erste Male* Mainz. Wiesbaden. Weingartner is taking Cockaigne on *tour* with the Kaim Orchester! The overture is also down at Boston, Chicago & Pittsburg – 3 different orchestras! *Things is humming*.'

Increasing success in no way impaired Elgar's sense of humour. Henry Ettling, a wine merchant and friend of Richter's, whose main delights were to play timpani and act the magician (hence his 'Uncle Klingsor' nickname), received a characteristic jape from Elgar. It centred on a fictional Letitia Barnett, whose address was Propriety Villa, 147 Precise Gardens, Parallel Road. Elgar wrote on 26 October:

> I much regret to hear that someone does not think the lovemaking in 'Cockaigne' strictly *proper*: this must be *Mrs. Barnett*! Perhaps she means the harmony, if so I never learnt enough to correct it; but if she means *morally*, a bit of Mendelssohn always makes anything right for the English. So I enclose a new *Coda*.

The 'moral coda' took the form of combining the lovers' music of *Cockaigne* with the Mendelssohn *Wedding March*. 'Mrs. Barnett' persisted in her criticism of Elgar and produced a final attack: 'I enclose a temperance card: if you could get Dr. Elgar to sign it & give up writing music I should be grateful.'

During October 1901 Elgar was asked to provide the major novelty for the 1903 Birmingham Festival. He was now ready to tackle the 'Apostles' project, and the idea was readily accepted. He told Edwards of *The Musical Times* that the subject of the apostles had thrilled him since boyhood, 'regarding them from their human side, as men, not as theological figures'. And he remembered how his old headmaster, Francis Reeve, had described them, as 'poor men, young men, at the time of their calling: perhaps before the descent of the Holy Ghost not cleverer than some of you here'. Elgar was to be his own librettist. He greatly admired Charles Jennens's *Messiah* text, compiled from the King James Bible. He wanted to avoid the pitfalls of Capel Cure's *Light of Life* book, and what he called the 'crude sanctified rhymings' of the traditional Victorian oratorio. There was, moreover, the compelling example of Wagner.

Before beginning on the oratorio, Elgar needed new sketchbooks. He put his request to Jaeger on 6 November 1901: 'My sketch books

[6] Birthplace Museum.

are rotten – I know the sketches are & so do you "*& Mrs. Barnett says so too!.*"' He asked for eight oblong books, to be bound in '4 different colours'. Eventually there were 'eight tints'. It was characteristic of him that he began by using Sketchbook II, dating it 14 November; Sketchbook I was dated five days later. It was in this book that he explained his use of the letter 'K', scrawled across so many of his manuscripts: '*Mem*: The ridiculous word "Koppid" meant that I had copied it fairly enough for anyone to read: I used the word to prevent confusion with the word "*copied*" which was used by the professional copyist.' At the beginning of Sketchbook IV Elgar wrote: '(Old Daddy Jaeger had these books made for me – (I paid for them) Alas!'

He was not yet ready for his biblical venture. Instead he wrote an extended concert piece for the pianist Fanny Davies, a distinguished pupil of Clara Schumann. She gave its première on 2 December, but Elgar was not entirely satisfied with it and never prepared it for publication. Nevertheless he gave it the provisional opus number '41'. The Elgars had just been for another stay at Ridgehurst, where a congenial fellow guest had been Laurence Binyon from the Department of Prints and Drawings at the British Museum, who was later to inspire Elgar to *The Spirit of England* and the *Arthur* music. Elgar had also recently met 'Ernest Newman', the music critic who had evolved from the bank clerk, William Roberts. Newman was planning an extended article on Elgar for *The Speaker* of 21 December. He felt Elgar was wasting his time on provincial choral festivals, but was thoroughly convinced by *Gerontius*. He thought Elgar distilled a feeling of England similar to that of our greatest poetry: 'Dr. Elgar's music suggests a broad and open relation to life, a moral purpose deep, steady, and universal – something peculiarly characteristic, one loves to think, of English poetry at its best, from Shakespeare to Wordsworth.'

Now it was for Germany to assess *Gerontius*. Buths not only mounted the Düsseldorf performance on 19 December, but had also translated the poem into German. After initial doubts, the Elgars decided to attend the concert, which was an unqualified success. Elgar was fêted, as he told his sister Dot: 'The laurel wreath is a yard in diameter with crimson ribbons – we bring it home';[7] and it was a novel experience to be addressed as 'Verehrter Meister'. He made the essential point in a letter to Alfred Littleton: 'As to the performance; it complete bore out my own idea of the work: the Chorus was very fine & had only commenced work on Nov. 11 – this disproves the

[7] Birthplace Museum.

idea fostered in Birmingham that my work is *too difficult.*' Littleton responded gratifyingly: 'We are ordering the full score and wind parts of "Gerontius" to be engraved.'

On returning to England, Elgar was depressed, as he explained in a letter of 3 January 1902 to Jaeger: 'The horrible musical atmosphere I plunged into at once in this benighted country nearly suffocated me – I *wish* it had completely.' He had heard from Edward Speyer that Strauss was to conduct *Cockaigne* in Berlin. Elgar added some tempo markings (later printed in the full score) for Strauss's guidance. But Charles Stanford wrote 'a belated line of much congratulation to you anent Düsseldorf. I am so glad they behaved well to you.' Stanford was planning the Variations at Cambridge and *Cockaigne* at the Royal College of Music.[8] For the moment Elgar was creatively nostalgic, working up the two *Dream Children* pieces for orchestra from earlier sketches, and producing an *Ave verum corpus* from a *Pie Jesu* written fifteen years before for the funeral of William Allen, his solicitor employer.

As 1902 progressed, Elgar became ceremonial. Plans were well advanced for the *Coronation Ode* to be performed in June. A. C. Benson, son of a former Archbishop of Canterbury and now teaching at Eton, had sent Elgar an outline of the text in December. Following a suggestion more probably from Clara Butt than the king himself, Elgar's peroration would be based on the trio tune from *Pomp and Circumstance* no. 1. Benson hoped to provide suitable words, though the metre was difficult: 'if you could string together a few nonsense words, just to show me how you would wish them to run, I would construct it, following the air closely'. Jaeger was sceptical of the idea: 'I say you *will have to* write another tune for the "Ode" in place of the "March in D" tune ... that drop to E & the bigger drop afterwards are quite impossible in singing ANY words to them   They sound downright vulgar.' Elgar took the risk.

Another *Pomp and Circumstance March* had been shaping in Elgar's mind. What eventually became the trio of no. 3 was written out on 7 February; at the time Elgar headed it as if for no. 4 and added 'I. A. Atkins gewidmet'. Atkins used it as a voluntary in Worcester Cathedral the following day. Novello now wanted a new version of *God save the King*. Elgar avoided 'anything *clever* or harmonically ingenious' and also requested instrument names in 'plain English', with a resurrection of 'Hautboys' and 'Kettledrums'.

Boosey was to publish the *Coronation Ode*, which was completed on 1 April. But the following day Benson wrote in some disquiet: 'One

---

[8] Birthplace Museum.

other point; it struck me suddenly on a lonely walk yesterday that there was not a word in the Ode about Queen Alexandra. This is a grave omission.' The gap was filled by 'Daughter of ancient kings'. Elgar was a strong supporter of Arthur Boosey in his furtherance of the copyright acts then going through parliament, and the firm appreciated too the 'invariable kindness and patience' that converted 'the paths of publishing into ways of pleasantness'. In the case of the *Ode*, progress was also being made 'on the translation into fee-fi-fo-fum' (tonic sol-fa).

Gerontius was now planned for two important performances, one at the Lower Rhine Festival on 20 May, the other at the Worcester Three Choirs Festival on 11 September. The latter was the more controversial. The problem was Cardinal Newman's poem in the setting of an Anglican cathedral. Elgar wrote to Father Richard Bellasis on 27 April: 'Now some objector has written to the Bishop & has stirred up strife: the Committee has drawn up a list of small *omissions* of words.' Suggested changes involved leaving out the litany of the saints; substitution of 'Jesus', 'Lord', or 'Saviour' for 'Mary'; 'souls' for 'souls in purgatory'; and 'prayers' for 'masses'. The changes were accepted by both Worcester and the Birmingham Oratory. It was now, with the tiresome negotiations done, that Elgar decided to give the MS full score of *Gerontius* to the Oratory. He made the gift soon after the Worcester performance, dating it 'Sept. 17: 1902'; he added: 'I offer this M.S. to the Library of the Oratory, with the deepest reverence to the memory of Cardinal Newman whose poem I have had the honour to set to music.' The Düsseldorf performance was a notable triumph. Elgar had been vexed with Strauss for taking so much time over the Liszt *Faust Symphony* that the *Gerontius* rehearsal was curtailed. But Strauss made ample amends at the banquet after the performance. *The Times* of 23 May reported the gist of Strauss's speech: 'I raise my glass to the welfare and success of the first English progressivist, Meister Edward Elgar, and of the young progressivist school of English composers.' Strauss and Buths also presented Elgar with a copy of Beethoven's death mask.

The Elgars stayed in Germany till 3 June, touring much of the time with Rodewald, seeing the Leipzig Hotel Sedan where he had lodged in 1883, and visiting Bach's birthplace, Eisenach. There Elgar corrected proofs of the *Coronation Ode* and sent a postcard to his father, feeling 'rather small' in the presence of the great cantor. Strauss's speech had caused something of a stir in English musical circles and had not been well received in all of them. To Jaeger Elgar expressed exasperation on 11 June: 'I always said British musicians were several kinds of fool & ignoramus – but this is worse than usual from them.'

Rehearsals for the *Coronation Ode* were proceeding, and Elgar attended. But back in Malvern he resumed cycling and became the countryman again. On 21 June he rode to Bredon and Kemerton, then back by Pershore. Alice's diary records that he also looked for William Allen's grave and 'found the stone had fallen down the night before'. It seemed a bad omen, and the diary entry for 24 June noted an unexpected development: 'E. out cycling again, Heard the dreadful news of the King's illness & postponement of Coronation.' King Edward needed an emergency operation for appendicitis. To Jaeger the following day Elgar seemed indifferent: 'Don't, for heaven's sake, *sympathise* with me – I don't care a tinker's damn! It gives me three blessed sunny days in my own country (for which I thank God or the Devil).' He had heard about it 'at a little roadside pub: I said "Give me another pint of cider" '.

Later in the same Jaeger letter Elgar wrote, 'I have been thinking mighty things!' His thoughts were now turning to *The Apostles*. A letter to Atkins on 2 July informed him that he had been 'Biking wildly', 'playing Bach – who heals & pacifies all men & all things', and was 'now plotting GIGANTIC WORX'. That was a day he also 'rode to Longdon Marsh', source of inspiration for many *Apostles* ideas, and 'saw Heron fishing'. Again G. H. Johnstone undertook the commercial dealings with Novello, striking a hard bargain, and making the point that Boosey was waiting in the wings. Littleton wanted to see some of the score before deciding; but this was impossible, since it did not exist.

For the nights of 11–12 July Elgar was in Hereford to rehearse the local Three Choirs contingent in *Gerontius*. Again he commemorated Dan in the visitors' book, this time 'wistful (outside the cathedral)', with five Adagio bars, *mesto* and then *dolce lusingando*; the music was incorporated eventually in 'For the Fallen', last number of *The Spirit of England*. After a *Don Giovanni* in London, Elgar went on to Bayreuth for the last time. He had been invited by Archibald Ramsden, a piano dealer known to the Elgars as the 'President' because of his position in the U. B. Quiet Club (a society in which talking 'shop' was forbidden). They saw *Der fliegende Holländer* and *Parsifal*. Of the *Ring* Elgar saw only the first three operas, as he was unwell and left Bayreuth early.

On the last day of July Alice noted that Elgar 'Began to be very busy collecting material'. This was for *The Apostles*. Elgar's researches towards the libretto were absorbing, time-consuming, and productive of sufficient ideas for half-a-dozen oratorios. He described his method to F. G. Edwards: 'For more than a year I read no end of books on divinity, in order to get thoroughly in touch with my all-absorbing

subject.' He added that to get the particular nuance he was after 'I
have spent two whole days hunting for a suitable text'. For the first
time since autumn 1889 Elgar was having serious eye trouble, but he
could report some improvement when he wrote to Jaeger on 3 August,
as well as something on *The Apostles*: 'it's too philosophical for your
cheap publisher's side of your mind but just the thing for the "real"
A.J.J.'

Elgar was diverted from the oratorio by the writing of two songs,
In the Dawn and *Speak, Music* to words by Benson. On 1 September
his mother died; three days later Alice reported the funeral as taking
place on a 'Beautiful sunny peaceful afternoon' though she did not
herself attend. The *Dream Children* pieces were first performed that
evening at Queen's Hall under Arthur Payne. Alice thought the
Worcester Three Choirs *Gerontius* 'Most beautiful, most wonderful in
Cathedral'; and Granville Bantock wrote to Ernest Newman about it:
'If Elgar never writes another note of music I will say that he is a
giant, and overtops us all.' Elgar commemorated the performance with
a postcard to F. G. Edwards; he drew on it some demons and arrows
pointing to 'Former abode of Bowdler'; he apologized that the demons
did not resemble Edward Vine Hall, whom he considered had stirred
the bother over Cardinal Newman's poem. During the festival Elgar
also made a *Falstaff* sketch. The fanfare-like motif did not appear in
the completed work, but the project was simmering.

Despite his own Irish Protestantism, Stanford had pleaded strongly
for the inclusion of *Gerontius* at the 1902 Sheffield Festival, as 'the
first English composition to be given at a Lower Rhine Festival'.[9]
Despite wretched toothache, Elgar conducted it there on 2 October.
Later that day came the première of the *Coronation Ode*, which could
hardly fail in the context of the postponed coronation and the king's
subsequent recovery. At dinner the following evening Alice was taken
in to table by Charles Stuart Wortley, the local member of parliament
whose wife, another Alice, was to be a main inspiration for later Elgar
works. On 5 October 'E. had gas & the tooth out. E. conducted
"Gerontius" all the time he was under gas.'

The *Coronation Ode* was performed in London on 26 October. The
last chorus had to be repeated, and 'Land of Hope and Glory' was
now launched on its remarkable career. Two further performances in
the capital generated equal enthusiasm. The main sign that Elgar still
had *The Apostles* and compilation of its libretto in mind was the
purchase of a typewriter at the end of October. Jaeger was introduced
to it at once: 'I have brought this infernal machine down home to try

[9] Birthplace Museum.

if I can make head or tail of it. so I think I can't do better than worry your dear old Moss-head with one of my first attempts.' On 2 November Elgar sent to Novello *Weary Wind of the West*, a partsong required as test piece for the 1903 competitive festival at Morecambe. Canon C. V. Gorton was the inspiration behind the festival, and Elgar had an immediate rapport with him when eventually they met. Indeed it was to Gorton that Elgar was increasingly to turn for advice on his oratorio librettos. For the moment, however, he consulted Capel Cure. Elgar's text ideas for *The Apostles* were still very fluid. The Prologue was shaping; Scene I was to open with Christ at prayer in the mountain; of the individual disciples Judas's character was being developed first; many disparate ideas were to be shaped into a 'pastoral scene'. The suggestions were put before Capel Cure in a letter of 3 November, with specific request that he should sketch for Elgar a 'fields of corn' scene.

During November Elgar completed his five male-voice partsongs from the *Greek Anthology* op. 45. It was also the month that the Meiningen Orchestra under Fritz Steinbach came to London; the only English work in their programmes was the 'Enigma' Variations. Much of Elgar's social life during the period of the concerts, including a meeting with the painter John Singer Sargent, was organized by an increasingly good friend, Frank Schuster. Elgar wrote to Sargent on 26 November: 'I appreciate *your* art very much, but I thought you would not want to hear an ignoramus discourse on it, so I was tongue-tied – nervously, in your presence.' Schuster reported the same day that Paderewski had been asked who was Elgar's teacher and had replied '*Le Bon Dieu*'.

Success in London made Worcester music-making the paler. The programme for the twelfth concert of the Worcestershire Philharmonic Society, eventually conducted by Granville Bantock, included 'The Shepherds' Farewell' from Berlioz's *The Childhood of Christ*, three Palestrina motets, some Josquin and Benevoli. Elgar reacted angrily to lack of rehearsal progress, and on 27 November wrote a curt letter to Martina Hyde, one of the secretaries: 'I do not see how it is possible to give a fair performance of the choral portion of the programme; under the circumstances I cannot conduct the concert announced for the 11th Dec., and, as a consequence, it is unnecessary for me to come to any more practices.' Alice reported 'General consternation'. In London there was more musical excitement, with the first performance of Strauss's *Ein Heldenleben* on 6 December. Elgar told Jaeger that 'Strauss tore himself out of the crowd & said to me "Freund, sind Sie zufrieden?"' Elgar had replied, 'Ja! gewiss!'. He wrote to Strauss, addressing him as 'Richard Coeur de Lion': 'I rejoiced to see and hear how the audience appreciated your gigantic work & your genius.' Alice called *Ein Heldenleben* 'Very astonishing'. Elgar's response was to sketch music for a sequel to *Cockaigne*, to be subtitled after James Thomson's poem 'City of Dreadful Night'. Some of the music went to the slow movement of the Second Symphony, another idea to the unfinished Third Symphony via the unwritten *Last Judgement*.

Towards the end of the year 1902 Elgar wrote about the *Coronation Ode* to Benson: 'I did not intend the thing to lie on the musical antiquary's shelves, but wanted the "people" – in the best sense of the word – to enjoy themselves: – and they *are* doing so.' He then changed the subject to his 'serious music' and said he was 'working at it now'.[10] With most of *The Apostles* still undefined, Elgar began composition of the Prologue and sorting of musical material. He had certain themes to hand from the Welsh holiday; Rabbi F. L. Cohen came up with 'Shofar' suggestions and recommended Pauer's collection of *Traditional Hebrew Melodies*; at the home of Adrian Mignot in Liverpool Elgar had come across the gradual 'Constitues eos' and the antiphon 'O sacrum convivium'.

Two of Elgar's 1902 Christmas gifts provided both inspiration and distraction. The *Encyclopaedia Britannica* offered many ideas for the *Apostles* libretto, and Elgar was reading far and wide. To Dorabella he signed himself 'Isaac Newton Elgar', to Nimrod he was 'Paracelsus Elgar'. He told Jaeger he now knew 'who was Aaron's mother-in-law's first cousin's "bootblack"', and that there was a butterfly in his study helping *The Apostles*: 'I'm sure the beast is a familiar spirit – Angel Gabriel or Simon Magus, or Helen of Tyre or somebody.' These were all characters considered in connection with the 'Apostles' project. The other present was Ellis's translation of the Wagner prose works, in which the *Jesus of Nazareth* scenario offered ideas for Judas. He was also soon to receive from Schott the full score of *Parsifal*.

At the beginning of 1903 Alice Elgar had frustrations of her own: 'tried to get "Pinnock's Analysis Old Testament" for E. Was first offered a game & then a Scripture puzzle!' The first batch of *The Apostles* went to Novello on 21 January. This took Elgar as far as 'The Dawn'. In the depths of winter he could not always get to Longdon Marsh, as he told Jaeger on 5 February: 'the weather is too cold for me to go and sit in the marsh with my beloved wild creatures to get heartened up and general inspiration'. The following day Elgar 'sent off his beautiful wayside scene', a second scene of *The Apostles*

[10] Birthplace Museum.

much changed since its original conception. By now proofs of the vocal score had started to arrive, providing renewed stimulus for the Mary Magdalene episode. Interest in the new work led to another interview with F. G. Edwards for *The Musical Times*; Scene III was still not complete, but Elgar showed no sign of abandoning his original scheme of going on 'till we arrive at Antioch'. At the start of April *The Apostles* and a new bicycle were both causing concern, as he explained to Frank Schuster: 'my work is all behind & my life a worry at present – also my bicycle – new – collapsed with ME ON IT'. The Judas scene made good progress during the month, but Ernest Newman got a foretaste of the crisis ahead in a letter of 14 April: 'I am sadly tired out and this vast view from my window makes me feel too small to work: I used to feel that I "expanded" when I looked out over it all – now I seem to shrink and shrivel.'

At the end of April the Elgars were committed to the Morecambe competitive festival. Their first impressions of Morecambe on 30 April were depressing, but Canon Gorton and his wife proved congenial in a house well stocked with pictures and books. *The Banner of St George* was a set piece for the massed choirs, and the new partsong, *Weary Wind of the West* produced a standard of singing far higher than Elgar had anticipated. Elgar recognized in Gorton the expert in Anglican doctrine he needed for the 'Apostles' project, and he came away with a reproduction of *The Temptation of Christ* painted by the Russian Ivan Kramskoi in 1872. Kramskoi said of the picture: 'This is no Christ, it is the image of the sorrows of humanity which are known to all of us.'[11] For Elgar this was his 'ideal picture of the Lonely Christ' he was then trying to realize in music.

Johnstone was concerned that the Birmingham chorus had not yet started on *The Apostles*. Novello tried to be helpful by promising 'half the work', though with no more idea than Elgar had what that might involve. It was clear Elgar must modify his scheme. He now proposed a new chorus, 'Turn you to the stronghold', as conclusion to Part I, and apologized optimistically: 'I am sorry for all this delay but I think all will now go on smoothly. Pt.II will end at the Ascension and Pt.III (short) will conclude the work.'

There were plans for a *Gerontius* in Westminster Cathedral on 6 June 1903. This would be London's first opportunity to hear the work. Stanford warned about the acoustics of the new building and commiserated with Elgar. Littleton investigated and thought the fears exaggerated. Ebenezer Prout wrote to Elgar for tickets, adding that

[11] Quoted in G. H. Hamilton, *The Art and Architecture of Russia* (Harmondsworth, 1954), p. 246.

'Your work has *seized on* me as no other composition by an Englishman that I have ever seen'.[12] Gerontius was to be sung by Ludwig Wüllner, who had earned golden opinions in Düsseldorf. Justifiably Jaeger warned of a 'foreigner's *English*', which did indeed cause problems. Hubert Parry reacted to the cathedral as 'very imposing indeed and good for sound too', but the Catholicism of the work was oppressive: 'it reeks too much of the morbid and unnatural terrors and mysteries engendered by priestcraft to be congenial – vivid though it certainly is'.

Back at Malvern, Elgar wrote to the Stuart Wortley daughter, Clare, about Longdon Marsh and his 'friend the heron – who stands fishing on one leg'; he said they were 'the only two people who know much about the lonely marsh & we both love it – he catches frogs & I don't; that's all'. During June Elgar's anxieties over *The Apostles* continued. He finished the 'Ascension' chorus on the 25th; but now Jaeger was seriously concerned about the proximity of the first performance on 14 October. He could only remind Elgar of the *Gerontius* débâcle three years before. Scoring had still to be done, so Part III would have to be abandoned. Alice Elgar went to Novello in London and Johnstone in Birmingham with the tidings that *The Apostles* would now end at the 'Ascension'. Elgar wrote to Littleton on 28 July: 'of course all financial arrangements are at an end & must be reconstructed as *you* please entirely'.

Much of the Part I scoring was done at Rodewald's Welsh home, Minafon, at Betws y Coed. Elgar amused himself by wrestling with Welsh and trying out his new acquisition on some of the Novello staff. Jaeger was to write an analysis of *The Apostles* and was urged to spend some time at Rodewald's. This he did. Elgar urged caution over Jaeger's signposting of leitmotifs: 'I should not call that theme (?) anything It only adds to the sort of "life of the passage".' Occasionally Jaeger complained that a motif was missing where he expected it and asked for its insertion. Elgar might concur or not. Of Jaeger's admiration there was no doubt: 'Your work grows on me *tremendously* & by leaps & bounds It's *great* stuff & quite wonderfully original & beautiful.'

Scoring was complete on 17 August, and Elgar rounded off his work with three lines from William Morris's *Earthly Paradise*:

> To what a heaven the earth might grow
> If fear beneath the earth were laid,
> If *hope* failed not, nor *love* decayed.

[12] Birthplace Museum.

Granville Bantock came the next day, when they 'all walked on the hill & E. sent up the kite into the clouds'. At this stage Elgar was himself planning to write notes on the libretto. He was again delving into 'all his books on Scripture & so happy with them'. Elgar reacted from *The Apostles* by turning to algebra: 'it's better fun & no audience!' Yet the work should have all possible exegesis: there would be Jaeger's analysis, an 'Interpretation' by Canon Gorton, and Elgar's libretto notes.[13] As he told W. G. McNaught, writer, editor and successful adjudicator, 'the Messiah has had 150 years of explanation, commentary and analysis & Elijah we have heard dissected ever since our babyhood'.

Jaeger was much exercised in getting orchestral parts ready in time: 'THREE copyists you have killed (momentarily) with your beastly music!!!' Elgar gave his wife a vocal score of *The Apostles* on 7 October. He inscribed it with the Bliss Carmen words he later put on the full score of *The Kingdom*, and in it were pasted four photographs of Longdon Marsh.[14] In view of Richter's failure with *Gerontius*, Elgar had always been determined to conduct *The Apostles* himself. Atkins sent his good wishes: 'Everything promises well, and with your own dear old mystic self at the helm all should be right. Above all, I pray for poetic insight. Look lovingly at the chorus and they *must* give you their best.' From their first rehearsal the Birmingham chorus felt it had a debt of honour to pay off, and the performance on 14 October did the work justice. Richter thought it was the finest religious work since the *Missa solemnis*. Parry was more cautious, considering the 'Mary Magdalene episode finely conceived. Judas inadequate'. Jaeger's praise was judicious yet heartfelt: 'If you get conceited I'll come and spank you & put your dear noble nose on all the pages which I cant & wont & never shall get used to in them there "Apostles".' Elgar made a diary note on the performance day that Grey Tick won the Cesarewitch. On their way to the station after the festival, the Elgars called in at St Philip's Church (now Birmingham Cathedral). Elgar described how they 'walked up it to see the stained glass & on turning round were struck by Burne-Jones' Ascension (It is mine – or mine is it.) the sun shining thro' it   Very impressive ending to our glorious week'.

---

[13] BL, Add. MS 47904B; Elgar's notes were never printed.
[14] In possession of Raymond Monk.

4

Duties professorial and religious (1903–1907)

The autumn of 1903 brought sadness to Elgar. He had to give up the tenancy of Birchwood, his tree-girt retreat the other side of the Malvern Hills. On 4 November a card came from Rodewald that he seemed to be recovering from a bout of illness. Three days later the Elgars heard he was unconscious and there was no hope for him. Elgar went to Liverpool on 9 November, only to find his friend had just died. He was broken-hearted and wrote wretchedly to Jaeger: 'What I did, God knows – I know I walked for miles in strange ways – I know I had some coffee somewhere – where I cannot tell. I know I went & looked at the Exchange where he had taken me – but it was all dark, dark to me.'

The success of *The Apostles* led Frank Schuster to wonder about an Elgar Festival at Covent Garden for March 1904. H. V. Higgins of the Covent Garden syndicate put the idea to Elgar, suggesting three concerts, to include *Gerontius*, *The Apostles*, and a miscellaneous programme, perhaps with *Caractacus*: 'Does such a scheme smile upon you?'[1] The plan was that Richter should conduct, and Elgar agreed. He in his turn had a proposal for Higgins. In reaction to the vast creative effort of *The Apostles* Elgar now suggested a 'Rabelais' ballet. Higgins was intrigued, and the heading 'Rabelais' occurs now and again in Elgar's sketchbooks; but the project failed to take shape.

In London en route for Italy, Elgar was depressed. As he wrote to Atkins on 17 November, he was loth to leave Malvern and Worcester: 'I've been into the Cathedral, which I have known since I was four & said "farewell" – I wanted to see you. I am sad at heart & feel I shall never return!' With the help of 'Tomaso Cooko' the Elgars reached Bordighera in northern Italy on 28 November. The people in the hotel were 'not very enchanting'; none the less Elgar met the Archbishop of York, lending him a copy of *The Apostles* and the 'Interpretation' by Gorton. Bordighera proved to be merely an 'Anglicised paradise', the haunt of 'nursemaids calling out "*Now*, Master Johnny!"' Accordingly,

[1] Birthplace Museum.

62

the Elgars moved to the Villa San Giovanni at Alassio. The weather was villainous and the mosquitoes were troublesome; but 'E. bought some music paper Looked hapsy in his study'.

It was hoped Elgar might produce a symphony for the Covent Garden Festival, but his immediate task at Alassio was to orchestrate the op. 26 partsongs, *The Snow* and *Fly, Singing Bird* for performance by Henry Wood at Queen's Hall. Novello was now anxious to secure an exclusive contract with Elgar. Littleton broached the matter, and Elgar acknowledged the proposition on 26 December: 'I will not reply to your very sweetly expressed proposition now: this is only to thank you for the thought & for putting it so kindly before me.' It was many months before Elgar finally accepted.

At the start of 1904 it was clear the symphony would not materialize. He told Jaeger his change of plan on 3 January: 'this visit has been, is, artistically, a complete *failure* & I can do nothing: we have been *perished* with cold, rain & gales ... I am trying to finish a Concert overture instead of the Sym'. Four days later Elgar wrote to both Richter and Schuster about the overture, suggesting 'In the South' as title. Carice and Rosa Burley had joined the Elgars, and now there were visits to 'Moglio Church & back by the old mule track'; to 'Andorra by train'; to the 'Roman Bridge', and up to the church of St John the Baptist: 'shepherd there was watching his flock, sheep & goats, *lovely* sight & view'. The name 'Moglio' was transcribed into a musical phrase for the overture; place was also found for a shepherd's song and the tramp of ancient Rome. He dedicated the work to Schuster and said that he 'wove the music on a summery day in the Andora valley'.

While at Alassio, Elgar met Joseph Armitage Robinson, the Dean of Westminster. Troyte was told about the meeting: 'he is a real good sort I think & approves of much of my libretto notions & we jawed over the remainder of the Apostles which is still in the womb of time (classic phrase)'. Robinson later sent articles relevant to the project,[2] and Elgar noted many of his ideas when planning *The Kingdom*. Release from the uncertain weather of Alassio came from an unexpected quarter: Elgar was invited to dine with the Prince of Wales at Marlborough House; King Edward would be present and there was to be a 'Smoking Concert' afterwards. Elgar accepted and told Jaeger he hoped to 'bring most of the new score for you to go on with'.

The evening at Marlborough House on 3 February was enjoyable and a success: 'the King talked music to E. & took him out 1st after dinner'. The party then drove to Buckingham Palace for the concert

[2] Birthplace Museum.

by the Royal Amateur Orchestra. Elgar conducted the *Pomp and Circumstance March* no. 1, which the king immediately encored. In reply to a letter from Atkins welcoming his return, Elgar extended '*two* fingers (royally) unto you'. He ascribed the regal gesture to his 'recent frequentations!'

In the South now proceeded at Craeg Lea. On 8 February he 'wrote splendid "Romans"'. Scoring was quickly done, and the last pages were despatched on 22 February. There was now intense pressure to have everything ready for the first rehearsal in Manchester on 9 March. Four days before, 'All the Overture came for E. to correct'. Richter was insistent that Elgar must conduct *In the South*; it was indeed the only possible course, since Elgar was in possession of the score and parts till the last moment and himself took them to Manchester. Jaeger realized the importance of the Covent Garden Festival to Elgar's career, but also issued an affectionate warning: 'You *will* have festive times next week! Don't let 'em spoil you, you "dear, innocent guileless Child," as dear old Hans calls you in his fatherly, loving way.' Elgar responded on the day of the Manchester rehearsal with mock reserve: 'Dear Mr. Jaeger: The time has come when I think all familiarity between us should cease ...'. Jaeger was then urged to turn the page and read as follows: 'Dearie Moss: What an old frump you are! – whenever anything of mine is to be done you beg me not to be conceited & not to forget my old friends.'

The Elgars stayed at Schuster's for the festival. The strain took its toll on Elgar: 'dreadful headache, in bed all the morning ... Still precarious till evening'. This was on 13 March, when Schuster gave a splendid pre-festival dinner party and 'proposed E.'s health in the most touching way with his heart in his voice'. Elgar failed to reply, seeming abstracted and remote from the proceedings. The king and queen came to *Gerontius* on 14 March, as also for *The Apostles* the next evening. Queen Alexandra came alone to the first performance of *In the South*, but sent for Elgar, who reported on the royal patronage to his father: 'the King came twice & the Queen 3 times! It has all been a most gigantic success & they have made a huge fuss of me.' Nothing like it had been done for an English composer before; Jaeger had called the première of the Variations in 1899 an historical concert and could only dub this 'an Historical *week*'.

On 18 March the Elgars were guests at Lord Northampton's. Arthur Balfour, the prime minister, was there and raised the matter of a knighthood; Elgar discussed mainly the copyright laws. He pursued the matter in an interview for the *Daily News* a week later: 'While the world of fashion, as well as the middle classes – were honouring the art at Covent Garden, at the other end of the town our legislators were heaping indignities on it by whittling down the Musical Copyright Bill by inserting clauses which will make it quite inoperative.'

As token of ripening friendship, Elgar received from Alice Stuart Wortley an engraving of Cardinal Newman's portrait painted by her father, the Pre-Raphaelite John Everett Millais. Elgar acknowledged it on 25 March with real pleasure, '& we value it the more as it comes from you'. Of other 'friends' Jaeger was suspicious: 'You ought to be left alone with your work: you have enough in hand for 10 years! When will You do it if these fools & Rogues & snobs worry you so?' Elgar was always easily distracted, but for the moment it was not so much snobs as shrimps. He was stocking an aquarium for his daughter and visiting local ponds. He explained his activities to Jaeger on 1 April: 'I am up to my eyes in work & a shrimp has had a baby in my tank & between times I have to nurse them in a teaspoon!' Alice Elgar was later to record 'Atrocities going on in Aquarium'.

During April, at the proposal of Parry and Stanford, Elgar was elected to the Athenaeum Club; and at the end of the month he was again at Morecambe, where 'The Wraith of Odin' from *King Olaf* was one of the competition pieces. There were further travels when the Elgars attended a performance of *The Apostles* under Steinbach in Cologne on 22 May (Jaeger was 'quite pink with happiness'), and when Elgar received an honorary doctorate at Durham. Meanwhile Alice Elgar 'saw letter from A. J. Balfour locked it up safes'. Elgar returned from Durham on 22 June and thought initially the letter might be on the subject of copyright. 'Then he opened the letter & found H. M. was going to make him a Knight. D. G.' The next day Elgar went to his sister Pollie's at Stoke to tell his father; one of his nieces took a photograph of the occasion. The immediate result was 'between 80 & 90 telegrams', 'about 80 letters by 1st post', and further '*Shoals* of letters'. Jaeger considered the knighthood richly deserved, 'for no one can have lived a life more earnestly devoted to the highest & best & purest in life & in art'. Carice felt that Lady Elgar had regained her rightful social position.

A move from Malvern to Hereford was imminent. Elgar 'rode to Hereford most of the way', and on 1 July 1904 they spent their first night at 'Plas Gwyn'. There was sadness at Malvern and in Worcester. Rosa Burley had seen the new house and wondered whether the increased grandeur was right for a 'sensitive and highly strung artist'; she also knew joint cycle rides would be rarer. For Ivor Atkins 'This meant that the Friday meetings which had been such a feature in my life were to cease'; over the previous five years, 'as the weeks had passed, I had seen a steady succession of masterpieces unfold themselves before me'.

The Elgars had to be in London for the investiture on 5 July, when the 'King smiled charmingly & said "Very pleased to see you here Sir Edward" '. The previous evening there had been a public meeting of the Musical Defence League, at which Elgar spoke briefly and simply:

> My life, ladies and gentlemen, has, as you know, been a self-made one. London called me from my country home, and *you* have made me what I am. But you call other composers from their homes to you, and you allow the law to deprive them of their livelihood. That is all I have to say.

As a correspondent, Elgar was not in cheerful mood over the next weeks. Jaeger was told 'It's all very well to talk to me about doing Sextetts & Symphonies & all the things I *want* to do, but tell me what & who is going to keep a roof over our heads?' Richter was informed that 'Work has not yet commenced here and I sometimes wonder if I shall ever invent any more music'. He had written bitterly to Lord Northampton, who would have none of it. Just back from Bayreuth, he had seen *Parsifal*, which he found 'ennobling & soul-stirring – Its only rival is the Apostles'. He elaborated the point: 'You have moved men's souls to the highest truths of Christianity & then you say in a fit of depression "*as ever* unprofitable".'

Elgar's only original contribution to the Gloucester Festival in September was a cadenza for Harford Lloyd's Organ Concerto. An American admirer, Samuel Sanford, professor of the piano at Yale University, and recently heir to a fortune, presented Elgar with a Steinway upright; and Robert Buckley's biography of him appeared. By the end of September Novello gave striking evidence of Elgar's standing with the firm. Full scores were to be engraved of *The Black Knight*, *The Light of Life*, *King Olaf*, *The Banner of St George* and *Caractacus*. Elgar expressed his pleasure to Alfred Littleton on 15 October: 'I have been thrilled by receiving proofs of various full scores of my things & I understand that many of them are coming out: I send you an especial word of thanks.' He wrote also about Birmingham plans for 1906: 'if the new oratorio is ready *they expect it* – they will give two performances, preceded by the Apostles – 3 performances, I mean programmes to me alone!' But there were also other matters afoot at Birmingham.

Granville Bantock came to Plas Gwyn on 22 October to discuss with Elgar the foundation of a chair in music at the university of Birmingham and the possibility of Elgar's being the first professor. It was a matter that caused Elgar much agony. The university was keen on the idea. The professor of German argued the case at Plas Gwyn, then Bantock returned on 17 November with the secretary of the Midland Institute. At the time Elgar was finishing *Pomp and Circumstance* no. 3; four days later he took it to Boosey in London and then consulted Littleton about the Birmingham chair. He 'advised acceptance'. As so often in Elgar's life, a personal attraction was the deciding factor. On 25 November he was taken to see Richard Peyton, prospective founder of the chair. Elgar liked him, and the following day he accepted.

Frank Schuster had stayed with the Elgars in mid-October. He arrived in his Fiat car, and Lady Elgar noted that from an excursion to Monmouth they came back 'in 55 mins.' Schuster sent a handsome thank-you for his stay, a sundial for the Plas Gwyn garden. When acknowledging it Elgar decided it was 'very human, – it *lies* all the morning & tells the truth, repentantly, all the afternoon ... Also it is feminine & only beams & smiles in sunshine'. The following month he and Schuster went briefly to the Continent. The immediate objective was *The Apostles* at Mainz under Fritz Volbach. It was also done at Rotterdam, and then *In the South* was conducted by Steinbach in Cologne. Elgar sent Jaeger some impressions on 8 December: 'At Mainz the *real* effect of the shepherds *outside* was beautiful & quite justified my "stage direction".' This referred to the night scene in the mountain where Elgar suggested in his full score that the oboes and cor anglais should be 'Outside the Orchestra'.

Jaeger's health was giving grave concern, and his condition had so far deteriorated that he was ordered to Switzerland for the mountain air. He was dreading the journey on 11 January 1905, but three days before he left for Davos he was more concerned about Elgar: 'I fear greatly we shall get less & less out of you. This is the danger of success artistic & social! (especially social, of course).' His conclusion was that 'England *Ruins* all ARTISTS'. As if goaded to action, Elgar made a diary note, 'Strg orch piece'. This was the first mention that the Introduction and Allegro was under way. The idea had been Jaeger's. He wondered whether Elgar might not write a work to display the virtuosity of the newly formed London Symphony Orchestra. He had floated the scheme on 28 October 1904: 'Why not a brilliant *String* Scherzo, or something for those fine strings *only*? a real bring down the House *torrent* of a thing such as Bach could write ... You might even write a MODERN FUGUE for Strings.' Elgar had been at work on the Introduction and Allegro less than a fortnight when he reported progress to Jaeger on 26 January: 'I'm doing that string thing in time for the Sym. orch: concert. Intro: & Allegro – no working out part but a devil of a fugue instead. G major & the sd. divvel in G minor – with all sorts of japes & counterpoint.'

At the same time as writing the 'string piece', Elgar was sitting for a portrait by Talbot Hughes, now at the Royal College of Music. There was a further interruption for an honorary doctorate at Oxford.

Parry's Latin oration affirmed that 'in a common bond of appreciation the distant Muscovite was at one with the distant American'. The Elgars' host in Oxford was the Warden of New College, W. A. Spooner, whose delight in word-play had given the language its original 'spoonerisms'. It was not surprising they were 'Charmed with the family Spooner'. When Elgar conducted the Variations in the Sheldonian Theatre the following evening, it marked the beginning of his close association with the London Symphony Orchestra.

Parts of *Pomp and Circumstance* no. 3 had now to be corrected. The timpani part was entrusted to Lady Elgar, and she was much praised for playing 'drum part of March on brass tray with E.'s spectacle case'. Elgar then turned to the writing of a libretto for Ivor Atkins, to be called *A Hymn of Faith*. Elgar felt the subject apposite, in view of recent 'correspondence & preaching about "Do we believe?"' The Talbot Hughes portrait had also inspired him to try his hand with oils. Lady Elgar told Jaeger on 1 March that he was painting 'strange symbolical pictures a la Böcklin, & Segantini & Blake!' She thought a picture he had done 'of a river with sombre trees & a boat crossing' very suggestive, and hoped he would explain the symbolism to Jaeger.

For the double première on 8 March 1905 of the Introduction and Allegro and *Pomp and Circumstance* no. 3 Elgar was in wretched health. Lady Elgar had to go to Queen's Hall with a 'bag of restoratives'. The 'string piece' made less than its proper impression, but Jaeger heard from Lady Elgar about the thrilling qualities of the new March: 'the most pacific friends were ready to fight'. The inaugural lecture at Birmingham on 16 March seemed to have a similar effect.

Atkins from Worcester and Sinclair from Hereford were both there, and the former gave his impressions: 'The Lecture was a little discursive and largely taken up with an uncompromising survey of Music in England at that time.' It was stirring stuff, but 'as Elgar lashed out fiercely at musicians and critics alike, we both (Sinclair too) fidgeted in our seats, becoming more and more anxious as the lecture proceeded about the effect of his words in the musical world at large'. Lady Elgar claimed he held his audience breathless; Rosa Burley considered the occasion 'one of the most embarrassing failures to which it has ever been my misfortune to listen'. Parry reported that Stanford 'was in a great rage about Elgar's inaugural address'; and some months later Mackenzie was ready 'to discuss the recent pronouncements by Elgar which rouse his ire greatly – and no wonder!' When the storm broke, Elgar wrote to Jaeger that 'It really makes one disgusted with English musical life to see the way everybody (except Kalisch who heard me speak) misquotes me!' The reception of the lecture made every such further occasion a penance for Elgar. His fame caused his every word to be noted; his continuing insecurity meant that many of those words were injudicious. Yet in practical matters his advice was sound. He wanted to build up the library, suggesting the Bach and Beethoven complete editions and subscription to series in course of publication, such as the volumes of the Purcell Society.

At Hereford Elgar acquired a new confidant. It was on 15 May that Carice and her cousin May Grafton 'brought up lovely white "Peter rabbit"', named after Beatrix Potter's creation, 'who was very naughty'. Elgar took Peter most seriously, purchasing a book about the keeping of rabbits, later elevating him to adapter of texts and dedicatee of his music. That first day the Elgars 'played about with Peter all the aftn. everybody!' When Ivor Atkins came to try the *Hymn of Faith*, Elgar was busy making a hutch.

Professor Sanford was anxious that the Elgars should make a first visit to the United States and that Elgar should receive an honorary doctorate at Yale. The idea of the States did not greatly attract Elgar, and he was determined that any work he did there should be well paid. He had made this clear in a letter to Littleton about possible concerts there in 1906: 'I will not go for less than Weingartner who has £2,500 (not dollars) for sixteen concerts: they can either take me or leave me.' Before departure on 8 June they had again attended the Morecambe Festival, where *King Olaf* had been splendidly performed.

Initially they were 'Much impressed with N. York – & Harbour & magnificent river'. The most important of the new acquaintances was Julia Worthington, who was not only a generous hostess to them in New York but became also a close friend. The degree ceremony was on 28 June, at which the 'Meditation' from *The Light of Life* and *Pomp and Circumstance* no. 1 were played on the organ. There were negotiations with Cincinnati that Elgar should conduct at their 1906 festival. These were also pursued by Novello, who were told of 'authorization to engage Sir Elgar's services for the sum of *one thousand pounds*'. Novello corrected the figure to £1500. As the American visit neared its end, the New York summer and its humidity became increasingly intolerable. Elgar was so worn down he told Littleton, 'I doubt if there will be anything of me to sail'. They began the journey home on 11 July, accompanied by flying fish, porpoises, a shark, and Professor Sanford.

Musically there was little to show for the summer. Jaeger wondered whether he would be writing an analysis for the sequel to *The Apostles*. To this Elgar replied brusquely: 'I know nothing about Apostles pt. 2. or any analysis: if it is ever finished I imagined you might take on the analysis *if* properly recompensed.' In the middle of the month Elgar began sketching a setting of Callicles's final song from Matthew

Arnold's *Empedocles on Etna*. It was a project that engaged Elgar's attention repeatedly, but the planned music was diverted to other works, such as *The Music Makers, The Spanish Lady* and the Third Symphony. Jaeger tried again on 25 August, saying that Alexander Siloti had requested first performance of the 'symphony': 'I wish I could lift the veil surrounding that much talked of & long expected Symphony.' Instead Elgar produced a partsong, the *Evening Scene* to words by Coventry Patmore. He told Littleton it was 'quite a short thing & will do for artistic singers but I fear it's not a gold mine & it certainly isn't a pot boiler'.

Elgar's boyhood friend Hubert Leicester was now mayor of Worcester. He was determined to demonstrate local appreciation by offering him the Freedom of the City. The ceremony on 12 September was fixed to coincide with the opening of the Three Choirs Festival. Canon Gorton was there, arrayed Elgar in his Yale gown and praised Leicester as 'a king among mayors' when writing to his wife in Morecambe; he admired the 'lightness of touch & happy phrasing' in Elgar's speech, and noted there had been only '8 Freemen, the first was Lord Nelson'. Elgar had paid eloquent tribute to his mother: 'I was brought up in a knowledge of literature and English and many of the things which my mother said to me I have tried to carry out in my music.' His father watched the procession from above the shop, and Elgar stopped briefly as a sign of respect. There followed a performance of *Gerontius* in the cathedral. At the Wednesday evening concert Parry heard the Introduction and Allegro for the first time, finding it 'very ecstatic with the usual rits. and accelerandos and spasms'.

Frank Schuster was at the festival, and told Elgar about a cruise he was joining as guest of Lord Charles Beresford, commander-in-chief of the Mediterranean fleet. An invitation came for Elgar too and after some hesitation he accepted. Elgar's absence allowed his wife to invoke assistance from Jaeger: 'Now could you, without trouble, help me in this. I am anxious to Collect all Edward's sketches, rough Copies &c, together, as I know they are of great interest.' In his reply Jaeger touched on the splendour of Elgar's fame: 'The triumph is *yours* no less than his!' He knew what stimulus Elgar would get from the distant view of Athens and the Acropolis: 'Only! – What about "Apostles Part III" for B'ham next year? I begin to fear that we shall hope in vain to see our soaring expectations fulfilled.'

The Mediterranean was indeed stimulating, and Elgar kept a diary for the month he was away. The fortifications of Corfu reminded him of Böcklin. At Phalerus there were seventeen ships of the British navy, and as they left on the *Surprise* Elgar took a 'long, long look, for the last time' at the Acropolis. On board Elgar wanted some shin of beef, and language difficulties forced him to show the steward his shin: 'What a good thing you hadn't wanted rump-steak.' At Lemnos the fleet made a '*grand* noise anchoring'. There was a lovely journey to Çannakale, 'Passing Troy & the Hellespont'. A delicate political situation now meant transfer to an Austrian liner for the passage to Istanbul. Dolphins kept up with them, but they rammed a large local boat, causing eight men to drown. On 25 September there was a 'Glorious sunrise. & the minarets of Stamboul began to come into the mist – wonderful! wonderful!' The evening was equally impressive: 'in the sunset the Bosphorus & Stamboul were insanely beautiful'. The weather was such that Elgar thought providence 'kinder to Moslems than to Xtians'.

They were at Smyrna, the modern Izmir, on the last day of the month. Elgar was much excited by the bazaar: 'This was my first touch with Asia. & I was quite overcome. the endless camels made the scene more *real* than in Stamboul. the extraordinary colour & movement, light & shade were intoxicating.' After visiting the tomb of St Polycarp, they dined with the commander-in-chief on the *Bulwark*, where the band played *Sérénade lyrique* and *Salut d'amour*. Elgar noted that Smyrna was one of the seven churches of the book of *Revelation*; but after lunch the next day they 'drove to the Mosque of dancing dervishes'. Officials of the small mosque received them in style: 'Music by five or six people very strange & some of it quite beautiful – incessant drums & cymbals (small) thro' the quick movements'. The dancing was less exciting. When they left Smyrna on 3 October the weather broke: 'Awful squalls all day. Awnings taken down. Everyone ill.' They left the *Surprise* at Patras, and from Corfu on 8 October there were the 'last views of Greece & the isles like clouds floating in a large sky'.

Elgar reached London on 12 October. Immediately he went to the 'East End & tried to get Eastern food'; 'then back to this dreary civilization'. Elgar's displeasure found vent the next day in an ill-tempered letter to Gorton about Ernest Newman: 'I do hope you will throw him over entirely: his influence is bad (& despicable) on all with whom he comes in contact.'[3] This was to some extent coloured by Newman's dismissive view of *The Apostles*, which Elgar was about to conduct in Norwich: 'and the last music I had heard was the Dervishes in Smyrna!' Fritz Kreisler, the Austrian violinist, was also to play at the Norwich Festival. While Elgar was still abroad Kreisler had given an interview to the press: 'If you want to know whom I consider to be the greatest living composer, I say without hesitation, Elgar.' The

[3] Birthplace Museum.

immediate result at Plas Gwyn was that Elgar made sketches for a violin concerto, already defining themes that would go into the completed op. 61. The sketches were dated 22 October 1905 and presented to Kreisler 'with admiration and gratitude' about the time of the first performance in November 1910. There were pre-echoes also of the Second Symphony. Elgar told Ivor Atkins about a theme he'd called 'Hans himself!' in honour of Richter; it was to feature largely in the Symphony's finale.

Jaeger was again ordered to Davos for his health. Elgar wondered on 29 October whether Schuster might provide 'Nimrod' with a fur coat: 'It does not matter how old or shabby it is as he doesn't want it to show off (poor dear) but only to slumber in out of doors.' He added that he was 'killed with the University'. An offer that Elgar prudently declined came from the corporation of Hereford. They held out to him 'the highest honour in their power', the mayoralty. Elgar asked Hubert Leicester whether his being a Catholic would cause problems, but then decided the duties were both honorary and arduous. A new interest began to surface before the end of the month; on 30 October he went into town and 'bought chemicals'.

The first of the Birmingham lectures was on 1 November. Elgar spoke on 'English Composers', making the point that they had achieved little respect abroad. The fact that Elgar himself had won considerable renown made his views seem insensitive, even mischievous, and Stanford was sufficiently irked to counter them in *The Times*. A second lecture on 8 October dealing with the Third Symphony of Brahms was less controversial, though critics were bewildered that Elgar should make such a strong case for absolute music when most of his own works had been illustrative.

Music for the *Apostles* sequel was shaping, and Elgar played some of the 'new tunes' at Frank Schuster's in the presence of the Stuart Wortleys. But the lectures were not the only distraction. He was now booked for a conducting tour with the London Symphony Orchestra. Brahms's Third Symphony was one of the main works on the programmes, and after the Manchester performance Adolph Brodsky, who had given the première of the Tchaikovsky Violin Concerto with Richter, 'came in weeping saying Oh if Brahms cd. have heard yr. rendering, there cd. be nothing more poetic'. From Birmingham Elgar wrote 'in wretched spirits' on 22 November; and that day Dorabella arrived at Plas Gwyn. Elgar returned the following midday, tired and with a bad cold. The 'Apostles' project was now a major worry. But that evening, in a highly nervous state, he worked hard at Mary's soliloquy in what was to be Scene IV of *The Kingdom*. Dorabella described the tension in the house.

Tea was put outside the study door, but Elgar took none. Over dinner he said nothing, then 'banged the study door and turned the key'. Later Dorabella and Lady Elgar made tea: 'While we were drinking our tea we heard the piano at last! ... It was really most wonderful hearing the scene as it grew, phrase by phrase: once a reminder of something in *The Apostles* – the Lady and I looked at one another – and then it was all new again.' Eventually the music stopped and they heard the key turn: ' "Hullo! You still up? and Dorabella? and tea! Oh, my giddy aunt! This is good!" ' Elgar then asked Dorabella to turn over for him, while he played through the evening's work. She saw the words, 'The sun goeth down; Thou makest darkness, and it is night'.

The next day Elgar's cold and depression were worse, and on 26 November Lady Elgar felt that the fate of the new oratorio was 'trembling in the balance'. Elgar again had to compile a lecture, on 'English Executants' for 29 November. He began concentrated work on it only the day before. The result was hectic activity the following morning: 'E. frantically busy with lecture, A. & May writing it out till time to start. Worked all the way in train.' Two days later Robert Buckley came to Plas Gwyn 're storm raised by misleading quotations from E's lecture'. Lady Elgar was now afraid he would be assassinated. There was solace in the chemical experiments, which he demonstrated to his neighbour, Count Lubienski. But there was only a week between the lectures, and the rushed preparations were repeated when the subject for 6 December was 'Critics'. Back in Hereford Elgar discovered a remote spot that was to inspire much music. He and Carice went for a walk on 7 December and 'found old bridge in Lugg meadows'. 'Mordiford Bridge' was a name inscribed on more than one sketch. The last lecture of the current series, 'Retrospect', was given on 13 December, prepared with less haste and causing less controversy.

Next day Lady Elgar reported to the ailing Jaeger in Switzerland that 'now he is turning to Music again which is a great joy'. She also made a rare reference to Peter Rabbit: 'he is a very dear person & has a hot water bottle every night for fear he shd. be cold!' Elgar, in better spirits, wrote to Schuster about Carice and his theory about his own origin from the Scandinavian 'aelf-gar': 'Carice is going to a fancy dress ball & will personify her own name – Elgar – the fairy-spear. Can I hire for her, *for little* price, a nice looking spear with an electric light at the end which she could put on & off?' Charles Kenyon, who wrote under the pseudonym 'Gerald Cumberland', was at Plas Gwyn on 23 December, and a week later Lady Elgar had some suggestions for the article he submitted. She enlarged on 'one of the contradictions you mark in the outset', and continued: 'although devoted to Nature &

73

the Country (& from wh. he could bear no *long* separation) he keenly enjoys the Society & higher Social recreations which await him in great Cities & is equally at home in the house of Princes as in the fields'.[4]

For the new oratorio Elgar already had some scenes drafted. The Dean of Westminster had sent proofs of his article on the 'History of the Apostolic Age' in *The Cambridge Companion to the Bible*. In this Elgar noted the essential distinction between the formation of 'Jewish Christian Churches' and 'Churches wholly or in Part Gentile'. Armitage Robinson dealt first with the 'Church within the Walls of Jerusalem'. For this section Elgar had music that was originally to have appeared in Part III of *The Apostles*. There was already a start to Scene I incorporating part of the 'O sacrum convivium' antiphon. Some of Scene III, 'Pentecost', and the 'Lord's Prayer' were also legacies from the 1903 plan. Yet at the end of the year, when writing to Walford Davies on 31 December, Elgar was again in low spirits about the project: 'I am the same depressed (musically) being & the same very much alive (chemically & every other 'ally) mortal; keen for everything except my avocation, which I feel is not my vocation by a long tract of desert.'

On 4 January 1906 Elgar sent to Novello 'the first scrap of the new work'. This was the section starting at cue 18, which was to have begun Part III of *The Apostles*. Elgar now decided on a radiant and glowing Prelude for the new work; its sketches contained also acid stains from chemical experiments, but he despatched it on 12 January. Despite considerable progress, five days later Elgar was 'Turning against his work'. Yet he was pleased to hear that Novello was sending proofs to Jaeger: 'I am so delighted to know that the firm send the stuff on to you. So far it is the best thing I've done *I know*.' Despite Elgar's apparent optimism and lining up of friends such as Alice Stuart Wortley and Frank Schuster to receive and admire proofs, Lady Elgar had to deal with a major crisis on 29 January. She now had to undertake another mission to Novello and the Birmingham chairman. Elgar wanted to give up the work altogether but 'then E. said A. might say he hoped to do half'. Alfred Littleton now lived at Hatteral, within easy reach of Plas Gwyn, and proved sympathetic. Mr Johnstone was 'Very nice about it all and ready to accept a morning's part instead of a whole day'. Elgar's present scheme would take him nowhere near what he had originally planned for *The Apostles*.

Towards the end of March Lady Elgar was busy settling what switches and plugs would be needed at Plas Gwyn for the arrival of

[4] Birthplace Museum.

electricity. Then she was back at a musical task, preparing full score pages by 'ruling &c all the available proofs'. Elgar was by then completing St Peter's sermon, and sent the end of Scene III to Novello on 27 March. They left Liverpool for the States on 6 April. The shipboard company was dull. They were placed at the captain's table, '& who next us but Prof. King terrible bore – A. most discouraging to him – Soon ceased talking to her'. There was rough weather but Elgar found a sheltered spot for them to watch the turbulent sea: 'Gorgeous sight. Crested waves like snow mountains, flying rainbows, bars & ponds of emerald.' It was thick fog as they approached New York, but Sanford met them.

At Cincinnati there were 'crowds of reporters & photographers. E. not very gracious'. On 18 April he was at a choral rehearsal of *The Apostles*: 'Chorus knew their parts but very unpoetical & not as if they understood the words. E. *very* kind & good.' In spite of noise at the Country Club where they stayed, Elgar began orchestration of the new oratorio and probably completed Scene I during his time in the States. There were rehearsals of the Introduction and Allegro and of *Gerontius*. The orchestra was initially recalcitrant in the first, and soloists did not know their parts for the second. On 1 May came news that Elgar's father had died. Schuster wrote that 'there is no sting in *such* a death, and it is perhaps as well that the long farewell was spoken when you thought it only an "auf wiedersehen"'. After a trip to Niagara ('down by lift & went underneath') and meeting with Andrew Carnegie in New York, the Elgars left for England on 18 May.

It was a fine afternoon on the way to Hereford: 'the Church bells sounded so sweet & lovely sounding across fields as we stopped at the little country stations'. With the Birmingham commission weighing heavily upon him, Elgar now suggested to Hubert Leicester that the county might like him as its Unionist parliamentary candidate. The idea got no further. Birmingham did not yet know the title of the new work, but with Littleton's help a decision was made for 'The Kingdom'. With two more scenes to write, Elgar seemed 'unfit for anything'. His doctor ordered him to New Radnor in Wales, where he 'began a little composing' and wrote the introduction to Scene IV. Encouragement came from Arthur Benson, who had just heard *The Apostles* and called Elgar 'a great magician, like Merlin, like Virgil', thinking of him 'in the isle full of noises, sounds & sweet airs &c where you dwell with such as Prospero'. In a letter of 25 June Elgar explained to Littleton that he would finish composition by the end of July, the new sections could be printed in August, and the chorus could learn them in September. Then Elgar slipped and injured his knee. He told Benson he was temporarily 'minus one arm & one leg & much brain!' Despite this setback, which necessitated an immediate return to Hereford, Elgar kept to his timetable. Julia Worthington and Professor Sanford were both at Plas Gwyn in the first half of July, but Lady Elgar ensured *The Kingdom* should be protected even from Jaeger: 'the new work will be about his best, and in time convincing even to pagans, but you must PLEASE not worry or hurry him in any way'. Composition was finished on 23 July, and on the following afternoon Elgar walked with Carice to Mordiford Bridge, 'Very serene at conclusion of this part of the work'.

A visit to London included lunch with Professor Sanford, when fellow guests were the eminent singers Caruso (who had been performing in *Tosca*), Tosti and Maurel. Orchestration of *The Kingdom* was resumed on 29 July, and Elgar reached p. 362 of the full score, the end of the work, on 31 August. The title page contained a quotation from the Canadian poet, Bliss Carman: 'I would write "A Music that seems never to have known / Dismay, nor haste, nor wrong".' In its composition *The Kingdom* had certainly known both dismay and haste; the wonder is that it suffered so little from them. Jaeger was to write his analysis of the work, and in a letter of 24 July Elgar mentioned a further 'Apostles' instalment: 'You might hint that perhaps a further section is contemplated (it's partly written) dealing with the church of the Gentiles.' Elgar had many libretto ideas for such a continuation, but musically there existed only brief sketches for a 'Simon Magus' scene.[5]

The first orchestral rehearsal of *The Kingdom* was at Manchester on 25 September: 'The players broke into uncontrollable applause now & again & Dr Richter sd. when A. asked him if he were zufrieden – "Zufrieden, aber es ist wieder ein grosses Werk grossartig"' ('satisfied, but again it is a great work, sublime'). For the first performance at Birmingham on 3 October 1906 there was an 'Enormous audience. Some standing room (guinea each) allotted'; there had been 'a special train from London'. Frank Schuster expressed the view of those to whom the 'Apostles' project was of major significance: 'You have been entrusted with one of the greatest messages ever sent to mankind. Do not falter, do not fail, but God willing, go on and deliver it unto the end.' Ernest Newman, now appointed to the *Birmingham Daily Post*, expressed forcibly an opposing view: 'The wisest thing for him to do now is to abandon the idea of a third oratorio on the subject and turn his mind to other themes. These may bring him new

---

[5] See Robert Anderson, 'Elgar's Magus and Projector' in *Elgar Studies*, ed. R. Monk (Aldershot, 1990), pp. 118–33.

inspiration and a new idiom; at present he is simply riding post-haste along the road that leads to nowhere.'

Reaction set in, and by the end of October Elgar was 'dreadfully depressed'. Further university lectures were scheduled. On 1 November he spoke about 'Orchestration'; the morning involved 'Copying by A. at white heat of haste'. What was to be the last of Elgar's Birmingham lectures, on Mozart's Symphony no. 40 in G minor, caused even more distress. He went to Birmingham alone on 8 November, and returned 'most wretched. Small room, more people than cd. well find place – no light for piano &c&c&c'. A visit to London included Puccini's *Tosca* and *Fedora* by Giordano at the opera, and Bernard Shaw's *Man and Superman* at the Court Theatre. Elgar's eyes were again giving serious trouble, with inflamed lids. He was ordered to rest them and therefore to give up Birmingham lectures for the time being. Depression lifted at once. He wrote to Sir Oliver Lodge, principal of the university, offering to 'pay back stipend & resign'. Lodge replied that he need only get better.

Elgar decided on a Welsh cure at Llandrindod Wells. On 8 December he and Lady Elgar tried 'to find Roman remains but they seem to have disappeared'. He recounted his experiences to Sidney Colvin, Keeper of Prints and Drawings at the British Museum. Some aspects of the cure had been weird: 'we met like ghouls in the pumproom at 7.30 a.m. in the dark: mysterious & strange; hooded & cloaked we quaffed smoking brine & sulphur & walked thro' dim-lit woods, sometimes in snow'. Still Elgar was little better, and it seemed essential to go further afield and try Italy again. On Christmas Day Elgar wrote of their decision to Atkins: 'Our plans have been upset, revised, coddled, altered, married, rebuilt, rejuvenated, & a lot more. Now it is settled that Alice & I go on the *Orontes* on Friday.'

The destination was Naples, and they departed on 28 December via Gibraltar and Marseilles. A main pleasure of Naples was the proximity of Canon Gorton, who was acting as chaplain to the English church on Capri. There were joint expeditions to Pompeii, 'great billiards' in the evening, and much interest in the feeding of an octopus at the aquarium. But Naples was cold and they decided for a month on Capri. There Elgar struck up novel musical friendships, as he explained to Carice: 'I have been playing duets & trios with the barbers'. Initially he had played violin to a barber's mandoline; then a second barber came with a guitar. Inspired by their performance, Elgar wrote 19 bars of a trio for the unlikely combination and inscribed it 'for the *Barbers*'. There were walks to Anacapri, where on one occasion Elgar was found 'pale & shivering', to the Villa Tiberio, and to Axel Munthe's 'San Michele'; Vesuvius was snow-capped, the winds were keen and Elgar had a '1st Arsenic' treatment for his throat. A telegram had come from Carice, and on 26 January Elgar wrote her a playful letter: 'The first word in your telegram is "bln" & I have adopted it: when anything happens, – nothing ever does happen here apparently – I shall say "Bln". It's difficult to say & may mean anything awful but still I will say *BLN*.' The Elgars left for Rome on 12 February, staying with the Slingsby Bethells, their hosts of previous years in Garmisch.

There was to be another American tour in 1907, and when the Elgars returned to Plas Gwyn on 26 February, it was imminent. This time Elgar went alone, to conduct the oratorios in New York and an orchestral concert in Chicago. He departed on 2 March. On arrival Elgar sent a cable containing the word 'anemone'. This may have been a code word for their separation, referring back to Alice Elgar's poem *Fly, Singing Bird*, and in particular to the lines

> Say I wait where anemones blow,
> Weary wait, till with waiting, I
> Fail, and failing, I sigh.

Elgar never took much pleasure in America. He wrote to Mrs Gorton from New York on 14 April: 'After our sweet & delightful time in Capri it is a hideous change to be in Western America: here, in New York, I have that dear & wonderful woman, Mrs Worthington, to speak to: she sends her love.' Julia Worthington was vividly described by the father of the poet, W. B. Yeats: 'She is a sort of Duchess over here. Socially clever and a friend to all the distinguished people – She is an intimate friend of the musician Elgar.' He was in Hereford again on 27 April, and Lady Elgar could hardly contain her delight: 'Such intense joy to have E. back – must look & touch again & again to be sure it is real.'

There was the Morecambe Festival once more at the beginning of May, and by now Elgar was 'rather tired of it all'. None the less he enjoyed the male-voice singing of 'Yea, Cast me from the Heights' from the *Greek Anthology* partsongs. Before the end of the month composition was resumed. For inspiration Elgar turned to some of his early church music, refining an *Ave Maria* and *Ave maris stella* as companion pieces for the *Ave verum corpus* of op. 2. Elgar wrote affectionately of them to Littleton: 'They are tender little plants so treat them kindly whatever is their fate.' The approach of his fiftieth birthday on 2 June 1907 seemed little cause for rejoicing, as he told Jaeger: 'I have my pipe & the bicycle & a heavenly country to ride in – so an end. I take no interest in music now & just "edit" a few old boyish M.S.S. – music is off.' This was far from true, even though Elgar had a new distraction in a boomerang. The birthday was 'Trying to him as usual', but he used it to compose the partsong *Love*, with words by Arthur Maquarie. Elgar wrote 'C.A.E. on it – wh. made A. feel very unworthy & deeply deeply touched'. The end of the poem expressed all too accurately Elgar's precarious dependence on his wife:

> Let me ever gaze on thee,
> Lest I lose warm hope and so
> Cease to be.

Pomp and Circumstance no. 4 was also shaping. To Jaeger Elgar described the first part of the march as 'good: the middle *rot* but pleasing to march to'.

The day after completing the march, 'E. started bicycling, perhaps towards London'. Wind and storms held him up at Stratford-on-Avon and eventually made him abandon the attempt. From London the Elgars went on to Cambridge for a performance of *The Kingdom* in King's College Chapel. This was the occasion when Elgar said to Arthur Benson 'that it was no sort of pleasure to him to hear "The Kingdom", because it was so far behind what he had dreamed of – it only caused him shame and sorrow'. He asked for a seat near the door, so that 'he might rush out if overcome'.

The nostalgia that turned Elgar to his early church pieces was further nourished by a gift from his brother Frank of 'the old iron chest' that had been in the family home. Elgar worked on it so that 'the colours came out wonderfully'. He set about investigating his very earliest music, connected with the play the Elgar children had hoped might convince the 'Two Old People' that the fairyland this side of a brook was superior to the conventional world. In the midst of shaping the little tunes towards the *Wand of Youth* suites, Elgar was also playing on 27 June the 'great beautiful tune' that was to form the 'motto' of the First Symphony; and on 2 August Elgar wrote a '*lovely* river piece. You cd. hear the wind in the rushes by the water'. This, too, was to play an important part in op. 55.

Elgar received an honorary MA at Birmingham on 6 July ('Delightful Neville Chamberlain', the future prime minister, was a fellow dinner guest); and Ernest Walker from Oxford, 'not mad about Nature' nor 'a thrilling visitor' but busy with *A History of Music in England*, came to Hereford for a night. For the moment the 'Children's Music' remained Elgar's chief concern. Originally designed as one suite, the pieces multiplied so that it seemed advisable to split the work into two. The first suite was finished on 11 August, and Littleton took it away to Hatteral. Lady Elgar explained that it was known as 'Brown paper music', 'as it has been carried upstairs at night in brown paper & never had a case like other ops'. A ten-day holiday in Wales ended with a hilarious journey back to Hereford on 22 August: 'Slow train – E. & C. had riotous games & E. fell full length along the bottom of the train! A. laughed so much she cd. not even urge him to rise before some one came down the corridor.' The Elgars went on to 'The Hut', Frank Schuster's house on the Thames near Maidenhead. There Elgar played the *Wand of Youth* music to Henry Wood, who gave suite no. 1 its first performance on 14 December.

During the Gloucester Festival the Elgars called on Hubert Parry, who lived nearby. Soon after, Elgar heard Parry's *A Vision of Life* and was greatly impressed, sending him a copy of the vocal score he had marked with some suggestions. Parry said he would 'meditate gratefully' on the criticisms and was himself conscious of 'inadequacies'. He recalled seeing Sir John Millais 'sitting under the trees in Kensington Gardens smoking his pipe', in a bad mood because there was 'a bit in that picture I can't get right – and it's no use shirking it'. Elgar hoped Nicholas Kilburn might perform *A Vision of Life* and recommended it also to Atkins: 'Will it not· do for Worcester? I don't know if the jarring creeds episode wd be grateful to a Dean and Chapter. Oh! ye priests.'

Littleton had been at Plas Gwyn on 22 September. On that occasion 'E. played booful new things to him – Vio.Concert. &c.& the *gorgeous new tune*'. This was again the opening of the First Symphony, as a later annotation makes clear. In Birmingham for a Richter concert on 16 October, the Elgars heard a 'Fervent appeal to E. to finish the Sinfonie – dear noble old man'. In fact Elgar approached the Symphony by a seemingly devious route. The Elgars heard the Brodsky Quartet in Malvern on 26 October, and he began the writing of a string quartet the same day. Surviving drafts of the quartet, which occupied Elgar through much of November, make clear that material of its 'Scherzo' and slow movement were transferred directly to the Symphony.

The winter was to be spent in Italy, and in London on the way Elgar attended a 'Most dreadfully dull' dinner given by the Worshipful Company of Musicians and saw *The Devil's Disciple* by Bernard Shaw, whom he thought 'very *amateurish* in many ways'. The play had scenery by Troyte Griffith, with whom Elgar had recently been in correspondence about a gravestone for his parents: 'As we bear an old Saxon name wd. it be too fanciful, if practicable, to take some Saxon thing for a model or rather type?' The party for Italy consisted of the three Elgars and May Grafton, and they arrived in Rome on 7 November. Elgar put his name down for French lessons at the Berlitz school, and his textbook has survived at the Birthplace. Lesson 12 inspired him to write in the bottom margin '*He not there has nothing of what*!!!', and he put five marginal lines as comment against another questionable proposition: 'Les animaux aiment généralement leurs petits, mais l'amour de notre mère est bien plus fort.' The sights were a constant enchantment, with vespers at St Peter's, 'as it was the anniversary of the dedication, & the relics were exposed', the Colosseum and Arch of Constantine by moonlight, and San Giovanni Laterano, where it was 'Lovely in the Cloisters – Monuments &c very trying'. Memories of Forli, the Elgars' first Malvern home, suggested a visit to the sacristy at St Peter's 'to see the Melozzo da Forli angels'.

Elgar wrote to Littleton on 23 November about the 'glorious view' from the flat at 38 Via Gregoriana: 'it is really one of the best situations in Rome & the walks on the Pincian are at our door'. He was uncertain how much work he would achieve: 'there are "voices most vociferous" & pianos most pianiferous in the street which is otherwise quiet'. Elgar had made two important decisions by 3 December 1907, the date of another letter to Littleton. He had been considering the matter of the third oratorio for the 1909 Birmingham Festival and now told Littleton he had 'written definitely & finally to give up the idea'. His other decision was to transform whatever was serviceable from the string quartet into the long-awaited First Symphony. Lady Elgar wrote on 9 December to Jaeger, now too ill even for Switzerland: 'He loves his Rome very much & loves going for long exploring walks, one day impressed by the Palatine, going back to the wonderful days of the Caesars, another day to the wonderful Churches & *their* associations.' She also mentioned the Symphony: 'When Pianos &c allow of any quiet, E. has been writing, & I TRUST you will hear the Symphony, yet, & many times.'

With his decisions made, Elgar characteristically turned elsewhere, to the writing of partsongs. For F. G. Edwards of *The Musical Times* he set *How Calmly the Evening*, a poem by T. T. Lynch. Alice Elgar provided the words of the op. 52 *Christmas Greeting* written for the boys of Hereford Cathedral with accompaniment for two violins and piano. There were also two marching songs, one written at Littleton's suggestion to words by de Courcy Stretton, the other a 'Manuscritto Racommandato' that set Bret Harte's *The Reveille* at the urging of W. G. McNaught. He completed the year with the four partsongs of op. 53, to words by Tennyson, Byron, Shelley, and himself. The last was called *Owls*, and he dedicated it to Carice's now Italianate white rabbit, Pietro d'Alba.

Quite by chance Elgar heard on 30 December that A. C. Benson had been in Rome for a fortnight and was leaving the following day; he asked him to call after dinner, and Benson wrote an account of the visit:

Elgar

E. in dress clothes – we were not – came eagerly out to fetch us in ... He looked well, with his pale face, high-bridged nose, quick movements. But he said his eyes were weak & he cd. only work an hour a day. With all his pleasantness & some savoir faire, one feels instinctively that he is socially always a little *uneasy* – he has got none of Parratt's courtesy or Parry's geniality ...

Lady E. *very* kind but without charm, & wholly conventional, though pathetically anxious to be *au courant* with a situation ...

... E. lighted us down the long stairs. The worst thing about him is the limp shake of his thin hand, wh. gives a feeling of great want of stamina.

5

Massive hope and elevated mood (1908–1911)

The Symphony was started, but how far it progressed before the Elgars left Rome on 5 May 1908 is unclear. Lady Elgar's and Carice's diaries make no mention of it. The New Year had hardly begun when May Grafton was summoned home to her father, who was gravely ill. Will Grafton died soon after. Julia Worthington arrived, now known as 'Pippa' after Browning's drama *Pippa Passes* (it was probably Gorton who gave her the name; he was something of a Browning expert). In the second half of January Elgar was 'laid up for a fortnight with severe cold & influenza'. Then Lady Elgar went down, so that the only musical activity reported by the end of February was correction of partsong proofs. There were opera visits in March, twice to Rossini's *Barbiere*, then *Tosca* and *Die Meistersinger* in Italian; in Florence they saw an 'inane' new work, *Fausta* by Bianchi. After a week in Florence, they returned to Rome on 3 April. There was a general strike in the city, about which Elgar wrote to May Grafton on 8 April: 'Only *one* private carriage ventured out on Friday (Princess Roastpig I think) & the Minister for War sent a message to say if she *must* go out he wd. send an escort with her – but she had better not!' This was Princess Rospigliosi, on whom Lady Elgar called.

The Brodsky Quartet, perhaps hoping for a new work by Elgar, gave concerts in Rome from 11 April. After a family expedition with Pippa to the Villa d'Este and the Villa Adriana, Elgar wrote to Atkins in some financial gloom: 'Things do not pay, alas! I do not mind this for *myself* & wd gladly throw over the whole ghastly phase of respectability to be able to write my big things.' On 23 April Elgar saw the musical treasures owned by Giovanni Sgambati, protégé of Liszt. He described them in a letter to Jaeger:

> Sgambati (dear man) has some wonderful things – given him by Liszt the first copy of the score Siegfried Idyll sent by Wagner to Liszt in Rome with a little writing on the title. Also the first *exemplum* of *Faust* Berlioz sent by B to Liszt! & above all (1868) the full score Meistersinger sent by W. to L. with words on the title 'De profundis clamavi!' at the top a date &c. below & *Richard*. How wonderful to see & touch.

Before leaving Rome Elgar wrote to Atkins, wondering whether he would like him to conduct the second *Wand of Youth* suite at the 1908 Worcester Festival. This was to be a first performance, and he would also 'write a few notes for the programme book'.

The Elgars arrived at Tilbury on 16 May. On returning to Hereford, Elgar took instant pleasure in his home and countryside, though there was a sign of things to come on 1 June: 'E. depressed about bicycling on account of Motors.' Jaeger had less than a year to live; but his importance as Elgar's musical confidant and most perceptive critic was again demonstrated in the ten days that led up to work on the Symphony. He was always ready to counter gloom, and on 13 June he wrote a fine letter to Lady Elgar, touching on the op. 53 partsongs, and underlining Elgar's essential greatness as he saw it: 'These pieces are so much more than stereotyped partsongs. They are wonders, pieces of E's very being, of his heart and soul.' His reaction to Elgarian depression was forthright: 'E. MUST be great in his works, & great in his contempt of the world which may not repay him as is his due.' Jaeger had recently heard Delius's *Appalachia*, which he considered a typical example 'of the crazy "colour" school'. By contrast he saw Elgar's development 'more and more as a strong, original melodist'. Forgetting for the moment even his 'own' variation and risking offence to Lady Elgar, Jaeger continued:

> To me E. has only begun his career as a *great* man, as a genius. Excepting, say, the prologue to 'King Olaf' (one of the finest things I know), his early works (before Gerontius) do not sound the note of *Genius*. Gerontius & the 2 oratorios are full of it. So I look forward to E's future with high hopes.

That day, 13 June, marked also the first mention in Lady Elgar's diary of the work in progress: 'E. writing beautiful Symphony; and June 1908 was the fiftieth anniversary of the Indian Mutiny's collapse, so that her father General Roberts was once more resurrected in the British press. Elgar was engrossed in the Symphony for the rest of the month. Diary entries plot the course of the work: 'E. wrote all day, possessed with his Symphony' (29 June); 'E. loth to Go & leave his Symphony & the baby bunny' (2 July, when leaving for London); at The Hut 'E. played his Symphony. F. quite wild with enthusiasm. Max Beerbohm there too' (5 July); 'E. settling down to his Symphony again' (8 July, when back in Hereford). He wrote on 13 July to Antonio de Navarro about his attitude to the new work: 'I am busy with a symphony – twenty years ago I should have thoughtlessly said "my" symphony: but I have lived long enough to know nothing is mine – certainly not the sounds one is permitted to weave together.'

On 15 July he wrote his programme note for *Wand of Youth* suite no. 2, and also thought over the Roman experience in a letter to Walford Davies: 'Rome was deeply interesting to me & I long to return: but I could not reconstruct the ancient period or the renaissance: I could only efface the present by peopling the place with folk living from 1650 to 1800. Evelyn, Horace Walpole etc. etc.' A contemporary letter to Troyte again took up the matter of a tombstone for his parents: 'can't I have something nice? must two honest old burghers have a *trade*-memento – bought by the dozen?' He wrote again on 19 July, mentioning Shaw's *Getting Married* that he had recently and pleasurably seen and the Symphony as viewed by Peter Rabbit: 'Do come over: I am writing heavenly music (!) & it will do you good to hear it & Peter's criticisms are rather monotonous & samey although I can have no doubt they are sound: yours would come fresh.' Below the signature he added the remark: '"Most prayers are inverted imprecations" – are they?' He continued in high Miltonic vein: 'It was very hot & riding we felt like ghosts of hippogriffs grazing charred grass upon the meads of hell.'

Elgar on top creative voltage was as apt for verbal as for musical wonders. On 19 July he sent F. G. Edwards, who lived at Potters Bar, some notes on the new *Wand of Youth* suite and made further exuberant sallies: 'Who was Potter & why did he possess a Bar?' Elgar theorized:

> This is my theme: I cannot conceive that Potter kept a tavern; the occupation is too common to be identified in this *public* way
>
> Potter surely did not levy toll at a private 'pike': a sort of sedentary highwayman? the thing is not possible
>
> I conceive Potter as a philosopher: high & serene musing on & clarifying problems far beyond human knowledge; I see him brought face to face with some impenetrable riddle before which the mighty intellect – even that of Potter – quailed, paled & failed.
>
> Surely this was Potter's Bar.

Elgar had not done. Two days later he made further attempts to unravel the mystery:

> I *am* aware that soap & music are given to the world in bars; surely you will not contend that Potter was a musical composer because he has left one bar? In our young days we spoke of Purcell's Ground & thought it covered the whole ground; we say Bach's Mass, or Beethoven's Violin Concerto; those great men having left behind them one only of the compositions named – always in the possessive case. But Potters *Bar*! produce the bar & we can judge its musical value.
>
> I hold it were trifling on your part to suggest that Potter, whom I assume to have been a man of intellect, made soap: even if he did condescend to

soap he must necessarily have made more than one bar. I wish you would treat Potter seriously; if you really believe that there were many Potters in the district, artists in china, first prove to me that the parish affords a clay proper to the use of potters.

By way of postscript Elgar burst into heraldry:

Potters bar can have no heraldic significance: ignorant novelists speak of a bar sinister, a thing which cannot exist, & the simple bar is to 'obvious' an ordinary to be associated solely with Potter. The same objection wd. hold in the case of two Potters or a thousand Potters. Potter was acutely English; this I am prepared to swear; the equivalent of barre in French is *bend* in English: we should then have Potter's Bend ...

There is no diary mention of the Symphony on the two 'Potter' days, but during the rest of July Elgar was 'working at speed' or 'very hard'. The diary entry on 5 August has 'E. trying to finish his Scherzo. Very badly all P.M. distressingly so'. Five days later, however, Elgar was ready to take the first two movements to Novello for printing. On that same 10 August Littleton wrote to his production manager, C. J. May, about the Symphony: 'You will remember that Elgar wants the score to be got into as small a number of pages as can reasonably be done to avoid continual turning over.'

There was an enforced week's break for a concert at Ostende. Elgar conducted *In the South*, *Wand of Youth* suite no. 1 and the Variations; he also accompanied *Sea Pictures* for a Tilly Koenen who 'did not know her Songs but made some effect'. A partial hearing of Delibes' opera was not a success: 'To Lakme in evg. Most shocked – left after 2nd Act'. Back in Hereford, on 18 August Elgar was 'feeling his way to his Symphony again'. Four days later he was 'playing La Tosca, & going on orchestrating slow movement'. Except for a letter to Littleton on 'the worst side of the U.S.A. character' that Elgar had experienced, correspondence amid progress on the Symphony continued cheerful. He commented to Atkins on a new addition to the Worcester Cathedral organ: 'I am glad the 32 feet which after all is $\frac{1}{3}$ of a centipede (environs), goes well'. To Schuster he took further one of the 'Potter' ideas: 'I am resuming chemistry & made soap yesterday between fits of scoring (not scouring!) the symphony. I have been vainly trying to persuade Carice to wash with it – strange how little encouragement I get!'

The most important letter of all was despatched on 29 August, when Elgar resigned the Birmingham professorship. Acceptance had been a bad mistake and had caused him much needless agony. Peyton, the founder of the chair, naturally felt time had been wasted, but Granville Bantock at the Midland Institute was waiting as obvious successor. At the Worcester Festival the text of *Gerontius* was still 'Anglicanized': Tilly Koenen was to have been the Angel as also Mary Magdalene in *The Kingdom*, but again she did not know the music, as Elgar informed Atkins: 'I saw the terrible woman this a.m. & worked hard – but – she is impossible.' She was replaced, but 'The Tame Bear' and 'The Wild Bears' of the new *Wand of Youth* suite made their effect: 'all mad over bears & singing & acting them'. Lady Maud Warrender bought a toy bear to increase the jollification of the Elgarian party. For the rest of September Elgar concentrated on the finale of the Symphony and took it to Novello on the last day of the month. Jaeger had already been asking for more: 'Make *no pause* when the Symphony is finished. By that time you should just be in the *right mood & trim to go on* with Part III of your sacred Trilogy.'

The first London performance of *Wand of Youth* suite no. 2 gave occasion to congratulate Peter Rabbit on a scoring hint, probably in 'The Wild Bears'. He received a note: 'Your idea – the vigorous entry of the drums was splendid Thanks.' Lady Maud Warrender came to stay at Plas Gwyn, and on 7 November she sang *Pleading*, the new song dedicated to her; Elgar orchestrated it six days later. Elgar was also busy with much chemistry and the fitting-out of his laboratory, called the Ark, in the garden. He had just heard that 'The Elgar Sulphuretted Hydrogen Apparatus' was to go into production, and wrote to Jaeger on 11 November of his varied activities: 'I have many proofs of the Sym to finish & some diagrams of the machine to *draw* & send to the makers by this post so goodbye.' This marked the climax of his fame as a chemist, in pursuance of which he had acquired many books. John Attfield's *Chemistry General, Medical, and Pharmaceutical*, for instance, was profusely annotated and is now at the Birthplace. Various experiments were marked and presumably performed. He was bidden to 'Heat a few grains of ammonium chloride with about an equal weight of calcium hydroxite'. Another involved the 'Preparation of Red or Mercuric Iodide by Precipitation'. In the Birmingham lecture on 'Critics' Elgar had defined Bernard Shaw chemically, pointing out that in his writing 'there was always a substratum of *practical matter*, or to put it chemically to volatile and pellucid fluid, held in solution, matter which was precipitated into obvious solid fact by the intro-duction of the reader's *own common sense*'. Elgar wrote '*Expln*' in the margin against information that '*Nitrogen Iodide* is formed when excess of aqueous ammonia is added to a solution of iodine in potassium iodide'. And indeed it is well known that an Elgar experiment resulted in the violent explosion of the Plas Gwyn water butt.[1]

---

[1] See William H. Reed, *Elgar as I Knew him* (London, 1936, 2/1973), p. 39.

Meanwhile Jaeger, now often confined to his bed, had been playing the Symphony's slow movement from Karg-Elert's newly printed piano arrangement, and wrote to Elgar on 26 November, addressing him as 'My dear, great Edward'. He explained that he 'was allowed to come down today for the first time for a month, and I spent some happy quarter Hours over your Adagio in the Symphony'. He considered it 'not only one of the greatest slow movements since Beethoven', but also *'worthy of that master'*. He thought it Elgar's greatest achievement so far, 'written by a good pure man, & only such a character can feel & invent such music'. Elgar was nervous about the first rehearsal at Manchester on 3 December. He felt so unwell he was 'doubtful if going till last minute'. Once there he 'stood up by Dr. Richter & showed what he wanted & did splendid good'. It was Richter who had insistently urged on Elgar the writing of a symphony, and Elgar had responded with a work he hoped worthy of a man who had been closely associated with both Wagner and Brahms, and thus intimate with 'the greatest'. The dedication to Richter as 'True artist and true friend' told its own story; Richter saluted the work as the finest of modern symphonies, and not just by an Englishman.

The Symphony's first Manchester audience on 3 December agreed with Jaeger about the quality of the Adagio. Lady Elgar reported that 'after 3rd movement E. had to go up on platform & whole Orch. & nos. of audience stood up – Wonderful scene. also at end.' Robin Legge of the *Daily Telegraph* claimed to have 'discovered old Papa Hans Richter and Sir Edward Elgar hugging each other like a couple of bears and gaily waltzing round a table in the middle of the room!' The critics, at Manchester and after the 7 December London performance, recognized Elgar's achievement. The *Daily Mail* considered the Symphony as 'perhaps the finest masterpiece of its type that ever came from the pen of an English composer'. Parry, with his four symphonies already behind him, thought the work 'Very interesting, personal, new, magnetic. A lofty standard'. Jaeger, who had written his last letter to Elgar three days before, extolling the Symphony as a whole, managed to attend the London performance and described its conclusion to Dorabella: 'After that superb Coda (Finale) the audience seemed to rise at E. when he appeared. I *never* heard such frantic applause after any novelty nor such shouting. Five times he had to appear before they were pacified. People stood up and even *on* their seats to get a view.' A fine pen-portrait of Elgar at his moment of triumph appeared in *The Clarion*. He seemed

> a tall, thin man with a slight stoop, black hair turning grey; a thin, ascetic face, yet the face of a fighter if it were not for the earnest eyes and brow of the mystic; a resolute chin, the lower half of the face showing indomitable

energy, yet it is the face of a student. Elgar's bearing is aloof and dignified, yet also distinctly diffident. Altogether a curious and lofty personality, intensely English, yet with a touch of something strange and apart.

Lady Elgar was able to maintain the mood of exaltation back to Hereford, where they arrived on 11 December; she even echoed Jaeger's hope for the third oratorio: 'Glorious sunshine in our hearts all the afternoon & wonderful sunset, seemed a good omen. The sunset I pray, presaged the 3rd Pt. of "Apostles", it was like the Civitas Dei pinnacles, towers set in gold.' If a sunset over golden Mainz inspired Wagner to the *Meistersinger* Prelude, the Hereford sunset had no such effect on Elgar. In a Christmas Day letter to Frank Schuster's sister Adela he said the Symphony was 'making a very wild career' and uplifting everybody but himself: 'I wish it uplifted me – I have just paid rent, Land Tax, Income Tax' and there were 'children yapping at the door, "Christians awake! salute the yappy morn"'. To Alice Stuart Wortley he was even more Scroogelike: 'I am dulling in the house with a cold which is depressing for me & *I mean to make it so* for all around me.' All that he could report about the Ark was that it was 'silent & deserted & Mozart's portrait has curled up & fallen into the Hydrofluoric acid'. He was mulling over 'memories mostly of the New world geographically & musically – that Symphony *is* a new world isn't it?' And he implored her, 'Do say yes'.

The year 1909 began well, with Elgar himself conducting the Symphony in London; he 'looked Nobilmente as he were his Music'. But gradually his spirits sagged, and he hoped to revive them with a cure at Llandrindod Wells. He 'liked the Sulphur water' and sent 'Peter Rabbit, esq. Mus D' a card addressed to his 'Stallag[g]io'.[2] There seemed little improvement, but he tried Llandrindod again. Lady Elgar now felt they would have to go further afield, and the solution came through Julia Worthington, who suggested they should join her in a villa she had taken at Careggi, outside Florence. The news inspired Elgar to write words for a 'Patriotic Song', which Boosey considered too ephemeral and 'political' for publication; and on 24 March he tried out on Troyte some etymology: 'I have an idea that Troyte after all is derived from detritus & not truite – altho' the reason you liked Schubert's Forelle may be that you are derived from the same root or rather Quelle I suppose.'

On 9 April Elgar crossed to Paris; Lady Elgar and Carice followed eight days later, and Pippa joined them on the 18th, when Elgar also wrote to Gorton: 'Paris *is* alive &, in a curious way, inspiring: all cities are built on seven somethings. Rome on seven hills Hereford (!)

[2] Birthplace Museum.

on the cardinal virtues I suppose very much buried & Paris certainly on the seven deadly sins – which makes life worth *looking at* if not worth living.' At Careggi music returned. Lady Elgar went hunting for music paper and parasols; almost at once Elgar wrote 'some beautiful new music'. To Alice Stuart Wortley she described the 'very nice spacious Villa, the hall in Roman days was the Atrium & in later ages, it was one of the Medici Villas; the great Medici Villa where Lorenzo died is close by. I trust you will hear E.'s impressions, tonally, some day.' Elgar had new ideas for the Violin Concerto, and made extensive sketches for the slow movement. The start of the Second Symphony was also shaping, and there were ideas for the Larghetto and Rondo. One of Elgar's quainter ambitions was to 'get the (1000000) frogs in the Vineyard into the Score of Sym II – a fine sound'. Another project was described in a letter of 18 May to Canon Gorton: 'I have been writing some things a big part song to *fine* words by Cavalcanti – translated by Rossetti.' This was *Go, Song of Mine*, which Elgar dedicated to A. H. Littleton; he also wrote the *Angelus*, probably to words of his own, for Alice Stuart Wortley. While at Careggi Elgar heard that Nimrod had died; he wrote to Mrs Jaeger on 21 May: 'The news came as a great shock & I cannot realise that the end is come. I am overwhelmed with sorrow for the loss of my dearest & truest friend.'

They left the Villa Silli on 28 May. The monuments of Pisa made a great impression: 'E. quite carried away. Went again & saw it again all in full moon. So quiet & lovely.' They were nine days in Venice, where Elgar adumbrated ideas for the middle movements of the Second Symphony, struck, as he later explained to Charles Sanford Terry, by 'the contrast between the interior of St. Mark's at Venice, & the sunlit & lively Piazza outside'.[3] He told Littleton that the cross-rhythms at the start of the Rondo came 'from some itinerant musicians who seemed to take a grave satisfaction in the broken accent of the first four bars'. The return journey took them to Richard Strauss in Garmisch, who lived in a 'Nice house, beautifully fitted & kept'. Access to manuscripts was controlled by Frau Strauss, who hid the necessary key under her skirt.

Elgar's first composition once home was an *Elegy* for strings. This was requested by Littleton to commemorate Rev Robert Hadden, who had been warden of the Worshipful Company of Musicians. It is still played annually, on or near St Cecilia's Day, to remember those of the Company who have died during the year. At the beginning of July Elgar was 'getting ready for cycle excursions & looking up sketches'.

[3] Notes held at the Athenaeum Club.

The cycling took him initially to his sister Pollie at Stoke; the sketches gained an increasing hold on him so that by 19 August Elgar was 'possessed with his music for the Violin Concerto'. Fritz Kreisler spoke again to the press: 'Sir Edward Elgar promised me a concerto three years ago ... But I can't get the first note out of him.' Elgar was also concerned about a memorial concert for Jaeger, and wrote to Richter on 2 August: 'I have been asked to enquire if you would be disposed to conduct several pieces by the London Symphony Orchestra? The proceeds would be for poor Jaeger's widow and children who are badly off.' Elgar's own child caused consternation at the end of August by catching scarlet fever and putting Plas Gwyn in quarantine just before the Hereford Festival.

Hereford had the first performance of *Go, Song of Mine* on 9 September. Ivor Atkins had already commented on it as 'one of the VERY BEST things you have ever done'. With the festival over, Lady Elgar was still busy with quarantine matters, 'trying to make house very safe'. Her efforts were such that she 'Burnt paws with too strong Carbolic – rather scared'. At the beginning of October Elgar was 'thinking of his new Symphony'. He had heard Richter rehearse the 'Eroica', and wrote to him on 3 October: 'I am very busy writing No. 2 !! (E♭ key perhaps inspired by Eroica).' But a conducting tour took Elgar away, as far as Aberdeen. To Schuster he cursed the tour: he only wanted to be at home.

Elgar returned to Plas Gwyn and an Indian summer on 5 November. He wrote to Alice Stuart Wortley of his delight: 'I only sit in the sun in my study looking like Hans Sachs without his beard & stoutness.' He went on to contrast Hereford with the cities of the tour: 'It *is* lovely here – the air so pure & soft after the loathèd North with all its mysteries of commerce – I saw locomotives building & torpedoes & other nasty maleficious things: now it is warm & lovely & feels & looks like an ashamed summer.' As so often when writing to Frank Schuster, Elgar sounded dejected on 25 November. He mentioned the doctor who was treating him: 'the poor man thinks it's nerves over composition – when its only heartbreak for something or somebody else'.

With the Violin Concerto and Second Symphony in temporary abeyance, Elgar now planned a cycle of songs to words by Gilbert Parker. Six poems were chosen, but only three were set. Parker wanted no payment; it was enough 'to have the master of English Music enshrine my words and give them a chance of life beyond their own moment.'[4] The rest of the year was devoted to song, with the

---

[4] Birthplace Museum.

composition of *A Child Asleep* for the baby son of the singer Muriel Foster (Mrs Goetz), *The Torch* to passionate words effortlessly adapted by Pietro d'Alba (the Italianate rabbit), and a resurgence of the trio tune from *Pomp and Circumstance* no. 4 to words by Alice Elgar. Her subject was 'Kingsway', the grandiose London street that had replaced the slums north of Aldwych and been officially opened by Edward VII in 1905. The words scarcely enhanced the tune, but Elgar took the setting to Arthur Boosey and was able to send a 'Rejoiceful telegram'; it said 'Song causes delight', and Lady Elgar received three guineas for copyright of the verses.

As a Christmas gift the Speyers of Ridgehurst sent Elgar miniature scores of Haydn, Mozart and Beethoven quartets. He replied on 15 December with gratitude and touching evocation of his youthful studying days 'when the world of music was opening & one learnt fresh *great* works every week'. Now that he understood 'all the mechanism of composition, the old mysterious glamour is gone & the feeling of *entering* – shy, but welcomed – into the world of the immortals'. He wondered whether 'our passage into the next world shall be a greater & a fuller experience of the same warm, loving & *growing* trust – this I doubt'. When summing up the year, Lady Elgar mentioned the death of not only Nimrod, but also Basil Nevinson.

For the Jaeger memorial concert Elgar decided to orchestrate the three Parker songs he had completed as his op. 59; there was also work on the Violin Concerto and the Romance for bassoon and orchestra. But the Elgars were much saddened by another death, that of Professor Sanford on 6 January 1910; he was one of the few Americans for whom they had genuine affection. By 20 January Elgar was ready to try the slow movement of the Violin Concerto with Lady Speyer, the Ysaÿe pupil Leonora von Stosch now married to Sir Edgar Speyer, a merchant banker who was also chairman of the Queen's Hall syndicate. They repeated it four days later, on the evening of the Jaeger concert. Lady Elgar noted the success of the concert: 'Richter conducted splendid performance of Vars. He turned to the Orch. spreading out his arms as if to draw every sound & made the Nimrod gorgeous. Songs went well, the 1st not quite the reading, great ovation & repetition of No. 2.' Muriel Foster had sung the songs and Elgar conducted them.

On 2 February Elgar sent Sidney Colvin's wife Frances a copy of *Go, Song of Mine*. He enclosed also another poem, 'The River', adapted by Peter Rabbit: 'With it I send a specimen of my dear friend Pietro d'Alba in his most, or *almost* most pessimistic mood. To read it one wd. think the carrot crop had failed or some other catastrophe acutely affecting the rabbit world was toward.' The Stuart Wortleys heard the

Andante of the Violin Concerto, again played by Lady Speyer, on 6 February. The following day Elgar expressed doubts to Alice Stuart Wortley about the movement: 'I am not sure about that Andante & shall put it away for a long time before I decide its fate. I am glad you liked it.' Alice Stuart Wortley became ever more closely associated with the work. It was she who persuaded him to continue, and on that same 7 February he sketched the music of cue 2 in the opening Allegro to link the themes already devised under the inspiration of Kreisler. He sent her the new theme:

> I am putting the enclosed (written in dejection as Shelley says) in to the Concerto I think & hope; I made it the other evening & like it myself very much. Please tell me (this is what I began to write to you for) what passage in Puccini I have annexed – I cannot place it – but you must tell me at once so that I can remove it. I only *know* 'La Tosca' altho' I have *heard* 'Butterfly'

This tune, and the main second subject of the Allegro, became 'Windflower' themes for Elgar, a name he transferred to Alice Stuart Wortley herself.

Success brought a new asperity into Elgar's business dealings. Novello handled his conducting engagements, and he resented the fact he was paid half what Richter received. In a letter of 12 February to the Novello company secretary, Henry Clayton, he contrasted his own fee with that paid to an eminent man from abroad: 'They had these three really *trying* concerts from me for 75£ – then paid Debussy about 200£ for a concert which only ¾ filled the house.' He did not see why he 'should earn money for people to spend on others'. Towards the end of February Elgar was in London again and often at the theatre. He saw Galsworthy's *Justice*, *Misalliance* by Shaw, a Barrie double bill of *Old Friends* and *The Twelve Pound Look* with Meredith's *The Sentimentalist*, and *The Madras House* by Granville Barker.

At the beginning of March the Elgars moved into a flat they had taken at 58 New Cavendish Street, London. A main attraction to Elgar was the splendid library. It provided the backdrop to a letter of gloom for Adela Schuster: 'I am like a sham book in a library, only a name, & useless for wit or wisdom.' On 15 March he went with Lady Maud Warrender to Strauss's *Elektra*. It was conducted by the composer, who received £200. Elgar was much impressed by the opera but thought also of *Othello* and 'kept on saying The pity of it! the pity of it – going back to murderous horrors'. The evening was probably inspiration for an 'inverted aphorism' Elgar delivered to Charles Graves at the Athenaeum, that modern musical genius might be defined as 'an infinite capacity for giving pain'.

On 30 March Elgar went to stay with Adela Schuster in Torquay as prelude to a motoring holiday with her brother Frank. They made for the Stuart Wortley house at Tintagel on 3 April, as Elgar described in his own diary: 'Snowstorm on crossing the moors – arrd. at Tintagel about 3.30 Sent in wrong names to the Wortleys – Frank's joke.' According to Clare, the daughter of the house, conditions were not favourable: 'The afternoon of their arrival, we all walked down to the sea in the "Cove", below the Castle ruins; and saw it all in very bad weather, at its most stern and forbidding.' The diary suggests Elgar was not unduly impressed: 'Coast fine but not as fine as Llangranog', which he remembered from the summer of 1901. But one evening the sun shone, and it was then, wrote Clare Stuart Wortley, 'that the austere yet lyrical beauty of the Tintagel country really showed itself to Sir Edward at last'.[5]

Elgar returned to London on 11 April and Dorabella came to dinner. He played her the Larghetto of the Second Symphony, which struck her sombrely: 'The whole movement seemed to me to tell a tragic story of anxiety and sorrow, fears and hopes.' Elgar summed up the motor tour for Adela Schuster on 14 April:

> I have very dear memories of Torquay, then my mind is full of S. Cross at Winchester, then the dignified calm of the close at Salisbury: next the rocky coast we have seen in Cornwall & the desolation of the Lizard Oh! it was a confusion of interest & makes a background for present sorrow.

The nature of the sorrow was unclear. Sir Edgar Speyer had in fact sent Elgar a cheque the previous day, the fruit of a speculation. Elgar, who was negotiating with Sir Edgar about the first performance of the Second Symphony, felt he could not possibly accept the money. Lady Elgar considered it a 'Very human kind touching episode – Dear of Sir Edgar & of course perfect of Edoo!'

There was progress on the Violin Concerto, and reports of it went to Alice Stuart Wortley, the 'Windflower'. On 20 April he was 'ablaze with work & *writing hard*; you *should* come & see (& hear it!)'. Lady Elgar was inviting many people to tea; Elgar could play them Symphony or Concerto as he wished. Jaeger's widow came and the Hugh Blairs; the *Daily Telegraph* art critic Claude Phillips and, on 24 April, the Windflower herself (with Mary Trefusis, the former Lady Mary Lygon, calling later in the evening); the following day there was Gertrude Walker, a memory of long ago. Three days later Elgar had been 'working hard at the Windflower themes but all stands still until you come & approve!'; on the morrow he was depressed: 'It is so dreary

---

[5] Notes written for Carice Elgar Blake; Birthplace Museum.

today & the tunes stick & are not Windflowerish – at present.' Elgar sent the Windflower sketches, 'giving her', as her daughter explained, 'what she most liked, themes & MSS'.

On 1 May Elgar sent a sketch of the second 'Windflower' theme. He enclosed with it a *Daily Telegraph* article by their mutual friend, Claude Phillips. It described Titian's *Nymph and Piping Shepherd* in the Vienna Kunsthistorisches Museum:

> it is twilight, and soon will be night, with the lovers, who dally still in the sombre air shot with silver. The poetry of the early years has come back, intensified by something of added poignancy, and of foreboding that is tinged it may be, with remorse. This last passion has something that the earlier passion had not; in one sense it is nearer to earth and earthiness; in another it is infinitely higher and more far-reaching.[6]

What exactly was the significance of this cutting to Elgar we cannot know; all that is certain is that it was sent to the 'stepmother' of what he called his 'too emotional' Concerto.

On 3 May Elgar received a telegram saying simply, 'All over very painless'.[7] He communicated at once with Frances Colvin:

> I write to tell you how very sad we are to-day: my dear old friend Peter left this life this morning quite suddenly & painlessly: Why should I tell you this! Because I want to write to somebody (– ? everybody) and say how really grieved I am & then only two people in the world would understand & you are one.

It seemed 'terrible to think how many human beings could be spared out of our little life's circle so much easier than my confidant & adviser Pietro d'Alba'. Three days later there was warning of another death: 'Terrible news only too true – So difficult to believe the King was really dangerously ill.' King Edward VII died on 7 May, making the times seem 'too cruel & gloomy'; none the less, as he continued to Frank Schuster, 'I have the Concerto well in hand & have played (?) it thro' on the P.F. & it's *good*! awfully emotional! too emotional but I love it.'

A casual meeting in Regent Street brought W. H. Reed of the London Symphony Orchestra to assist with the Concerto. He came to New Cavendish Street for the first time on 28 May and has left a vivid description of the occasion:

> I found Sir Edward striding about with a number of loose pieces of MSS. which he was arranging in different parts of the room. Some were already pinned on the backs of chairs, or fixed up on the mantlepiece, so we started

---

[6] Research communicated by Brian Trowell.
[7] Birthplace Museum.

without any loss of time. I discovered then that we were playing a sketchy version of what is now the Violin Concerto. The main ideas were written out, and to use one of his own pet expressions, he had 'japed them up' to make a coherent piece.[8]

When writing to thank Reed two days later, Elgar was anxious to complete the first movement and was 'only waiting for the final "flourish"'. He enclosed a 'truly diabolical effort', and hoped Reed would have a chance to play it to him before the Elgars had to vacate the flat at the beginning of the next month. Reed came, and on 1 June the opening Allegro was ready for Novello. Elgar hoped for another period at The Hut to finish the Concerto, and told Schuster he 'had best invite its stepmother to the Hut'. And he did. Elgar spent a week there, and wrote to Alice Stuart Wortley after she left, enclosing a windflower with the letter: 'I have made the end serious & grand I hope & have brought in the real inspired themes from the Ist. movement ... the music sings of memories & hope.'

It took Elgar some time to 'find' himself back in Hereford. He told the Windflower in a letter of 23 June that the finale seemed to be getting out of hand: 'I am appalled at the last movement & cannot get on: – it is growing so large – too large I fear & I have headaches.' Reed was summoned for 30 June and described how 'Passages were tried in different ways: the notes were regrouped or the phrasing altered. The Cadenza was in pieces; but soon the parts took shape and were knit together to become an integral part of the concerto.' Elgar was tireless in investigating all possibilities, and 'bubbling over with enthusiasm when the quest was ended and he had found what he had been seeking'.[9]

On 1 July Kreisler at last saw the Concerto he had been awaiting for five years. Lady Elgar reported that he was 'much impressed. He said at one passage "I will shake Queen's Hall"!' The completed work was sent to Novello in piano score on 6 July, and there was much competition over which orchestra should give the first performance. Elgar was bewildered by the confusion as the London Symphony Orchestra, the Queen's Hall Orchestra, the New Symphony Orchestra and the Philharmonic Society vied with each other. The Elgars went briefly to Cornwall, staying with Colonel and Lady Mary Trefusis. Later, in Bournemouth Elgar saw Parry and Mackenzie but 'Did not speak to Stanford who fled when he saw E.'

He returned to Hereford on 9 July and four days later wrote to the

---

[8] W. H. Reed, 'The Violin Concerto', *ML*, xvi (1935), p. 31; repr. in *An Elgar Companion*, ed. Christopher Redwood (Ashbourne, 1982), p. 251.

[9] W. H. Reed, *Elgar as I Knew him*, p. 29.

Windflower: 'All radiance again – the Concerto-orchestration dances wildly along.' By the middle of the month it was decided that the first performance would be given by Kreisler on 10 November under the auspices of the Philharmonic Society. Elgar was to receive £100, with another £100 for a second performance on 30 November. After a *King Olaf* in York, the Windflower came to Plas Gwyn: 'Seemed perfectly happy here. & quickly adopted the current vocabulary'. On 5 August Elgar reported the end of his task to Charles Sanford Terry: 'I have put the last note to the last movement in the full score and have lit a pipe.'[10] Julia Worthington was staying at the time.

The Elgars then visited Severn Grange, now taken over by a younger Whinfield. At Foregate Street Station they were joined by Mrs Fitton and launched on a nostalgic few days. Elgar was able to tell his hosts 'things about the house they did not know. Old Mr. W. used to consult him where to put pictures & things.' The next day 'Ysobel' of the Variations came to lunch and in the evening Elgar rowed his wife and Mrs Fitton on the lake. Lady Elgar thought it was probably malarial, and also wrote to the Windflower. She said that Kreisler had sent 'the *most* deeply & movingly enthusiastic appreciation' of the Concerto; and that the Severn Grange garden seemed 'more like a Maeterlinck fantasia than any English place'.

Alice Elgar went to London and wondered about a flat in Mount Street; she decided it was 'rather nice but might feel like a cage – for her booful Eagle bird'. Meanwhile the 'Eagle bird' was digging potatoes and setting Psalm 48. He particularly enjoyed the verse that described how 'the kings were troubled, and hasted away'; he called them his 'flying Kings'. Then on 2 September Elgar went to London for a run-through of the Concerto with Kreisler in the Novello boardroom. Sanford Terry turned over. Elgar had hoped the Windflower might do so, but he told her about the occasion: 'I have played it for 3 hours with Kreisler & it is tremendous.' Both Reed and Kreisler were at the Gloucester Three Choirs Festival in September, and both played the Concerto to a small, invited gathering. Reed's performance was on 4 September: 'I knew every note of the concerto, and exactly how he liked it played: every nuance, every shade of expression; yet I felt a little overwhelmed at being asked to play the solo part at what would actually be the very first performance before an audience.'[11] Robin Legge, critic of the *Daily Telegraph*, heard Kreisler and Elgar rehearse on 8 September: 'If we were not making history I am a Dutchman'. He added that 'Kreisler is crazy about it & so am I – it will be a huge

---

[10] Letter with first proofs of full score; BL, Add.MS 62000.
[11] Reed, *Elgar as I Knew him*, p. 30

success. (Poor old Stanford!)' He sketched Elgar as 'a remarkable person. Full of nerves but, oh so genuine & so musical & so keen & warm & enthusiastic'. Legge continued about the Concerto's slow movement: 'What the Adagio means *au fond* to Elgar I cannot guess of course, but at the end of it the tears were pouring down his face. The whole man & his life is in his composition ... No wonder we love his music & him – he is the personification of sympathy.'[12]

Sanford Terry arrived at Plas Gwyn on 7 October and helped with proofs of the Concerto. The dedication was to go to Kreisler; but Elgar added separately a quotation in Spanish, 'Aquí está encerrada el alma de . . . . .', referring originally to the 'licendiado Pedro Garcias' in Lesage's *Gil Blas*. Terry was there when Elgar was pondering the quotation and noted his impressions at the time: 'I have not the slightest doubt that it is his own soul which the Concerto enshrines. In the first place it will be noticed that he originally wrote "del" before the blank, an indication that the name to follow was a masculine one.'[13] While Terry was watching, he changed the 'del' to 'de la', but then consulted a Spanish friend whether 'del' would leave the sex undetermined. He was told it would and changed the word back. The five dots of the blank were not always five; but they have given rise to much speculation. Alice Elgar affirmed that they referred to Julia Worthington; other female suggestions have been Alice Stuart Wortley, Adela Schuster, Alice Elgar, or Elgar's former fiancée, Helen Weaver. In gratitude for his help, Terry was given first proofs of the Concerto full score, and on 11 October he wrote to Alice Stuart Wortley: 'It is a *glorious* work, & *what* a glorious man he is! When I leave Plas Gwyn I always feel like a schoolboy facing the awful blackness of a return to school.'

Kreisler played the work on two more occasions with Elgar at the piano, and made some slight alterations to the solo part. At Plas Gwyn there was arduous collation of the orchestral parts and full score. Troyte gave an impression of the hectic activity: 'They played the violin concerto one Sunday at Hereford from 10 o'clock in the morning to 11 o'clock at night only stopping for meals. Elgar objurgating Novellos whenever he found a mistake.'[14] The performance on 10 November 1910 was indeed a triumph. Dorabella hinted at the tension: 'The place was simply packed. Kreisler came on looking as white as a sheet – even for a player of his great experience it must have been a nervous moment – but he played superbly.' Terry noticed one lapse in

---

[12] Letter from Robin Legge to his wife; Birthplace Museum.
[13] Notes by C. S. Terry; BL, Add.MS 62000.
[14] MS reminiscences; Birthplace Museum.

Kreisler's otherwise splendid performance: 'His magnificent interpretation of the work was the theme of all. Save at one point his memory did not fail him throughout.' Lady Elgar interpreted the applause in her own way: 'Enthusiasm unbounded – *Shouts* – E. walked backwards & forwards bringing Kreisler but England wanted *him* & he had to come by his souse.' No subsequent Elgar première received such acclamation.

There was now pressure for completion of the Second Symphony, as Elgar had contracted to conduct in Canada and the States from the second half of March. Another foreign commitment took the Elgars to Krefeld in Germany, where he conducted the First Symphony on 17 December. He wrote to the Windflower the day before the concert: 'some things sound odd – the Hautboys are so different (& rough)'. It was arranged that she should come to Plas Gwyn for Christmas, when Lady Elgar was able to record a more successful time than usual: 'Very pleasant evg. E. showed his robes &c & then played new *Symphony*. A very dear day – E. so much happier than ever before over Fest.' The Symphony now possessed him, but on 30 December he had to be in Liverpool to conduct Kreisler in the Violin Concerto. He took the opportunity of going to the Walker Art Gallery to see 'his favourite picture of The Pot of Basil' by the Windflower's father, Millais. Called 'Isabella', the painting illustrated a poem by Keats about the doomed love of young Isabella and Lorenzo. So ended 1910, during which the Elgars had been much in London and had decided they should now leave Plas Gwyn, the three cathedral cities, and the West Midlands.

For much of January 1911 Lady Elgar was house-hunting; but it was the Windflower who accompanied Elgar to Hampstead one day and came across the house that would eventually be his London home. She viewed it and wrote a description of 'Kelston', an artist's house designed by Norman Shaw, architect of her own place in Chelsea. In imitation of Hans Richter, Elgar had acquired a date-stamp during the course of 1910. His fascination with this new gadget, used to stamp sketches and drafts of the Symphony, means that the progress of the work can be followed in unusual detail. A sketch at the Athenaeum Club is dated 25 November, and first movement dates continue till 21 January 1911. There were interruptions: Ivor Atkins came to discuss the new edition of the Bach *St Matthew Passion* that Novello was to publish under their joint names; Oscar Wilde's son Vyvyan Holland called, and there was much talk of books. The immediate result was a letter to Littleton of 10 January: 'I am all behind with my work & I have grave fears for the 2nd Symphony, but I must decide its fate next week.' He had to be in London for another Violin Concerto performance with Kreisler, but managed good work on the Symphony there.

Back in Hereford progress was swift, and on 28 January Lady Elgar could report the first movement finished: 'Very wonderful & gorgeous – He was hardly over a fortnight scoring & writing this from his sketches!' To the Windflower Elgar wrote that he had 'recorded last year' in it, adding 'I have worked at fever heat & the thing is tremendous in energy'. While Elgar wrote out the Larghetto, Lady Elgar was away for three nights, still house-hunting. Her absence was so unusual that she remarked on it in the diary: 'A had never been away for one night since marriage when E. was at home.' The Larghetto was ready on 6 February soon after her return: 'A. hears lament for King Edward & dear Rody in it – & all human feeling.' He had written to Frances Colvin at the beginning of the month, referring to the Shelley words, 'Rarely, rarely comest thou, / Spirit of delight' that he was to add at the end of the MS full score. He then quoted more Shelley, from *Julian and Maddalo*:

> I do but hide
> Under these notes, like embers, every spark
> *Of that which has consumed me*

'Hide is hardly the right word is it for this case?'

While in London for a Violin Concerto performance under Henry Wood, he went over Kelston, the Hampstead house, and Lady Elgar wrote about it to Alice Stuart Wortley on 11 February: '*if* he really likes it, wh. he does, I feel he must have it, & have a proper room to dream dreams of loveliness in'. Soon after his return to Hereford came news that Hans Richter, already so much associated with the Symphony, was retiring. Elgar wrote at once on 13 February: 'I see in the Telegraph an announcement which gives me a great pain. More than half my musical life goes when you cease to conduct.' Two days later Lady Elgar noted the result of more concentrated work: 'finished his Third wonderful brilliant movement. Really marvellous only 7 to 8 days writing it from his sketches with so much composing as well orchestration.' Elgar gave his own description to the Windflower: 'very wild & headstrong it is with soothing pastoral strains in between & very, very brilliant'.

Before beginning what he called 'the great serene movement', Elgar conducted the *Romance* for bassoon and orchestra in Hereford; and that morning there came a deputation from the London Symphony Orchestra led by Edwin James, soloist in and dedicatee of the *Romance,* asking Elgar to succeed Richter as the orchestra's conductor. He accepted. Scoring the Symphony's finale took the last week of February; it was finished on the 28th, 'a day to be marked'. Lady Elgar's estimate of the work was just: 'It seems one of his very greatest works, vast in design & supremely beautiful.'

In the second week of March the Elgars went to Brussels, where Elgar conducted the First Symphony. He told the Windflower about it: 'We have had a most triumphant performance to-day Ysaye created a sensation by leading the orchestra *himself* in my honour.' The planned departure to North America on 18 March had to be postponed, as Elgar was unwell. John Pointer of Novello came to Plas Gwyn, and proofs of the finale were read at Elgar's bedside. A heartfelt letter of 16 March went to Richter: 'Your influence for all that is noble and good in our Art is deeply felt, and you have transformed the musical taste of this country to something higher and better than could have been imagined.' A postscript mentioned the Second Symphony: 'I hope you may hear it some day – it was meant for you to like.'[15] And Elgar was now able to write to Littleton about the dedication of the Symphony: 'H.M. the King is pleased that I shd. dedicate the Symphy to the memory of the late King Edward – it was intended to dedicate it to him.' The case had been furthered by Lady Mary Trefusis, a lady-in-waiting to Queen Alexandra the Queen Mother, who wrote to the king's private secretary: 'As Elgar is the greatest living composer in any country, the work would be worthy of such a dedication.' Another task completed was an anthem, *O Hearken Thou unto the Voice of my Calling*, to be performed at the coronation of George V in June.

Transatlantic impressions were no more favourable than before. The tour was with a choir assembled by Henry Coward from the best singers of the Sheffield and other northern choral societies. He wrote to Frances Colvin from Toronto, 'in this awful place', with 'every nerve shattered by some angularity – vulgarity & general horror'. He had seen an announcement about Sidney Colvin's edition of Robert Louis Stevenson's letters, had been 'looked after *well* & *motherly*' by Julia Worthington in New York, but was 'longing for home'. Elgar conducted a number of *Gerontius* performances, had always a *succès d'estime*, and sometimes more; but his thoughts were elsewhere, as is clear from a letter of 26 April to the Windflower: 'I loved having your letter from Tintagel & all the sea was in it.' Offers had been made for further visits to the States: 'I said nothing in the world wd. induce me to spend 6 months here – not $10,000,000 – this they do not understand.'

Elgar was more than happy to be at Plas Gwyn again. He found two windflowers growing by the door of the Ark, his garden laboratory, and sent them to Alice Stuart Wortley: 'It is lovely to be back, & all the world is more lovely than ever – my swallows are here & the

---

[15] Birthplace Museum.

garden full of birds & nests & buds & blossoms & the air full of divine scents – after U.S. it is heavenly beyond words.' He also told her that a miniature score of the Symphony had arrived: 'advance copy – it looks lovely'. He inscribed it the same day, 11 May, to his daughter Carice, embellishing it with a drawing of three tufted creatures with long noses in procession across the front cover.

Before the Symphony rehearsals began, Elgar made some progress with the op. 65 *Coronation March*. At the rehearsal on 20 May Lady Elgar felt it was 'Wonderful the way one cd. hear E.'s very soul in many parts'. When it came to the performance on 24 May 1911, the Symphony made less than its proper impact. Lady Elgar blamed a 'dull indiscriminate audience'. W. H. Reed remembered that 'He was called to the platform several times, but missed that unmistakable note perceived when the audience, even an English audience, is thoroughly roused and worked up, as it was after the Violin Concerto or the First Symphony'. Elgar could only remark, 'What is the matter with them, Billy? They sit there like a lot of stuffed pigs.' Elgar may have paid the penalty for nothing more than the serenity of the last pages: concert hall applause has always varied in accordance with the volume of the final note. But the effect on Elgar was devastating. Repeat performances within the next weeks were so ill-attended that Elgar would take no fee from the orchestra.

The *Coronation March* was completed and the Elgars were invited to the ceremony. Then, on 17 June, 'E. was looking at letters. He suddenly looked up & said "It is the O.M." What a thrill of joy – A. cd. see the pleasure in his face.' The Order of Merit had been founded by Edward VII at *his* coronation; there were only twenty-four British members. At a rehearsal in Westminster Abbey there was the 'procession, peers in robes &c – Some of them & Mary Trefusis saw E. & called out their Congratulations, very nice'. That evening Elgar went to a Shakespeare ball in a costume of the Henry V period. The following day Lady Elgar 'bought veil & feather in *case* of going to Westminster Abbey'. Something was amiss, and by the end of the day she could only add, 'Felt it was impossible for E. & A. to sit 7 hrs. in those seats'. The places they had been allotted were in the south aisle of the nave, from where little of the ceremony would be seen. Sir Edward decided neither of them would be there. The diary for Coronation Day, 22 June, told Lady Elgar's reaction: 'A. very tired & dreadfully disappointed, in bed till afternoon.' Elgar gave some account to Atkins the next day: 'Now we are in the thick of coronation things & a free fight is on as I refused to go to the Abbey – I loathe a crowd even to crown a King.'

Elgar's bitterness was compounded by disappointing royalty figures from Novello, and he wrote to Littleton on 27 June about the exclusive agreement in force since 1904: 'I feel compelled to send a formal letter to the firm giving notice that our agreement – or whatever it was – must end – I believe twelve months' notice is required.' Littleton replied with dignity and generosity. After expressing 'some surprise and regret', he went on: 'I shall always be proud of the connection of our house with the production of your works – particularly of your earlier works when publishers were not so accessible to you as they naturally would be at the present time'. Novello waived any question of notice for termination of the agreement, and Elgar was now free to place works where he wished. In fact all his remaining major works appeared under the imprint of Novello.

The Elgars were much exercised by the prospective Hampstead house. Many friends saw over it, and Rosa Burley was there with Elgar on 17 July; she found it 'one of the strangest afternoons we ever spent together and I have never known the duality of his character so strongly marked'. She doubted whether the house was financially possible but realized Elgar meant to live there:

> On the one hand he clearly took a natural pride in the importance of the house with its fine panelling, its long music room, and its great staircase at the head of which Alice would stand to receive her guests. But on the other hand he wanted equally clearly to make me feel that his success meant nothing to him and that there was always some lovely thing in life which had completely eluded him.

Atkins was again rehearsing *Go, Song of Mine* and was equally moved: 'Tears are a poor tribute, but you exact them always with your best music.' Elgar's reply expressed concern that the significance of the Order of Merit should be properly understood: 'Worcester people (save you!) seem to have small notion of the glory of the O.M. I was marshalled correctly at Court & at the Investiture *above* the G.C.M.G. & G.C.V.O. (the highest Lord Beauchamp can go!) – next G.C.B. in fact. Such things as K.C.B.'s are *very cheap* it seems beside O.M.' Lady Elgar's father, General Roberts, had been a KCB.

The edition of the *St Matthew Passion* had been mainly Atkins's work, but he came to Plas Gwyn for a session on the preface at the end of July. It was Carice's twenty-first birthday on 14 August, when Elgar was absent at The Hut. From her earliest years she had not featured much in her mother's diary, but Lady Elgar now assessed her character: 'grown very helpful & wise & very charming. A very fine lofty character – strong feeling of duty – & full of bright spirits – Sorry not enough scope for those always.'

To complement the *St Matthew Passion* at the 1911 Worcester

Festival, Ivor Atkins conceived the idea of having a chorale played from the cathedral tower before each part. Elgar wondered whether the players would agree but eventually produced the arrangements, describing himself on the score as 'incited to the doubtful emprise by the wiles of Ivor Atkins'. At the festival Elgar produced a handbill of 'Side Shows' that were to take place 'in Contemptuous Defiance of the Dean and Chapter'. He also recaptured his youth and nourished an essential part of himself when he went 'down to river & reeds where the wind sang to him amongst them'.

There was much conducting in the autumn, notably in Turin and for the first concerts with the London Symphony Orchestra as Richter's successor. After a bout of sickness and giddiness, Elgar left for Italy on 14 October to conduct the Variations and Introduction and Allegro, both works prepared by Toscanini. He met Debussy there and renewed acquaintance with Richard Strauss. The first LSO concert was on 23 October. It began with the *Meistersinger* Prelude, Kreisler played the Elgar Concerto, and it included Brahms's Third Symphony and Liszt's *Die Ideale* in honour of his centenary the previous day. *The Times* particularly admired in Elgar's Brahms 'the way in which he kept the whole thing light'. At the start of the second concert on 6 November was the *King Lear* overture of Berlioz. Elgar's score, now at the Birthplace, shows he had difficulty deciding what key the trumpets were in. They are in C, then E; but at one point Elgar hazarded '? in F'. There was more Brahms, when Donald Tovey played the Second Piano Concerto, 'with feeling', thought Lady Elgar, 'but not great enough'. The *Daily Telegraph* put things more pointedly: 'Surely it can have been on the very rarest occasions that such incongruous elements could possibly have met on the concert platform as were represented by the cold, even chilly, classical Mr. Tovey and the strongly, almost sensuously, emotional Sir Edward Elgar.' In Beethoven's Seventh Symphony a cautious *Morning Post* considered Elgar 'dignified yet emphatic in the right way'.

Negotiations for Kelston had dragged on through much of the year. That Lady Elgar made no diary entries from 30 November to the end of December is an indication of her intense activity and concern. Hers was the Trust that had to be broken to help finance the purchase, and it was her relative William Raikes who had been closely involved in the complex negotiations. On Christmas Eve she wrote to the Kilburns 'that on Friday (22nd), quite suddenly! completion was achieved so the *long* trying worry over the new house business is I hope at an end'. Till now Elgar had been used to rented homes; he was about to enter the first house he had ever owned. He did what he could to pretend it was in Worcestershire: Kelston, a Somerset name, was changed to 'Severn House'.

6

Siromoris becomes a youth (1912–1915)

On the first day of 1912 Elgar became a Londoner and Lady Elgar was content: 'Entered E.'s own house – May it be happy & beautiful for him.' According to Norman Shaw himself, the front door panels were 'filled with men in armour on horse and foot, doing all sorts of mysterious things'.[1] It was a chivalrous portal. Elgar signified his new status by signing himself to the Windflower with a palindrome, 'Siromoris'. This became the telegraphic address of Severn House. On 3 January Elgar told the Windflower the new home was even quieter than Plas Gwyn, where they heard trains; the only inconvenience was probably due to the previous owner's (Edwin Long) having been an artist: 'the heating apparatus we can't manage well & get too hot (I think, entre nous, it was designed for the comfort of Long's nude ladies!)' Edward Speyer offered to have book shelves erected at his own expense; Elgar told Speyer he had informed his books, now mostly lying on the floor: 'which attitude, after all has been known to express high exaltation – or the after effects!'

The first music to come out of Severn House was both metropolitan and imperial. Elgar had been approached by Oswald Stoll in connection with a masque to be produced at the London Coliseum on 11 March 1912. It was to commemorate the last of the Delhi durbars, held in 1911, when George V was crowned Emperor of India and announced the transfer of the capital from Calcutta to Delhi. Hence a cast in *The Crown of India* headed by India and her most important cities, a herald called 'Lotus', St George, and many Moghul emperors. Hence also Delhi's taunt to Calcutta:

> thou wast a swamp
> One hundred years ago; when I a Queen
> Enthroned for forty centuries had been!

Terms were advantageous and, after misunderstandings with Novello, the masque was eventually published in piano score by Enoch. During

---

[1] Letter of 14 May 1903 from Norman Shaw to Reginald Blomfield.

its composition Elgar's health had been poor. He told Frances Colvin on 1 February that his books were still on the floor: 'I have followed them more than once having fallen through this gout in my eyes & head.'

Elgar was also committed to a larger project. Since March 1904 it had been public knowledge that he was interested in setting Arthur O'Shaughnessy's *Ode: We are the Music Makers*. The Birmingham Festival, deprived of an Elgar novelty in 1909 (there had been hope of more 'Apostles' music), now wanted a major choral work for 1912, and the 'Music Makers' idea was revived. Elgar told Robin Legge there would be an important part for contralto solo. Soon after the masque opened, Frances Colvin wrote her appreciation: 'your music is gorgeous & gave one just the right thrill. I longed to stop those women [the cities of India] shrieking & just have the music, & the wonderful colours to look at, it would be superb!' In reply Elgar celebrated the commercial success of the masque, the more welcome because of Severn House expenses: 'When I write a big serious work e.g. Gerontius we have had to starve & go without fires for twelve months as a reward: this small effort allows me to buy scientific works I have yearned for & I spend my time between the Coliseum & the old bookshops ... I found a lovely old volume "Tracts against POPERY" – I appeased Alice by saying I bought it to prevent other people seeing it – but it wd. make a cat laugh.' He wrote from Severn House, but another Severn was in mind: 'My labour will soon be over & then for the country lanes & the wind sighing in the reeds by Severn side again & God bless the Music Halls!' During the run of *The Crown of India* Elgar received from the Duke of Argyll suggestion for an opera about St Columba. The only snag was the saint's dislike of women, so strong 'that he wd. allow nothing of female sex – not even a cow – in Iona!'[2]

The successful run of the masque ended on 23 March; but it was some time before Elgar could go to the West Midlands. The noises in his ear were increasingly troublesome, and his doctor Sir Maurice Anderson sent him to a specialist. The result was a month in what he called 'Cold Storage'. But he managed to complete the op. 67 setting of Psalm 48, *Great is the Lord*, and wrote about it to Clayton at Novello on 29 March: 'it is very big stuff of Wesley length but alas! not of Wesley grandeur'. The enforced idleness was wearisome, and Elgar was much distressed by the loss of the liner *Titanic* on her maiden voyage. It was not until 2 May that Lady Elgar could report some musical stirring: 'E. free all day – Got out sketches &c.'

[2] Letter at the Birthplace Museum.

With less than five months before the première of *The Music Makers* on 1 October, Elgar was hard pressed. His sketchbook researches were more comprehensive than usual, and the Ode absorbed ideas originally intended for much earlier works. On 29 May Elgar was even wondering about the wind quintets of his novitiate and wrote about them to Hubert Leicester: 'I wonder whether you would lend me the old *Shed*-books: I should very much like to see some of the old things & perhaps copy some of them.' Again Alice Stuart Wortley received evidence of the work's progress. She was sent part of the introduction, enigmatically headed 'the complete understanding': she then received the 'Novissima hora' quotation from *Gerontius* near the end of the setting; eventually there were vocal score proofs of the first eight pages: 'I hope you will like it.'

During the composition Elgar went to a concert on 12 May conducted by Siegfried Wagner and was 'Much bored'. Four days later he and Carice were at Golder's Hill and heard a band playing *Sea Pictures*; 'E. cd. not think *what* they were playing.' At the beginning of June the Elgars saw an 'Airship in far cloudy distance', presage of trouble ahead. There were tea parties at Severn House; outside the Elgars' closest friends were such guests as Laurence Binyon, Ignac Paderewski, Leopold Stokowski and Henry James. The last named reminded Elgar of a passage in *Curiosities of Law and Lawyers*, which he carefully underlined: '*His stop for a word, by the produce, always paid for the delay.*'

Finishing the vocal score of *The Music Makers* plunged Elgar into abject misery. He wrote to Alice Wortley the next day, on 19 July: 'Yesterday was the usual *awful* day which inevitably occurs when I have completed a work: it has *always* been so.' He had hoped for 'open air & sympathy & everything to mark the end of the work'; instead he 'wandered alone on the heath – it was bitterly cold – I wrapped myself in a thick overcoat & sat for two minutes, tears streaming out of my cold eyes and loathed the world'. After a visit to The Hut he turned aside from the Ode and orchestrated instead the two op. 60 songs, *The Torch* and *The River*, as well as Alice's *The Wind at Dawn*. When the Windflower went to Bayreuth, she took with her a set of vocal score proofs of the Ode to show Hans Richter. Elgar wrote to her there on 12 August and mentioned the place-name he had written at the end of the MS vocal score: 'We saw Judge's Walk transfigured by the evening sun from miles away thro' my field glasses – but it looks *fearfully* desolate – desolate.' The orchestration was completed on 20 August, and he added to the full score the same Tasso quotation he had adapted for the final page of the 'Enigma' Variations: 'Bramo assai, poco spero, nulla chieggio.'

A conducting engagement in Harrogate took Elgar north through fields sodden by a wet summer. He told the Windflower on 29 August that he 'wept during the Variations my friends seemed so far away'. Lady Charles Beresford was there, and on this occasion Elgar found 'Society' refreshing: 'Of course Harrogate thinks itself very fashionable & more than chic – & the ladies dress up terribly. Lady C. shews her contempt for the whole thing by wearing a hat at dinner & a curious sac-like robe something like a waterproof – the Majestic Hotel visitors are very much hurt I think.' They then went into one of the 'salons', where 'somebody began to sing. Whereupon Lady C. uttered a shriek & we fled! it was all very amusing.' As the letter continued, he turned to music: 'I have written out my soul in the Concerto, Sym II & the Ode & you know it & my vitality seems in them now – & I am happy it is so – in these *three* works I have *shown* myself.'

At Hereford to rehearse *The Dream of Gerontius*, Elgar also went to look at Plas Gwyn, wanting to see, as he told the Windflower on 1 September, 'if the swallows are still cared for'. He found the loft repainted and the windows tight closed, 'so my companions of eight years found no welcome this year & have had to seek new homes'. At the Three Choirs Festival Muriel Foster sang the newly orchestrated songs, *The Torch* and *The River*, and Elgar took her for a drive to Broadheath. Again the Bach chorales were sounded from the cathedral, as Lady Elgar noted: 'very beautiful but people paid no attention & wind carried sound away'.

In Birmingham on 28 September Lady Elgar listened to Henry Wood rehearsing Delius's *Sea Drift*, 'but cd. not endure either work *or* the Conductor'. There was an interesting juxtaposition at the première of the Ode on 1 October in Birmingham Town Hall. After the interval came the first English performance of Sibelius's Fourth Symphony. Delius heard both works and wrote to his wife Jelka about them: 'Elgars work is not very interesting – & very noisy – The chorus treated in the old way & very heavily orchestrated – It did not interest me – Sibelius interested me much more – He is trying to do something new & has a fine feeling for nature & he is also unconventional.'[3] Parry thought the Ode 'mostly commonplace'. Critical reaction was generally guarded: it was felt there was little substance in O'Shaughnessy's claim for the music makers as harbingers of worlds to come; that Elgar's self-quotations from some of his finest works were hardly more than a private indulgence serving merely to show up the comparative poverty of the new music. Robin Legge in the *Daily Telegraph* made the point neatly: 'Where the poet speaks in general terms, Elgar

---

[3] Lionel Carley, ed., *Delius: a Life in Letters 1909–1934* (Aldershot, 1988), p. 93.

appears to look at the personal aspect of the matter.'

After a brief holiday in the Lake District, the Elgars returned to see *Captain Brassbound's Conversion* by Shaw and *The Winter's Tale*. During the next weeks there were sittings for a portrait by Philip Burne-Jones, son of the artist whose stained glass the Elgars so much admired in what was now Birmingham Cathedral. Elgar thought the portrait 'weak-kneed', and that Burne-Jones had made him 'stand like himself'. Elgar was soon to conduct the César Franck Symphony, with which he was unfamiliar; so he got Alice Stuart Wortley to play it as a duet with him. The only 'new' music before the end of 1912 was the reworking of a very old piece from the 'Shed' books, now orchestrated as *Cantique* op. 3 and somewhat lost at its first performance in the Albert Hall on 15 December.

Elgar was now determined to have a billiard table, for which the sale of the Gagliano violin would assist. Lady Elgar took it to Hill of New Bond Street, but 'felt such a traitor to the thing she loves vesy muss'. Another Elgar purchase caused different unease. A dog called Jock came to Severn House on 19 November but was dismissed at the end of the month as 'not quite trustworthy we feared'. On Boxing Day they saw with the Windflower *John Bull's Other Island*, and Lady Elgar approved: 'Most delightful. The noble & ideal left in instead of the poison of other B. Shaw.'

In January 1913 another Aberdeen terrier lasted even less time: 'Dreadful tragedy he was only here about 2 hrs & was lost – dear thing.' Next day Elgar went to the Battersea home for lost dogs 'to try to find the Wow', but had no success. Again it was decided to go abroad. A suggestion of the Riviera did not appeal, and eventually they went by ship to Naples, from where they moved on to Rome. A letter of 17 February to Carice makes clear that her mother, now in her mid-sixties, was feeling her age. Elgar referred to his wife as the 'Paint' when writing: 'I have wandered all about the whole of Yesterday & seen most of the old spots – of course theres the old difficulty – the Paint can't walk & loathes it & wants to do everything & – nothing.' Before leaving Rome on 22 February, the Elgars heard that Julia Worthington was gravely ill.

Italy had done little for Elgar; nor did Wales in the first half of March. Lady Elgar was saddened, but went to Tenebrae at the Brompton Oratory on Maundy Thursday and took comfort 'near their marriage altar ... that love is untouched after these years to E. & A.' The next day she thought of her own home: 'the Redmarley people gardening as they always did on Good Friday'. Elgar had another commission to fulfil, for an orchestral work at the Leeds Festival of early October 1913. It was to be *Falstaff*, a piece long contemplated,

with some sketches made soon after the turn of the century. On Easter
Saturday, 22 March, Elgar touched the new work but was also 'busy
with Heraldry'. Four days later he wrote an embittered and hurtful
letter to Kilburn, who had encouraged him to further creative endeavour: 'You say "we must look up?" To what? to whom? Why?

> "The mind bold
>   and independent
> The purpose free
> Must not think
>   Must not hope" –

Yet it seems sad that the only quotation I can find to fit my life comes
from the Demons' chorus! a *fanciful* summing up!!' Whereas Lady
Elgar recorded Elgar's frequent visits to the church at Belmont near
Plas Gwyn, in London she seems to have gone to Spanish Place, to the
Hampstead church, or to the Dominicans without him.

Elgar tried to lift his spirits in Worcestershire, going to his sister's
at Stoke on 2 April. Lady Elgar at Severn House discussed the Nobel
prize with a friend: 'Pray it may be given to E.' He returned after a
fortnight away, looking better and with 'nice out of door colour'. He
was practically involved with *Gerontius* and some very young demons
on 23 April, as he told Clayton: 'There was no applause when the
work ended – in the enormous room half the people knew nothing
about it – *each person brought a baby*! (which cried – *all* of which
cried continuously).' This was a performance at Mountain Ash in
Wales. Back in London he vented his spleen to the Windflower about
arrangements for the Royal Academy dinner on 3 May: 'After all I did
not dine at the R.A. – I went in, found they had omitted my OM &
put me with a crowd of nobodies in the lowest place of all – the
bottom table – I see no reason why I should *endure* insults – I can
understand their being offered! to me.'

On 25 May, a day when Henry James came to tea again, Elgar was
'beginning to turn to Falstaff'. The Windflower had been sent one
Falstaff sketch the day after he returned from Stoke; she now received
a copy of Prince Hal's theme, marked just this once 'nobilmente'. With
composition under way, Elgar was himself again. The family was
much saddened by the death of Julia Worthington on 8 June, but then
went on to The Hut, with the 'Garden like a Paradise'. Elgar stayed
on to work at *Falstaff*; the others returned to London for a film about
Wagner. Their way to the cinema was impeded by the funeral of a
suffragette, but the film was impressive: 'Very harrowing, creditors
interrupting composition &c. Splendid how possessed he was with his

works, & no opposition stopped him.' With Elgar much had been different.

When he returned to Severn House on 17 June, Lady Elgar had a slight accident. She ran to meet him in the music room, slipped, and fell on her back. Elgar, too, had a setback when the LSO informed him that his services as permanent conductor would no longer be required. This he felt keenly. Visits to the opera proved a successful diversion. He saw *Boris Godunov* at Drury Lane, with Chaliapine making his London début in the title role; the next evening was *Pelléas et Mélisande* at Covent Garden: 'E. liked much'; later there was *Tosca*. With the music for Justice Shallow's Gloucestershire orchard fresh in his mind, Elgar thought lovingly of the days round Malvern and Longdon Marsh, and wrote to Rosa Burley:

> Yes I remember all the sweetness of it – the syringa, then the beans & the limes. I suppose I shall never see it all again or cycle over the old places. How lovely the marsh must be – I envy you your seeing it & living in it all again. During the two moments I have spent in M. – all the people seem to disappear & only the eternal hills & the memories of the old loveliness remain.

Falstaff was making sure progress, with Elgar orchestrating direct from many a bald line of MS sketchily laid out for keyboard. On 17 July he gave an interview to 'Gerald Cumberland' and expressed his delight in *Falstaff*:

> I have, I think, enjoyed writing it more than any other music I have ever composed, and perhaps, for that reason, it may prove to be among my best efforts ... I shall say 'good-bye' to it with regret, for the hours I have spent on it have brought me a great deal of happiness.

Three days later Chaliapine came to Severn House, and there was talk of an Elgarian *King Lear*. Nothing came of this, nor of various suggestions Sir Sidney Colvin made in a letter the same day. He was staying at Thomas Hardy's, 'and this is a line to say that my embassy is successful, in so far as I find the old man not only willing but keen to co=operate on an opera with you'. Ideas included *The Trumpet Major*, *The Return of the Native*, and a section of *The Dynasts*, a nineteen-act drama about Napoleon. This last, Colvin thought, would involve 'bringing on big cosmic forces (choruses, perhaps invisible, of the Pities & the Years) as well as historic personages & events'. Elgar was intrigued, but for the moment *Falstaff* was responsibility enough and *Lear* was a strong temptation. Colvin had every reason to be excited: 'But this is thrilling news indeed. Chaliapine in the last act of

Ivan of course IS King Lear: and the conjunction of you two over that theme ought to be something tremendous.'

The Elgars went to The Hut on 26 July. Colvin was there for more operatic talk, and the Windflower to speed *Falstaff*. W. H. Reed helped with bowing the string parts and Elgar wrote to thank him: 'I am glad you are haunted by *Falstaff* – such a fat ghost can do no harm.' This was on a printed card to the effect that Elgar was abroad and would deal with matters when he returned, now altered to read, 'SIR EDWARD ELGAR is fast asleep: your communication shall be laid before him when he wakes!' The Elgars were to leave for a holiday in Wales on 5 August, and during the last London days Elgar was under great pressure to reach the end of the new work. On the morning of departure Elgar was down at 4 a.m. to complete the score: 'A. made him tea &c &c & finished his great work Falstaff – D.G.'

There were proofs to correct in Wales, and an analysis of *Falstaff* to write, so Elgar was fully occupied. Lady Elgar was not altogether happy with Wales. One day she was 'furious with the uncourteous people'; on another, when the weather was misty, 'mountains & sea like phantoms & little ships like vague ghosts', she experienced her usual '*rage* with Welsh official who wd. not answer directly'. They saw with pleasure Conway and Carnarvon castles, the Menai Bridge; and there was 'much paddling'. Departure on 1 September found Lady Elgar 'Sorry to leave the Sea delighted to leave the disagreeable Welsh'.

At the Gloucester Three Choirs Festival in September Elgar conducted the *Coronation March* and gave his wife the chance to describe him on the rostrum: 'he looked so beautiful in order & robes & part of Court Suit & the sun lit him up as he stood'. Again he heard *Messiah* and was 'much affected by it & the wonderful sound of the Hallelujah Chorus rolling round the wonderful Cathedral'. *Falstaff* orchestral parts only arrived from Germany on the morning of the first rehearsal, 22 September. Part of the first performance day at Leeds, 1 October 1913, was spent at Fountains Abbey; Elgar went with Carice, the Windflower, and her daughter Clare. Back in Leeds for the evening concert, Elgar first conducted Bantock's *Dante and Beatrice*, which Lady Elgar thought 'long and dreary'. *Falstaff* came after the interval, and she felt he 'rather hurried it & some of the lovely melodies were a little smothered but it made its mark and place'. The applause had not been enthusiastic, and Elgar was very depressed. Perhaps the performance had not been ideal, as Robin Legge confirmed in the *Daily Telegraph*: 'I do not think even Elgar has ever written more complicated music, and it is for this very reason that I wish a greater conductor than he had explained his complications last night.' *Falstaff* fared no better in London under its dedicatee Landon Ronald, who gave three performances of it before the end of the year. C. W. Orr was at the first and noted 'an array of empty benches!' Parry was at the second and thought the work 'Full of his mannerisms and distortions, but a genuine product of his orchestral subtlety'. But from Bayreuth Hans Richter wrote to his friend, Marie Joshua: 'During the summer he sent me the number of the "Musical Times" which contained a communication of the Work accompanied by music themes. And what Themes! So entirely unmistakable Elgar-like! Instinctively I raised my "Conductor's-Arm" and conducted what I read.'

Musically the rest of the autumn was fallow. After Leeds Elgar did some work on 'Callicles', the Matthew Arnold setting. Social standards at Severn House were maintained as far as human failings allowed. One guest was 'much shocked at maid's depravity not drawing curtains'. The Elgars saw two more Shaw plays, *Androcles and the Lion* and *The Doctor's Dilemma*. Much of Elgar's intellectual energy went towards the diary entry of 21 November: 'E. solved Cryptogram. Very wonderful of him.' He was busy with it again the following day; but the achievement had quite a long history behind it.

Robert Buckley's biography said of Elgar: 'During journeys amuses himself with cryptograms'. He had collected articles by John Holt Schooling in the *Pall Mall Gazette* of January to May 1896. These dealt chronologically with various types of cipher 'From Late-Elizabethan Days' until 'the present day'. There was simple substitution of classical names for current ones, with Queen Elizabeth as Penelope and Sir Robert Cecil as Solon; a musical cipher from the reign of George II, which produced an absurd melodic line and arbitrary rhythms from 'I have received yours of the sixteenth'; the numerical cipher of the Russian nihilists; and finally a declaration by Schooling that 'the meaning of the cipher which now follows will never be solved by any one'. Elgar's progress towards the key-word 'COURAGE' can be seen on a discarded sketch for *Cockaigne*; and in the 'cryptogram box' now at the Birthplace are nine sheets of lucid explanation how Elgar solved the insoluble problem. Elgar in his turn felt that the coded missive he had sent Dorabella in July 1897 could likewise not be solved. The symbols used by Elgar on that occasion perhaps derived from the description of Ogham writing in the Book of Ballymote, a manuscript of the late fourteenth century. The message has baffled many.[4]

Some plans for 1914 took exciting shape towards the end of the year. Henry Embleton dined at Severn House on 1 December and propounded a scheme for *The Apostles* at Canterbury the following

[4] See Eric Sams, 'Elgar's Cipher Letter to Dorabella', *MT*, cxi (1970), p. 151.

June. Ivor Atkins wanted Part 3 of the 'Apostles' project for the 1914 Three Choirs Festival. Elgar was discouraging: 'I longed to complete the *Apostles*, but you see the fee you offer wd be the *only* return for a whole year's work.' There was no relenting when he wrote again on 29 December: 'the Lord desireth in these his days the pleasant degradation of Man (how foolish wd be an empty Hell to its maker!)'. He ended by hoping that 1914 might be 'of a better & wholesomer flavour than 1913'. More immediately hopeful was a contract with W. W. Elkin for two small orchestral pieces on a similar scale to *Salut d'amour*. Their first performance would be in the studios of the Gramophone Company, with the discs aiding sales of the sheet music. *Carissima* was composed in December and dedicated to Muriel Foster's sister, wife of Jeffrey Stephens from the Gramophone Company who had been largely responsible for the scheme.

Another instrumental piece occupied Elgar at the beginning of 1914. He had sent Alice Stuart Wortley ideas for a piano concerto, and on 10 January she came to try them over. For the rest, January was devoted to choral music. He started *Give unto the Lord* for St Paul's. He also completed five 'choral songs', so called at McNaught's suggestion and published as opp. 71–3. *Death on the Hills* op. 72 was started on 20 January and described by Lady Elgar as a 'weird & wonderful part song'. The following day was the trial recording session for *Carissima*, and the Gramophone Company was sufficiently aware of its significance to send Elgar a selection of records and the first of many gramophones he was to receive from them. It caused much pleasure at Severn House: 'we listened to it for the greater part of the aftn. Chaliapin as Boris the most wonderful.' That same day, 24 January, Alice Elgar read her husband *Two Summers*, a short story she had written in 1884 about a country lad recruited for Waterloo. Elgar was very moved by the tale, and Lady Elgar was briefly pensive: 'A. felt this a *great* appreciation – regretted muss not to have written more. Consoled by wise dictum "the care of a genius is enough of a life's work for any woman".' Four days later came the recording of *Carissima*, firstfruits of an association that was to continue till the end of Elgar's life. On the last day of January the Elgars attended a *Parsifal* rehearsal at Covent Garden. This was to herald the first London performances of the work Wagner had restricted to Bayreuth (and Munich for the private delight of Ludwig II). The grail and other Munich props had been lent for the occasion, but the diary was unimpressed: 'Such long[u]eurs quite unnecessary – & Orchestration unsatisfying'.

If Novello wanted the choral songs, Elgar wanted a good price for them. He wrote to Clayton on 3 February: 'Would the firm be disposed to give me a sum down, say one hundred & twenty five Guineas free of restriction & an immediate royalty of 25%?' Alfred Littleton had recently lost his wife, and unexpectedly married his nurse. Lady Elgar considered this 'a heartbreaking humiliating trial for the daughter Rose'. His gradual detachment from Novello meant that his brother Augustus was assuming the main executive power. Hence his letter to Clayton about the choral songs: 'I sent you a wire this morning saying must agree Elgars terms. I don't think we ought to hesitate a moment. The price is high amounting to extortion, but the point is that plenty of other houses would jump at the stuff at the price.' If the partsongs caught on, there was money to be made. The future must look after itself, but his present policy was clear: 'I don't want any more Elgar symphonies or concertos, but am ready to take as many partsongs as he can produce even at extortionate rates.' The question of whether Novello would want such a song as *The Chariots of the Lord*, completed during February, did not arise; it found a natural home with Boosey.

At the beginning of March Elgar was asked to add his signature to those of Lord Milner, Lord Roberts, Kipling and others, as one of 'twenty distinguished men' to protest against Home Rule for Ireland. The setting of Psalm 29 was less controversial, but on 6 March Lady Elgar reported a characteristic situation: 'E. much inclined to play with anything to avoid working at Anthem.' Elgar was committed to some adjudication in the Isle of Man at the beginning of April. Before sailing from Liverpool he saw his favourite *Isabella* by Millais and told the Windflower about it: 'it is hidden away for fear of Suffragettes – but I got in by persuasion & a card: bless you for having such a father & bless him doubly for having such a daughter'. The first impression of the capital, Douglas, was dreary, but at Government House Elgar was on top form, amusing and at ease. The adjudication went well; only the orchestra in *The Banner of St George* seemed 'extraordinary', with a cornet blasting 'irrespective of anythg!'

Troyte, whose office was in the Malvern Priory gateway, was approached by Elgar on 1 May about prints of Worcester, its cathedral, and the surrounding area: 'I have six good ones (1777) & Buck 1732 & some cathedrals of different ages. Oh! I have nearly $\frac{1}{2}$ doz: of your gateway including a Turner! with lightning – very terrible Have you any of these?' A week later it was the Elgars' silver wedding day; they celebrated it four days on with Act 1 of *Die Meistersinger* (the conductor Nikisch's daughter was the 'rather dreadful' Eva) and dinner at Lady Elgar's club. Elgar saw books and prints of Worcester when he stayed with the Leicesters at the beginning of June. The son, Philip Leicester, described him: 'E. looked well but very grey. Has aged somewhat since I last saw him. Very jolly and chatted away about old times in most vivacious way.' He mentioned a priest who had called on Mrs Elgar at Forli: 'Insisted on coming in & told her he did not want to interfere "if she was doing her washing or anything of that sort." He roared with the fun & said "fancy *Alice* doing the washing".' Young Leicester said that Elgar smoked 'incessantly. Carried a supply of pipes in a little green ladies' handbag'.[5]

On 18 June the Elgars made for Canterbury; he met Henry Embleton and the Leeds chorus that evening. *The Apostles* on the morrow seemed to Frank Schuster 'the greatest musical experience he had ever had'. Embleton now wished to build on this success. He came to Severn House on 30 June and had a long talk with Lady Elgar: 'He said beautiful things & made proposals about the 3rd Part of The Apostles in such a beautiful & delicate way like a friend who really loved E. & his work. E. had a talk when he came in & they clasped hands at parting, E. consenting. A feeling of quiet joy settled on us.' If *The Last Judgement* was ever written, it now seemed it would be for Leeds rather than Birmingham.

There had been another recording session on 26 June, for *Pomp and Circumstance* 1, *Salut d'amour*, and two of the *Bavarian Dances*. The recording technique of the day demanded a much reduced orchestra from Elgar's norm; and a record side of roughly four minutes frequently meant cuts. Gramophone royalties were such that Elgar always made the adjustments willingly. The Elgars both worked at the task on 25 June, and on the morning of the recording it was still a matter of 'E. working, A. helping, till nearly moment of starting drive to Hayes'.

There was a *Gerontius* rehearsal in Worcester on 9 July, and Elgar went the previous day to the Leicesters. He and Philip walked round the city after dinner. He called on his sister Lucy Pipe: 'All he could talk of for a few minutes after was her deafness which he thought such a dreadful affliction.' They went round St George's Square, down Thorneloe and along Stephenson Terrace: 'Here we stood some time, gazing out over Pitchcroft & over to Malvern, the lights of which were faintly visible in the dusk. He turned to me at last & said he was so glad I liked Worcester. Said he loved the old town & the old houses & hoped it might remain unspoilt & unchanged.'

Over the next months little was to remain unspoilt and unchanged. The Elgars left for Scotland on 19 July, partly retracing the route of Elgar's 1882 holiday. This time they were also in Iona, and Lady Elgar assessed the cathedral: 'in imposing position but looks so plain & distressingly *Protestant*'. St Columba would doubtless have protested her presence. By 25 July they had reached Achnasheen, well west of

[5] MS notes; Birthplace Museum.

Inverness, with 'Great mountains desolate & bare'. As the days went by Elgar and Carice contentedly fished; for the other member of the party it was less satisfactory: 'Really, dearly, A. found it rather monotonous!' At the beginning of August 1914 the war clouds were darkly menacing, and the Elgars were cut off from news. They were very anxious: 'Feared the government wd. not take action & feared betrayal of Belgium & treaty.' When war was declared on 4 August, Lady Elgar had no doubts: 'Our conscience is clear that we tried all means for peace & waited at our own disadvantage in patience & forbearance.' The problem now for the Elgars was how to get south, as public transport had already been commandeered. He told the Windflower that the Lovat Scouts had been through the village and 'rode off into the moonlight by the side of the loch & disappeared into the mountains'. Eventually a charabanc rescued them and they returned to London via Inverness, Perth and Edinburgh.

There was a brief Elgar première at Queen's Hall on 15 August. This was *Sospiri*, dedicated to W. H. Reed. It seemed to Lady Elgar 'like a breath of peace on a perturbed world'. And 'Land of Hope and Glory' launched on its wartime career: 'Enormous audience rose Shouts'. Marie Joshua, German on her father's side, was sure of her loyalties: 'I love this great England which has sheltered me so long & which has a conscience even in politics.' She was deeply upset when she heard that Hans Richter had renounced all English degrees and honours. Elgar considered that the war would ruin him financially, but the whole family was determined to aid the cause. Elgar enrolled as a special constable at the Hampstead police station: 'When some of the police or rather the one taking his name saw the O.M. he sd. "there are not many of them going about" '. The king was impressed that 'upwards of 30,000 inhabitants of the Metropolis' had answered this call. Elgar touched on his duties in a letter of 25 August to Schuster:

> Carice spends her whole time in *practical* ways – learning nursing &c &c.
> I am a s. constable & am a 'Staff Inspector' – I am sure others cd. do the work better but none with a better will. I was equipping (serving out 'weapons') & taking receipts & registering my men for hours last night: this morning at six I inspected the whole district.

He went on to give an idiosyncratic view of the hostilities:

> Concerning the war I say nothing – the only thing that wrings my heart & soul is the thought of the horses – oh! my beloved animals – the men – and women can go to hell – but my horses; – I walk round & round this room cursing God for allowing dumb brutes to be tortured.

117

Elgar now corresponded with Benson about the possibility of new words for 'Land of Hope and Glory', 'since the people have adopted our effort as the 2nd. National Anthem & it does good'. He sent an initial suggestion:

> Leap thou then to battle,
> Bid thy hosts increase;
> Stand for faith & honour,
> Smite for truth & peace.

Benson obliged at once, but got the rhythm wrong. Elgar then wondered about ideas from the American John Hay and his poem 'The vengeance is God's'. Benson was not sure what there was to revenge: 'we have hemmed in Germany tight all round for years, in the Goodnatured unsympathetic way in which we Anglo-Saxons *do* treat the world, & the cork has flown out'. Elgar clarified his meaning: 'Of course there's no vengeance &c&c: it was the idea, tersely put, "If it's God's work (Heaven knows there's enough *praying* being done) it is our place to do it" – an admonition to shirkers.' Benson persevered, and the final version was published in *The Times*.

There was anxiety at Severn House over the destruction of Louvain, the loss of Boulogne, a German advance on Paris; then the Elgars heard of the 'destruction of Reims Cathedral – Much upset. Felt must go & see Westminster Abbey was there'. Lady Elgar noted that 8 September was the day *Gerontius* should have been performed at the Worcester Festival 'but for Hun Kaiser'. The Three Choirs Festivals were now in abeyance till 1920, but publicity had been printed, and on the back of a 1914 programme Elgar made some notes about 'Antichrist' ideas for the third oratorio. He completed *A Soldier's Song* to words by Harold Begbie. Clara Butt sang it at the Albert Hall, but Elgar withdrew it and effectively suppressed it. On 22 September Elgar went for a brief stay in Stoke, a journey that became a wartime habit. He travelled with soldiers who had been wounded at Mons and gave them tea.

Lady Elgar's initial war work was to teach French to soldiers at Chelsea Barracks, and Elgar filled in time by painting heraldic shields to decorate the billiard room. But his thoughts were very much in the Three Choirs heartland when he wrote to Ivor Atkins on 26 October: 'We are fighting for the *country* & I wish I could *see* it.' His nostalgia turned to the cathedral and its surroundings: 'If it is sunshiny just go round to the W. end & look over the valley towards Malvern – bless my beloved country for me.'

The ravaging of Flanders was the inspiration behind Elgar's first major war music. A poem by Emile Cammaerts spoke of the dreams that would retake Liège, Malines, Brussels, Louvain, Namur, and finally make triumphant entry to Berlin. Cammaerts was married to Tita Brand, daughter of Elgar's first Angel in *Gerontius*. She had translated the poem, and with her he negotiated a setting for reciter and full orchestra. With arrangements made, Elgar went again to the West Midlands. In a letter of 13 November to the Windflower he said he had been for a day in Worcester, sitting 'in the old library in the Cathedral among the M.S.S. I have often told you of – the view down the river across to the hills just as the monks saw it & as I have seen it for so many years'. It seemed curious that he 'played about amont the tombs & in the Cloisters when I cd. scarcely walk & now the Deans & Canons are so polite & shew me everything new – alterations   discoveries &c. &c.'. The *Carillon* première on 7 December could not but be a success in the emotion of the moment, and Cammaerts wrote his gratitude the next day: 'I cannot let this day pass without thanking you again for your glorious work. I have met a good many Belgians to-day and they all wonder how you managed to share so completely our pain and our hopes.'

Zeppelin airships had bombed Ostende, and fear of air raids had blacked out London. The darkened city appealed to Elgar, as he told the Windflower on 11 December: 'How beautiful it is in the still quiet streets without the trying brilliant lights: all seems so muffled – a muted life to me and so sweet & pure.' As the year ended, Elgar wrote to Antonio de Navarro that the war had 'closed some vistas, opened others & has shifted many narrow points of view, but it has tightened friendships'. And Lady Elgar closed her 1914 diary: 'Year ends in great anxieties but with invaluable consciousness that England has a great, holy cause'.

Suggestion for a significant Elgar choral work came from Sidney Colvin in January 1915: 'Why don't you do a wonderful Requiem for the slain – something in the Spirit of Binyon's For the Fallen, or of that splendid passage of Ruskin's which I quoted in the Times Supplement of Decr 31?'[6] Binyon had already made a reputation as a war poet with *The Winnowing-Fan* published at the end of 1914. For the moment Elgar was otherwise engaged, buying Piranesi prints of Trajan's Column in Rome and indulging in obscure literary research at the British Museum. On this occasion he was after a portrait of the minor poet, Edmund Smith (1672–1710) and investigating a *roman à clef* by Mrs Delarivière Manley, who had bigamously married her cousin and been mistress of the Fleet Prison's warden. As Elgar told

---

[6] *Modern Painters*, vol.3, chapter xvi; final paragraphs on the Crimean War.

Colvin, 'this grubbing delights me and I will proceed to more reputable pursuits when this is done'. Such grubbing became an increasing delight.

Carillon was to be recorded on 29 January; it was also to be the *pièce de résistance* in a tour Elgar was to undertake with the LSO. He wrote to Carice about a journey back from Bradford: 'I hated the train and, as Vasari says of the monk who saw his grapes being stolen, I stood up & "said many things *which are not in the mass*".' Perhaps to avoid other similar occasions he resigned from the Special Constabulary on 22 February. Following Colvin's suggestion, Flgar had begun sketching music for three of Binyon's poems. He then heard that 'For the Fallen' was already being set by Cyril Rootham of St John's College, Cambridge, and that Novello had already agreed to publish it. After a meeting with Rootham, Elgar decided he could not proceed, and wrote to Binyon on 24 March 1915:

> I have battled with the feeling for nearly a week but the sight of the other man comes sadly between me and my music. I know you will be disappointed, but your disappointment is not so great as mine for I love your poem & love & honour you for having conceived it.

Two days later Lady Elgar summed up the result of 'Wrotham's disappointed face' as 'Sad loss for the world'.

That was not the end of the matter. The project already had powerful allies. The Handelian R. A. Streatfeild came to Severn House on 5 April. He induced Elgar to join the Hampstead Volunteer Reserve; he was also distressed that Elgar had given up 'For the Fallen' and was 'quite *angry* too – (quite right.)' Streatfeild eventually persuaded Novello to publish both Rootham and Elgar; and Sidney Colvin was 'overwhelming in his attack on E. to go on'. Now another scheme took shape. On 13 April Elgar had a visit from Emil Młynarsky (1870–1935), former director of the Warsaw Conservatoire and now conductor of the Scottish Symphony Orchestra. He wanted Elgar 'to write something for Poland as he did for Belgium'. The next day Elgar resumed the Binyon music '& loved it himself – there is hope'.

At the end of the month the Elgars saw six Shakespeare plays in Stratford. There was an 'interesting & rather original' Shylock in *The Merchant of Venice*, too much slapstick in *The Merry Wives of Windsor*, *Romeo and Juliet* ('Mercutio *very good* – Too harrowed after his death'), a *Twelfth Night* which was rather 'too rough', *Richard III* ('Grew depressed & weary of it – So steeped in crimes'), and finally a *Coriolanus* that was '*Most* interesting & absorbing'. Elgar was also keen to get some shooting practice. He had written to the Windflower the previous month: 'My hand is shaky: I have just been doing rifle exercise.' Now he spent some time at a rifle range: 'E. much excited about shooting – Hit target at 600 yards, wonderfully good as he never tried a rifle before.' General Roberts would have had to agree.

Elgar was making good progress with the Binyon music. He completed 'For the Fallen' first, though it was intended as third part of *The Spirit of England*. After scoring it in June, he inscribed it *'to the memory of our glorious men, with a special thought for the Worcesters'* and put it aside. The war was also taking many civilian casualties: the passenger liner *Lusitania* was sunk on 7 May (a 'truly German deed') and six people were killed in a Zeppelin raid on London (*'Brutes'*). Elgar had also all but finished his Polish work, and on 2 June, his birthday, he took it to the publisher William Elkin. He had incorporated in *Polonia* some national themes and tunes by Chopin and by the great contemporary pianist and composer, Paderewski. Lady Elgar attended the rehearsal on 7 July, the morning of the first performance, and remembered what Rodewald said about the Elgar orchestra: 'Such a wonderful *sound*, as dear Rody used to say, *his* sound, drums like guns'. The concert had apparently been badly advertised and was poorly attended.

Arthur Bliss, already a promising composer, wrote to Elgar on 12 July, just before his battalion departed for France. He expressed gratitude for the hours of pleasure Elgar's music had given him and described his luggage plans: '2 lbs out of the modest 35 that I am allowed to take out with me as necessary kit are taken up by the scores of your variations and second symphony.' By mid-July Elgar had another war work ready. This was *Une voix dans le désert* involving the recitation of another Cammaerts poem about suffering Belgium. This time there was a central 'song' about the return of spring, when the churches of Antwerp, Ypres and Nieuport would reopen.

After a stay at The Hut and visit to the Stoke Poges churchyard where Thomas Gray had written his *Elegy*, Elgar tried over for friends in London the new recitation and also entertained them with excerpts from George Tolhurst's *Ruth*, perhaps the worst of all oratorios. There was a run of *Carillon* at the London Coliseum in the first half of August, but no more original music that summer. At the beginning of September Elgar went alone to the Lake District. He wrote to Troyte that the weather was exceptionally lovely: 'I won't say divine because "le bon Dieu suffers from megalomania & thinks he's the Kaiser." (This is from Paris.)' Lady Elgar travelled up on 10 September, and they met at Ravenglass, almost on the west coast. The Stuart Wortleys were staying nearby, and the Elgars were with them for ten days. When about to arrive, Elgar enciphered the word 'Walls' by means of the Russian nihilists' numerical square and wrote the message 'am coming'.[7] They went to Furness Abbey and admired 'the great open arches & recumbent figures of Knights in armour with hand on sword'. Lady Elgar's Catholic ire was stirred by a visit to Calder Abbey, which was 'ruined by that Hun Henry VIII like Furness'. There were bonfires and the taking of a wasps' nest, which remained a legend in the Stuart Wortley family.

Carillon continued to fulfil the needs of the moment. On 9 October Lady Elgar reported on a new reciter, Lalla Vandervelde, daughter of the Speyers of Ridgehurst: she looked 'very picturesque a type as it were of suffering Belgium'. Oswald Stoll had auditioned her against 'the tinkling sounds of the untuned piano which Sir Edward was belabouring as energetically as its decrepitude would allow'. Stoll wanted the background to be a burning village. Lalla preferred to stand 'outside the drop curtain, which was bright red. As I should be dressed in black the contrast would be striking, and I could use the curtain to lean against, or to clutch – for "business"'.[8] Arthur Bliss remembered an occasion when she recited it to cadets at Prior Park. The evening was supposed to be a 'diversion', but she had given them poems by Claudel and Maeterlinck. In *Carillon* Bliss did what he could as pianist 'to support the ringing voice of Madame Vandervelde but it was the last frenzied cries of "à Berlin, à Berlin" that established the evening as a real "diversion"'.[9]

A telephone call from Robin Legge on 9 November raised the suggestion that Elgar might write music for *The Starlight Express*. The play was an adaptation of Algernon Blackwood's 1913 novel *A Prisoner in Fairyland*. Had the war not intervened, the play might have been produced by Basil Deane (later associated with Delius's and Flecker's *Hassan*) with music by Clive Carey. The production was now the responsibility of the Canadian-born Lena Ashwell, who had taken a lease of the Kingsway Theatre from 1907. She had appeared there earlier in 1915 as Margaret Knox in *Fanny's First Play* by Bernard Shaw; he both praised and scolded: 'Even your squawks are priceless. I love to hear you say "Quahtly," and should cry with disappointment if you said "quietly." ... You will play girls of 18 for the next ten years. Your Margaret is a great joy.'[10]

She was now determined on Elgar's support: 'The play is half reality & half fairyland & it is your help in fairyland I want so much. There is a great mystic quality in the play which I am sure will help

---

[7] Birthplace Museum.
[8] Lalla Vandervelde, *Monarchs and Millionaires* (London, 1925), p. 116.
[9] Arthur Bliss, *As I Remember* (London, 1970), p. 46.
[10] Dan H. Laurence, ed., *Bernard Shaw: Collected Letters 1911–1925* (London, 1985), p. 292.

people to bear the sorrows of the war'. Lena Ashwell came to Severn House on 10 November and made a favourable impression – an impression confirmed the following day when she had given them a box to see her in *Iris Intervenes*: 'Much thought as well as amusement in it. The only play or novel in which a woman has the sense to say "Nothing wd. make me believe it" A. clapped.' Elgar's interest was aroused, and on 12 November he was 'busy thinking out the music'. The next day 'Lena Ashwell came & E. settled to do or adapt his music for her Play. She was moved to tears by E's music from The Fountain.' At this stage Elgar was uncertain how far he might write original music or adapt parts of *The Wand of Youth*, from which he had played to Lena Ashwell. The 'Starlight' story readily recalled aspects of the Elgars' childhood play as he now remembered it.

Blackwood came to Severn House on 15 November and immediately charmed the Elgars with his tale about 'rearing a horse to run in the Derby on dried milk'. A concert in Leeds gave opportunity for more talk with Embleton, who now wanted *The Spirit of England*, when completed, for York Minster; Embleton then left for a night journey to Newcastle to pay his colliers, and Lady Elgar amused him by saying she would be anxious the money might run out.

The timetable for *The Starlight Express* was now very tight. Elgar looked over sketches originally conceived for other works; he called the procedure 'labour exchange'. Sir Thomas Beecham had been expected some days ago but had not turned up. He now arrived on 21 November for discussions about *Une voix dans le désert*: 'had long talk with E. in Library & came into tea & ate cakes & drank cold water'. Friendship with Blackwood ripened; after dinner he would join in 'Very pleasant nice out of the world talk late round the fire'. It was wet on 9 December, but Elgar set out 'to try & find an organ – went to all sorts of wonderful places in London – no success'. Four days later Lady Elgar laid aside the diary and made no entry for 13 days; it was a 'Breathless time with Starlight Express'.

With the music done, Elgar wrote to Sidney Colvin on 20 December: 'it has been a real joy to me to have something so pure & simple to do & Blackwood is an unusual man – & sympathetic to me'. But his pleasure was disturbed by a letter from his colleague:

I hear that Mr. Wilson, the artist, has designed the Sprites in the spirit of Greek fantasy – Lamplighter a quasi-Mercury, Gardener as Priapus, or someone else, and Sweep possibly as Pluto. It is a false and ghastly idea. There is nothing pagan in our little Childhood Play. It is an alien symbolism altogether.

The Hellenism was abandoned, but Blackwood then reported trouble with the costume for the Organ-Grinder, whose 'Piedmontese brigand appearance with those ghastly tight breeches' was equally inappropriate.[11] Elgar was now so concerned on Blackwood's behalf and his own that he refused to conduct the first performance on 29 December and would not even attend. But there was another reason. Two days previously Lady Elgar's taxi had been in collision with a car, and she had been badly concussed. She wrote it up in her diary later, having been told that 'she spoke most politely & behaved with much dignity', though she remembered nothing. *The Starlight Express* ran for a month, and Robin Legge considered it a success, though pruning would have helped, as '$3\frac{1}{4}$ hours is too much'.[12] Despite his disapproval of the staging, Elgar was often there.

Lady Elgar summarized the year 1915: 'D.G. much success in many ways to England – Sad losses & awful atrocities by the Germans who have become more diabolical than ever.' These war months had shown Elgar responding to what England and her allies expected of him but turning for spiritual strength always towards Worcester and the West Midlands. Finally he had seized a chance to resurrect the childhood memories of Broadheath with its *Wand of Youth* ideas. He felt rejuvenated by *The Starlight Express*, and it remained his most extensive work of the war years. At the end of the full score he drew five scurrying mice and a couple of cats, signing himself as 'ae. 15', aged fifteen.

[11] *Starlight Express* correspondence; BL, Add.MS 69834.
[12] Birthplace Museum.

7

Sorrows national and personal (1916–1920)

The run of *The Starlight Express* finished on 29 January 1916, and Elgar was much saddened. That same day saw the première of *Une voix dans le désert* in a triple bill with *Cavalleria rusticana* and *Pagliacci*; Beecham conducted the operas, Elgar his own music. The immediate future of *The Starlight Express* now lay with the Gramophone Company; it was the first venture under the terms of a new and generous contract with Elgar. As soloists he wanted Charles Mott, who had already performed in the play, and Agnes Nicholls, his first Mary Mother in *The Kingdom*. She remembered that Elgar was 'very excited about these records, and if I may say so, very pleased with the way I did it'. Blackwood was staying at Severn House when the records came; they were judged '*Very* good'.

The latter part of February was spent on orchestrating 'To Women', the second part of *The Spirit of England*, and plans were advanced for the printing of the two sections now ready. Cyril Rootham was thoroughly dismayed, and it fell to Streatfeild to take up the matter again on 28 March. Rootham maintained that Elgar's withdrawal the previous year 'was intended to be final, that he had no right to resume work upon his setting of the poem, and that he broke his word'. Streatfeild pointed out that Binyon had not given Rootham exclusive rights on the poem; but Rootham's conviction that Elgar had behaved dishonourably never ceased to rankle.[1]

Elgar was delighted when Edward Speyer sent him an article he had written on watercolours of the Mozart family. He acknowledged it on 13 March and asked about an anecdote that the boy Mozart had triumphantly complied when given the figured bass of a Vivaldi concerto to realize. Elgar then mentioned the Vivaldi parts his own father had, on which Elgar too had practised figured bass. He went on to cite evidence that might link the Elgar parts with those shown to the young Mozart: 'I always like to think we own the very book that the Wonder Child played from.' On 18 March there was lunch

---

[1] Rootham's widow still remembered the matter with bitterness in the late 1940s.

with Lady Cunard. Binyon was there, and Elgar had further converse with Beecham. Lady Elgar did not approve: ' "Thomas" afterwards – Very phantasmagoric, & not appealing to us *at all*'. Personally this did not matter; musically it was a pity that England's greatest composer was never seriously taken up by her greatest conductor.

At the beginning of April Elgar had influenza. He had planned a visit to Stoke, but collapsed on the train and was taken to a nursing home in Oxford. 'To Women' and 'For the Fallen' were to be given their first performance on 4 May at Leeds, with John Booth and Agnes Nicholls. Lady Elgar was apprehensive: 'E. far from well. It seemed quite cruel for him to travel, so unfit for exertion.' The new works were well received, and Ernest Newman wrote eloquently about them: 'Only out of an old and a proud civilisation could such music as this come in the midst of war. It is a miracle that it should have come at all, for Europe is too shaken just now to sing.'[2] London first heard them in a series of charity concerts arranged at Queen's Hall by Clara Butt for 8 to 13 May. On each occasion the *Spirit of England* music was to be followed by *The Dream of Gerontius*. Lady Elgar thought the 'King seemed very fidgety & unKinglike in demeanour' when the royal couple came on 10 May: 'They had to catch a train at 4.45 – & I cd. *feel* E. hurrying & feeling the constraint of their want of interest – The King was said to be much affected by "For the Fallen" but Gerontius was evidently too long for him.' But the week of concerts made £2700 for the Red Cross. Streatfeild now wrote to Lady Elgar 'that we ought to have "The Fourth of August" as soon as possible'; yet a year was to pass before Elgar could decide how best to set Binyon's stanza beginning 'She fights the fraud that feeds desire on lies'. The apparent depravity of the enemy was a real stumbling-block.

Elgar had bought at auction some stone fragments supposed to be from the tomb of King John in Worcester Cathedral. He wrote about them to Atkins on 26 May: 'I wonder what you think? I *rescued* them on the chance of their being genuine & Canon Wilson & the Dean accept them.' On Elgar's fifty-ninth birthday husband and wife went to Worcester and then in different directions, he to Stoke, she to the Novarros at Broadway. They were equally shocked on 6 June to hear that HMS *Hampshire*, carrying Lord Kitchener at the Tsar's invitation to Archangel, had struck a mine and sunk with all hands. Elgar mentioned the disaster when Percy Scholes came to Severn House on 29 June in connection with an article for *The Music Student*. He said that any musical nation would have insisted on British music for Kitchener's memorial service rather then the Chopin funeral march.

---

[2] *The New Witness*, 11 May 1916.

This was also the occasion when he played Scholes some of his earliest music, and Scholes later organized a competition for the completion of an organ fugue in G minor.

Elgar returned to Stoke for the second half of July. He lunched one day with the Windflower at Droitwich, showing her 'our bit of forest' and his sister's home, 'The Elms'. His own Alice never visited it, a fact he was to recall after her death. But on 1 August he arranged to meet Lady Elgar for a stay at Bridgnorth. It was a happy reunion: 'Both had such real excited joy in meeting. He had a garland of clematis & threw it over A.'s head'. They went on to Ullswater in the Lake District and Lady Elgar reported an incident while they were on the water:

> A storm came on & E. & A. sat at end of bench on boat very close together & vesy hapsy under one umbrella, & a man who had been standing by talking to another suddenly said, putting his face close to theirs, 'You are *lu*vers still like me & my wife.' A. rather speechless with surprise, E. said in a sweet way 'I hope so.' it was quite sincere & very touching.

Elgar hated coming back to London. Still he was unwell, and Sir Maurice Anderson suggested electric cautery for the throat: 'E. bore it so *splendidly*.' On 6 September he wrote to the Windflower, again at Tintagel: 'Make the most of the sea & the Arthurian land.' Two days later the Elgars were en route for the Berkeleys at Spetchley Park. It was a Catholic household, and the chaplain was in his Dominican robes at dinner. At Mass, Lady Elgar thought 'Mr. Berkeley & his son looked just like "Donors" in the old pictures, serving for the Bishop'. Ernest Newman happened to be in Worcester, and it was suggested he should come over and see Elgar: 'As I was nearing the Hall I was hailed by someone from the lake. It was Elgar. He brought the punt to the bank and conveyed me to the middle of the lake, where I passed with him one of the golden afternoons of my life, talking about this and that.' Newman summed up his impressions: 'Elgar, for all his comprehensive interest in life, was at heart, I have always thought, an "escapist".' Elgar inscribed his host's copy of *Gerontius* with a memory of his schoolboy days. Where the Soul of Gerontius sings about 'The summer wind among the lofty pines', Elgar wrote, 'In Spetchley Park, 1869'. He went briefly to Stoke and wrote to the Windflower about Spetchley, a 'lovely place where I played as a child, $3\frac{1}{2}$ miles from Worcester'. He continued: 'I am very sad – & cannot *rest* even here, so after *one* night I restlessly go home.'

Back at Severn House there were only oblique references to original music. Jack Littleton of Novello (Alfred's son) proposed a '*Toad* &

Verklärung' symphony. Elgar had come home with a toad one day:

> E. bought it of some boys for 2d. He did not think it was happy with
> them – He put it in the garden & calls it Algernon as he met A.B. [Algernon
> Blackwood] at the time – He puts his head out of the window & says 'do
> you think he will come out if I make a noise like a worm?' – Algernon
> invisible.

McNaught wanted Elgar to write a 'Bugle' symphony that might
appeal to the whole army. Of visitors to Severn House, Yeats gave
little pleasure when he came to tea with Lalla Vandervelde: 'There
seemed a lack of sympathetic spark, A. *could* not arouse a word from
him.' More welcome was the Windflower on 26 October, who again
played part of the projected piano concerto. That music was seriously
in the making was clear three days later when Clara Butt arrived to
sing some of 'The Fourth of August', the missing movement in *The
Spirit of England*.

The Violin Concerto was to be recorded by Marie Hall, an Elgar
pupil of the Malvern days. On 13 November Elgar was busy rescoring
the work and abbreviating each of the three movements to take a four-
minute side; the cadenza was to have a side to itself, and for the
'Aeolian harp' accompaniment Elgar wrote a special part for concert
harp. Before the recording on 16 December there was news that Hans
Richter had died in Bayreuth eleven days previously. The sadness of
his anti-British stance was softened by a letter from Sidney Loeb about
a recent communication from his father-in-law: 'Give my love to my
friends and all the artists who worked with me. They are with me in
my waking hours and in my dreams, and my thoughts of them are
always good and pleasurable.' They heard on 18 December that Charles
Stuart Wortley was to be made a peer, and two days later Elgar wrote
to the Windflower: 'I am out of bed for the first time since Saturday &
I use the first minute to send you love & congratulation on the event, –
I gave you a coronet long ago.' He assumed that nothing essential had
changed: 'But you are still the Windflower I think and hope.'

On 21 January 1917 Lady Elgar was at the Albert Hall to hear the
slow movement of the Second Symphony played in memory of Sir
George Warrender, an Elgarian friend since the Mediterranean cruise
of 1905. Elgar went instead to the Royal Court Theatre 'to see Lalla
in B. Shaw's horrid little play'. Lalla Vandervelde was playing the
Lady in the première of *Augustus does his Bit*. At the beginning of
February 1917 the war took a decisive turn: 'Diplomatic relations
between America & Germany broken off. *at last*.'

More original music came from a suggestion inspired by Alice Stuart
of Wortley (her new style). Elgar had only just emerged from his sick

bed on 7 February when 'Ina Lowther came to lay the Chelsea Ballet idea before E.' The plan was for a short work as part of a war charities matinée. The scenario was to be based on the design of a fan drawn in sanguine by Charles Conder. Pan and Echo from the classical world were to wreak havoc amid a group of eighteenth-century amorous mortals. Elgar's decision was quickly made and his health quickly mended. He wrote next day to the Windflower: 'I am better & am doing the Ballet – or *think* of doing it – but where are you? I wanted to tell you the theme & *every note* must be approved by you.' After his signature there was a playful suggestion: 'I thought of using up *your Piano Concerto*! (Labour exchange!) but you would not allow that would you?' While at work on *The Sanguine Fan*, Elgar was saddened by two deaths. George Sinclair, of the bulldog Dan, died on 8 February, and Elgar wrote to Atkins that he had 'just opened the paper & seen the sad, sad, sad news of Sinclair. I am overwhelmed & sorrowful.' Then it was his Uncle Henry, his father's partner and successor in the Worcester shop, who died on 24 February.

In March Elgar started at once on the four Kipling settings that were to be known as *The Fringes of the Fleet*. A conducting engagement in Leeds took the Elgars to the Queen's Hotel, where they had often stayed in peace time. Elgar described the present situation in a letter of 6 March to the Windflower: 'The *service* here is beyond belief – e.g. I ordered breakfast at 8.40 sole & porridge – at 9 o'c the young lady came back to say they had no sole: I sd. What have you? She didn't know: then she went away for $\frac{1}{2}$ an hour to find out'. Among the results were '*two* pint jugs of *cream*, no serviettes.' When they left for London the next day, history was unfolding dramatically: 'Startling news on opening paper at station Revolution in Russia & Czar deposed – May it have all success!'

The orchestra for *The Sanguine Fan* was initially less than adequate: 'Made A. start from her seat at some of the noises they made'. At a rehearsal George du Maurier, who was taking the part of Pan, said that Elgar would 'become absorbed in his music & keep him standing on one leg while he dwelt on a note!' At the performance on 20 March the ballet shared the programme with some unworthy items, as Elgar wrote to Atkins: 'The Fan Ballet was lovely & you *must* see it – some of the entertainment was a disgrace – low & *vulgarly uneducated*.' He also mentioned some MSS they had been discussing for the cathedral library; he hoped to present the full scores of both *Froissart* and *The Light of Life* (Worcester commissions), but for the moment could not trace them.

At the end of March Elgar was working to complete *The Spirit of England*. He told the Windflower that 'the Binyon Big thing is in full blast', and on 12 April Elgar informed Binyon that the piano score was done: 'I sent *The Fourth of August* to the publishers today so that our work, complete in three divisions, will appear some day. Thank you for allowing me to set your splendid poems.' At Queen's Hall there was a repeat performance of *Une voix dans le désert* and the première of Elgar's third wartime recitation, *Le drapeau belge*, again to a belligerent poem by Cammaerts.

Yet letter after letter shows Elgar's thoughts far from London. He wrote to the Windflower on 13 April: 'It is nice to know that you love *my* Stratford: I wanted to take you a walk beyond the mill by the river.' Next day he dealt with Worcester topography to Atkins and coincidentally described the house that was to be his last home: 'The Red House still exists & is now called Marlbank ... If the old Red House (which has oak floors etc) had been more free from surrounding new buildings I wd have ended my days in it – it *is* for sale.' Then on 17 April Colvin was given the results of spring weather at The Hut: 'The river has risen very suddenly & poor Frank's "river border" of choice flowers (a few come & more to have come) is quickly being eroded by the cruel, crawling foam & sails, piecemeal, down the black stream.'

Severn House was sufficient for Lady Elgar, but she was well aware that Elgar and his music needed more. After the arrival of *Fourth of August* vocal score proofs and completion of her task of laying out the full score pages, she went to Sussex on a journey of exploration with Carice. While Elgar was at Stoke, they viewed a cottage near Fittleworth on 2 May: '*Lovely* place, sat in lovely wood & heard nightingale, turtle doves, & many other dicksies & saw lizards.' Lady Elgar had doubts because the cottage was 'so very cottagy but large studio & *lovely* view & woods'; she decided on renting it for June. It was now a matter of moment whether Elgar would like 'Brinkwells'. Back from Stoke, he began orchestrating *The Fourth of August* on 8 May and took four days over it. The Kipling songs were also well advanced, so that Elgar approached Oswald Stoll about the possibility of performances at the Coliseum. The idea appealed. There was a repeat of *The Sanguine Fan* at the Palace Theatre on 22 May, when Lady Elgar took more pleasure in the music than in those listening: 'Most things dull – a *very* heavy dull audience – Why shd. Philanthropy make ladies so oppressively stupid? The Ballet a perfectly lovely gem.' The day was likewise memorable for a first run-through of *The Fringes of the Fleet*.

On 24 May Elgar was free for Brinkwells. On the journey they all but failed to dismount at Pulborough, the nearest station. Then Lady Elgar missed the turning to the cottage, 'but a kind farmer's daughter showed them a short cut'. Elgar was enchanted with his new retreat, which made him once more into an instrumental composer and largely relieved him from wartime words, whether bellicose, patriotic, dutiful, mournful, or escapist. Alice Elgar wrote at once to her namesake: 'I am delighted to tell you that Edward's first exclamation was "It is too lovely for words".' There was a carpenter's bench with tools, and Elgar quickly knocked up '2 rustic footstools'.

They returned to London on 4 June, with the Coliseum performances of *The Fringes of the Fleet* a week away. Elgar went to Harwich to get correct naval kit for his 'sailors' and then wrote to Schuster on 7 June about Brinkwells and the forthcoming show: 'we went to Sussex & it is *divine*: simple thatched cottage & a (soiled) studio with wonderful view: large garden *unweeded*, a task for 40 men. The "Navy" turn will come off at the Coliseum next Monday.' Elgar explained that the admiralty was 'taking great interest in it & on *Monday* NIGHT we hope to have a great show of Admirals & gold lace in the front row'. *Fringes* had a long and successful run at the Coliseum. There were war alarums of various kinds. On 14 June Elgar was at the theatre, and Lady Elgar was not far away at the National Gallery. An air raid was threatened, and the public was herded into the basement of the Gallery: 'A. cd. not bear not being with E. if raid came so an official let her out at some back door & she "sprinted" up to Coliseum.' Charles Mott, leader of the four baritones, was called up and threatened with drill parades. The work was dedicated to Lord Charles Beresford, who personally interceded for Mott, and was taken on stage by Elgar to meet the singers. One morning Elgar bought some herring as extra props, and on 25 June he produced an unaccompanied partsong, 'Inside the Bar', to words by Gilbert Parker. The five pieces were recorded on 4 and 27 July.

At the outset of a tour with *The Fringes of the Fleet*, Elgar wrote on 17 August to Colvin from Manchester about a French edition of Athenaeus set in Baskerville type: 'I am always interested in these sorts of fr. books, as B, who was a Worcester man, altho' he worked in Birmingham, sold his types to Paris & from them the first collected edn. of Voltaire was printed.' Lady Elgar was staying with 'W. M. B.' at Hasfield Court and was in nostalgic mood: 'Thought so much of E. & when he was at Hazeldine & our walks there – Willie Baker motored me over to Hazeldine – Rather gray & rainy but not much rain – Lovely & thrilling to see it again.' She even wondered about what might have been: 'Want the upper room (the old spare room) for E.'s study'. After conducting the *Fringes* in Leicester, Elgar returned to Severn House on 26 August and to a new worry: 'It seems atrocious but mean spirited R. Kipling wants to stop "The Fringes" continuing.'

Ten days at Brinkwells provided a break, but still Kipling was causing trouble about his poems: 'cd. not get satisfactory answer or explanation from him – wretched creature'. A week of *Fringes* at Chiswick proved a sore trial, as Elgar told the Windflower on 18 September: 'I "got thro" the Chiswick week but had to be taken down & brought back every evening – I mean *convoyed* as I was so giddy. This morning I feel better for the first time – Next week Chatham. I fear the Songs are doomed by R.K. he is perfectly stupid in his attitude.' Chatham was an important naval base, and the week was much disturbed by the war, its air raids and gunfire. The performances were to have started on the evening of 24 September, but the first had to be cancelled. The Elgars escaped to Canterbury for a day, where memories of the 1914 *Apostles* consoled them. Lady Elgar took up for her namesake the Chatham tale of raids and 'star shells' on 27 September: '*Crowds* in the streets not minding at all & on Monday evg. at the picture Palace wh. E. has to pass through on his way, they were sitting there & singing Land of Hope & Glory in all the firing, joining in Chorus – rather fine & touching.'

At the beginning of October Elgar managed a few days with his sister at Stoke; but the main event of the month was the first performance in Leeds of the complete *Spirit of England* on 31 October. Agnes Nicholls did all that was expected of her, but Gervase Elwes had almost no voice. There had been no time to find a substitute, Elgar told the Windflower, 'so after all – he just came on to the platform & whispered a few phrases & spoke it: just like praying'. The London première was on 24 November. The previous day's rehearsal at the Albert Hall caused Lady Elgar displeasure: 'Had to wait while Stanford did his common songs & a *dreadful* new one. Then the great music began – E. looked like the High Priest of Art.' Parry in his turn derived little pleasure from *The Spirit of England*: 'Very poor stuff for the most part. Justified choral writing. Like a sentimental part-song.' But priest and acolyte still had their sense of humour. Alice Elgar had seen an advertisement which began, 'GENTLEWOMAN, young, bright, husband in Mesopotamia ...'. Elgar enclosed it in a letter to Schuster the day after the concert, suggesting that 'the way to get "bright" is to send yr. husband to Mesopotamia'. He added an afterthought: 'Oh! I forgot; I've been ill for ten days.' Yet his health continued a problem. On 29 December Sir Maurice Anderson brought Dr Hale White from Guy's hospital for a consultation. Nothing was organically wrong: 'Urged smoking, golf, change'.

Elgar wrote to Troyte Griffith on 10 February 1918 describing his recent reading. He had also come across some lines of verse written

for Edinburgh University prize poems. One subject had been Neb-
uchadnezzar: 'Two lines in the grass-eating episode are splendid and
very useful anyday now, –

> "Said, as he chewed the unaccustomed food, –
> It may be wholesome, but it isn't good."

A useful "grouse".' Another title was 'The River': 'After the usual
source, the rill and the increasing flow we arrive at the climax, the
cataract.

> "The water, wildly leaping in mid-air,
> Left the astonished river's bottom bare".'

On 15 February Elgar had his first lunch at the home of Bernard Shaw
and his wife Charlotte. And two days later 'Quite a nice quiet man'
came to Severn House to go through *In the South*. This was Adrian
Boult, who later did much for Elgar's music when its reputation was
less secure than now.

Elgar continued unwell, and on 6 March Sir Maurice pinpointed the
trouble: it was tonsillitis, and Elgar agreed to an operation, entering
the Dorset Square Nursing Home eight days later. The operation was
a success, though Carice remembered that 'He was in a great deal of
pain for several days; they were not anything like the sedatives that
we have now, but nevertheless he woke up one morning and asked for
pencil and paper and wrote down the opening theme of the "Cello
Concerto".' At the time the 9/8 theme had no fixed destination, but
he copied it out as 'a thank offering to a good Windflower'. Perhaps
at this stage the theme was associated with Lady Elgar's diary entry
for 25 March: 'E. began a delightful Quartett. A remote lovely 1st
subject. May he soon finish it.' The same day Elgar wrote to McNaught,
wanting to know more about the 'Grosshändler' Tost, to whom Haydn
dedicated a dozen quartets and wondering about 'merchants' nearer
to Hampstead: 'Do ENCOURAGE, say, Selfridge, as a useful Grosshändler, to order some quartets from me.'

On 2 May they could return to Brinkwells. Elgar delighted in a
useful legacy from *The Fringes of the Fleet*: 'Navy boots great joy for
wet woods'. Elgar described his Brinkwells routine in a letter of 12
May to the Windflower: 'I rise about *seven* work till 8.15 – then dress
Breakfast – pipe (I SMOKE again all day!) work till 12.30 lunch (pipe) –
rest an hour – work till tea (pipe) – then work till 7.30 – change
dinner at 8. bed at 10 – every day practically goes thus.' Elgar's pursuits
were thoroughly rural: he was killing snakes, weeding, clearing the
fowl run, and fishing. He was also engaged in practical work about
the cottage, making a door-stop, setting up the sundial once presented

by Frank Schuster to Plas Gwyn, making a birch broom (it proved too heavy), painting a water tub. Lady Elgar read Lytton Strachey's *Eminent Victorians*: 'Very interesting – annoying sometimes by unworthy flippancy, ignoring the passion of aspiration & worship entirely.' But war echoes from across the Channel came even to Brinkwells, and Lady Elgar noted on 30 May: 'Bad war news this & succeeding days Incessant gun fire (distant cannon).'

Composition resumed with a setting of Kipling's *Big Steamers*, requested by the Ministry of Food. In view of the *Fringes* problems Alice Elgar considered it 'Very magnanimous to set anything more of R. Kipling's but he said, "anything for the cause"'. There were a number of guests at Brinkwells, including Lalla Vandervelde, the Windflower, Muriel Foster, and on 18 July Algernon Blackwood. He was shown the gnarled 'sinister trees' in Flexham Park and an 'Octopus' beech tree. He was adjudged by Lady Elgar 'Exactly the Brinkwells guest – He did wonderful feats with leaping pole, jumping up to top of gate head of lane & standing on the top of it'.

Elgar's chamber music year began to shape with the arrival of a piano at Brinkwells. This was on 19 August, as Lady Elgar reported: 'Much excitement – the piano arrived, in Mr. Aylwin's waggon ... It sounded so well – not the worse for journey. May it result in booful new works.' Elgar was able to tell Rosa Burley that he had 'a rabid attack of writing music', so that the Violin Sonata was complete within the month. Probably the slow movement 'Romance' was defined first. Five days after the piano came Lady Elgar referred to 'wonderful new music, different from anything else of his. A. calls it wood magic. So elusive & delicate'. They heard on 26 August that the Windflower had broken her leg at Tintagel; Elgar's response was the broad cantilena at the core of the Andante. Landon Ronald came two days later. By now Elgar had begun 'orchestrating 9/8' and Ronald was introduced to the works in progress: 'He heard the new music after lunch & loved the mysterious Orch. piece & wants it dreadfully, & much liked the Sonata.' During the last three days of the month W. H. Reed was at Brinkwells to try over the completed movements, with Elgar listing in his own 1918 diary their activities: 'fiddled, fished & fooled'.

After a brief stay in London and at Ridgehurst, Elgar resumed the Sonata, embarking on a movement he described to the Windflower as 'very broad & *soothing* like the last movemt of the IInd Symphy'. On 6 September Elgar offered the dedication of the Sonata to Marie Joshua. She was unwell at the time and hesitated to accept. Four days later she died unexpectedly. The music written after hearing of the Windflower's accident was now incorporated into the finale as well, as 'a wonderful soft lament'. The Sonata was nearly complete, and on

15 September another project was started: 'Wrote part of Quintet wonderful weird beginning same atmosphere as "Owls" – evidently reminiscence of sinister trees & impression of Flexham Park.' The following day Lady Elgar continued her account: 'E. wrote more of the wonderful Quintet – Flexham Park – sad "dispossessed" trees & their dance & unstilled regret for their evil fate – or rather curse – wh. brought it on – Lytton "Strange Story" seemed to sound through it too.'

The partsong *Owls* had set Elgar's desolate poem of 1907, but obviously the trees of Flexham Park were taking on a new significance. It may have been Blackwood who associated the trees with Spanish monks deprived of life while performing impious rites. Elgar seems to have told his biographer Basil Maine that 'the trees are their withered forms'. A consignment of Bulwer Lytton novels arrived at Brinkwells on 3 September. Among them was *A Strange Story*, dealing with occult happenings in a village setting.

Elgar extended the territory of Brinkwells on 16 September by acquiring for £3 'the Underwood below garden house'. This now demanded much chopping and clearing of paths; at one point a chip flew into his eye and inflamed it badly. Still very much the countryman, he wrote to Colvin on 26 September: 'I have never seen anything so wonderful as the sun climbing over our view in golden mist. I see now where Turner found such sights as Norham Castle etc.' He told the Windflower that London had no appeal: 'I have had – at the thought of town life – a recurrence of the old feelings & have been just as limp as before the nursing home episode.' It became clear on 8 October that Elgar was now working at the String Quartet: 'E. possessed with his wonderful music, 2nd Movement of 4tet.' This 'Piacevole' became a favourite of Lady Elgar's; already the next day, her seventieth birthday, she called it 'gracious and lovable'.

A wen had to be removed from Lady Elgar's brow, and this meant a month's stay at Severn House. The Sonata was played by Reed and Elgar to an invited audience on 14 October, and again to the still housebound Windflower. Elgar wrote to Ernest Newman on 21 October about the new chamber music, including the 'incipient Quintet' – I only mention this because I should like to dedicate the last named to you if it is ever finished'. Now that the war was almost over, Laurence Binyon had written a 'Peace' Ode and sent it to Elgar for possible setting. The reply on 5 November was not enthusiastic: 'I do not feel drawn to write peace music somehow – I thought long months ago that I could feel that way & if anything could draw me your poem would, but the whole atmosphere is too full of complexities for me to feel music to it.' He admired much of the poem but regretted 'the appeal to the Heavenly Spirit which is cruelly obtuse to the individual sorrow & sacrifice – a cruelty I resent bitterly & disappointedly'. Ivor Atkins dedicated his *Organists of Worcester Cathedral* to Elgar, who acknowledged it and admitted that 'Alice's "little" operation on her forehead turned out to be of more importance than we thought: she is all right now'.

News of the Armistice came on 11 November: 'E. put up our Flag, it looked gorgeous.' Carice was at the Coliseum, where 'Land of Hope and Glory' was sung twice; but her parents returned at once to Brinkwells. Two days later Elgar resumed the String Quartet: 'Wrote music & tried to recover the threads (*broken*'. After taking up the Quintet again, he completed the 'Piacevole' on 26 November. There was a *Falstaff* performance at Queen's Hall on 5 December which the Elgars attended: 'Mr. Saunders, leader, said he never enjoyed playing so much & had a lump in his throat at the end.' They returned to Fittleworth the next day, and on 8 December Elgar was 'writing last movement of Quartet – Very impassioned & carrying one along at a terrific rate'. As the movement proceeded, it seemed to Lady Elgar 'like Galloping of Squadrons' and 'like a mighty force'.

Her enjoyment was rudely interrupted by news of a burglary at Severn House. She decided she must be there, and departed early on 17 December: 'A. left in pony carriage at 6.15 – Beautiful stars on pale blue sky, brilliant moon.' She found that the major depredations seemed to have been on Elgar's clothes and the wine cellar; everything was reported to the police, and she was back at Brinkwells that evening. A week later the Quartet was complete and the parts copied out for W. H. Reed. Elgar left for Severn House on Boxing Day, finishing his 1918 diary notes with a table of fish caught; Lady Elgar listed the books she had read at Brinkwells.

When she returned to Severn House, Lady Elgar found that much silver had also been stolen. With the Sonata, String Quartet and Piano Quintet first movement complete, it was decided to have a play-through at home on 7 January 1919. Elgar wrote to Newman about it two days before: 'your Quintet remains to be completed – the first movement is ready & I want you to hear it – it is strange music I think & I like it – but – it's ghostly stuff'. The occasion was a success, and again Lady Elgar remarked on her favourite movement: 'the Piacevole like captured sunshine'. On 12 January Elgar was busy with the 'apotheosis' of the Quintet and was going to *The Provok'd Wife* by Vanbrugh in the afternoon; he remarked on the juxtaposition to Sidney Colvin: 'I am hard at it now & I think my proposed afternoon's entertainment will help in a nondescript sort of way – a change of mind anyhow!' Not everything at Severn House was ideal. Elgar was

muttering 'this is no home for me!' and on 18 January Lady Elgar
went to the town hall 'to remonstrate on Coal allowance' and drew a
picture of 'Sir E. sitting in ice cold studio with no food'; that evening
a 'much augmented allowance was notified'. The following day the
chamber music, now including the Adagio of the Quintet, was played
at Lord Charles Beresford's.

Elgar's London was summed up for the Windflower on 26 January:
'No music & interruptions by the thousand – I think of the holy peace
of Brinkwells in the early morn.' The unexpected death on 6 February
of R. A. Streatfeild, gratefully remembered for his diplomacy over the
Binyon setting, cast a gloom; it was 'a real loss of a devoted friend'.
But three days later the Quintet was finished. There was a dance on
18 February at Severn House for Carice, with Arthur Bliss among the
guests. When the Elgars lunched at Cheyne Walk soon after, the
Windflower produced a cast of Chopin's hand, 'so strangely like E.'s'.
A lunch on 4 March at the artist Roger Fry's was less successful.
Bernard Shaw was there and wrote an entertaining account of how
Elgar, nettled by Fry's remark suggesting the equality of all arts,
launched into a ferocious defence of music's supremacy.

More music was planned at Severn House for 7 March. This time
the three chamber works could be played complete. Arthur Bliss turned
over for Elgar in the Sonata, but was embarrassed what he should say
at the end: 'Was my disappointment due to the far from brilliant
performance or to the belief that its musical substance had little in
common with the genius of his earlier masterpieces?'[3] Bernard Shaw
was there on his first visit to the Elgars' home, and wrote a detailed
account of his reactions to the Quintet. Four days later Elgar told
Newman that the gathering had been 'bowled over' by the Quintet,
and that though he was not 'foolish enough to be swayed by intimates',
yet 'the "thing" likes me much'. And he sent on Shaw's letter for
Newman's perusal. The Elgars went to Liverpool on 14 March, he to
conduct *Gerontius*, she to admire the growing Anglican Cathedral as
'a wonderful building on such a wonderful site'. Elgar then fulminated
to the Windflower about the miseries of post-war society: 'It is *awful*
here – all dreadful *U.S.* Americans – the lowest of the human race – &
a jazz band. I am dreadfully unhappy at everything.' It was to be
increasingly so.

A major inspiration at the beginning of April was the arrival of
some Piranesi prints. Elgar described to his wife their effect on him:
'when one has looked at the great massive bridges one cd. not *think*
of small things, & after tiresome letters about trivial things looking at

---

[3] Bliss, *As I Remember*, p. 24.

these made one think *great* again'. About this time Elgar was busy with some 'Air' songs to words by E. F. Benson. He had discussed the project with Oswald Stoll at the Coliseum, and he seemed interested. Elgar was writing the music on 17 April, and a week later he wrote to the Windflower about it: 'I expect to be working at the "Air" (Benson) turn if the Coliseum take it on. I have much *sketched* & playable & wanted you to hear it.' The 'Air' scheme, perhaps a follow-up to the 'Sea' of *Fringes*, came to nothing.

Frank Schuster organized a private performance of the Quartet and Quintet at his Westminster home on 26 April. Some members of the press were present, and this was a trial run for the first performance with the same team of Albert Sammons, W. H. Reed, Raymond Jeremy, Felix Salmond and William Murdoch. Reed also played the slow movement of the Sonata. E. J. Dent was there and wrote afterwards to Elgar saying how deeply he was 'impressed with your Quartet & Quintet on Saturday afternoon. They are both intensely characteristic of yourself, especially in the slow movements, which one gets hold of easiest at a first hearing.'[4] He seems later to have changed his mind somewhat.

While Elgar was putting the final touches to the Quintet, 'painting' it as he said, Messrs Hill lent him a violin that had once belonged to Mozart. On 6 May Elgar went to The Hut, and Lady Elgar accompanied him as far as Paddington Station. She had both the Mozart violin and the Quintet MS with her: 'Afraid to put either down so with fiddle case in one hand & music under her arm, walked higher up to get taxi'. When the instrument was returned, 'Mr Hill smiled visionarily & was so pleased the Violin had been here'.

A few days at Brinkwells prepared the Elgars for the chamber music concert at the Wigmore Hall on 21 May. Lady Elgar noted that the 'faithful band' was 'much in evidence' and how interesting it was 'to watch the *delight* creeping over faces'. H. C. Colles in *The Times* longed for 'the contrast of a more virile mind, something less purely visionary and more touched by hardness'. Elgar seemed only to be looking to the past: 'What has he to say now, and have the years stamped their meaning on him in any profound way?'

On the last day of May the Elgars and Windflower heard the Portuguese cellist Guilhermina Suggia at Queen's Hall: 'Wonderfully picturesque looking in bright green & vivid claret silks – Disappointed with her playing.' The Augustus John portrait of Suggia was four years away, the Elgar Cello Concerto as many months. The first diary mention of such a work is on 2 June 1919 when Algernon Blackwood

---

[4] Letter at Birthplace Museum.

and Landon Ronald came for dinner and an evening of plate pool: 'E. played some of the Concerto to Lan who loved it at once.' The main tune of the first movement had been in Elgar's mind for well over a year, but when the concerto idea took shape is not known. Elgar now worked at speed. Felix Salmond became the Concerto's coadjutor. He was at Severn House on 5 June 'to try Cello Concerto'; five days later he was there again. The Windflower came too, and later W. H. Reed, 'quite enthused with the new work "the only man", he said, "who can write a slow movement" '. On 12 June Muriel Foster took the Elgars to the Russian Ballet, and they heard some Stravinsky: 'Bored with Oiseau de Feu – such a deadly story & manufactured music'.

They left for Brinkwells the next day. On 22 June Elgar was 'finally revising the beautiful 3rd movement of Cello Concerto, "Diddle, diddle diddle" '. This suggests what is now the second movement; perhaps Lady Elgar was in error, or Elgar had not yet finally decided the order of the work. Four days later Elgar wrote to Sidney Colvin: 'I am frantically busy writing & have nearly completed a Concerto for Violoncello – a real large work & I think *good* & alive.' He than asked if the Colvins would accept its dedication: 'Your friendship is such a real & precious thing that I should like to leave some record of it; I cannot say the music is worthy of you both (or either!) but our three names wd. be in print together.' Elgar 'did much orchestration of Cello Concerto' on 28 June, the day the Bedham Chapel School bell rang the news that peace had been signed: 'Very touching hearing this remote tanging little bell, all Bedham cd. do but proving itself alive to the great event & chained up as its Link in our great Empire.'

On 5 July Felix Salmond joined Elgar for a play-through of the Concerto to a group of friends at Severn House. There followed a week's stay at Ridgehurst, and he wrote for his host a notorious jape, his 'Op 1,001' dated 10 June. After a chorus of 'unintelligent smokers', Edward Speyer was to be woken by the orchestra '(furioso)' and then to deliver an irate recitative in the composite bass-baritone character of 'Sarastrowotanbasilioklingsohrdalandmarcelorovesobiterolfscarpia'. This third number, to the text 'Kindly, kindly, kindly do not SMOKE in the Hall on Staircase!' was fully orchestrated by Elgar, with thick clouds drawn up the score over the offending word. The day of Elgar's return to Severn House, they were again at the Russian Ballet. Once more there was Stravinsky, and the reaction was the same: 'Bored with Petrushka'.

Back at Brinkwells, Elgar may have added something to the Concerto on 22 July: 'E. went to Music room before breakfast & wrote wonderful passage – most haunting. Then made stand for the coffee pot!' Elgar copied out for Edward Speyer the final bars of the Concerto in full score, showing at the same time how much the solo part was altered before reaching its definitive form. The Elgars had again to be in London to identify some of the property stolen from Severn House; he also conducted for a peace pageant at the Coliseum. 'Land of Hope and Glory' and the *Imperial March* were played, during which Britannia was shown 'acknowledging all Colonies & dependencies &c. Very imposing'. Felix Salmond came to Brinkwells on the last day of July: 'Enchanted with the place. – After tea played Concerto & after dinner – It sounded perfectly beautiful – It is a flawless work.' Elgar now asked Salmond to give the first performance; his reaction was reported by Lady Elgar: '*thrilled* with the thought of playing the Concerto for the 1st time & wildly excited about it, did not sleep all night thinking about it'.

With the Cello Concerto almost complete, Elgar wrote to the Windflower about future plans on 3 August: 'I want to finish or rather commence the Piano Concerto which *must* be windflowerish so I hope you will come but somehow I know you will not.' In fact she did arrive, on 20 August; but the projected work made no progress. At Severn House there was a shock, as some 'dear wavy trees' had been cut down for the making of a neighbour's garage. Elgar went at once to The Hut, where William Rothenstein made a drawing of him. While he was there, the *Times Literary Supplement* published on 4 September a letter he had written dealing with the pseudonyms adopted by the 'Quadruple Alliance' of Walpole, Gray, West and Ashton. Elgar's main contention was that these names derived from contemporary plays: 'I think it probable that "Celadon, Courtier," in Dryden's *Secret Love*, was the original of Walpole's assumed name.' Paget Toynbee, original editor of the letters, was delighted with Elgar's discoveries and wrote the next day:

> Your suggestion as to the source of 'Celadon' seems to me likely; and I think it quite probable that Voltaire's 'Orosmane' may account for the puzzling 'Orosmades'. It is a satisfaction to have the Viscontina identified and I am pleased that you have been able to produce a 'Cindaraxa' – I hunted in vain.[5]

Elgar sent a cutting from the *TLS* to the Windflower, 'which will not interest you'; but it was she who had originally given him the books, '& I wd like to let you know how much I loved having them'.

Two days after returning from The Hut, Elgar was at a memorial service on 13 September for Lord Charles Beresford. He then had to attend the trial of two ex-policemen, responsible for the Severn House

---

[5] Letter pasted into the edition of the Walpole letters; Birthplace Museum.

thefts: 'The two burglars each sentenced to 5 yrs. penal servitude.' The return to Brinkwells was initially gloomy, with no music afoot. A railway strike aroused Lady Elgar's ire: 'they ought to be shot – worse than the worst enemies – & they have *no* excuse'. A visit to Lady Leconfield at Petworth House was also unsatisfactory. She seemed bored showing them the pictures and rather hustled them: 'After seeing the Turners, we sd. goodbye & found ourselves in the Hall with no one to show us out.' Walford Davies tried to urge Elgar towards opera; his reply was negative: 'I have never found a subject I cared about – I wanted something heroic and noble but I am only offered blood and lust in the way of libretti.'

The Cello Concerto première was on 27 October, at a concert launching the LSO's first post-war season. Albert Coates had chosen to conduct the 'Forest Murmurs' from *Siegfried*, the Skryabin *Poème de l'extase* and Borodin's Second Symphony. In the event Elgar's rehearsal time was cruelly curtailed, and Lady Elgar expressed herself forcibly: 'The *new* work, Cello Concerto, never seen by Orchestra – Rehearsal supposed to be at 11.30. *After* 12.30 – A. absolutely furious – E. extraordinarily calm – Poor Felix Salmond in a state of suspense and nerves – Wretched hurried rehearsal – An insult to E. from that brutal, selfish, ill mannered bounder A. Coates.' The final rehearsal was no better: 'That *brute*, Coates went on rehearsing "Waldweben" Secy. remonstrated, no use. at last just before one, he stopped & the men like Angels stayed till 1.30 – A. wanted E. to withdraw, but he did not for Felix S.'s sake – Indifferent performance of course in consequence.' Lady Elgar was no calmer next day: 'Still furious about rehearsals – *Shameful* Hope never to speak to that brutal Coates again.' Ernest Newman did not pull his punches in the *Observer*: 'never, in all probability, has so great an orchestra made so lamentable a public exhibition of itself'.

Elgar retreated to his sister's at Stoke, then on to Worcester, where Philip Leicester described him at sixty-two: 'He looks older. His hair & moustache are now more white than grey. His face is paler. Otherwise he seems unchanged. The same low voice, rapid earnest speech, keen sense of humour, & quick movement.' The next day he spoke about the Severn House burglary and the court case: 'Said that he usually sympathised with the criminals – "they are the only poets in these days".' He mentioned the case of a young man who had seduced a girl of seventeen from an unhappy home and run away with her. He thought it odd that, while we instilled into our young pagan theories of love as found in the classical writers, 'when two young people have the courage to defy convention & follow the poets to find perfect bliss, you send the boy to gaol & the girl home to her parents'. The ideas were already a little Shavian.

From 15 November Elgar was twelve days in Belgium and Holland. On arrival he sent an 'Anemone' word to his wife; she, however, was sufficiently unwell for Sir Maurice Anderson to order her to stay in bed. The Violin Concerto and First Symphony were enthusiastically received in Amsterdam, but he told the Windflower that the prices were awful: 'everything double what it wd be in London'. Belgium gave little pleasure as Lady Elgar reported on his return: 'Brussels gay, lavish clothes, gay shops, much eating! What we did apparently forgotten.' He wrote to Troyte about the new buildings the Belgians were putting up: 'the suburbs of, say, Wigan are noble compared to these atrocities'.

In that same letter to Troyte, Elgar mentioned his wife's health: 'I write for Alice who has been very ill (chill inside) & is still a very very poor thing She gets up at mid-day now but it will be some time before she is about again *and*, she is a very bad patient!' The Gramophone Company wished to record the Cello Concerto as soon as possible. Four days after the première it was discussed at a meeting: 'The newspaper critics and private reports agree that this is the finest cello concerto of recent years.' There was then the question of soloist. Salmond was not one of the company's artists; Suggia's fee was excessive; finally the twenty-seven-year-old Beatrice Harrison was chosen. All movements except the Adagio were cut; for Lady Elgar the occasion on 22 December was sad, as ill health meant it was 'the only time A. did not go with him'.

Before the year's end the first number of a new periodical, *Music and Letters*, appeared; it contained an extensive article on Elgar by Shaw, who at once placed Elgar among the greatest: 'The names are up on the shop front for everyone to read. ELGAR late BEETHOVEN & CO., Classics and Italian and German Warehousemen. Symphonies, Overtures, Chamber Music, Oratorios, Bagatelles.' Certain things, Shaw felt, could be said without hesitation. One was that 'his range is so Handelian that he can give the people a universal melody or march with as sure a hand as he can give the Philharmonic Society a symphonic adagio such as has not been given since Beethoven died'. He defined Elgar's orchestration as 'an absolutely new energy given to the band by a consummate knowledge of exactly what it could do and how it could do it'. Shaw then extended his argument:

> The enormous command of existing resources which this orchestral skill of his exemplifies extends over the whole musical field, and explains the fact that though he has a most active and curious mind, he does not appear in music as an experimenter and explorer, like Scryabin and Schönberg.

He took music where Beethoven left it, and where Schumann and Brahms found it.

He detected in Elgar 'the stigmata of what we call immortality'; and among the recent crop of English composers, 'so far, Elgar is alone for Westminster Abbey'. Lady Elgar was delighted, and wrote appreciatively to Shaw; Elgar took exception to a disparaging remark about Parry, and addressed a letter of 7 March 1920 to *Music and Letters*, in which he referred to 'the many occasions on which Parry advised me and encouraged me'. Shaw approved, merely commenting: 'I hope you did not take his advice as well as his encouragement.'

In the first half of January 1920 Elgar lunched twice with the Shaws, once in London and once at Ayot St Lawrence. It was 'Quite a refreshment for E.' He also saw *Arms and the Man* with Lalla Vandervelde. He was busy with a preface for *Musical Notation* by H. Elliott Button, a Novello editor he had known at least since *Gerontius* days. He gave further evidence of his 'active and curious' mind: 'Printing, and all that belongs to it, has had a fascination for me since I was first permitted to pull a lever in Leicester's offices in Worcester fifty years ago; with the same thrill I touched a similar machine in the Musée Plantin in Antwerp a month back.' On 13 January Ivor Atkins mentioned in a letter to Lady Elgar her husband's Worcester visit the previous November: 'Everybody was enchanted with E. E.'s all-round fitness. He went about the place like a Grand Seigneur, dealing with everything and everybody with Royal sureness of touch.' Lady Elgar had mended slightly; Elgar told Atkins that she had 'been out once for ten minutes – the first time since Nov. 2nd'.

Elgar was approached about music for the dedication of the Cenotaph in Whitehall, and he noted in his own diary for 13 January, 'Worked on Cenotaph stuff'. He decided on a revised version of 'For the Fallen' that would omit three verses and the solo part, curtail the orchestral introduction and rewrite the middle section. He wrote to Binyon on 26 February when it was finished; Novello was wondering what it should be called: 'they suggest "With proud thanksgiving" or "England mourns" – something from the poem. I said I wd. ask you about it.' The first title was chosen, and the vocal score was published in May 1920 as 'especially intended for the performance at the Dedication of the Cenotaph and similar ceremonies throughout the country'. Its accompaniment might be 'for Military or Brass Band, or Organ or pianoforte'.

Elgar was delighted by a suggestion of Sidney Colvin's that he should be proposed for the Literary Society, to which Wordsworth, Matthew Arnold and Lord Lytton had once belonged. Elgar expressed his pleasure on 5 February: 'I am overwhelmed with emotion over the Literary Society: thank you for the book of biographical details: what a gorgeous crowd of shades & realities; a real thrill. Thank you again. I now feel so humble, syntaxless & void of grammar.' A new interest was the cinema, to which Elgar became increasingly addicted. He saw *King Solomon's Mines*; was fascinated to observe 'a dead man acting' (this was George Alexander, in a film made shortly before his death); watched Bernard Shaw being filmed; and on 5 March he went 'to Cinema in Denman St. to see film of ME'.

Lady Elgar managed to attend a recording session on 24 February but had not the strength to stand at an 'Incursion of Royalties, Crown Prince of Roumania. *Sad* looking little thing.' She was afraid she might be taken for a Bolshevist. Elgar was melancholy that his sister's house at Stoke was to be sold over her head and that she would have to move. To the Windflower his grief took also a personal turn: 'Everything I have ever loved & wanted has been denied me but I hate to think of my sister, after 37 years, being turned out.' He went with the Windflower to *Pygmalion*; and then to Shaw's *Candida* with Muriel Foster.

By the middle of March Lady Elgar was very unwell; but she heard the Second Symphony conducted on 16 March by the thirty-year old Adrian Boult. It was the last time she was to describe an Elgar performance: 'After 1st movement great applause & *shouts*, rarely heard till end & great applause all through. Adrian was wonderful At end frantic enthusiasm & they dragged out E. who looked very overcome, hand in *hand* with Adrian at least 3 times.' After a rehearsal Elgar had written to Boult: 'don't be afraid to let the first movement go & the Celli in the opening of the finale might play *out free* almost'. He was equally perspicacious after the performance: 'I am most grateful to you for your affectionate care of it & I feel that my reputation in the future is safe in your hands.' Lady Elgar was wholehearted in her praise: 'You made it so clear & irresistible that I feel sure it penetrated straight to the minds & hearts of numbers who had failed to understand it.'

The day after the concert Elgar went to the Speyers at Ridgehurst; Lady Elgar saw Sir Maurice Anderson 'who gave her new meddies & relieved her mind of some anxiety'. She made only one more diary entry, on 18 March. Elgar was made a member of the Institut de France, and she commented: 'How beautiful to have this & the Symphony success. So thankful.' Elgar later added a few words: 'My darling kept this book by her bedside, but wrote no more'. She managed to attend a concert of the three Elgar chamber works on 23 March, and Elgar noted it: 'My darling's last concert all my music. thoughts of the 30 (weary fighting) years of her help & devotion.'

Elgar had been in Leeds conducting *Gerontius*; on his return he found Lady Elgar in a bad way. He wrote to the Windflower on 26 March: 'Carice & I are in much trouble of mind about poor dear Alice who seems really very ill & weak & does not improve.' She could retain no food. The next day Elgar lunched at the Savile Club, and left a note for 'Lady Elgar': 'Darling wife. I thought you wd rather I went to my lunch so I have started: zu was asleep. I shall be back vesy quick. I tissed zu paws (bofe) Yr own Eddoo.' He had signed himself as the 'E.D.U.' of the Variations for the last time. She suffered much pain, and by 6 April was delirious, so that Elgar 'cd. not understand her words'. The end came on 7 April: 'My darling sinking Father Valentine gave extreme unction. Sir Maurice called at 12.30 Sinking all day & died in my arms at 6.10 pm (Summer time).' Fox Strangways had been busy during the afternoon in the library writing an obituary for *The Times*.

The funeral on 10 April was at St Wulstan's, Little Malvern, in the shadow of the hills Alice Elgar had known since childhood. Philip Leicester described the occasion:

> All was quiet in the little church. The coffin lay solitary before the altar. The priest sat at the side. The score or so of mourners were still in their places. In the wee organ loft Will Reed and the three other members of the L.S.O. were playing the *String Quartet*. Very lovely and peaceful, the last tribute of the fiddlers. Then they buried her outside, close to the church, E.E. seemed very grey, old, and grief-stricken.

It happened that Charles Stanford was at Malvern convalescing at the time. He attended the funeral and caused Elgar bitter resentment. It was Frank Schuster who arranged the playing of the 'Piacevole' movement from op. 83. Two days later Elgar expressed his thanks for the music: 'it was exactly right & just what she wd. have loved'. He then meditated a little on the location of the grave: 'The place she chose long years ago is too sweet – the blossoms are white all round it & the illimitable plain, with all the hills & churches in the distance which were hers from childhood, looks just the same – inscrutable & unchanging.'

8

Silence rarely broken (1920–1934)

His wife's death was a shattering blow to Elgar, and it was long before he recovered. Messages of sympathy poured in, but a couple of sentences from Clayton's letter of 9 April went to the heart of the matter: 'What you will do without her, & her help, it is impossible to imagine'; and he continued: 'I only hope that your terrible misfortune will not overwhelm you.' Elgar wrote to Schuster from Stoke, where he had taken refuge: 'Here my dear A. never came so I can bear the sight of the roads & fields.' He recalled deep hurts: 'I am plunged in the midst of ancient hate & prejudice – poor dear A.'s settlements & her *awful aunts* who wd. allow nothing to descend to any offspring of *mine* ... simply because I was – well – I.' For the first post-war Worcester Festival Atkins dearly wanted a new Elgar work; the plea was turned down on 6 May: 'you cannot fathom the loneliness & desolation of my life I fear'.

He corresponded with Troyte about the headstone for Lady Elgar's grave, touching on heraldic matters. He wanted the motto 'Fortiter et fide' to go in: 'it suited dear A. so well'. Henry Embleton called at Severn House on 21 June, so anxious for the third oratorio that he followed up the interview with a cheque for £500. But Elgar retreated to Brinkwells. Even there betrayal seemed to come from some of the places he held dearest, as he told the Windflower on 18 July:

> It seems odd that Stoke was advertised last Saturday week (the sale) – the *same* day Birchwood Lodge (the old Worcester Cottage) advertised & *sold* – I wanted it; and then in Country Life *same day*!! all the Wye fishing where I used to lie & fish & write & dream & where you & I walked once.

A brief stay at The Hut and another at Ridgehurst only proved that the post-war world was uncongenial to the dispirited Elgar. He reported to the Windflower about 'some extraordiny females, friends of the youth whom F. introduces as his "*Nephew*"'. This was 'Anzy' Wylde, a New Zealand officer who had lost a leg at Gallipoli and was eventually to be given The Hut. Ridgehurst provided 'a German lady &

her daughter who sang to the Germans in Brussels!!!' There was one German with whom he wished to resume contact. Adrian Boult was to tour on the Continent with the Second Symphony, and Elgar asked him to greet Richard Strauss for him.

Elgar planned to attend the Three Choirs Festival, and even to conduct. In his diary for 1 September he made a note about 'bespectacled soloists' in the London rehearsals for *Gerontius*, a work that Atkins now regarded as 'the Festival stay in the years to come'. Elgar performed with undimmed vitality, and Atkins was full of gratitude and admiration: 'You ought even in the most difficult moments to find some rest and anchorage in the thought of your works and their heaven-sent message. They are great, but what I like is your vigour. You are about as lively as Vesuvius and equally disturbing.'

Yet the fundamental gloom continued. He marked Frank Schuster's score of the Variations with crosses against those of the 'Friends pictured within' who had died. He put a cross against his own 'E.D.U.' as well. When the nineteen-year-old Jascha Heifetz came to tea at Severn House, Elgar was sufficiently impressed to invite him back and copy out one of his early violin studies as a gift. This was a 'Third-finger Exercise', written when Elgar was having lessons from Pollitzer. At the end of the year a facsimile of it was published in the *Daily Telegraph*. Heifetz played the Violin Concerto at a Philharmonic Concert on 25 November, and a couple of days later Elgar responded to congratulations from the Windflower: 'Thank you: yes, it was a tremendous display – not exactly our own Concerto: – as to the noise afterwards – none of it was for me or my music – the people simply wanted Heifetz to play some of his small things with piano.'

Elgar and Carice went to *The Beggar's Opera*, of which the long run was certainly a sign of debased times. And so were the changes at the Shakespeare Hotel, Stratford. Elgar and Carice lunched there on the way to Stoke by car, and he told the Windflower on 23 December they could never go again: 'the dear old Hotel is in new hands & much enlarged; – *smart* (!) waitresses with *very short skirts*'. In the dining room 'they were jangling rag-time at two o'c', and there was to be a three weeks' carnival with 'JAZZ BAND specially imported'. Before the end of 1920 Elgar had used his influence towards a knighthood for Atkins and offered to act as 'mentor as to the Court business'.

Elgar's niece Madge Grafton came to Severn House at the beginning of 1921 for an orgy of theatre and cinemas, while a microscope filled other empty hours. Slides were made of 'all the leaves in the garden' according to Carice's diary; another of '16 gramophone needles', fifteen used and one unused; then oyster shells were examined, till a 'Horrible

insect appeared'. In March came a slight move towards music. Clayton
wrote that an Albert Hall concert was planned for 7 May 'to celebrate
the Jubilee of The Royal Albert Hall, & the Royal Choral Society'.
The idea was to include music by all those who had conducted the
Society, from Gounod to Elgar himself, who was to be represented by
'Land of Hope and Glory' and *With Proud Thanksgiving*. The Binyon
piece would now have to be scored for full orchestra, a task readily
undertaken. Elgar also found himself stimulated to a more ambitious
project.

For almost a year Carice had tried to take her mother's place. In
one respect she had done better: Elgar had been encouraged to have a
dog called 'Meg'. But there was to be a fundamental change in the
household. Carice was proposed to by a farmer, Samuel Blake, and
Elgar gave his consent to their marriage. He was to lose Brinkwells
too, as the owners wanted it back. But on 17 April Carice noted that
Elgar was 'playing Bach fugues', and two days later he was 'busy
orchestrating Bach Fugue in C minor'. He had chosen the 'Fuga' from
the organ work BWV537. A first version of the virtuoso score was dated
'Ap. 24: 1921'; but Elgar had a profusion of more brilliant ideas and
copied out the score completely again. It was finished a month later
when he was already at Brinkwells; but he preserved the original date
of 24 April for the amplified version. He explained his aim to Atkins:
'many arrgts have been made of Bach on the "pretty" scale & I wanted
to shew how gorgeous & great & brilliant he would have made himself
sound if he had had our means'.

It seemed for a moment as if greater things might follow. Elgar
wrote to Troyte Griffith on 9 May, telling him of Carice's impending
marriage and making a suggestion for his own future. He wanted
accommodation at Malvern Wells: 'It is possible that I may be finishing
the III part of *The Apostles* & I want to be quiet & uninterrupted
generally.' He summed the matter up: 'What I feel now is that I am
not young! and I want to complete the *great* work; – that I want to
be near my dearest one's grave – and that I want you not too far off.'

Because of poor royalties, especially on his smaller works, Elgar was
anxious that Novello should compound their value and make an offer
for outright purchase. Clayton replied on 10 June that no one could
accurately foretell the future, but the figure they had come up with
was '£500 for the lot!!' Elgar rounded off his reply with a sentence of
some obscurity: 'I never really belonged to the musical world, – I
detest my slightest necessary connection with it & should be glad to
have done with it and get back to my (deceased) dogs & horses!'

A visit to one of Shaw's finest plays, *Man and Superman*, was
followed up by an invitation to the Shaws and some of the cast to

lunch at the Café Royal on 17 June: 'Father made amusing & brilliant speech.' It had been decided that Severn House should be given up, and Elgar faced the task of sorting his music. Carice described the proceedings on 2 July: 'Very busy day – turning out stationery cupboard – Father went through all his sketches, M.S.S. etc sad work. Destroyed much & got all in order. At it all day.' The task continued on the morrow, and a week later the MSS were relabelled and put away.

Elgar was busy with another letter to the *TLS* on 17 July. It was part of a correspondence on Walter Scott's 'use' of Shakespeare. Elgar made his points under three headings: direct quotation; reference; assimilation. The most telling examples of Scott's practice could be found in *Kenilworth*, which 'in addition to presenting Shakespeare the man, contains quotations (more or less correct) both in the text and as chapter-headings, and some "references" to *Twelfth Night*'. Then came the opening of the Gramophone Company's new premises at 363-7 Oxford Street, for which Elgar made a notable speech. He thought it a pity that the directors of His Master's Voice had not adopted St Dunstan as their patron: 'The legend is that St. Dunstan, after playing a hymn on his harp, hung up the instrument in his cell; a little later the harp repeated the tune without human intervention; I apprehend that this must have been the very earliest example of recording.' He now felt that a 'gramophone with a first-class selection of records should be placed in every school in the country'.

A last visit to Brinkwells had had no regrets for Meg, the Aberdeen terrier. Elgar told the Windflower she had brought various toys into the house: 'but two dead snakes are a little beyond what we wished for in our wildest dreams'. Volkert at the London branch of Schott the music publisher now sent Carice £500 as a wedding present, 'in memory of Mother'. This was a happy gesture in view of the inspiration and great success of *Salut d'amour*, issued by Schott so many years before. On 21 August they finally left Brinkwells.

At the Hereford Three Choirs Festival Elgar conducted *The Apostles*. Among the audience was Siegfried Sassoon, who later came across Elgar by chance. He wrote of the encounter in his diary, unable to equate the man and his music: 'Could this possibly be the man who composed that glorious work – this smartly dressed "military"-looking grey-haired man, with the carefully trimmed moustache and curved nose?' Elgar 'admitted that the final climax in *The Apostles* had been "pretty good". I suppose he is very "English" – always pretending and disguising his feelings.'

Elgar conducted *Falstaff* at a Queen's Hall Promenade Concert on 22 September; this was Bernard Shaw's first hearing of the work: 'It's magnificent, and perfectly graphic to anyone who knows his Shake-spear. All the other geniuses whom I venture to admire let me down one time or another; but you never fail.' He mentioned Strauss's *Till Eulenspiegel* and *Don Quixote*: 'this ought to be played three times to their once'. He then made a general point: 'Composing operas is mere piffle to a man who can do *that*. It is the true way to set drama to music.' Elgar then sent him a copy of his *Falstaff* article from *The Musical Times*. In a letter of 29 September Shaw took issue with him over Theobald's emendation at Falstaff's death of 'and a Table of greene fields' to 'a-babbled of greene fields'. Elgar had accepted this, but Shaw preferred 'His nose was as sharp as a pen on a table of green frieze.' He said he had seen a man's nose look exactly like that.

Carice had been on the lookout for a service flat that might suit her father. She found 37 St James's Place, and Elgar signed the lease on 15 October. Hers was the task of clearing Severn House. The remains of General Roberts's Indian armoury, swords, daggers, musket and shield, went initially to the Victoria and Albert Museum, and then to Monmouth. Elgar told the Windflower that the 'end of Severn House was more *radiant* than the beginning'. Another house plan got short shrift. Sir Edwin Lutyens, architect of the Cenotaph in Whitehall, to say nothing of the New Delhi foreseen in *The Crown of India*, had conceived an idea for the forthcoming Empire Exhibition of 1924. Elgar told Troyte he 'had a circular asking me to contribute a microscopic MS. to help furnish a *Doll's House* Castle or some-thing, wh: he designs to present to the Queen'. Elgar refused 'tout court'.

The première of the Bach Fugue under Eugene Goossens on 27 October was such a success the work had to be repeated. As a measure of thanks Elgar organized a lunch at the Royal Societies Club; Arthur Bliss was invited too, and remembered the occasion: 'The luncheon went a bit awkwardly with Elgar at his most nervous; then, when the coffee came, he suddenly told us the reason of our being gathered there. He wanted Howells, who was not present, Goossens and myself each to write a new work for the Gloucester Festival of 1922.'[1] The results were *Sine nomine* by Howells, *Silence* by Goossens, and what was later to be called *A Colour Symphony* by Bliss.

In mid-December Elgar was in correspondence with an irritated Colvin about Bernard Shaw: 'I don't think we shd. have "liked" Aristophanes personally or Voltaire (perhaps) but I cannot do without their work. GBS's politics are, to me, appalling, but he is the kindest-hearted, gentlest man I have met outside the charmed circle which

[1] Bliss, *As I remember*, p. 71.

includes you – to young people he is kind.' Elgar then recalled his own boyhood:

> I am still at heart the dreamy child who used to be found in the reeds by Severn side with a sheet of paper trying to fix the sounds & longing for something very great – source, texture & all else unknown. I am still looking for This – in strange company sometimes – but as a child & as a young man & as a mature man, no single person was ever kind to me, so my heart goes out to any man or woman of such assured position as G.B.S. who helps others.

He also likened Shaw to Charles Churchill (1732–64) of the biting verse: 'About the brains & the enormous Churchillian satire I do not speak now – but they have my deepest admiration.'

Carice was married to Samuel Blake on 16 January 1922 at St James, Spanish Place, where her mother had frequently worshipped. Six days later Elgar arranged a lunch for Richard Strauss, in London for the first time since the war; to this were invited Bernard Shaw, such younger composers as Arnold Bax, Arthur Bliss, Rutland Boughton, Eugene Goossens, and John Ireland; Adrian Boult came too. Though financially not in the same league as Strauss, Elgar now had a new three-year contract with the Gramophone Company under which he was to have a retaining fee of £500 per annum for a minimum of four recording sessions. The Bach Fugue was already recorded, and it may have been at this lunch that Elgar suggested Strauss should orchestrate the Fantasia that went with it. Strauss demurred, and Elgar undertook the transcription himself.

Bernard Shaw had become a staunch ally. A performance of *The Apostles* on 8 June was wretchedly attended, and in the *Daily News* Shaw castigated London society:

> It would be an exaggeration to say that I was the only person present, like Ludwig of Bavaria at Wagner's premières. My wife was there. Other couples were visible at intervals. One of the couples consisted of the Princess Mary and Viscount Lascelles, who just saved the situation as far as the credit of the Crown is concerned.

Six other people in the stalls, he thought, probably had complimentary tickets.

In his new flat 'Chez Holy Jim' Elgar was no distance from the London Library, which may have aided a letter to the *TLS* of 10 August 1922. This time Elgar wrote about Jonathan Swift's residence in Bury Street, just across the road from him, and of a misreading concerning his rent, which Swift described as 'plaguy deep', rather than 'dear'. Many authorities had got this wrong, including *The Cambridge History of English Literature*. In September Elgar was on home ground, conducting both *The Apostles* and *The Kingdom* at the Gloucester Festival. The former resulted in 'record attendances & collections'. After the latter a memorial to Parry, who had died in October 1918, was unveiled in the Cathedral. Stanford was there, and he and Elgar shook hands. The Fantasia and Fugue was given its first performance; but Elgar told Atkins he had not at all approved of Skryabin's *Poème de l'extase*: 'To think that Gloucester Cathedral should ever echo to such music. It is a wonder that the very gargoyles don't come tumbling down.'

The idea of the third oratorio came to the surface again. Immediately after the festival Elgar wrote to Atkins. He wanted timings of *The Kingdom*, and it may have been now that he contemplated making certain additions to the work, as indicated in his vocal score: 'I have some thoughts upon the subject & belike, its successor.' He got Mary Clifford, niece of a former servant at Severn House, to do some typing for him, 'a lot of libretto for Part III of The Apostles'. When Carice visited him on 1 November, 'Father played some of new music – 3rd pt of Kingdom Piano Concerto'. Both were put aside.

The suggestion for the first original music Elgar was to write since the death of Lady Elgar came from Laurence Binyon, whose *Arthur* was to be produced at the Old Vic on 12 March 1923. Binyon wanted incidental music for the play from Elgar. By 28 January Elgar was virtually committed and wondered whether he might try and sketch the music at Carice's home near Guildford: 'Will you send me a wire as soon as you can on receipt of this just saying "Yes dearest father" – or "No, you drivelling old blighter".' She said 'yes'. Elgar brought a microscope and stayed at Carice's till 10 February. At first he was unwell and the music would not 'go'; he was then diverted by gathering 'pond weed' for the microscope. But progress was made, and twice Carice wrote in her diary, 'Father busy all morning'. He wrote to the Windflower on 19 February: 'I have worked at the Binyon music & have nearly finished it – one or two Windflowerish bits – but it is short.' Elgar started rehearsing at the Old Vic on 2 March. To the *Sunday Times* it seemed a quixotic venture: 'Fancy the greatest composer in England conducting 10 musicians in the Waterloo Road!' Elgar described his impressions to the Windflower: 'We tried the entr'actes on Friday evening – a curious sound I think from such a small but very good-hearted seven.' The *Sunday Times* had more the following week: 'Degas missed a wonderful picture as England's greatest composer, his face half-lit by the light in his pipe, waited at the conductor's desk while the stage hands struggled with the scanty properties.' Elgar conducted on the first night, but insisted on five extra players, which he paid for himself. The *Arthur* run stimulated

Binyon to thoughts of another play. The canonization of St Joan in 1920 had focused literary attention upon her, and Sybil Thorndike urged Binyon to dramatize the subject. But Bernard Shaw got in first, so that Binyon abandoned the idea and perhaps also deprived the world of some Elgarian music for St Joan.

Elgar now realized his wish to return to the West Midlands. He kept the London apartment, but on 26 March he signed a lease for Napleton Grange, just outside Worcester. He moved on 7 April 1923 and arranged with his sister Pollie that one or other of his Grafton nieces should take charge of the household. He celebrated with a communication to *The Times*, published on 28 April: 'The little group of anemones called windflowers are happily named too, for when the east wind rasps over the ground in March and April they merely turn their backs and bow before the squall.' And when rain threatened, 'the petals shut tight into a tiny tent, as country folk tell one, to shelter the little person inside'. Carice came to Napleton Grange on 1 May and they hoped to visit 'R.B.T.'; but her diary told otherwise: 'Went to see Townshends at Oxford – great shock found it was his funeral.'

Yet Elgar was in his element, as he wrote to Ernest Newman: 'In my own land I am a boy again – I wish you were here.' He put it differently to Colvin on 27 May: 'I have no news & have settled into senile slipperdom.' It was not quite the whole story. By the end of May he had orchestrated three works to be heard at the 1923 Worcester Festival. There were two anthems, Battishill's *O Lord, Look Down from Heaven*, and Wesley's *Let us Lift up our Heart*, as well as the Overture in D minor to Handel's Second Chandos Anthem. Elgar wrote to John West about the Handel on 16 July: 'I have known the overture from the old two stave organ arrangement since I was a little boy and always wanted it to be heard in a large form – the weighty structure is (to me) so grand – epic.'

At the beginning of June Elgar was asked to write a piece for the new carillon of forty-seven bells in the 151-foot tower erected to the war dead in Queen's Park, Loughborough. He obliged, only reserving the right to arrange the piece for organ (a task begun but not ended). A C minor Fugue of his own, now laid out for piano but later to be incorporated in the *Severn Suite*, was dated 29 June. Two male-voice partsongs followed in July, *The Wanderer*, mainly to words probably found in Isaac d'Israeli's *Curiosities of Literature* (Elgar supplied the first stanza himself), and *Zut! Zut! Zut!*, setting of a marching song by 'Richard Mardon', who was wholly Elgar. Novello hesitated about their publication. John West was unimpressed by the marching song: 'I am sorry to say this is rather *cheap* for Elgar – *cheap* without being sufficiently *interesting*'. There was disagreement about terms, and the correspondence dragged on. Elgar wrote peevishly to Clayton on 8 August: 'Just tear up the M.S.S. – or return them to me & I can do so.' Novello was unwilling to destroy an Elgar manuscript, and agreement was eventually reached.

In the midst of this distasteful episode Elgar entertained himself with another summer letter to the *TLS*, published on 2 August. He wrote to cap a considerable correspondence about some nonsense lines beginning 'poluphloisboisterous Homer of old'. Tennyson had admired the original Homeric line in *The Iliad* and the 'loud-resounding' adjective descriptive of the sea. Elgar points out that Tennyson was probably reminded of it when he saw it in an essay on *Locksley Hall* by 'an almost forgotten writer', George Brimley.

After the Worcester Festival, during which much of his music had been performed and he unveiled a memorial window in the cloisters to five of the Cathedral organists, he wrote to the Windflower: 'The Kingdom, Gerontius & For the Fallen are not bad: I think I deserve *my peerage* now, when these are compared with the new works!!!' This was not Elgar's last plea on the subject, but on 10 October he mentioned other matters: 'I have been to *12* theatres since I retd: I am so desperately lonely & turn in to see anything'. He then touched on the possibility of a long journey. This was to be what the Booth Line advertised as 'A unique cruise 1,000 miles up the Amazon' in a ship of considerable comfort. He made his decision, and on 15 November left for Liverpool to embark on SS *Hildebrand*. He returned on 30 December full of his experiences, as told to W. H. Reed: 'the Amazon impressed him less than the fact that in South America, in places with quite a small population, the opera house was the handsomest and most important building in town'. An Elgar opera, Reed claimed, was now a matter for serious discussion.

The immediate task of January 1924 was more occasional work. Elgar received a letter from Walter R. Creighton: 'You may remember me as a small boy who once studied the violin with you in Worcester. But now I am what is called the Controller of the Pageant of Empire which is being held in the Stadium at Wembley during the Exhibition.' He specified the main request: 'What we want is a March of Empire from you which will be the Leit Motive going through the three days programme.'[2] Elgar started at once, writing to the Windflower on 10 January: 'I have "composed"! *five* things this week – one about "Shakespeare" you will love when I shew it to you – slight & silly.' They planned to attend on 18 February the London opening of Shaw's 'Metabiological Pentateuch', *Back to Methuselah*; Elgar wrote on 12

---

[2] Letter at the Birthplace Museum.

February: 'Shaw sent me the play (or plays) long ago & I am most anxious to see it, them, *you* or rather *you* them it.' The next day he could only express astonishment that the Cello Concerto was proposed for the 1924 Hereford Festival: 'I am studying the programme & am dumb: *I say it!!* how about that scherzo in the cathedral?'

Sir Walter Parratt, old friend of the Elgar family and Master of the King's Musick, died on 27 March. Next day Elgar wrote to the king's private secretary: 'If there is to be a new appointment may I suggest, without presumption, that I should feel it to be the greatest honour if I might be allowed to hold the position?' It was not certain that the post would be continued, but Elgar felt strongly: 'To abolish it at this moment would have a very deterrent effect on the prestige and progress of British music especially abroad.' Elgar was finally offered the position on 25 April, with 'a nominal salary of £100 per annum'.

The Wembley project went ahead, with a musical programme that Elgar described as 'short & lurid'. The king wanted 'Land of Hope and Glory'; and the *Imperial March* of 1897 was to be played instead of the new *Empire March*. The exhibition was to be opened on 23 April, St George's day, and Elgar described for the Windflower a rehearsal at the Wembley Stadium: '17,000 men hammering loud speakers, amplifiers – four aeroplanes circling over etc etc – all mechanical & horrible – no soul & no romance & no imagination'. There was one consolation: 'at my feet I saw a group of real *daisies*. Something wet rolled down my cheek.' Twice in the letter he brought up the question of a peerage. The *Daily Mail* reported the opening: 'The Lord's Prayer was recited reverently by the multitude. Sir Edward Elgar, a lonely figure in black poised in his lofty pulpit, raised his baton. The massed choirs above him sang "Jerusalem".'

After another meeting at The Hut, Siegfried Sassoon gave a diary account on 5 July of the two Elgars he had encountered. One was the Elgar who played for him in the music room, touching on the Mozart A major Piano Concerto κ488, Bach organ fugues and the solo violin Chaconne, before proceeding to *Death on the Hills*, the *Te Deum* and *Light of Life*: 'Quite sketchy unpianist playing, but the rhythmic sense of course wonderful'. Elgar said of the Schubert Rondo brillante for violin and piano, 'the best *natural* music ever written'. Sassoon summed up:

It was splendid to see him glowing with delight in the music, and made me forget (and makes me regret now) the 'other Elgar' who is just a type of 'club bore'. At lunch, regaling us with long-winded anecdotes (about himself), he was a different man. The real Elgar was left in the music-room.

The Pageant of Empire opened at Wembley on 21 July and ran until 30 August. Each of the three days in the programme began with the *Empire March*, so that it became the opening music for representations of 'Henry VII and John Sebastian Cabot', 'The Days of Queen Elizabeth' and 'George III and the departure of Captain Cook'; it was heard a fourth time at the end of 'A Pageant of New Zealand'. Apart from the Elgar songs to texts by Alfred Noyes, which were distributed over the three days, *Sursum corda* was played during 'The Pageant of Canada' on the first day; the *Imperial March* concluded 'The Days of Queen Elizabeth', 'Land of Hope and Glory' made the finale of 'The Pageant of South Africa', and 'The Early Days of India' brought the second day to an end with a considerable chunk of *The Crown of India*. 'A Pageant of Heroes' on the final day was notable for a rare performance of *With Proud Thanksgiving*. Among some eighty musical items Elgar's name featured twenty times; for the rest it was a remarkable hotchpotch.[3]

During much of August Elgar was in Scotland, retracing earlier routes and wondering whether to go on to St Kilda and Shetland. While he was away both Frances Colvin and Claude Phillips died. Back for the Hereford Festival, he had had driving lessons from Percy Hull, the cathedral organist. Elgar wrote his thanks on 1 October: 'I am more than ever convinced that Austin is short for St. Augustin'. Not all had gone well since: at his sister Pollie's Perryfield home he was '*demonstrating* in the garden & backed into a row of logan berries – they fell never to rise again'.

He was saddened by the death of Fauré on 4 November and wrote to Schuster about it: 'he was such a *real gentleman* – the highest type of Frenchman & I admired him greatly. His chamber music never had a chance here in the old Joachim days I fear; I may be wrong but I feel that it was "held up" to our loss.' He ended by offering to do what he could for a performance of the Fauré Requiem at the Three Choirs Festival, but the work had to wait till 1937 for a first British hearing.

By the end of 1924 the canine establishment that was to last the rest of Elgar's life was in place. He described it to the Windflower: 'Marco is the loveliest Spaniel I have ever seen – quite a silly baby & cries for nothing. He loves riding in the car. Mina – the little cairn – is a love & so sharp.' One day, perhaps to entertain a child, Elgar made use again of cryptic symbols similar to those in the Dorabella letter of 1897. He showed how they could be made to write 'Marco Elgar' and also 'a very old cypher'.

[3] Programme at Birthplace Museum.

At the beginning of 1925 Elgar informed Atkins that he had resigned from the Athenaeum Club, and could therefore not sponsor Atkins's membership as he had intended. He said the committee had 'admitted a person whom I think unfitted for membership & my action was short, sharp & decisive'. This was Ramsay MacDonald, the first Labour prime minister. Initially the year contained 'nothing but dogs & cars'. To these were added crossword puzzles, but there was no music until July, when he wrote *The Herald* and *The Prince of Sleep*, a couple of partsongs. This year's *TLS* letter (6 August) took up a phrase from Boswell's life of Johnson. Elgar thought that 'I'll have a frisk with you' sounded 'somewhat strange from Johnson'. He wondered whether it was an echo from Vanbrugh's *The Provok'd Wife*, in which Sir John Brute (played by Johnson's friend, David Garrick) used very similar words.

Elgar was given the Royal Philharmonic Society's gold medal at a concert on 19 November consisting of the Bach transcription, the Variations, Cello Concerto, *Falstaff* and *In the South*. The presentation was made by Henry Wood, who had received his medal four years before. Elgar told the Windflower it was 'a *dreadful* evening – such a sparse audience. I *was* glad when it was over'. He returned also to the leitmotif of the peerage: 'I cd. not help thinking of your scheme of aggrandisement of the undersigned when some of the big, brilliant passages resounded.' At the end of the year he had to have an operation for haemorrhoids, which kept him in South Bank nursing home, Worcester from 23 December until 14 January 1926. He then went to a consultant physician in Birmingham. Dr Arthur Thomson judged Elgar 'a neurotic who most of all wanted reassurance'. He further told Jerrold Northrop Moore: 'Again and again he would come in depressed, as if all useful life was over; and after reassurance, he would brighten up perfectly'. During their conversations Elgar confessed that 'the serious business of the day' was making up his 'betting slips'.

Henry Embleton was still anxious for the third oratorio, and on 23 March 1926 Carice noted: 'Father full of writing Apostles III'. He was to conduct both *The Apostles* and *The Kingdom* at the Worcester Festival in the autumn, and the Gramophone Company wished to experiment with recording them by the new electrical process. But the dean and chapter would not consent. It was proposed to include some *Parsifal* in the programme. Canon Lacey protested about this in the *Worcester Daily Times* of 15 March, and Elgar weighed in: 'As to the "delirium of sensual love and that craving for the refreshing ministrations of the white-robed angels", has Canon Lacey forgotten John Donne who, after experiencing the same travail, ended his life in the same Church of England of which Canon Lacey is such a distinguished, if a somewhat disingenuous, ornament.'

Lord Stuart of Wortley died on 24 April and Elgar wrote briefly to the Windflower: 'I can say nothing in this dreadfully sad time except that my thoughts are with you always & my good wishes.' Elgar was at his most perverse over the Worcester Festival orchestral concert. Atkins had hoped for a suite from the *Arthur* music and had included it on a programme proof; by the side Elgar wrote 'alas! no.' Then Atkins wondered about *Sospiri*, which elicited an unhelpful reply: 'I have not the remotest notion of what *Sospiri* is, was or will be.' *Dream Children* was suggested next, and Elgar again professed ignorance: 'As to "Dream Children", I have no recollection of them – or it. But I do not want them or it done.' In the end *Dream Children* was allowed. On 9 September Elgar conducted *The Kingdom*. He seemed unmoved by the music and irritated by the singing so that, until 'The sun goeth down', his conducting was perfunctory. Then Agnes Nicholls brought him back to form. He was none the less pleased to receive the Three Choirs cheque, as he told Atkins on 29 September: 'Three tails wagged (profusely) at the sight of the cheque and the owner's prophesied *Bones*.'

The peerage remained an obsession. He mentioned it again to the Windflower on 26 November: 'I should like to know if "it" is entirely dead – my birthday (70) next June is to be "recognised" by concerts in the musical world & I do not want this or these & shall *squash* them unless the other thing turns up.' There was no peerage, but the birthday celebrations went ahead. Elgar conducted *Gerontius* at the Albert Hall on 26 February 1927; the Gramophone Company attempted to record the performance live, and was able to issue two discs. They also wanted a major recording to mark the birthday. The Second Symphony was chosen, though an earlier acoustical version had been out only eighteen months. It was recorded complete on 1 April; Elgar's playing time was two minutes longer than before.

Siegfried Wagner was in London during April with his wife Winifred, future adherent of Hitler and the Third Reich. Schuster gave a dinner for them, to which Elgar was invited: 'Siegfried does not alter in "style" at all – his wife is a great discovery – charming.' Later in the month Elgar collected the Atkins family for 'a most exciting day at the Croome Races'; as described by Wulstan Atkins, 'He and my mother had a wonderful time going into the paddock, examining the horses, discussing form, odds, etc, and placing bets on every race. I can see Elgar now, immaculately dressed, with grey top hat and racing glasses.' There was a last flicker about the peerage on 6 May: 'As to

your little aggrandisement plan, I have definitely ruled it off the map!'
It was as well.

Elgar could now turn his thoughts to the distant past. Carice was
at Napleton towards the end of May. Together they went 'to Abbots
Morton to see Mrs Jenner'. This was Gertrude Walker, friend of the
days before Alice Roberts, who now, after some acting and choir
training in the parish, was breeding golden setters. On 30 May he
reminded Volkert at Schott that it was fifty years since he had bought
from him violin pieces prescribed by Pollitzer: 'Much has happened
since then – I have had some satisfaction & even pleasure in my life
but have no pleasant memories connected with music.' On the evening
of 2 June Elgar conducted the BBC Chorus and Orchestra in a
programme of his works. He closed the broadcast with a very personal
valediction: 'Good *night*, everybody. *Good* night, Marco.'

As his personal birthday offering, Frank Schuster had the three
chamber works performed on 26 June at 'The Long White Cloud'
(Anzy Wilde's new name for The Hut). Two days later Elgar expressed
his thanks and added: 'of course that Slow movement in the Quintet
is too much for my eyes &, I think, yours'. To the Windflower, who
had not been there, he said simply, 'the Quintet is not of this world'.
To a younger member of the audience, Osbert Sitwell, Elgar and his
contemporaries hardly seemed of this world either. He had glimpsed
'through an hallucinatory mist born of the rain that had now ceased,
the plump wraith of Sir Edward Elgar, who with his grey moustache,
grey hair, grey top hat and frock-coat looked every inch a personification of Colonel Bogey, walking with Frank Schuster'. The
devotees 'listened so intently to the prosperous music of the Master,
and looked forward to tea and hot buttered scones'. Outside glossy
cars waited to take them home: 'some of the motors were large and
glassy as a hearse.'

Another anniversary was to be celebrated that summer. Festivities
on 1 July were to mark the Diamond Jubilee of Confederation in
Canada. 'Land of Hope and Glory' was to be sung by 1000 voices as
climax of the musical programme, and this was to be combined with
the opening of the carillon in the Peace Tower of Ottawa's parliament
building. Elgar was requested to 'write a counter-melody to the chorus,
in crotchets, to be performed on the carillon during the singing'.[4] He
obliged, with a descant mainly in quavers. The bells were cast in
Croydon, and a test performance of the obbligato was given there in
the presence of W. H. Reed and Wulstan Atkins.

Since the previous October there had been negotiations through

---

[4] Letter at the Birthplace Museum.

Leslie Boosey over a possible film to be called 'Land of Hope and Glory'. Initial offers seemed to Elgar inadequate, but when he received a cheque in July, his interest was aroused and he told Boosey he 'wd. go so far as to write some original music, if this wd. call attention to the Film'. He added a postscript: 'I could make a rare "pasticcio" out of the four marches, the Coronation Ode, Cockaigne, & if necessary, for quiet effects the Songs.' It is perhaps a pity he did not do so. In the end no new music was written, though Elgar conducted a performance of the film when it opened on 11 November.

The 1927 Three Choirs Festival was at Hereford. Elgar wrote for it *A Civic Fanfare* to greet the mayoral procession into the cathedral; there was no other original music that year. But Hereford had proved more accommodating than Worcester in the matter of recording, so that more *Gerontius* and excerpts from *The Music Makers* were taken live. Elgar now had to move from Napleton Grange, and took a six-month lease on Battenhall Manor on the outskirts of Worcester. He wrote to the Windflower about it on 14 December: 'I wish I could have given you a Christmas here – it is a real Yule-loggy house & you wd. have met, in spirit, Oliver Cromwell, Charles I & II & a lot of agreeable restoration ghosts.' Then came the New Year honour: 'I am very sorry to tell you that H. M. has offered me the wretched *K.C.V.O.* (!!!) which awful thing I must accept.' This particular vexation was soon overtaken by a greater sorrow: Frank Schuster died on 27 December after a short illness. Elgar wrote at once to Adela Schuster: 'By my own sorrow – which is more than I can bear to think of at this moment (a telegram has just come) I may realise some measure of what this overwhelming loss must be to you.'

Schuster had made special mention of Elgar in his will, and on 10 January 1928 Adela Schuster could give the full facts:

> The sum Frank left you in his will is £7000 – (but there are death duties to come off this.) and the words in which he makes the bequest are there: 'To my friend, Sir Edward Elgar O.M. who has saved my country from the reproach of having produced no composer worthy to rank with the Great masters'.

When Shaw heard about it he thought that 'Schuster really deserves to be buried in the Abbey, though he overlooked ME'. He resented the chancellor's death duties: 'I grudge Churchill his share. Why don't they make us duty-free instead of giving us O.Ms and the like long after we have conferred them on ourselves?'

Elgar's time at Battenhall Manor was running out, and on 21 April he moved to Tiddington House, with garden down to the river, at Stratford-on-Avon. An early action was to deal with the paintings:

'Decided to cover all portraits with "chintz" or something.' April was a good time to arrive in Stratford. Shakespeare's birthday, traditionally on 23 April, was the occasion for a festival of plays. Bernard Shaw went with Elgar to *The Merry Wives of Windsor* and *Richard III*; the Elgar household persisted with *Henry IV Part 1* (seen twice) and *Julius Caesar*. Elgar was an ardent Shakespearean, and his set of the plays was much marked. He noted references to music, underlining such stage directions in *Timon of Athens* as 'Trumpets sound' and 'Hautboys playing loud music', or in *Antony and Cleopatra* 'Sound a flourish, with drums'. He marked profusely so famous a passage as Lorenzo's speech in Act 5 of *The Merchant of Venice* (Vaughan Williams was later to use it in his *Serenade to Music*). He hazarded an emendation to Shylock in the previous Act, wondering whether the 'woollen bag-pipe' should not be 'wauling'. *The Two Gentlemen of Verona* contained a line that struck home with Elgar: 'For Orpheus' lute was strung with poets' sinews.' In two of the major tragedies Elgar took issue with Shakespeare. He considered *Hamlet* to have the 'finest opening ever written'; it was 'marred only by Bernardo's misplaced "poetry" '. He thought 'the high (unnecessarily high) tone weakens Horatio's address to the Ghost'. Against *Macbeth* there was a similar complaint: 'I cannot stand Macduff's speech "Confusion etc". – much too wordy for the moment; – but Macduff is always melodramatic.'

Shaw sent Elgar an advance copy of *The Intelligent Woman's Guide to Socialism and Capitalism*; in reply to an Elgar query, he wrote a postcard on 30 May putting Elgar's achievement in context: 'Your products have the extraordinary quality of being *infinitely consumable* without diminution or deterioration. I should have done a chapter on the Economics of Art; but it would have been too long.' There was the possibility of more music when Elgar received on 24 May a request from Gerald Lawrence about a Bertram Matthews play he was to produce in November. The subject was Beau Brummell, depicted in the play 'as a gentleman who is ready to sacrifice his life, his career, his friendship with the Prince Regent, to save a woman's honour'. This twist to the story of fashion's arbiter appealed to Elgar, and he accepted.

Elgar's brother Frank, in charge of the High Street shop in Worcester for so many years, died on 7 June. The day after the funeral Elgar saw *Show Boat* in London. By the end of the month he had purchased his own boat for trips along the Avon, some of which were photographed. Now at last he mentioned to the publisher William Elkin the idea of an *Arthur* suite; but it went no further. Ivor and Wulstan Atkins visited Elgar on 14 July; on this occasion he was much interested by Wulstan's account of drilling at the Firth of Forth in connection with a proposed road bridge. He wondered if he might have rock samples to cross-section for the microscope. Leslie Boosey wanted some new patriotic words for the trio tune in *Pomp and Circumstance* no. 4 to replace Alice Elgar's *The King's Way*. Elgar juggled with the words Boosey sent, but by 10 June he had given up: 'I cannot by any help of Providence, or Old Nick, make them fit. One other thing: I think the *pronounced* praise of England is not quite so popular as it was; the loyalty remains but the people seem to be more shy as to singing about it.' Boosey persisted, and wondered about Kipling; Elgar countered with Alfred Noyes, who produced an acceptable *Song of Victory*.

At the end of October Elgar sent Novello a setting of Ben Jonson, the carol *I Sing the Birth was Born Tonight*. By now the *Beau Brummell* music was ready, and Elgar directed the first rehearsal on 3 November. Carice reported: 'Very poor performers but Father made them do it somehow.' Two days later came the first performance, when the Theatre Royal in Birmingham was rather 'empty on acct of fog'. Hopes of a London run did not materialize. A final musical scheme of 1928 made no headway. Elgar wondered whether a major Shelley poem would be suitable for the Worcester Festival. The Dean considered the suggestions and wrote to Atkins: 'I have looked through the two poems you mentioned – "The Demon" and "Adonais" – As poems they are beautiful – "Adonais" is the best, but it is frankly pagan. I have been trying to see if it can be twisted into a Christian poem. It is not possible.' He went on to urge a subject as suitable as *Gerontius* (when expurgated) had proved. Elgar wrote greyly to Atkins accepting a verdict he must have known to be inevitable: 'Weather dull & dogs bored.' The question of renewing American rights in *Gerontius* was now raised by Novello. Elgar replied on 14 December: 'I presume that the work is worthless, or as nearly valueless to me in the U.S.A. as it is in England.' Novello had to agree.

By contrast Bernard Shaw burst boisterously into 1929 with a letter of 2 January: 'Lazy! I've not only begun a new play but finished it. Not since The Messiah has a work hurled itself on the paper so precipitously.' This was *The Apple Cart*, to be performed at the Malvern Festival in August. Shaw continued with an exhortation: 'Your turn now. Clap it with a symphony.' There was no sign of this at the moment, but a friend of longer standing urged Elgar to break what would soon be virtually a ten-year silence since the Cello Concerto. Ivor Atkins passionately wanted the third oratorio: 'I know you to be a sleeping volcano. I want you, for the sake of all of us who love you and your music, to cause yourself to erupt.' He chided Elgar's inactivity: 'I could weep to see you keeping silence as you do. One day succeeds another and you will not break it. And yet I *know* that the old magic is there. You cannot keep back the little flashes that show me that it is *there!*' Then came the final request: 'Why not the Third Part? it *is quite* possible.' Atkins had voiced what many wished to say; Elgar's response was to orchestrate Purcell's *Jehovah, quam multi sunt hostes mei* for the Worcester Festival.

Elgar's protestations that nobody wanted his music had no basis in fact. Critical fashion might have swung away from him, but Ronald Taylor has shown that broadcasts of his music were not only very frequent but covered an extraordinary range of his output.[5] On the Continent the situation was different. Despite former successes, Elgar did not return to Germany after the war. His old friend Fritz Volbach made the position clear in a March 1929 article for a Munster periodical, *Am Weg der Zeit*:

> Elgar was well on his way to gaining a permanent place here in Germany when war broke out. It abruptly snapped the threads which had been woven. When peace came, he had been virtually forgotten. His works appeared only occasionally. The younger generation of musicians had no interest in him, for however modern he was, he was no inconoclast or atonalist.'[6]

On 17 April Elgar clarified to Leslie Boosey the politics of 'Land of Hope and Glory', defining who might use it: 'all right about Lady Rodd & the *conservatives* – don't let any blasted labour rogues or liberals use the tune!' He was pleased that Arthur Bliss should dedicate his *Pastoral* to him and he wrote on 9 May that he had enjoyed a broadcast of it: 'the transmission or reception (I know nothing of the workings of the BBC with aerial sprites) was not good. But I could judge that your work is on a *large* and *fine* scale, and I like it exceedingly.' He also approved the arrangement for solo viola by Lionel Tertis of the Cello Concerto.

By 12 August Shaw was 'up to the neck in rehearsals' at Malvern. He told Elgar that Barry Jackson, originator of the festival, had 'reserved the front row in the theatre for distinguished guests, which really means you'. He said Jackson had wondered about an Elgar overture for *The Apple Cart*, but on investigating the costs realized he would be 'lucky if he came out of the affair with a shirt on his back'. Shaw put his own view 'that six bars of yours would extinguish (or upset) the A.C. and turn the Shaw festival into an Elgar one.' Shaw told Elgar that the Malvern librarian wanted him 'to open some sort

---

[5] See Ronald Taylor, *'Music in the Air: Elgar and the BBC'* in *Edward Elgar: Music and Literature*, ed. R. Monk (Aldershot, 1993), pp. 327–55.

[6] See 'Fritz Volbach on Elgar Part II', translated by Philip J. Titcombe, *ESJ*, vol.5 no. 2 (1987), pp. 4–7.

of Shavian exhibition he has sharked up at the public library'. Elgar obliged on 17 August, alluding to Shaw the music critic: 'He was a musical critic and a good one in those dull days when the two Universities and the Colleges of Music used to do nothing but sit around and accuse one another of the cardinal virtues.' Shaw was heartfelt in his response:

> Although I am rather a conceited man and I feel I could carry my head high compared with any other artist in England, I am quite sincerely and genuinely humble in the presence of Sir Edward Elgar. I recognise a greater art than my own, and a greater man than I can hope to be.

For the Worcester Festival Elgar took the house on Rainbow Hill he had mentioned to Atkins twelve years before; and Harold Brooke of Novello came there to film him with the dogs. Since Marl Bank was for sale, he decided to buy what was to be his last home. When asked by a professor of singing at the Royal Academy of Music for information about *The River*, its geographical position, the nationality of the translator and so on, Elgar put a brief note on the letter: 'Mr d'Alba died some years ago.'[7] Elgar had been approached during the summer for a 'March of Praise' to celebrate George V's recovery from a serious illness. In the end he decided to write 'A simple Carol for His Majesty's happy recovery', adapting an old tune to words by the Elizabethan George Gascoigne.

Elgar now suggested a novel recording idea: he wanted to experiment with some improvisations at the piano. This he did on 5 November, and five pieces were successfully taken. Towards the end of 1929 Elgar was much concerned with the Musical Copyright Bill then before parliament. The bill was not passed, but one pleasing result of the controversy was a David Low cartoon showing Elgar as a street musician with a score of *Gerontius* at a Salvation Army harmonium, and Bernard Shaw singing at his side. By way of Christmas greeting Elgar celebrated his dog-centred life and chose a Walt Whitman poem beginning:

> I think I could turn and live with animals, they are so placid
>   and self-contained;
> They do not sweat and whine about their condition;
> They do not lie awake in the dark and weep for their sins ...

For many years Elgar had been pressed by Herbert Whiteley to produce a competition piece for brass band. Since 1930 was the twenty-fifth Crystal Palace competition, he decided to take up the challenge

---

[7] Letter at the Birthplace Museum.

and was able to write to Whiteley on 16 April: 'I sent off the final portion of the score to-day & when destroying my untidy M.S. I thought you might like to have the first recorded thought of the piece which you called into being.'[8] The *Severn Suite* was now complete in Elgar's first version. The dedication was offered to Bernard Shaw, who readily accepted on 25 May: 'Naturally I shall be enormously honoured: it will secure my immortality when all my plays are dead and damned and forgotten.'

This reawakened creativity led to another new work, *Pomp and Circumstance March* no. 5, which was with Leslie Boosey by 2 May. The work was dedicated to Percy Hull, the last of the Three Choirs cathedral organists to be so honoured. Through the agency of Landon Ronald, Elgar had opened negotiations with a new publisher, Keith Prowse. The terms eventually stipulated that 'the Composer will in each year during the period of this agreement compose and submit to the Publisher manuscripts of not less than three songs or pieces'. In return Elgar was to receive £250 annually plus royalties and a proportion of any broadcasting and recording fees. By the end of 1930 Elgar had sent Keith Prowse a revised version of the unpublished Piano Sonatina he had written for May Grafton in 1889, a new song, *It isnae me*, and the *Nursery Suite*.

At the beginning of July Carice was at Marl Bank and recorded visits to the races. This interest of Elgar's was encouraged from the cathedral precincts, where Lady Atkins was chairman of the Worcester City Corporation Race Committee. There was a hint at the end of August that Elgar's zest for the outdoor life, whether with dogs or horses, might in future be restricted. Carice noted in her diary for 31 August: 'Heard Father had lumbago.' The back pain was troublesome that autumn, and meant Elgar had sometimes to sit when conducting at the Hereford Festival.

He was not fit enough to attend the Crystal Palace performance of the *Severn Suite* on 27 September, but Bernard Shaw compiled a detailed report the following day: 'I heard the Severn Suite yesterday only eight times, as extreme hunger and the need for catching the 5.10 train at King's Cross forced me to surrender before I had ceased finding new things in it.' He thought Elgar should drop 'the old Italian indications and use the language of the bandsmen'. He suggested 'Remember that a minuet is a dance and not a bloody hymn'; 'Steady up for artillery attack'; 'NOW – like Hell'. For Elgar's physical troubles he suggested an osteopath.

At the end of September Elgar looked back sixty years in a foreword

[8] Letter at the Birthplace Museum.

to Hubert Leicester's *Forgotten Worcester*. He quoted the words of some 'unbrilliant university' man about him: 'I am said to have "left the humdrum atmosphere of Worcester for" – etc. I object to this. I deny that any atmosphere could be exactly humdrum while Hubert Leicester and myself were of it and in it.' He recalled the school journeys to Littleton House: 'It is pleasant to date these lines from an eminence distantly overlooking the way to school; our walk was always to the brightly-lit west.' With such thoughts recently in his mind, Elgar worked at the *Nursery Suite*. When well on with it, he wrote to Sir Frederick Ponsonby on 11 October: 'I am completing a miniature Suite – *Nursery Suite* – four little childlike (not childish) movements. I should very greatly appreciate the honour if I might be permitted to dedicate the music to the Duchess of York and the Princesses Elizabeth and Margaret.'

The New Year burst upon Elgar with a letter of 2 January 1931 from Shaw containing a substitute second verse for the National Anthem. Shaw had written anonymously to the Dean of Worcester, unable to 'stand the grotesque contrast of your gorgeous new orchestral garment for the National Anthem with its disgraceful old literary rags'. Shaw felt that the dean suspected his authorship and that, if he raised the matter with higher authority, 'instead of being made a bishop, he would be thrown down the stairs of Buckingham Palace'. In fact the dean approached Elgar about it in his capacity of Master of the King's Musick. Elgar wrote a very unecclesiastical reply: 'I have no views: – the Old "Confound their politics" in the National address to the Almighty would have the effect – if the Almighty ever took any notice of anything, which of course he never did, does, or will do – of putting the whole Government in Hell.'

An enquiry from the county surveyor of Herefordshire about Elgar's interest in Mordiford Bridge elicited from him on 16 January a note about his working methods: 'Most of my "sketches", that is to say the reduction of the original thoughts to writing, have been made in the open air. I fished the Wye round about Mordiford & completed many pencil memoranda of compositions on the old bridge, of which I have vivid and affectionate memories.' As a result of the correspondence Elgar became a vice-president of the Council for the Preservation of Rural England.

In May 1931 Elgar was approached by Basil Maine, a Cambridge man who had studied under E. J. Dent and later became music critic for the *Daily Telegraph* and *Sunday Times*, about a proposed book on Elgar's life and works. Elgar replied ambiguously on 11 May: 'if anyone is bold enough to publish such a book as that proposed I shd. be delighted to know that you were writing it; I can say no more than that I never read anything about myself if it is possible to avoid doing so'. When published in 1933, Maine's was the most serious study of Elgar to date, retaining its supremacy till well after the Second World War. The study was timely, for Elgar's position in English music had recently aroused controversy.

The Cambridge professor, Dent, had published as early as 1924 an article on modern English music in Guido Adler's *Handbuch der Musikgeschichte*. He associated Elgar closely with 'the works of Liszt, which were abhorrent to Conservative academic musicians. He was, moreover, a Catholic, and more or less a self-taught man, who possessed little of the literary culture of Parry and Stanford.'[9] He made a general point: 'For English ears Elgar's music is too emotional and not quite free from vulgarity.' The orchestral works were described as 'animated in colour, but pompous in style and of a too deliberate nobility of expression'; the chamber music was now 'dry and academic' (a change of view since 1919). The article was reprinted in 1930, and now Philip Heseltine (Peter Warlock) organized a response. Such younger composers as John Ireland, E. J. Moeran and William Walton added their names to those of Augustus John and Bernard Shaw. Their essential point was simple: 'At the present time the works of Elgar, so far from being distasteful to English ears, are held in the highest honour by the majority of English musicians and the musical public in general.' Shaw made his own contribution: 'Elgar holds the same position in English music as Beethoven in German music'.

Elgar recorded the *Nursery Suite* on 23 May. The last movement had to be retaken, and a second session was planned for 4 June, attended by the Duke and Duchess of York. Elgar had written two days previously to Sir Frederick Ponsonby: 'I shall be very grateful to you if you find it possible to convey to His Majesty an expression of my sincere thanks for the honour which I am informed by the Prime Minister is to be bestowed on me.' He was to become first baronet of Broadheath. Hugh Allen, the Oxford professor, congratulated him in terms of the turf: 'This is splendid news & the proper way to celebrate Derby Day for the money is put on the right horse & it is a bad day for the Bookies.'[10]

Despite much back trouble through the summer, Elgar conducted at the Gloucester Festival such major works as *Gerontius* and the Violin Concerto, as well as the *Nursery Suite*, and later for a Promenade Concert the Second Symphony. A plan to take the *Sanguine Fan* ballet

[9] See Brian Trowell, 'Elgar's Use of Literature' in *Edward Elgar: Music and Literature*, pp. 182–326.
[10] Letter at the Birthplace Museum.

to Canada put Elgar in touch with the young composer-conductor Constant Lambert. He mentioned 'the too great length of some of the *dances*' and urged Lambert to 'deal with it unmercifully'; he also congratulated Lambert on his most recent success, compounded of jazz and South American sultriness: 'May I take this opportunity to say how much I have enjoyed your "Rio Grande" & how highly I think of it.'

On 7 November Elgar was rehearsing *Gerontius* in Croydon and asked to be introduced to Vera Hockman, a violinist who had caught his attention. It was to become an important friendship. Five days later was the official opening of the new recording studios in Abbey Road in the presence of such notables as Bernard Shaw, Barry Jackson and Landon Ronald. Elgar was filmed as he came in, and the main business of the day was *Falstaff*. Shaw wrote afterwards about Landon Ronald: 'he knows your scores by heart, and suffers agonies in his longing to conduct them himself. He wants to make more of every passage than you do. A composer always strikes an adorer as callous.'

Elgar was now exercised about the three new works to be submitted to Keith Prowse by the end of 1931. He had been approached by Stephen Moore, a local schoolmaster, about some unison songs but was uncertain what words to set. He settled finally on three poems by Charles Mackay, *The Rapid Stream*, *When Swallows Fly*, and *The Woodland Stream*. Carice and Troyte were at Marl Bank for Christmas, and the gramophone listening harked back to 'my ideal' of younger days, in the form of three Schumann symphonies.

Shaw launched 1932 with a characteristic sally, having previously lent Elgar £1000. He was heading for South Africa on the *Carnarvon Castle*, and wrote on 7 January: 'Why dont you make the B.B.C. order a new symphony? It can afford it.' It was also rough at sea: 'Yah! the ship has pitched fiersomely, and all but shot Charlotte into the fireplace.' Ernest Newman was at Marl Bank and became unsuccessfully involved with Elgar's racing and betting activities: 'I am sorry your horse behaved badly – you chose well: with this is the epic, classic history of the race.'

The new Shakespeare Memorial Theatre was to be opened in Stratford that year, and Keith Prowse wondered about an overture from Elgar. But he put a different suggestion to Novello: 'I proposed to use excerpts from *Falstaff* for the performance of "Henry IV" at the opening.' In the end Elgar was so upset by the architecture of the building, considering it 'an insult to human intelligence', that he abandoned all schemes.[11] Instead he orchestrated the funeral march

[11] Letter at the Birthplace Museum.

from Chopin's B flat minor Piano Sonata during March, and went on to score the *Severn Suite* for full orchestra, giving the movements such local names as 'Worcester Castle', 'Tournament', 'Cathedral' and 'Commandery'. On 25 April Carice noted another local matter: 'Old Bridge going to be put up'. The bridge over the Severn at Worcester was being widened, and its iron railings would be redundant. Elgar had two lengths set in concrete for the Marl Bank garden.

Shaw wrote on 3 May ascribing to Elgar a popular hit of the day: 'The perfect simplicity, elegance, and effectiveness of Monah betrays the master's hand.' He then queried: 'Have you really been leading a double life as a composer? And if so, why aren't you rolling in money?' Elgar replied at once: ' "Monah" – that is the version by Jay Wilbur, is a sheer delight & has displaced pro: tem: a lot of weary Bach Brahms & others.' Later in May Elgar received a royal request for music to be sung at the unveiling on 8 June of a statue to Queen Alexandra, mother of the then king. The words of *So Many True Princesses* were by the poet laureate, John Masefield, and the work was performed by the boys of the Chapels Royal, the choir of Westminster Abbey, and military band. The *Daily Telegraph* reported: 'Sir Edward Elgar has taken up his baton, and the wistful melody of his music rises and falls as the little puffs of wind in the June sunshine carry it back and forth.'

While in London, Elgar discussed with Wayne Daley at Keith Prowse a project that was to absorb many of his remaining days. Elgar wrote to him on 10 June: 'I was very glad to see you again & to have your views about the third Symphony.' Elgar was now seriously contemplating Shaw's suggestion. A postcard of 29 June from the same source pursued the subject: 'Why not a Financial Symphony? Allegro: Impending Disaster. Lento mesto: Stony Broke. Scherzo: Light Heart and Empty Pocket. Allo con brio: Clouds Clearing.' Rumour spread, and Walter Legge, editor of *The Voice*, wrote to Elgar on 4 August: 'I have heard, on what I believe to be very reliable authority, that you have practically completed a third symphony. Is there any truth in this rumour?' Elgar replied cagily: 'there is nothing to say about the mythical Symphony for some time, – probably a long time, – possibly no time, – never'.

The Gramophone Company had long hoped that Kreisler would record the Violin Concerto; but now Fred Gaisberg, manager of the recording department, had other news: 'I have just spoken to Yehudi Menuhin on the telephone'. The sixteen-year-old violinist wanted to play the work to Elgar, record it, and perform it publicly, since he had 'fallen madly in love with it'. The pianist Ivor Newton described their first meeting at Grosvenor House: 'Menuhin and Elgar discussed the music like equals, but with great courtesy and lack of selfconsciousness on the boy's part.' They next met for the recording sessions on 14 and 15 July. Test pressings were played at Marl Bank to an audience that included Bernard Shaw, Lawrence of Arabia (now also going under the name Shaw) and Vera Hockman. She described how they 'all sat, spellbound at the glorious sounds, G. B. S. with bowed head, sometimes softly singing with the music; Aircraftman Shaw serious and silent, looking straight ahead with those unforgettable blue eyes which seemed to see into the life of things'.

Basil Maine was invited to Marl Bank to gather material for the biography. He arrived on 11 June and made notes on Elgar's conversation. His personal antipathy to Beecham was clear; he was described as 'dishonest & doesn't know it'. Stanford's 'bad, green teeth' were remarked, and his habit of butting rudely into a conversation, on the assumption that the subject was himself. He mentioned the 'complete' Voltaire that had formed part of his youthful 'hay-loft' library, and quoted Mozart's verdict on him as 'one who died like a dog & serve him right'.

As dedicatee of the *Severn Suite*, Shaw received records of the orchestral version. He wrote on 11 July: 'What a transfiguration! Nobody will ever believe that it began as a cornet corobbery. It's extraordinarily beautiful.' He now had the three newly published volumes of *Music in London* to send to Elgar: 'Resurrection pie from the nineties'. Elgar in his turn looked forward to Shaw's latest play: 'Can't you engineer that I sit *with you* for the first performance of *Too true to be good* "my last chance".' Not everyone approved of the Shavian influence on Elgar. Mary de Navarro, for instance, was to inform her bishop: 'I pulled him up soundly on saying he was making a new religion by taking all the "nots" from the Commandments & putting them into the Creed, but that was when he was very intimate with Shaw.'

There was also contact again with one of his oldest friends, Charles Buck. The British Medical Association had returned to Worcester after fifty years, and Elgar wrote to remind Buck of 'the dear old days'. Buck replied at once and recalled the occasion when they had been 'carrying my parrot over to Settle with a stick pushed through the cage when the bottom fell out' and they all but lost the bird. In his next letter Elgar protested ignorance of anatomy: 'I never could learn anything about the human form & to this day if you offered me £1,000,000,000 I cd. not tell you where my liver, or Kidneys, or any damn thing lies.'

At the Worcester Festival Elgar implied in conversation that the Third Symphony was all but finished, yet public indifference made it hardly worth his while to continue. Shaw took the matter up on 30 September with Sir John Reith, Director General of the BBC, reminding him of the £100 gift from the Philharmonic Society to Beethoven in his last illness. Shaw called this 'by far the most creditable incident in English history'. He continued: 'You could bring the Third Symphony into existence and obtain the performing right for the BBC for, say, ten years, for a few thousand pounds. The kudos would be stupendous.'

Now that music interested him again, Elgar was characteristically embarked on another major project. It is uncertain when the idea of making an opera from Ben Jonson's play *The Devil is an Ass* first possessed him. He knew his Jonson as well as he knew his Shakespeare, and had clearly been busy making a libretto long before his approach to Barry Jackson in 1932. A letter to Jackson of 23 September makes clear his thinking: 'My feeling has always been that the Elizabethan (for short) dialogue is splendid for recit.' He then outlined his magpie method with the text: 'for lyrical moments I had marked out several things from the Masques, but I cannot find (at this moment) my "cut up" copy of Gifford's edn. – I had adumbrated two acts exactly as you say'. Three days later he wrote again: 'I had suggested, to myself long ago, that Wittipol might be a woman (contralto, as in Rosenkavalier) this might upset the disguise however: of course the contralto business gives a lovely air of *unreality* (in the best sense) to anything e.g. Handel's operas.'

Elgar was also engaged on smaller things. He sent Keith Prowse two piano pieces, *Serenade* and *Adieu*, on 29 September, adding that 'they can be adapted to any "arrgt." you think fit'. And by 5 December the firm had received *Mina*, provisional title for what was to seem a miniature tribute to Elgar's smallest dog. A 12 October letter from Aircraftman Shaw linked Elgar's symphonic past and future: 'your 2nd Symphony hits me between wind and water. It is exactly the mode that I most desire.' He then looked ahead: 'the news of your 3rd Symphony was like a week's sunlight. I do hope you will have enough enthusiasm left to finish it.'

An Albert Hall performance of the Violin Concerto with Menuhin took place on 20 November. The *Daily Mail* hinted at a moving occasion: 'Side by side they carried their audience away from the world of reality on the wings of music; the boy with his life before him – the man with so much of his life behind him, a life of high endeavour and notable success.' A plan to repeat the Concerto in Paris the following May filled Elgar with doubt: 'The attitude of the press I feel sure would be that dear Yehudi was making a mistake in appearing with a musician of very inferior Calibre (me).'

The major celebration of Elgar's seventy-fifth birthday came in three

BBC concerts at the end of the year, on 30 November, 7 and 14 December. Elgar directed *Cockaigne*, the Violin Concerto with Albert Sammons, and the Second Symphony. Landon Ronald conducted the First Symphony, and on the evening of the last concert announced that the BBC was commissioning the Third Symphony. Fred Gaisberg wrote the following day: 'We would certainly like to record it immediately before or after the inaugural performance.'

Shaw had recently sent Elgar a copy of *The Black Girl in Search of God*. Elgar coupled his thanks with distress that the Shaws were soon to be away for a long time on 'a devastating world journey'. They departed on 16 December. Meanwhile Elgar too was busy with a fable involving God, to be sent as his Christmas and New Year greeting. He envisaged 'a gorgeous, illimitable, golden corridor', in which 'several of the Higher-Beings were in waiting'. They were disappointed with God's new world. But then a 'vast Purple Shadow filled the space and Lucifer sat'. He looked forward to earth, its inhabitants, and its religions. The rest were despondent, until a 'pleasant and not unmirthful' sound was heard. After drawing back a curtain, the archangel Michael reported: 'HE is pleased. – HE laughs – He has made, (Michael whispered) – a Puppy!' Now only Lucifer was concerned, for he knew 'that through the ages Man could be serenely happy with his DOG'. This was Elgar's most elaborate tribute to Marco and Mina.

At the beginning of 1933 opera and symphony were proceeding in tandem. On Christmas Day at the Philip Leicesters' Elgar had looked ahead: 'Now, you all open your Christmas crackers, and I'll put the sound into my new Symphony.'[12] For the opera Elgar had ransacked early sketchbooks and unpublished music, using whatever still appealed and seemed serviceable. But the symphony was the more pressing, and he wrote an encouraging report to Reith on 25 February; he hoped to start scoring soon: 'I am doing the best I can & up to the present the Symphony is the *strongest* thing I have put on paper.'

But the international scene was again darkening, as he observed in a letter to Adela Schuster on 17 March:

I am in a maze regarding events in Germany – what are they doing? In this morning's paper it is said that the greatest conductor Bruno Walter &, stranger still, Einstein are ostracised: are we all mad? The Jews have always been my best & kindest friends – the pain of these news is unbearable & I do not know what it really means.

He mentioned the 'new things which may be heard one day – if there are any listeners allowed to live'. Later in the year Elgar was to have

[12] MS notes at the Birthplace Museum.

chaired a banquet for Bruno Walter in London; but ill health prevented him, and his place was taken by Beecham.[13]

The Shaws returned from their world tour in April, and Elgar expressed his pleasure: 'the world seems a cold place to me when you are both away'. While Carice was at Marl Bank that month, something very untoward occurred: 'Came back & found Father very bad – had to send for Dr. & he came 3 times in evening.' It was apparently sciatica. He now approved a BBC plan to postpone the symphony by six months: 'I like your idea to announce the Symphony for the May Festival of 1934.' He detailed the symphony's movements as 'Allegro', 'Allegretto', 'Adagio', 'Allegro', though still uncertain about the order of the central two.

The Paris performance of the Violin Concerto had been fixed for 31 May 1933. Gaisberg suggested they went by air: 'From Croydon to Le Bourget it usually takes from an hour and a half to two hours, depending on the wind.' Elgar had another idea: 'I do not know how far away *Delius* lives, but I should like to see him.' There was an *Apostles* to conduct in Croydon and then he went on to Newmarket. That May Elgar was in communication with many leading bookmakers and had been assigned for the placing of bets such *noms-de-plume* as 'Elhamboy', 'Alectryon', 'Elmusic', 'Elbow', 'Elshie', and the ever-resonant 'Siromoris'.[14] With the Paris trip imminent, Elgar wrote for reassurance to Shaw; the reply asked, 'How does the symphony get on? Dont you think you could get two into the time? Remember, you have to catch up on Beethoven.'

Gaisberg described the flight on 28 May: 'Elgar enjoyed it with just a tinge of anxiety as he would grip the rails when we struck some air pockets on his first flight.' But he completed a crossword during the journey. After rehearsing the Concerto the following morning, Elgar and Gaisberg made for Grez-sur-Loing. Gaisberg described the paralysed Delius as sitting 'very upright, with his hands resting on the arms of a big rolling chair. Illuminated by the afternoon sun, his face looked long and pale and rather immobile. His eyes were closed.' He and Elgar discussed work in progress (Delius was busy with the Idyll, aided by Eric Fenby) and literary preferences (Elgar was for Dickens and Montaigne, Delius for Whitman and Kipling). Elgar wrote an account of his visit for the *Daily Telegraph* of 1 July. He gave his general impression of Delius: 'He is very much amongst us; little escapes his alert intelligence of what is of interest or value in contemporary art – music, painting, literature.' Delius wrote later to Ernest Newman: 'It

---

[13] See Bruno Walter, *Theme and Variations* (London, 1947), p. 333.
[14] Letters at the Birthplace Museum.

was the first time that the real Elgar was revealed to me and that I could talk intimately with him and that I had the opportunity of appreciating his fine intellect and affectionate nature.'[15] They drank champagne to celebrate.

Back in Paris, Elgar was decorated the following day by the French president, who also attended the concert. He complained to Atkins about the embrace with a waxed moustache, and wrote also to Delius: 'my meeting with you was the "clou" of my days in Paris: the boy played wonderfully but that is natural to him'. The return flight was on 2 June, Elgar's seventy-sixth birthday. Next day it was announced in the Birthday Honours that he was created KCVO. The summer of 1933 was unusually hot, and 'the exuberant sun' was a trial to Elgar. But on 17 August he conducted the Second Symphony in London and had a buoyant conversation with Gaisberg: 'Elgar joyfully announced to us that his Third Symphony was practically complete, a Piano Concerto was nearly finished, and he was half way through an opera.' On paper this was hardly so.

From 26 August Gaisberg spent the weekend at Marl Bank. The dogs dined either side of Sir Edward, and Gaisberg heard parts of the opera. He summed up his impressions of the Symphony: 'The whole work strikes me as youthful and fresh – 100% Elgar without a trace of decay.' He then made an important psychological point: 'His secretary Mary Clifford says he has not done much recently on the Sym. and seems to prefer to work on his opera. I think he misses the inspiration and driving force of Lady Elgar. Some sympathetic person, lady or man, of strong character should take him in hand and drive him on.'

The Hereford Festival heard the first performance of the Cello Concerto in Tertis's new version for viola; Elgar conducted. Carice's diary of 20 September struck an ominous note: 'Heard Father had bad turn but all right again.' Nine days later he was 'bad with sciatica'. On 7 October he had to go to South Bank nursing home for an exploratory operation. He informed Reith at once, offering to repay his advances in case the Symphony should not be finished. The operation on 8 October revealed that cancer had already spread far through Elgar's body, and that further surgery was not to be attempted.

The correspondence with Delius continued. Elgar wrote from South Bank on 13 October: 'I am supposed to be improving and want to share a few more years with you and hear your "brave transluminary things" and to see and talk once more with the poet's mind in the poet's body – you in fact.' Delius had received some records from

[15] Carley, ed., *Delius: a Life in Letters 1909–1934*, p. 432.

Gaisberg and was particularly enjoying the Introduction and Allegro, 'a special favourite of mine', and *Falstaff*, 'so full of life and in its changing moods so human, vigourous and natural'. Grez kept Elgar supplied with barley sugar 'of the holy and sanctified manufacture'. Elgar told how in New York he had been urged to 'lead a private prayer meeting' for the failure of Strauss's *Salome*. Delius remembered 'the beautiful singing in 4 part harmony of the negroes in their own quarters at the back of the orange grove'. He had harsh views on 'this Jazz rot that has come from New York to Europe'; he thought it 'a *horrible travesty* by New York Jews'.

Shaw sent a copy of his latest play, *On the Rocks*, with 'proofs of its terrific preface'. He urged him to 'read, or get Carice to read you the part about Socrates, Jesus, Joan and Galileo, because it ends with a quotation written expressly for you'. The quotation began 'Wonderful! Counsellor!' Shaw also negotiated with Reith so that Elgar could be relieved of anxiety about the symphony: 'The very pleasant arrangement made by you in the goodness of your heart for my peace of mind & betterment last year was turning out to be my greatest worry & disappointment'. Elgar was also gratified to hear from the clerk of the Worcester Races course that next April an 'Elgar Plate' race would be run.[16]

Elgar improved sufficiently to be moved home on 3 January 1934, and at Marl Bank he had his last recording session. Elgar's sick-room was linked to the Abbey Road studios in London. He was able to comment on the playing of the Triumphal March from *Caractacus*, and at one point he said, 'Who could have written such a beautiful melody?' He also wanted the 'Woodland Interlude', then insisted on a repeat 'very much lighter and a slower tempo'. When *Mina* was recorded, he was able to criticize that too on 15 February; but that was the end of Elgar's music-making. He had exacted a promise from Reed that no one should 'tinker' with the sketches of the Third Symphony; the last entries in his diary, fixtures he was unable to attend in November and December 1933, concerned not music but the Worcester Races. On 8 February Carice wrote to the Windflower: 'I am sorry to say Father has been going downhill the last 3 weeks very much'. He died on the morning of 23 February 1934, and the Windflower said what needed to be said: 'He is our Shakespeare of music.'

---

[16] Letter at Birthplace Museum.

9

Secular choral works

It was Elgar's cantatas of the 1890s that first took his fame beyond Worcester and its neighbourhood. Small orchestral works had been heard in Birmingham and indeed London, and *Froissart* had consolidated his local reputation at the Worcester Festival of 1890. When Elgar submitted his first cantata to Novello in September 1892, he consciously attached it to current fashion: 'I would point out that the present work is of a class much in request – chorus & orch:- & that the poem set is picturesque & popular at the same time presenting no great difficulty to the performers.' He had also just returned from Bayreuth, with his Wagnerian enthusiasm intensified, and the sounds of the Wagner orchestra fresh in his ears.

The Black Knight

Press notices of the *Black Knight* première were favourable and perceptive. *Berrow's Worcester Journal* noted the increased scale of Elgar's ambition: 'He has done himself eminent credit with instrumental suites and other trifles, but he has not previously ventured upon so large a work as a cantata.' *The Musical Times* felt it revealed

> qualities in the composer which are bound to bring him rapidly to the front. His themes are striking and picturesque, and his command of the means whereby they can be made the most of is very considerable. The result is a work displaying power, charm and musicianship in a high degree. Its orchestration also is excellent.

The Longfellow text has been much criticized. Yet its gaucheness (it was supposed to be an improvised translation of Uhland's German) does not militate against it as a musical libretto. The brisk narrative, a tale of a prince and princess pursued ruthlessly to an untimely end, proceeds in pithy, sometimes almost telegraphic, lines. The rhythms vary to the point of uncertainty, and rhymes can be as approximate as 'whole' and 'cool', or 'utterly' and 'die'. There was indeed no verbal straitjacket such as Elgar was to meet later in *The Music Makers*. His imagination could be fired to the limit of his technique. The poem came from his mother's favourite *Hyperion*; its setting was among the firstfruits of his marriage. Again the contemporary critic of the *Worcester Herald* saw to the root of the matter: 'Mr. Elgar has gone to the days of chivalry for his conception, and in his delightfully descriptive writing brings before us the imposing grandeur, the mysticism, and the romance of the period – a rare achievement in this prosaic age.' Elgar might have penned the criticism himself.

On a sketch of the work Elgar expressed his diffidence: 'Music by Edward Elgar if he can'. Yet the opening was shown to have a curious inevitability. In the fourth of his early sketchbooks, dated to April 1879, he remarked an odd coincidence. The theme he thought he had 'composed' in the summer of 1889 already existed ten years before: 'how strange', he wrote. Elgar divided Longfellow's ten six-line stanzas into four scenes, all of two stanzas except the last.

Scene I is set at Pentecost, with a 'luxuriant Spring' about to break forth, and the king's son as all-conquering hero of the joust. Elgar takes the first three lines of the poem as his first section, launching in full panoply with an eight-bar phrase in a G major already grandly Elgarian (Ex. 1). To counteract the falling melodic line there are two upward leaps of a major sixth, and the downward striding bass underpins enough dissonance in the inner parts to spice the diatonic

Ex. 1

177

harmonies. The 'woods and fields', always dear to Elgar, conjure an affectionate *cantabile*. A swift modulation to B minor launches the second stanza, in which 'Drums and trumpets' flash fanfares across the score. For 'the play of spears', when all comers are defeated by the royal prince, the *molto marcato* choral lines gather triplets and dotted rhythms till the sopranos at the top of their range resume the opening of 'Pentecost'. A quick wrench to a *pianissimo* pedal is the first shadow that Elgar casts over the music, his hint that 'the Feast of Gladness' may turn out ill. The G major of the opening returns in opulent bombast but fades through a finely graded last paragraph to end quietly.

Scene II follows without a break, and begins with a miniature march in C, still festive in character (Ex. 2). The broken rhythm of its second beat is an Elgarian hallmark that anticipates other more resplendent marches. The arrival of 'a sable knight' hardly disturbs the texture

Ex. 2

until his 'name and scutcheon' are demanded. With no soloists in the work, the narrative is entirely choral, so that 'I am a Prince of mighty sway' comes out in powerful octaves, screwed up by semitones. These words also gather to themselves a Klingsor-like motif that is to characterize the sinister stranger. As he rides into the lists, the heavens darken, the castle rocks, and a climax is reached in descending chromatic minims from the chorus over an orchestral bass plunging by tritones. The whole section is intensely dramatic, but the music thunders on way beyond the availability of any new words, so that Elgar can merely repeat again and again the meagre supply Longfellow has given him. The movement ends with the motif of the stricken prince, until the stranger leaves the lists *pianissimo*, his work done.

The 'high hall' of the royal castle is the setting for Scene III. A lengthy orchestral introduction in D major uses two main themes. The first of them develops a B minor pendant over a dominant pedal; this consists of a one-bar figure that rises and falls in sequence with unchanging rhythm. Elgar's spaces were often to be filled thus. The choral entry, when 'Pipe and viol call the dances', gives the basses a sinuous tune in G that stretches to thirteen beats in a largely unaccompanied section. The sinister stranger and his motif return at the words 'Waves a mighty shadow in'. He asks the king's daughter to dance, and Elgar ends the section with four chords so mysterious that he wondered whether to introduce the sound of Mozart's basset-horn at this point. The dance, a 'measure weird and dark', has Neapolitan inflexions and, to travel geographically, a Moorish melodic flavour, with stroke of metal beater on cymbal. The princess's flowers fade to the music that described her brother's grounding in the lists.

The four stanzas of Scene IV open with an A flat march, again instinct with dotted notes and triplets, as the guests come to the 'sumptuous banquet'. An arching melodic phrase describes the knightly pride of the gathering. In a new C minor section, obsessive repeated notes define the king's anxiety for his children. With twist to G minor and a quickening of the tempo the dark knight takes a beaker till harshly insistent orchestral chords announce his speech: 'Golden wine will make you whole'. The penultimate stanza, as the children bid their father farewell, is largely for unaccompanied chorus. A violin solo, suggestive of lessons learnt in Bayreuth, heralds their death. The king's outburst in the last stanza, that Death (for it is he) has taken the children 'in the joy of youth', brings back with telling irony the 'Pentecost' motif. The Black Knight's message is stark: 'Roses in the Spring I gather.' Towards the end the music quietens and slows, until the final bars enshrine a mystic orchestral climb into the heights such as would later close *Gerontius*.

Scenes from the Bavarian Highlands

If the bold drama of *The Black Knight*, for the most part admirably realized, revealed a composer learning quickly some important Wagnerian lessons, the 'Bavarians' hinted at the melodic freshness and rhythmic piquancy of Dvořák. The work traded joyously and touchingly on the experiences of three consecutive summers in south Germany. The six poems by Alice Elgar all celebrated some place visited during the holidays, and the music was Elgar's distillation of the *Schuhplatt'l* dancing they had witnessed and the rustic part-singing they had heard. It was very much a joint achievement.

Much of the music has a carefree spontaneity, yet it is subtly wrought. Here Elgar inexhaustibly devises new melodic tags from only a handful of basic ideas: by 1895 he was already master of the thematic processes that would produce the 'Enigma' Variations in four years' time. 'The Dance' was set at Sonnenbichl, which Elgar described in a letter of December 1900 as 'a wooden Gasthaus in the mountains & a favourite beer resort of mine (Munich beer)'; the strong rhythm of the opening ländler alternates with brisker music as the rustic couples 'hasten to the dancing'. Wamberg is celebrated in 'False Love'. The orchestral introduction yodels in cross rhythm, and the first half of the piece praises serenely the sweet voice of spring and 'my sweetheart true'; but there is a rival at the door, and Elgar deals in tender sadness with the infidelity of the girl. The 'Lullaby' at Hammersbach, 'a small village at the foot of the Höllenthal', combines thistledown orchestral caresses with a slumber song of touching simplicity for the altos. The lure of the far-away zither is resisted, and the mother stays with her child, hushed by new orchestral counterpoints.

'Aspiration', a reflection on the Baroque chapel at Sanct Anton, is the only song in quadruple time, and the most solemn. Elgar conjures up both the stillness of winter, and the warmth of God's protecting hand. 'On the Alm' is subtitled 'True Love', and the scene is Hoch Alp, dominated by a mountain peak. The men's voices begin unaccompanied, as they describe the girl dwelling on a hill pasture to tend cattle. Her lover must bound up the heights and hope for a joyous welcome. 'The Marksmen' and their shooting club at Murnau make an ebullient finale, with a strong imitative middle section as the men return with their prizes to claim the reward of love. In his programme note for the première Elgar offered 'this work as a tribute of esteem and affection to my many friends among a noble and simple people'.

Scenes from the Saga of King Olaf

Elgar's use of thematic 'labels' in *The Black Knight* had been distinctive and effective. The motifs had been striking and well differentiated; he had also shown subtlety in their development and combination. But in the Bavarian holidays of 1893 and 1894 Elgar wondered anew at Wagner's art: his rich orchestral palette, as apt to the Rhine depths as to fire-girt mountain peaks; his ability to paint the varied phenomena of nature or probe the obscurest psychological twist; the wizardry that could devise textures appropriate to the descent of the Grail or to snarling schemes hatched in the entrails of the earth.

Elgar took what he wanted from Wagner into his own art. The subject of King Olaf might well have attracted Wagner; but whereas Wagner searched always for the ultimate human significance of saga, myth and legend, Elgar's episodic work has quite a different aim and achieves a different success. Elgar could now make a dramatic point with speed and precision, had enriched his harmonic vocabulary, and shows in *Olaf* a virtuosic skill in the use of his leitmotifs that he rarely equalled in his later works.

After the success of *The Black Knight*, Longfellow again seemed a reasonable choice for the basis of a major work, and Elgar was attracted by his colourful treatment of Olaf Tryggvessön's career. Longfellow followed the bardic tradition of singing his hero's fame in isolated episodes, of which there were twenty-two. Here, in 'The Musician's Tale' from *Tales of a Wayside Inn*, was a sprawling text far from the succinct drama of *The Black Knight*. To make his libretto, Elgar cut up different editions of Longfellow, altered the order of the sections, abbreviated, thought out the musical divisions of the text, and gradually refined his conception of Olaf. There is robust humour and crude brutality in Longfellow; Elgar played this down, hoping to emphasize the very muscular Christianity of Olaf as against the bloodthirsty Odin-worship of Norway.

Elgar was working at the libretto from January 1894; the commission from Charles Swinnerton Heap for performance at the North Stafford-shire Festival of October 1896 concentrated his mind. It was then he involved his neighbour Harry Acworth in the project, to supply connecting recitative texts between the episodes, and to remodel four Longfellow scenes. If the versification was Acworth's, the drift of the argument and its emphasis was often Elgar's. From Longfellow's catalogue of troublesome women, only Gudrun, claiming her murderous dagger is a bodkin, remained unchanged. The haughty Queen Sigrid is insulted by Elgar's Olaf less outrageously than in Longfellow, and Thyri is sufficiently tamed to sing a love duet. Longfellow had luxuriated in the spray-drenched clash of Olaf's final sea fight, multiplying its characters and stretching it over five episodes. Acworth drastically curtailed it, locating his scene on 'The bosom of the troubled deep', into which the vanquished Olaf sinks. The conclusion, with Olaf's mother at prayer in the convent at Drontheim, was retained.

Elgar prefaced his score with an explanatory note: 'In the following Scenes it is intended that the performers should be looked upon as a gathering of skalds (bards); all, in turn, take part in the narration of the Saga and occasionally, at the more dramatic points, personify for the moment some important character.' So the soprano soloist represents all three women wooed by Olaf; the tenor is Olaf himself; the bass is the pagan Ironbeard and sings all the Acworth recitatives. The chorus sets the various scenes and carries the bulk of the narrative in the manner of *The Black Knight*. Elgar was embarked on a ninety-minute work, the most ambitious of his career hitherto, with eight major sections between Introduction and Epilogue.

Elgar's music-making had a new-found freedom. Some movements, such as the Introduction, are ternary in structure, ending in the key they began in, though often wide-ranging in their tonality. Others follow the drama with bold key-relationships and rely for coherence on the telling use of leitmotifs. The thematic elements of *King Olaf* make use of some thirty motifs, many labelled by Elgar himself when supplying notes to Joseph Bennett for his analysis of the work. Rising motifs, often spanning a fourth or sixth, are associated with Olaf and his new Christian religion; motifs of equivalent descent represent the pagan forces. Elgar's sense of drama is powerfully developed and tension remains high. Indeed, Jaeger remarked in December 1897 that he felt 'the absence of a developed broadly melodious lyrical movement' and that Elgar was *'always* "at it" '. This was an occasion when Elgar rightly ignored Jaeger's criticism. Nor did he expand the Epilogue, which Jaeger considered too short.

Elgar's skill at defining atmosphere was a strength of *The Black Knight*. In *Olaf* it is movingly apparent from the outset. The remote world of the sagas is evoked in a mist-shrouded G minor, in which the stepwise descent spanning a series of fourths is balanced by the upward minor sixths of the violas, so that Elgar's idea of the conflicting religions is unobtrusively outlined from the beginning (Ex. 3). The middle section is based on a fine sweep of modulating melody building from one-bar units over a largely chromatic descending bass. 'Sagas' resumes on E flat, but is soon in a G minor that sharpens the third for the final bars.

The 'God of Thunder' recitative releases lightning flashes from Elgar's orchestra as it leads to a fragment of canon and the key of B flat minor. 'The Challenge of Thor' launches a *pianissimo* ostinato that spans the descending fourth and insists, with emphatic second beat, on the god's eternal 'fastness and fortress' in the Northland. The blows of Thor's hammer are struck with descending fourths in the bass and forceful last-beat triplets above. His gauntlet and girdle are similarly described as the music climbs tone by tone from A to E flat major and back to the B flat minor of the ostinato. Violins flicker with the Northern Lights across the score, and the ostinato moves from bass to treble. 'Force rules the world still' propels the music over an ever wider range of keys until mention of the Galilean god brings a sudden *pianissimo* and an awed hush to the 'Hammer' motif. Thor ends the movement with his *fortissimo* challenge: 'Gauntlet or Gospel'.

Olaf is said to have been converted in the Scilly Isles and confirmed at Andover. His return to Norway is described by Elgar in a movement (no. 3) that climbs from the five flats of Thor's B flat minor towards the F and G sharp (A flat) major of his thoughts about his mother Astrid. Elgar runs a considerable risk by introducing new motifs at every section of the movement: but thrice he recalls the darting Northern Lights and maintains such impetus that the sequence of the journey seems as inevitable as that of Siegfried to his destination on the Rhine. The movement is for tenor solo, whose line abounds with the upward leaps of Olaf's energetic Christianity. A brief recitative introduces the 'Sailing' motif in F minor. Elgar moves quietly to the subdominant as Olaf 'stood as one who dreamed', then to C minor for the Northern Lights as they 'glanced and gleamed' on his armour. Elgar closely follows Olaf's thoughts, as he relives his childhood's exile with Astrid. A change to 12/8 (a rhythm that can be facile in Elgar) limns Olaf's 'Beauty' in impetuous phrases. The climax is reached at 'Thus came Olaf to his own'. Thor's ostinato returns in B flat minor, the challenge is reissued, and Olaf is back in Norway.

Ex. 3
'Sagas'

A recitative leads to 'The Conversion', the first Acworth reworking of Longfellow. The confrontation between the faiths is boldly managed by Elgar. Olaf proclaims his martial Christianity over a persistent triplet figure. Ironbeard will have none of it. He and his men recall Thor's hammer and reject the new religion with increasing emphasis in A, B and C sharp (D flat). Olaf demands that Ironbeard and his daughter Gudrun go through the fire of the pagan gods. Ironbeard in his defiance recalls the night fires of Thor and others of the god's motifs as he points to the golden image of his deity. The chorus hurls itself into the fray *doppio movimento*, as Olaf shatters Thor's image, and a 'housecarle' lays Ironbeard low. The final choral hymn nods towards Mendelssohn, but owes more, with its impassioned sweep and melodic turns, to the Wagner of *Lohengrin*.

Gudrun's motif makes clear she is Ironbeard's daughter. Heard on three cellos at the outset of the recitative (no. 6), it dominates the 'Gudrun' movement. The moonlit night is evoked on muted violins and harp, while 'its tide of dreams' recalls the motif of Olaf's shipboard dream. Gudrun's evil intent is symbolized in a retrograde version of her theme. As she approaches Olaf with a dagger, her eyes are fixed on the cairn that covers her murdered father. Elgar's pleasant 9/8 does little to express the coldness of 'the dagger's kiss', but the remote chord to which Olaf sleeps brings inspiration back. His awakening and the duet of recrimination are excitingly done. As Gudrun is dismissed, her motif dies away and is reduced to fragments.

'The Wraith of Odin' is a choral ballad dealing eerily with the arrival of a one-eyed stranger and uttering obsessively the sinister refrain, 'Dead rides Sir Morten of Fogelsang'. Olaf's rising intervals are prominent in the movement, and brief thematic snatches refer to the pagan gods and 'Sagas'; but the pace is such and the narrative so gripping that the ordered skill of the piece is only gradually apparent. The resource with which the monotone of the refrain is varied shows Elgar at top voltage. When the singers stay silent, the timpani twice tap its rhythm.

The 9/8 of 'Sigrid' has both charm and menace. The maidens of the haughty queen describe with joyous excitement, in Acworth's words, the fording of the river by the approaching Norwegians and the iron beat of their horses' hooves. Olaf's greeting to Sigrid, with falling sixths and fourths, suggests religious trouble ahead; but the orchestra, *grazioso molto*, constructs a marvellous paragraph of varied repetitions that underpin the initial exchanges between king and queen. Soon they are hurling insults about each other's faith, till Olaf rejects utterly a 'heathen dame', and also casts in her teeth her lack of beauty and youth. His glove, thrown towards the floor, strikes the queen on the cheek, and the maidens urge Olaf's departure. They foresee Olaf's doom, and use with nice irony a phrase from the introductory recitative (no. 10) to hint that Sigrid is both 'wronged and weak'. Her final outburst to the same music, 'Sigrid yet shall be Olaf's death', implies nothing of the sort.

In the world of the Norse sagas, womenfolk come and go; Elgar now tackles Olaf's third relationship. Thyri left her former husband, King Burislaf, 'after a week and a day'. Rumour, a 'little bird in the air', is busy with gossip about her past, and the possibility of marriage with Olaf. This is the stuff of another choral ballad with refrain of good practical sense:

> Hoist up your sails of silk,
> And flee away from each other.

At the outset of the recitative (no. 12), which presages the infectious waltz rhythms of the ballad, the descending stepwise fourth in the horn spells out the future refrain. Most of the gossiping is done by the choral women, initially in G. The men launch the refrain, of which the repetitions take it to B, D sharp (E flat) and on to G, climbing by major thirds, a favourite Elgarian procedure. The cunning with which Elgar shortens the refrain when it recurs bears closest inspection. A rollicking waltz sauced with grace notes first appears in the heightened excitement of B major; at the final 'flee away from each other' it has resumed G major, and ends the movement with magnificent panache.

Acworth wrote the words for the Olaf-Thyri duet, following Long-fellow in as far as Olaf's new queen is more interested in getting her lands back than in Olaf's gift of angelica. Elgar's lilting 6/8 deals well with her as she observes the return of spring. At Olaf's 'Thyri, my beloved' the musical temperature drops for the first time in the work, but Thyri brings vitality back with motifs from the preceding ballad. Olaf too recovers to the extent of adopting the grace-noted waltz. If king and queen resort too frequently to octaves in their passionate outpouring, there is excitement enough to hint at the opera that might have been.

A choral recitative (no. 15) to Longfellow's words relates that Thyri's brother, King Svend the Dane, has now married Sigrid. At the outset Sigrid's 'Vengeance' sounds on violins and bass clarinet. Motifs such as 'Sagas' and Olaf's 'Sailing' are finely fitted into the rich narrative texture, but Sigrid is monomaniacal for satisfaction. 'The Death of Olaf' is Acworth's text. After an orchestral introduction, Elgar continues in C major with music he originally wrote for a *Millwheel Song* to words of his wife. As the Danish ships are sighted, the key-signature changes to C minor, and a version of Thor's ostinato underpins the structure. Many motifs are recalled in the surge of the music, but Elgar makes graphically clear that the 'Woe for Norroway' is Sigrid's curse. As Olaf's ship is sunk, there are reminders of the wailing wind and dashing foam that accompanied his initial return to Norway.

The Epilogue returns to Longfellow, with Olaf's mother at prayer in the convent of Drontheim. She listens to the imagined voice of St John the Divine. The three soloists begin his message:

> It is accepted,
> The angry defiance,
> But not with the weapons
> Of war that thou wieldest.

The music is Thor's, hushed now to acquiescence; Olaf's rising fourth occurs only at 'Patience is powerful'. Yet it is his interval that dominates the start of the unaccompanied partsong 'As torrents in summer'. Longfellow's last two stanzas begin with the words 'Stronger than steel / Is the sword of the Spirit'. It is here that Elgar's nerve deserts him, and he retreats into the comfortable clichés of his period (Ex. 4). Having managed the varied episodes of the saga with consummate skill, Elgar fails the final test of asserting the triumphant religion. Mendelssohn at his weakest could do little worse, and the music of

Ex. 4

'As torrents', returning in orchestral magnificence, is not strong enough for Longfellow's 'God is still God'. By a happy stroke Elgar returns to the music of the Introduction, offers a masterly précis of it, and thus rounds off his saga, making it 'more complete'.

The Banner of St George

In 1897 Novello wanted a popular cantata for Queen Victoria's Diamond Jubilee, and Elgar, after the success of *King Olaf*, seemed a man fitted to the task. As an occasional piece for a high-noon empire, it is perhaps above the average; as a product of Elgar's fortieth year it is well below *his* average. As in *Olaf*, it is the final section that threatens to kill the work. *Olaf*, stocked with robust characters and packed with stirring incident, can easily survive. *The Banner*, with the pallid Sabra as helpless heroine, a pantomime dragon, and a saint who strives with embarrassing sentimentality for 'the martyr's fadeless crown', need break its silence seldom.

As with *The Black Knight*, the narrative is choral, with only the princess as optional soloist. At once Elgar sets the scene: daily from 'his dank lair the awful dragon comes' to claim a maiden from Sylene. The B minor of the opening launches a melodic line that descends through a seventh to represent the dragon's threat. At mention of 'the comely daughters' of the city, the music moves to D major in a tender strain of mourning worthy of the situation. Sabra's emergence from the palace endows music that lacks strength with an air of injured innocence. Mention of the dragon draws from low strings, bassoons and tuba a motif descriptive of the monster as he waits, 'His breath a pestilence'. Sabra's words of self-sacrifice elicit from Elgar music beautiful yet facile, an inadequate response to a predicament worrying enough if taken seriously.

Shapcott Wensley, the librettist, gave Elgar an impossible task at the beginning of Scene II. Sabra's robes as she faces death are 'spotless as the virgin snow', and 'snow-white lilies deck her sunny hair'. Elgar responds with busy weaving of motifs previously heard, but inspiration not unnaturally eludes him. St George arrives 'at foaming speed' with a fine clatter of hooves, and Elgar easily matches the bombast of his opening speech. There is little excitement in the dragon's approach, but his motif dwindles convincingly when he 'Lashes the earth in vain, and dies'. The people of Sylene rejoice in an ecstatic transformation of the dragon's music, perhaps more exuberant than seemly. The sentiments of the Epilogue, a glorification of England's flag, belong to an age now far distant. Elgar finds the level of the words, and is content to remain there while energetically thumping the tub. Perhaps the Diamond Jubilee was not altogether beneficial to his burgeoning muse.

Caractacus

The six scenes of *Caractacus* comprised Elgar's longest work to date. Having collaborated on *King Olaf*, Acworth was now sole author of the libretto, descriptive of Caractacus in his last stand against the Romans and in his transport to honourable retirement at the hands of the Emperor Claudius. The setting is Elgar's own countryside, with the Herefordshire Beacon as traditional site of the British camp, and the fatal battle somewhere along the River Severn (Habren). Acworth provides Caractacus with a daughter, Eigen, named after a Malvern neighbour; and her betrothed is Orbin, a member of 'the half-priestly order of minstrels'. In addition there is an Arch-Druid, a Druid Maiden, along with hosts of Druids and Druidesses. After the première, Acworth was charged with prolixity. Longfellow, for all his faults, fed vitality into his verse; Acworth signally failed to do so. In fact he wrote more than Elgar set, and some of his least felicitous lines remain in the printed libretto, tactfully bracketed. But what more than anything vitiates the scheme of the work is the manufactured conclusion in which the Roman Empire, having 'crumbled into clay', gives place to its greater successor, that of Britain. The dedication to Queen Victoria set the seal on a protracted and inappropriate burst of patriotism.

There are numerous stage directions in libretto and scores; and at the beginning of Scene I, for instance, Caractacus and the British host are entering camp at night. Elgar wondered about an overture for the work but decided in the end on the 26-bar introductory march in C minor. The choral 'Watchmen, alert' acts as binding refrain to the movement, but almost at once 'the Roman hosts' are mentioned, and the motif of the foreign power, with third-beat triplet, is heard in the wind. Two bars on they have 'girdled in our British coasts', and the strings span the wide intervals of the patriots' theme. There is much reliance on augmented fifths as the contraltos bid the forces sleep before the battle. 'Britain' is enunciated *tutta forza* and canonically by the chorus as the last of the men gather 'On these green mountain tops'. When Caractacus steps forth, his opening music echoes some of the army's sounds, but then he 'proceeds to the foot of the mound by the Spring of Taranis', the Druid god. In E flat he hymns the natural beauty of the scene in an arching five-bar phrase. Elgar is now on home ground, and the reflective side of the king's character finds in him a ready response. Less happy is the F minor of Caractacus the warrior. The king describes in triplets the 'thund'ring car' that he has

driven over the ridges of war to the discomfiture of Rome. He ends
with the motif of Britain in E flat and now triple time to hint at
ultimate safety after 'one last endeavour'. Caractacus has not gripped
Elgar's imagination as Olaf did. Indeed the most powerful music Elgar
wrote for Caractacus does not appear in the work at all. It featured
in a letter to Dorabella in response to news from her about the
Wolverhampton Wanderers footballer, Malpas. A reporter had written,
'he banged the leather for goal'. Elgar dashed off an impetuous
recitative for the king, with final plunge down a diminished seventh,
to the text, 'We bang'd the leather for goal!' That was the way to deal
with Romans.

The entry of Eigen, whose theme has an expressive octave dip at
mid-point, establishes E minor. As the dialogue with her father
develops, Elgar introduces a motif with falling sixths and sevenths,
which he described for the analyst Herbert Thompson: 'this is what I
call a conversation (domestic love) tune – used to knit all else together'.
Orbin's theme is heard as Eigen explains he is waiting for her while
she wanders through the camp. He enters, and bids Caractacus listen
to Eigen's prophetic tale. She begins, in 12/8 and B major, a gentle
nature piece over a dominant pedal, with trills for 'the birds singing'
and 'the songs of the forest'. She and Orbin had met a Druid Maiden,
who had begun her fateful message to the king with the words:

> When the voices of earth
> At the midnight are still ...

This was the point where Elgar first intended the use of saxophones
in *Caractacus*. Thirty years later, in a speech to the Gramophone
Company, he claimed this as the idea of 'a bold and daring spirit'.
The problem of getting players and the expense had made him give
up the plan. The Druid Maiden's instruction is that Caractacus must
lure the Romans 'deep in the forest', and his eventual triumph will be
on the mountain heights. A concerted movement for the three soloists
culminates in a powerful octave declamation of the Druid Maiden's
message. Spirits of the Hill encourage Caractacus to cast his cares
aside, and the sentries repeat their hushed refrain.

Scene II, at 'The sacred oak grove by the tomb of the Kings', begins
in innocent charm. The Arch-Druid urges a mystic dance on his
followers. Acworth incites the Druidesses to 'Loose your locks, your
bosoms bare', but Elgar preserves a studied decorum. The B flat
'Invocation' to the god Taranis has a certain portentous power, though
its references to the sacrificial knife thrice reddening with a victim's
life tend to shift sympathy towards the Romans, who disliked human
sacrifice. The reading of the omens follows, to a motif initially in B

flat minor on solo violas and cellos. Orbin can see only gathering shadows, and eventually the Arch-Druid decides to suppress the prophecy and let Caractacus go to battle fired by a Druid blessing. Caractacus and his men enter to four trumpets and timpani hammering at the chord of F sharp minor and a clatter of percussion. The Arch-Druid enrols the organ as well as he mounts his throne and delivers to the words 'Go forth, O King, to conquer', the fullest version yet of Britain's theme. Its dubious quality is hardly improved by a choral pause on its top note; but for the moment it is at the service of dramatic irony. The music that accompanied Caractacus's entry is inverted to mock the promised triumph, but soon the king launches with splendid vigour on the rough and raw sentiments that take him to war in the three stanzas of his 'Sword Song'. In increasingly exciting music Orbin urges Caractacus to forget the omens and roundly bids the Arch-Druid tell the truth. As Druids and Druidesses, the chorus unites to drive Orbin forth. He remains defiant; the chorus, martial again, echoes the 'Sword Song', then finally returns to the sacred oak and bids Taranis doom the apostate. Elgar has remained on top form.

Scene III is set at the 'Forest near the Severn', which Elgar describes in a lovely G major landscape. A sketchbook idea from 1887 underlies the opening theme (Ex. 5a), and the music continues the more fragrant for its happy use of sequence (Ex. 5b).

Elgar described it to Herbert Thompson as 'all forest sounds (written in *our own* woods) which I hope you will see one day'. These were the woods round Birchwood Lodge. Acworth now directs that in 'the distance youths and maidens sing while they weave sacred garlands'. Elgar introduces their innocent partsong with chromatic chords he suggested might be scored 'for four Jaegers'. An extended 'nature' aria for Eigen takes some time to leave its tonic pedal; the music becomes fresher when it absorbs ideas from the orchestral introduction. Eigen is awaiting her beloved, but Elgar omitted Acworth's expectant conclusion:

> With joyous feet I fly
> To find my rest upon his breast,
> And in his heart to die.

Orbin recounts the Arch-Druid's duplicity, and the garland wreathers resume. Eigen's 'Thine in death' over a chromatically descending bass is set to a Tristanesque phrase Elgar called 'endless devotion'. The love-duet, starting in E minor and ending in G, modulates widely and subtly. If it relies much on sequence and again on too great a use of octaves for the soloists, it is the one section of the work that might have helped towards the opera Elgar later wanted out of *Caractacus*.

Elgar returns to his ravishing forest music, but the last vocal phrase had to be adjusted in proof, as he explained to Jaeger: 'I quite forgot to give the poor wretches time to breathe.'

Ex. 5
'Woodland Interlude'
(a)

(b)

Scene IV reverts to the Malvern Hills, and over proofs of the introductory bars Elgar wrote 'so sad'. Maidens are brooding in a G minor that darkens to B flat minor on rumours of 'battles lost and won'. Eigen enters to a recapitulation of part of her Scene I nature music. The Druid Maiden has foretold to her the British disaster leading to the eventual triumph in the 'forum of Rome'. The defeated army appears and recounts the course of the battle in a powerful D minor Presto. The persistent 7/4 of Caractacus's 'Lament' was suggested, Elgar told Herbert Thompson, by the first line of the words.

This is special pleading. More significant is his remark on the thematic link between the opening of the 'Invocation' to Taranis and the 'Lament'. He claimed not to understand the 'workings of my limited mind ... but I did it unconsciously'. The triplets followed by the drop of a fifth suggest also the might of Rome, as Caractacus appeals to his dead warriors to justify his conduct in the fight.

The setting for Scene V is the Severn, with 'British captives embarking on the Roman galleys'. The part now given to the Bard was originally intended for the Arch-Druid; Elgar presumably considered him too discredited to be allowed to sing again. Elgar informed Thompson he had written the music by the Severn: 'I made this on the banks & its rather like'. Harp and lower strings describe the lapping of the waters over which the Bard declaims a new motif of slavery. The mainly D minor movement has a lengthy orchestral postlude leading to the dominant of C and an *accelerando* towards the Roman forum.

Elgar claimed not to be able to analyse the 'Triumphal March' of Scene VI. All he said to Thompson was: 'It generally represents the noise & glitter of the Scene.' Acworth gave Elgar his cue for the four trumpets that 'scream aloud', the 'cymbals sharply ringing', and a brilliant part for the glockenspiel. The chorus has taken the music to C minor, and as 'Eigen, Orbin and Caractacus pass', the 'slavery' motif is heard. The march concludes as the 'Emperor fills the curule chair'. Caractacus's hands are unbound and he pleads his case, nowhere more eloquently than when he mentions his native woodlands. There, Elgar explained to Thompson, 'he breaks down & chokes – thinking of his woods – as I do when I'm away from Birchwood'. Eigen and Orbin join the plea with motifs from their past. The citizens of Rome cry death to them, but Claudius is impressed, and the motif of 'endless devotion' dominates the quartet of now liberated captives and emperor. The opening of the work is recalled, and with the words 'Britons, alert!' Elgar prepares for what he headed 'Modern Britain. A March'. It is difficult to be unmoved by Elgar's conviction, but equally difficult not to shudder at the words he set. Dramatically the situation is impossible, and yet again a jingoism that was deeply felt prevented Elgar from transcending the limitations of his period.

Coronation Ode

Caractacus, conceived in the afterglow of Queen Victoria's Diamond Jubilee, occurred to Elgar as a possible offering for her successor's coronation. When asked by the Covent Garden authorities for a suitably festive work, he suggested *Caractacus* as basis for an opera. In the end he set A. C. Benson's *Coronation Ode*. Inevitably an occasional work, it appeared again at the coronation of George V; elsewhere much of it can only seem an opulent curiosity. Apart from the four soloists, chorus and orchestra, Elgar also specified on the MS full score organ and military band. In the third section, where Benson urges that Britain's sons be 'Strong to arise and go, if ever the war-trump peal', Elgar adds a marginal note: 'Trumpets, Cornets Trombones &c. (as much brass at this pitch as possible)'. But at the end of a sketch for the work he relieved his feelings by setting 'Strong in faith and freedom, we have crowned our Kat!' On this occasion he added 'Fine del Sheddo', numbering the work among the playful effusions of his youth.

Benson had little time for Edward VII, regarding him as an 'ungraceful, small-minded, gross (though admittedly "kindly") man'; Elgar rated him more highly. None the less the six sections of Benson's *Ode* are always efficient, and sometimes more. The king is to be crowned with life, might, peace, love and faith in the first five stanzas, with God very much in charge of the sixth. Elgar launches in the same key as the end of *Caractacus*, his E flat of ceremony and patriotism. The lengthy orchestral introduction has a succession of grand tunes sumptuously scored with soaring strings and sonorous brass. But amid the splendour Elgar achieves a moment of magic in the sixth stanza with the quiet introduction of the trio tune from *Pomp and Circumstance* no. 1.

'Daughter of Ancient Kings' was a tribute to Alexandra of Denmark, the king's consort. Benson pointed to her old-established family in a country she never ceased to love; and as 'Mother of Kings to be', she was rightly shown in a domestic rather than public setting. Elgar's simple chords, heartfelt and very beautiful, were equally appropriate. He summed it up for Thompson: 'We are allowed to show a personal affection to our Queen'.

Benson's third section beseeches for Britain military and naval power in the cause of peace. Elgar responded more to the 'war-trump', 'battle-thunder', the 'scream of the flying shell' in a grandiloquent movement for bass solo and male chorus of little musical value. In Elgar's words: 'No 3 is frankly military, or rather naval & military & means "fight"'. Benson invokes in no. 4 the various arts as 'Airy powers of Earth and Sky'. Music comes first as 'sweetest child of heaven', and Elgar responds worthily to the art he might affect to dismiss but never touched without deep emotion. Benson moves on to the 'Music of the poet's heart', then the teachings of the 'Painter–poet'. Elgar enshrines Benson's conclusion in gentle chromatics for solo quartet: 'Only let the heart be pure.'

The Boer War was still being waged while Elgar worked on the

Ode; hence Benson's two stanzas, 'Peace, gentle Peace', which comprise the fifth section. Elgar set them for unaccompanied chorus and soloists, with just the lightest touch of orchestra, in music of tender simplicity. The verses are among Benson's weakest, but Elgar acknowledged the very real desire for peace, even if its expression was flat. Benson's problem in the final section was to find words for the march tune that already existed; his eventual solution provided the *Ode* with one section at least that needed no coronation for its performance. Elgar's finale begins quietly with contralto solo; but ceremonial fanfares crown its conclusion, in praise of an island 'Throned amid the billows, throned inviolate'. Whatever the fortunes of the island, 'Land of Hope and Glory' has so far proved inviolate.

The Music Makers

Having become increasingly 'political' in his secular choral works over the years, Elgar changed direction entirely with *The Music Makers* of 1912. O'Shaughnessy's *Ode* had been published in *The Athenaeum* of 30 August 1873, and its author was one of the more unlikely figures to have been employed by the British Museum. Recommended there by Lord Lytton, of whom he was a courtesy 'nephew', Arthur O'Shaughnessy (1844–81) was under constant threat of dismissal. Edmund Gosse described him as 'a sort of mystery, revealed twice a day. In the morning, a smart figure in a long frock-coat, with romantic eyes and bushy whiskers, he would be seen entering the monument and descending into its depths, to be observed no more till he as swiftly rose and left it late in the afternoon.' The antiquities of the museum fired O'Shaughnessy's imagination, as is clear from at least one stanza of the *Ode*.

The poem had considerable fascination for Elgar. He was always sensitive to the appeal of dreams, and responded readily to the poet's idea that the music makers and dreamers of dreams were also 'the movers and shakers of the world'. O'Shaughnessy has two rhyme-schemes for the nine stanzas, and by means of them he divides the *Ode* into three. Through musical reminiscence and recapitulation Elgar respects the scheme, though in more fundamental ways he is hardly faithful to the poem's intent. O'Shaughnessy held his past and future in balance:

> For each age is a dream that is dying,
> Or one that is coming to birth.

Elgar put most of his emphasis on the past, using quotations from his own greatest works to make of his setting a personal document of almost painful intensity.

Self-quotation had been successfully tried by other composers. Mozart had used a *Figaro* tune at Don Giovanni's banquet; Wagner's Hans Sachs had heard the sad tale of Tristan and Isolde. But it was Richard Strauss who expanded the device into a whole section of *Ein Heldenleben*, which Elgar heard at its English première in 1902. Moreover, Strauss gave him a full score of the work, and Elgar labelled the quotations as far as he could identify them. Ernest Newman was to write the programme note for *The Music Makers*, and Elgar counselled on 14 August 1912: 'Please do not insist on the *extent* of the quotations.' But he was glad Newman liked the idea: 'after all art must be the man, and all true art is, to a great extent egotism & I *have* written several things which are still alive'. He felt that O'Shaughnessy's ' "music makers" must include not only poets and singers but also all artists who feel the tremendous responsibility of their mission to "renew the world as of yore" '; 'therefore', Elgar continued, 'the atmosphere of the music is mainly sad'.

This was to misinterpret the *Ode*. O'Shaughnessy is by no means pessimistic, but Elgar seized on the fact that at least three of the stanzas, having found hope in the future, make a regretful farewell to the past. Such lines as 'And their work in the world be done', 'That ye of the past must die', 'And a singer who sings no more' turned Elgar towards his own hurts and griefs so that the setting tends to fragment the poem. He explained his practice to Newman: 'Occasionally I have departed from a general interpretation of the words, as an orator leaves the broad view of his subject to give a particular instance.' The argument was specious; Elgar knew perfectly well what the poet was driving at: 'The mainspring of O'Shaughnessy's Ode is the sense of progress, of never-ceasing change: it is the duty of the artist to see that this inevitable change is progress.'

At the outset of the orchestral introduction in F minor there are two main ideas, the first entwined with chromatics and steadily falling (Ex. 6a), the other diatonic and gradually climbing (Ex. 6b). Both are short-breathed, rely heavily on sequence, and are rhythmically akin; for Alice Stuart Wortley the whole passage was labelled 'the complete understanding'. After a brief transition, Elgar introduces the first six bars of the 'Enigma' theme from the Variations. The scansion is altered to fit twelve bars in the prevailing 3/8 and the harmonies are spiced, but the bass line remains. Elgar expounded to Newman the significance of the theme: 'it expressed when written (1898) my sense of the loneliness of the artist as described in the first six lines of the Ode, to me, and it still embodies that sense'.

Ex. 6

(a)

(b)

The choral entry at O'Shaughnessy's first stanza is quiet but arresting (Ex. 7). Elgar called it 'a sort of "artist" theme', and it recurs to mark off each third of the poem. Elgar explains thus his next reference: 'at "We are the dreamers of dreams", the theme quoted refers to a particular Dream'. It is indeed the start of the 'Judgment' motif from

196

Gerontius. There is not time for its solemn implications to sink in before the opening of *Sea Pictures* underlines the 'lone sea-breakers' and 'Enigma' returns for 'sitting by desolate streams'. If any test were needed for the unity of Elgar's creative imagination, it is here: the disparate ideas dovetail happily, and it is only their associations that conjure up thoughts of an enigmatic judgment by the sea. The first choral climax, *fff*, comes at 'movers and shakers / Of the world for ever', and a thrice echoed 'for ever' dies away to 'Enigma'.

Ex. 7

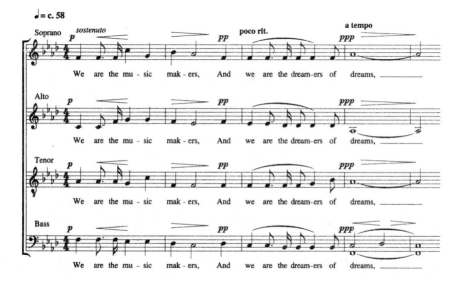

The second stanza describes the power of 'deathless ditties' to build 'great cities', initially in C minor.

> And out of a fabulous story
> We fashion an empire's glory

suggests other quotations to Elgar. With imperial taps on the side-drum he turns to Britain and France, with 'Rule Britannia' and the 'Marseillaise' in quick succession. He told Newman he did not regard them 'as being peculiarly fabulous stories (although under the present government "Rule Britannia" has been made the most foolish of all national boasts), but as examples of the things "music makers" have achieved'. He drew Newman's attention to the way the tunes 'go together & the deadly sarcasm of that rush in horns & trombones in the English tune'. This was to 'comicalise' it. Prolonged diminished sevenths for 'dream' are facile enough, but 'Can trample a kingdom down' uses a whole-tone idea Elgar originally planned for the 'Praise to the Holiest' sequence in *Gerontius*.

'Callicles' provided the modulating figure for the start of the third stanza, 'We, in the ages lying'. It continues with two broadly developed sections. The first describes how the world-losers built Nineveh and Babylon, overthrowing them with tidings of the future. The orchestra in D minor insistently repeats a strong one-bar melodic phrase until the mirth that constructed Babylon culminates in a cascade of woodwind and string chromatics meant originally for Judas in *The Apostles*. The tidings given to the ancient world concerned 'the new world's worth'. Elgar used here a rich texture of ascending and descending scales interspersed with seventh leaps first considered for 'And that a higher gift than grace' in *Gerontius*. Again diminished sevenths do duty for dying dreams. A new theme that takes the sopranos by a series of bold steps from middle C to top A quickly subsides to an echo of the *Gerontius* 'Grace' motif. With a third of the poem done, the chorus quietly resumes the opening 'Artist' motif to the original words, 'We are the music makers', ending in F minor.

The second tune from the orchestral introduction to the work takes over in its original A flat for the fourth stanza. The chorus words, 'A breath of our inspiration', attach a deeper significance to the music. The stanza introduces a plethora of new themes. 'A wondrous thing of our dreaming' evokes violin arabesques designed for the 1907 string quartet. Descending chromatic harmonies over rising consecutive fifths at 'Unearthly, impossible seeming' lead to an outburst of energy as the 'soldier, the king, and the peasant' work together 'till our dreams shall become their present'. The 'soldier' sets the tone, exploiting in a rousing G major Elgar's fondness for second beat accent and fourth beat triplet. The quiet coda to this section had its origin in a playful 'duo' sketch, in which characters labelled 'He' and 'She' exchanged their snatches of tune till they fell asleep.

The fifth stanza marks the centre of the Ode; and musically this is the core of the work, if only because Elgar is principally concerned with two of his grandest inspirations, 'Nimrod' and the coda to the Second Symphony's finale. Elgar separates the stanza from what has gone before by a pause, a change of key, and the introduction of the soloist. It is also the stanza in which Elgar most obviously diverts O'Shaughnessy's sense to his own purpose. Elgar chose to apply the second half of the verse to Jaeger ('Nimrod') and himself, as he told Newman: 'Here I have quoted the Nimrod Variation as a tribute to the memory of my friend, A. J. Jaeger: by this I do not mean to convey that his was the only soul on which light had broken or that his was the only word, or look that wrought "flame in another man's heart".' It is grand to hear the alto soloist give such heartfelt meaning to the inspired strains of 1898, and lead by a new twist to a choral statement in the subdominant of which the climax, at the words 'Wrought flame', is the incandescent quotation from the Second Symphony. On a sketch of the music for the alto solo's pronouncement that soldier, king and peasant had 'no divine foreshowing' of their future land, Elgar wrote 'Climactic tragedy', thus drawing aside the whole cast into his private world.

In the sixth stanza O'Shaughnessy expounds the results of the 'flame in another man's heart'. Elgar's music is immediately less inspired, managing a feverish orchestral energy, heavy with accented passing notes in the melody and climbing chromatics in the bass. As there comes to pass 'The dream that was scorned yesterday', Elgar is again at an *fff* choral climax. At this dynamic, and with the orchestra similarly reinforced, the chorus recalls the opening words of the *Ode* to a slight variant of the 'Artist' theme and thus demarcates the end of the second third of the poem.

The bustle resumes towards another *fff* climax and the rumbustious return of the soldier, king and peasant. But Elgar ends quietly, meditating on what the new dream may bring the world, 'for its joy or its sorrow'. The word 'sorrow' lingers as the first theme of the work returns, giving a new sadness to its meaning, and the music subsides into the shifting chromaticism of the 'unearthly' chords.

The *Gerontius* 'Grace' music returns in A flat for the seventh stanza, more fully developed than before. As Elgar reaches the last lines of the stanza, in which O'Shaughnessy refers again to the loneliness of his music makers, dwelling 'A little apart', the 'Enigma' theme makes a final appearance. But this time 'Enigma' is insufficient; Elgar quotes also from the Violin Concerto, first the second subject's continuation in the opening Allegro, then the *nobilmente* passage in the slow movement that he told Ivor Atkins he wanted engraved on his tombstone.

The dreamers of O'Shaughnessy's eighth stanza remain apart, and the 'Artist' theme quietly takes over its original F minor. A quick *crescendo* evokes the motto theme from the First Symphony, now in B flat, as the intrepid cry of the dreamers sounds 'out of the infinite morning'. The orchestra's military response makes clear that soldier, king and peasant are still co-operating. As conclusion to the stanza Elgar briefly recapitulates the music from the second stanza that built the 'world's great cities'; and the whole-tone scale, having previously trampled a kingdom, now deals effectively with the death of yesterday's men and women.

The last stanza greets the comers 'From the dazzling unknown shore'. The alto solo launches on a bold phrase, and the orchestra recalls the 1907 quartet arabesques. As the alto continues with 'Bring us hither your sun and your summers', to the second tune of the introduction, the music is indeed 'mainly sad'. The theme is developed by variation and extension more fully than previously, with lovely interchanges between soloist and chorus. Imperceptibly Elgar goes back to the seventh stanza words, emphasizing yet again the loneliness of the music makers as the ravishing paragraphs succeed one another. The 'unearthly' chromatic chords descend in sequence by steps of a tone for O'Shaughnessy's last two lines:

> Yea, in spite of a dreamer who slumbers,
> And a singer who sings no more.

The last quotation is 'Novissima hora' from *The Dream of Gerontius*; it alternates with the first theme of the Ode as the chorus repeats its long-drawn 'no more'. O'Shaughnessy's end is almost dismissive, concentrating mainly on 'the dazzling unknown shore'; Elgar's extended *envoi* can only grieve for the 'dreamer who slumbers'. After a long silence, the chorus gives final utterance, *ppp* and getting quieter, to the 'Artist' theme of music makers and dreamers of dreams.

The Spirit of England
The three Laurence Binyon poems Elgar chose to set appeared very early in World War I. By 21 September 1914 they had been published in *The Times*, and by the end of the year they had been collected as part of *The Winnowing-Fan*. 'For the Fallen' was the poem that first fired Elgar, and he orchestrated the three sections of the work in reverse order. He claimed he had been held up over 'The Fourth of August' because of indecision as to how to set the stanza beginning 'She fights the fraud that feeds desire on / Lies ...'

Ernest Newman wrote programme notes for the three sections, and on 17 June 1917 Elgar described 'The Fourth of August' as 'the simplest of all as I felt the subject shd. be treated so'. Binyon invokes the 'Spirit of England, ardent-eyed', and Elgar begins in G with a theme he linked to 'courage and hope'. Its obsession with a rising sixth in so many of the initial bars is hopeful enough, if also monotonous; and the soloist's emphasizing the uppermost note with a pause adds the further risk of vulgarity. The second verse, 'the cares we hugged drop out of vision', begins in C with a tendency towards swagger. As often with Elgar, a boldly imagined sequence saves the situation. The upward sevenths of the third verse, 'For us the glorious dead have striven', are more subtly managed, mainly with the aid of modulation; but the return of the opening music at 'Among the nations nobliest chartered' merely magnifies its faults. Indeed the best music in the movement is reserved for the sixth stanza, the one that troubled Elgar so long. His decision was to quote from the Demons' chorus in *The Dream of Gerontius*. This solution to the problem might have occurred to him at the series of concerts in May 1916 when nos. II and III of *The Spirit of England* were performed immediately before *Gerontius*. Elgar told Newman he had been hoping for 'some trace of manly spirit' among the Germans: their conduct of the war prevented him from inventing 'anything low & bestial enough'; but Cardinal Newman had invented a hell 'where the great spirits gibber & snarl *knowing they have fallen*'. As the demon Huns disappear, the orchestra quietly resumes the G major of the opening and the soloist leaps an octave at the words 'Endure, O Earth!' (Ex. 8). This combination recurs also in 'To Women'. Lovely

Ex. 8

modulations lead flatwards to seven magical bars for unaccompanied chorus. The end, restating the first verse *nobilmente e grandioso*, is less admirable. Easily the weakest of the three movements, 'The Fourth of August' is stylistically at odds with itself.

'To Women' is in A flat, a semitone above the first movement, shifting uneasily between major and minor. Elgar divides Binyon's six verses with much subtlety. The first pair is for solo voice and orchestra, and Elgar's inspiration is at once on a higher plane, in music of grave and solemn beauty. The second verse varies the vocal line, and at 'Not with the marching drums and cheers' contrives to end a semitone lower than the first verse, so that it cadences into G minor. The pace quickens for 'Swift, swifter than those hawks of war', a stanza that Elgar headed 'aeroplanes'. The 'threatening wings that pulse the air' are graphically portrayed in the orchestra. Elgar now takes the last three stanzas as a unit, beginning each with similar sounds of war. Halfway through Binyon's fourth verse Elgar slows to the original tempo and prepares again for A flat minor and a choral version of half the opening solo. In verse five Elgar moves the climactic 'From hearts that are as one high heart' up a semitone. Will the arching phrase cadence this time in A minor? In fact Elgar extends it in sonorous sequence to make fifteen bars instead of the original eight and cadences again in A flat. The whole process has been masterly, and in this grand paragraph, which also involves the chorus, Elgar has used most of Binyon's last verse. Only the final four words are left out, and at this point Elgar reverts to 'The Fourth of August'. He explained to Newman that the three movements are 'slightly connected by the recurrence of themes or portions of them'. He pointed out that 'the *cantabile* in the orch. is the main subject of "The Fourth of August" – the words here "*BUT not to fail*" warranting the use of the theme associated with the courage and hope of the first poem'. The octave leap is there too, and the flatward modulations that this time come full circle to A flat minor. With a repetition of Binyon's last urgent phrase (Ex. 9), Elgar inserts also 'a "premonition" of the climax of no. III'. A quiet orchestral coda closes the movement.

'For the Fallen' is screwed up another semitone, to A minor. For Elgar's setting Binyon wrote an additional stanza, beginning 'They fought, they were terrible', which brought the total to eight. Elgar has four main sections, of two verses each, the last recapitulating the first. A lengthy orchestral introduction, heavy with tolling bass, and lightened by ascending scales that quote the sixth of bulldog Dan's moods as he waited 'wistful outside the cathedral', presents most of the first section's material. The orchestra makes to repeat the introduction, and the chorus enters quietly at the third bar. At the words 'Flesh of her flesh

Ex. 9

they were' comes the 'premonition' from the previous movement. Fanfare figures introduce 'Death august and royal', and the scales are explained by the phrase 'Sings sorrow up into immortal spheres'. The first section ends with the 'premonition' now *fortissimo* supporting words Elgar well understood: 'There is music in the midst of desolation.' Five bars of the introductory music act as closing ritornello into D minor.

Elgar described the next section to Newman: 'the whole movement here is a sort of idealised (perhaps) Quick March, – the sort of thing which ran in my mind when the dear lads were swinging past so many, many times'. Apart from a loud chordal refrain with triplets in the bass, the music is eerie and spectral, illustrating rather 'They fell with their faces to the foe', and 'They fell open-eyed and unafraid'. It is a ghost army. Again the orchestra has the stuff of the matter.

The third section changes to triple time and slows the tempo again. Binyon wrote 'They shall grow not old, as we that are left grow old'; Elgar changed it to 'They shall not grow old'. The two verses, but for scoring, are virtually identical in an allusive E minor, with orchestral melody and harmony rich in semitones (Ex. 10a). Violins and oboe

Ex. 10a

204

share much of the thematic material. The solo voice joins the melodic line at 'We will remember them', climbing to a remotely harmonized F natural at the end of each stanza. Elgar begins the last two stanzas with a 'Quasi Recit.' for soloist and chorus. There follows a nearly exact recapitulation of the introduction's music, but for additional bars of modulation. The ascending scales now carry the words, 'As the stars that shall be bright when we are dust', and the 'premonition' is presented in opulent splendour to illustrate the next line, 'Moving in marches upon the heavenly plain'. With steady *diminuendo* Elgar returns to the opening figure and its tolling bass for the last line and its echo, 'To the end they remain'.

With Proud Thanksgiving

Binyon's 'For the Fallen' and Elgar's setting of it became a national threnody for the rest of the war years. The poem was the best of the three that made up *The Spirit of England*, and it was a natural choice for the dedication of the Cenotaph in Whitehall two years after the end of the war. Elgar's reworking of 'For the Fallen' to make *With Proud Thanksgiving* was a fascinating exercise in recomposition. The introduction is cut by fourteen bars, and Elgar abbreviates wherever possible. The chorus begins loud instead of soft, and the writing is more full as the verse proceeds. The result is an opening section of concentrated power. The phantom March is omitted and 'They shall not grow old!' becomes a passage of simple block harmonies in E major, not minor, perhaps more consoling now that the slaughter was for the moment done (Ex. 10b). By means of two downward semitone

Ex. 10b

shifts 'Moving in marches upon the heavenly plain' is now in D major rather than the E of 'For the Fallen'. A subtle touch restores the original tonality, and A minor concludes a movement quite as fine as the original and more homogeneous.

So Many True Princesses

There is a lovely pendant to Elgar's choral music in the 1932 ode to the memory of Queen Alexandra. John Masefield's four stanzas are a touching tribute to a woman noted for her beauty, and Elgar's setting, for choir and military band, is much more than the formal offering from a Master of the King's Musick. His instinctive chivalry is here poignantly expressed in graceful melodic shapes as eloquent as they are apt. He approaches the B flat of his long introduction with Schumannesque shyness. The words are set with the suppleness of long experience, and Elgar begins them in a subdominant E flat, making the fine paragraph take in also the first line of the second stanza. Four bars of the introduction intervene before 'But this most lovely woman and loved Queen' leads to the quiet glimpse of D major that also brightened the orchestral ritornello.

The third stanza reverts to E flat and the gentle music of the first verse at 'Here, at this place, she often sat'; and Elgar lets the sounds fade gradually away as 'the day-long multitude' gives place to night. A hushed reference to the ritornello builds to the affirmation of the last verse, 'Now here we set memorial of her stay', again in E flat, but leading via the ritornello to the final tonic of B flat. Elgar's reluctance to abandon the last line, 'And won our hearts and lives within them still' conjures ravishing music. Elgar's homage to the royal household is here, and only here, a very personal and almost private matter.

10

Oratorios, *The Dream of Gerontius* and other religious works

By 1895, when Elgar received his first oratorio commission, the English tradition for such works was not at its most fresh. Bernard Shaw, subsequently one of Elgar's firmest friends and loyallest of supporters, wrote not a word about him in his days as a professional London music critic. But he had much to say on the typical festival sacred offering and summed up his view that in 1894 the 'modern oratorio is mostly a combination of frivolity and sensuality with hypocrisy and the most oppressive dulness'. It cannot be said that in his first effort Elgar escaped all these charges.

The Light of Life
This 'short oratorio' was Elgar's second Three Choirs commission, after the *Froissart* overture of 1890; and it remained the largest work Elgar was to write specifically for one of his native cathedrals. Edward Capel Cure, the librettist, was both a cellist and a composer; his partnership in the new project showed him confident enough to advise Elgar about its layout. No. 8, for instance, 'Doubt not the Father's care' he thought might be for solo or quartet, whereas Elgar noted at once on the draft libretto '*Female Voices?*' But Elgar took up his idea of a double chorus in no. 9. *King Olaf* and *The Light of Life* were virtually written simultaneously. A comparison between the two shows how inhibiting to Elgar the oratorio tradition and the desire for success within it proved. The musical cogency and power of the saga all but redeems its episodic libretto; the oratorio manages some moments of drama, but the meditations on them are often bland, or even dull. When preparing the libretto for composition, Elgar wisely tipped the balance towards drama. He cut four of Capel Cure's more jejune commentaries on scripture. Perhaps there was also a touch of playful, quasi-Shavian, hypocrisy in Elgar's musical treatment. In an interview with Robert Buckley of 31 July 1896 he exposed his contrapuntal flank: 'The British public would hardly tolerate oratorio without fugue. So I tried to give them one. Not a "barn-door" fugue, but one with an

independent accompaniment. There's a bit of canon, too, and in short, I hope there's enough counterpoint to give the real British religious respectability!'

Having reduced Capel Cure's nineteen numbers by three, Elgar took further steps to make the work less sectional. The first six numbers, dealing with the blind man and the reasons for his affliction, are not closed but lead one into another. The next four describe the actual healing and the reaction of the man's neighbours; again Elgar links the movements, writing 'Segue' at the one final cadence. The rest of the work is concerned with the incredulity of the Pharisees and Jews, their reviling of the healed man, and his eventual belief in Jesus. Here the links are less close, with the final 'Light of the World' chorus thematically separate.

The opening 'Meditation' for orchestra reviews some of the most important themes in the work: the first (Ex. 11), in G minor and portentously Wagnerian, is associated with the Levites and their

Ex. 11

quotations from Psalm 136; the second, at the change into triple time, accompanies the blind man's initial prayer; a third in the tonic major and 9/8, sequential in itself, and building to a climax by sequences a major third apart, signifies 'Blindness'; 'Jesus as healer' in C minor has chromatically woven inner parts; and finally, reverting to 4/4 and G major, comes the motif of 'Light'. It must be said there is little individuality or strength in the 'Blindness' snippet, and 'Light', of which Elgar makes many ingenious transformations, has a would-be nobility (Ex. 12) that does not quite make the grade.

The choral entry of Levites, for men alone, is unobtrusive, subtle and beautifully judged. The blind man utters his G minor 'prayer' in music originally meant for the Ophelia song that was to have been op. 21 no. 1. The contralto narrator introduces no. 3 and begins the account of the miracle from *John* ix on which the libretto is based.

Ex. 12
'Light'

The music moves down a tone to F minor, and the disciples begin a strict 'canonette!', as Elgar called it. A motif of 'God's Word' sounds ominously in the bass as, in Capel Cure's libretto, the disciples quote *Job* to the effect that a perfect man will not be cast away, nor will the evil be helped. The theme appears once more in association with the Lord's ordinance to Moses concerning the Sabbath in no. 11.

The words of the mother's plea for her son in no. 4 involved Elgar in controversy. He set Capel Cure's

> Hadst Thou a son, O Lord, how could'st Thou bear
> To see him made Thy curse?

Edward Vine Hall, former precentor of Worcester Cathedral, considered these words 'absolutely irreverent'. Capel Cure proved obstinate, but eventually Elgar had them adjusted. There is Mendelssohnian fluency and discreet anguish in the music as the mother upbraids God for her son's condition. The easy transition between one motif and the next tends to reduce their significance, so that however helpful to Elgar, their meaning will largely escape the listener.

The words of Jesus in no. 5 are scriptural and to some extent cut the theological knot by explaining that the man is blind so 'that the works of God should be made manifest in him'. The final chorus of the first section, 'Light out of darkness' has Elgar's 'Canonic intro' on the 'Light' motif in a modulation from G to A flat. At the choral entry, 'Light' continues in powerful augmentation; but comfort is too easily won as it closes in F minor and prepares for a 'Passion' motif for women's voices in parallel thirds illustrative of Christ's sufferings. There is little compulsion in the new idea and, as Capel Cure's last stanza draws its questionable moral, Elgar remains respectable if not convinced.

The second section begins at no. 7 with the narrative of the miracle. The biblical words 'he spat on the ground, and made clay of the spittle' were Capel Cured so as more to befit Worcester Cathedral; nor would susceptibilities be ruffled by Elgar's charming bits of canon in the succeeding duet for the women. At the Pool of Siloam the blind man is healed in a quick blaze of F sharp major and 'Light'. The neighbours and others question his identity in modulating orchestral bustle. Eventually comes Elgar's miniature C minor 'fugue' on a text that, with his boasted lack of schooling, he clearly relished: 'The wisdom of their wise men shall perish.' The one passage of eight-part writing rises from G major to a blazing climax on E at the words 'shall see'. Elgar called the succeeding E flat aria for the man that was blind 'visionary': it is also commonplace.

The final section starts with the Pharisees in an obsessive D minor. Healing on the sabbath is their charge against Jesus, and they invoke Mosaic law to the 'God's word' motif. Elgar explained the intervention of the female chorus: 'The idea was, roughly, that the women should side with the Mother.' Both groups demand to see the healed man. The forthright 'He is a prophet' leads to the only alto aria, another piece that shows Elgar both prisoner and victim of his period. With what Elgar called 'a jolly touch of sarcasm' the now-sighted man taunts the Pharisees in no. 13, considering it remarkable 'that ye know not whence He is'. The enraged Pharisees cast him out in their original D minor, in which key the mother and her allies forcibly attack them as unfaithful shepherds of the flock. When they reach the tonic major, the women adopt the accent of reformed Flowermaidens in addressing the duties of a good shepherd. The final encounter between Jesus and the healed man introduces a last motif of 'Yearning' or 'Longing', beautifully dovetailed in the orchestra at the man's confession of faith. Jesus declares himself the good shepherd in an aria starting in B major and ending in E flat. The last chorus reverts to the G major of the 'Meditation' and the comfortable Anglicanism of the 1890s. However disappointing, it is perhaps a proper ending for a work that retreated so far from the achievement of *King Olaf*.

The Dream of Gerontius

There was little in Elgar's output before 1900 that could prepare his admirers for *The Dream of Gerontius*. Among the cantatas, *King Olaf* had shown his technique the equal of a vivid imagination; the 'Enigma' Variations had proved him capable of a masterpiece; but there was nothing in the Anglican cathedral works, such as *The Light of Life* for Worcester or the Hereford *Te Deum and Benedictus* remotely to hint at the stature of *Gerontius*. At last, in Cardinal Newman's poem Elgar had found the 'book' that was not only dramatic, coherent and moving in itself, but that had a general application far beyond anything Elgar had previously essayed.

Newman wrote *The Dream of Gerontius* early in 1865 and dedicated it to the memory of a fellow Oratorian, John Joseph Gordon, who had died thirteen years before. By the time Elgar came to know the work, it had become linked with another Gordon, the hero of Khartoum. The fact that General Gordon had been reading the poem during his lonely vigil greatly impressed Newman's Oratory at Birmingham. The markings Gordon had made against various passages did the rounds of the Catholic priesthood; but his evangelical Anglicanism gave the poem a far wider currency. The copy Elgar gave his future wife in 1887 was from the twenty-second edition. Gerontius was perhaps not an exclusively Catholic everyman.

Cardinal Newman was both poet and musician, a keen violinist who considered that a poetical view of experience was a Christian duty. An early poem of his, 'Lead, kindly Light' (from the *Lyra apostolica* of 1836) had been set to music some forty times before his death. Indeed *The Dream of Gerontius* had been offered to Dvořák in 1887 as a suggestion for a Birmingham commission. The poem has numerous references to music. Elgar seized on many of them, accepting the challenge of such lines as

> I cannot of that music rightly say
> Whether I hear or touch or taste the tones.
> Oh! what a heart-subduing melody!

Doubtless he also pondered similar moments of daring imagery, as when the pavement of the Judgment House, made up of 'blessed and immortal beings', hymns 'their Maker's praise continually'; the lintels of the presence-gate echo the mighty Angels' praise of the Incarnate God; and ultimately the golden prison of purgatory will open its portals,

> Making sweet music, as each fold revolves
> Upon the ready hinge.

Elgar's reverence for Newman's poem was absolute. Yet it was too long for his purpose and had to be cut. The Cardinal's Part II was four times as long as his Part I; Elgar's abbreviated text made it only twice as long. Many angelic choruses were sacrificed; Elgar, with a mezzo-soprano in mind, eliminated references to the maleness of the Angel; but as late as 7 May 1900 he consulted Jaeger about a lengthy section of dialogue in Part II: 'tell me if you think those *conversations* between the Angel & the Soul are *wearisome*. I went thro' the libretto with a priest from the Oratory & we cut out *all* we thought possible. But I know the poem too well & you, (as an outsider, as it were), might see if you could further curtail it.' Jaeger took no action.

Conversant with Catholic liturgy and practice, Elgar fully recognized how much of Newman's poem echoed phrases hallowed by long use in the Church. At the Elgar Birthplace, for instance, is a copy of *The Catholic's Vade Mecum or Manual of Prayer* that he gave his recently converted wife in November 1889, six months after their marriage. The 'Bona Mors' section, dealing with a 'good death', has many a phrase taken straight over into the poem, most notably in the Assistants' choruses of Part I, 'Holy Mary, pray for him', and 'Be merciful, be gracious'. This was reason enough for Elgar's keeping Part I of the poem almost intact. Elgar was anxious too that his setting should have similar links with Catholic tradition. He wrote to Hubert Leicester on 20 February 1900 about a book that used to be at St George's, Worcester, and that he would like to consult: 'an odd volume containing some Gregorian things (we did the Te Deum) & Benediction services'.

With *Gerontius* Elgar followed his usual practice of sending portions of the vocal score to Novello as he completed them. Printed scores and parts were needed for choir rehearsal, but not the whole work at once. Elgar liked the reassurance of proofs to correct; their arrival and perusal were often a spur to more composition. With a work such as *King Olaf*, episodic from the outset, the method worked splendidly. The wonder is that it worked equally well with *Gerontius*. If there are a couple of moments where seams show, the fault may lie in this serial method of production. Elgar usually worked under pressure, and certainly he worked best so.

By the time of *Gerontius* Elgar had absorbed all he needed from Wagner and transmuted it through personal alchemy into a fully formed style of his own. *Gerontius* was unthinkable without Wagner, and indeed without *Parsifal*. But Elgar's independence is clear at once. The lone thematic line of the opening, emerging from silence, might seem common to both works. Whereas Wagner is rhythmically elusive, with slow syncopations and avoidance of any clear accent until the third bar, harmonically he is manifestly in A flat. Elgar's slow pulse makes no denial of the bar-line, yet the beginning is tonally ambiguous. The first notes, A, G sharp, might be establishing a key-centre on A minor, and it is only gradually that D minor emerges. The ambiguity is at the heart of Elgar's conception (Ex. 13). When this 'Judgment'

Ex. 13

(a) *Parsifal*

(b) *The Dream of Gerontius*: 'Judgment'

motif (Jaeger's terminology is handy for this work and the later oratorios) is heard again more briefly in Part II at the words 'I ever had believed', Elgar makes the initial A into a tonic and adjusts the passage so that it can remain in A minor. As the Angel tells of St Francis and the stigmata, 'There was a mortal who is now above', the vocal line defines the opening B once more as a dominant. The subtlety is admirable, and the psychology apt. As in the Prelude, the St Francis version ends on a major chord, with the slow process of judgment leading to eventual transformation. Gerontius's earthly belief, on the other hand, remains static, ending in the minor key with which it began. The sureness of Elgar's rhythm at the start of the work is equally important, and the first four bars achieve their maximum intensity in the sequence of massive chords that lead, in Part II, to the Soul's momentary vision of God.

The initial oscillation in the 'Judgment' theme between semitone and tone informs much of the work's thematic material. It is concentrated into the 'Fear' motif (Ex. 14a), inverted at the core of 'Prayer' (Ex. 14b), and contributes to the restlessness of 'Sleep' (Ex. 14c). The third and fourth bars are equally productive. They provide the notes of 'I am near to death' in Gerontius's opening solo (Ex. 15a); they are inverted to provide the first notes of the Prelude's orchestral bass entry (Ex. 15b), a version that also leads into the repetition of the 'Sleep' motif at cue 5 and can be found in the notes of the 'Committal' theme

(Ex. 15c). Such dense motivic logic shows Elgar as master of devising themes that are distinctive, easily recognizable, yet have close interconnections. Wagner had shown the way; Elgar followed with comparable skill.

Ex. 14
(a) 'Fear'

(b) 'Prayer'

(c) 'Sleep'

Ex. 15

(a)

(b)

(c) 'Committal'

The form of the prelude is finely judged. It is the only opening to an Elgar religious work that is other than a stately procession of themes to be developed later. Of the six main themes heard before the central 'Committal', three, however chromatic, have basic tonal stability. That much may be said of 'Judgment', 'Sleep' and 'Miserere' (Ex. 16a). The other three, 'Fear', 'Prayer', and 'Despair' (Ex. 16b) are modulating motifs responsible for much wandering tonality. In this

Ex. 16
(a) 'Miserere'

(b) 'Despair'

extensive opening section 'Fear' and 'Prayer' are initially dovetailed. 'Despair' and 'Prayer' are much developed and are responsible together for the first mighty climax of the work. The second climax is built from the fourfold repetition of the impassioned 'Committal' theme, one of the grandest of Elgar's inventions. Its phrasing is subtle, owing much to the three-bar section at its core, and completely avoiding the rhythmic monotony that can too closely fetter other Elgar tunes. The basic 'Committal' theme is extended first by five bars, then finally by nine bars in a beautifully graded *diminuendo*. A baleful stroke on the gong recalls the sickbed of Gerontius and heralds a much-shortened recapitulation. There is no reference to 'Prayer' or 'Despair', both so strongly featured in the first section. The other motifs appear in different order. 'Sleep' is intertwined with 'Fear', now in 3/4 and so adjusted as to move in three steps from D major to D flat. An abbreviated 'Miserere' on B flat leads to 'Judgment' at its original pitch. The first note is now parsed as a dominant, with timpani taps and double bass pizzicato sounding the tonic in the far depths. In this sombre but succinct survey of his material, Elgar also omits six central bars from 'Judgment' to round the Prelude.

In his analysis of *Gerontius* Part I Jaeger gives thirty-three music examples and names fourteen motifs. An Elgar letter to Herbert Thompson of 5 June 1902 refers to the analysis as 'practically authorised by me as far as the choice of themes is concerned, but not always the actual naming of them'. Wagner was similarly cautious about Wolzogen's labelling. Whether 'Christ's Peace' was approved by Elgar is not known; but Jaeger was the first to be delighted by the motif's long-range effects. First heard in the initial solo of Gerontius at the words 'And Thou art calling me', it is repeated orchestrally in the next bar. It appears again as part of the chorus 'Be merciful, be gracious', where the music moves to the dominant, E flat. The opening words are 'By Thy birth, and by Thy Cross', on a new theme memorable for its leap of a sixth. Here Elgar has three themes at play over a two-bar period, and launches on six bars of triple counterpoint (Ex. 17). 'Christ's Peace' is initially on woodwind and violas in the midst of the texture, its expressive new extension reinforced by the tenors at 'By Thy death and burial'. When the theme ascends from violas to first violins, tenors again emphasize the extension. It is next given to lower strings and chorus basses, where the extension is treated in sequence so as to rise through two more bars to the climax. At 'Save him in the day of doom' the sopranos and upper instruments have the theme in a passionate G minor. Throughout the passage Elgar has so organized the texture that each line in the contrapuntal web stands out with maximum clarity. The persistent quavers, mostly staccato in the bass and typical of the movement hitherto, are interrupted by rests. But it is a lovely moment when these detached quavers move into the top part and the choral sopranos transform them into an expressive vocal line at the words 'By Thy rising from the tomb, By Thy mounting up above'. Elgar's craftsmanship is here marvellously at one with his imagination. 'Christ's Peace' returns at the end of this section, first as a middle orchestral part, and then on top. At the end of Part I Elgar resumes his three themes at cue 76. Even now he was not quite finished with 'Christ's Peace'. He introduced the motif once more as coping-stone for the final chorus of *The Apostles*.

Other aspects of this 'Christ' theme occur in Gerontius's 'Sanctus, fortis' declaration of his creed. When he confesses 'Manhood taken by the Son', the oboe sounds the motif in its original key and shape; the orchestra at once expands it and modulates with it. 'In that Manhood crucified' again invokes the oboe for a doubly expressive version of

Elgar

Ex. 17

the first two bars. With the entry of the heavy brass and darkening of the harmony, clarinets and strings use it to illustrate 'Him the strong'. Its shape also underlies the final cry of Gerontius, 'To the God of earth and heaven'. In this form Gerontius later beseeches angelic help, such as came to Christ 'In Thine own agony'. Elgar's melodic, contrapuntal and theological flexibility with Jaeger's 'Christ's Peace' far outdistances its label; if the words of 'ye humble analyst' cannot possibly contain all implications of Elgar's musical thoughts, the rough blueprint they provide remains a useful key to understanding.

One of Elgar's major achievements in *Gerontius* is to differentiate so completely the atmosphere of Part I from that of Part II. The most extensive link between the two parts is the music of the destructive powers. Part I has significant pre-echoes of the sizzling Demons' chorus in Part II. The first instance is at Gerontius's onset of terror at the words 'a visitant is knocking his dire summons at my door'. Then at greater length comes the passage beginning 'And, crueller still', in which many of the later diabolical motifs are briefly rehearsed. These moments of heightened horror find a natural place in the fevered atmosphere of Gerontius's sickroom.

There are other motifs integral to Part I that have also an essential function in Part II. Take the case of 'Fear'. After the Prelude, it occurs in Part I again only to provide hectic detail to the onslaught of the 'bodily form of ill' that 'Floats on the wind, with many a loathsome curse' (Ex. 18). In Part II it recurs in its original form, twice repeated and twice lifting the tonality a major sixth, when the Angel explains that the Soul's present lack of fear is because he 'forestalled the agony' during life. The demons recall its headlong 'hectic' version when they rail at God for giving their forfeit crown 'To psalm-droners'. Perhaps fear has changed to awe when Elgar traces the outline of the theme twice within the House of Judgment. The first occasion is just after the Soul has sung of the 'grand mysterious harmony' that floods him. At this point Elgar omitted a considerable portion of Newman's poem. The Angel explains that they have reached the stairs that 'rise towards the Presence-chamber'; and there the Angels of the Sacred Stair hymn the 'great Creator in His sickness' at Gethsemane, when soothed by the Angel of the Agony. In such a context Elgar made his transformation of the 'Fear' motif. It recurs again at the end of the great 'Praise' chorus, when the Soul is near to judgment and the Angel of the Agony will plead for him.

In the exalted regions of Part II any echo from the hothouse and priestly world of Part I makes telling effect. Elgar places such echoes with unerring skill. When the Soul confides in the Angel that in life 'the thought of death' and judgment was 'most terrible', the orchestra

Ex. 18

Floats on the wind, with ma-ny a loath-some curse,

retraces exactly, but for the final chord, the last four bars before Gerontius's opening 'Jesu, Maria' (Ex. 19). The sidestep to, and momentary hovering on, the remote chord of E flat is equally mem-

Ex. 19 (a)

Allegro ♩ = 108

the thought of death And judg - ment was to me most ter-ri-ble.

221

Ex. 19 (b)

orable on both occasions. When the Angel explains that the momentary 'sight of the Most Fair' will gladden but also pierce, Elgar recalls, in the rarefied beauty of three solo cellos, then three solo violas, the last words of the dying Gerontius, 'Novissima hora', and their music. Again, when at Jaeger's instigation the last sections of the work had achieved their final order, the 'one moment' of divine vision releases a last passionate reference to the same motif at 'Take me away'.

An early reminiscence of Part I was to have occurred in the Soul's first speech. Elgar eventually omitted such Newman lines as

> And then I surely heard a priestly voice
> Cry 'Subvenite' ...

but he had provisionally set them, with a backward look at the 'Proficiscere' chords (Ex. 20). These chords come later, when the Soul says 'I hear the voices that I left on earth'; they are followed by the

Ex. 20

steady tread of 'Go, in the Name of God' as the Angel explains that

> It is the voice of friends around thy bed,
> Who say the 'Subvenite' with the priest.

Elgar's omission of the earlier reference was right. It was too soon in Part II to recall the earthly scene, and it would have detracted from the realization that all of Part II up to 'the veiled presence of our God' had miraculously taken place within an instant of time.

It was Elgar's own decision, at the Soul's 'I go before my Judge' to introduce the Voices on Earth singing again 'Be merciful, be gracious; spare him, Lord'. Elgar's only hint was a final 'Ah!' from the Soul in Newman's poem, followed by four dots, with another four dots before the Angel's 'Praise to His Name!' Thus indeed did Elgar banish 'the busy beat of time'. What was already an Elgarian stroke of genius was made the more telling by the use for these words of the 'Kyrie' music from Part I, followed by 'Proficiscere'. The harp and pizzicato strings show too that within 'Proficiscere' were always hidden the initial semitones of 'Judgment'. Sound here achieves the ineffable. Judgment done, the Soul longs to be 'in the lowest deep':

> There will I sing, and soothe my stricken breast,
> Which ne'er can cease
> To throb, and pine, and languish, till possesst
> Of its Sole Peace.

The theme of the song will be the same prayer for mercy uttered in Part I with the words 'Sanctus fortis, Sanctus Deus', and backward glance as far as the 'Miserere' theme of the Prelude.

Part I is characterized by a variety of marching rhythms, symbolizing the slow tread of approaching judgment, Gerontius's attempts to 'play the man', the solemn dignity of the Church militant and its priesthood, the grand invocation of ecclesiastical worthies as Gerontius is dismissed from the world, and the processional route towards 'the Holy Mount of Sion'. All the choruses are in quadruple time. In Part II it is different. The heavens favour triple time, and so it was that Gerontius had made his Part I confession of faith to the Godhead three in one. Not even the demons are totally quadruple. Their derision of the saints and the 'sordid aim' of any aspiration towards heaven is snarled out in triple time. Except for brief moments when they underpin the narrative, or the extended duple chorus of 'O loving wisdom of our God!', the varied groups of Angelicals always have three beats to the bar. It is the same with the Souls in Purgatory, who have yet the strength to affirm, 'from age to age Thou art God'.

223

The overall key scheme of the two parts is simplicity itself. Both aspire to the benediction of a final D major, with wandering tonality characteristic of many sections. Part I launches from the D minor of the Prelude to move initially flatwards. Certain motifs have their own key associations. 'Sleep', for instance, is often in D; 'Committal' favours G minor. The flatward move begins with the B flat entry of Gerontius (his usual Part I key centre); it continues with the E flat of the 'Kyrie', A flat of 'Be merciful, be gracious', E flat minor of 'Rescue him', while the litany of what Elgar called his 'sporting prophets' reaches the remotest point from D of A flat minor. By an enharmonic change Elgar now recapitulates the 'Kyrie' music in E major, the 'brightest' moment in Part I, to be repeated similarly in Part II. The D major of 'Sleep' for the death of Gerontius is darkened to his own B flat at 'Proficiscere', as the Priest dismisses his soul from this world. With the address to the Trinity, D major is established, to be again deflected to B flat at the choral entry. 'Committal's' G minor leads on to a final B flat at the choral 'Proficiscere', and the ultimate goal of D major is reached over a dominant pedal as the chorus begins the processional 'Go on thy course'.

Part II begins in F, a key touched only in passing throughout Part I. At the first words of Gerontius, 'I went to sleep', the D major of the restless Part I 'Sleep' motif returns, but now in association with the calm freshness of the new heavenly music. Gerontius's novel sensations take him to A flat, and at the 5/8 'Jape' from E flat via G and C to the radiance of E major. This is the point where Gerontius first senses the Angel's singing, fitting sequel to the 'Kyrie' music of Part I, last heard at 'Rescue this thy servant' in the same key. The Angel's basic C major tilts towards E minor and major as the narrative proceeds. The quiet refrain of 'Alleluia' and triumph won always ends in C, the ultimate key of the Angelicals' worship in the final 'great blaze' of 'Praise to the Holiest'. Much of the dialogue between the Soul and Angel, involving the return of 'Judgment' and 'Fear' is in A minor. Again Elgar travels as far as possible tonally for the serene warmth of E flat at 'A presage falls upon thee', and the ensuing duet. The demons abide by their G minor.

The sequence of 'Praise' choruses reverses the procedure of Part I. Starting in E flat with the 'Least and most childlike of the sons of God', the great hymn sheds its flats until it reaches the magisterial splendour of C major. Echoes of the sickroom and 'Proficiscere' recall A flat, and the solemn tread of 'Subvenite' takes the music to D flat. That is the key for the Angel of the Agony and his 'ghastful' enharmonic changes. By solemn steps, as Gerontius goes before his Judge, minim chords descend towards the A flat minor of the Old Testament figures in Part I. Again the chorus moves enharmonically to sing in E major the 'Kyrie' music of the Voices on Earth, linking those rescued in ancient times with the present plea for mercy. The Angel's final 'Alleluia!' is in A minor, revealed as dominant of D minor, the key of 'Judgment' and the awesome chords of the approach to the vision of God. The climax is overwhelming, but within a few bars the music achieves the key signature of two sharps, not used since the last chords of Part I. Initially, at the second 'take me away', the key is B minor. D major is finally established with the psalm of the Souls in Purgatory, and remains the focus throughout the 'Angel's Farewell'. A reference to 'Angels, to whom the willing task is giv'n' recalls the 'Angel' motif and its constant hints of E. The 'Praise to the Holiest' of the distant Angelicals, again an Elgarian interpolation, begins in the C major to which it earlier aspired. But D major gradually envelops the whole ensemble and steers it steadily towards the sevenfold Amen that ends the work.

In *The Light of Life* Elgar was praised for his orchestration, less for his choral writing, and least for the solo parts. *Gerontius* has all three aspects in perfect focus. The variety of Newman's rhythms was a considerable help towards the vocal layout, and Elgar increased the impression of variety by the cuts he made to the poem. Much blank verse went, notably in the first speech of Gerontius and in the lengthy Part II exchanges between the Soul and Angel. Newman's 'Praise to the Holiest' verses all have the same rhythm; there are thirty of them but Elgar kept only twelve. Newman ranges from such hexameters (with additional 'Amen') as 'Moses from the land of bondage and despair' to the terse diabolical trisyllables of

> Low-born clods
> Of brute earth.

Newman's rhymes are equally resourceful. Sometimes he piles them on, as Gerontius is to be delivered

> From the perils of dying:
> From any complying
> With sin, or denying
> His God, or relying
> On self, at the last.

Then there are such regular schemes as those in 'Firmly I believe and truly', or more loosely in 'Praise to the Holiest'. Most subtle of all is the Angel's first song, with its seven-line stanzas (the sixth line is 'Alleluia'); here the rhyming lines are one and five, two and seven, three and four. The ingenuity clearly appealed to Elgar, and the poem's considerable bravura was a constant stimulus, quite apart from the compelling nature of its message.

The word-setting for Gerontius himself is exemplary. The imaginative splendour of this tenor part can best be appreciated by studying the gradual steps through which it was achieved. An early version of 'Firmly I believe and truly' is not only harmonically commonplace; it also has none of the Italianate fervour so convincing in the finished work. The first verse, for instance, has lower tessitura, no rests, limping rhythm, and no orchestral overlap at 'by the Son'. The inspiration of the revisions could not be more vibrantly apparent (Ex. 21). It was with justifiable pride that Elgar said to Steuart Wilson of this whole section: 'Verdi wouldn't have been ashamed to write that tune'. After

Ex. 21

the Soul's vision of God in Part II, the exaltation of 'Take me away' persists through 'and in the lowest deep' so that a top A is again sung on 'lowest'. It was not always so. The original version, dubbed by Jaeger 'weak whining' crept by semitones to the lower A. In the part of the Priest and the Angel of the Agony the range is less and movement more conjunct, as befits their awesome dignity. The Angel, entering so unobtrusively in mid-motif, shows time and again with what subtlety Elgar could now weave a vocal line round a basically orchestral idea. At the recurrence (cue 24) of the 'Fear' motif, for instance, the Angel's phrase mounts towards the radiant arch of 'now thou dost not fear', only to descend with equal inevitability in the succeeding bars. When 'Judgment' is used to underpin the St Francis story, the voice part is a wonder of natural declamation, and quite different from Gerontius's line above the same theme some pages back. Here too Elgar made improvements as he went along. In the final farewell the words 'Be brave and patient on thy bed of sorrow' originally descended by step; the drops of a fourth were an afterthought.

The choral parts are so crafted that leads are carefully prepared. Though much technique is required, as the initial performers found to their cost, choir entries are not difficult. The idea of the semi-chorus may have come from the layered voices Wagner deployed in the dome of the Grail Hall for *Parsifal*. Elgar originally specified eighteen singers, but in 1928 he felt twelve would do, or even eight; but they must be 'very "simple" voices without the slightest vibrato'. There are magic moments when the semi-chorus emerges from the full choral sound, as in the resumption of the opening 'Kyrie', at the recital of the ancient prophets, or in the closing pages of Part I. A further subdivision occurs in Part II where the female voices of the semi-chorus have a major share in the Angelicals' music. The choral writing has magnificent range, from the prayers of the Assistants to the fierce hubbub of the Demons and massive eight-part splendour of the 'Praise to the Holiest' climax. The discreet doublings in 'Be merciful, be gracious', the octaves of the climax and, above all, the boldness of the tenor lines show profound knowledge of choral effects. The disposition, too, of the choral Amens in the Old Testament litany, a remote moment of modal calm, is as subtle as it is simple. At the other extreme are the grand sonorities of the choral 'Go, in the name / Of Angels and Archangels' and the mounting excitement of the 'Praise' choruses. In the layout of the two finales Elgar had little guidance from Newman, who gave all the words in Part I to the Priest, and in Part II to the Angel. The precise deployment of soloists, semi-chorus and chorus was Elgar's, and for both sections he wrote a verbal 'Plan' before setting to work. In neither case did he follow his original scheme completely, but the outline was there on which to found the vast architectural structure Elgar had in mind. There has been much criticism of the Demons' chorus. If there is a fault, it derives not from the composer but from inadequate performance. Newman's Demons knew their Milton as

> The primal owners,
> Of the proud dwelling
> And realm of light –

So does Elgar, and finely captures

> The mind bold
> And independent ...

The hissing sibilants of the fugue and harsh ejaculations of the repeated 'Ha! ha!' need only total conviction from chorus and orchestra to realize Elgar's vision.

'Orchestration unsatisfying' was the Elgars' verdict on *Parsifal* in January 1914. When Elgar begins *Gerontius* on violas, he doubtless knew this was the one stringed instrument Wagner omitted at the start of *Parsifal*. As already in the cantatas and the finale of the Variations, Elgar here uses the organ as an additional orchestral resource and marshals in addition a vast array of percussion. These instruments are used not only in the Demons' chorus but for many touches of colour throughout the work, for example the gong in the Prelude, the timpani roll with wooden sticks at the first utterance of Gerontius, a single stroke on bass drum at 'Tainting the hallow'd air', the shattering sextuplet on the timpani at 'O Jesu, help!', again the gong in Part II at 'which would make me fear Could I be frighted', the side-drum roll as the Demons assemble, and their ultimate summons on the triangle a bar before 'Low-born clods'.

The 'deep hideous purring' on the low flutes has often been remarked. Equally memorable are the oboe solos at 'Manhood taken by the Son' and 'Manhood crucified' in 'Sanctus fortis', the winding clarinets of 'This silence pours a solitariness', the infernal hammering on bassoons and double bassoon of 'We are now arrived / Close on the judgment-court', with the plunging descent of the tuba against *col legno* violins a few bars later. There are notable moments for the horns, as when they take the melodic lead halfway through 'Sanctus fortis', sonorously reinforce 'Christ's Peace' near the end of Part I, and launch the E flat 'Praise' section at 'Glory to Him, who evermore'. Muted trumpets back the evil emanations of Part I; and the Demons' chorus relies much for its proud anger on the imperious challenge of the trumpets, and their clangour. The trombones have their traditional hieratic role at the Priest's 'Proficiscere' and in the portentous chromatics associated with the Angel of the Agony. Special string effects are the fifteen-part divisi across almost six octaves and against pulsating harps at Gerontius's ' 'Tis this strange innermost abandonment', the muted mysteries that start Part II, and the rustling arpeggios in the upper instruments and harps against whispered pizzicatos at the first utterance of the word 'Praise'.

It was not clear in October 1900 that in *The Dream of Gerontius* Elgar had written his choral masterpiece, let alone his greatest work. At the time his Catholic faith was real, and this was the only major Catholic text he set. Every aspect of his musical technique was fully developed, and his staggering virtuosity was at the service of a lofty ideal he believed in. Everything in the work bears the mark of total conviction, points are made with precision and without exaggeration, and ends and means are perfectly matched. Strauss saw the work as progressive, and indeed Elgar's daring can still astonish; but after almost a century *Gerontius* seems timeless, and Alice Elgar has been proved right, as she very well knew when writing to Mrs Kilburn on the day the orchestration was finished: 'It seems to me that E. has given a real message of consolation to the world.'

The Apostles
If it was the difficulty of compiling a biblical libretto that deflected Elgar from the 'Apostles' project at the end of 1899, the problem remained central in the evolution of what was none the less Elgar's grandest design. At the outset he seems to have envisaged only one work; but the setting of the scenes he had in mind so outstripped his original time-span that one oratorio was clearly insufficient. His method was largely improvisatory, a procedure daring and risky, but very Elgarian. When starting *The Apostles*, Elgar thought he knew how it would begin and how it would end; he was vague on what might intervene. Ultimately, with two oratorios complete, Elgar was nowhere near his original goal.

Elgar had no doubt how he should set about the libretto: it would be based on the King James Bible, with recourse to the Revised Version on occasion, and the vivid imagery of the Apocrypha. He gathered quite a library of books on theology and biblical exegesis, many still at the Birthplace. Robinson's *Harmony of the Four Gospels* enabled Elgar to build an eclectic narrative, choosing a verse from here or there, a phrase, or sometimes even a single word. Pinnock's *An Analysis of New Testament History*, of which paragraph after paragraph was marked as relevant to the scheme, provided Elgar with a framework, and Archbishop Whately's *Lectures on the Characters of Our Lord's*

Apostles both confirmed and stimulated Elgar in his ideas of characterization. Another powerful influence from the past was Longfellow, whose 'Tower of Magdala' episode in *The Divine Tragedy* helped to shape Scene III of the completed *Apostles*. The work planned for Birmingham in 1903 was to start with Christ's reading from *Isaiah* in the synagogue at Nazareth; it would end at Antioch, where his followers were first called Christians. Compilation of the libretto began in earnest in July 1902, leaving fifteen months till the first performance. As pressure increased, Alice Elgar became much involved with libretto matters. Using Cruden's *Concordance to the Bible*, Elgar could both pursue and clarify a train of thought. He would chase up references, note the most promising, and get his wife to write them out in full. Gaps in her diary denote periods of heaviest labour on the task and her own essential involvement.

Even with the experience of the cantatas and *Gerontius* behind him, Elgar seemed to have little idea how the proportions of text and music would eventually match. Hitherto his judgment had been exercised in shaping and cutting texts that already existed; in this he had shown much skill. Now the outline was vague, and it is difficult to imagine how many different scenes Elgar envisaged if he were to fulfil his original purpose. *King Olaf* had been episodic; *The Apostles* threatened to be more so. It gradually became clear to Elgar as he clothed the text with music that his proposed scheme was unworkable. After many a crisis of confidence over the two oratorios, *The Kingdom* finally reached a point he had hoped to pass well before the end of *The Apostles*.

Elgar's task was indeed formidable. The apostles themselves were to be central, or rather those three he 'had attempted to individualise', Peter, John and Judas. He had already shown in *Caractacus* that, after the manner of Greek tragedy, he preferred high drama to be reported rather than enacted. His initial dilemma was how to portray Christ adequately and yet keep him from centre stage. Elgar appreciated the problem from the outset. He originally planned an actual prayer for Christ when he 'went out into a mountain to pray'. The text was assembled, hints for the music jotted down; but then the scene was abandoned. As the work progressed, and the tragedy of betrayal, Peter's denial, the crucifixion and death was unfolded, Jesus was given only a few words. 'Crucify Him!' becomes a cry of 'the People (remote)' inserted into the final monologue of Judas; Golgotha is the scene of a meditation between Mary Mother and John; and even the resurrection is alluded to obliquely by an angelic choir in such a way it involves no human reaction. Jesus returns briefly for the ascension, bidding the apostles baptize and teach all nations. The danger, which Elgar certainly did not avoid, was so to distance his characters from the gospel events that their own verisimilitude was at risk.

In the compilation of the libretto Elgar's scholarship sometimes took him too far. In the Prologue, for instance, he might have been wise to imitate Longfellow and confine himself to the *Isaiah* quotation in *Luke* rather than cite the original to produce the arcane ideas of giving 'them that mourn a garland for ashes, the oil of joy for mourning'. The *Apostles* text relies greatly for commentary and meditation on the Old Testament and Apocrypha. It is when wandering through these sources that Elgar shows how little he has escaped from nineteenth-century habits of oratorio text-making. The authority of quoted scripture is simply not enough to make dramatically relevant such lines as 'a bruised reed shall He not break', 'Thou has trodden the winepress alone', the Magdalene's description of herself as 'the grape-gleanings of the vintage', or Judas in his dire affliction remembering Job's complaint: 'Sheol is naked before Thee, and Abaddon hath no covering.' Elgar's difficulty was the age-old one of how to supplement biblical narrative to make a full-length work. To look no further than Bach, the two Passions can hardly glory in the verse of Brockes or Picander; indeed the stanzas provided by Capel Cure for *The Light of Life* are neither notably better nor worse. Elgar certainly avoided the bathos of the versifiers, but he could not in his *Apostles* text always carry conviction.

Elgar's Gregorian discoveries in Liverpool, 'Constitues eos' and 'O sacrum convivium' were crucial for the music of the 'Apostles' project. The first promised power to the apostles, the second celebrated their fellowship in communion. Both were originally intended for *The Apostles*, but 'O sacrum', being designed for the 'Peter' scenes and the 'Church in Jerusalem', was postponed till *The Kingdom*. Many of the themes of *The Apostles* can be derived from 'Constitues' (Ex. 22a). The chant moves mainly by tones and semitones, but with thirds represented too; the largest interval is a perfect fourth. The opening 'Spirit of the Lord' motif, for instance, can be found in the last notes

Ex. 22
(a)

of the Gregorian music (Ex. 22b). 'Christ, the Man of Sorrows' is there

(b) 'The Spirit of the Lord'

(though not the chromatic descent of the inner part that produces its characteristic false relation) (c); the 'Pastoral' idea that sets the scene

(c) 'Christ, the Man of Sorrows'

for Christ at prayer reproduces much of 'The Spirit of the Lord' (d);

(d) 'Pastoral'

and the 'Apostles' theme itself is derived from the opening of the chant (e). When presented with so many thematic interconnections, Elgar would doubtless have replied 'I did it unconsciously'; and it would be tedious to spell out the many other examples that abound in the work.

(e) 'Apostles'

Again Jaeger was responsible for labelling the themes. Since the *Gerontius* analysis he had gained in confidence, yet he agonized much over *The Apostles* and was often baffled by it. His interest in the motifs became obsessive. Take the three-note tag he called 'the Preaching and Teaching theme' (Ex. 23a). A later point in the vocal score greatly

Ex. 23 (a) 'Preaching' (x) and 'Gospel' (y)

worried him: 'But where it should be writ large, on p. 101 last two bars, it don't turn up!!! though the Apostles do largely. Is the "Preaching" in the orchestral score or can you add it?' (Ex. 23b). Elgar's answer to both questions was 'no'. Jaeger's zeal in finding names for every snippet of music gave Ernest Newman an easy chance for just ribaldry. His attention had been drawn in the analysis to 'a little figure of three notes' much used in the storm of Scene III: ' "the Ship" motive is no more suggestive of a ship than it is of a banana or a motor-car'. Newman had of course been misled precisely as Elgar feared, and Jaeger is to some extent responsible for the impression of patchiness *The Apostles* has often given to commentators, who have observed the apparent number of Elgar's themes rather than their kinship.

Yet Elgar's method was not as satisfactory as in *Gerontius*. There, themes had been developed in the Prelude so as to assume a musical life and significance of their own before acquiring additional meaning from the words. And a theme such as 'Judgment' or 'Fear' had been used flexibly and subtly throughout the work, with varied harmonic implications. In *The Apostles* so many of the motifs are static. Their meaning is explicit, the more so on repetition; but musically they refuse to take wing. A motif such as 'Christ's Prayer', mysterious and aloof at early appearances can only stale in unvaried repetition, and almost collapses under the weight of *fff* hammering in the otherwise finely conceived 'Ascension' movement. Ernest Newman reserved his harshest criticism for the Introduction to Part II in *The Apostles*, roundly calling

Ex. 23 (b) 'Gospel' (x) and 'Apostles' (y)

it 'the most unsatisfactory piece of work ever put together by Elgar', in which 'the musical interest diminishes to vanishing point'. Newman's charge was simply that the forty bars of the piece consisted of one motif after another juxtaposed without necessary connection, so that only a 'crude pictorial continuity' had been achieved. The case is not overstated, and the tired chromaticism of some of the motifs robs them of whatever novel appeal they may have had when Newman wrote.

As completed on 25 June 1903, *The Apostles* consisted of a Prologue followed by seven scenes. All the main musical ideas of the Prologue had long-range influence, not only on the rest of *The Apostles* but also on the future *Kingdom*. At one point Elgar also looked back, quoting the 'Light' motif from *The Light of Life* at the words 'recovering of sight to the blind'. Such allusiveness was natural to Elgar and often served him well. Here there is no disruption to musical thought or texture and the reference is readily subsumed into an exciting *crescendo* towards the first great climax of the work. The Prologue is by definition expository, so the threefold repetition of 'Comfort', with the winding chromatics of its inner part, and twofold 'Church' are acceptable, if already symptomatic of musical procedures that endanger much of *The Apostles*.

As in *The Light of Life*, the recitative music that starts Scene I is functional and unobtrusive. In later scenes appropriate motifs are incorporated to point the meaning; but here only the tiny ritornello at start and finish shapes the piece. Yet this recitative shows in miniature how Elgar planned many of his movements. Extemporizing his way from scene to scene, he defined many a section by just such a simple *ABA* scheme. This is immediately clear from the ensuing 'Night' introduction, framed by its 'Pastoral' reeds. The 'Dawn' depends much on local colour. The shofar, a Jewish liturgical instrument of ram's horn with probable history back to the Exodus and with persistent interval of a rising sixth, is integral to the scene. Equally so is the call of the 'Watchers', based on a Jewish penitential chant and the authentic tune for Psalm 92. The antique cymbals, tambourine and triangle that add some 'oriental' colour to the psalm interludes sound quaint rather than satisfying. More significant is the fact that the shofar's sixth coincides with Elgar's 'Light and Life' theme conceived on the Welsh holiday of 1901; and the fortuitous but happy way the traditional Jewish themes develop the data of 'Constitues eos'. The dawn itself is a moment of orchestral splendour that cannot quite silence doubts about the wisdom of declaiming 'Christ's Prayer' *fff* on trombones, tuba and organ. The ensuing ensemble with the first hint of dissent from Judas ('We shall eat of the riches of the Gentiles'), mingles grandiloquence with touching sincerity. Christ's 'Behold, I send you forth' is uttered against a choral setting of the last phrase in 'Constitues eos'.

After many changes of plan, Scene II confined itself to the Beatitudes and the comments of the onlookers. Elgar quoted in the notes he hoped to publish with *The Apostles* a sentence from Hillard's *Life of Christ* to emphasize the importance of these teachings: 'they sum up the revolution Christ is going to cause in men's ideas of goodness'. And he added a comment of his own about the nature of the audience's response: 'I have purposely made the listeners interpret the words in many cases too literally, that is, more in accordance with their own feelings at the time than with later enlightenment.' The scene now becomes a rural interlude of quiet instruction and meditation. The thematic threads on which the movement is based are contained in the eleven bars of the orchestral introduction, the 'Wayside' motif, in which the rhythm is the constant factor controlling the flow of the melodic line, and the 'Beatitudes' motif itself, always recognizable, but varied in its shapes and direction. Elgar follows the text of *Matthew* for eight Beatitudes; the ninth is omitted here and reserved for Mary's soliloquy in *The Kingdom*. Elgar spreads his music thinly, perhaps too thinly, in his determination that Christ's words should have unimpeded sway. He later made the 'Beatitudes' theme into an Anglican chant for Canon Gorton.

Consecutive fifths and anguished chromatics set the scene for 'The Tower of Magdala'. For text Elgar begins this Scene III with the apocryphal book of *Baruch*. He favoured the Apocrypha if only because it was less familiar than the canonical books of the Bible. The sagging chromatics of the penitent Magdalene give place to a choral vision or 'Fantasy' about her past life, which has an evanescent good cheer somehow insufficient to justify such an abasement of self-pity. The storm on Galilee gives the Elgarian orchestra its first opportunity since the 'Dawn' to indulge itself to the full and hurl another *fff* at a natural phenomenon. The concerted utterances of terror by the disciples serve to separate Judas slightly from the rest, but musically this section fails to satisfy until the Magdalene's question: 'Who maketh the storm a calm?' Then, for a few precious pages Elgar emerges as a great composer, making glorious music from a motif, dubbed 'Ardent Longing' by Jaeger and introduced almost inconsequentially towards the end of Scene II (Ex. 24). From the outset it was a modulating motif, and Elgar subdivides it, extends its elements, and treats it with compelling symphonic logic and skill. A new 'Conversion' theme continues on the same high level and contributes to a musical oasis all too rare in *The Apostles*. As if to emphasize the point, the apostles could hardly be more commonplace in their reporting to Christ that some say he is the Baptist, Elias, Jeremiah or one of the prophets. The introduction of 'Peter' themes before Christ's pronouncement that he is to be the rock of the Church is significant more for their future in *The Kingdom* than for any present effect. A brief solo for Mary the Mother is a heartfelt moment of touching simplicity, a tiny but concentrated tripartite structure. Elgar commented on the next section in a letter to Canon Gorton of July 1903: 'I have put the words of Simon "This man, if he were a prophet" – for the Women (always the hardest on their own sex).' He put it even more succinctly on a sketch: 'Women mocking (brutes!)' The forgiveness of the Magdalene was to have been followed at once by the betrayal and Judas scene. Part I, though, was already long enough. Elgar was now in the extraordinary position of having defined his three chosen apostles only by scattered lines in ensemble, apart from Peter's failure on the water and his declaration about the nature of Christ. It might well have given him pause that so far, with an hour's playing time used up, he had produced only a half-hearted heroine. He decided to conclude Part I with a smooth-flowing chorus of generalized comfort in 'Turn you to the stronghold'. The climactic 'Blessed is he who is not fallen from his hope in the Lord' looks back thematically to the Beatitudes and on to Mary's soliloquy in *The Kingdom*, while the succeeding passage contributes also to the setting of the Lord's Prayer.

The choral recitatives of Scene IV that lead to the taking of Jesus

Ex. 24
'Ardent Longing'

in Gethsemane have more dramatic than musical virtue, and the succession of vaguely military motifs are no more than Elgarian clichés. Musical interest increases when Peter is questioned by the servants in the palace of the high priest. The new motif of 'Questioning', with its

Elgar

Ex. 25
'Questioning' (x) and 'Fellowship' (y)

repeated slither into the depths of Peter's soul (Ex. 25), dovetails naturally with other motifs and culminates in an ironical hint of 'The Spirit of the Lord' at his final 'I swear by the Lord; I know not this Man'. The virtually unaccompanied female chorus telling of Christ's turning to look at Peter is a lovely passage in its own right and also has important implications for *The Kingdom*.

Scene IV comes to an end with the 'Temple' episode. Singers inside chant relentlessly the more implacable verses of Psalm 94 while Judas ponders the enormity of his deed. After a brutal exchange with the priests, Judas responds to Psalm 94 with part of Psalm 139 from outside. Whether it is psychologically right for a man in the depths of despair to search for a suitable biblical quotation is less significant than Elgar's occasionally striking an inapposite musical note. The framing music of 'Whither shall I go from Thy Spirit' is altogether apt in its dragging weariness. But the 'Light and Life' motif that leads with such freshness to the refulgent dawn of Part I is hardly appropriate to Judas's 'Then shall my night be turned to day', seeing that all he wants is darkness. Wagner knew marvellously how to summon irony to music: Elgar is less adept. Again, the motif that Jaeger oddly called 'Indifference' is a happy enough illustration for the words 'the breath in our nostrils is smoke', but in context it is goodnaturedly frivolous. Despite the real terror in the cries of 'Crucify Him!' and the tense drama of the final bars, the bold conception has been inadequately realized. In the same letter to Gorton of July 1903 Elgar put forward his view: 'To my mind *Judas'* crime or sin was *despair*; not only the betrayal, which was done for a worldly purpose. In these days, where every "modern" person (Ibsen &c, &c) seems to think "suicide" is the natural way out of everything my plan, if explained, may do some good.'

Scene V, 'Golgotha', has an initial theme on strings that represents the last of Christ's 'words' on the cross. Elgar gave his reason to Canon Gorton: 'I chose this rather than either of the other "last words" because it permits me to use much of the rest of the Ps (22) in the Ascension chorus.' At 'sabachthani' Elgar thought he had repeated the 'Angel of the Agony' chord in *Gerontius*; in fact it is a slightly lower order of dissonance. The dialogue between the Virgin Mary and John the favourite disciple is introduced by a new chromatic motif on horns, 'Mary's Grief', that suggests a return to the 'Tower of Magdala' atmosphere. The rest of the material, however, has strength in its sorrow, and the allusions to the Angel's night solo in Part I are natural, apt and expressive. Particularly touching is Mary's twofold recourse to recitative.

'Light and Life' appears again, to start the third day, with the opening of Scene VI, 'At the Sepulchre'. Its quiet confidence is justly invoked, and again the dawn 'reacheth even unto Hebron'. This time angels interrupt the sunrise with a semi-chorus of Alleluias from the female voices. The freshness of the writing in the rest of the movement, often in only two real parts, is sheer delight, with varied phrase lengths, enough sequence to aid memory, and a simplicity that is never facile. The wonder is that after *Gerontius* Elgar still had so much angelic music in him.

Scene VII, 'The Ascension', follows straight on. At the outset the apostles are still musically and theologically unimaginative, but Jesus's final speech, as well as giving a résumé of many crucial motifs, prepares at 'Go ye therefore and teach all nations' for the music that will launch the impetuous vitality of the Prelude to *The Kingdom*. Elgar once more shows himself a genius with the ensuing ensemble. The contralto beautifully smooths the false relation in the 'Christ, the Man of Sorrows' motif as the cloud receives Jesus into heaven, and the angelic Alleluias bind together in symphonic splendour themes first associated with Peter's opening solo in Scene I, with a section of 'Turn you to the stronghold', with Mary Magdalene's sense of sin, and with 'Christ's Prayer'. This last motif merges in effortless counterpoint with the 'Peter' theme to make a profound theological point in terms that are supremely musical. The central section, beginning at 'I have done Thy commandment', uses the 'Man of Sorrows' theme as binding agent while it surveys elements of the passion. The return of the Alleluias brings a last new theme, 'Christ's Glory', that modulates widely over its seven-bar span. The climax repeats *fff* and with a full orchestral battering the thematic combination that had just been wondrously done *pp*. At the only 'nobilmente' of the score, Elgar declaims 'The Spirit of the Lord' *tutta forza* with a top B flat appoggiatura to give new emphasis to the high-point. The Alleluias calm the music and finally entwine themselves with 'Christ's Peace' from *The Dream of Gerontius*, which now achieves its ultimate fulfilment.

The Kingdom

In a letter to Elgar written within a fortnight of the *Apostles* première, Capel Cure expressed curiosity about the sequel: 'Pentecost we have already discussed & I know how magnificently you will develop its musical possibilities – but after that, what next?' Canon Gorton, then Elgar's main Anglican helper, wrote to him on 10 February 1904: 'I have constantly in mind your future development of Apostles. What will you do with S. Paul?' This was an open question. It was still Elgar's ambition, though, that the project should eventually find its

Elgar's father, William Henry, at
about the time of his marriage in 1848

Elgar's mother, Ann Greening, at
about the time of her marriage

3   Elgar's birthplace at Lower Broadheath, outside Worcester, photographed in 1952

The five surviving Elgar children in about 1877 when Elgar was twenty. Back row to r.), Dot, Frank, Pollie; in front, Lucy and Edward

5 'The dragon is resting now': a drawing dated 20 March 1897 to commemorate completion of *The Banner of St George* five days before

6 Elgar at about the time of *The Dream of Gerontius*; he is wearing a diamond tie-pin given him by his wife

7　Lady Elgar at her desk; taken at Plas Gwyn, Hereford

　Hans Richter, 'True artist and true friend', who launched Elgar's international career

9 The front door panels at Severn House, as pictured in *The Architect* (14 March 1890) two years after it was built

10 A gathering of distinguished musicians at festivities celebrating the centenary of Bournemouth in July 1910. Back row (l. to r.), Hubert Parry, Edward German; front row, Elgar, Dan Godfrey, Alexander Mackenzie, Charles Stanford

1 Elgar at the Marconi Studio in 1930

12 First page of Elgar's draft of the Second Symphony, showing his 'Spirit of Delight'

way to Antioch. In the interview with Rudolf de Cordova of May 1904 he went even further:

> It was part of my original scheme to continue The Apostles by a second work carrying on the establishment of the Church among the Gentiles. This, too, is to be followed by a third oratorio, in which the fruit of the whole – that is to say, the end of the world and the Judgement – is to be exemplified.

The Kingdom as completed has a strong narrative thread, based on *Acts* i, ii and iv. It was Elgar's intention that this should represent Part I of the new work, ending with the 'Breaking of Bread' and the 'Lord's Prayer'. Part II could then continue the exploration through *Acts* until chapter ix, when the disciples were first called Christians at Antioch. Elgar had a libretto planned for three of the projected Part II scenes, those dealing with Simon of Gitta, the Centurion Cornelius, and the city of Antioch itself. Canon Gorton's question about St Paul was partly answered in Elgar's mind: he should be a prime witness at the stoning of Stephen; his conversion would also be treated.

Composition of *The Kingdom* caused Elgar much anguish, but from the outset the new libretto was likely to have a better balance between narrative and comment than that of *The Apostles*. With a trilogy in mind, Elgar was now embarked on the central work, and was engaged in long-term musical thinking. But his procedure was the same as with *The Apostles*, except that there was now a useful legacy to hand from the earlier work. Some music intended for Part II of *The Apostles* as originally planned was already written. The antiphon 'O sacrum convivium' had been invoked to set the scene for 'The Upper Room'; part of 'Pentecost' was composed, and the setting of the Lord's Prayer was complete.

The antiphon now needed a Prelude, and Elgar embarked on the most extended and satisfying piece of symphonic writing in the whole 'Apostles' project. The inhibitions of *The Apostles*, the too great reliance on motifs alone to sustain interest without adequate musical development, the wearisome nature of some of the motifs and the enervating effect of too much penitence – all this is forgotten in a glorious sweep of orchestral sound that makes one of Elgar's most exciting openings. 'Peter' motifs, reminders of his questioning and denial and 'Christ's Loneliness' come from *The Apostles*; but they are caught up in the grandness of musical thought; and it is the themes of 'New Faith' and gratitude for the final Communion that linger in the memory. In a letter of 21 July 1906 Elgar told Jaeger that 'the whole thing is intentionally less mystic than the A! – the *men* are alive & working & the atmosphere is meant to be more direct & simple'. The

241

result is nothing but gain, and this time Elgar himself took a large hand in the labelling of themes. Jaeger was now a very sick man, and the draft analysis he submitted for *The Kingdom* was much cut and modified by Elgar. This meant only a dozen new names for motifs, though Elgar's invention is quite as rich as in *The Apostles*.

In Scene I the Disciples and Holy Women are assembled in the Upper Room at Jerusalem. In their 'Aspiration' theme at the outset (Ex. 26) Elgar indulges a favourite rhythm at the words 'Kingdom of God', happy sign that his heart is in this music-making. A main feature

Ex. 26 'Aspiration'

of the ensemble is the easy inevitability with which Elgar incorporates the modal harmonies of the antiphon into his tonal structure. 'O sacrum convivium' (Ex. 27) itself is treated with utmost flexibility.

Ex. 27 'Real Presence'

242

Initially stated in full, and recapitulated thus by Peter at 'He took bread and blessed it', it is subsequently chopped and changed in rhythm so that even in précis the references are clear and the atmosphere is captured. Another fine inspiration is the 'Concord' motif (Ex. 28), hardly more than a thematic tag, but capable of great resource in modulation and as binding agent in this and other movements. Motifs

Ex. 28 'Concord'

from *The Apostles* are passed in review without halting the impetus of the music, so that the whole finely woven tapestry is as impressive in its overall design as in the intricacy of its detail. The concluding 'Amen', half tonal, half modal, puts an appropriate seal on the whole ensemble.

Peter's recitative about the necessity to choose a replacement for Judas, culminates in the triumphant ring of the 'Resurrection' Alleluias, and continues the impression of the opening chorus. The music of the 'Apostles' project, dormant in Elgar's mind for more than two years, was now such an integral part of his thinking that he could conjure with it at will. Launching on *The Kingdom* appears to have been a musical release similar to that of Wagner's when starting *Siegfried* Act 3. Jaeger failed to see the relevance of the choice by lot of Matthias; for this he earned a stern rebuke from Lady Elgar in March 1906: 'instead of "Matthias" meaning nothing to us, it is the type of Everything wh. can still infuse heroism, self sacrifice & great thoughts into all those who are not dead to such things.' The contrapuntal play with motifs, in diminution, by topping and tailing, and in summaries, displays virtuoso skill until it leads from four bars of pedal A to the intense drama of the interrupted cadence at 'O ye priests'. It is a rerun, and no less effective for that, of the choral entry in *Gerontius* at 'Go, in the name / Of Angels and Archangels'. As occasionally in Elgar, the 'Nobilmente' marking at 'to stand before the congregation' is almost

243

a warning: these choral octaves, if not made to sound noble will undoubtedly be vulgar. The orchestra is sometimes thinking ahead of the words, as when the 'Spirit of the Lord' motif unobtrusively accompanies the words 'For it is not ye that speak'. Recapitulation of the choral material begins in E flat rather than F, an Elgarian 'jape' he also took over into the symphonic music, and the climax is approached by a thrilling choral version of the Prelude's start, rousing the sopranos to top B flat, and stretching over a dozen bars. As the choral notes lengthen for the final 'the Spirit of your Father', the violins have a *pp* augmented version of 'to stand before the congregation', this time truly *nobilmente* if not so marked.

The overspill of music from *The Apostles* offered practically nothing for Elgar's Scene II. He wanted a quiet interlude between the massive splendour of 'O ye priests' and the drama of Pentecost. During the first months of 1906 Elgar put specific questions to Canon Gorton about this scene. Gorton had helpful advice and also approval of Elgar's judgment: 'you could if you preferred make it the morn of Pentecost. Again, as to Beautiful Gate, you are quite right, it was the Gateway which led into the court of the women so that the holy women are in place there.' So time and place were settled for this 'piacevole' duet between the two Marys. The text has a minimum of narrative; there is just the reference from *Acts* iii to the man lame from his mother's womb. The rest is again comment, mainly from the Old Testament and Apocrypha as in *The Apostles*: but the texts are warmly apposite, avoiding extreme flights of fancy and ideas that jar. In this way Elgar had learnt much since *The Apostles*. It is the same with the music. The three-bar phrase that begins the movement and acts as binding ritornello never returns in the same form; twice it has two bars, and lastly has four. There is now a lovely *cantabile* version of the 'Watchers' music from *The Apostles*, having shed all the heartiness of its earlier appearances. It is subtly modified as the movement proceeds, so as to combine with 'Light and Life' at 'the temple might sound from morning'. The lame man's motif, chromatically sad and a little gangling in the bass (Ex. 29), has not a trace of self-pity. In her central solo Mary the Mother makes for the only climax in the movement: otherwise the duetting overlaps a little, is sometimes artfully dovetailed, and thrice closes a section with a brief phrase in unison. An idea Elgar discussed with Gorton was the equation of Pentecost with 'the day of the First-Fruits'. Thus the 'Pentecost' motif pre-echoes prominently in the movement.

Scene III, initially in the Upper Room, is the central point of *The Kingdom* as eventually modified for Birmingham, and therefore the central point of the whole trilogy as Elgar now conceived it. The

Ex. 29
'Pity' (x) and 'Watchers' (Y)

coming of the Holy Ghost made possible the spread of the Church not only within Jewry but widely among the Gentiles. This was the crucial moment prophesied by Christ in the 'Ascension' movement of *The Apostles*, and also the moment referred to by the young Elgar's headmaster, Francis Reeve, when he described the apostles as 'perhaps before the descent of the Holy Ghost not cleverer than some of you here'.

The tenor recitative shows Elgar in virtuoso control of his motifs. The even quavers of 'Concord' lead to 'Pentecost' insistently combined in canon with its own diminution. The 'Apostles' Faith' motif, not heard since the finale of *The Apostles*, establishes itself briefly, then combines with 'Concord' and merges imperceptibly into the 'Apostles'. The transitions are effortless and show both the kinship between so much of the thematic material and Elgar's wondrous skill in handling it. The next step seems equally inevitable, the emergence of 'The Spirit of the Lord' for unaccompanied male chorus (Ex. 30). In the two dozen bars from the beginning of the movement Elgar has been equally at home with a Wagnerian art of transition and a Brahmsian process of developing variation. The quiet orchestral awe of 'Pentecost' is emphasized on muted strings, organ, and in the mysterious pulse of the bass drum. A mystic chorus of female voices is accompanied by a persistent quaver figure in the orchestra that refers constantly to 'The Spirit of the Lord'. The high-point of expectation is reached when the unaccompanied six-part mystic chorus freely develops 'The Spirit of the Lord' till it recalls the appoggiatura climax first heard near the end of *The Apostles*.

The announcement by the contralto solo of the 'rushing of a mighty wind', and the tongues 'like as of fire' gives Elgar a glorious opportunity for orchestral display. The 'Pentecost' motif hurtles from the top of the texture to the bottom, and flashing semiquavers coruscate over the score till a triple hint of the 'Apostles' motif proclaims the impassioned march of 'He, who walketh upon the wings of the wind' as a glowing new counterpoint (Ex. 31). Amid varied phrase lengths the march strides tonally from A flat, via E and A to the *nobilmente* climax of the mystic chorus in F, with the 'Gospel' motif. To celebrate the arrival of the Holy Ghost in a sublimated march could not be more Elgarian, and conviction animates every note of the score. The narrative reference to 'Jews, devout men' elicits from the orchestra two bars of the Temple psalm rhythm in Scene I of *The Apostles*. It is there for the hearing, but this time Elgar does not bother with details such as the antique cymbals.

The scene shifts to Solomon's Porch, where the multitude expresses its amazement at the gift of tongues in a set piece of dazzling brilliance.

Ex. 30
'Concord' (w); 'Apostles' Faith' (x); 'Apostles' (Y); 'The Spirit of the
Lord' (z)

Ex. 31

The sharp comments of the crowd are hurled from voice to voice while the orchestra is busy with an emphatic angular figure that darts through the texture. The reiterated 'What meaneth this?' brings from John the soaring march phrase, 'He who walketh upon the wings of the wind', while the orchestra reiterates the 'Apostles' motif. This last reminiscence was in fact added by John Pointer at Novello (with Elgar's approval) on the analogy of the combination at Peter's entry some bars later. The people ascribe the apostles' inspiration to drink: 'These men are full of new wine'. This was a sentence Elgar originally assigned to Simon of Gitta, the Samarian sorcerer who tried in *Acts* viii to purchase from Peter the power to bestow the Holy Spirit, and who was to have been Peter's great antagonist if *The Kingdom* had proceeded along the road to Antioch. The final cry of 'What meaneth this?' is answered differently. The orchestra stills its headlong rush and quietens through a descending whole-tone scale to 'Christ, the Man of Sorrows'. Thus the people had their answer. Elgar now shows further piercing insight. Over the motif of 'Christ's Prayer' Peter, about to launch on his first sermon, recalls to himself the words of Jesus foretelling Peter's threefold denial before cockcrow: 'I have prayed for thee, that thy faith fail not' (Ex. 32).

Ex. 32
'Christ's Prayer' (x)

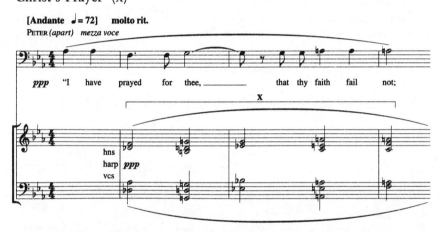

It has been held against Peter's sermon that so much of it is based on musical motifs from the past. Half the actual words of the sermon in *Acts* quote verses from the Old Testament, since citations from Joel, from David, and yet again David were the best weapons in Peter's armoury for convincing his Jewish audience. So nothing could be more appropriate than to address 'all ye that dwell at Jerusalem' in a musical phrase from the Temple's morning psalm. Indeed Peter, the 'rock', turns his thoughts to the future 'Church' and the inspiration of 'Pentecost', as he prepares to quote Joel with the words 'It shall come to pass in the last days'. Throughout most of Joel's prophecy the orchestra is busy with the 'New Faith' theme, not heard since the work's Prelude. The majestic flow of the paragraph is interrupted at 'and your young men shall see visions, and your old men shall dream dreams'. Here Elgar had a major change of plan that exemplifies his determination that Peter (and he himself) should not be too much concerned with the past. His original idea, pursued as far as the MS full score, was to set the words to the 'Angel's Farewell' music in *Gerontius*, indeed the dream of an old man. But with scoring complete, Elgar sensed the associations were wrong, and substituted the four radiant bars that now so justly illuminate the text. A bar of 'New Faith' punctuates the sermon at crucial points, but the flashbacks are equally well judged. At the first mention of Jesus, Peter's inner thoughts turn to the wayside teaching and the music of the 'Beatitudes'; Christ's 'mighty works' remind of the miracle when he walked the Sea of Galilee; mention of the crucifixion conjures 'Eli, Eli' and other motifs from Scene V of *The Apostles*. The rest of the movement is concerned with *Kingdom* music. When the people's conscience is stirred by Peter's account of Christ's death and resurrection, their bewilderment develops passages heard in the Prelude.

Peter's message, 'Repent, and be baptized' (Ex. 33) is delivered to a magisterial tune not heard before. Where a great tune was required,

Ex. 33

Elgar produced it. His pleasure in it is demonstrated by the exuberant semiquaver counterpoint he devised for the lead up to the climax of the choral restatement. It takes the four horns stepwise to a top D. This was sufficiently near the limit of the instrument's practical range for Elgar to write about the passage to Adolf Borsdorf, first horn of the LSO. He wanted to know if it was ' "asking too much" of four Horns in unison to play this passage, in moderate tempo'. The reply was encouraging, and the resulting bravura raises the question whether Elgar's kingdom was not rather in the orchestral world. The final ensemble is approached by recapitulation of the 'expectancy' music before the arrival of the Holy Ghost. Some 'largamente' bars require a sensitive conductor to save Elgar from himself, where the previously *pp* becomes *ff*; but sonorous sequences on 'Pentecost' mingle with a combination of the 'Gospel' and 'Apostles' motifs until 'New Faith' and now triumphant Alleluias give 'Pentecost' the just and well-earned accolade of 'nobilmente'.

Elgar now returns to the Beautiful Gate and calls his next movement 'The Sign of Healing'. Its composition gave Elgar much worry, coinciding as it did with his return from America, sickness, and an unpleasant accident. The three themes of the orchestral introduction to Scene IV are all new, though the first has a 'Pentecost' tailpiece. In a letter to Jaeger of 7 July 1906 Elgar called the first a 'new Baptism (*refreshing*) theme' (Ex. 34a). The second he was very pleased with: 'That *surprise*

Ex. 34
(a) 'New Baptism'

or rather quiet astonishment theme is all right, eh?' It was a theme (b) that for some reason Elgar associated with Ivor Atkins, to whom he

(b) 'Surprise'

wrote about it on 3 October: 'Some themes go with my friends: in my mind this goes with you: but it *feels artistic & striving, educated* (!) and *courteous* only to a limited degree.' The third new motif (Ex. 34c) was to be associated with 'wonders and signs done by the Apostles'.

There are two points of action in the scene. The first is Peter's healing of the lame man, accomplished amid an intricate network of motifs that are yet subsumed into the excitement of the moment. The

(c) 'Signs and Wonders'

ensuing chorus combines motifs from the music of Scene II with the sharp rhythm of the people's incredulity at the speaking with tongues. Peter's explanation of the miracle has new-found confidence, is tonally fluid, and involves a survey of motifs as quick as the apostle's thought. The F major of John's 'Unto you', lyrical and impassioned, has such strong Neapolitan leanings first time round that it settles second time into G flat. With the entry of Peter the emotional temperature rises but the musical quality lowers, and only some lovely Straussian sideslips towards the end go some way towards salvaging an exuberant but dubious piece of duetting. The 'refreshing' theme now has the strength of a giant, with the horns exulting once more in their top D.

A contralto recitative narrates how 'the priests and the Sadducees' put the apostles in ward because of their preaching the resurrection of the dead. This is the scene's second moment of action; but it is the last words of the biblical verse 'for it was now eventide', that stirred Elgar's imagination. The text for Mary's soliloquy, from many sources, is finely compiled. The first 'stanza' is mainly from different psalms; for the central section Elgar took a sequence of phrases he found in *The Topical Bible* under 'Persecution', with sub-heading 'Of the Righteous'. The violin solo introduction in C minor uses two bars of the Jewish 'Hymn of Weeping'. Rabbi Cohen described it as an 'example of the plaintive elegies chanted, or rather crooned, in the dim-lighted synagogue on the fatal 9th of Ab, the anniversary of the destruction of both Temples'. Elgar goes on briefly to cite also the 'Hymn of Parting'. This ritornello underpins Mary's opening psalm-thoughts. It is followed by another in G minor, based on a retrograde version of Mary's 'goeth down'. It leads to the ninth Beatitude, left over from Scene II of *The Apostles* and sung to a phrase Mary had used there also. The 'Persecution' texts recall many earlier motifs, including one of Peter's as the orchestra anticipates his martyrdom at the words 'Some shall they kill and crucify'. A final 'Beatitude' comes from the first of Peter's epistles. After reference to 'Comfort' from *The Apostles*, Elgar drives the music to a fine climax by means of the exultant 'Christ's Glory' motif. The word 'Kingdom' has not appeared in the libretto since the initial 'Seek first the Kingdom of God'. Now Mary refers to it twice. On the first occasion, with the 'Gospel' and other motifs prominent, she sings of the 'Gospel of the Kingdom' which 'shall be preached in the whole world'. This is a saying of Jesus reported by Matthew, who follows it with hints about the end of the world and the second coming. The other reference, 'the Kingdom and the patience' is to *Revelation*. About this last phrase Elgar felt very strongly. Julius Buths's German version had not made the connection adequately, and Elgar wrote to Novello on 13 October 1906: 'Will you please *insist* that *Patience must* be in even if we alter the phrasing of the music completely.' He had checked that the Luther Bible had 'Geduld'. The phrase is sung to an incandescent version of Christ's 'Beatitudes' motif; for Elgar it obviously represented an essential element in Christ's 'schooling' of the apostles. There follows the fullest statement of the 'Church' motif since the Prelude of *The Apostles*, and in the same key of E flat. It leads through a long *diminuendo* to a return of C minor, the opening violin solo, and Mary's initial meditation. A brief hint of the second ritornello closes the scene.

Scene V returns to the Upper Room, where the 'Concord' theme leads exultantly to the return of the 'Seek first' music and the splendour of 'Christ's Glory'. Peter reports their interrogation by the chief priests and elders, a passage about which Elgar wrote to Gorton in August 1906: 'I have a terrible moment when Peter says "they took knowledge of us *that we had been with Jesus*" [vocal score p. 156] here there is a momentary suggestion of the Denial & the Servants: an instantaneous revelation of Peter's mind impossible in any other art than music.' The following chorus in which 'they lifted up their voice to God with one accord' is buttressed by 'Concord'. Elgar wisely avoids the next verse in *Acts* iv, 'Why did the heathen rage, and the people imagine a vain thing?'; but there are new vocal lines and much choral imitation to illustrate the rulers' 'threat'nings'. At the sentence 'grant Thy servants to speak Thy word with all boldness', Elgar refers to an ardent motif not previously heard in *The Kingdom*. It appeared in Scene I of *The Apostles* to the words, 'He hath chosen the weak to confound the mighty'. A brief recapitulation of the start of the chorus allows 'Concord' to reintroduce a fragment of 'O sacrum convivium', preparing modally for the age-old 'Breaking of Bread'.

At this point Elgar took his text not from a biblical source but from the *Didache*, an ancient manual of prayers discovered in a monastery at Constantinople in 1873. Apart from one new phrase for the soloists, the music relies mostly on 'Concord' and 'O sacrum' until the moment when the orchestra, accompanying John's 'Give thanks first for the cup', begins to recapitulate much of the Prelude's last section. In connection with this Lady Elgar wrote to Novello on 29 June 1906: 'Sir Edward wd. be glad to have by return of post pages 7 & 8 "The Kingdom" any old proofs wd. do, he has none of those pages.' They were the last two pages of the Prelude in the vocal score, and a comparison between them and the final sections of *The Kingdom* movingly reveals the thought processes of a great composer. All seems the same, yet a bar is lost here, ordering of the phrases is changed, a counterpoint (for instance, the final soprano 'Thou, O Lord') is given new prominence, so that all is familiar yet subtly different.

The setting of the Lord's Prayer dates from the days of *The Apostles*. Canon Gorton advised about its placing: 'I hope the Lord's Prayer is not coming until *after* the descent of the Holy Spirit. It is the prayer of fellowship and sonship. by which we pray Abba, Father, which dedicates the Temple not made with hands.' Elgar approaches it with a last proclamation, much of it unaccompanied, of the 'Church' theme, as the faithful are gathered 'into Thy Kingdom'. The prayer itself has two references to the 'Kingdom', but its main motifs are the 'God the Father' chords first heard in *The Apostles* when Peter declares Christ to be the 'Son of the living God', and 'The Spirit of the Lord'. The setting of 'and forgive us our trespasses' recapitulates 'For he will forgive their iniquity' in 'Turn you to the stronghold' at the end of *The Apostles* Part I. As the solo and choral voices fade one by one into silence, 'New Faith' in augmentation closes the work and brings to a rapt conclusion Elgar's greatest choral work since *Gerontius*.

The Last Judgement

When Jaeger wrote his analytical notes to *The Kingdom*, he described it as dealing with the 'Church in Jerusalem'; he went on to say that a 'third section, having for its theme the Church of the Gentiles' was contemplated by the composer. What Elgar now envisaged it is impossible to say. Did he seriously consider setting out a third time on the journey to Antioch? He already had material to hand. His libretto notes cautioned him not to confuse Antioch in Pisidia ('? wrong place the other Antioch') with the capital of Syria. Association with the Mary Magdalene music of *The Apostles* was suggested by a verse from *Isaiah*: 'And the harp, and the viol, the tabret, and pipe, are in their feasts.'

An obvious occasion for production of the third oratorio was the

1909 Birmingham Festival, but Elgar turned to the First Symphony instead. Friends continued to press for the completion of the trilogy; in moments of optimism Elgar envisaged it too. He wrote, for instance, on his fifty-third birthday to Littleton, expressing the view that so long as he could get the requisite quiet Novello should eventually have *The Music Makers*, Second Symphony, the Violin Concerto '*and* the IIIrd Oratorio'. Whatever had been Elgar's intentions immediately after *The Kingdom*, the 'Church of the Gentiles' was now abandoned, and Elgar was thinking along the lines of a draft letter to the Rev W. E. Torr, in which he described the work as 'beginning with the Strife (Antichrist) ending with judgment & the Heavenly Kingdom'.

Elgar was now concentrated mainly on the book of *Revelation*. Wherever he read, his musical imagination was also at work. Among the books Elgar annotated for the project was a copy of *Revelation* in *The Century Bible*. Against the opening of chapter iv, 'After these things I saw, and behold, a door opened in heaven', Elgar wrote '? *begin*' by the side. He also condensed, by means of crossings-out, much of chapter i as a solo for John. He underlined the words 'kingdom and patience', already used for Mary's soliloquy in *The Kingdom*. The phrase 'sound of many waters' was similarly treated and ringed, with 'Gerontius' in the margin; Elgar was reminded of his music to Newman's lines,

> It floods me, like the deep and solemn sound
> Of many waters.

An editorial note referring to 'the Sun of Righteousness' caught Elgar's attention and recalled John's solo in Scene IV of *The Kingdom*. The Demons of *Gerontius* were conjured up by the verse dealing with 'a pale horse: and he that sat upon him, his name was Death; and Hades followed him'. So Elgar was using the same procedure with the third oratorio as he had with the others. Wherever the words suggested a musical idea, he noted it. Interest of a different kind was stimulated by editorial comment on the verse mentioning 'the dogs and the sorcerers'. Elgar ringed his beloved 'dogs' and underlined the note: 'By "dogs" are meant impure, lascivious persons.'

At a time when he was still thinking of Antioch, Elgar drew up an overall scheme for the trilogy, showing the development of the different characters and their interconnections. Peter was eventually to become the 'Spirit of robust faith', John the 'Spirit of trusting love'. Judas was linked with Simon Magus, and then Antichrist. Judas was also to have offshoots into the world of female wickedness, leading to Sapphira who was responsible for financial trickery in *Acts*, and so on to the barren women. All the Judas group was heading for 'Everlasting fire'.

In the third oratorio Jesus was characterized by the challenging sentence, 'Worthy is the Lamb'.

There was no commission deadline for *The Last Judgement*, as the work was to be called, and Elgar clearly derived pleasure from compiling libretto ideas. Bloodcurdling texts for Antichrist were culled from the Old Testament. *Revelation* was further explored in a translation by R. H. Charles, published in 1922. New music was also devised. By the end of the 1920s a considerable body of material had been assembled for *The Last Judgement*. But the commission for the Third Symphony in December 1932 redirected much of it. The projected opening for the Symphony, for instance, was probably an Antichrist idea. The end of the development incorporated a sketch headed 'Hell followed him'. A solo viola part in the scherzo of the Symphony was formerly for tenor, presumably the oratorio's John. The start of the slow movement was a motif dear to Elgar. It seems to have been intended originally for the sequel to *Cockaigne*; it is then specifically headed 'The Judgement'. The shofar was to reappear in the oratorio in connection with the last trumpet, and a sombre passage, in which the shofar plays an inner part, was also transferred to the Symphony's Adagio. Music of considerable strength, much of it dating to Elgar's ripest maturity, had been gathered for the completion of the trilogy. Its ultimate silence is to be regretted.

Early church music

Elgar's earliest music for the church was written for St George's, Worcester, and its notable choral tradition. To honour his church's ambitions and to pit his own powers against two revered masters, Elgar composed in July 1873 his Credo on themes from Beethoven symphonies, and later adapted a Mozart violin sonata movement into a Gloria. The Credo began in Beethoven's A minor with the Allegretto of no. 7; but Elgar transposed the ensuing A major into F, and by the time he reached 'Et incarnatus' the slow movement of no. 9 was in A flat. This flatward tendency was Schubertian, but also already Elgarian. He signed the work 'Bernhard Pappenheim', either from a curious name seen on a German map, or because his Credo was indeed 'pastework'. The Gloria is mainly interesting for the formal changes made. Elgar wanted three additional quiet bars (in the second movement of κ547) for 'bonae voluntatis' and added them; in the recapitulation he cut eight bars at 'Tu solus sanctus'.

Settings of such Catholic texts as *Salve regina* and *Tantum ergo* followed, and in 1877 Elgar wrote an E minor Credo of his own. At 'et vitam venturi saeculi' he anticipated the future of others rather than himself by trying out an outlandish progression from E minor to E minor. He wrote hymn tunes, one of which, 'Drake's Broughton', recalled a favourite Worcestershire haunt, found its way into the *Westminster Hymnal* of 1898, and was later incorporated into the 'Aubade' of the *Nursery Suite*. A work of some significance was the *Domine, salvam fac reginam* of 1879, Mozartian in style but with modest harmonic adventures outside the Classical mould. Two settings of *O salutaris hostia*, both strophic and perhaps from 1880, were Elgar's earliest Catholic church music of any size to be printed. That in F, with pleasant dovetailing between voices and organ, appeared in the *Complete Benediction Manual* (1898), the other in E flat, with some pleasant and prophetic quasi-modal harmonies, became no. 21 in *Modern Music for Catholic Choirs* (1889).

A body of litany chants was written in 1886, among which four for the Virgin Mary were published with dedication to Father Thomas Knight of St George's. The motets later published by Novello (1902 and 1907) as Elgar's op. 2 also date from this period. The *Ave verum corpus* was originally conceived in January 1887 as a *Pie Jesu* in memory of William Allen. Elgar was dubious about its originality, noting at the end, 'Very like "Love divine" in Daughter of Jairus Stainer'. For publication he revised the simple but shapely tune so as to alternate solo soprano with four-part choir; he also added a final six bars of highly expressive cadence. Elgar then assessed it to Jaeger as 'too sugary I think but it is nice & harmless & quite easy'. The *Ave Maria* in B flat begins in a melodically fluent 6/8. The piece is subtly put together, with words and music counterpointing each other unexpectedly, so that there is an ambiguity as to whether Elgar means three or four stanzas. In *Ave maris stella* Elgar again distributes the words cunningly. The organ begins with a three-bar phrase that is repeated to the title words. But these words recur six more times, with placing as ingenious as are the rhythmic dexterities of the piece.

The most impressive of Elgar's St George's works is *Ecce sacerdos magnus*, written in some haste for a visit of the Bishop of Birmingham on 9 October 1888. Elgar wrote to Buck about it four days later: 'the leading paper says, the new composition was "exquisite" so I suppose 'twas good enough'. It was orchestrated five years later for the dedication of a new chancel in November 1893 at St Catherine's of Siena, Birmingham. Perhaps the first theme is a stately reminiscence of the Benedictus from Haydn's *Harmoniemesse*. The steady rhythmic figure of the accompaniment is an Elgarian favourite at whatever speed. The main theme is of four bars; its successor has three and is weighted with expressive suspensions. The climax is reached with the main theme in the dominant and the addition of the heavier orchestral instruments. Towards the end Elgar turns flatwards and finishes plagally in a work that achieves grandeur with the simplest means.

Te Deum and Benedictus

The rather odd idea of combining two morning service canticles in one work was presumably G. R. Sinclair's. As with *The Light of Life*, an Anglican cathedral did not inspire a masterpiece. The work is built on grand, festive lines, but the thematic material has little distinction and is far below the standard Elgar had already set himself. The orchestral (or organ) introduction has insistent rhythm, subjected to sequence and a repetition of the sequence. If the build-up to the choral entry is conventional, it is a nice Elgarian touch to place 'God' at the bottom of the initial clause. Now, too, phrase lengths have variety, with the odd bar slipped in. There is very little word repetition, so that the lengthy text is covered with despatch. The cherubim and seraphim revert to sequence, as does the threefold repetition of the word 'Holy'. As a good Catholic, Elgar states the 'holy Church' text five times, while other parts are busy pursuing different clauses. He reaches his first *fff* climax with the choir at 'Thou art the everlasting Son' with a virtual augmentation of 'holy Church'. Characteristically Elgar shuts down at once to *pp* as the oboe leads to a sinuous orchestral theme in thirds and tied triplets tenderly evoking the clause about 'the Virgin's womb'. Elgar makes a nice contrapuntal and theological point by combining to perfection his 'All the earth' music and 'holy Church'. The opening motif of the work returns for 'Day by day we magnify Thee', and an unimpressive sequence at 'We worship Thy name' is twice repeated to prepare in rather threadbare style for a final 'Day by day'. The most that can be said for these sequences, and there are more of them at once, is that they make a naïve claim to represent 'world without end'. The *Te Deum* text ends quietly, and Elgar recollects the main motifs of the piece in choral tranquillity till an orchestral postlude bids them affectionate farewell over a long *diminuendo*.

The lyrical 12/8 of the *Benedictus* makes as if to begin in A minor before easing into F; it is initially in strong contrast, with much of the choral writing virtually unaccompanied. But perhaps the themes already look back to the *Te Deum* when the sopranos reach 'That we should be saved from our enemies'. The broken vocal line traces the shape of 'holy Church', with its stepwise descent and falling fifth. Certainly the quiet modulation to D major resumes the sinuous thirds that treated before of Christ's birth. As the tempo quickens, reminiscence gives place to the first hint of large-scale recapitulation. 'Prophet of the

Highest' recalls 'We praise Thee, O God' and the opening idea of the *Te Deum* in a recourse to *fff* far from the prevailing mood of the *Benedictus*. The quiet 12/8 pulse moves flatwards for 'the tender mercy of our God', but once the *Benedictus* words are done, the *Te Deum* mood prevails. The 'Gloria' begins with cymbal crash and *fff* tutti. Elgar rehearses once more the *Te Deum* sequences, now familiar if not distinguished. The work ends with a non-thematic rising scale on mainly chromatic triplets, a favourite Elgarian way of bringing down the curtain.

Psalms

Elgar began *Great is the Lord* (Psalm 48) soon after completing the Violin Concerto. Echoes of the greater work strayed into the psalm setting, which he dedicated to Armitage Robinson, now Dean of Wells. Elgar was as eclectic with the words of the psalm as he had been with the oratorios, selecting from different versions, and sometimes paraphrasing. The setting is very sectional. It opens in a D major apt to lose its C sharps with a strong unison tune in a bluff 3/2 on the lower voices. The description of Mount Zion brings in the upper voices and an access of charm. Repeat of the initial tune carries a descant with reminders of the Violin Concerto finale. At 'For, lo! the kings assembled themselves' the character changes completely with marcato quavers in the accompaniment and disjointed declamation for the voices. Elgar gives a very realistic setting of 'pain, as of a woman in travail', and stirs up quite an east wind to break 'the ships of Tarshish'. He relishes, too, the discomfiture of the kings as 'they hasted away'. An A flat bass solo (as far from D as can be) is interesting for its phrase lengths but little else. 'Let mount Zion be glad' is antiphonally jolly in a 6/4 dance rhythm. The concluding 'For this God is our God' reverts to the opening music and accents the words to emphasize the latent chauvinism. Too many pedal points throughout the setting and too much unison writing suggest Elgar was not fully engaged in this work. The 200th anniversary of the Royal Society deserved better.

Give unto the Lord set Psalm 29 for the 1914 Sons of the Clergy service in St Paul's Cathedral, and is a finer piece. It begins *nobilmente* in the *Kingdom* key of E flat, and has some of the oratorio's power and drive. The three-bar opening is at once arresting, and the characteristic rhythm of 'worship the Lord in the beauty of holiness' has the robustness of Anglican good sense. The voices are contrapuntally bold in a psalm that becomes increasingly elemental. The Lord is very much on the rampage, thundering, breaking the cedars, dividing the flames of fire, shaking the wilderness, stripping the forests; and Elgar follows graphically, modulating to B minor, D minor and C minor before settling on B minor for the central 'In His temple', a lovely, intimate passage into which Elgar inserts a quiet reminiscence of 'Worship the Lord'. The music works round to E flat and a recapitulation of the opening, enhanced but not improved by a couple of pauses on top notes. Writing in 1914, Elgar is emphatic that 'the Lord shall give His people the blessing of peace'. But confidence ebbs, the music changes from command to prayer, and ends with a gentle sequence on the notes Elgar had so questionably emphasized at the recapitulation, reiterating again and again a plea for 'the blessing of peace'.

Minor religious pieces

Another Elgar offering for the coronation of Edward VII was the hymn *O Mightiest of the Mighty* to words by the Rev S. Childs Clarke in an unusual metre (10.10.10.8). Elgar told Jaeger he did not relish the task: 'That Hymn is all "wrong" – hymns always are.' But he said he would try, and by the end of the letter it was done: 'I enclose a tune – there are 10,000 people can do this sort of thing better than I can'. Perhaps it was not Elgar's fault that the tune does not work equally well for every verse.

At the end of 1908 Jaeger came up with an idea from his sickbed. He had received the Elgars' 1897 Christmas card, an F major setting of 'traditional words', *Grete Malverne on a Rock*. Jaeger thought it a 'very nice & *quaint* "carolly" tune', and Novello asked Shapcott Wensley to devise four new verses in the original rhyme scheme. He obliged, and gave new life to an unpretentious piece of quiet beauty. Elgar had achieved a slight modal flavour by ending five of the eight lines on a minor chord.

In April 1909 Elgar sent Novello two single and two double chants for the Anglican psalter. The first two were for Psalm 95 (the *Venite*), the others for Psalms 68 and 75; all were published in *Single and Double Chants by Various Composers* (1909). More significant was the *Angelus* of May that year. It was the first product of the Elgars' stay at Careggi, which also had associations for the Stuart Wortleys, who had told them about a favourite monastery on the way to Fiesole. A sketch for the piece shows considerable variation in the words, more than could occur in revising a translation. It is likely, then, that this version of the 'Tuscan dialect' was Elgar's own. He dedicated the work to the Windflower, but expressed some doubts: 'I was afraid the simple words might be too papistical for you – or for your family.' To the quiet chimes of a 'Hail Mary', persisting through the first two lines of both stanzas, the miracle of Christ's birth is told in music of a restrained beauty.

The words of the offertory for the coronation of George V were verses 2 and 3 from Psalm 5 beginning 'O hearken Thou unto the voice of my calling'. They were sung while the king made offering of bread and wine for the Communion. Elgar produced a work of tender devotion, with introduction that buttressed the music and subtly informed much of the setting. The searching harmonies achieve a hard-won consolation with no hint of complacency along the way.

The harvest anthem, *Fear not, O Land*, a setting of words from *Joel* ii.21–4 and 26, dates from late spring 1914. The work was not orchestrated, and Elgar needed help in marking the organ part; he wrote to John West about it: 'two manuals scourge me a great deal'. Beginning robustly, Elgar quietens to show affection for the 'beasts of the field'. There are fine imitative entries when 'the pastures of the wilderness do spring', and warm sequences for encouragement of 'the fig tree and the vine'. The anthem ends in the accents of the opening and the strong assurance that God 'hath dealt wondrously with you'.

The carol to words by Ben Jonson, *I Sing the Birth*, is one of the simplest and most beautiful of Elgar's settings. The bulk of the narrative is carried by solo baritone and alto in contemplative phrases rounded by modal alleluias. The piece is gently conceived and perfectly executed with an austerity and economy of means unusual for Elgar.

Instead of a march or Kipling setting to celebrate George V's return to health, Elgar wrote a '*Partsong Carol* sort of thing' to George Gascoigne words. As basis for the five stanzas he used a hymn tune from his early days. There is no awkwardness in the underlay, and the forthright tune is subjected to nice expressive point when the word 'dolours' is extended through a long tenor note, the 'little birds which sing so sweet' chirrup cheerfully in imitation, and the 'rainbow bending in the sky' is set in place with rapt authority. Elgar described it to Walford Davies as 'just a simple tune that's all'.

11

Dramatic music, partsongs and songs

Except for *The Spanish Lady*, all Elgar's dramatic works, whether incidental music for the theatre or wartime recitations for the concert room, were written at the request of others. The opera hoped for by Elgar's friends did not materialize. Of the stage subjects he tackled, those most attuned to his spirit seemed to be *Grania and Diarmid* and *Arthur*. *The Starlight Express* is a special case, the touching result of a link between Elgar's nostalgia for youthful innocence and an impossible farrago of a play. If nowhere is a masterpiece in sight, and many of these pages seem a waste of creative effort, yet among them are moments of Elgarian strength or tenderness that mean they can certainly not be written off.

Grania and Diarmid

Diarmuid and Grania, a play by George Moore and W. B. Yeats, was produced at the Gaiety Theatre, Dublin in October 1901. Yeats later remembered 'the life-wasting folly of it all' and saying to himself that 'an unperturbable goat waiting to take its place in some pastoral scene was the only sensible creature among us when I heard an actor say, "Look at that goat eating the property ivy"'. It was Moore who approached Elgar for music, particularly 'for the death of Diarmuid'. Then he wanted horn calls, and finally a song for the Druidess Laban to sing as she spun the thread of fate: 'Is it to[o] late to scribble a few notes under the words for the actress to sing at the wheel? Surely not, half an hour will do it.'

Elgar's Funeral March has notable grandeur, with modal harmonies chromatically enriched and a fine tune over a quietly treading bass, reaching a powerful climax till a gong stroke starts its slow decline. Moore was delighted: '*I have heard the music.* There is nothing in Wagner more beautiful and it is quite original – How you do hold on to that wailing phrase and what extraordy effects you get out of it.' Yeats, too, referred to its 'heroic melancholy'. Elgar later drew together the fragments of incidental music, with oscillating string chords, and solos for low flute and clarinet, into a connected whole. For the song 'There are seven that pull the thread', Elgar devised a simple, obsessive vocal line and recalled the string chords of the incidental music. Moore wanted Elgar to go on to an opera on the subject. His parting shot was a letter of May 1914: 'I can no longer believe, if I ever believed it, that you were wise in refraining from writing an opera.'

The Crown of India

Perhaps the Delhi Durbar of 1911 had provided mainly for 'the rather arrogant assertion of the British Raj'. The presence of George V as king–emperor and even more the interminable file of native princes ensured glamour, and it was the occasion to announce transfer of the capital from Calcutta to Delhi. Hence Lutyens's grand imperial architecture for a new city, and hence Elgar's *Crown of India*.

The first of two tableaux in Henry Hamilton's Imperial Masque for the Coliseum was entitled 'The Cities of Ind'. Elgar's festive overture opens with 'The sinful youth of Dan' (from April 1903); it ended with a D minor presentation of India's motif, then a more stately 'Sacred Measure'. The scene displayed a temple with view of the Taj Mahal at the back; on stage was an Indian crowd, including a 'native musician with a tom-tom' and a pair of 'snake charmers with pipes', all incorporated into Elgar's score. A double line of nautch-girls filed on, for whom Elgar provided a 3/8 piece of languorous movement in A minor, with oriental swirls no less authentic than those Strauss provided for Salome. When India greets the twelve great cities of her land, her speech is basis of a melodrama, with musical snatches mainly from what is to be the 'March of the Moghul Emperors', but also watery noises for the Ganges. Agra's song quotes from the 1905 piano piece *In Smyrna* and from the introduction's 'Sacred Measure'.

Trumpets proclaim the entry of Calcutta, attended by Commerce and Statecraft. Elgar has a 3/4 E minor movement, obsessive with triplets, for her. The same calls usher in Delhi, with Tradition and Romance as attendants. To stake her claim as capital Delhi summons the witness of the four greatest Moghul emperors. The D major march that grandly brings them on is Elgar's most considerable contribution to the masque. Calcutta invokes 'John Company' in a stately E flat minuet representing the Honourable East India Company. British worthies such as Clive, Warren Hastings, and Wellesley salute Calcutta. Delhi now summons the patron of England's chivalry:

> Thou that in Cappadocia's gloomy gorge
> Did'st beat the Dragon down – Appear, St. George!

The saint is firm and four-square in G major, with hints of the 'Crown of India' march to come. But St George is too chivalrous to select one of the cities for capital and leave her rival in distress. So King George must make the ultimate decision. The saint launches into a jingoistic song about 'The rule of England'. The exhortation to 'Lift aloft the Flag of England' recalls *The Banner of St George* in verses that are perhaps worse and music that is no better. In the last verse there is a momentary quote from 'Land of Hope and Glory'.

The scene for the second tableau symbolizes the Durbar, with distant view of Delhi. Warriors have a powerfully rhythmic G minor dance; then India enters with her cities and the Moghul emperors. At the announcement of George V, a 'Fanfaronade of trumpets' introduces the 'Crown of India' march, the core of which is another choral performance of 'Lift aloft the Flag of England'. India greets the king as 'Kaisar-i-Hind'; then Elgar gives Queen Mary a touch of diatonic freshness as India pays homage to one who brings the 'breath and beauty of some woodland way' to 'our swooning Indian heats'. After the homage of the native princes, the judgment is pronounced:

> The Majesty of Ind his will proclaims:
> Delhi to be his capital he names:
> And, of his Empire, further makes decree
> Calcutta shall the Premier City be.

It was a diplomatic master-stroke, eminently deserving the final 'God save the Emperor'. Whether it was to hasten or postpone the First World War must remain an open question.

Carillon

The German onslaught on Belgium in 1914 aroused much righteous anger in England as well as admiration for her king, Albert I. The Belgian poet Emile Cammaerts captured the mood of the moment in a series of poems later gathered into *Chants patriotiques et autres poèmes*. Elgar was eventually persuaded to treat three of them. Rosa Burley claimed to have influenced the manner of his setting: 'I ventured to suggest that he should not try to tie himself to the metre of the words, as he would have to do if the piece were treated as a song or a choral item, but that he should provide an illustrative prelude and entractes as background for a recitation of the poem. This he did with immense success.'

Elgar's MS copy of the *Carillon* poem, given him by Cammaerts, was headed 'Après Anvers' and dated October 1914. Lady Elgar's diary reinforces the point: 'Much distressed at fall of Antwerp'. The poem urged the Belgians to guard the pride of their defeats, to dance on the city ruins, bury their sons as the dying leaves scent autumn woods, bid the earth send dreams of future conquest as far as Berlin, and sing finally of the pride of charity. Elgar has the Belgians sing and dance to a sub-Polovtsian theme, more sedate than Borodin yet of similar cast. But beneath its triple metre is Elgar's four-note descending 'carillon', starting each time on a different beat of the bar. The shattered towers of Belgium continue an obstinate life with their bells in this score. The lengthy introduction is more rousing than subtle but the work has moments of Elgarian tenderness, notably at the burial sequence, and jubilant fanfares to anticipate the fall of Berlin. *Carillon* achieved a 'succès boeuf'.

Une voix dans le désert

The mood is here very different. Cammaerts's poem is liberal with place names, meaning little now but of great significance at the time. There is mention of the 'twinkling fires' along the Yser, to which the Belgians retreated after the fall of Antwerp; then 'a flight of crows along the railway line', an embankment held by the Belgians just west of Ostende; when retreat forced opening of the sluice gates, there was a 'low thatched cottage standing out of the floods alone'.

At the start of *Une voix* Elgar uses side drum and muted strings to conjure a miasmic air of desolation and dread. The music is fragmentary and atmospheric, the 'crows' are vividly described, as also the fires by the river, and the sound of 'boots along the muddy road'. It is scene painting intensely and economically realized, with the horror of war made palpable. A brief consoling phrase in the orchestra (Ex. 35) strikes the more warmly into the bleakness of the hostile background, and it is this phrase that plays an important part in the central song

Ex. 35

of the peasant girl, who has remained in the cottage with her father, waiting for spring when 'graves will flower'. A tap on the side drum, and the narrator briefly resumes the chill phrases of the opening. Elgar's recapitulation is laconic and stark, with just a hint of hope to finish. For many, this was the essence of war.

Le drapeau belge

The third Cammaerts poem was devoted to the national flag of Belgium, with its colours of black, yellow and red. Black was for 'the tears of mothers' in the first verse, for 'the veils of widows' in the second, and in the third 'the mourning ashes'. The other colours were similarly treated. The title page of the MS full score describes the work as 'Marche Militaire', which is apt enough for this least ambitious, and strophic, third recitation. But just where Cammaerts issues his imperious summons, 'To the glorious flag my children', Elgar embarks on a miniature 'trio' tune, for clarinet, oboe, then violin in delicate sequence. It is a moment of poetry the more moving for its gruesome context.

The Starlight Express

It was not only Lena Ashwell, producer of *The Starlight Express*, who felt the play would 'help people to bear the sorrows of the war'. Elgar's 1915 had included *Polonia*, *Une voix dans le désert*, and exhausting runs of *Carillon*. Having just conducted *Wand of Youth* suite no. 2 in Bournemouth, Elgar too was ready for escape. He took to the play at once. It not only banished the war; he could once again explore his own youth.

The play dealt with an English family, 'wumbled' because the grown-ups are without sympathy. The children organize a secret society in the belief that while they sleep, their spirits can wander the sky and gather the 'star-dust' of sympathy. Their main accomplice is cousin Henry, who brings as passengers on the Starlight Express a group of

Sprites, 'thought alive' from memories of his own childhood. By day 'they have only a slight air of strangeness and mystery to distinguish them' from types in the real world. By night they become 'super-tramp, super-sweep, etc., mysterious swift, singing creatures with their strange musical call not unlike a birdcall. They are blue-shadowy, or faintly luminous.' Algernon Blackwood's whimsical imagination did not translate easily into theatrical reality. It was both an inspiration to Elgar and a means of diverting him into a project that turned out pretentious and naive.

The Sprites needing music from Elgar were the Laugher and the Organ-Grinder. The latter introduced each Act, and his first song is a plea to enter the children's 'garden of sweet surprise!' Most of the song's music was newly composed, its movement symbolizing the turning of a barrel-organ handle; but Elgar also included some 'Little Bells' (*Wand of Youth* no. 2). As the work progressed, this theme represented for Elgar the sleep that changed the vision of the world and during which the starlight or star-dust of sympathy could be gathered. The Act 1 scene is the Campden family home in Switzerland, 'The Den' at Bourcelles, with cowbells heard in the distance. It was to be a 'muddled, comfortable-looking room, as untidy as it can be without looking absurd'. The father, an unsuccessful writer, is short of inspiration; the mother is harassed in the household; and all expectation is on the arrival of Cousin Henry the following evening.

The Organ-Grinder's song for Act 2 tells of the 'fairy that hides in the beautiful eyes' of children 'who treat her well'. The music was a waltz tune that Elgar told Blackwood dated from long before. The scene is now a pine forest at night with the star-studded sky above. Cousin Henry tells the children about the Pleiades, described by Blackwood in the programme as constantly hunted by Orion, 'for they have the softest light of all the Constellations and the finest Star-dust'. In the production these were seven young girls 'in clinging dresses of silver, on which play different lights giving the effect of an opal, or a pigeon's breast'. The Organ-Grinder then sings a curfew song to 'waft the fairy call' into the dreams of the sleeping children. Elgar now wrote what he called 'two minutes (tiptoe tune)' to 'mark the passage of time' till the children in their dream should stand before the Star Cave. The Starlight Express brings the Sprites, coming for the star-dust in the cave. Among them is the Laugher, the 'universal solvent of despair'. The rest of Act 2 concerns the 'unwumbling' of village inhabitants and the children's parents. Elgar calls on further numbers from *The Wand of Youth*, the 'Sun Dance', 'Fairy Pipers' and 'Moths and Butterflies'.

The Organ-Grinder's song for Act 3 speaks of tunes that bring token of 'a long-forgotten day'. The scene is once more the family home, and the father is close to inspiration as he muses that 'the source of our life is hid with Beauty very, very far away'. The final scene is again the forest at night, where sympathy has won through. The stars are now a single star pointing to the place 'where a child was born', and Elgar closes the work with a setting of *The First Nowell*.

The Sanguine Fan

Lena Ashwell was also connected with Elgar's next dramatic project. The *Sanguine Fan* ballet was to help fund her 'Concerts at the Front'. The scenario based on the fan design envisaged a woodland clearing with bright sunlit sky beyond. To the right was the era of Louis XV, to the left the world of Greek mythology, represented by Pan and Echo; Eros, god of love, linked the two sides of the fan. It has ingredients that might have attracted a Hofmannsthal and Richard Strauss. For Elgar it was another escape from the war, this time into territory he had not previously explored. France of the eighteenth century offered opportunity for pastiche; and the myth of Pan and Echo, involving unsuccessful wooing by the god and the transformation of the nymph into a disembodied voice, in fact made the scenario more dramatic than the fan implied.

The action centred on a shrine with a 'somewhat disfigured statue of Eros'. Pan has his syrinx (Elgar's clarinet) and Echo her flute. As Pan sinks down in sleep, a young man in courtly dress approaches the statue and waits expectantly. Two ladies make for the shrine and, after initial courtesies and the dropping of a fan within a fan, the young man makes off with one of them. Echo wakes Pan by throwing flowers in his face. Cross at first, he falls in love with her and makes music till he plays himself asleep. The human couple has quarrelled, and the young man curses Eros. A peal of thunder presages disaster. Echo now takes Pan's pipes and entices the young man away. They dance passionately and Pan wakens to wrathful jealousy. As the god of 'panic', he could inspire terror, and in his fear the young man flees to the shrine of Eros. The god of love now takes his revenge and strikes him down with a flash of lightning from his torch. Echo can only turn to Pan, who relents and carries her off to his woodland haunt. The mortal girl kneels by her stricken lover; Pan pauses a moment, looks back at them, and 'laughs sardonically'.

Elgar responded at once to a subject that seemed hardly Elgarian. Pan as inventor of the syrinx might not be a musician after his own heart; but at least he was a musician. Elgar wrote deliciously and with much fantasy for both Pan's clarinet and Echo's answering flute. Indeed

269

the wind solos throughout the work have a late Straussian poise and charm. The orchestra for the March 1917 Chelsea première consisted of Echo's flute on stage, single woodwind, two horns, harp, percussion and strings. Elgar had in fact scored the work more fully, doubtless hoping for more ambitious productions. A slow minuet evokes the eighteenth century, but there is much intensity in the enactment of Pan's passion, and the drama is excitingly maintained. The framework was artificial, but Elgar gave of his best to the ballet, distinguishing nicely between the human victims and the gods who do not care. He found sadness in both worlds. The surface filigree gave the score elegance and period charm; but it was deeply felt, and the subject proved not altogether escapist.

The Fringes of the Fleet

The four Kipling poems that made up *The Fringes of the Fleet* as originally performed are mostly energetic and breezy. Elgar had long owned a copy of the *Barrack Room Ballads* and early criticism had often linked his name with Kipling's. Elgar's setting turned out a very successful piece of war work, as popular in its way as *Carillon*. The suggestion for the music came from Lord Charles Beresford, friend and admirer from the days of the 1905 Mediterranean cruise, and Elgar found tunes catchy enough to match the robust jauntiness of Kipling. The verse had little distinction; nor has the music, except in the case of the third song, 'Submarines'. The idea of these strange craft in the depths of the sea, 'In the belly of Death', captured Elgar's imagination, and he produced sombre, slow-moving music to match the throb of engines working dangerously and secretly on their sinister mission. He devised a special orchestral effect, the rubbing together of two sand-paper blocks to depict the muffled swish of the water as the submarine's hull passed through. By the end of June 1917 Elgar had added a fifth song, a glee-type setting of Gilbert Parker's 'Inside the Bar' for the four baritones unaccompanied. The poem pursued its cheerful way till the throwaway threat of the last two lines:

> And God help the lubber, I say,
> What stole the sailor man's bride.

Elgar deftly twisted his nonchalant encore piece to end in wry ambiguity. With these songs of sailors dressed for the sea but sitting at their ease outside an English pub, Elgar captured the national mood. It was indeed his last popular triumph.

Arthur

Laurence Binyon's *Arthur: a Tragedy* touched much of the essential Elgar. The play was based on Malory's *Morte d'Arthur*. Chivalry was as instinctive to Malory as it had been to Froissart, and in Binyon's play she seemed again to lift 'her lance on high'. Elgar felt the epic heroism of the tale, and certain details must have struck him at once, as when Elaine asks Launcelot about his wounds and he replies:

> By the black winter waves
> Under Tintagel's towers, that blow was dealt.

The play was to be performed at the Old Vic Theatre in March 1923, and Robert Atkins the producer requested from Elgar an overture and music between each of the nine scenes to introduce the main character in the next section. The Old Vic orchestra was small, comprising flute, clarinet, cornet (or trumpet), two first violins, one second, viola, double bass and piano. Elgar supplemented the orchestra for the first night at his own expense, and also supplied more music than initially required. He added considerable stretches of 'melodrama', and an exeunt piece for Launcelot's forces in the battle of Scene VII.

Elgar begins his overture with chords of deep foreboding, and follows them with a 'Windflowerish' motif for Elaine, the young girl doomed to die for love of Launcelot. But the main B flat theme denotes 'Chivalry', proud in its prancing step and obstinate in rhythm (Ex. 36).

Ex. 36

In Scene II Arthur is concerned with treachery at court, and Elgar makes a powerful and painful climax from 'Chivalry' before restating it *nobilmente* and presenting it in augmentation as a sombre 'Arthur' theme in G minor. Scene III is introduced by chords that descend in sequence to further development of the 'Elaine' music. The most extended prelude is that to Scene IV, which takes place at Westminster. A banquet is held, at which Queen Guenevere's honour is impugned by the king's nephew Mordred. A flamboyant theme for 'King Arthur's fellowship' launches the music in D major, and leads to a fine symphonic development for Guenevere's motif. There follows the A minor 'Banquet' music that Elgar was to consider later for both his opera and the Third Symphony. With the skill of long experience Elgar modifies his motifs in accordance with the psychological twists of the drama. After the banquet has broken up in confusion, a barge carrying the dead Elaine appears, and her music rounds off the scene.

Elgar's introduction to Scene V, in the queen's tower at night, is on muted strings beneath a sad cantilena for solo violin. Guenevere's thoughts are doom-laden and concentrated into a triplet motif of 'Fear'. This is the scene of the play's catastrophe, in which Launcelot is surprised in the queen's company and slays all the conspirators but Mordred. Scene VI in the king's tower follows without entr'acte, but Scene VII has an extended battle introduction with chromatic motif on marcato minims. This is a lengthy piece, developing 'Chivalry' into a hectic fanfare, that combines with 'Elaine' music and also Guenevere's 'Fear' motif. It makes a contrapuntal web of some complexity. There are contrasting trumpet calls for Launcelot's army and Arthur's, and Elgar directs the singing of 'Ecce sacerdos magnus' to its traditional chant for the arrival of the *episcopus ex machina*. By Scene VIII Guenevere is in the convent at Amesbury, for which Elgar devised a slow 'Gregorian' motif, repetitive, and confined within the interval of a fourth. Arthur's visit to the queen, his departure and the report of his death in Scene IX (introduced again by the 'Gregorian' theme) evoke the G minor augmentation of 'Chivalry' that had always stood for Arthur and the heavy burden of kingship. The foreboding of Elgar's opening was justified, and he brings down the final curtain with the same sad series of chords.

Beau Brummell

Elgar and Beau Brummell are odd bedfellows indeed. Yet there had always been something of the dandy about Elgar, and the ruinous old age of the sometime royal favourite, withering towards his end in the early days of Queen Victoria, struck some chord in the disillusioned composer. There was nothing of the rowdy spendthrift in Bertram Matthews's play, and Elgar's music is elegant, courtly, and 'mainly sad'. Only the Act 1 Minuet was published, a piece of considerable charm, rising to an eloquent climax and dying away with much regret. A motif for Brummell himself, portly on the cello, alternates bars of 4/4 and 3/4. A Lento piece for muted strings has graceful melodic lines and was later to be subsumed into *The Spanish Lady*. The same applied to the Act 4 Introduction, a *mesto* movement expressing extended sorrow for times past.

The Spanish Lady

The subject of Elgar's final choice for an opera seems equally unlikely. Ben Jonson's *The Devil is an Ass* satirizes the foibles of London society with wit and some bitterness. There is nothing here of the heroism and idealism that Elgar claimed to have been seeking in a libretto. Perhaps a hankering for the 'Rabelais' ballet still lingered. With the eventual help of Barry Jackson, a complete libretto for *The Spanish Lady* was produced. Elgar had ranged through the works of Jonson, taking lyrics from here and there to soften the hard-edged prose of his chosen play. Other writers were eagerly scanned for suitable passages, so that the American John Hay, Alfred Noyes of *The Pageant of Empire*, and Dora Wilcox as printed in *The Oxford Book of Australasian Verse* were also raided. Indeed, if any justification were needed for Elgar's election to the Literary Society, the libretto of *The Spanish Lady* produces it.

On a sheet of manuscript paper Elgar compared the singing range of his main characters with those of Puccini's *Tosca*. He had ambitious ideas for the work, telling Barry Jackson it was 'going to be a Grand Opera, and it is going to be very grand, and it is going to out-Meistersinger the Meistersinger'. Musically Elgar was as eclectic as with the libretto. The only number partially scored is a 'Bolero' that began life in 1879 as a 'Polonaise' for violin and piano dedicated to the Powick asylum pianist. As well as going back to his earliest sketchbooks, Elgar gathered into the *Spanish Lady* folder themes considered for 'Callicles', the piano concerto, and a projected organ sonata. He made use too of some *Arthur* music, considering the Guenevere theme as an ingredient in the overture and for Act 2 scene ii. Arthur's fanfare on the battle field was appropriated for Trains, 'a small cheeky youth', and its hectic version from the Scene VII introduction as a 'Blast' for the debauched Everill. Motifs from *Beau Brummell* were also to be incorporated. There was much new music too, the last dated example being a march idea of 16 September 1933.

Less than half the proposed numbers have any indication of voice part, but two songs, 'Still to be Neat' and 'Modest and Fair', both to words from Jonson's *Epicoene*, were sufficiently complete for publication after Elgar's death. Elgar worked hardest at an Act 1 duet for the 'projector' Meercraft and his cousin Everill, an extended piece copied many times. Thematic ideas for it came from the Simon Magus scene considered in 1906 for *The Kingdom*. Another duet, for Manly and Lady Tailbush, has links with a sketch for *The Last Judgement*. Of the more than thirty instrumental pieces Elgar assembled for the opera, few were assigned a precise place within the two Acts. Much of the music has vivacity and charm, but W. H. Reed, who played the

273

pieces with Elgar and heard him discuss them, remained mystified: 'if I am ever asked what it was all about, I shall have to confess that I have not the faintest idea'.

Partsongs

Elgar's finest music is not usually to be sought among his smaller works, but the partsongs are a notable exception. They provide an immediate refutation of the early view that he did not write well for voices; it is only very rarely that he miscalculates an effect. Whereas in the songs he tended to avoid the greatest poetry, here he was prepared to set Henry Vaughan, Byron, Shelley and Tennyson, to say nothing of his own skill in the words he wrote for *Owls*. The result is a body of music that ranks high in Elgar's output, and an occasional partsong that can be numbered among his best works.

O Happy Eyes, to words Alice Roberts had written in 1888, was composed in November 1889, while the Elgars were at Oaklands. The third stanza, with delicately wrought sequences, has a fine tenor part, beautifully illustrating 'And lightly kiss' and going on to hold a legato line against staccato chords in the other voices. The end is long-drawn-out in a sweet final sigh of content. *My Love Dwelt in a Northern Land* was conceived at the same time. Andrew Lang consented to the use of his poem with such a 'very bad grace' that Alice Elgar devised alternative words lest final permission failed to come. In the third stanza tenors and basses are *divisi*, and over a steady pulse of two quavers and two crotchets, sopranos and first tenor give a chill description of the moon 'white o'er wood and lawn'. The words are subtly deployed so that they and the music repeat at different points. The last stanza repeats the opening of the first two, but also incorporates the essence of the third at 'The grass above my love is green'.

The *Spanish Serenade* op. 23 dates from May and June 1892. The first version was for accompaniment of two violins and piano; Elgar scored it on 12 June for 'muted strings, tambourine & all sorts of games!', as he told Charles Buck. The text was from Act 1 scene iii of Longfellow's play *The Spanish Student*, and on his MS full score Elgar quoted the stage direction: '(Scene. A street in Madrid. Enter CHISPA followed by musicians with a bagpipe, guitars & other instruments.)' The student Victorian has organized the musicians to serenade Preciosa, a gypsy. His servant Chispa considers the singers too many: 'Do you think we are going to sing mass in the cathedral of Córdova?' Despite the refrain, 'my lady sleeps!', Preciosa is wide awake on the balcony. The A minor introduction has some characteristically Brahmsian rests and a 'Spanish' rhythm Elgar was planning to use again in the Third

Symphony. The monotone of the voices' start gradually develops into the warm harmonies of the sensuous refrain: 'She sleeps.' Elgar designed his partsong in a miniature sonata form, with repeated exposition, and now in the third stanza a development with fragmented accompaniment, generous sequences, a thwarted cadence into C sharp minor, and a long held note on Elgar's beloved 'Dreams'. The last verse recapitulation closes into an A major coda that is constantly tugged towards the minor. Elgar wrote about it to Jaeger in August 1904: 'if young England could turn out as *neat* a piece of work as that – there wd. be some hope for it!'

The two op. 26 partsongs, *The Snow* and *Fly, Singing Bird*, both used words of his wife's. They were written towards the end of 1894 for two violins and piano, then orchestrated at Alassio in December 1903. Again Brahms is suggested by the E minor figuration at the start of *The Snow*. Moves towards a major key court danger, and there is no avoiding it when Elgar accelerates towards a maestoso injunction that the soul should not sow its 'gifts to fade like snow'. Neither words nor music have quite deserved such an access of emotion. The major section of the third stanza almost saves the situation by neatly transforming the introductory violin figure in the closing bars. *Fly, Singing Bird* has an exuberant 6/8 movement until the slower sequences of 'Tell my love that I wait'. This time the second and third verses are run together with compositional cunning, and inconsequential pizzicato on the strings prepares the punctual end.

Elgar closed the century with his 'Partrigal' of February 1899 to celebrate Queen Victoria's eightieth birthday. *To her Beneath whose Steadfast Star* was to be included in a book of *Choral Songs by Various Writers and Composers*. Elgar's writer was Frederick Myers, who in 1881 had described his encounter with George Eliot on the subjects of God, immortality and duty. She had declared 'how inconceivable was the *first*, how unbelievable the *second*, and yet how peremptory and absolute the *third*'. The following year Myers became a founder member of the Society for Psychical Research. This explains his odd lines about the future reunion of the queen and Prince Albert:

> Till soul with soul the Wife hath found
> Her mystic-wedded home.

Elgar begins beautifully, but soon the English force far 'Their worldingathering way'. Imperial sentiments were hardly manageable on this scale. Whatever Myers envisaged by his 'mystic-wedded home', the words brought the tender best out of Elgar. But the 'blue tide's earthengirdling wave' defeated him, and he produced some of the most rudderless bars of his career.

There were few partsongs in the oratorio years. *Weary Wind of the West* was a test-piece for Morecambe from November 1902. The four verses by Thomas Brown, a Manx poet, were of no great quality. They presented Elgar with many a pathetic fallacy but also some good opportunities for musical illustration. The 'distance dim' is repeated tellingly, and the word 'sobbing' is expressively set. If the calm of the first two verses is finely caught, Elgar enjoys equally the onset of the wind as it comes 'with a rush to the shore'. There is a moment of real technical difficulty, when the sopranos hold a top G *ppp* and *diminuendo*, supported by only quiet threads of sound below.

The *Greek Anthology* partsongs of op. 45 make up only one of three sets Elgar had in mind on texts from the ancient epigrams. The five male-voice songs he completed all have anonymous verses, except *Feasting I Watch* by Marcus Argentarius. Four are so short atmosphere has to be established at once. *Yes, Cast me from Heights of the Mountains* begins impetuously, ranging from the *ff* mountain tops to the *pp* ocean depths. Mysterious harmonies illustrate the man broken by Eros, and the lightnings of Zeus return to the opening music. *Whether I Find thee* deals with the endurance of love, whether the woman's hair is fair, dark, or eventually grey. Elgar has only two tiny motifs for the six lines. The first settles on 'fair', expands upwards for 'raven', and still further for 'Love'. A second deals with the passage of time in stepwise ascent; and the 'Love' form of the first turns the hair grey. It is neat and psychologically apt. *After Many a Dusty Mile* suggests distance covered by contrasting the ascending upper voices with an ostinato bass descent. As the traveller rests, a wind passes through Elgarian pine trees. The middle section has the rhythmic chirp of grasshoppers, first from tenors, then basses. At the end we learn it was the voice of Pan, benign in the grasshopper's rhythm, which counselled the cool rest. This finest of the songs ends *ppp*. The slightest is *It's oh! to be a Wild Wind*. The lover wishes to be a wind caressing his lady or a rose at her breast. Success comes in a languid and sequential three-bar phrase. Garnett's translation of *Feasting I Watch* is more pompous than the deft original, but Elgar enjoys the 'constellations' pageantry', and expands to some bars of imitation as the singer wreathes his hair and warbles to the harp. The grandiloquent end hardly clarifies the meaning of the poem, but nor did Garnett.

The *Evening Scene* of August 1905 was a complete contrast. It reminded Jaeger of Schubert's *Der Leiermann*. It suggested to him 'a *wide expanse* of country for the "Scene", such as fills the soul with a sweet melancholy'. Coventry Patmore's words from *The River*, with only a line and a half to regret in the three stanzas, were such as to rouse the countryman in Elgar. The slow, falling phrases in D minor over drone pedals drowsily evoke 'curfew-time', its gnats, dismal owl and voiceless bat. The second stanza is much in two parts and starkly moving octaves, as the 'river seems to think'. The 'distant, dream-like sound' of the flies' 'weary tune' in the last stanza takes the music into a rapt remoteness as it dies almost to nothing. The far baying of 'an old guard-hound', momentarily on a passing dissonance, magically closes the scene.

Elgar wrote *Love* on his fiftieth birthday and dedicated it to Lady Elgar. The F major setting of Maquarie's poem is simple, deceptively so, since the first two phrases are of three bars and five. 'Thus I looked to heav'n again', the start of the third verse, moves to the brightness of A major; but it is at the end, with the basses' fourfold repetition of 'Cease to be', and the tenors' tracing of an expressive melisma on 'cease', that Elgar's craftsmanship is most in evidence. He described the partsong to Littleton as 'unimportant but perhaps worth printing'. It came out as op. 18 no. 2, a companion to Alice Elgar's *O Happy Eyes*.

The Elgars' stay in Rome from November 1907 produced a wondrous harvest of partsongs. The first was to words by T. T. Lynch sent by F. G. Edwards, who wanted a supplement for the January *Musical Times*. Elgar obliged, sending the strophic music on 2 December: 'Here's the little setting of those simple words – homely but "*felt*".' The three stanzas of *How Calmly the Evening* each had an emotional centre for Elgar. In the first it was the descent of evening 'as still as a prayer', where the words are repeated and extended. The second spoke of man in contemplation of his worth 'and its brevity feeling'; the last was a key word for Elgar to linger over. In the final stanza it is 'rest' that detains the music for repetition before sinking to its quiet end.

In *A Christmas Greeting* Lady Elgar contrasted Italian vines with English apples, the dark Tiber feeling 'the weight of ancient crime' with the Wye flowing 'in mist and silv'ring rime', the sun of the south with northern snow. Elgar set it for the boys of Hereford Cathedral, with two violins and piano. The instruments again make a Brahmsian start with a touch of added aspiration. The boys begin afresh in a lilting 6/8 with scintillating accompaniment, and a rising violin scale announces Lady Elgar's Christmas message: 'Friends, in storm or calm'. At the end of the second stanza Elgar modulates to accommodate the pifferari who 'wander far' and have brought with them the Pastoral Symphony from *Messiah*, which haunts the third verse. A pleasant brief postlude rounds the fourth stanza.

On Christmas Day itself Elgar put his signature to a very different work, *The Reveille* for male voices in D minor. It was a magnificent achievement. The words, by the sometime American consul in Glasgow,

Bret Harte, pitted the summons of 'the quick alarming drum' against the man communing with himself. The war 'tramp of thousands' urged on by the drum dominates the first stanza. Insistent rhythm is everything, and the crisp virtuosity of the writing gives the impression of a mighty host on the move towards the stanza's abrupt end. The doubts of conscience in the next three verses are finely expressed, but the relentless drum dissonantly intervenes with a 'Come!', quieter than conscience or with shrill persistence. In the last stanza Elgar incorporates words from the first to reinforce the mighty summons, 'My chosen people, come!'; but his moment of maximum power is the thrice repeated 'throbbing' to describe 'the great heart of the nation' in its agony of decision. The final acceptance is matter-of-fact and muted. When writing to Littleton on 27 December, Elgar hoped the setting was not too 'disastrously complicated & harsh'.

The partsongs continued in January 1908 with the four published as op. 53. The first was to sensuous words by the young Tennyson from *The Lotos-Eaters*. The poetry is slow-moving, sultry and dense with heavy sounds; Elgar's setting admirably captures their atmosphere. *There is Sweet Music* is an eight-part work, with all voices divided. To Ivor Atkins he explained that the work was 'in two keys at once!' The female voices were in four flats, the men in one sharp. He was pleased with the result: 'It will sound very remote & will please village choirs'. There was much antiphonal writing so that moments of bitter-sweet dissonance were limited. Elgar's other device was to notate enharmonically, so that the voices might coincide aurally however distinct they seemed visually. It was none the less a ravishing *tour de force*. McNaught thought that crotchet = 44 was too slow; but it is just right for Elgar's hallucinatory music. Syncopations further dislocate the pulse, and time signatures changing from the basic four crotchets to two, five, ten, and back. The word-distribution is masterly. The opening 'male' bars cover six of the eight lines making up the 'exposition'. Soporific repetitions of the lines including the word 'music' increasingly hypnotize; 'Than tir'd eyelids upon tir'd eyes' settles to an arching phrase for all the men's parts. The 'development' covers the other five lines in music that faintly echoes a passage in the finale of Schubert's String Quintet. The held C flat in the women's voices as music 'brings sweet sleep down from the blissful skies' allows the men to begin their G major 'recapitulation', much foreshortened. The alternating A flat and G chords of the last bars on the word 'sleep' are Elgar's Neapolitan cadence in its most telling yet quietest form.

The next partsong, *Deep in my Soul*, set the first two stanzas of Medora's song from Byron's *The Corsair*. As Conrad, her pirate lover, remarks: 'sure thy song is sad –'. The piece is no less searching than the last, and again Elgar has produced a tripartite slow movement, tonally perhaps even more elusive. The last section repeats the first stanza and its music, but by no means exactly. The start is in E flat, but a threefold repetition of 'Deep in my soul' modulates so that the climax 'Save when to this my heart responsive swells' has reached A major, at furthest remove from E flat. By swift steps Elgar resumes the opening phrase, on the basses, now scanned as in A flat minor. The tonal migrations are repeated so that the first section ends on a bare D sharp to the words 'silence as before'. The second stanza, 'There in its centre' interprets D sharp as E flat and launches on phrases yet more sombre and broken. Melody struggles to shape itself at 'Which not the darkness of Despair can damp', but largely in vain. The final section parses the opening phrase differently again, in A flat major. Elgar takes the climax this time in B major. The basses keep their last note as B sharp, while the rest of the voices fade 'into silence as before' on an E flat chord. Elgar's daring is here the equal of his artistry.

The third partsong, dedicated to W. G. McNaught, took words from Shelley's *Ode to the West Wind*. 'This poem', wrote Shelley, 'was conceived and chiefly written in a wood that skirts the Arno, near Florence, and on a day when that tempestuous wind, whose temperature is at once mild and animating, was collecting the vapours which pour down the autumnal rains.' Elgar set the fifth and final section, adding Shelley's exordium, 'O wild West Wind!' Again in E flat, this is the only Elgar partsong to begin 'Nobilmente,' and the only one in op. 53 that occasionally yearns for an orchestra. The soaring phrases for 'The tumult of the mighty harmonies' almost break the medium. Shelley's three-line stanzas are split with admirable variety, and accents differently placed. Elgar avails himself of this freedom, ending his first section in A flat minor halfway through the second line of the second stanza, and having given touching, hushed expression to 'a deep autumnal tone'. Elgar begins to recapitulate at the start of the fourth verse, 'Scatter, as from an unextinguished hearth', yet not from the actual opening of the piece. The original material is subtly disguised, with powerful augmentation at 'The trumpet of a prophecy'. A coda plays with Shelley's last line, 'If Winter comes, can Spring be far behind?', further invoking the wind and striding to a grand conclusion.

Most remarkable of the set is *Owls*, dedicated 'To my friend Pietro d'Alba', Carice's white rabbit. The words are by Elgar himself; he subtitled the poem 'An Epitaph'. 'What is that? Nothing' begins the first two of the three stanzas, and nihilistic terror haunts the whole poem. In the first verse it is the falling leaves that rustle and end 'Dead at the foot of the tree'; in the second it is 'A wild thing hurt in the night'; in the third there is a 'marching slow of unseen feet' until the bier stands 'at the foot of the tree'. Elgar's setting is in a shifting C minor. The falling semitones of 'Nothing' dominate much of the broken music (Ex. 37). The second stanza is raised a semitone to C sharp minor but continues sombre as before. The beginning of the last substitutes a *molto espressivo* 'Ah!' for 'Nothing'; the ensuing material is presented in augmentation as the most agonized of all Elgar's marches. The end, *mesto*, the last 'Nothing', is as inconclusive as the first. When Jaeger asked about the piece, Elgar wrote on 26 April 1908: 'As to "Owls" – it is only a fantasy & means nothing. It is in wood at night evidently & the recurring "*Nothing*" is only an *owlish* sound.'

Ex. 37

Elgar's last Italian partsong, and perhaps the greatest, was written at Careggi in May 1909. *Go, Song of Mine* has words from a canzone by Guido Cavalcanti, 'first friend' of Dante, but whose father is among the *Inferno* heretics. The poem was translated by Dante Gabriel Rossetti as 'A Dispute with Death'. The last words of Death are 'Let pass thy soul in peace'. The pleadings finished, the soul asks God that it may 'weep within thy will a certain space'. Elgar set the final words of the poem, bidding man absorb its lesson. The work opens in B minor with a solemn chanting of the first line, rising only a semitone on the word 'go'; the second line heads back whence the song began, to a held F sharp. The tenors make a new start with the rising eloquence of 'Say how his life began', and the music builds to an intense climax. The work glows with increasing radiance as it mounts in aspiration with the 'unerring spirit of grief' until the searing beauty of the sequence at 'His soul, being purified'. Perhaps Elgar intended a hint of the *Tristan* 'Liebestod' at this point, perhaps not; the phrase is unforgettable in Elgarian terms, with steady descent of inner chromatics and diatonic bass against a melodic line that is as much common currency as Wagnerian. The end is exquisitely judged, with reference again to the opening and a whispered B major chord for the final 'Go'. A. H. Littleton received the dedication.

A request from Sir Walter Parratt for music to commemorate the death of Queen Victoria produced *They are at Rest*. Words by Cardinal Newman were acceptable for the occasion, and the first performance was at the Frogmore royal mausoleum on 22 January 1910. The poem is one of Newman's happiest and, as so often with him, asks for music to illustrate 'that hymn which Seraphs chant above'. The setting is mostly quiet, with twofold repetition of 'They are at rest' to start and end the piece. The two stanzas are managed strophically, with a tender hovering near the atmosphere of *Go, Song of Mine* when Newman conjures the 'mountain grots of Eden' and its equivalent in the second stanza. The 'fourfold river' of paradise inspires Elgar as movingly as any of his local streams 'as it murmurs by'. The long-drawn cadence is Elgar's final tribute to a sovereign he had celebrated more noisily in years gone by.

January 1914 matched the partsong productivity of 1907 in Rome. Elgar wrote two pieces to words by Henry Vaughan and three to translations from the Russian. The Vaughan verses came from his *Silex Scintillans or Sacred Poems* of 1650. Elgar set only the last of Vaughan's three stanzas in *The Shower*, op. 71 no. 1. The first word 'Cloud' is Elgar's own, a substitute for Vaughan's 'Yet', but justly chosen. There are only six lines in the E flat setting, dedicated to Frances Smart of Malvern. The first section uses three of them, with block chords and modulation to F minor. The second section repeats words and music except for the pattering inner parts descriptive of the rain and adjustments that send the arching phrase of the third bar a tone higher than before. The last section is the longest, involving repetition of all the words, and takes the quavers higher still at 'God would give a sunshine after rain'. Elgar lingers long over the last four words, allowing tenors as well as sopranos a brief glimpse of the sun in a melting cadence.

Elgar called the second Vaughan partsong *The Fountain*; it was published as op. 71 no. 2 and dedicated to W. Mann Dyson of Worcester. Again he used only part of a poem, a stanza and a half from the middle of *Regeneration*. Elgar's setting is in D, but sidesteps briefly to B flat at 'Chequer'd with snowy fleece' and eventually reaches a chord of F sharp. In this key Elgar expounds the central antithesis of his excerpt: 'Thus fed my eyes'; and Vaughan continues 'But all the Eare lay hush'. Elgar set instead 'all the earth' and ends his first section on a long held F sharp. The second deals with the 'little fountain' and the 'music of her tears', described in a rising scale figure moving from voice to voice. It wanders through various keys back to D, where 'the music of her tears' adopts the rhythm and eventually the notes of the beginning. The end is *ppp*, marked in Elgar's sketch 'murmurando'.

Elgar dedicated his op. 72 *Death on the Hills* to Frances Colvin, and described it to the Windflower as 'one of the biggest things I have done'. The words were by Rosa Newmarch translated from the Russian of Apollon Maykov. In the first D minor motif, describing 'dusky shadows' on the hill slopes, descending fourths predominate. A rising semitone asks the question whether it is the wind or rain that lashes them; the fourths answer that it is 'Death who rides across the hills'. The two motifs offset the rhythmic chanting as the cortège of the old, with the young riding in front and babes on Death's saddle, are sombrely described. As the female voices urge with gathering speed the plea of young and old, Elgar abandons D minor and instructs the upper voices (using only the lighter tenors) to sing 'with a thin and somewhat veiled tone'. The victims want the village road, so that the old may get water, the young play, and the little children gather flowers. After moving uneasily between B minor and G in his hollow prayer, Elgar settles to obsessive repetition of the words in A minor. They are to be sung with 'firm, sobbing accents, and great expression'. Death uses his heavy motif on the bass line to avoid the village road lest 'wife might see her husband' and 'mother see her son'. The fateful opposition gradually slows to the exhaustion of the last A minor chord. The scene is powerfully imagined. In December 1921 Elgar wrote to Atkins about it: 'It is, I declare, courageous of you to frighten your people into singing "Death on the Hills" – I *should* like to hear it & I know you wd get every bit of drama out of it – my ears have never quivered to it yet.'

Love's Tempest (op. 73 no. 1) is also to Maykov–Newmarch words and dedicated to Sanford Terry. The poem is less gripping than the last, and so is the setting. Elgar's bare fourths and fifths finely suggest the silence of the 'sapphire ocean'. Initially in E flat, the passage is repeated even quieter a semitone higher. So far there is only magic; but in the 'roaring, seething billows' of a C minor tempest Elgar's fierce accents and virtuoso surging bass demand too much of the singers. Himself unsure, Elgar asked McNaught whether he should not repeat the word 'roaring': 'will it give them more chance to breathe & roar more lustily?' No change was made. The second stanza describes a heart quiet till 'your image' arose, causing tumult 'Wilder than the storm at sea'. This time the C minor 'tumult' rises to a *grandioso* climax that exceeds the merits of both words and music.

The last of the Newmarch translations was *Serenade*, op. 73 no. 2, the original words by Nikolai Vilenkin (pseudonym 'Minsky'). Elgar's obsession with dreams takes a new twist: now they are 'all too brief' and once broken 'come not again'. A four-bar phrase in G minor, staccato and fragmented, acts as refrain throughout. Sopranos carry the burden of the two verses, as dark clouds sweep the sky and the prisoner 'dreams of freedom's rescuing'. The folly of scattering glad dreams that 'haunt your slumbers deep' is suggested by a strain of mounting intensity in E flat minor. The piece ends with a quiet repetition of the refrain; Elgar dedicated it to Percy Hull.

Elgar knew the worth of these five partsongs, and Novello had to acquiesce in his valuation. Robin Legge in the *Daily Telegraph* of 14 March 1914 had no doubts either: 'In the matter of sheer originality and individuality Elgar has never reached a higher mark; that itself is remarkable considering the smallness of the form'. It was now to be almost ten years before Elgar returned to the partsong. The war had intervened and the death of Lady Elgar. Moreover, Novello estimated Elgar quite differently in the summer of 1923.

None the less, Elgar's four last partsongs are also on a very high level. The origin of the words set in *The Wanderer* was an anonymous poem published in *Wit and Drollery* of 1661. Elgar adapted the version appearing under the title 'Tom O'Bedlam's Song' in volume 2 of Isaac D'Israeli's *Curiosities of Literature* (with 'Memoir' dated 1848 by Benjamin Disraeli), and added his own first stanza. The verses move sadly between sanity and madness, and there is terrifying beauty in Elgar's male-voice setting. The quiet first stanza in A minor sets the tone, and the rest add variations to it. 'The moon's my constant mistress' begins the third verse, and this is more tender still. The next verse 'With a heart of furious fancies' signals an outburst of energy that reaches an agony of intensity at 'To the wilderness I wander'. At the end poor Tom is summoned to tourney with 'a knight of ghosts and shadows' way beyond 'the wide world's end'. Elgar can only sympathize at the thrice repeated 'Methinks it is no journey'.

Despite reluctance at Novello, Elgar next produced *Zut! Zut! Zut!* to his own words under the pseudonym Richard Mardon. This was a march for men, much of it spectral, which Elgar also headed 'Remembrance'. It was his last tribute to those he had celebrated in 'For the Fallen'. The steady tread bursts into feverish energy at 'How we worked and drilled together' in the first stanza, and at 'How fiercely they fought for freedom'. But there was no triumph in this D minor piece, and the march plodded doggedly away to silence. Novello was even less impressed, but finally gave Elgar half what he originally asked for the two partsongs.

A Song of Union, one of Elgar's pieces for the 1924 *Pageant of Empire*, was written originally for SATB. It is a march in Elgar's boldest manner, with swaggering melodic line above an imperiously descending bass. It hymns the 'love that linked our realms in one', a sentiment to be encompassed only by a good dose of panache. Elgar returned to a restless and elusive E flat for the first of his 1925 partsongs. He chose verses from *A Life-drama* by the Glaswegian poet, Alexander Smith. It described the death of a 'grim old king'. Elgar's sombre music for male voices bounds from key to key as the royal 'blood leapt madly when the trumpets brayed'. Rhythms, too, closely follow the words. Elgar becomes lyrically involved when describing the white steed that 'seemed to mourn with its drooping head'. The music stirs to its initial energy as the dying monarch hears 'his old victorious banners flap the winds'. A stark unison announces the king's readiness to join the dead: 'I come'. A burst of imitative counterpoint accompanies the soul as it 'fled and shrieked through all the other world', and the agony is twisted to its highest point as the herald proclaims to the dead, 'My master comes!' Atkins was right to describe *The Herald* as 'one of the most thrilling things you have done'.

In his setting of Walter de la Mare's *The Prince of Sleep*, also 1925 but for mixed voices, Elgar begins with a quiet whisper of searching harmonies. The last words of the first stanza, 'in a lonely place' conjure music of brooding sensitivity. The next two verses, now in 3/4, describing the prince's garb as 'grey of lavender' and his eyes shining 'faint in their own flame' are run together in music of gentle parallel movement. In the fourth stanza Elgar reserves a moment of magical inspiration for the 'muffled calls' of the golden flocks as they graze at evening. The last verse resumes the mood of the opening, and to conclude Elgar repeats the whole of the first verse so that he ends once more in his 'lonely place', to which for inner strength he often had recourse.

Unison and children's songs

The *Marching Song* to words by Captain de Courcy Stretton was a special request from Alfred Littleton towards the end of 1907. It came into its own seven years later at the outbreak of war under the title *Follow the Colours*, when it was issued as a unison song with optional male chorus. It is in Elgar's sturdiest manner, with a tune that is effective but not obvious: it belongs, though, to other days. *The Birthright*, a unison song for boys with parts for bugles and drums, was written just before the First World War. Elgar headed his sketch for it 'Scouts', which was apt enough. It is a brisk little march of no great individuality. Horatio Parker, professor of music at Yale, requested three pieces for a series he edited. Elgar produced during the war *The Brook* for two-part choir, *The Merry-go-round* for unison children's choir, and *The Windlass Song*, a cheerful and effective piece for unaccompanied mixed voices, with enough sequence to stick in the memory. A last wartime effort was *Big Steamers* to words by Kipling. Elgar outlined his aim: 'The occasion seemed to call for something exceptionally simple and direct, and I have endeavoured to bring the little piece within the comprehension of very small people indeed'. The unison song is simple enough but by no means trite, and has some sensitive harmonic touches: by 1918 Elgar was bored with brashness.

In the fallow year of 1922 Elgar was stirred to begin two songs with chorus on Worcestershire subjects, both to words of Ethel Anderson. *The Ballad of Brave Hector* was about 'a restive hound' who 'chased the bunnies round & round'. Elgar made two incomplete drafts of the song. Nor did he finish *The Worcestershire Squire*, described by the author as 'a gallop, with four jumps and the gasp a crowd gives when a man's down'. A *jeu d'esprit* of 1924, *The Bull (in May Week)*, was a setting of words by Lord Frederick Hamilton in praise of the Cambridge hostelry on Trinity Street. Elgar's D major setting for male voice, optional chorus and piano, is sprightly and properly rumbustious. From the same year, *The Heart of Canada*, one of the *Pageant of Empire* songs, has a unison refrain to verses contrasting Britain and the youthful Dominion: 'Thou art old and she is young'. Elgar's setting is competent and sturdy, but of no significance beyond its occasion.

Three unison songs for children were the result of a request from Stephen Moore, son of the vicar of Claines, who wanted a competition piece for the Worcester City Schools' Music Festival. Elgar turned to the poetry of Charles Mackay, a volume he acquired in March 1932. He began by setting two 'river' pieces, *The Rapid Stream*, with its innocent refrain, 'Why hurry to the sea?', and *The Woodland Stream*, a more complex piece linking the 'lustre of our lives' with the heaven reflected in the flowing water. Moore chose the latter for competition, and at the end of 1932 Elgar added another song, *When Swallows Fly*. The verses of all three poems touched subjects long dear to Elgar, and the music was his last tribute to the childhood that had so richly nourished his own imagination.

Solo songs

Elgar's solo songs rarely approach the level of the partsongs; indeed he wrote to William Starmer in August 1921 that 'I am not a song writer although a few of such things have achieved some popularity'. He deliberately avoided first-rate poetry, and it is ironical that the music to his one projected Shakespeare setting, Ophelia's Mad Song from *Hamlet* Act 4, eventually carried words by Edward Capel Cure in *The Light of Life*. The sentiments of the verses chosen rarely transcend their period, for Elgar was aiming often enough at the ballad audience of the miscellaneous concert. From 1900 the majority of Elgar's songs were published by Boosey, the arch-purveyor of such music. The central group of Elgar songs is *Sea Pictures*, the only cycle he managed to complete. There should also have been a cycle of six Gilbert Parker songs, and another pair to the two adaptations of op. 60 by 'Pietro d'Alba'. The sketchbooks abound with songs begun and then abandoned: inspiration was often there, but not the energy wholly to capture it. Elgar's piano parts are serviceable rather than idiomatic, accompaniments more than equal partners with the voice. Sometimes the vocal melody is too long doubled by the piano, as if Elgar was thinking in terms of a vocal score 'reduction'. Apart from the three 'cycles', the only other song Elgar eventually orchestrated was the very successful op. 48 *Pleading*.

Yet Elgar's first song, *The Language of Flowers*, written for his sister Lucy's twentieth birthday and dated 29 May 1872, promised well. The words by the American poet James Gates Percival treat charmingly of such plants as the rose, the bay, the cypress, forget-me-not, and their significance. The song is through-composed, and Elgar's melliflous line is much varied in the five stanzas. But it is the keyboard writing, flexible and accomplished in prelude and postlude, and closely following the words, that hints at a song composer who never fully materialized. Another unpublished song of the 1870s, *The Self-banished*, sets words by Edmund Waller. Elgar makes a tripartite form from the five verses by repeating the second one at the beginning of the last section. Again there is a notable, Mendelssohnian piano introduction, which also marks the divisions of the song. The smooth 9/8 of the first two verses agitates to a 12/8 description of the fever that has spread throughout the lover's 'tainted blood the fire'.

A Soldier's Song of 1884 to words of C. Flavell Hayward was originally published as op. 5 in 1890; it was reissued by Boosey as *A War Song* in 1903. It starts as rumbustious Valkyrie music in the minor and 9/8. Unfortunately Elgar marches into the major at 'Glory or death'. Despite Valkyrie resumption and a touching slow-down for 'Now the warfare is o'er', the song remains a lost cause. An American poet who interested Elgar over many years was Colonel John Hay (1838–1905), who eventually became secretary of state. Elgar's first Hay setting was perhaps *A Phylactery*, with 'memento mori' refrain, a poem that resurfaced in the *Spanish Lady* libretto. The song was never completed, but Elgar sent Hay a copy of *Through the Long Days* ('Giggleswycke', 1885), and it was acknowledged as 'most appropriate and beautiful'. It has deft touches, beginning as if in the subdominant, modulating sensitively, and with subtle bridging of the third and fourth stanzas. The poet of Elgar's next song was Charles d'Orléans, who married the widow of our Richard II and was for twenty-five years a prisoner in England. Elgar set a version of the four stanzas by Louisa Stuart Costello, making a tripartite design with middle section in the tonic minor. A poem from the age of chivalry stimulated Elgar to a show of the grand manner in the month of his meeting Alice Roberts. The title was *Is she not Passing Fair?* and at the end of the manuscript was a cryptic word-square.

A Song of Autum, perhaps written in 1887, set four stanzas by Adam Lindsay Gordon (1833–70). Apart from the opening motif with its touch of syncopation, Elgar adheres obsessively to the crotchet and two quavers of Schubert's 'Wanderer' theme. It is easy to see why the poem, with its garlands withered at 'the falling of the year', appealed to Elgar; and there is considerable artistry in his deployment of the syncopated figure, sometimes to introduce a verse, sometimes in the middle of one. R. H. Barham (1788–1845), better known by his pseudonym Thomas Ingoldsby, wrote *As I Laye a-thynkynge* on his deathbed. Elgar's setting (1887) enters Barham's pseudo-medieval world, with its antique spelling and sentiments that are sadly-gay, through music nicely balanced between make-believe and involvement in the poem's alternating moods. Elgar manages to be at once graceful and poignant, as the singing of a 'Birde' follows the vicissitudes of human life and finally takes the spirit of a deserted lass to a nest among the stars.

The Wind at Dawn (1888) was Elgar's first setting of a poem by Alice Roberts. It was written eight years before, about 'a country saying that such & such weather will ensue if the wind goes out to meet the sun'. The four stanzas have sun and wind rising to fullest strength. Elgar does likewise, having dismissed the moon in the darkness of the minor key. The *grandioso* climax suggests an access of confidence rather than judgment. The virtuoso piano part has turbulent semiquavers to stir the wind. Simon Wastell's *Like to the Damask Rose* is again a very Elgarian poem. Man is likened to the rose, the sun, the shade, the gourd of Jonah, all of which must yield to time. A second stanza extends the catalogue to reach the dying swan. Elgar's introduction is formal, with a hint of the Baroque; but he beautifully illustrates the brief phrases of the poem to make a highly successful work. *Queen Mary's Song* is dated 1 July 1887. The verses come from Tennyson's play about Mary Tudor. The queen herself sings them, having heard that Calais has fallen and in the conviction that Philip of Spain now hates her. The piano has a plaintive 6/8 melody over spread 'lute' chords. Voice and keyboard dovetail their sad phrases, and all is well while the minor key prevails. The shift to the tonic major jars. Schubert could thus intensify emotion; Elgar dissipates it, and only recovers heartbreak in the final bar.

The Poet's Life sets words by Ellen Burroughs. The first stanza describes the poet in his happiness, ignored by the world, heard only by two lovers. In the second, his sorrow made him sing for God alone, and the heartbreak brought fame. There is little distinction in the poem, and little in Elgar's music. The keyboard exordium is no more than complacent, and its *grandioso* goal of reputation in the last bars sounds an empty note of self-satisfaction. There is far more subtlety in *The Shepherd's Song*, completed in August 1892. Barry Pain's four verses are simple and direct, about the joys of summer, 'the strong life of the sea', and poppies on the hillside; the beloved must answer 'in the dreamtime'. Elgar's quiet accompaniment, with legato melodic line and internal pedals, suggests the contented drowsiness of summer. The third stanza, with staccato semiquavers for the 'bright red poppies' builds to a considerable climax. The winding homeward road of the last verse resumes the earlier calm to end *ppp*. Elgar wrote *Rondel* in January 1894. It sets a poem by Froissart in Longfellow's translation. Elgar reproduces easily the accents of courtly love, in an Allegretto scherzando that is both serious and playful. He makes subtle use of the first line, 'Love, love, what wilt thou with this heart of mine?' It recurs twice in the poem; Elgar ignores the scansion by using 'Love' once only, but letting the accompaniment recall the original setting. With two 'Loves' to spare, Elgar ends with a climactic repetition of the first line *in toto*.

The first song of op. 31, a setting of *After* by Philip Bourke Marston (1850–87), is more profound. It was written on 21 June 1895 during work on the organ sonata; but the second stanza almost prophesies Elgar's devastation after his wife's death. The song starts with the tender simplicity of folksong; but at the third verse words 'long, long years to weep in', Elgar's agony surfaces, and for the first time a song approaches the level of the best partsongs. The emotion is powerfully controlled and sustained to the end. In *A Song of Flight*, op. 31 no. 2, Christina Rossetti (1830–94) covers some of the same ground as *The Wind at Dawn*. Again the sun leaps to the day and the winds sweep to their goal; we too should make for our home 'beyond the stars and the sea'. The keyboard introduction has teasing cross rhythms that obscure the prevailing 4/4 to come. There is access of urgency in the third stanza, as we are pressed to 'race for the promised prize'. The last two lines resume the pace of the opening but with dynamics writ large. The fourth section of 'A baby's death' in *A Century of Roundels* by Swinburne (1837–1909) was set by Elgar in 1887, but not performed till the Diamond Jubilee year of 1897. Elgar called the song *Roundel*. The song's mellifluous and sentimental line is fitting vehicle for Swinburne's jejune speculation about the new life that may be lighting the 'little little eyes' of the dead child. Swinburne essays nothing beyond verbal conceits; Elgar does better, but not well enough.

Sea Pictures, completed in 1899 soon after the 'Enigma' Variations, was designed for the Norwich Festival and Clara Butt, then still in her twenties. The starting-point for the cycle was the *Lute Song* to words by Alice Elgar published in 1897. The music may go back some eight years more, when it seems Elgar had originally wanted words by Andrew Lang. For the new context Alice Elgar substituted waves for wind, foam-flakes for blossoms, and joy was sea-swept. The five poems Elgar assembled make an odd assortment. None is first-rate, and the best are the least pretentious, those by Alice Elgar and Richard Garnett.

The cycle begins with 'Sea Slumber Song' by Roden Noel (1834–94). It refers to Kynance Cove near the Lizard in Cornwall. The opening approaches E minor from the subdominant, balancing arpeggio figures with a quiet undulating motion to portray the sleeping sea birds. The murmuring song of the sea turns to a slow ground-swell in E major, the shifting of the water repeated in the accompaniment bar by bar. The central section, delicately poised between C major and its dominant, paints the foam glimmering on an elfin shore. The final section repeats the first, and the recurrent 'good night' takes the music dreamily from E major to A flat and C in a reference to the central elfin music.

'In Haven' was now a reminiscence of an early holiday Alice Elgar had in Capri. Elgar sets the poem strophically, moving in each verse from C to A minor and back, with a brief moment of Neapolitan tension at the end. The vocal line spans only an octave, and the accompaniment remains calm despite the threatening words in each stanza. In an idyllic tribute to his wife Elgar puts all his emphasis on the last lines and the enduring power of love. On the MS full score he called her 'Bag poet'.

'Sabbath Morning at Sea' is part of a poem by Elizabeth Barrett Browning, with the five verses making uneasy transition from the progress of a solemn ship, via an onshore church service she cannot attend, to the higher place where saints keep an 'endless sabbath morning'. The poet's too easy invocation of 'God's Spirit' produces from Elgar uncomfortable bluster, amid reminiscences of the 'Sea Slumber Song' that are more or less apt. The introductory bars come from an early sketchbook and probably date to 1883. The ground-swell of the first song is prominent in the C major of the opening two stanzas. The section ends with four pompous bars heavy with last-beat triplets in the accompaniment for the word 'glory'. The tonality shifts to B major in the next verse and a new idea manages to keep the triplets under control. After a D flat fourth stanza, the movement's introductory bars usher in the final stanza and pervade it. The music is that of the third verse now *grandioso* to its detriment, and the triplets are frankly vulgar.

Richard Garnett's (1835–1906) delicate fancy about 'the land where corals lie' makes a subtle antithesis to Alice Elgar's poem: love must now give place to the exotic charms and colours of nature at the bottom of the sea. The C major peroration of the previous number is eased into B minor with two bars of octave introduction to the simple accompaniment that gives the song its character. Elgar's invention is happy, subtle and playful, leading to a final B major cadence *ppp*.

The last poem is by Adam Lindsay Gordon, and Elgar chose four and a half stanzas for 'The Swimmer'. The verse is often harsh and crude, with such rhymes as ghastly / mast lie; crimson / dim sun. A pedal A prepares for D major through descending scales fiery with augmented intervals. A confident tune emerges in rising sequences, only to be dashed aside by the turbulent declamation of the first stanza. Elgar's formal plan is clear. After the central half-verse has recapitulated in the original C the middle section of 'Sea Slumber Song', the last two stanzas echo the first two, though with ingredients reordered and a triumphant coda to bolster the aim of the last words and arrive where 'no love wanes'. The materials consist of dramatic recitative, vivid arpeggio figures lashed by stabbing chords, another D major tune of descending sequence, and rising chromatics over a dominant pedal.

Dry those Fair, those Crystal Eyes was written in 1899 for a gift album in aid of Charing Cross Hospital. Elgar chose verses by Henry King (1592–1669), Bishop of Chichester and friend of Izaak Walton. The unepiscopal conceits of the two verses urge a girl to stop her tears lest her admirers become enamoured of sorrow. Elgar's setting is strophic, and a simple vocal line is accompanied by gentle chords. By repeating the beginning of the third line in verse 1, and the whole of the second line in verse 2, Elgar shows a subtle understanding of the poem. Adrian Ross's *The Pipes of Pan* could not be more different. The nine rollicking stanzas explore ancient tales of the goat-foot Pan, how the nymph Syrinx became his musical instrument, and how in time of war he can cause panic. Ross's achievement is to have found nine rhymes for Pan and inspired Elgar to a 12/8 movement that never loses its sense of direction, with variety in phrase lengths and detail of the accompaniment. Elgar takes the verses in groups of three, initially two minor, and one tonic major; in the last triptych, descriptive of armies on the battlefield, he gives the first stanza a triumphant turn to the major. *Come, Gentle Night* (1901) was written against the background of a burgeoning *Cockaigne* and inhabits a very remote world. The words by Clifton Bingham are a plea for rest by one weary of his work and longing for the quiet shadows of night. The three verses are through-composed, and Elgar preserves the essential simplicity of the message while ringing changes on the detail. The last stanza, 'Come, holy night!', has heartfelt repetition of its opening words at the end. About the same time Elgar set *Always and Everywhere*, a translation by Frank Fortey of a poem by Zygmunt Krasiński (1812–59), a Polish patriot who went into Parisian exile after the Warsaw uprising of 1830. Better known for his plays, Krasiński had also a considerable lyric gift. The title recurs as a refrain to verses of a doomed but passionate love, and Elgar manages a song, heavy with tolling bell in the accompaniment, that probes deeper than most.

Elgar's next two songs, to words by A. C. Benson in *The Professor*, were published as op. 41. The six stanzas of *In the Dawn* celebrate the understanding that can grow between man and woman as secret thoughts are shared. Parting suggests 'vales of misery'; to have loved puts the soul 'among the stars'. The first two verses share the same music over pulsing quavers, with the last line extended in tender sequence by the piano. The music moves to the warmth of the flattened mediant, and the thought of separation raises the key another minor third. The stars are eventually reached in the calm of utter quiet.

The elusive rhythms of Benson's *Speak, Music* stimulated Elgar to a protracted essay in 15/8. The three stanzas spoke of fancies 'too fleet for me', hopes for 'something more true than death', and longings for 'all that the poet, the priest cannot say'. The song is confined almost entirely to one-bar phrases, depending much on an ostinato heard at the outset. Elgar told Benson this was the better of the two songs, and he dedicated it to Antonia Speyer of Ridgehurst.

Speak, my Heart (1903–4) also has words by Benson. The song was originally written to words by Adrian Ross meant for a musical, *A Country Girl*. When the copyright could not be obtained, Boosey approached Benson for a 'parody' text. He responded with three verses of village wooing. The stanzas' last line reflects the lass's attitude; they end 'Silence, my heart!', 'Courage, my heart!' and 'Speak, my heart!' Elgar's first two verses are virtually identical in the freshness of their banter. The third has the lad more serious and slower in the supertonic minor. The girl whispers slower still, and the song ends cheerfully with an abrupt bang. The verses of *In Moonlight* were chosen by Elgar himself to go with the 'Canto populare' of *In the South*. They are the second and fourth stanzas from a Shelley poem beginning 'The keen stars were twinkling'. Despite a sequential introduction based on the overture's main theme (it recurs at the climax), the song is a failure. The words fit only clumsily, and in its new context the lovely tune has lost its magic and gained nothing. *Pleading* (1908) resulted from Arthur Salmon's sending Elgar some poems of his, *A Book of Verses*. Elgar intended to set also 'The Haven of Desire', of which a sketch exists. Elgar thought well enough of his song to orchestrate it and dedicate it to Lady Maud Warrender. The poem touches many of Elgar's concerns, speaking of dreamland's hills, fallen leaves, 'faith grown fainter', and memory 'smoulder'd to a dull regret'. After two introductory bars, a telling phrase beautifully encapsulates the first line. The music is terse and concentrated; not a word is repeated, not a note is superfluous.

The three songs of op. 59, to poems by Gilbert Parker, came from a volume called *Embers*. As well as the three set, Elgar chose also 'Proem, 'The Waking' and 'There is an Orchard' towards his proposed cycle; of these only sketches exist. *Oh, Soft was the Song* should have been no. 3. In the absence of the first and fourth songs it is impossible to say how closely Elgar would have knit the cycle. The large-scale reminiscences of *Sea Pictures* would almost certainly not have featured; but the intervals contained within a descending fourth such as open no. 3 are an obvious hallmark of the completed songs.

'Oh, soft was the Song' actually began the second verse of Parker's poem 'At Sea'. Elgar crossed out the first verse. The repeated semiquaver figure of the introduction is quickly dropped and recurs only in the penultimate bar. Indeed the significance of the song lies in its constantly varied vocal part. From Parker's five lines of uneven length Elgar contrives a semblance of three verses, each starting with virtually the same phrase though shaping differently. The motto fourth is all-pervasive in *Was it some Golden Star?* Elgar marks the song *fantastico* as he pursues through four stanzas Parker's imagined knight addressing his supposed queen. The first verse has virtually half its bars unaccompanied, a rarity in an Elgar song. Interplay between voice and piano is cunning. At the beginning of the second stanza, for instance, the keyboard accompanies with a phrase from the vocal line of verse 1, and at the start of verse 3 they swap parts as the song reaches its climax. The mood is playful, the technique masterly. In *Twilight* the descending fourth has a tolling seriousness to accompany the insistent 'Adieu!' and more besides; indeed it is rarely absent. Parker's three stanzas tell of the setting sun and creeping mist, that the passing years are as a broken song, and that some day the veil between what is and what might have been could be drawn back. The words are instinct with Elgarian nostalgia and go to the making of a highly expressive song. The music of each verse is substantially the same, but subtleties of verbal stress make each one a bar longer than the last. The final cadence devises a strange harmonic question out of the descending fourth.

Muriel Foster had sung the Parker songs at their première, and it was for her infant son that Elgar wrote *A Child Asleep* to verses by Elizabeth Barrett Browning. The setting of the four verses (Elgar selected nos. 4, 5, 9 and 12 from an original twelve, and added the opening words of the poem) follows his ideal scheme of repeated exposition, development and recapitulation. Some of the poet's conceits are far-fetched, but Elgar transmutes them into an essential innocence in the spirit of his dedication: 'This Simple Song (For his Mother's singing) is made to Anthony Goetz (Ae. I)'. His birthday was 26 December. A tiny rosalia at the end of all verses except the third tenderly enshrines the 'summer sun', then 'music all the day', and the final dismissal, 'go in peace'. *The King's Way* (1909) was in stark contrast. The triumphant success of 'Land of Hope and Glory' prompted speculation whether the trio tune of *Pomp and Circumstance* no. 4 might not do equally well. Yet the construction of a new London street was hardly the stuff of permanent rejoicing, and Alice Elgar's mention of the former roads on which the 'sick and poor sink sadly down' might sooner raise a tear than a cheer. Indeed the idea of alternative words was mooted in 1928, and Alfred Noyes produced a *Song of Victory*. It had a further lease of life in the Second World War as *Song of Liberty* to words by A. P. Herbert.

Elgar began another cycle of songs before the end of 1909. This time they were to be to his own words, with the help of Carice's Peter Rabbit. Four songs were planned but only two written to become op. 60. *The Shrine* and *The Bee* are known only by their names, but the words of the completed pair were ascribed to 'Pietro d'Alba (from a folksong – Eastern Europe)'. The first, called *The Torch*, is a passionate, declamatory love-song, of an intensity rare for a rabbit. The torch will light the beloved through the lonely track of the dark wood and across the ford at the cold stream. The setting is laconic, making in one direction to the flattened submediant, in the other to a major chord on the mediant. The ending in the minor offers little hope. The second of Peter's folksong adaptations was *The River*. It told the bitter tale of a river that would have overwhelmed the enemy if still in flood; instead, it sank below its normal level. The refrain word 'Rustula!' occurs thrice in each verse, *ad lib* and out of tempo. The impetuous introduction recurs between verses, never exactly and always abbreviated. For the rest the accompaniment is chordal, harmonically simple till the chromatic twists of the gradually sinking river. The final 'Rustula!' is deadly quiet.

The *Arabian Serenade* (1914) is Elgar's only attempt at a vaguely Spanish idiom in solo song, and it works well. The poem comes from *Songs of Childhood and Other Verses* by Margery Lawrence. The alternating chords of the accompaniment, slipping from minor to major and back, simulate the clangour of the guitar. The song moves purposefully till the imperious recitative at the start of the last verse invites the girl to a feast between the purple sea and the wood. The eloquence of the end rises to high passion. *The Chariots of the Lord* of early February 1914 is entirely worthy of the words. These came from *Hymns of the Early Church* by Rev John Brownlie which translated some from Latin and Greek but contained also 'several original pieces'. One can only hope that Elgar's swashbuckling poem was 'original'. *Fight for Right*, written for Gervase Elwes in 1916, is little better. The William Morris verses from *Sigurd the Volsung* paint a picture of wartime topsyturvydom that is apt enough; but Elgar's introductory march sets a tone of undistinguished bravura that is effortlessly maintained throughout the song. A choral refrain rams home the message that 'great are the wrongfully dead'.

Six of the songs written for the 1924 Pageant of Empire were for solo voice. This was Elgar's first collaboration with Alfred Noyes (1880–1959), whose seafaring muse appealed to him. *Shakespeare's Kingdom* described the youthful poet's arrival in London with a 'scroll of quiet songs' in his knapsack. It was the third verse that caught Elgar's imagination, when Noyes described the 'Spirits of light and music' that trod 'the April air'. Elgar's favourite rhythm is prominent, and repeat of the words involves a dramatic modulation a semitone down. The second song, *The Islands*, hymned New Zealand with an all-purpose diatonic robustness. He used the same music indeed for *Sailing Westward*, the fifth song of the group. *The Blue Mountains*, in praise of Australia, is quietly effective without having penetrated far into Elgar's imagination. *Merchant Adventurers*, which follows, has a G minor verse, vigorous and redolent of salt spray. The refrain (also arranged for SATB) settles into a complacent E flat to celebrate England's 'glory everlasting, in the lordship of the sea'. Elgar returned to these words when planning the libretto for the first scene of *The Spanish Lady*. The penultimate song, *The Immortal Legions*, begins sombrely, in heartfelt gloom for the legions of the dead. Noyes repeats words from *Sailing Westward*: 'Are there worlds beyond the darkness?' and Elgar sets them as before. This music recurs in the refrain of final triumph, when the dead are awarded due glory, honour and thanks.

Elgar's last published song, *It isnae me*, sets a simple text of northern regret by Sally Holmes. He responds with a sufficiency of Scotch snaps, a vocal line that does not stray beyond an octave, and an eloquent use of silence, slightly altering the end of the poem so as to incorporate effective verbal echoes of earlier lines. Elgar had always enjoyed tinkering with his texts; as here, his adjustments were often for the better.

12

Marches, major orchestral works, transcriptions

If all Elgar's greatest orchestral works were written between 1899 and 1919, marches of one sort or another stretch through his whole creative life, from jottings in the early sketchbooks to the handful being considered for inclusion in *The Spanish Lady*. Indeed, with the exception of *In the South*, the long line of orchestral works from the Variations to the Cello Concerto all pay tribute at some point to this most fundamental means of Elgarian expression. What the waltz is to Richard Strauss, the march is to Elgar.

Marches

Elgar's marches have often been reckoned among his 'musical crimes'. His own attitude was unequivocal, as he explained to Rudolf de Cordova in February 1904. Perhaps Alice Elgar's military relatives peered quizzically over his shoulder as he said 'I have some of the soldier instinct in me'. Certainly he cultivated the impression. Referring among other works to the *Imperial March* of 1897, he clarified his position:

> I like to look on the composer's vocation as the old troubadours or bards did. In those days it was no disgrace to a man to be turned on to step in front of an army and inspire the people with a song. For my own part, I know that there are a lot of people who like to celebrate events with music. To these people I have given tunes. Is that wrong?

The *Imperial March* op. 32 was first in the long series that reached its end in *Pomp and Circumstance* no. 5 of 1930, a series so successful and apparently definitive that William Walton had grave doubts when the BBC asked him for a coronation march in 1937: 'he wondered if, after Elgar, one could write such a thing'.[1] The *Imperial March* was a Novello commission, and the firm plied Elgar with criticisms and suggestions when his initial draft was submitted. His reaction was

[1] See Susana Walton, *William Walton: Behind the Façade* (Oxford, 1988), p. 72.

entirely satisfactory, for he produced a ceremonial piece that instantly catches the intention despite its quiet beginning. It was the first great occasion of national rejoicing he was asked to celebrate, and he did so with brilliance, flair, and dignity. The great tunes were to come later, but Elgar marshals his fanfares, his strings soaring with warm melody against glowing counterpoints in the horns, the imperious summons of the side drum, and the broad touches of humour with the easy mastery of a man in his element. The apparent confidence is yet tinged with the wistfulness that constantly haunts Elgar; but when the central episode returns *grandioso* towards the end, on this occasion it is justly so.

When talking to de Cordova about the *Pomp and Circumstance Marches*, Elgar expounded his aim: 'I do know we are a nation of great military proclivities, and I did not see why the ordinary quick march should not be treated on a large scale in the way that the waltz, the old-fashioned slow march, and even the polka have been treated by the great composers.' For his title Elgar went to Shakespeare's *Othello*. There is some irony in his choice. It comes from the speech in Act 3 scene iii in which Othello, crushed by new knowledge of Desdemona's supposed infidelity, takes leave of his military profession:

> Farewell the neighing steed, and the shrill trump,
> The spirit-stirring drum, the ear-piercing fife,
> The royal banner, and all quality,
> Pride, pomp and circumstance of glorious war!

When all-out war came Elgar's way, it seemed far from glorious. But during the distant Boer War Elgar had few doubts and was prepared to take verses by the botanist Lord de Tabley as overall motto:

> Like a proud music that draws men to die
> Madly upon the spears in martial ecstasy,
> A measure that sets heaven in all their veins
> And iron in their hands.

Elgar paid his tribute to the marching feet, and the ideals for which they marched. He celebrated his achievement to de Cordova: 'I have written two marches of which, so far from being ashamed, I am proud.'

There was reason for pride. In the first march he had what he called 'a tune that comes once in a lifetime'. When he first played the march to Dorabella in May 1901, he pointed to the start: 'What note does it begin on ?' She replied 'E flat', and Elgar continued, 'Yah! there's a joke!' The E flat exordium lasts eight bars; then Elgar settles firmly into D major and a series of two-bar phrases that may be responsible for Stanford's preferring the A minor march when he heard both for the first time. This main section of the march now sounds a little factitious, despite the enharmonic cunning of the return to E flat before preparing the trio tune. As Henry Wood wrote: 'Little did I think that the lovely, broad melody of the *trio* would one day develop into our second national anthem.'[2] In the subdominant warmth of G major the downward tendency of the melody is balanced by the diatonically rising bass. The sixteen-bar tune begins to sport Elgar's favourite rhythmic tag in its third strain; it becomes the more prominent as the tune repeats with an eight-bar addition and climactic upward leap of a seventh. Recapitulation of the march is exact until the abbreviated preparation for the trio, now in the tonic D, with side drum in constant attendance, tambourine *ad lib*, and first entry of the organ. The great tune is finally dismissed in a flurry of chromatic scales. Arnold Bax remembered the première as a foggy night: 'Sir Henry's back and the faces of the orchestral players were as figments in the baseless fabric of a dream.' But the end of the march worked wonders: 'The very fog was disturbed into dense and delirious whorls and eddies.'[3]

The second march, in A minor, was very different. Dedicated to Granville Bantock, it begins with a brief flourish to introduce the first theme, initially conspiratorial, but rising in sequence and dynamics to a hammered climax and cadence in G. The second theme, in E minor, begins as an insistent call to arms, with a triplet quaver pendant that assumes considerable importance later. The tune develops lyrically, and the triplets enrich the inner parts. An eventual return to the opening cadences into A major for the trio. The triplets are now in the bass and become an ostinato accompaniment to the sprightly woodwind tune, of which the rhythm is equally obstinate. Its repetition involves the strings in a cantabile extension and a couple of three-bar phrases. After wholesale repeat of march and trio the end comes in a series of dramatic gestures and prolonged side drum roll. Four days after the première Jaeger was delighted: 'The tunes, damn them, Keep buzzing in my empty head, & the orchestral effects, harmonies & all your Monkey tricks dance about & within me. The things are splendid & will make your name Known everywhere.'

The trio tune of *Pomp and Circumstance* no. 3 was already dedicated to Ivor Atkins in February 1902; but the march was not complete till autumn 1904. This C minor march is the most elusive of the set, darkly coloured with the addition of a third bassoon and tenor drum. The

[2] Henry Wood, *My Life of Music*, p. 154.
[3] Quoted in Reginald Pound, *Sir Henry Wood* (London, 1969), p. 79.

Ex. 38

opening is spectral, with only disjointed fragments of theme hinting at some future tune amid the dogged persistence of rhythm (Ex. 38). Two bars of rapid *crescendo* lead to the most protracted *fff* in the marches and a jagged theme punctuated by brass salvos. The deadly quiet of the opening is resumed till a powerful tune unites the fragments in cogent melody. The A flat trio makes a playful theme from the previously jagged rhythms, lightly scored with solo wind and staccato strings. The recapitulation of the march is shorn of its first eight bars and the trio tune returns glorified in C major. This march has the longest coda of the set, returning to C minor and reviewing in a different order the main themes.

The fourth march in G was completed on 7 June 1907, dedicated to G. R. Sinclair and first performed under Henry Wood on 24 August 1907. The originality and persistence of the opening rhythmic figure dominate the march section. Just when Elgar starts risking monotony with his two-bar phrases, he slips in one of three bars. The expansive C major trio tune is the first to be marked 'nobilmente'. As with 'Land of Hope and Glory', the melody has already run its course once before reaching its climax. Many attempts have been made to fit words to the tune; 'Land of Glory and Hope' would make a reasonable start. After recapitulation it is the original march rhythm that drives the piece to its triumphant conclusion.

Pomp and Circumstance no. 5 followed after a very long gap and was dedicated to Percy Hull. Elgar conducted the first performance when he recorded it at Kingsway Hall on 18 September 1930. Alone of the marches its first C major section is in 6/8, a youthfully ebullient and jaunty paragraph in which rhythmical accents are constantly changing. After so skittish a start, the splendour of the A flat trio tune is a surprise. It is the greatest and subtlest of them all. The constant return to C might be the end rather than beginning of a phrase, so that always there is an air of ambiguity about the four-bar sections, emphasized by the *sfp* on the top C. Elgar's rhythmic hallmark appears in the fourth bar, but it is in the second limb of the tune that Elgar's imagination soars, far beyond words to be set or indeed words to describe. It is the highest art (Ex. 39). After recapitulation, with the

Ex. 39

trio tune *nobilmente* and in utmost glory, the 6/8 brings down the curtain fast.

Elgar told de Cordova he intended a sixth march, 'a Soldier's Funeral March'. This was not to be; but there are two further marches, different again from the *Pomp and Circumstance* set. The *Coronation March* of 1911 begins sombrely with a 3/4 theme that originated in the Rabelais ballet project. Despite the gorgeous colouring, the march never quite shakes off a brooding anger that occasionally gives the work a Mahlerian touch. It is far from festive, and the fanfares and rushing strings that bring back the opening in the prevailing 4/4 have a hectic feverishness about them. This was a coronation Elgar preferred not to attend.

The *Empire March*, written for Wembley in 1924, is the most overtly brilliant of all. Elgar follows up the audacity of his Bach transcription with scoring to banish any suggestion of post-war economy and remains unrivalled in his command of sumptuous orchestral sound. The music is forthright and apparently brimming with self-confidence. There is a good trio tune, livened with nice touches of imitation as it proceeds. The percussive splendour of the end was a brave attempt to mend times that Elgar knew were thoroughly out of joint.

Concert overture, *Froissart*

Elgar, soon to be a father, set about his overture for the Worcester Festival of 1890 with considerable zest. Diary entries suggest that the music was started on 6 April and acquired the title 'Froissart' on 25 May. Froissart and his writings were very much after Elgar's heart. Vivid chronicler of the fourteenth century, he travelled far, was endlessly curious, and remembered avidly. He loved dances, carols and minstrelsy, was partial to dogs and hawks, enjoyed the uncorking of bottles and gorgeous apparel, and was zealous for the virtues of chivalry. On his way to King David of Scotland, he rode along the Roman wall, equated Carlisle with the Carlyon of King Arthur, came back along the banks of the Severn and passed by 'l'escole d'Asque-Suffort', or the University of Oxford. Elgar followed him in his journeys, marking in his copy of the chronicles such a passage as 'dead horses and other carrion were thrown by the engines into the castle to poison them by their smell'. Travelling in the south of France with a knight and good raconteur, Froissart's delight overflows: 'Sainte Marie! How pleasant are your tales, and how much do they profit me while you relate them! And you shall not lose your trouble, for they shall all be set down in memory and remembrance in the history which I am writing.'

Such vitality was irresistible, and Elgar set out to capture it. A movement of 340 bars in all, *Froissart* was easily Elgar's most ambitious orchestral work to date. Indeed its adventurous sonata structure had no precedent in his output. The wind quintet movements had been Classically 'correct', but this was music-making of a different order. There are hints of Brahms, perhaps, and Wagner in the overture, but most of all it is the spontaneity and panache of Dvořák that has influenced Elgar. Yet the composer himself emerges as a commanding personality in his own right. Even the first four semiquavers, important later in the work, are an Elgarian hallmark (Ex. 40a), cropping up

Ex. 40
(a) *Froissart*

again as late as the Piano Quintet first movement (b) and in the finale

(b) Piano Quintet

of the Cello Concerto (c). The fanfares and cascading arpeggios on

(c) Cello Concerto

strings became another stock in trade, but there is clear tribute to Wagner and his ubiquitous 'love' motif (Ex. 41a) in the seminal phrase

Ex. 41
(a) *Rheingold*

for trumpets and trombones (Ex. 41b). The Andante adumbrates three

(b) *Froissart*

distinct ideas. The first descends by mainly arpeggio steps into the depths before covering wider and wider intervals to reach the D from which it began. There follows a march motif on B flat horns. The third is a theme that starts chromatically and again describes the shape of Wagnerian 'love'. Against the accompaniment of continuous dactyls at the Allegro moderato, the Wagner tune expands to include a falling seventh and is developed imitatively between the violins. A tutti statement of the arpeggio and march themes from the introduction ends the first subject group, and a gradual *diminuendo* is managed with the repetitive charm of Dvořák. The second subject in F derives equally from the first tune of the introduction and the love theme, and there are many quick Elgarian hairpins, those sudden accesses of passion he made so much his own.

Elgar's attitude to development was idiosyncratic. This is the only one of the three overtures to attempt extended manipulation of the exposition's data; the others introduce new and largely independent material. Here there are five closely knit sections. Elgar begins in D flat, answering the first theme of the introduction with the second subject. Impetuous semiquavers have taken the music to G minor, and the second section starts with a double bassoon solo, woodwind flashes of the Wagner theme, and rising chromatics on violins. Again the texture owes something to Dvořák. Descending arpeggios and an upward scale rush into the E minor third section and the introduction's march at full volume. The fourth section has a Dvořákian augmentation in F of the introduction's arpeggio and successor phrases. The development's final section is extended dominant preparation with fragments of the Wagner motif flashed across the score until the impetuous scales embody it upside down and lead into the recapitulation.

If the logic of the development was diffuse, the recapitulation is notably succinct. By various short cuts Elgar reaches the second subject in twenty-five instead of sixty bars. With the cello as protagonist, the tune is now more richly scored. The coda starts with a tamed version of the march against a magical background of six-part violins. Over a dominant pedal the Wagner motif takes over in the wind, while the initial semiquavers of the work build to a brief summary of the essential materials and a final *stringendo* to the end of Elgar's first orchestral success.

Concert overture, *Cockaigne*

The medieval Cockaigne was a land of luxury and idleness, where the rivers flowed wine, the houses were cakes, roast birds wandered the streets for the eating, and buttered larks fell from heaven. Boileau applied the name to his own capital: 'For the rich Paris is a land of

Cockaigne.' Elgar's 'London Town' is teeming with vitality, bubbling with humour, full of incident and rich variety. Elgar told Richter about the overture in August 1901: 'here is nothing deep or melancholy – it is intended to be honest, healthy, humorous and strong but not vulgar'. He saw the work through the eyes of a young couple, strolling the streets of the city on a fine afternoon and wondering at the sights.

Elgar puts London's high spirits together bit by bit, with a series of pithy themes, atmospheric scraps that only gradually coalesce into a full-blooded statement *fff* of London as 'the goodliest of thy neighbours', to quote Thomas Dekker. Elgar's first printed use of the word 'nobilmente' (it appears earlier on 'Enigma' sketches) characterizes the fine tune descriptive of London strong in character, and confident in its strength (Ex. 42). Its two bars are extended by sequence both melodic and rhythmic until a three-beat motif from the middle of the tune disrupts the prevailing four in a bar. The music sinks towards E

Ex. 42

flat, and the strings gently sing the love of the young couple (Ex. 43). The octave of the beginning and its following semitone come from the heart of London in its strength. The tune soars to span a twelfth, and develops a lovely Schumannesque pendant, passed from instrument to

Ex. 43

instrument till increased emotion takes the tune. It dies away to the music that introduced it, and immediately young London cocks a snook at its elders with their confident theme in diminution. It was the procedure of the Nuremberg apprentices in *Die Meistersinger*, though Elgar claimed in a late letter that he recognized the idea first in Delibes's *Sylvia*.[4] Even if the London lads' cheekiness has a touch of adolescent woe in the slithering chromatics of the countersubject, they adventure from E flat to G minor to B major, bouncing up each time by a major third till they resume E flat with their own brand of brilliance. A codetta reviews London's high spirits and fades out to a reminiscence of the young couple's love.

The start of the development, initially in B flat and then straying far, quietly explores strong London in its stillness. The rhythm is again confounded, this time in a sequence that takes six steps to resume the E flat from which the development set out. The Schumannesque pendant sheds its fragrance till the solo clarinet gives first hint of an approaching band. The development is now frankly episodic. Thematic links can be rummaged for, but the primary impression is of novelty. With an onrush of sleigh bells and triangle, the band blares along the street, bumptious on cornets and trombones. G-string violins take it through C minor and E flat till it returns yet more grandiloquent on the full orchestra. Youthful London is delighted, and the battery hammers out the three semiquavers of high-spirited London. As the band retreats, a pedal F supports it in a remote G flat. The bass rises by semitones, but the acoustic trick of distance keeps the disappearing band always off-key. The young couple strays into a church to a theme distinctive by its final triplet in each bar. The tune and its countersubject can ultimately think of nothing but sequences; it is then that young London starts poking irreverent fun at them. Gradually Elgar produces an exciting contrapuntal web from London's youth and London's lovers as the church is left behind. The music of the opening high spirits builds up with much brass emphasis, and the recapitulation is taken in mid-crowd.

Now the young couple return in the overture's C major in resplendent scoring. The band thunders in again even more noisily, proclaiming with maximum emphasis that Elgar had recently learnt a great deal (perhaps too much) about the trombone. The one theme that has not yet returned in its original form is the 'nobilmente' of confident London. By a stroke of genius Elgar puts it into the key of E flat that has so warmly dominated the music on behalf of the young lovers and the initial mockery of the lads. It is a moment of generous understanding for which some sequential tedium and vulgar tromboning can be readily forgiven. Elgar

[4] Letter at Birthplace Museum.

suggested to Joseph Bennett he might be prudent to listen to the overture at the other end of a telephone.[5]

Concert overture, *In the South*

This concert overture was Elgar's 1904 substitute for his still-postponed symphony; but in the event his Italian experiences coalesced into the longest symphonic movement he had yet written, extending to fourteen bars short of 900. Elgar was not pleased that Jaeger should mention Strauss when analysing the new work. He wrote on 13 August 1904: 'I do not think I should put that about Strauss at the beginning – not necessary – S. puts music in a very low position when he suggests it must hang on some commonplace absurdity for it's very life.' Yet *In the South* was as autobiographical in its way as the contemporary *Symphonia Domestica*, if less overtly so, and musically more cogent. Excursions from Alassio discovered Moglio on its steep hillside where, as Rosa Burley was to describe, 'the returning inhabitants would walk rapidly down hill and suddenly disappear into their homes like rabbits into a burrow'. One could roll home, and Elgar took up the idea: 'Moglio, Moglio, roglio, roglio', making it into music for his 'Fantasia Overture' as he originally called it. Much else of that winter went into the work.

The opening, however, was due to Dan the bulldog. The theme went back to July 1899 and commemorated 'Dan triumphant (after a fight)' and was to continue ' 'till the next dog comes along'. Dan had the theme in F major, a key Elgar used less than the present favourite E flat, the key also of Strauss's *Heldenleben*, which may have suggested the new context. In jottings sent to Percy Pitt for the Covent Garden programme Elgar called the theme 'Joy of living (wine & macaroni)' and went on to characterize it as 'Maybe the exhilarating *out-of-doors* feeling arising from the gloriously beautiful surroundings – streams, flowers, hills; the distant snow mountains in one direction & the blue Mediterranean in the other'. The supreme energy of the theme, itself rising in giant-step sequence, generates counterpoints by the dozen and can take in its stride sequences by the score. The first subject group continues with a *nobilmente* passage combining an impassioned descending melodic line with the slow twist of rising chromatics in the inner parts. For the 'pitiless Pitt' Elgar elaborated on the background to his transition themes: 'A shepherd with his flock straying about the ruins of the old church – he piping softly & reedily and occasionally singing.'

[5] Letter at Birthplace Museum.

After two 'shepherd' bars (Ex. 44a) 'Moglio' answers (b) and is

Ex. 44
(a)

(b)

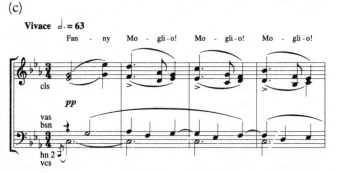

gradually developed into 'Fanny Moglio' (c). The three ideas are

(c)

interchanged to settle over a dominant pedal into F minor. The pedal continues into the second subject group, starting in a much chromaticized F major (the movement's supertonic). The scansion of the tune is elusive; Elgar described it as 'E.E. & family musing' and adjudged it 'not bad' (Ex. 45). A passionate repeat leads to a closing theme that combines the 'shepherd' with the falling fourths in 'Fanny Moglio', while the clarinet adds a brief reminder of Dan.

Ex. 45

The 'shepherd' and 'Moglio' are further worked at the beginning of the development until 'Fanny Moglio' joins them and moves with quickening pace towards the *grandioso* of the local remains. Elgar claimed that *In the South* 'follows generally the ordinary overture form: new matter (the Roman section & the Shepherd's song being introduced in the working out section'. Elgar noted the impression of the Roman ruins: 'the massive bridge and road still useful, and to a reflective mind awe-inspiring'. On the score he quoted Byron's *Childe Harold* about

> a land
> Which *was* the mightiest in its old command
> And *is* the loveliest.

Impressive as it is, this is the section of the overture that has worn least well. The piled discords, intensifying rhythms and insistent

308

repetitions become increasingly tedious. They close in D flat, and there follows initially in C minor another unsatisfactory episode of little musical substance. Elgar called it 'strife' and wanted to 'give a sound-picture of the strife and wars ("the drums and tramplings") of a later time'. Jaeger was baffled: 'I couldn't get the "Hang" of it (the "*meaning*" I mean).' Elgar now resumes the development on as high a level as he had started it. He wrote of 'the Shepherd singing softly his Canto-*popolare* & the peace & the sunshine once more take the chief place in the picture'. The whole passage (Ex. 46) is introduced

Ex. 46

with magic touches on the glockenspiel and has a tune of sublime simplicity, first in C on solo viola, then romantically in E on horn till the violins take over. There are reminders of Dan, calm beneath an Italian sky, and even of the warfare stilled. The viola resumes in D and leaves the tune in mid course, suspended on G.

As the third of E flat, this note launches the recapitulation. By omitting for the moment the whole of the *nobilmente* section and curtailing the transition, Elgar is soon at the second group, now in E flat but with a tiny glint of E major towards the end. The coda is superbly contrived. The *nobilmente* begins *ppp* and *tranquillo,* but is extended through a long *crescendo.* The movement gathers speed, Dan is afflicted with stretto across the bars, and ultimately combines with the *nobilmente* in full-dress splendour. The brass hammer at the subdominant, 'Fanny Moglio' flashes across the score, there is a timpani roll, and Dan has the last word.

That timpani roll is probably Jaeger's responsibility. He made a characteristic complaint on 24 February 1904: 'Why the Divel have you a *silent Bar* in your Coda (Overture)? You WILL play pranks with Your Kodas. Foolish boy!, unsagacious neophite! Weber, Beethoven Wagner Knew better. It's never too late to do the wrong thing, however.' Elgar responded four days later: 'By the way the bar's rest is practically $\frac{1}{2}$ a bar: why quote Beethoven if you don't know the 2nd or 5th Symphonies for instance?' He signed himself 'Jaeg*ee* (the hunted)'; but he added the timpani roll. The overture was dedicated to Frank Schuster; in a letter of 22 February 1904 Elgar claimed that the ingredients of the work were 'mixed up in an orchestral dish which with my ordinary orchestral flavouring, cunningly blent, I have put in a warm cordial of spice of love for you'.

'Enigma' Variations

The mystifications with which Elgar surrounded the Variations for Orchestra op. 36 brought him more bother than he anticipated and raised in the public mind questions to which the answers can be only conjectural, even if Elgar knew what they were himself. The 'dark saying' and the theme which 'goes' have produced 'solutions' as various as *Auld Lang Syne*, 'Dido's lament', the slow movement of Mozart's 'Prague' Symphony, and ideas as disparate as 'friendship' and 'Bach'.[6] Perhaps there is something to be said for concentrating rather on the points Elgar clarified. When writing a note for a 1911 Italian performance, Elgar made mention of his friends: 'It may be understood

[6] See the bibliography.

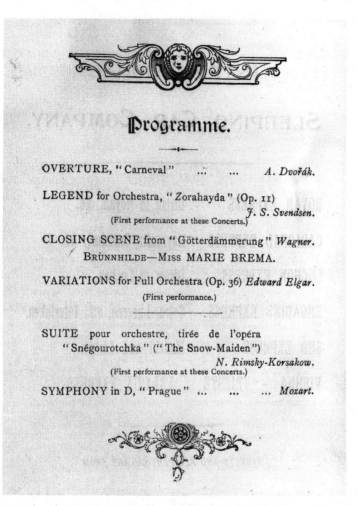

Programme.

OVERTURE, "Carneval" ... ... *A. Dvořák.*

LEGEND for Orchestra, "Zorahayda" (Op. 11)
J. S. Svendsen.
(First performance at these Concerts.)

CLOSING SCENE from "Götterdämmerung" *Wagner.*
BRÜNNHILDE—MISS MARIE BREMA.

VARIATIONS for Full Orchestra (Op. 36) *Edward Elgar.*
(First performance.)

SUITE pour orchestre, tirée de l'opéra
"Snégourotchka" ("The Snow-Maiden")
N. Rimsky-Korsakow.
(First performance at these Concerts.)

SYMPHONY in D, "Prague" ... ... *Mozart.*

Programme for the St James's Hall concert of 19 June 1899: the proximity
of Edward Elgar and Mozart has inspired one 'solution' to the 'Enigma'.

that these personages comment or reflect on the original theme & each
one attempts a solution of the Enigma, for so the theme is called.'
Again, in 1929 Elgar wrote helpful notes to accompany pianola rolls
of the work, making essential points about his tripartite theme and
their implications for what followed. He first drew attention to the
rhythm: 'The alternation of the two quavers and two crotchets in the
first bar and their reversal in the second bar will be noticed; references
to this grouping are almost continuous.' He then mentioned an

important interval: 'The drop of a seventh in the Theme (bars 3 and 4) should be observed.' Finally there was a textural matter in the middle section: 'At bar 7 (G major) appears the rising and falling passage in thirds which is much used later (Ex. 47)'. Elgar might also

Ex. 47

have referred to the ubiquitous intervals of a third and a fourth in the first section, the conjunct span of a fourth in the second, and the alternation of G minor and major in the three sections, with the final major chord. In the programme note for the 1899 première Elgar had warned 'that the apparent connection between the Variations and the Theme is often of the slightest texture'. That is both enigmatic and misleading. In a work as close-knit and thematically integrated as the Variations such a 'warning' could not be more wide of the mark.

Elgar had heard the Brahms–Haydn Variations at the Gloucester Festival a month before he began his own work; but he does not follow such a rigorous model. Yet in the supreme resource of his thematic evolutions Elgar could hardly be more Brahmsian, and in imaginative flair he is more than his equal. As well as a very plastic theme, Elgar had the added stimulus of human portraiture, so that the Variations became the first of his masterpieces overtly dependent on people around him. Just as Wagner always needed a dramatic idea or visual image to fire him (he could make little of the American Centennial March, which conjured up only its 5000 dollar fee), so Elgar gave of his best when the spirit of some place or the soul of some person sparked invention.

Two bars after the end of the theme G minor is resumed to introduce 'C.A.E.', Alice Elgar, for whom he designed 'romantic and delicate additions' to the theme. The scoring is affectionately wrought, as is Elgar's 'whistled' call on oboe and bassoon to signal he had come home. A bar is inserted to launch the middle section in E flat. The return to the third section is disguised by an interrupted cadence and *largamente* counterpoint from the heights; but the theme is there. The variation is extended by the conjunct parallel thirds of the middle section, and the final chord becomes four extra bars in G major.

The subject of Variation II is H. D. Steuart-Powell, amateur pianist who had played duets with Parry at Oxford during their student days and, later, piano trios with Elgar. Here the falling thirds and fourths of the theme are chromatically at sixes and sevens. Elgar claimed this was a humorous travesty of Steuart-Powell's 'characteristic diatonic run over the keys before beginning to play'. The first section of the theme appears eventually on cellos and basses, is enamoured of the falling sevenths for four extra bars, and the final bar stretches now to ten bars of *diminuendo*.

R. B. Townshend is depicted in Variation III as a whimsical character in amateur dramatics with his 'low voice flying off occasionally into "soprano" timbre'. He was also an explorer, prospected for gold, taught classics, translated Tacitus, and wrote many books. The only one now remaining among Elgar's library at the Birthplace is his

Inspired Golf (1921). His variation, starting in the tonic major, gives the oboe an initial stutter, inverts intervals, and plays merrily across bar lines so that six bars become seven. The second and third sections are repeated. The second is much expanded, but the parallel thirds and falling fourths are there. Tonally the A sharp that featured momentarily in the transition to 'C.A.E.' is now parsed as the third of F sharp over a dominant pedal. It is a delicious side-step. F sharp minor moves by sequence to G minor, and the third section can resume in G major. As Elgar points out, there has been 'growing grumpiness in the bassoons'. R.B.T.'s nephew maintained they represented his uncle's tricycle or galloping over a western prairie.

William Meath Baker, lord of Hasfield Court, was brother-in-law of R.B.T. He was an enthusiastic climber and supporter of the Three Choirs Festival. Variation IV represented W.M.B., having assigned carriages for his many guests, as he '*forcibly* read out the arrangements for the day and hurriedly left the music-room with an inadvertent bang of the door'. Back in G minor, the variation has no melodic rests in the theme. Except for 'the teasing attitude of the guests' on canonic woodwind, all is loud and peremptory. The first section is virtually unaltered in its breakneck course. In the major second section, an original single bar has become two, so that proportions are much altered. To compensate, the 'guests', chattering in canon at a crotchet's distance and a fifth below, pre-echo the third section over ten bars. W.M.B. returns *fff* with renewed emphasis.

Variation V concerns Richard Penrose Arnold, son of the poet Matthew Arnold, grandson of Dr Arnold of Rugby. He deserted family traditions, retiring in his early forties from nothing in particular. Elgar enjoyed the fact that 'His serious conversation was continually broken up by whimsical and witty remarks'. The music is in C minor and major, a subdominant move from G, and is the first of the variations to be linked with the next. The pattern follows that of III, with second and third sections repeated; but here so much detail is changed that the whole is written out fully. The opening six bars are in double counterpoint, with G-string violins propounding an opulent counter-subject to the theme below. A solo flute gracefully concentrates most of the second section's matter into one bar, and R.P.A.'s wit is represented by woodwind parallel thirds. The third section inverts the first with discreet adjustments. Finally the clarinet winds down to abbreviated hints of section one and quiet entry of the trombones.

The subject of Variation VI is Isabel Fitton, whose name Elgar olde-Englished into 'Ysobel'. Elgar taught her the viola and noted that 'a phrase made use of throughout the variation, is an "exercise" for crossing the strings'. The variation remains mostly in C, with hint of the dominant in the first section, and subdominant in the second. Written out repeats make virtually five sections, but the 3/2 time signature implies a stretching of resources. At the outset violas and cellos play with Elgar's short–short–long figure; bassoons and clarinets do likewise and have a firmer grip of the theme. The second section has chromatic touches and a delightful extension of the parallel thirds to fill the longer bars. The counterpoint on viola solo in the third section acknowledges the thirds of the theme. The repeat of the second section has an Elgarian rush of emotion that accounts for his describing the movement as 'pensive and, for a moment, romantic'.

The Troyte Griffith of Variation VII was more sensitive than his music suggests. Architect, water-colourist, and trusted friend over many years, Troyte also indulged in 'maladroit essays to play the pianoforte'. These, said Elgar, made the basis of his variation, with the 'uncouth rhythm of the drums and lower strings'. The first section of the theme is represented by the manic cross-rhythms of the opening in C, the parallel thirds of the second section are at once recognizable, and falling thirds do duty for the last section. At a spanking Presto the twelve bars are over in a flash, and Elgar shrewdly repeats them. The heavy brass thrusts the second section into C minor and an upward rocket of a chromatic scale completes the first half of the variation. Elgar now performs an almost exact da capo, except that the cross-rhythm appears once only, and a brusque coda on the theme's first section tells us why.

Winifred Norbury of Variation VIII conducted village choirs and was closely associated with Elgar as a joint secretary of the Worcestershire Philharmonic Society. A niece described her as 'very sedate and calm, rather like a kind governess with him, but had a sense of humour and I believe he purposely kept on being tiresome till he had got the laugh – like a rather deep bell'.[7] But Elgar hinted that the music was more 'suggested by an eighteenth-century house', the Norbury home at Sherridge; yet it is for W.N. that 'a little suggestion of a characteristic laugh is given'. The music is now back in G, and the first section of the theme is gracefully arched over four bars in a long series of rising and falling thirds and fourths. Elgar repeats the pattern with subtly inverted rhythm. The woodwind trio is W.N.'s laugh as start to the second section, which continues with expressive appoggiaturas on top and hints of the first section below; it too repeats with an additional pair of appoggiatura bars. The third section recapitulates the first to conclude on a held violin G.

Elgar's Nimrod, as enshrined in Variation IX and in *The Music*

---

[7] Communication from Roger Fiske.

Makers was the companion of his rise to greatness. It was his gift to recognize genius and to spur it. The correspondence between the two reinforces Elgar's statement that 'Something ardent and mercurial, in addition to the slow movement' was needed to 'portray the character and temperament of A.J. Jaeger'. The immediate inspiration had been a discussion about Beethoven slow movements, and Elgar responded with his noblest one to date. The rhythmic pattern most typical of the theme is ubiquitous, and the E flat tonality is taken from the heart of 'C.A.E.'. Melodically, too, the music is closer to the theme than any of the variations since 'C.A.E.', and it is for 'Nimrod' that Elgar reserves the full expressive potential of the falling sevenths. It is they that extend the first section in both its initial presentations. The parallel thirds of the second section are here inverted on violas and cellos, and continued into the depths. The third section (Ex. 48) takes up again

Ex. 48

the second version of the opening music, working by repetition to a climax with flattened sixth, and by a further surge to the *largamente* of the last bars and the very Elgarian *diminuendo* beyond *pp*.

Dora Penny, step-niece of W.M.B., acquired her 'Dorabella' nickname from Mozart's *Così fan tutte*. The 'dance-like lightness' of Variation X was directly suggested by Dorabella's delight in devising dances to Elgar's piano-playing. Elgar called the movement 'Intermezzo', and here his 'warning' about the connection between theme and variations might have some application. Perhaps the double bars in the music are the clearest indication to his thinking. There are two, and each marks the start of the theme's second section. In the very extended first section the fluttering violins mark the climb of a third and a fourth with the initial notes of each group, and the chattering wind reply in the span of a falling third. The entry of the solo viola spells out stepwise elements of the second section, but the delicate figuration persists, taking the music from B minor to F sharp minor and through the remotest regions so far reached in the Variations, gradually back to G and a restatement of the Intermezzo's start, adorned this time on low flutes with an inverted hint of the second section. At the double bar the second section begins in earnest with the upward surge on violas to G minor, with the diatonic steps of the theme taken in contrary motion (Ex. 49). The first close is into B flat,

Ex. 49

then D minor, then back to G via a Neapolitan cadence, and on to the third section, which is the low flute version of the opening. At the next double bar the second section repeat is shortened, and a final four bars flutter to the end.

George Robertson Sinclair of Variation XI was organist of Hereford Cathedral, and notable on the pedals;[8] but Elgar's explanation of the music was canine: it had 'nothing to do with organs or cathedrals, or, except remotely, with G.R.S. The first few bars were suggested by his great bulldog Dan.' Back in the G minor of 'W.M.B.', the cascading strings of the first bar represented Dan 'falling down the steep bank into the river Wye'; the panting compression of the theme's first four bars on bassoons and basses was Dan's 'paddling up stream to find a landing place'; then came the D major flash of the second section, and Dan's 'rejoicing bark on landing'. Perhaps Dan gives five more A major barks as the brass resumes the first section in that key. A central portion of the movement busily works Dan's paddling through the strings till the start of the variation is recapitulated in the home G minor. An impetuous coda combines the first section's thirds and fourths above, with seventh-league strides below.

Basil Nevinson, the cellist of Variation XII, was at Oxford with Variation II, and both knew Alice Roberts before her marriage. Trios with Elgar were a natural development. Elgar refers to B.G.N.'s 'scientific and artistic attainments'. These were an amateur interest in entomology and devotion to music. A possible career as a barrister was not taken up. A solo cello begins and ends the G minor variation with a thoughtful paraphrase of the theme's third and fourth bars. The full band of cellos now launches on a version, with initial rests, of the theme's first four bars that expressively ornaments its essential structure. A move to repeat this in the relative B flat major gathers emotion enough to move in sequence through D minor and nearly related keys towards the second section in B flat. Here the upper voices have the original shapes, while the cellos continue with a counterpoint describing disjunct and conjunct thirds. The third section resumes the initial tune but without rests. There is no B flat repeat, but the melody rises in sequence to an impassioned climax and a fade-out as complete as that in 'Nimrod', so that a solo cello can re-emerge to close the movement.

The three asterisks at the head of Variation XIII conceal the name of Lady Mary Lygon of Madresfield House, a member of one of the great local families. She directed amateur choirs, and was associated with Elgar over the Madresfield Musical Competition. He presented

[8] See Ian Parrott, *Elgar* (London, 1971), pp. 46–9.

her with a bouquet at Foregate Street Station on 11 March 1899, when she left Worcester for Australia. Subtitled 'Romanza', the variation is in G, with prolonged voyages to remote tonal parts. The five plus five bars of the opening gives a new pacing to the theme, in which rising and falling thirds are ubiquitous, whereas the melodic fourths always fall. The central section, with its side drum sticks (or a couple of coins) on timpani, suggests 'the distant throb of the engines of a liner'. While violas in A flat preserve the 'alternation' of quavers and crotchets that Elgar remarked when describing his theme, a solo clarinet quotes the second subject of Mendelssohn's *Calm Sea and Prosperous Voyage* Overture. In a letter to Jaeger Elgar doubted the wisdom of the quotation, suspecting that reminiscence hunters might start other hares. On a proof of the keyboard version he cut out the inverted commas and lowered the second note of the phrase by a third, thus echoing the start of the variation. But Mendelssohn returned: A flat darkens to F minor and heavy brass take over the 'Calm Sea' theme. The opening paragraph is resumed, and an E flat coda sends the liner further on its way to Australia (or New Zealand),[9] which with a G major chord feels quite like home.

The finale, 'E.D.U.', is a self-portrait. Occasionally Lady Elgar wrote 'Edoo' in the diaries, her abbreviation for the German Eduard. Elgar said the movement was written 'at a time when friends were dubious and generally discouraging as to the composer's musical future'. It became an emphatic statement of his own confidence. The two shorts and a long of the theme's beginning are tightened to a new rhythm and build through a succession of arpeggios to a triumphant G major statement of its essential elements. Immediately, as often later, the movement turns to E flat, the key of 'Nimrod' and the middle section of 'C.A.E.', for a brief reminder of 'Nimrod'. The opening paragraph, ending *fff*, has dealt with figures from the theme's first section. In C major, over a chromatically descending bass, Elgar turns to the second section (Ex. 50), which generates fine new counterpoints culminating in a descending scale in dotted notes over a tonic pedal. The scale continues against the theme of the first section in its 'Nimrod' form, grouped in 3/2 across the 2/2 bars. Elgar treats the falling sevenths in sequence, then stretto, till he resumes the arpeggio introduction, initially in E minor. Eventually Elgar's 'homing' call is heard on the woodwind and the first seven bars of 'C.A.E.' are recapitulated in the original G minor. When this gracious music has run its course, the second section with all its new counterpoints is resumed. A dominant pedal, rushing scales, and the G major triumph originally brought the

---

[9] See Cora Weaver, *The Thirteenth Enigma?* (London, 1988), pp. 66–72.

Variations to an effective if laconic end. As first planned, the finale would in fact have been longer, as Elgar intended more Mendelssohnian reference to Lady Mary Lygon in the subsidiary E flat. Largely owing to persistence of Jaeger, the movement was indeed lengthened and glorified by the addition of an organ part. Elgar turned once more to C.A.E., immediately introducing the *largamente* counterpoint that had marked the climax of her variation and then reverting to 'Nimrod', with the sevenths bestriding a magisterially descending diatonic bass. The music of the finale's G major triumph sidesteps to B flat and E flat; then Elgar embarks on his final conflation of the theme's 'Nimrod' manifestation, while the diatonic bass moves steadily down-under. A last G major triumph, last excursion to E flat with the theme in augmentation, last *sforzando* chord, and Elgar had flung wide the gates to international fame.

Ex. 50

Symphony no. 1 in A flat

Nimrod was doubtful whether he would ever hear an Elgar symphony. His health was wretched when he wrote to Richter's son-in-law Sidney Loeb on 17 November 1908, hardly more than a fortnight before the première of op. 55: 'Isn't it cruel of fate to debar me from hearing Elgar's symphony for which I have been waiting for so long? For it is exactly 10 years this month that Elgar wrote to me that a "Gordon Symphony" for which I had sent him a synopsis was "possessing" him, but he could not yet write it down.'[10] Richter himself and many others had urged Elgar towards a symphony, and in his 'Retrospect' lecture at Birmingham on 13 December 1905 Elgar had issued his own challenge: 'I hold that the Symphony without a programme is the highest development of art'. When he eventually settled to the First Symphony, it took him hardly more than a year.

Two bars on the note A flat and the motto is launched 'Nobilmente e semplice'. Elgar wrote to Ernest Newman about the theme on 4 November 1908:

> It is, perhaps obvious that the opening theme is intended to be simple &, in intention, noble & elevating (I do hate to attempt to describe what I feel): the sort of *ideal* call – in the sense of persuasion, not coercion or command – & something above the everyday & sordid things: the theme does not become triumphant in the Ist. movemt. but emerges in the end as the conquering (subduing) idea.

A. J. Sheldon thought it 'such a theme as the Knights of the Grail might have kept step to in their solemn progress through Monsalvat'.[11]

The motto may be simple in presentation, mainly in two parts, diatonic with hardly an accidental in sight (Ex. 51). Yet the structure of the tune is subtle and complex, its initial units making a seven-bar phrase, with the long notes variously placed across the bars; and in

Ex. 51

the fully harmonized version some elements are omitted while others are repeated. The motto dies away to the A flat note from which it arose, and at the Allegro all is turbulence. The four flats are reduced

---

[10] Jaeger–Loeb correspondence; in possession of Richard Westwood-Brookes.
[11] See A. J. Sheldon, *Edward Elgar* (London, 1932), p. 48.

to one, and in a letter to Jaeger of 19 September 1908 Elgar claimed to have 'thrown over all key relationships as formerly practised'. At the same time he pointed out: 'I am not silly enough to think (or wish) that I have *invented* anything: see Beethoven's late Quartetts passim.' Having redefined his A flat enharmonically, Elgar now moves into a stormy, seventh-infested area that he said 'gives a feeling of A minor', the flat supertonic. Perhaps he had particularly in mind Beethoven's C sharp minor Quartet op. 131. There the opening fugue in the tonic is followed by the Allegro molto vivace movement in D major. Elgar told Jaeger that 'the signature of one flat means nothing – it is convenient for the players'. The first theme of the Allegro (Ex. 52)

Ex. 52

rises mainly by thirds to a climax in the fourth bar; its subsequent descent also features thirds. A subdominant restatement of this first subject develops an important countermelody that is a long time revealing its true significance. It was such cryptic procedures that baffled even Jaeger at the first performance he heard. In a letter to Sidney Loeb of 9 December 1908 he considered the first movement: 'E has *not yet* attained to that big symphonic sweep of the *true symphonist*.' He suspected that repeated hearings were necessary: 'I know the beauties are there, but they are not "stated" in Billposter fashion, with Tchaikovskian brutality in the way of doubling parts to get a thick, fast, palpable tone for every theme.'[12] Twelve days later he had heard the work again and could write very differently: 'That puzzling first movement is now clear as daylight to me, and very striking and dramatically beautiful it is.' Even so the cryptic countermelody (Ex. 53) hints at much to come.

Ex. 53

A change to 6/4, scanned initially as three times two, launches the transition. The thirds of the first Allegro theme now fall, and crotchet inner parts settle to semitone oscillation. Over a pizzicato bass moving in thirds and hinting at the first half of the first subject, the transition begets a lyrical phrase at cue 11 with change of rhythm to two times three and melodic shape deriving from the second half of the first subject. In the midst of what seems improvisatory freedom, Elgar never loses sight of his thematic data. Elgar felt the fifth bar at this point to be 'sad & delicate'. The second group begins in F with a return to 2/2 and quaver arabesques for the moment in the background. It is a graceful, soaring theme (Ex. 54), relying on the stepwise movement of the motto and falling thirds of the transition. The richly scored

Ex. 54

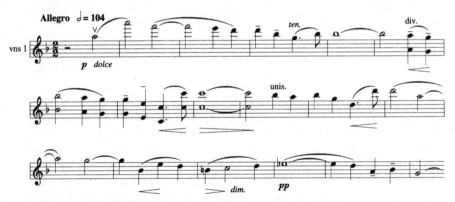

restatement sidesteps briefly to D flat, a moment of tender withdrawal into a quiet private world. A change to 6/4 brings back the chromatic

[12] Richard Westwood-Brookes Collection.

obsessions of the transition. The woodwind concentrate on a wide-leaping figure which gradually tightens its intervals so as to take the shape of the first subject, of which the outline is still in the ascendant in the *con fuoco* quavers of cue 16. The 'sad & delicate' theme is blared on the brass *tutta forza*, repeatedly, in an agony of woeful augmentation that is thoroughly 'Billposter' in fashion. Elgar draws his double line, and the exposition is done. Elgar scored the Symphony thus far before finalizing the rest of the movement.

The development begins with a faint echo in C, on muted horns, of the motto's first phrase. It is clear from Elgar's earliest sketchbooks that development within sonata form was initially a problem. It is as if pleasure in his themes almost precluded analysis of them and fragmentation. The small-scale perfection he achieved time and again in maturity, whether in partsong or lighter orchestral piece, only underlines the point. Initially this development seems episodic, and its close thematic thinking is almost too carefully concealed, with Elgar the mystery-maker too successfully at work. He now concentrates on figures that have hitherto played only a fleeting part in the movement, turning first to the cryptic countermelody of the exposition. Having established its identity, Elgar expands it into a tune of generous potential. The oscillating semitones of the transition lead to a theme built from the quaver arabesques supporting the second subject that develops a penchant for falling thirds. Hints of the first subject are intertwined also into a dreamlike web of sound. The lyrical phrase from the transition is fired to an incandescent climax, and out of its embers arises at cue 24 what Elgar called a 'restless, enquiring & *exploring*' idea. It is formed from the rising and falling semitones of the first subject, with intervals expanded to giant steps. The second subject returns, *grandioso*, in B minor over a dominant pedal. After further 'exploring' at half speed, a solo violin makes a new counterpoint to quaver arabesques and hints of the first subject in falling thirds and rising semitones. A veiled reference to the motto on clarinet and cello makes the point that D major, at furthest remove from A flat, can also feel the influence of the 'great beautiful tune'. The cryptic counter-melody now further explains its *raison d'être*: it combines with a slowed version of the quaver arabesques and then forms a bass for the return of the Allegro's first subject (Ex. 55).

Elgar decided early in his sketches on this start to the recapitulation. He told Newman of his pleasure at the thematic combination, which suggested both A minor and G major: 'I have a *nice sub-acid* feeling when they come together'. After some short cuts, Elgar re-establishes an allusive A flat before beginning the transition. The 'sad & delicate' theme has an extra three bars before the second subject returns in an

Ex. 55

unambiguous A flat, with a sidestep this time to E major. There is chromatic clatter from some 'Billposter' brass and an extension of the woeful augmentation to make the unobtrusive emergence of the motto the more telling. The cryptic countermelody now joins the motto in a final demonstration of its versatility. Elgar wrote to Newman about the orchestral layout at this point: 'I have employed the *last desks* of the strings to get a soft diffused sound: the listener need not be bothered to know *where* it comes from – the effect is of course widely different from that obtained from the *first desk soli*.' Once the motto has had its say (it is not 'triumphant' yet), the countermelody remains, then gives place to the 'exploring' theme. The quaver arabesques return, and they too make counterpoint with the motto. The last word is given to the 'sad & delicate' theme, now forgetful of all rhetoric. Elgar sent Richter instruction about the end of the movement and an extended passage in the development: 'Please *insist* that from four bars after **29** to **31** and from **53** to the end of the movement must be played in a veiled, mysterious way – a sort of *echo*: There is only one *f* (in the strings) for a moment throughout these two sections.' In a lengthy movement so apparently prodigal of material Elgar has yet demonstrated an underlying economy and tautness of thought as impressive as it is original.

Elgar

Elgar explained the F sharp minor of the Allegro molto second movement as derived from A flat via a seventh chord on its subdominant D flat leading to G flat minor viewed enharmonically. He summed this up for Jaeger: 'You will find many subtle *enharmonic* relationships & the widest *looking* divergencies are often closest relationships.' The progression to F sharp minor was

> a sort of *plagal* (?) relationship of which I appear to be fond (although I didn't know it) – must folks run through *dominant* modulations – if that expression is allowable & I think some of my twists are defensible on *sub*-dominant grounds. All this is beside the point because I *feel* & don't invent – I can't even invent an explanation.

The F sharp takes a little time to settle its key. The flying semiquavers suggest D major, with implications for the slow movement. But at the end of the seven-bar scurry, woodwind arpeggios clearly define F sharp minor. A strutting march tune invades the music with another seven-bar phrase athletically jointed; this made no appearance in the 1907 string quartet sketches. It gains mightily in confidence until eventually the quavers augment, and in a few deft moves Elgar shifts the tonality to B flat major for his 'wind in the rushes' music (Ex. 56). This did

Ex. 56

feature in the string quartet, but now it is delicately scored, with touches of pizzicato, a little doubling on the solo violin, and quiet rippling on the harp as accompaniment to the flute tune in a passage of sunlit magic. The tune gathers a counterpoint warmed with chromatics and enlivened with triplets. Clarinets in thirds complete the material of an idyll that Jaeger thought 'simply haunting in its truthfulness – most exquisitely treated by a master's supreme art'. The music reverts to F sharp minor, and the thirds continue as counterpoint to the resumed bustle of semiquavers. The march is now additionally aggressive, absorbing the semiquavers, and even launching the return of the 'river' music *fortissimo*. But this retrieves its own dynamic and develops generous aspirations in a rising sequential passage over a long paragraph. The semiquavers return again, with the thirds as counterpoint below. A long coda quotes all aspects of the movement, and steadily reduces the tension till only a held F sharp remains with broken echoes of the march beneath.

Elgar described to Newman how the slow movement evolved from the Allegro molto: 'You will notice that the rapid violin figure opening the second movement becomes slower (triplets) then in quavers & lastly in crotchets & eventually becomes note for note the theme of the Adagio.' The opening bars of the D major Adagio are just as in the 1907 quartet; but Elgar gave Newman another clue to his close thematic thinking: he instanced the entry of the horns with 'a veiled reference to the opening theme – it may be too obscure to strike anyone but very keen observers as you are!' Elgar's intention is indeed obscure: perhaps he had in mind the start of the first movement Allegro plus a fragment of the motto. The precise reference is not so important as the hint of how Elgar set about the writing of a symphony. The flying semiquavers are now spread over the slow tempo in ever-varied patterns so that a bar of the original makes two and a half bars, or one and a half, then two (Ex. 57). But the loveliest moment is the Adagio's refusal in the seventh bar to touch the top A of the original but rather to transpose down a semitone all the intervals of the bar into the remoteness of B flat minor. The first section of the Allegro molto tune is completed halfway through the thirteenth bar, and then,

Ex. 57

in even semiquavers, inner parts launch on the second section. It is an astonishing transformation and, unlike many such examples, a complete success. The music closes into F sharp minor, and the woodwind arpeggios of the Allegro molto are now adapted to string arabesques.

Fanciful figuration across the orchestra leads to solemn Brahmsian harmonies that pass from horns to trombones in a moment of expectation till timpani taps usher in the second subject in A. The lower parts transform in stately manner the fanciful shapes just heard, while the new theme, compounded of rising and falling sixths, describes a series of arches soaring higher and higher. The two themes work in sonorous double counterpoint before dissolving into the figuration from which one of them arose. In the brief central section clarinet and solo violin devise yet more fantastic ideas, until the music gradually settles to the Brahmsian harmonies that now prepare recapitulation. The first subject changes direction in the fifth bar, with the cor anglais taking the semitone sideslip momentarily into F minor. The second subject is initially in C sharp major, a semitone lower than might have been expected, and as surprising in its way as the A minor Allegro of the first movement. Half a dozen bars of the fanciful figuration restore the tonic, and as coda theme Elgar introduces an idea dating from 1904. When originally sketched, the theme carried a *Hamlet* quotation, 'The rest is silence'; now it sums up the movement's essence by combining in one melodic sweep the descending steps and wide intervals of the two strands that made up the second subject. The fantastic shapes of the clarinet are heard again and the triplets of the last bars on muted brass recall a moment from the first subject. From the outset Jaeger had no doubts about the Adagio: 'That movement I consider the most beautiful, and perfect message of peace, chaste feeling, aloofness from all things mundane and common that has been given to the world since Brahms penned the marvellous Adagio in the "Clarinet Quintet".'

The D minor of the Lento introduction to the finale is established almost at once. This is the anti-key to the work's A flat. The 'exploring' theme adumbrated in the first movement emerges from the depths and is treated imitatively. A sombre march figure is propounded on staccato bassoons and pizzicato cellos. Elgar told Newman this figure was 'really sort of foreshadowed at **96** in the clarinets &c' (second subject of the Adagio), and that 'the germ of this is of course in the introduction'. Elgar also wanted Newman to make a special point of 'the Clart entry "*romantico*" [actually *dolcissimo largamente*] two bars after 108'. This theme leads to the 'motto' on the last desks of upper strings with the march as glum counterpoint. A move to F minor recapitulates the 'exploring' idea and the march. A sudden *crescendo* brings A flat, a diminution of the 'exploring' motif, and the 'last desk' motto in its home key, surrounded in a chromatic haze of sound. The key cannot long hold its own. It changes to F flat (E major), with the march as bass. The 'romantico' works towards the dominant of D minor, and the music is poised for the finale's main tempo.

This D minor Allegro (the one-flat signature means what it says) begins determined and square-cut. The dotted crotchet–quaver figure is repeated forty times in the twenty bars that go to the first subject. The constant rise and fall of the theme maintains interest, but it is not one of Elgar's most distinguished paragraphs. The 'romantico' strides across the score from F major with passionate intensity, disrupting tonality and rhythmic flow with a series of triplet crotchets. The second subject at cue 114 (Ex. 58), unstable in key but uniting the rhythm of the first subject with the triplet crotchets of the 'romantico' motif at different places in the bar, has fine Brahmsian momentum and subtlety.

Ex. 58

Yet Elgar inserted it only after he had fully scored the finale. It gives place to 'romantico' and the dour persistence of the march, building insistently from D minor through F, A flat minor, C sharp minor, and E major till it comes full circle to a rumbustious D minor climax of blaring brass. A full-scale return of the first subject at this point makes of the movement the only sonata-rondo in Elgar's output.

The march is in full possession as the development opens, fragmented, in contrary motion, strident and obstreperous, until triplet crotchets emerge from long held notes on horns and trumpets. The dialectic now treats aspects of the second subject caught up equally in the maelstrom. Elgar checks the tempest at a stroke, just as he touches D minor again. A sudden C flat in the bass spells out the notes of the march, and the motto, again entrusted to the last desks, makes a shadowy return in A flat minor. The final episode of the development is the most wondrous. For the moment the march has done its worst, and at this point Jerrold Northrop Moore aptly quotes an Elgar letter to Neville Cardus: 'You do not see that the fierce quasi-military themes are dismissed with scant courtesy.'[13] The march is now transformed into a flowing cantabile in E flat minor. It is treated with fine canonic resource, twice at the seventh below, twice at the ninth above, with a third attempt in full sonority broken off. Indeed the 'coarser themes are well quashed!'

The first subject resumes in E flat minor. In both symphonies Elgar enjoys 'recapitulating' away from the home key so as to blur formal divisions and preserve the ambiguities so dear to him. The 'romantico' launches in E flat major, a tone below the equivalent place in the exposition, whereas the second subject returns a major third below. He continues with adjustments here and there so that the march builds from F minor, a minor third above the exposition. It follows the previous tonal pattern, ending in a very unquashed F minor. Elgar has now reached the relative minor of A flat, and his long-distance tonal thinking can be fully appreciated. D minor had to be dismissed as completely as the coarser themes, so there was no place for it in this recapitulation. Elgar's 'romantico' motif burgeons in augmentation on the horns and fully justifies its original title. It is combined with itself in the former note values, chases its tail in diminution, forms into descending arpeggios, and builds to the moment when the motto indeed appears as the 'conquering (subduing) idea'. The arpeggios continue to flash through the first strain of the grand tune, which then gathers to itself all the instruments in acclamation. Figures from the end of the first movement return, and a précis of the finale's second subject speeds towards a last spelling-out by the brass of the motto's first five notes.

To Walford Davies Elgar wrote of the work: 'There is no programme beyond a wide experience of human life with a great charity (love) & a *massive* hope in the future.' To Ernest Newman he was more

[13] Jerrold Northrop Moore, *Edward Elgar: a Creative Life* (Oxford, 1984), p. 539.

forthcoming. Absolute music must be, he felt, 'a reflex, or picture, or elucidation of [the composer's] own life. The listener may like to know this much & identify his own life's experience with the music as he hears it unfold.' And of the Symphony itself: 'As to the phases of pride, despair, anger, peace & the thousand & one things that occur between the first page & the last, as I said before, I prefer the listener to draw what he can from the sounds he hears.'

Symphony no. 2 in E flat

In the early 1900s Dorabella recalled seeing at Craeg Lea 'one fat book with "Symphony" on it'. She asked Elgar if he would play something from it. He complied, and she heard 'odds and ends; bits and scraps; and sometimes a good deal more'. If these fragments belonged to either of the completed symphonies, it was more probably to no. 2. At the time of the *Apostles* première Elgar wrote a playful letter to Richter on 11 October 1903 about an excursion near Birmingham: 'You will be pleased to hear that we are quite safe after our motor journey.' Elgar then claimed that six babies had been run over, two men knocked down, seven dogs killed, miles of fencing carried away, and canal bridges damaged. He summed up: 'all the incidents are being worked into the Symphony in E♭ dedicated to Hans Richter'. The E flat Symphony became no. 2 and has strong Richter links in the finale; but the dedication went to the memory of King Edward VII, since Richter already had the First.

Elgar explained to Charles Sanford Terry how he set about such a work: first he fixed the climax of each movement; then he arranged 'the great mass of fluctuating material which *might* fit into the work as it developed in his mind to finality'. The essential point was that the same 'oven' should have cast it all and thus ensure ultimate unity.[14] Lady Elgar wrote the word 'Ghost' on what she called the '1st. sketch of Symphony No. 2';[15] this was the eerie music that launches the first movement development at cue 24. The undulating chords at the start of the Larghetto had been discarded from Scene II of *The Kingdom* and had also been considered for a projected partsong, *Israfel*. Experiences in Venice lay behind much of the two central movements. The serene opening of the finale had been conceived at Alassio. Rosa Burley heard the tune there and did not think much of the 'phrase that was repeated sequentially *ad nauseam*'; but she remembered it in 1911: 'The moment that the orchestra began the last movement I found that

[14] MS notes at the Athenaeum Club.
[15] Sketches and drafts at the Birthplace Museum.

my mind had been whisked back to the holiday at Alassio over seven years earlier, to the memory of twelve men delivering a small piano at the Villa San Giovanni and of Edward's sitting down and playing the first tune that came into his head'. The transition theme of the finale had been invented by the autumn of 1905, when Ivor Atkins wanted to hear it; Elgar had dubbed it 'Hans himself!' in honour of Richter. 'Careggi' is written at the end of the Symphony's keyboard draft, because of ideas that occurred during the 1909 holiday, and 'Venice' appears on the printed full score; to both places was added 'Tintagel', where Elgar visited the Stuart Wortleys in April 1910.

A motto from Shelley, 'Rarely, rarely comest thou, / Spirit of Delight', headed the keyboard draft and ended the MS full score. Elgar appended a drawing of the 'Spirit' on the draft, a Piglet-like creature with antennae. He explained to the Novello chairman that the whole of the poem was applicable to the Symphony and outlined his purpose: 'The spirit of the whole work is intended to be high & pure joy: there are retrospective passages of sadness but the whole of the sorrow is smoothed out & ennobled in the last movement.' In conversation with Canon W. H. Temple Gairdner, Elgar agreed that 'the whole thing represents the "passionate pilgrimage" of a soul; that the last movement represents the final issue of his "passion" in noble action, and that the last two pages is apotheosis and the eternal issue of the soul's pilgrimage'.[16]

The Symphony is more concentrated than the First, less inclined to pursue the implications of a theme to its limits. It makes an impressive unity, though Elgar implied otherwise to Terry. He did not intend to make 'the new Symphony an organic whole by means of such a connecting-motif as that which opens and ends the Symphony in A♭. He wanted it to be the frank expression of music bubbling from the spring within him.' At the outset the orchestra gathers on the dominant and uses it as a springboard for one of the most exciting of all symphonic openings. Like the First Symphony it begins 'nobilmente', but this time with what Elgar described to Littleton as 'an assemblage of themes' (Ex. 59). The method is rather that of the Violin Concerto,

Ex. 59

¹⁶ William H. Temple Gairdner, *W.H.T.G. to his Friends* (London, 1930), p. 157.

the moulding of a huge paragraph from detachable units presented for the moment with irresistible impetus as a continuous outpouring of fiery melody. No motto maybe, but as Elgar wrote: 'The germ of the work is in the opening bars – these in a modified form are heard for the last time in the closing bars of the movement.' The initial bars marvellously vary the 12/8 rhythm so that it is only in the sixth bar that any of the patterns repeat. The first semitones in the work, F sharp to G, stand out clearly and are structurally important, as are the figures in the two bars that surround them. There is an early touch of the subdominant, audacious writing for the horns and trumpet, and a three-bar phrase before the music stabilizes to a series of sequences initially over an ornamented pedal C. Semiquavers proliferate across the score as the headlong impulse continues till at last they break up the flow of melody and upper strings make prominent a motif that will later assume a 'ghostly' shape. As the music quietens for the first time, the second subject group begins. It starts on a chord of G, but the theme is tonally elusive with momentary glints of various keys so that a restatement starting in E flat has little sense of homecoming. A motif on the cellos (Ex. 60), involving a descending semitone then

Ex. 60

tritone, is more suggestive of the dominant B flat and is accompanied by the rising semitones of the movement's second bar. Presumably because of its structural importance, Elgar drew particular attention to this motif: 'I wish the theme at **11** to be considered (& labelled) as the second principal theme.' The elusive theme returns with expressive counterpoints on oboe and clarinet that echo the second half of the cello motif. Tension builds to an *impetuoso* hammering across the beats and a passage of utmost brilliance over a bass moving in tritones. The climax is reached in a *maestoso* rethinking of the cello motif. A winding codetta theme with falling tritone dies away to harp harmonics and semitone echoes.

The 'ghost' then launches the development with descending semitones, thirds that span octaves, over a bass moving in tritones (Ex. 61). The motif, new yet anticipated in every aspect, engages in spectral dialogue with aspects of the first subject until a slowing of the tempo

Ex. 61

combines the 'ghost', Elgar's 'germ of the work', and a strange new cantilena on the cellos over an insistent E bass. The MS full score makes clear that the cantilena evolved its expressive independence only in the last stages of composition; its original shape was tied more absolutely to aspects of the 'ghost' (Ex. 62). A tender oboe solo twines over the last bars of this considerable contrapuntal feat. Elgar wrote on two occasions about this passage. To Littleton he described it as

Ex. 62 (a)

'remote & drawing some one else out of the everyday world'. He bade him 'note the *feminine* voice of the oboe, answering or joining in'. With the movement only just complete, Elgar hoped that Ernest Newman would enjoy parts of the Symphony, and particularly mentioned this section, 'which might be a love scene in a garden at night when the ghost of some memories comes *through it*; – it makes me shiver but perhaps it will miss its effect in playing'. The oboe solo is followed by a lingering and pensive reference to the 'germ of the work'. Littleton was told to 'note the happiness at 30 – real (remote) peace'. The night scene is resumed a third lower, this time with rhythm that includes insistent quaver taps on the side drum. Elgar now felt 'the atmosphere broken in upon & the dream "shattered" by the inevitable march of the Trombones & Tuba pp'. A pedal on C is established, ornamented as before, and with sequential figures from the first subject above. But this time it is not the C natural of the exposition but C sharp. Elgar gives the impression of gathering his forces towards recapitulation, and at cue 37 he would seem to have plunged *in medias res*. But he is in E major, not E flat, and the ensuing bars preserve an ambiguity similar to that of the finale of the First Symphony. It is some time before the bass sinks to B flat and Elgar launches on a prolonged and exciting passage of dominant preparation with flashing strings and virtuoso brass.

The actual moment of recapitulation could not be more emphatic, with hammered timpani and the 'germ' declaimed by the brass in rhetorical splendour. Elgar covered so much ground in his 'false' recapitulation that he can now move swiftly to the semiquaver break-up of the melodic flow and the second group, starting this time on F and repeating in D flat, a tone above and below the movement's tonic. Progress is as before to the A flat of Elgar's 'second principal theme', again on the cellos but subtly extended by a bar. The *impetuoso* is punctually reached and leads to a slightly shortened *maestoso*. It is only with the winding codetta theme that E flat is finally established. The brief coda to the movement refers in tender and wistful augmentation to a phrase from the first group, momentarily recalls the 'night' scene with timpani roll and pizzicato dactyls on the basses, and gathers powerful impetus for final arpeggios and a chromatic soaring into the heights.

The Larghetto was also described to Littleton: 'The second movement formed part of the original scheme – before the death of King Edward; – it is elegiac but has nothing to do with any funeral march & is a "reflection" suggested by the poem.' The C minor opening chords might recall the first movement sequences over the C pedals; for Elgar they carried also echoes from the 'Beautiful Gate' at Jerusalem and of Israfel, the angel in the Koran 'who has the sweetest voice of all God's creatures'. The theme of the slow march, with its solemn tromboning and off-beat timpani taps, refers directly to the opening notes of the Symphony, but has an expressive central section initially on the violins' G string. A melancholy transition motif, mainly on woodwind and involving triplet quavers, leads to the second group. This begins in remote calm on three-part strings and an F major with strong tendencies towards A minor. The restatement on wind gathers new counterpoints and richer harmonies till a passage of strenuous string dialectic retreats suddenly to remotest regions for a prolonged sequential episode adorned with pulsating wind and mysterious scales on the strings. This section has its origin in ideas for the second *Cockaigne* Overture, to be subtitled after James Thomson's poem, 'The City of Dreadful Night'. Its climax ushers in a phrase of passionate intensity, *nobilmente e semplice*, now in a fully established F major. It lingers through a long-drawn cadence and returns to the triplets of the transition. These do duty, in a handful of bars, for a bridge between exposition and recapitulation.

A solo oboe takes the triplets to itself in a winding threnody above the solemn tread of the march, heavier with multiple *divisi* arpeggios on the strings. This is where, Elgar told Littleton, 'the feminine voice *laments* over the broad manly Ist theme'. The proportions of this first subject group are now considerably varied, with the march and all its sorrowing paraphernalia extended by four bars and imposing also on the central section that now closes through A flat minor into the doubtful E flat of the second group. 'Dreadful Night' runs its awesome course as before, but the *nobilmente* climax rearranges its material so as to generate a passage of goldshot scoring with a searing intensity rare even in Elgar. It reverts to the original cadence, which conjures as start to the coda a two-bar reminiscence of the work's 'germ', perhaps 'like a woman dropping a flower on the man's grave?' queried Elgar to Littleton. Its triplet quavers lead naturally to the transition theme that had not been heard in the recapitulation. The march resumes briefly over a new figure that emphasizes every beat of the bar. The framing chords are heard once more and Elgar's elegy dies to silence.

The Rondo in C, starting playfully enough, contains within it the most terrible of Elgar's symphonic climaxes, hinting at an almost Mahlerian annihilation. The thirds and octave leaps of the Presto theme recall at once the first movement's 'ghost' and its semitones hint at the strange cantilena of the night. A restatement follows in E, and the rhythm breaks across the beats in a pair of seven-bar phrases. A sonorous theme in the tonic minor for strings in octaves is as regular in rhythm as the opening had been capricious. It moves upwards in quiet sequence till it develops an expressive oboe pendant. The skittish rhythms of the first bars return in compulsive chase through the orchestra and eventually generate a powerful new theme of impetuous energy (Ex. 63). An early sketch shows that at one time Elgar thought of linking this tune to the second 'Windflower' theme of the Violin

Ex. 63

Concerto. It now gives place to the main Rondo idea, *ff* with varied phrase lengths and the restatement in an unstable E flat. It closes into a woodwind breath of the countryside that tends towards D major and carries on exchanges with a sequential string figure more garrulous than significant. Reappearance of the Rondo theme brings with it a sense of foreboding in an outline of the 'night' cantilena that suggests also the Rondo itself in augmentation. The 'night' gradually takes its first movement form over an E flat pedal in Elgar's 'shattered dream' version, with repeated quavers more and more urgent on timpani then bass drum. As the theme repeats on trombones and tuba, it gathers to itself the side drum in steady *crescendo*, the Rondo rhythm in menacing flashes, and wild manifestations of the 'ghost'. The shattered dream has taken on the terror of waking nightmare, as Elgar explained to an orchestra he was conducting: 'Now, gentlemen, at this point I want you to imagine that my music represents a man in a high fever. Some of you may know that dreadful beating that goes on in the brain – it seems to drive out every coherent thought.'[17] The 'ghost' figure calms the music sufficiently to banish from it the incessant throb, and confidence returns with the sonorous string tune. Rondo rhythms chase through the score again, and eventually a coda reduces them to insistent and near-manic repetitions till there comes an inversion of the first movement's end, with a chromatic hurtling to the depths.

'The last movement speaks for itself I think: a broad sonorous, rolling movement throughout – in an elevated mood.' So Elgar explained it to Littleton. The first tune relies for its effect on subtle rise and fall of the melodic line within a fixed rhythm. It is a favourite Elgarian device with an inbuilt risk of monotony. Here the contours of the tune are so nicely varied from bar to bar that the result is a complete success; its last statement within the first group shows how flexibly the shape can be moulded and how the slightest tightening of the rhythm can herald drama in so leisurely a context. The transition theme, 'Hans himself!', presents itself in various guises of A flat and moves by imposing sequences, with last minute tonal sidesteps, to the dominant B flat and its second group, the only *nobilmente* of the movement. The tune is grandly sonorous, and its restatement receives additional radiance from a brief glimpse into B major. From its high point it dies away in one of Elgar's loveliest sequences that he also remembered for *The Music Makers* of the following year; a cadential reminder of the first subject switches abruptly to A major and the start of the development, again as far from E flat as the First Symphony's D minor was from A flat.

[17] Bernard Shore, *The Orchestra Speaks* (London, 1938), p. 135.

Initially there is imitative treatment of the 'Hans' theme, combined with aspects of the first subject (in triplet quavers or the original dactyls) and a capricious concoction of arpeggios and scales. The phrases are mostly of three bars, but stretto reduces them to two bars, then one. As B minor prevails, Elgar's counterpoints include the first theme, a fragment of 'Hans' culminating in a long held top B on the first trumpet, and a stepwise theme on rising crotchets. This last engenders a quaver motif also integral to the development's thematic mix. The high trumpet note was the subject of an exchange between Elgar and Ernest Hall of the LSO: 'Sir Edward asked me at a recording why I held my top B♮ over to the next bar, & I replied that I was so pleased to get the note I didn't like to leave it. His reply was, – I intended to write it so, but thought it would be too high to hold.'[18] With B minor still as tonal centre, an apparently new theme joins the development cast at cue 152. Its rhythm is nearest to that of the codetta at the end of the second group, but it is only gradually that it is seen to fit as cunningly as its companions in Elgar's contrapuntal web. On a sketch Elgar called it 'Braut's bit', so presumably Lady Elgar approved. The first bassoon hints almost at once that it will combine with the 'Hans' rhythm; then the first theme establishes its claim to relationship. As the music turns towards C minor, a melding of the first theme's rhythm and the rising crotchets is answered by the arching shape of the quaver pendant. Elgar headed a sketch of this passage with a quotation from Shakespeare's Sonnet 66, 'Art tongue-tied by authority'. Finally the quavers receive the imprint of the first theme's rhythm in a series of timpani taps.

Thus the recapitulation is launched, with 'Braut's bit' still in attendance. Imaginative readjustments bring back 'Hans himself!' in E flat. Its tonal sidesteps are a little extended to give the E flat of the second group a slight element of surprise, and now the final sequences are the more protracted in glowing pages of ravishing texture. So as to end 'in a calm &, *I hope & intend*, elevated mood', Elgar remembers the 'germ of the work' from the Symphony's start, enshrining it with the quiet scales and trills that hint at Beethoven's late piano music. The cadence figure returns momentarily, the first theme too, and Elgar's last chords before settling to E flat are a signal homage to the end of Wagner's *Tristan*. He first heard the 'Liebestod' at a Wagner memorial concert of March 1883 and wrote on his programme: 'I shall never forget this.'

In a June 1932 conversation with Basil Maine about the symphonies,

---

[18] Jerrold Northrop Moore, ed., *Music and Friends: Seven Decades of Letters to Adrian Boult* (London, 1979), p. 196.

Elgar considered the '2nd much bigger in idea than the Ist', but went on to explain that 'many of my friends did not dare to come round after the first perf. of E flat, they were so disappointed!' And he gave a main reason: 'Last movement of E flat, such sustained nobility – no passion as in Finale of A flat'. The peroration of the First was itself enough to bring down the house and launch a triumphal career. Jaeger understood the public's need for a loud end when writing to Alice Elgar in November 1900 about *Cockaigne* plans: 'Let him finish it with a *"Bang"* though, & give us a really rousing piece. We can all do with it.' On that occasion Elgar complied; the conclusion of the Second Symphony was very different.

Symphony no. 3 in C minor

The BBC commission for a Third Symphony, announced on 14 December 1932, was both an incentive to Elgar and an anxiety. The following August Fred Gaisberg, after hearing Elgar play, could report good progress: 'The work is complete as far as structure & design and scoring is well advanced.' The sketches and drafts tell no such tale. The full score of the opening Allegro molto maestoso was hardly begun. Nineteen pages had been laid out with clefs, key-signatures and bar lines for the exposition, but only the first two had been fully scored. The rest might contain as little as a fragmentary melodic line, until the first time bars for repeat of the exposition were reached; these contained fuller indications. A couple more pages was all that the first movement could show. Five full score pages had been set aside for the 'Scherzo', all but blank, and there was one finale page. That was the total.

In keyboard draft, however, the opening exposition was complete. Its two main subjects were probably separated by twenty years. The start was a powerful, pounding motif intended for *The Last Judgement* (Ex. 64a); the second subject was a new idea headed by Elgar 'V.H.'s own theme', an inspiration linked in Elgar's mind with Vera Hockman (Ex. 64b). Both themes relied for their effect, as so often before, on a persistent rhythmic figure maintained over different pitches. The codetta was to be based on an ingenious passage which W. H. Reed 'had to play countless times in every conceivable manner' to settle the bowing. The development was to incorporate a passage, again from the third oratorio, originally to have included four bassoons, such as Verdi had used near the start of the 'Libera me' in the Requiem. The reference on the sketch to '4 Fag' was crossed out.

The 'Scherzo' was to begin with the banquet music from Scene IV of *Arthur*, music that had lain dormant since 1923. The semiquaver figure was now to be accompanied by the rhythm Elgar had used as long ago as 1892 for his Longfellow setting in *The Spanish Serenade*.

Ex. 64

(a)

(b)

A slightly harsh progression in the *Arthur* version was smoothed out, and Elgar showed in other sketches how one of the episodes would lead back to the main theme, and how another would combine with the *Arthur* motif to provide the end.

The Adagio was to start with an idea originally planned for the second *Cockaigne* overture and that Elgar copied out for W. H. Reed on his deathbed. A sketch for the overture shows how Elgar would also have used it in diminution. Elgar described its significance in the Symphony as opening 'some vast bronze doors into something strangely unfamiliar'. The main theme of the movement again derived from *The Last Judgement*, and over it hovered reminders of the shofar that had featured so dramatically in *The Apostles* and would have heralded 'eternal dawn' in the successor work.

For the finale the most coherent body of themes had first been heard in *Arthur*. They were motifs associated with the idea of chivalry and more specifically with the king himself, as he wrestled with the political problems of his realm and the emotional turmoil of his marriage. Included too was the theme in augmentation last heard in the play as Arthur disappeared into the shadows en route for his final battle.

The music of the Symphony impressed listeners as different from Gaisberg as W. H. Reed, Basil Maine and Bernard Shaw. Perhaps the work was largely complete in Elgar's mind; certainly, as Gaisberg hinted, he missed 'the inspiration and driving force of Lady Elgar'. Equally certainly Elgar knew on his deathbed that no other hand could complete the Symphony and no one else must ever 'tinker with it'.

Falstaff

Elgar had long contemplated a work about Shakespeare's Falstaff. He wrote the name of the fat knight at the beginning of the first Jaeger sketchbook, dating from 1901; and it is there that can be found a sketch for cue 119, jostling with music for *The Apostles* and the projected 'Rabelais' ballet. Another 'Falstaff' sketch bears the date 'Sep 1902'; this, written during the Worcester Festival, was not eventually used for *Falstaff*, but may also have been considered under its other heading, 'Hudibras', as suited to Samuel Butler's presbyterian knight.

The stimulus finally to order his Falstaff ideas came during Elgar's work on *The Music Makers*. On 3 May 1912 Littleton told Elgar that Leeds wanted him to conduct at the 1913 Festival and that a new orchestral work could be commissioned. Having justified his claim in the Birmingham lectures for 'absolute music' by writing a couple of symphonies, Elgar now felt free to devise for himself a Falstaff 'programme'. It was to be a Falstaff very much after his own heart.

When Elgar decided he would himself write an explanatory essay about the new work, he emphasized that his Falstaff was based on the historical plays, the two parts of *Henry IV* and *Henry V*; the 'caricature' in *The Merry Wives of Windsor* was not relevant. Elgar had investigated much Shakespearian literature. He quoted a 1777 essay by Maurice Morgann on the complexity of Falstaff's character: he was 'at once young and old, enterprizing and fat, a dupe and a wit, harmless and wicked'. Above all the essential Falstaff was 'a knight, a gentleman and a soldier'. Elgar cited Kenneth Deighton, editor of the Macmillan Shakespeare, to the effect that Falstaff had been 'page to the Duke of Norfolk', had earned knighthood through military service, consorted with John of Gaunt and been praised by Prince Hal when he supposed him dead. In the Heinemann edition of *Henry IV* part I Elgar marked a passage of the introduction by George Brandes in which Falstaff's deterioration 'in ever worse and worse company' is charted so as to justify his rejection by the new king and former Prince Hal on his coronation day. Elgar informed Ernest Newman, who was to write programme notes for the première of *Falstaff*, about the work's scope: '*Falstaff* (as programme says) is the name but Shakespeare – the whole of human life – is the theme ... & over it all runs – even in the tavern – the undercurrent of our failings & sorrows.'

Elgar's analysis described the work as falling into 'four principal divisions which run on without break'. The scene of the first section is 'an apartment of the Prince's', with Falstaff and Hal in colloquy. To characterize the first Falstaff theme, with its strong leaning to the dominant of the work's C minor, Elgar invoked Morgann again, who described the protagonist as 'in a green old age, mellow, frank, gay, easy, corpulent, loose, unprincipled, and luxurious' (Ex. 65). The most

Ex. 65

unprincipled bit of the theme is the fourth bar, where the A sharp begins by sounding like a B flat. The second motif has Falstaff courteous and knightly, with lordly swagger in the huge string leap. The third theme scintillates in the wind instruments and is illustrative of Falstaff in discussion with his page: 'I am not only witty in myself but the cause that wit is in other men'. The corpulent Falstaff returns with cascading trills in high glee above. The 'true prince' has a fine E flat tune (Ex. 66), distinguished by upward and downward sevenths, with a touch of sternness when it turns to the minor and passionate intensity in its moment of contrapuntal imitation leading to a more fully scored restatement. Despite the lyrical contours of the theme,

Ex. 66

Elgar allows it little flexibility and virtually no development. Falstaff misjudged the young prince from the start. Corpulent Falstaff introduces a new aspect of his character as 'cajoling and persuasive' in an E minor theme that tempts towards a variety of keys before descending by glissando of an eleventh to an extended repeat. This Falstaff urges the prince to be governed by the moon, 'under whose countenance we steal', and play the highwayman. Other Falstaff themes jostle for position till the prince takes over once more, genial and without sternness. There is quick repartee between the two till the cajoling and corpulent Falstaff brings the first section to an end with a last question and final decision. As Elgar has it: 'Sir John is in the ascendant'.

The second section begins at the Boar's Head in Eastcheap. Elgar wanted the thematic material to 'chatter, blaze, glitter and coruscate'; it had been inspired by a sentence in Dowden: 'From the coldness, the caution, the convention of his father's court, Prince Henry escapes to the teeming vitality of the London streets and the Tavern where Falstaff is monarch.' Elgar propounds four tiny tavern motifs from cue 17, which can combine or scatter in any order and are distinct in shape and rhythm. A minim trill and skittish triplets depict the hostess, Mistress Quickly, 'a poor widow of Eastcheap', along with the moll Doll Tearsheet and perhaps the 'dozen or fourteen honest gentle-women'. On 2 September 1913 Elgar wrote to Troyte Griffith that his wife was 'horrified I fear with my honest gentlewomen – of course they must be in – do you think I have overdone them?'. For the moment they make only a couple of expostulations before Falstaff holds the stage, vast and confident, a 'huge bombard of sack', with a hint of hangover. For Elgar this is 'the Falstaff who sings, "When Arthur first in court," who shouts delightedly at the prospect of battle, "Rare words! brave words!"' There are sufficient doleful chromatics in the theme to remind also of 'the undercurrent of our failings & sorrows'. Elgar's tavern has hitherto been concerned with no particular Shakespearian incident, but the next main theme, with huge intervals treating Falstaff's 'boastfulness and colossal mendacity' is specifically connected with the double robbery at Gadshill. Elgar quotes Falstaff on the appalling odds against him: 'I am a rogue if I were not at half sword with a dozen of them two hours together'. Elgar's Gadshill episode, to which the boasting of cue 25 properly belongs, does not begin until cue 32; but Shakespearian chronology is less Elgar's concern than Falstaff's character. After 'boastfulness' has run its preposterous course, it is joined by Falstaff confident; and the tavern snippets, with the fourth gleefully contrapuntal on the bassoon family, subside towards Gadshill.

The conspirators assemble to a 'cheerful, out-of-door, ambling theme', interspersed with furtive, night-time noises. Scurrying strings and muted horn notes increase the tension. There are hints of the 'cajoling' Falstaff and the prince in diminution covertly disguised. The staccato version of the prince's theme, busy with the rush of quaver triplets, becomes more and more insistent until Falstaff and his gang are set upon and bereft, in eight battling bars, of the booty they have just taken from benighted travellers. Falstaff's boastfulness is reduced to scrambling diminution as he makes his escape, 'sweats to death, / And lards the lean earth as he walks along'. A frenzied fugato on the subject gets the discomfited Falstaff out of danger and ripe for a restoration of confidence. Thoughts of the Boar's Head mingle with the 'out-of-door' theme to end the episode with sufficient sense of recapitulation.

The honest gentlewomen now demonstrate at length, and with a psychologically apt repeat, their qualities of heart and soul. The cajoling Falstaff entwines himself with them for a moment, but his reply to them is the boastful theme uttered 'somewhat unsteadily but encouragingly' by the solo bassoon. There follows Elgar's 'trio section of uproarious vitality', based mainly on the quavers of the second tavern theme in combination with the hangover aspect of the confident Falstaff and some emphasis on 'failings & sorrows'. After more from the gentlewomen, the bassoon boastfulness becomes 'somewhat more incoherent, vague, and somnolent' till Falstaff is left 'fast asleep behind the arras, and snorting like a horse', with fragments of his corpulent theme sinking into ever deeper slumber. So ends the second section.

When already scoring *Falstaff*, Elgar estimated to the Austrian conductor Ferdinand Löwe that it would play for 'about 20 minutes'. Such an apparent miscalculation backs the evidence of MS material that the idea of the 'Dream Interlude' was a late addition to the work. There is no mention of it in Elgar's draft schemes for *Falstaff*. Scored for small orchestra, relying much on a solo violin, it is in Elgar's words 'simple in form and somewhat antiquated in mood'. It recalled a time described by Justice Shallow: 'Then was Jack Falstaff (now Sir John) a boy, and page to Thomas Mowbray, Duke of Norfolk.' And Falstaff himself claimed, 'I was not an eagle's talon in the waist: I could have crept into any alderman's thumb-ring.' The Interlude stays quietly in A minor, a very Elgarian addition to Shakespeare. The insistent minor ninths of its tiny introduction have lost their freshness; otherwise, it is a fragrant passage recalling to the sleeping Falstaff 'what might have been'.

The third section is Elgar's conflation of Henry IV's battles in 1403 and 1405, the first mainly against Harry Hotspur at Shrewsbury, the second to suppress rebellion in the north from the Earl Marshal Mowbray, the Earl of Northumberland, and the Archbishop of York. Elgar's schemes for the work mentioned Shrewsbury, but the 'scarecrow army' of 1405 was too good a musical opportunity to omit, and the analysis of the work discreetly sits on a historical fence. Elgar has Falstaff awake in an outburst of knightly energy and wit. Shakespeare pays tribute to his latent valour, speaking of

> a dozen Captains,
> Bare-headed, sweating, knocking at the taverns,
> And asking every one for Sir John Falstaff.

There are warlike fanfares on muted brass, and before their further clamorous onset Falstaff addresses the denizens of the Boar's Head: 'the man of action is call'd on. Farewell good wenches.' Falstaff recruits his scarecrow army from Justice Shallow in Gloucestershire, the 'cold soldier' Simon Shadow, the 'good scab' Thomas Wart, and the 'most forcible' Francis Feeble. Elgar represents them in the toneless sound of assorted percussion, and Falstaff trudges on. The warfare is graphic with tearing chromatics on horns and trumpets, and fragments of Falstaff motifs coursing bravely through the score. The battle won, and his scarecrows still intact, Falstaff decides 'I'll through Gloucestershire, and there will I visit Master Robert Shallow, Esquire'. It was Elgar country, and the scarecrow rhythm is now turned into spring-like melody, as the men return home and Falstaff continues to the sound of the Gadshill open-air theme. Shallow offers hospitality: 'Nay, you shall see my orchard: where, in an arbour we will eat a last year's pippin of my own graffing, with a dish of caraways, and so forth.'

This is the setting for Elgar's 'sadly-merry pipe and tabor music' of the second Interlude, again in A minor. The pipes are exchanged for sinuous seventh chords on the strings, and the sounds are as inconsequential as the songs Shakespeare gives to Master Silence in the play. When playing records of *Falstaff* to Basil Maine in June 1932, Elgar said of this Interlude: 'That's what I call music!' He turned the volume very low, 'then flashes out the succeeding episode'. The idyll is indeed interrupted. The year is now 1413, and news comes that Henry IV is dead. Pistol breaks the tidings to Falstaff and Shallow with jubilant sounds from Eastcheap:

> Sir John, thy tender lambkin, now is King.
> Harry the Fifth's the man, I speak the truth.

A pause of incomprehension, and the prince's theme is briefly heard. Falstaff promises generous preferment to his host: 'Master Shallow, my Lord Shallow, be what thou wilt, I am Fortune's Steward.' The boasting theme is splendidly augmented and *pesante* beneath exuberant arpeggios of jubilation. The night ride to London is a steady *stringendo* on the march to battle rhythm. Falstaff is urgent: 'I know the young King is sick for me. Let us take any man's horses: the Laws of England are at my commandment'.

The fourth section begins near Westminster Abbey on the new king's coronation day. Henry V approaches to the music of his 'stern, military character', and 'trumpet clangor sounds' prevail. In the midst of the expectation, Elgar has a new theme for Falstaff at cue 119, yearning and poignant, a very early idea for the work. Elgar presents it also as a counterpoint to the corpulent Falstaff of the opening: 'It shows my earnestness in affection'. The king advances to the staccato version of his theme last heard in the Gadshill episode, and cajoling Falstaff swells with excitement. At length the king arrives, and the Hal music now represents him as 'Glittering in golden coat ... and gorgeous as the sun at midsummer.' The theme is *grandioso* and gloriously scored; it is developed a little more fully than before but remains under Elgar's strict control. Falstaff is swaggeringly confident, then punctured and pleading, until he is 'inexorably swept aside by the King's brazen motto and the last pitiful attempt at cajolery is rudely blasted by the furious fanfare'. The king's words are cruel indeed:

> I know thee not, old man: fall to thy prayers:
> How ill white hairs become a fool and jester!

Falstaff is a broken man and 'is so shaked that it is most lamentable to behold'. Elgar paints his decline with a few deft strokes, as visions of Eastcheap flit across his mind. On his deathbed Falstaff's thoughts wander first to Gloucestershire in the string music of Shallow's orchard. The gentlewomen bring momentary cheer to his disordered mind, but he sinks back to the 'green fields' and a last fond memory of the prince, as if still 'bewitch'd with the rogue's company'. The corpulent theme breaks apart, a solo clarinet devises final consolation out of the 'failings & sorrows', and the brass signals Falstaff's end with a resolution on to C major. A muffled side drum salutes the fat knight; but Elgar gives the last word to the king in military mood, admitting that 'the man of stern reality has triumphed'.

Falstaff won acceptance slowly. Shaw and Delius were early converts of note, but Donald Tovey was one of the first to declare it Elgar's greatest work: 'If I want to understand anything in Elgar's music to which I find myself recalcitrant, I shall in future stand on *Falstaff* as on a mountain.'[19] The reasons for Tovey's approval are not far to seek. Elgar is again busy with 'friends pictured within'. The *Falstaff* characters are limned as certainly and economically as in the Variations. The form of the work is Elgar's own, suggested by episodes in Shakespeare, some illustrated more graphically than others, yet so translated into music that it achieves a valid independence. A broad knowledge of the *Henry IV* plays can only help understanding, but Elgar's sequence of events is not Shakespeare's, and his Falstaff is a skilful but very personal distillation from the infinite variety of the dramatist's creation. As in the symphonies, themes combine effortlessly; but here there is an overall freshness and spontaneity that never has to strive for effect. The action is swift and clear, but the emotional impact is no less.

---

[19] Donald F. Tovey, 'Elgar, Master of Music', *ML*, xvi (1935), p. 1, repr. in *Essays and Lectures on Music* (Oxford, 1949), p. 301.

Violin Concerto

The Concerto is planned on the grandest lines, with opening tutti almost a fifth of the whole first movement and characteristically longer than the development. One of its subtlest points is the A natural in the bass of the first bar (Ex. 67). The instant impression is maybe a concerto in F sharp minor, and it is not until the end of the second bar that B minor becomes a probability. The thematic units of the

Ex. 67

processional first paragraph are small, one of descending thirds, another a reshaping of the opening motif, but the more flexible for that. The first of the 'Windflower' themes (Ex. 68), in A minor at the outset, makes much play with Elgar's favourite rhythm, and moves swiftly

Ex. 68 'Windflower 1'

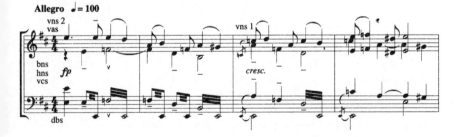

through D minor and G minor to settle on B minor. The second 'Windflower' theme (Ex. 69), starting in E and characterized by rising thirds, launches the second subject group. By a series of subdominant steps it touches the remoteness of E flat. Five bars with falling thirds restore B minor over a dominant pedal and continue in invertible counterpoint to 'Windflower 1'. The main first theme spins a new extension with virtuoso writing for the horns, and the falling thirds,

349

gathering appoggiaturas on the way, lead to the original shape of the first theme, now with A sharp in the bass.

Ex. 69 'Windflower 2'

W. H. Reed wrote of Elgar's 'joy on hearing the solo violin boldly entering in the first movement with the concluding half of the principal subject instead of at the beginning'.[20] Elgar reinforces his pleasure with a *nobilmente* for the soloist, which none the less preserves the crucial semitones of the first theme. The violin begins its rumination by turning part of its opening statement backwards, a point the violas emphasize. The falling thirds introduce a prolonged meditation on 'Windflower 1'. The reshaped first theme from the tutti is next discussed through flatward keys towards C minor, and sequential steps lead to G major and 'Windflower 2' for the start of the second subject group. The continuation of the theme has the soloist describing shapely melodic arches; when the strings take over, however, the solo violin

[20] William H. Reed, 'The Violin Concerto', *ML*, xvi (1935), p. 32; repr. in *An Elgar Companion*, pp. 251–2.

counterpoints the tune with an inner part, as happens also at the start of the Andante. The passage closes into a reminiscence of the Concerto's opening. Here the A natural in the bass makes an early move to F sharp minor possible and logical. Over a C sharp pedal the horns rethink 'Windflower 1' while the soloist creates new patterns from the first subject. The orchestra has further play with these patterns beneath violin semiquaver octave figuration. This passage originally had even more octaves: when asked by Elgar, Reed said it was playable at the speed; it was Fritz Kreisler who altered it. 'Windflower 1' returns to end the exposition, showered by a cascade of chromatic scales, and to launch the development in F sharp minor.

The fiery tutti deals first with 'Windflower 1', which develops a falling third and modulates swiftly by subdominant strides to reach 'Windflower 2' in G minor, then D minor and A minor. This second subject is now *ff* and given a new extension on the horns; meanwhile triplets on the orchestral violins emphasize the semitones of the first subject. Whatever one feels about the assumed Windflower grandiloquence, the sheer thematic virtuosity of the tutti can only exhilarate, as hints of both main subjects are pitted against each other in multifarious combinations. The headlong progress is steadied by the first theme on oboes and clarinets, with horns emphasizing the semitones. The solo violin carries the theme downwards in one-bar sequences against 'Windflower 1' on muted horns. In an orchestral meditation on 'Windflower 2', the soloist decorates the all-pervasive semitone in triplets. Cellos expand into an expressive turn not heard since the opening tutti, and the clarinets answer deliciously in a triplet arpeggio figure taken over from the soloist. As the tempo slows to *lento*, 'Windflower 1' is resumed in D major; increasing speed and a renewal of solo triplets bring back B minor at cue 30.

Perhaps this is Elgar's point of recapitulation, perhaps not. There is little feeling of being on home ground until eight bars later at cue 31, when Elgar has reached the unexpected A minor. As so often, Elgar enjoys covering his formal tracks with thematic material and tonality out of kilter. Sketches make clear that he worked hard at the passage, the bar of descending string scales causing particular trouble. Two short cuts bring back the second subject group, now in D, ten bars earlier than before. Again its return is obscured, as it enters first on the orchestra, while the soloist's semiquaver figuration persists. This time the second subject group conflates the version heard in the opening tutti (the romantic turns were a prominent feature) with the last six bars of the soloist's exposition, making the longest statement of the three. Elgar continues to dovetail material from the tutti and his rethought exposition. The recapitulation builds towards a pause and climax not on 'Windflower 1', as before, but on 'Windflower 2'. The coda begins powerfully with appoggiaturaed thirds, till Elgar gives the clarinet at cue 44 what he called 'an "affliction" of the opening phrase'. Here he wanted Reed's advice for the solo part: 'I think it is possible to make a good, festive noise but I am not sure about the bowing: whether it wd be best detached or slurred (*dug out*) in twos. Any wisdom you may have to spare will be thankfully received by your very grateful friend.' Lower orchestral instruments extend the first subject in mainly white notes over seven bars, then reverse the process with closer and closer diminution till the final utterance, under the soloist's octaves, enlarges the tune's main interval to a major sixth.

The 'semitone' aspect of the Concerto and emphasis at the end of the Allegro on C natural is preparation enough for the key of the Andante, the remote B flat. The direction 'semplice' gives a clue to the first theme, which might have been called 'Windflower 3', if the work had been composed in sequence. Tonally the second half tends towards D flat major round an internal pedal. The soloist enters to a repetition of the theme, initially with an inner part. A third statement is extended by sequence to make a five-bar phrase, as violin solo harmonics close into G. Reed played these notes in various ways before trying harmonics, 'the sound of which pleased him so much that that method of interpretation was instantly adopted'. The modal harmonies leading towards the second subject support a melodic shape that recalls the main theme of the Allegro. It closes on to a chord of E, where the solo violin gives an impassioned preview of the second subject. The process is repeated to end another minor third down, in D flat, already so well prepared. The instrumentation for the second theme is dark-hued, with the solo line supported by muted horn and a quiet entry of the three trombones. The violin embarks on an *ad lib* passage that again owes something to Reed. It ends with a 'sudden leap of a twelfth' taken on the G string. Reed recalled: 'The first time we tried it this way instead of going to a more reasonable position on the D string, the effect so electrified him that I remember he called out "good for you" when I landed safely on the E with a real explosive *sforzando*.' A brief reminder of the Andante's opening, still in D flat, launches the development.

Elgar and Reed had considerable discussion about the ensuing violin arabesques, 'whether they should be demisemiquavers or whether the groups should be written as broken triplets'. The transition theme returns in an emphatic D major, and the orchestra has its first *nobilmente* passage in a phrase that again owes something to the Allegro's start and that Elgar told Atkins he would like inscribed on his tomb. The arabesques return as before but this time end in B. The *nobilmente* theme is much delveloped, and modulates through D flat to B flat minor and reminiscences of the slow movement's main theme. A quiet echo of the *nobilmente* in B flat major prepares for recapitulation. This time the D flat of the first tune's second half takes over the last five bars completely and remains to start the transition. It is only one step of a minor third to the home key of B flat, where the second subject is properly domiciled. There are reminders of the development, and the coda begins with the opening theme once more, gathering up the main ideas of the movement, including the transition, the *nobilmente*, and the expressive turn characteristic of all three movements.

The measured tremolo that starts the finale oscillates between the first two notes of the Concerto, and the violin turns are an accelerated version of some of the work's most romantic moments. The succession of seventh chords gives no moment of harmonic repose, and the whole of this first paragraph is introductory, with only orchestral hints of themes to come. The main march tune begins in D on full orchestra, with accents falling differently across the bars. Beneath the soloist's semiquavers the music works round to B minor and slows towards a transitional theme Elgar dubbed 'ritterlich' (chivalrous). A tutti wrenches it to B flat in a powerful two-part statement that none the less closes on the dominant of E. An oboe anticipates the second subject and the solo violin emphasizes in double stopping the semitones so integral to the work. The stately subject itself has acquaintance with the contour of the Concerto's first theme, and the orchestra develops it beneath manifold embellishments on the solo violin. The dying fall towards the double bar again spells out the semitones and closes the exposition.

At this point there is no development, and Elgar launches at once on a full-scale recapitulation. The march theme, now in B major, is resumed in triple-stopped violin chords, and the chivalrous theme is given at once to the full orchestra, emerging somewhat cavalierly in F major from a top held E. It is now in double counterpoint and occupies centre stage for twice as long. The second subject begins in B minor, a welcome change of mode, and at the second double bar the coda begins. Again marked *nobilmente*, the orchestra repeats the slow movement theme Elgar desired for his tombstone. It is now developed still further and acquires a second *nobilmente* from the soloist. The finale's first subject interchanges with the chivalry of the transition until the music slows and the semitones of the work's opening become quietly insistent in preparation for the accompanied cadenza.

Elgar wrote to Schuster about this section: 'You will like the cadenza which is on a novel plan I think – accompanied softly by a few insts. & – it comes at the end of the last movement – it sadly thinks over the 1st. movement.' The pizzicato *tremolando* Elgar had devised to provide the desired sound was to 'be "thrummed" with the soft part of three or four fingers across the strings'. He described the result to Ernest Newman: 'The sound of distant Aeolian harp flutters under and over the solo'.[21] The first theme of the Concerto emerges on *ponticello* violins. The two 'Windflower' tunes are mulled over, falling thirds are prominent, and the semitones pervade many of the soloist's arabesques. There is brief reference to the Andante's *nobilmente*, and the cadenza ends with the music that first launched the soloist, again given the *nobilmente* that was always its due. The coda resumes the tempo of the finale and its music. Over an insistent crotchet bass, the *nobilmente* of the tombstone is now adapted, not quite happily, to the prevailing speed; but to crown the work cellos and horns proclaim the Allegro's opening theme in augmentation and a resounding B major.

Cello Concerto

The making of what Lady Elgar rightly called 'a flawless work' is little documented. There are sketches only of the first movement's 9/8 tune. It may be that the various stages of its shaping were among the materials destroyed by Elgar before leaving Severn House in 1921. This last of Elgar's masterpieces is altogether more reticent than the Violin Concerto of nine years previously. The orchestration is the same but for *ad lib* piccolo rather than *ad lib* double bassoon; yet it is much more subdued, as befits the nature of the solo instrument and the autumnal quality of the music. Indeed, use of the full orchestra is so rare that a review of the première suggested scoring for chamber orchestra would have been more practical. In the sketch Elgar copied for his Windflower, what is now the first tutti was marked *nobilmente*. This was not carried over into the finished work; but the solo cello's opening recitative begins thus, and the only two other such indications are in the solo part of the finale. If the second is almost too Falstaffian to be taken seriously, Elgar's conception of nobility was wide: in this sere and yellow mood he might well regret he had not verbally ennobled the fat knight himself.

The starting-point of the Concerto had been the 9/8 Moderato, of which the quietly swaying theme begins in a very uncertain E minor. So the initial recitative establishes the key boldly and unequivocally. The Moderato's supertonic start causes quiet subtleties. This section

[21] Letter of 18 September 1910.

consists of six statements of the six-bar theme (Ex. 70), with a tiny tailpiece down to E. The first statement, on violas and cellos of the orchestra, is unharmonized; the second has the solo cello over a pedal

Ex. 70

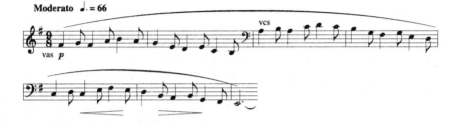

E with no great certainty about E minor; the third suggests B minor at first but in the last bar makes as emphatic an approach to E minor as has yet been heard: so much so that the next two sections begin melodically a tone lower on E, first with the soloist, then tutti. The last statement resumes the F sharp start and dies away to bare octaves on the lower strings. The middle section of the movement is equally simple in design and equally subtle. The whole, except for a couple of half bars, is in 12/8, a time signature that had sent Elgar on many an inconsequential amble in the past. Here all is beautifully poised and varied, with two E minor parts flanking an inner core in E major. The two-bar phrases follow one another with what might be monotonous regularity, had Elgar not injected them with hints of ambiguity. The last four bars before the change to E major might be two plus two bars or, by analogy with what has gone before, one plus three. The E minor flanks have their own characteristic rhythm, with semiquaver at the end of a 3/8 group; the E major core tends to have the semiquaver central. The E major bars contain a lyrical outpouring of melody shared equally between soloist and orchestra, with an immediate and abbreviated restatement following the half-bar. When the E minor flank returns, it too is shortened yet makes a powerful impression through a *largamente* access of passion that subsides as quickly as it arose. The 9/8 is resumed, this time for four statements of the winding theme. All except the third begin on the supertonic, but there are also new features. Initially there is for the first time a D sharp in the bass, and the orchestral strings have ghostly echoes of semiquavers given only to the soloist hitherto. A B minor statement remembers dotted rhythms from the E major core, and the E minor tutti breaks off dramatically to admit the soloist. The last section dies away as before, with pensive pizzicato notes to round the movement.

The 'scherzo' begins with a pizzicato version of the Concerto's opening recitative, alternating with rapid solo semiquavers that follow a pattern set in the Introduction and Allegro. Tonally E minor oscillates with G major, a minor third above; held notes on the wind strike a balance between the two until the strings tenderly interpret the B not as a third or fifth, but as a seventh on a chord of C. At the Allegro molto, with its gossamer semiquavers, G major wins the day; but already near the outset is a hint of the flattened sixth that will later assume importance. The semiquavers scurry from soloist to orchestra in playful chase and catch-can brilliance. The second subject is a brief but highly expressive epigram in E flat that checks the darting semiquavers for a moment of concentrated Elgarian emotion. What is virtually a restatement of the Allegro molto's material begins from a close in G minor. Elgar changes the order with unobtrusive skill, inserting bars here and there so that much seems new (especially the arching counterpoints on violins), though most is familiar. A deft sidestep suggests the second subject will come back in F; a further tiny adjustment ensures D, dominant of the movement. This time the epigrams close into F sharp minor, and the soloist speeds through delicate sequences towards a passage beginning in 3/2 that allows clarinets, violins and solo cello to spin a thistledown web from rhythmic transformations of the epigram. A faster coda hints at the subsidiary E flat and settles for a moment on the remoteness of A flat minor. The soloist concentrates on a *perpetuum mobile* of semiquavers, switches to a handful of pizzicato notes and ends with a tiny explosion.

The B flat major of the Adagio is again a minor third above the preceding G, far enough from E minor but by no means as remote as in the case of the Violin Concerto's Andante. The movement is framed by a pair of eight-bar paragraphs composed of three questioning phrases and ending in a half close. The glorious stream of melody on the solo cello (Ex. 71) is first characterized by octave leaps and various shapes within them; the second strain moves more by step over the span of a descending seventh complemented by a pair of sevenths aspiring to the heights. There, two quavers followed by two falling semiquavers look far into the future of the work. A cadence into the home key of B flat is interrupted by the age-old device of a diminished-seventh chord, expressively disguised, to herald the very unexpected A minor. With an inflow of warmth the orchestra transforms this into the major so that the cello repeats the whole of its B flat stream of melody in the new key. By a minute change, taking a seventh leap as minor rather than major, this restatement closes in G minor rather than a semitone higher. The orchestra quietly adjusts this to E flat, where the cello gives a gently sonorous résumé of the theme, pausing momentarily before B flat is again established and the concluding frame to the movement settles to its half close. This ending became a

Ex. 71

matter of correspondence between Elgar and Novello. If the Adagio were to be published separately, it was hoped Elgar would provide a full close. He experimented with an alternative on a fair copy of the piano score, but gave up, writing on 12 August 1919: 'I fear I cannot think of anr. ending for the slow movement – it will do as it is if played separately.'

The finale accepts the B flat of the Adagio, and by making it minor includes D flat as well. Four quick steps produce the dominant of E minor, so that the cycle of minor thirds is brusquely completed. The solo cello gives in quasi-recitative a *nobilmente* account of the movement's main idea and links it to reminders of the work's opening. The first theme of the Allegro non troppo, emphatic with dactyls, is launched resolutely by the solo cello in an E minor that avoids D sharp as long as possible. A tutti restatement is interrupted by the soloist, who begins a passage of wandering tonality that leads through an extended tutti of sequences descending by major thirds to the second subject in G major, as gnomic as in the 'scherzo'. It has to contend at first with a prominent flattened sixth (again shades of the second movement), and its expectant pause is answered by a disappearing slither into the depths.

The development begins in A flat with flowing cello semiquavers. An expressive counterpoint on the strings hints already at the agonized coda of the movement. Over falling fourths from the cello the woodwind resume the dactyls of the main theme, closing with cello pizzicato chords into F minor. After excursions elsewhere, the cello resumes A flat for a new figuration in triplet semiquavers. At cue 56 the orchestra produces a playful Schumannesque tag (such as he used in his own Cello Concerto) for spirited dialogue with the soloist. Schumann was still in some ways Elgar's 'ideal'. The triplet semiquavers resume in B flat, and gradually the cello develops a touch of ferocity as it takes snatches of the first tune into the heights. After emphatic dominant preparation on the orchestra, the main theme returns in Elgar's corpulent yet *nobilmente* version on all the cellos, with only skeleton E minor harmonies.

It is a hollow form of recapitulation, featuring a mocking trombone glissando and baleful minims on the horns. The cello embraces another key with almost every dactyl as it climbs through its range; this time the orchestral sequences stir the trumpets to a brazen comment at *fortissimo*, a brief moment of unregenerate Elgar. The second subject in C seems ready to slither as before. It does so once, but the second time it decides on an aerial excursion to a hovering harmonic. Against pizzicato cello chords the first subject makes its last extended appearance till the soloist transforms its dactyls into something at once more skittish but also hinting at its dissolution. A reiterated C sharp in the bass at slower tempo ushers in Elgar's final comment on the agony of the war and of himself. The searching harmonies, abstruse but at the same time direct in meaning, support a falling fourth and consequent chromatics. A climax of eloquence is reached as the chromatics and the fourth swap places. A change to triple time recalls the rhythm from the heights of the Adagio, and a rising seventh on the solo cello confirms the ancestry of a passionate passage that moves towards A flat through sequential steps shared antiphonally by soloist and orchestra. There the main Adagio theme, long-drawn in its sweetness, makes a last poignant appearance to close on the dominant of E minor. The opening recitative of the Concerto returns, this time punctuated by two unexpected chords from the full orchestra, and the main finale tune, obsessively grounded in E minor, closes a work as remarkable for its terseness as for its expressive power. Elgar himself felt that in some way the Cello Concerto marked the end of his creative life. In the list he made of all his works with opus numbers, he wrote against op. 85, 'FINIS R.I.P.'

Piano Concerto

Elgar's projected piano concerto remains fragmentary. Though in 1918 Elgar promised its first performance to Irene Scharrer and later talked to Harriet Cohen about 'Your poor old Concertochen',[22] the inspiration behind it was always the Windflower and her special touch as a pianist. The first diary reference to the work is on 10 January 1914: 'A.S.W. came & played the lovely Piano Concerto piece.' This is likely to have been part of the slow movement, in D major and 6/8. Seven pages of this exist, making a draft of thirty bars to be repeated, with a further thirty-four. Additional pages provide details of scoring, so that a performing version of the movement has in fact been produced.[23] Lady Elgar recorded on 26 January 1917 that Elgar played 'his lovely fragment of Piano Concerto over & over again' to Mary de Navarro. A fortnight later Elgar told the Windflower he had thought of 'using up *your* Piano Concerto' in the *Sanguine Fan* ballet; and he quoted in his letter the main slow movement theme.

There are hints for salient points in the first movement, including a rocking tune for muted violas and cellos. A possible start for the finale is preserved, in a solemn march figure marked 'Quasi recito.' Its most striking music, however, a powerful G minor idea, appears also to

---

[22] See Harriet Cohen, *A Bundle of Time* (London, 1969), p. 223.
[23] Edited by Percy Young.

have been considered for *The Spanish Lady*. Elgar's most determined expression in connection with the work occurred just after completion of the Cello Concerto. He wrote to Lady Stuart from Brinkwells on 3 August 1919: 'I want to finish or rather commence the Piano concerto which *must* be windflowerish so I hope you will come.' She did, but the concerto seems to have benefited little.

Transcriptions
The most sumptuous of Elgar's transcriptions is of the Bach Fantasia and Fugue in C minor for organ BWV537. It was the first occasion Elgar had written an orchestral work since the Cello Concerto and the death of Lady Elgar; it was as if he was determined not only to screw his own art to its utmost virtuosity but also to outmatch any conceivable rival. His success is total. Elgar changed the 6/4 of the Fantasia into 3/4, and nothing is more fascinating than the way he tackles the opening organ pedal held over so many bars. There is a steady pulse from alternate timpani and bass drum over the undulation of muted violas and cellos, over long-drawn double basses and eventually a pair of muted horns. Doublings are ingeniously contrived, and the scoring is wonderfully varied as the long pedal reaches the dominant. Wherever Elgar may seem to violate the part-writing, it will be found that the most prominent voices are scrupulously faithful to Bach. The Fugue is a *tour de force*. Initially it is the cunning with which Elgar gets the subject phrased as he wishes by selective doubling that strikes the eye (the ear accepts the result as sound logic). As the Fugue progresses, Elgar gives an increasingly strong kick to the tied note of the second bar. An isolated G minor entry has cymbal crash, harp glissandos and upper woodwind scales to mark the spot. Semiquavers hurtle through the score, percussion multiplies, trumpets break into demisemiquavers, and in the final bar the harps are to repeat their arpeggio 'as many times as may be required by the *ritenuto*' in the other parts. Elgar summed up his Fugue on 26 October 1921 for Ernest Newman: 'You will see that I have kept it quite solid (diapasony) at first; – later you hear the sesquialteras & other trimming stops reverberating & the resultant vibrating shimmering sort of organ sound – I *think*.'

The Handel transcription is of the D minor Overture from the Second Chandos Anthem, *In the Lord put I my Trust*. Handel admired the piece sufficiently to use the two movements, more richly scored, at the start of his Concerto Grosso op. 3 no. 5, and to transpose the fugue into F sharp minor as the third movement of the sixth Suite for Clavier (1720). Elgar first became acquainted with the music in an organ transcription during his days at St George's, Worcester. When he came to make his transcription, Elgar conflated Handel's orchestral and slightly longer keyboard version, and at the end he resumed some bars of the opening Largo. He also made a cut, as he explained in a letter of 16 July 1923 to John West at Novello: 'I have cut out *four* bars (the excision occurs halfway through the fifth bar of p. 13) – this does away with a weak repetition of the modulation into the dom. & a wandering excursion into treble regions – the pedal passage (on A here) is from the enlarged version of the fugue in F♮ minor.' The transcription is less exuberant than the Bach but no less effective. Elgar told West of his admiration for the piece: 'the weighty structure is (to me) so grand – epic'. Undoubtedly he responded equally to the lean effectiveness of Handel's three-part writing, so much after Elgar's own heart.

The third transcription is of the funeral 'Marche' from Chopin's B flat minor Piano Sonata op. 35. The suggestion for this seems originally to have come from EMI, but it was Boult at the BBC who put the matter to Elgar in a letter of 22 February 1932. The transcription was to form part of the BBC Symphony Orchestra's first recording venture, and in a lecture to the Royal Institution reprinted in *The Listener* of 28 December 1932 Boult explained that Elgar, with much gramophone experience behind him, 'took pains to keep a very open and clear score and resisted the temptation of adding too much to the richness and thickness of the texture'.

13

Smaller orchestral, string, chamber and instrumental music

In his smaller orchestral pieces Elgar rarely falters, with ends and means usually perfectly matched. Sometimes religious or nationalistic reasons may inflate an idea beyond its natural shape, but this occurs seldom. There are few dull pages, and Elgar's abundant melodic gift ensures a series of delightful pieces that exactly judge the extent of their welcome. The lighter Elgar has an ease and freshness that immediately stamps him as an accomplished miniaturist, perhaps the last in a long line of great composers to grace the salon as happily as the concert hall or cathedral. Elgar might protest about the 'necessity' to produce such music for financial reasons; his manifest skill in doing so illustrates a most attractive aspect of his music-making and gave great pleasure to himself and others throughout his creative life.

The Powick Asylum music (1879–84), though written for a variable orchestra with at best a bizarre wind section (piccolo, flute, clarinet, two cornets and euphonium were the norm), proved a useful introduction to the turning of effective trifles. The four sets of five quadrilles, with such titles as 'La brunette', 'Die junge Kokette', 'L'Assomoir' (the original Zola novel had two m's), and 'Paris', have variety, much vitality, and occasionally a secondary tune that hints at Elgar's future. The last section of 'L'Assomoir', indeed, was revived for 'The Wild Bears' in the *Wand of Youth* suite no. 2. The provision of attractive dance music was no bad discipline for any nineteenth-century composer, and Elgar passes the test with ease. The five polkas are at their best worthy of a Smetana and *The Bartered Bride*. 'Helcia' ends with the chords Elgar used later to launch 'Sabbath Morning at Sea' in *Sea Pictures*.

The *Three Characteristic Pieces* op. 10 had a lengthy history before reaching their final form in spring 1899. The second movement began as an 'Intermezzo moresque', first performed at the Worcestershire Musical Union under Vine Hall on 4 April 1883. At Birmingham later in the year it was announced as 'one of a set of three pieces'. Elgar corrected this to '4' on his own programme, but the four-movement

Suite in D was not heard in Birmingham till 23 February 1888. The last movement was the *Pas redoublé March* no. 2 of six years earlier that was also considered for Act 1 scene i of *The Spanish Lady*. The rest of the Suite was reworked for op. 10.

There are hints of Dvořák in both the first two movements, with their strong rhythms and vital colouring. The Mazurka is remarkable mainly for its wistful middle section, with a touching oboe solo. The 'Sérénade mauresque' is the most substantial piece, and its 'Moorish' flavour, considered 'Slavonic' by the 1888 Birmingham critic, is an early example of Elgar's penchant for 'Spanish' inflexions, with exotic intervals and pattering pizzicato. New counterpoints enrich the return, with mounting eloquence in the cellos till there comes a remote moment of near silence, made mysterious by the horns. Such a passage may date from 1899. The final 'Contrasts: The Gavotte A.D. 1700 and 1900' opposes to the elegance and charm of eighteenth-century pastiche a playfully energetic movement with chromatic counterpoints, cross-rhythms and an abundance of noise. The return of '1700' involves self-important augmentation; '1900' also attempts to boost its significance. Elgar described to Jaeger on 4 February 1899 the origin of 'Contrasts' in January 1883:

> I saw two dancers in Leipzig who came down the stage in antique dress dancing a gavotte: when they reached the footlights they suddenly turned round & appeared to be two very young & modern people & danced a gay and lively measure – they had come down the stage *backwards* & danced with their (modern) faces towards us: when they reached the back of the stage they suddenly turned round & the old, decrepit people danced gingerly to the old tune.

Lady Mary Lygon received the dedication of op. 10.

The 1884 *Sevillana*, dedicated to W. C. Stockley, was the second of Elgar's 'Spanish' pieces. He described it as 'an attempt to portray, in the compass of a few bars, the humours of a Spanish *fête*'. There are three main themes, the first of which returns at the end. All are in waltz rhythm, and for a while Elgar keeps up the Spanish atmosphere with some characteristic percussion. Elgar called the first section 'an imitation of a Spanish folk-song, played by the Violins on the fourth string'. The second, slower waltz, with its Tchaikovskian woodwind counterpoints, 'may (or may not) be taken to represent "un passage d'amour"'. The third waltz, with its cross-rhythms and energetic tromboning, has forgotten Spain: 'Something very like an *émeute* takes place during the progress of this, missiles are freely thrown, and at least one stiletto is drawn – but these are only modern Spaniards, and no tragic result follows.' The opening strain returns, there is some grandiloquence for the brass in the coda and early recourse to the side drum: 'somehow or other all ends happily.'

The main theme for the 'Andante religioso' that became *Sursum corda* op. 11 had origin in an abandoned violin sonata of 1887. Its new context was decided in December 1893 and it took final colouring for strings, brass, organ and timpani at Hugh Blair's request. The première in Worcester Cathedral was on 9 April 1894, and it was dedicated to H. Dyke Acland, Malvern bank manager and golfing companion. Wagner brooded creatively over the work, most notably in the fine exordium suggestive of Sachs meditating on Polterabend and at the climax of the central section when the brass recalls the solemnity of Titurel's exequies in *Parsifal*. The rising string sequences of the introduction maintain a fine standard of eloquence, which the main tune cannot quite match. It has a sinuous strength in its wide leaps and flexible shape, but the harmonies introduce a note of 'religiosity' characteristic of the weaker Elgar. Danger threatens when the tune is rescored in octaves, and is palpable when brass instruments reinforce it at the reprise. The central section is largely antiphonal between organ and strings. Emphatic brass triplets make a notable climax here; the rhythm recurs quietly on timpani alone to moving effect in the solemn postlude.

Such works as the op. 21 Minuet, originally for piano, and the violin pieces, *Chanson de nuit* and *Chanson de matin*, were to achieve their most lasting fame in versions for orchestra, but their origins lay elsewhere. Not so with the *Sérénade lyrique*, an exquisitely turned miniature that had its première on 27 November 1900, little more than a month after *Gerontius*. It was written for Ivan Caryll, who had achieved success with musical comedies at the Lyric and Gaiety theatres, and now directed a light orchestra. It is very much a string piece, with moments of shy intimacy and fine rhetoric for the cellos. The return after the shapely middle section is beautifully managed, with a telling chord on the harp. The piece is sentimental with the gentlest of touches and expires to a delicious coda.

Much of *Dream Children* op. 43 is of an intensity the more heart-rending for being so restrained in expression. Elgar wrote a baffling letter on 6 June 1907 about the work to F. G. Edwards:

> Now as to Dream Children; I really can tell you *nothing*! They (or it) were (or was) written for small orch: as published; the pianoforte is an arrangement. They were (or it was) written long ago, or rather sketched long ago & completed a few years back. I really know nothing of the first performance & I have never heard them (or it).

The sketches, whatever their date, were worked up in January 1902, and the first performance was given by Arthur W. Payne at Queen's Hall on 4 September of that year. No. 1 is headed 'Sorrowful Child's Suite', and on the full score is printed a quotation from Charles Lamb's essay *Dream Children*:

> And while I stood gazing, both the children gradually grew fainter to my view, receding, and still receding till nothing at last but two mournful features were seen in the uttermost distance, which, without speech, strangely impressed upon me the effects of speech: 'We are not of Alice, nor of thee, nor are we children at all … We are nothing; less than nothing, and dreams. We are *only what might have been*'.

That struck very deep with Elgar. In no. 1 he confides his profoundest sorrow to the clarinets moving in thirds or playing solo, with the strings muted throughout. The middle section maintains the air of grief and strange unreality, and the only moment of brightness is the *tierce de picardie* that ends the recapitulation. The ethereal waltz of no. 2 is again entrusted to the clarinet. The scoring suggests a disembodied Tchaikovsky, but the central section intensifies the sadness. Elgar can hardly bear to leave this mood of intangible regret and, after devising a bewitching resumption of the waltz, returns to it. A slow reminiscence of the waltz leaves the tune incomplete so that the opening of no. 1 can make its ghostly presence felt once more, ending again on a major chord.

Elgar was busy with *The Wand of Youth* in the summer of 1907. Originally he intended only one suite and had all thirteen movements fully scored by the time the family departed to Rome in late autumn. The work was a last turning to early sketchbooks before he embarked on the series of great orchestral works that brought him to the pinnacle of fame. The sketchbooks started in 1878 also contain copies of still earlier music. Annotations such as 'from the play (old)' or 'from children's opera' refer to the boyhood play with music the Elgar children are supposed to have devised to demonstrate the superiority of the young over the old. Elgar wrote a programme note for the second suite's première at the 1908 Worcester Festival, considerably flattering his youthful self: 'the music is now presented for the first time as imagined by the author: & in adapting to a modern orchestra these juvenile ideas the suggested instrumentation has been carried out as nearly as possible. Occasionally an obviously commonplace phrase has been polished but on the whole the little pieces remain as originally planned'. Elgar was playing with words as mischievously as his orchestra now plays with the boyhood tunes, interweaving them with sinuous counterpoints and decking them in piquant colours known best to a composer just past fifty.

If the Overture of the first suite (dedicated to C. Lee Williams) is launched with a boy's idea, it is instantly translated into tonal regions known to the man and followed by a burgeoning cantabile phrase characteristic of ripest Elgar. So it is with the rest of the suite. The lovely tune of the Serenade sings of long ago, but it is caught in a web of orchestral sound as delicate as it is cunningly calculated. These are indeed songs both of innocence and experience. If the Minuet, with its stage direction 'The two old people enter', leans heavily on a 'Menuetto à la Handel' copied into Sketchbook 5 of 1881, the flashing brilliance of the 'Sun Dance', deftly manoeuvring through cross-rhythms, is entirely of 1907. Until its central waltz, that is. Perhaps this was the music Elgar referred to, when describing the music for the Gramophone Company: 'To awaken the Old People, glittering lights were flashed in their eyes by means of hand-mirrors.' In 1907 he decided to be more graphic. 'Fairy Pipers' is the only other movement with a stage direction: 'Two fairy pipers pass in a boat, and charm them to sleep.' The outline of this piece and of 'Slumber Scene' may well go back to the 'play'. Indeed when writing about the recording, Elgar claimed authentic theatrical exigency:

> here we may note that the bass consists wholly of three notes (A.D.G.) the open strings of the (old English) double bass; the player was wanted for stage management, but the simplicity of the bass made it possible for a child who knew nothing of music on any instrument to grind out the bass. It may be added that the writer 'constructed' the double-bass himself and the monstrosity was in existence a few years ago.

The starting motif, on cellos and basses, of 'Fairies and Giants' was labelled by Elgar 'Humoreske a tune from Broadheath 1867' and is his earliest-known music. It now acts as an ostinato throughout much of the 'Fairies' section, gathering on the way a fine 1907 counterpoint. The 'Giants' are menacing in a fierce succession of semibreves. Their final diminution into Elgar's favourite rhythm does nothing to tame them.

The second suite March, a glum and dogged affair, comes from an early sketchbook; there too it has a semiquaver trio, though quite different from the waywardly attractive 1907 version, with its delicious woodwind runs accompanying the last bars and sonorous counterpoint on horns and violas. It was the March, Elgar said, that concluded the 'play' music. Again it was probably the central section of 'Little Bells' by means of which the old people 'were lured over the bridge' to fairyland. This, indeed, was a snatch of melody that Elgar loved; he used it also to great effect in *The Starlight Express*. The whirling accompaniment to the fleet carillon of the little bells themselves could be no part of a boy's vision. 'Moths and Butterflies' Elgar described as the oldest of the movements in the suite: 'I do not remember the time when it was not written in some form or other.' That applies to the main A minor tune, with its wrong note D sharp; such pendants as the lovely sequential flute solo came later. This movement, too, was used to tempt the adults across the brook. The 'Fountain Dance', with bass for a long time even simpler than that of the 'Slumber Song' in the first suite, has music which Elgar described as following 'the rise and fall of the jets; the water was induced to follow the music by means of the interior economy of a football'. 'The Tame Bear' performs to a tune that could have come out of Russia, where he too might have originated. At a concert performance in Bournemouth on 23 October 1915 Lady Elgar overheard a conversation and noted it in her diary: 'At the Tame Bear A. heard some one say. "they do not allow it now" So they understood the poor Bear – captive, made to dance.' Elgar has him dancing to the tambourine. Part of 'The Wild Bears' had featured as a Powick quadrille, part of the 'L'Assomoir' set. Now it hurtled recklessly as a rondo theme, generating episodes of equal exuberance. The second suite was dedicated to Hubert Leicester.

The Romance for bassoon and orchestra in D minor op. 62 was written for Edwin James, bassoonist of the LSO and its chairman. The work has the lyrical waywardness of the Violin Concerto, on which Elgar was working in January 1910, when the Romance was completed. Indeed the orchestra begins with a phrase that seems to have slipped out of the Concerto's first movement. In this work Elgar is not concerned with the comic possibilities of the bassoon; they could wait for *Falstaff*. It is not long before the bassoon, in the phrase that most haunts the memory, exploits Elgar's favourite rhythmic tag ♪ ♩ ♪, made pensive with pauses. The bassoon furthers the first section in a steady stream of melody on its initial figure. A central D major has the bassoon exploring a fuller range with much virtuosity, taking triplet ideas from the orchestra and handing them back. The recapitulation reverts to D minor, and the orchestra launches at once into a powerful version of the bassoon's opening solo. Much is dovetailed, so that reference can be made to the triplets of the middle section once more, and the orchestra ends a beautifully rounded work with a repetition of its Violin Concerto phrase.

Carissima, written in December 1913, was specifically designed for recording. It begins with a rising phrase spanning an octave, a characteristic Elgar shape. By judging the succession of intervals and placing of main accent with nice discrimination, Elgar avoids any hint of vulgarity. Indeed, at the outset the graceful tune seems almost fragile, though later it generates considerable warmth. The second idea, lighter still, yet gathers to quite a climax and inspires the opening theme to a profusion of tender new counterpoints. The coda makes affectionate reference to both main tunes.

Rosemary was the latest manifestation of a theme that had haunted Elgar since September 1882. It began as the trio tune of a Menuetto written at Giggleswick for violin, cello and piano. Later he reworked it as a piano piece, *Douce pensée*; now in 1915 it became a companion piece to *Carissima* for small orchestra. The modulations of the second half, to the keys of major submediant and flattened leading note, were in the 1882 original. What is new is the delicate four-bar introduction on the rhythm of the original minuet, the long-drawn sweetness of the extension into the coda, the momentary hovering on certain high points of the tune, and the shifting colours of the kaleidoscopic orchestration.

In *Polonia*, designed for a concert on 6 July 1915 to aid the Polish relief fund and dedicated to Paderewski, Elgar used ideas of his own and a number of Polish themes. After an initial throwing down of the gauntlet to establish A minor, Elgar hints at a dogged march rhythm that will later be prominent, following it with a broadly expressive tune made insistent by fanfares. A slackening of the tempo and a change of key to E brings the first of the Polish themes. Elgar's source was a copy of *Three Polish National Hymns* published in Moscow. At this point he used 'z dymem Pozarow' ('With the smoke of the buildings'), a song that became popular after the January 1863 uprising against the Russian tsar, Alexander II. It is heard first on cor anglais. The march now builds to a powerful climax, and the expressive tune dies away to a quiet repetition of its first bar. Beneath this Elgar quotes Chopin's Nocturne no. 11 in G minor, combining it half a dozen bars later with a theme from Paderewski's *Polish Fantasia* op. 19 for piano and orchestra. Elgar explained what he had done in a letter of 29 August 1915 to Paderewski: 'in the middle section I have brought in *remote* & I trust with poetic effect a theme of Chopin & with it a theme of your own from the Polish fantasia linking the two greatest names in Polish music – Chopin & Paderewski'.[1] Elgar develops the two themes, separately and in combination, at some length till the march reasserts itself more and more insistently and recapitulation begins with the expressive theme in A minor. The uprising song returns in A major. Modulations over the march rhythm lead to F, key of the final section, which is dominated by another of the national hymns, 'Jeszcce Polska nie Zginela' ('Poland is not yet lost'). Elgar embellishes the tune with rich harmonies and strongly wrought phrases so that his plea for the future of Poland comes to a rousing conclusion.

---

[1] Letter in possession of Richard Westwood-Brookes.

The *Severn Suite* op. 87 was Elgar's most sustained effort of original composition since the *Arthur* music of 1923. Written originally for brass band, Elgar's score was complete on 15 April 1930. The four movements were then submitted to Henry Geehl for revision and amplification. That was the version first heard at the Crystal Palace on 27 September 1930 and notably described by its dedicatee, Bernard Shaw. The work was indeed more than adequate for its competition première, and it bore Elgar's first opus number since the Bach transcription of 1921–2. In the version of the suite for full orchestra (1932) Elgar labelled the movements 'Worcester Castle', 'Tournament', 'Cathedral' and 'Commandery'. The suite does not achieve the freshness of much in Elgar's Indian summer. The Introduction is pompously effective, but the initial idea is too short-breathed to sustain all the repetition it gets; it is at its happiest when taking quiet chromatic twists at the centre of the movement. The Toccata bustles energetically on material that is more anonymous than Elgarian until galvanized into some powerful chordal rhetoric on the initial idea. The movement dies away to the restatement of a quiet subsidiary theme from the first movement. It is rare in Elgar to find a fugue untouched by some 'diablerie'. The 'Cathedral' movement is sober, serious, and a little dull. The final Minuet is based on music originally written for 'The Brothers Wind', incorporating ideas from *Harmony Music* no. 1 and *Promenade* no. 5. By way of coda the material of the first movement steals in quietly and chromatically. In the bass it gathers to itself staccato quaver hints of the Toccata, and ends with a *grandioso* presentation of the pompous beginning.

The *Nursery Suite* of 1930 was Elgar's farewell to the ideas of his own boyhood. *The Spanish Lady* was further to ransack the inspirations of his youth, but there they remain only fragmentary, whereas the suite came to full fruition. It was dedicated to the Duchess of York (the present Queen Mother), and the Princesses Elizabeth (now Queen) and Margaret Rose. The first performance was at a recording session of the suite on 23 May 1931, and the *Daily Telegraph* critic called it 'the sublimation of eternal youth'. The recording had to be completed on 4 June, and the suite was played again before the Duke and Duchess of York. Elgar wrote some programme notes five days later.[2] He said they were, 'Dashed off while the Footman waiting! *Unrevised*'. The 'Aubade', so effortlessly fresh, 'should call up memories of happy and peaceful awakings; the music flows in a serene way; a fragment of a hymn tune ("Hear Thy children, gentle Jesus" – written for little children when the composer was a youth) is introduced'. 'The Serious

[2] Repr. in Jerrold Northrop Moore, ed., *Elgar on Record* (Oxford, 1974), pp. 137–8.

369

Doll' was a 'sedate semi-serious solo for flute' that went in for notable virtuosity and involved also some solo writing for the violin. The wasp-like persistence of 'Busy-ness' had a 'suggestion of tireless energy', and Elgar drew attention to the 'fluttering theme' of the second subject. There is a middle section of manic accompaniment in search of a tune. Felix Weingartner was puzzled by the title of this movement: 'I understand that it is a quibble, but what is the sens of it? Is Ness perhaps a personal name?'[3] The muted waltz of 'The Sad Doll', again with violin solo, was to suggest 'a pathetic tired little puppet'. The dogged ostinato of 'The Waggon Passes' was self-explanatory: 'a remote rumbling is heard in the distance increasing in volume as the waggon approaches; the waggoners' song or whistle accompanies the jar and crash of the heavy horses and wheels, dying away to a thread of sound as remote as the beginning'. The shrieks of laughter attributed to 'The Merry Doll' were graphically illustrated. Elgar mentioned the 'bounding leaps' of this 'vivacious person'. 'Dreaming' recalled a leitmotif of Elgar's whole life and was meant to represent 'the soft and tender childish slumbers'. The violin cadenza introducing 'Envoy' was Elgar's farewell to his own instrument, brilliant, idiomatic, and warmly expressive. Its purpose was to introduce 'fragments of the preceding numbers'. Two of the dolls are recalled along with the dream sequence, leading this time to a reawakening of the dawn and the 'Aubade'.

Another work of 1930 was an oboe *Soliloquy* for Leon Goossens. Elgar left it in keyboard draft, and it was orchestrated by Gordon Jacob in 1967. The oboe is not here the pastoral pipe of other English composers; rather in its almost oriental flourishes and passionate rhapsodic flights it looks back to the Mediterranean cruise of 1905 and the mosque at Smyrna. It is framed with bars as delicate as anything in the antique world of *The Sanguine Fan*.

Mina was named after the smallest of Elgar's dogs, a cairn. The piece was sent to the publisher in early December 1932. In the following August Elgar suggested to Keith Prowse that its title was temporary but came up with no alternative. In the same letter he also hoped 'to send the full score with Solo Celesta (as I suggested to Mr van Lier) in a few days'. It is the bell sounds of the celesta that gently colour the rocking chords that frame the work. The slow, sad waltz continues for only a few bars until it breaks into a hesitant cross-rhythm, only to become sadder than before. Through the sorrowful sighs a clarinet weaves a chromatic counterpoint in ultimate heartbreak. The piece is brief enough, but it portrays the master rather than the cairn. It was dedicated to Fred Gaisberg, to whom Elgar gave the MS on 28 January

[3] Letter with MS full score; BL, Add.MS 58278.

1934, less than a month before he died. Gaisberg got a recording to him, which Elgar heard on 15 February. Carice wrote to Gaisberg the same day: 'he hopes you will not mind his saying that it is too fast'.

Works for string orchestra

The three movements of the 1892 Serenade for Strings op. 20 probably owe something to a suite Elgar had written four years previously and which the future Alice Elgar had celebrated in verse. She was also closely linked to the Serenade. Elgar began working at it on 31 March 1892; he made a piano duet arrangement of the completed piece, heading it 'Braut May 13: 1892' in honour of his wife. This score paid further tribute to her, perhaps in terms of Edward Lear's 'old person of Ware', whose mount was a 'Moppsikon Floppsikon bear'. Alice Elgar was now given a mock-German epithet, 'Sie ist so flopsikon'. Finally Elgar wrote that '(Braut helped a great deal to make these little tunes.) *signed E.E.*'

The 'little tunes' demand nothing in the way of special string effects. There is a handful of pizzicato notes, mutes are donned by all except double basses at the end of the Larghetto, and a solo violin separates from the rest for a few bars in the first and last movements. The violas more than once take the melodic lead, but the cellos are rarely in the tenor clef, and then only to double violins an octave below. Yet Elgar's impress is unmistakable, not only on the sensitive and idiomatic string writing, but also on the curve of the melodic shapes and the well-varied phrase lengths. If the final Allegretto becomes reminiscent almost too soon, that is the only regret in a work so perfectly proportioned.

The initial rhythmic figure on violas pervades much of the E minor first movement as accompanying and binding motif; occasionally it takes a melodic twist of its own. The broad span of the violin tune covers a seventh stepwise, and at its next statement an octave; mounting excitement in the coda stretches the interval to a ninth and a passionate threefold sequence. A second accompaniment figure of detached quavers takes over when the music closes into the relative major. Till now phrases have been dovetailed and emphases shifted with subtle effect. The first section returns to E minor and cadences quietly with flattened seventh. Transition bars on familiar rhythmic and melodic figures launch the central section in E major. The seventh is now taken by leap, and the seven-bar phrases are linked by a snatch from the transition. As the music modulates, Elgar anticipates the 'solo' and 'tutti' effects of the Introduction and Allegro. With the wide-leaping theme on lower strings and the detached quavers *ff* above, the first section is recapitulated minus half a bar. After the coda's sequential climax, the two accompaniment figures link to summon the flattened seventh cadence.

The C major Larghetto is also tripartite. It begins with a long-drawn phrase spanning an eleventh and including a seventh leap. The melodic ideas sensitively overlap, and there follows the finest tune Elgar had yet produced, aspiring, supple and shapely in its rising seventh and sixths till it begins to fall away from its quiet high point (Ex. 72). The

Ex. 72

central section in A minor is airily scored, using cellos sparingly and basses hardly at all. Fragments of the fine tune bind the phrases, and a 'Wagner' turn looks forward to Bayreuth the following summer. A restatement begins in E minor, leading by inexact sequence to recapitulation and the third section. The order is this time a mirror-image of the opening, with the fine tune, fully scored and reaching an eloquent climax, in first place. Two bridging bars of solemn marchlike tread, foretaste of a similar moment in the Larghetto of the Second Symphony, brings the return of the opening which, with five bars shed, quietly rounds the movement.

The Allegretto finale begins in G, and three introductory bars spell out both the span of a seventh and the falling fifth that launches the main tune. This too has a bold upward sweep covering a tenth, and moves sinuously through a four- and five-bar phrase till cellos and basses take over. They scan their paragraph as three times three bars, adding one extra to prove they have in fact reached a rerun of the introductory bars. Eventually a pizzicato chord recalls the end of the first movement transition and the initial rhythmic figure of the violas. Till the end all is reminiscence, with the wide-leaping theme again in

E major. The final curtain is a graceful succession of two-bar phrases, combining the viola rhythm with a falling figure that may indeed, as Jerrold Northrop Moore suggests, be a pleasurable anticipation of the Monsalvat bells in *Parsifal*, which Elgar was now studying for Bayreuth.[4]

Since Jaeger had played so important a part in the genesis of the Introduction and Allegro for string quartet and string orchestra, it was only right Lady Elgar should write to him not long after the première in March 1905. She described Elgar's most ambitious 'string thing' as 'quite fascinating. Many people think it the finest thing he has written, the 4t. comes in with so beautiful an effect, the peroration towards the end *is* fine.' The music of the peroration was based on an experience during the Welsh holiday of summer 1901. In his programme note for op. 47 Elgar claimed to have been thinking about 'writing a brilliant piece for string orchestra' even then. This was probably wisdom after the event. He described, none the less, a moment of inspiration:

> On the cliff, between blue sea and blue sky, thinking out my theme there came up to me the sound of singing. The songs were too far away to reach me distinctly, but one point common to all was impressed upon me, and led me to think, perhaps wrongly, that it was a real Welsh idiom – I mean the fall of a third.

The tune that was to play so expressive a part in the Introduction and Allegro was written in a sketchbook Elgar started towards the end of 1901. But there it is assigned to cor anglais, amid mention of other wind instruments. It next appears partly copied out for Alice Elgar and headed '*Pattern for Bag-Poet*', as if intended for a song to which she might write words.[5] Its presence in the 'string thing' was quite a late decision. In view of its origin, Elgar said the 'tune may therefore be called, as is the melody in the overture *In the South*, a *canto popolare*'.

Jaeger had urged Bach on Elgar, reminding him of a Brandenburg 3 they had heard together in Cologne. If anything, Elgar's rhetoric favours Handel rather than Bach, but he kept the Brandenburg key-centre. G minor and G major had always been a favourite juxtaposition of Elgar's, and the first chord of the piece, of thrilling resonance mainly on open strings, gets the best of both worlds by proclaiming a G with no third. Elgar's use of the string quartet, in contrast and association with the tutti strings, is mindful of concerto grosso conventions yet wondrously varied and subtle. Sometimes the two teams are antiphonal; sometimes they double each other. The quartet may reinforce the bass

---

[4] *Edward Elgar: a Creative Life*, p. 160.
[5] See Percy M. Young, *Alice Elgar: Enigma of a Victorian Lady* (London, 1978), p. 151.

of the ensemble; or at the solo viola's 'Welsh' tune, tutti violins may underpin the points of maximum expression with different and more continuous bowing. At the start of the Allegro it is the quartet that slurs over the beats while the orchestra articulates separately. Having launched the dashing semiquavers of the second subject in dialogue with the tutti, the quartet then confines itself to adding rhythmic spice, punctuating the orchestra as it drives with utmost brilliance to the climax and slow *diminuendo* of the codetta. Here all except the cello of the quartet are muted, and in unison they have an eight-bar reminiscence of the 'Welsh' tune. All four instruments are *pianissimo*, with second violin and cello *tremolando* and *sul ponticello*; the most telling contribution from the orchestra at this point is the pizzicato reference to the opening of the work from the first cellos. The central fugue has completed its exposition and more before the quartet enters at all. The cut and thrust of this section, its fantastic shapes and countershapes, belong to the orchestra. The quartet's function here is to make an important structural point: that the fugue subject is itself counterpoint to a theme in the bass near the start of the Introduction. Throughout the rest of the fugue, the quartet is mostly in unison or octaves. As the music calms towards recapitulation, the quartet regains independence and finally has some semiquaver references to the fugue subject. For most of the peroration at the end of the work, where Elgar's orchestral colours glow with ever more gorgeous richness, the quartet reinforces mainly in octaves. The patterns constantly change throughout the work, and Elgar's frequent bowings and fingerings, indications for harmonics and extended use of the G string, and brief recourse to *ponticello* all show a composer in total command of string technique.

Formally Elgar was his own master in the Introduction and Allegro. The elements of sonata form are there, but Elgar side-stepped the problem of development with his 'devil of a fugue instead'. The Introduction contains much of the work's thematic material, and Elgar makes the point by subdividing it into nine sections with a series of light double bars. Within Elgar's characteristic ebb and flow there is overall continuity, but he indicates the different elements of thematic data with nice precision.

The imperious start, magisterial in a body of string sound that reaches *fff* in the third bar, quickly establishes G minor and contrasts falling fourths with rising tones and semitones on insistent triplet quavers. The quartet emerges for the second section, which states in the minor the main theme of the Allegro. At its fullest extent the tune spans two octaves; here it falls a tone short. But the essential rhythm of the tune is established, with two crotchets at the centre of a fluid bar, the constant that steadies the wide range of the theme. In the third section it climbs downwards with changed rhythm and a bass counterpoint that is to gather importance in the Allegro and the fugue. At the overlap to the fourth section the first violins may be hinting at the 'Welsh' tune to come; more obvious are the octave statements on the quartet, first major then minor, of the Introduction's opening. Thematically sections five and six recapitulate two and three while modulating towards E flat. The seventh section, of only one bar, highlights the solo viola and a Neapolitan approach to E flat. Section eight is devoted entirely to the 'Welsh' theme, first on solo viola with impassioned quartet tailpiece, then on quartet and orchestra with the tailpiece extended by a further five bars through the *pppp* of the work's quietest moment to G minor, tempo primo and the final section. The opening of the work has generated a descending scale on the violas. Spelt backwards, this outlines the essential shape of the Allegro's semiquaver second subject. A series of held chords recalls the 'Welsh' tune on the quartet, and the Introduction poises its last chord on a secondary seventh.

The Allegro now makes on the orchestra a four-bar G major tune from hints in the Introduction, achieving effortlessly a two-octave span; its repeat achieves the top G climax a beat earlier and with full crotchet length. The orchestra gives prominence with a quick *crescendo* to the fugue's bass counterpoint. When the Allegro tune returns, it climbs with overlapping phrases to the highest point it ever reaches. Four bars of dominant preparation harp on the interval of a semitone and all is ready for the second subject group. Persistent semiquavers provide a new figuration. As in the second movement of the Cello Concerto, the melodic shape is defined by the second semiquaver in each group. The quartet takes the lead with three bars that first define D major, then go some way towards denying it by spanning the fifth from D to A upwards and downwards with an E flat and F natural. Eventually headlong scales usher in a *nobilmente* version of the Introduction's first tune over a striding quaver bass. Two-part writing is the norm over many of the ensuing bars as the melodic line, *con fuoco* and again *fff*, leaps dramatic sixths and sevenths. Brilliant violin scales that also find their way to the lower strings build the approach in chromatic ascent to the codetta. This has five bars of the Introduction's triplets, now augmented, and seven bars of the 'Welsh' tune. A light double bar proclaims the end of the exposition, and the 'devil of a fugue' begins in G minor.

If so inclined, one can find the 'Welsh' third and second group scales in the fugue subject. Elgar drew Jaeger's attention to 'all sorts of japes & counterpoint'. Once Elgar has three lines going, he is content to keep it like that. A new entry usually means the retreat of another voice, so that three-part texture is mostly maintained. The counterpoint from the Introduction is also fitted to the fugue subject. The first four semiquavers detach themselves and are bandied about in stretto. A 'Welsh' snippet on the quartet acts as clarion call to a new theme. The ensuing passage of triple counterpoint was carefully planned: it was a mixture of the new theme just evolved, the bass counterpoint from the Introduction, and a précis of fugal elements in running semiquavers. With three subjects for treble, middle and bass, Elgar had six possible arrangements. On his sketch for the passage he labelled them A to F and ticked them off one by one; the result was twelve bars of notable japes. When the fugue subject recurs *fff*, the texture is again reduced to two parts. Over a dominant pedal the quartet has first the fugue subject, then yet another expressive counterpoint instinct with falling thirds, while the orchestral violins creep down in chromatics towards the double bar that marks the end of the fugal section. The next seven bars are concerned with what Elgar in a sketch called 'return to 1st Sub'. The music has resumed G major and, after delicately showing the relationship between the fugue and the second group semiquavers, crosses a further double bar to signal the start of the recapitulation.

After the high imaginative flights of the fugue, Elgar can afford to be comparatively predictable. With the second group in the tonic G, Elgar has abbreviated here and there till the chromatic ascent towards the coda, where he spreads the process over an additional bar. Then comes Lady Elgar's sumptuous 'peroration' on the 'Welsh' tune. It is subtly put together, beginning with what had been the orchestral statement in the Introduction, with the fourth bar of the tailpiece turning back to a passionate restatement of its first two bars. Only now does Elgar resume the viola solo version, building its second half to the last *fff* climax of the work. The Allegro first subject returns, interspersed with semiquaver arpeggios and glancing momentarily at the key of E flat so structural in the Introduction. A dominant chord, open-string tonic from all the instruments, final pizzicato, and Elgar's splendid 'string thing' is done.

The MS score of the *Elegy* for strings has 'Mordiford Bridge' beneath Elgar's signature. The piece had other associations important to Elgar. It was sent to Novello a month after Jaeger's death, having been requested by Littleton to commemorate Rev Robert Hadden, a junior warden of the Musicians' Company; and it so happened that Hadden was the maiden name of Julia Worthington, with whom the Elgars had been staying at Careggi. It had therefore all the associations of place and person to inspire Elgar's best. He himself described it to Littleton on 25 June 1909 as 'quiet, somewhat sad & soothing'.

Littleton had called the piece a 'dirge', and Elgar took up with him the matter of its title: 'I have put Elegy on the copy but please alter it. I think I like Dirge best.' In this small work Elgar produced the most concentrated of his mourning pieces. The string writing is dense, and dissonant harmonies are more closely packed than usual. Some of the melodic lines hint at *The Music Makers*; here they have more cogency and grow inevitably towards the moment where a 'Wagner' turn releases tension. The shape is arched from its remote, rapt opening to an end that has gained serenity from passion spent.

Sospiri makes its effect differently. Originally intended as a 1914 sequel to the *Salut d'amour* of 1888, it was to be called *Soupir d'amour*. But in the writing it gained intensity and was eventually published by Breitkopf & Härtel, for whom Elgar gave it the German title 'Seufzer'. The MS score dedicates the work 'freundschaftlichst' to W. H. Reed and indicates that harp or piano, harmonium or organ are 'ad lib'. Perhaps a sketch at the Birthplace, headed 'Absence', clarifies its significance for Elgar. *Sospiri* is frankly a work of melody with accompaniment, for first violins and the rest. Yet from the outset, with dissonant entry over a held chord, it proves to be melody of a special cast. By means of syncopations or ties both first and second tune avoid strong beats, so that the themes float rhapsodically above the rest of the orchestra. Diatonic lines are constantly subjected to octave displacement so that wide intervals are the norm, especially in the second tune. The Birthplace sketch gives instruction for the recapitulation: 'the theme in octaves with full tone'; as elsewhere in Elgar, this results in a coarsening of the texture; but the second tune fares better, with an accompaniment of accented tremolos. As a whole *Sospiri* is more imaginative than successful, but it is easy to understand how the première, eleven days after the outbreak of the First World War, could seem to Lady Elgar a message of peace.

Early chamber music

From the age of twelve Elgar was determined to be a violinist, and string chamber music was one of his teenage pleasures. He copied and arranged many pieces for string quartet, including Bach fugues from the '48', Handel marches from *Hercules* and the *Occasional Oratorio*, overtures to *Messiah* and *Samson*, as well as the Overture in D minor to Chandos Anthem no. 2 that he was to orchestrate fully in 1923. Minuets from a Mozart piano sonata and the Beethoven Septet were joined by organ works from Geissler's *Tonstücke*. Most interesting of all was an 'imitation a Quattro through all the parts alternately', an original piece based on the second movement of Beethoven's Violin

Sonata in G op. 30 no. 3. He made also a collection of 'Christmas Pieces' for flute and string quartet that included the Adagio from Beethoven's Ninth Symphony, a Mendelssohn Allegretto from the *Lobgesang*, a Boccherini minuet and Chopin waltz, as well as two variations on *Adeste fideles* by Elgar himself. Another wind instrument was catered for in an incomplete Andante and Allegro for oboe and string quartet.

Music for 'The Brothers Wind' or the 'Sunday Band' was an admixture of original pieces and arrangements, with the former gradually predominating. A précis of the finale from Beethoven's A minor Violin Sonata op. 23 was a characteristic arrangement, but by Christmas 1877 Elgar had produced his cheerful *Peckham March*. An *Evesham* Andante continued the geography lesson and showed in its variations that Elgar was no mean bassoon player, ready to indulge in mild chromatics. The 'Harmony' or 'Shed' music was on a larger scale, with experiments in sonata form that revealed Elgar as already a master of writing for his instruments and skilled contrapuntist. The music is endlessly inventive, in anyone's style but his own. The merry chortling of no. 1 holds nothing but delight; no. 2 has Rossinian suavity with a development of happy resource and one theme that strikes a more solemn note; no. 3, in A minor, breaks off just as an oboe cadenza leads towards a passage of deeper and richer expression. A series of six *Promenades* continues the sprightly catalogue. No. 2 is called 'Madame Taussaud's' [*sic*] and interrupts its metropolitan strut with little explosions of glee. The scampering no. 3 has also an aspiring central tune. The dreamy start of no. 4 in octaves perhaps justifies its title 'Somniferous'; the teasing wit of its end could not be more alert. No. 5 shows Elgar slipping in a subdominant direction to prepare a delectable middle section. The last one, 'Hell and Tommy', manages amid the exuberance a musette-like drone. An Adagio cantabile, 'Mrs Winslow's Soothing Syrup', also belongs to this group; the medicine is comfortably administered, but some harmonic darkenings and chromatic twists suggest that the dose was not unqualified pleasure. There is also a sequence of four dances, Menuetto, Gavotte, Sarabande and Giga. The first has a strong *ländler* movement; the second features an athletic bassoon and ends deliciously; the Sarabande has an old-world elegance and some piquant harmonic touches; the Giga has a solemn middle to offset the sprightliness of the framing sections. The Sarabande was to have featured in Act 2 of Elgar's opera, at the entrance of the supposed Spanish Lady; Gavotte and Giga were also transferred to the opera folder.

There are four more *Harmony Musics*, on a scale Elgar had not previously attempted. No. 4, 'The Farm Yard', is a grand movement in C major with the imperious stamp of Beethoven upon it, both in its arpeggio first theme and the winsome appeal of its second. Discussion of the material tends to garrulity, but Elgar had now achieved a full-length sonata movement. In no. 5, 'The Mission', Elgar went further and completed his first four-movement work. The ideas in the D major Allegro moderato are characterful and piquant, with many points of imitation and subtle tonal shifts in the development. Beneath staccato chords for the rest of the group, the Minuet has a confidential counterpoint for clarinet that points to the future. A 'Noah's Ark' Andante in A minor floats rather sorrowfully; but the finale has more than 400 bars of exuberant chatter. The G major Allegro of no. 6, again an accomplished sonata movement, is followed by an Andante arioso with solemn tread similar to that of Haydn's variations in the F major String Quartet op. 77 no. 2. Elgar later revised it into his op. 3 *Cantique* of 1912. The last full-scale wind movement was written as late as the spring of 1881; it is among the most accomplished, but Elgar pursued the work no further.

When looking through this wind music in later years, Elgar wrote, 'I like the shed on the whole but the "Intermezzi" are "mine own children"!' Indeed these are the five movements most full of character. The first starts with Haydnesque imitations of Worcestershire farms, but manages also a tinge of sadness amid the wit. The G major Adagio of no. 2 intensifies the sorrow with much chromatic writing. In no. 3 there is skilful imitative writing and a beautifully contrived end. No. 4 has a delicious staccato part for Elgar as bassoonist and attains a succinct charm worthy of Tchaikovsky; while the last again exploits the bassoon and returns to Haydnesque high spirits in its teasing conclusion.

Wind instruments were also featured in two fugues, one in D minor for oboe and violin of 1883, the other for trombone and double bass written four years later. They show deft contrapuntal skill and the ability to devise themes striking in themselves and also apt for japes. Elgar explained that the first was written for Karl Bammert and Frank Elgar. He wrote on the MS score that they 'shared rooms at the back of my father's premises ... Occasionally, owing to the absence of a pupil, I found myself with half-an-hour's leisure; such restful moments I spent with a pipe in my brother's room & usually left some memento in M.S.; – this is one.' The other piece was a wedding present for a double bass-playing friend.

Behind the real achievement of the wind quintet music lay many attempts to write for strings. Indeed *Harmony Music* no. 4 is the splendid realization of a failed attempt to make a trio for two violins and cello out of the same material. Elgar's struggles can be seen in one of his early sketchbooks. Likewise the last of the 'Shed' musics brought to fruition a fragmentary string quartet that had broken off after thirty-nine sketchy bars. Most of the surviving quartet efforts launch into a minor key but do not achieve even an exposition. But two works in D minor promised more. The first evolved steadily through three of Elgar's 1878 sketchbooks to present a sturdy first theme with *pp* pendants and a mellifluous second subject in F over a dominant pedal. In this case the exposition was complete, and Elgar thought highly enough of the initial motif to copy it out for possible use in *The Spanish Lady*. He then labelled it 'on Stage Act II', and by the side wrote 'Beeth[ove]n'. The only quartet for which four movements were sketched was again in D minor, perhaps written in 1888. None of the constituent parts was fully worked out, but the Intermezzo in F was eventually completed to become no. 3 of the *Vesper Voluntaries* op. 14.

Yorkshire holidays at Charles Buck's provided the occasion for piano trios, and Elgar dated a Minuet and Trio 'composed expressly for his friend' 4 September 1882. The Minuet was later copied for possible inclusion in *The Spanish Lady*: the Trio became the piano piece *Douce pensée* and, ultimately, *Rosemary* for small orchestra. Another fragment, starting with a bold rhetorical gesture and more adventurous in layout, was started in 1886.

Chamber music hardly featured in Elgar's output again until the completed works of 1918–19. In correspondence with Jaeger of 1901 and later he mentioned a proposed string sextet, but nothing came of it. The start of a January 1907 piece for violin, mandoline and guitar was a *jeu d'esprit* 'for the Barbers' on Capri. Later that year Elgar was engaged on the string quartet that gave many ideas to the middle movements of the First Symphony.

Violin Sonata op. 82

Inspiration to shape Elgar's only completed violin sonata came with the arrival of a piano at Brinkwells. It was perhaps uncertainty about his ability as a keyboard composer that had inhibited Elgar from writing such a work till then. This is implied in a letter to Ivor Atkins of 23 September 1918: 'I have also made a table & have written a Sonata for Vn & Pf on it, & the latter (that is the piano part) requires much consideration & advice.' The piano layout turned out by no means ambitious, but economical and effective, causing no problems of balance. Elgar was pleased with the Sonata when done, describing it to Rosa Burley as 'concise & clear & passionate'.

Like Schumann so often, Elgar begins athwart his key, suggesting an initial A minor rather than the nominal E minor. The first subject group, with at least four thematic tags, gets a double airing. First time the violin leads, the piano, firmly in E minor, second time. The expressive second tune also begins in E minor. As this second group continues, it quietly transforms the first theme of the work, develops violin arpeggios and minim chords for the piano out of the second tune and finally, over an F sharp pedal, begins a long paragraph of chromatic working at a figure from the first group. There has already been so much thematic transformation that Elgar eschews further development and recapitulates at once. Proportions are varied and there are skilful short cuts. The second tune strongly asserts A minor, the movement's subdominant, and Elgar maintains his tonal ambiguity to the end of the extended coda.

Elgar described the Romance in a letter to the Windflower of 11 September 1918: 'a fantastic curious movemt with a very expressive middle section: a melody for the Violin – they say it's as good as or better than anything I have done in the expressive way: this I wrote just after your telegram about the accident came & I send you the pencil notes as first made at that sad moment.' Lady Stuart had broken her leg out walking at Tintagel. The 'fantastic' part of the movement, owing something to the weird witchery of the Brinkwells woods, twice ends in A major, but is happier in and around C sharp, with its curious pizzicato and fioriture (Ex. 73a). The central tune, in B flat via F, inhabits a completely different world and threatens to overwhelm the hesitant chromatics of the opening (Ex. 73b). It is long-breathed at the outset, capable of infinite expansion and reaches the only climax that looks in vain for an orchestra.

The E major of the finale has constantly to be reminded not to shed too many sharps. It too has strong subdominant leanings, as far as C. The serene, even flow of the opening tune is restated in A. An energetic transition theme starts in C and leads to a *poco sostenuto* second tune in a reluctant B minor that wanders passionately through a wide sequence of keys. A chromatic coda figure with an obsessive rhythm closes into G. Elgar now embarks on a resourceful development of the movement's every aspect, exploring hesitantly and with tenderness an isolated phrase from the opening tune. Recapitulation begins regularly, but the first tune and transition are truncated and lead to a second tune now laid out in opulent splendour for the two instruments, *con fuoco* and *appassionato*. This begins in A minor, with the subdominant pull characteristic of the Sonata, and remains throughout a tone lower than in the exposition. The chromatic closing figure steers the music towards the coda and a hushed return to the central theme of the Romance. It begins in E, but soon moves flatwards to reach a yet more

Elgar

Ex. 73a

Andante

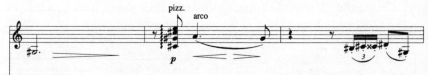

Ex. 73b

powerful climax closing into G. The opening tune of the movement and the transition motif take some time to establish a brilliant cadential E major with semiquaver figuration on the violin and broken octaves from the keyboard. A strong plagal leaning at the end sums up the Sonata's tonal thinking.

String Quartet op. 83

The MS score of the String Quartet contains a dedication to the Brodsky team Elgar had long admired. This was the fulfilment of a wish conceived some eleven years before when Elgar was apparently planning a 1907 quartet for these players. For some reason the intended dedication did not appear on the printed score. The airy textures of the 1918 Quartet gradually unfold the most consistently imagined and finely conceived of the chamber works. If a rest count is any indication of feeling for the essential interplay of good quartet writing, Elgar

383

scores highly; indeed he is never happier than when distributing his abundant invention for the four instruments into three parts.

As Elgar wrote, 'the quartet starts in rather a phantom-like way'.[6] Again nominally in E minor, the hesitant phrases and uncertain tonality of the opening generate motifs enough to propel most of the movement. The 12/8 signature, often risky for Elgar, is here a springboard for admirable flexibility. The opening bars return after the first climax and lead the music to the ambivalent G major of the second tune. A subtle shift moves it quietly to the remoteness of F, where it lingers tenderly. A powerful statement of the tune in its original shape thins the texture step by step until only the cello is left to prepare the development, which is unusually long for Elgar. Indeed the proportions of the movement, with development longer than exposition, a curtailed recapitulation, and coda half the length of the exposition, are one of its most satisfying features. The thematic data can be split apart in a variety of ways, can generate new tags, and be reassembled in different order. So, in a manner of speaking, development and reprise are dovetailed by Elgar. He brings back at the end of the development part of the exposition that had already wandered far enough from E minor to disguise its present purpose. A moment's pause, and the recapitulation is quietly begun. The second theme returns in E major, initially in broken phrases, and this time departs to an even more distant E flat. The coda powerfully draws threads together, remains tonally elusive, and subsides to a final E major chord. But the previous chord, separated by a comma, has prepared the key of the next movement.

The C major of the Piacevole is at the outset as secure as the first movement's tonalities were shifting. A six-bar phrase is extended by sequential steps and cross-rhythms a further sixteen bars, during the whole of which the first violin is silent. Its eventual entry an octave above the second violin only maintains the three-part texture. This theme was Lady Elgar's 'captured sunshine'. A transitional figure built from one-bar phrases treated imitatively wanders sharpwards and closes eventually on the dominant of A minor for the second subject group. This proceeds delicately by fits and starts, with the violins often in sixths, leisurely and unhurried until it subsides towards a bee-hummed drowsy phrase that repeats itself almost too often. A brief passage based on the bees' music, and the transitional figure leads to an *ff* recapitulation of 'captured sunshine'. There has been no formal development, but each exposition idea was very fully discussed before another was taken up. Now in recapitulation the first theme and

---

[6] Cohen, *A Bundle of Time*, p. 212.

transition are considerably abbreviated, but the second group, launched by an unobtrusive pun into D minor instead of A minor, pursues much of its course almost exactly. The coda plays lazily with 'captured sunshine', putting much emphasis on the supertonic. Again the last sounds, with the E of C major at the top, prepare for what ensues.

The finale is formally original and intriguing. Five introductory bars of energetic detached figures prepare for the grand sweep of the first tune, in E minor but with first strong accent on the supertonic. A slight hold-up leads to an important new theme with much syncopation that is transitional in so far as it modulates swiftly. There are reminders of first subject material and, as the note-lengths broaden, the first tune returns in E minor and this time develops headlong semiquavers. Is Elgar in the midst of a rondo? It might seem so, but in reality he has just completed a gigantic first subject group, with much Schubertian discussion along the way. The spacious second group is introduced by chromatic chords in an insecure A major. The main *dolce* tune is more stable but makes subtle tonal excursions as it proceeds. One of its elements becomes more and more prominent and then dominates the first section of the development. Elgar separates this section with a double bar and launches as if on a 'devil of a fugue' like the Introduction and Allegro. The whole section is unified with these continuous semiquavers first heard on the viola. Bandied from part to part they accompany the tail end of the second group until the transition motif gradually moves centre stage. At a momentary comma and sudden *ff*, it is this theme that begins the recapitulation, introducing reminders of the first subject as before. Further hints of it are heard over *ponticello* lower strings and lead to an extensive discussion of the second group's tail end. The main *dolce* tune now returns *teneramente* in C and, by an unexpected twist, finds E minor and at last the first subject, given in both its exposition manifestations. A brilliant coda combines the opening of the movement with the second group tail and then with the hurtling semiquavers of the development. The whole work is cogently thought and finely realized, as deft as it is original. If there is danger the slow movement may sag, Elgar's metronome mark is a useful corrective.

Piano Quintet op. 84

When writing about the Piano Quintet to Ernest Newman, its dedicatee, Elgar expressed doubts: 'I am not sure if I shd. publish it as pianists seem to require so much padding – passagework which is so commonplace & I have given none.' The work was first played complete at Severn House on 7 March 1919, and Bernard Shaw was present. In a letter written the following day he commented on the magic of certain keyboard effects: 'I have my doubts whether any regular shop pianist will produce them: they require a touch which is peculiar to yourself, and which struck me the first time I ever heard you larking about with a piano.'[7] The keyboard writing is indeed mostly above reproach, tactfully bolstering the strings and occasionally using full power in bold antiphonal effects. There is delicate figuration enough in the Adagio, and some brilliance in those bars near the start of the finale that Elgar called 'tadpoles' and 'straddlebug' passages. The weaknesses of the Quintet are more fundamental and concern the quality of the material itself. The situation is the reverse of the String Quartet: here the slow movement easily out-tops the other two.

The start could hardly be more impressive, with the chant fragments on the keyboard and chromatic figuration on the strings that brought to Shaw's mind the opening of Beethoven's *Coriolan* overture. The next, close-knit chromatic phrase (Ex. 74), with cello rising over a major seventh, grows from the previous section by augmentation or diminution according to whether one hears more nearly strings or piano. This motif is the work's motto theme. The ensuing 6/8 Allegro, still in A minor and as Brahmsian as anything Elgar wrote in his maturity, comes to as firm a full stop as the previous sections. After reference to the motto, the second, Spanish-flavoured theme is introduced. There is charm in its quiet swaying rhythm and harmonies on the flat seventh; again the string figuration of the opening is recalled. But the *crescendo* into E major launches one of the most dangerous passages in late Elgar. In a lighter context it would be in dubious taste; here it is a sorry lapse. When the dynamic drops, all is well again. The B minor coda restates the opening chant fragments now on the strings, with keyboard figuration, and then paraphrases the chant into a fine closing melody.

Shaw took exception to the beginning of the development, where Elgar devises an animated fugato on notes from the Brahmsian section. Shaw referred to 'a place where you start canonizing'. He complained of 'each voice repeating the phrase note for note at exactly the same distance in a quite blastedly and obvious manner'. And he offered advice: 'Couldn't you just knock it all silly and wonderful in a turn of the hand?' Elgar was sufficiently impressed with the letter to forward it to Newman, adding that he felt Shaw had mistaken the psychological drift of the passage at cue 10: 'it was meant to be square at that point & goes wild again'. The long *animando* builds considerable tension none the less, and thunderous semiquavers on cello and piano

---

[7] Laurence, ed., *Bernard Shaw: Collected Letters 1911–1925*, p. 592.

Ex. 74

develop the broken string phrases from the start of the movement. The Brahmsian material, after an *fff* climax, gradually resumes its original form in antiphonal exchanges, leading by broad descending sequences towards A minor.

And so the recapitulation begins with a much extended version of the Brahmsian passage. The 'Spanish' figure makes itself felt in the strings *con fuoco*, and the second group runs its course with extensions here and there. A lower dynamic keeps some of the earlier vulgarity at bay. Hints of the chant and its figuration return and flower into the continuous chant melody, now in D minor. The work's close-knit chromatic motto is resumed, and the movement closes with the fullest statement yet of the broken chant.

Shaw had no doubts about the Adagio: 'A fine slow movement is a matter of course with you: nobody else has really done it since Beethoven: at least the others have never been able to take *me* in. Intermezzos and romances at best, never a genuine adagio'. The E major movement starts with a spacious paragraph in which the viola leads an expressive eight-bar statement of the first theme. This is extended by imitation and sequence over a large area, with the final echo on the viola to closing pizzicato chords. A transitional passage starting in A combines broken chords on the piano with string syncopations, an impassioned melodic line and wide-ranging counterpoint on the cello. The procedure is repeated in B to reach C sharp and the second tune. This is a beautifully shaped sequel to the first theme, with smaller intervals, placing dotted notes and the main stress differently. After a cello continuation, the piano makes as if to repeat the transitional passage; but the syncopations take on a vitality of their own and launch a grand restatement of the second tune in F sharp minor. Elgar now note-spins for three blocks of four bars, the last block implying a resolution into F sharp. Instead Elgar slides unobtrusively to F major for a magical start to his development, with an imitative treatment of the viola tune's first four bars moving flatwards to E flat and C minor. Shaw doubtless approved the stretto that allows the four strings to compass the theme in twelve bars. Elgar develops with maximum eloquence the one dotted bar of the theme, and at the climax its essential shape is compressed into bars of paired quavers. Gradually, over a long period, the music calms and slows towards E major and the recapitulation. Much in the two main themes is cut or postponed to the coda. By a slight expansion of the transition the second tune is reached in the same C sharp minor of its original statement. Again Elgar diverts its final cadence by a semitone to begin his coda in C. During its course Elgar quietly recapitulates the last sixteen bars of the very first paragraph, a passage he had discreetly avoided at the start of the reprise. There is a last reference to the viola's first theme so that the beginning of the movement also shapes its end.

The finale begins with the chromatic motto of the work, at first quiet but repeated loudly, with the piano turning the original cello quavers into accelerating semiquavers over four octaves. The *con dignità* of the main Allegro tune is an attempt to make the best of a poorish job. Many a composer has run out of good ideas before starting a finale; here Elgar is no exception. Shaw was rightly 'exhilarated by the swing of the three-four', but it contains little of distinction and falls sadly away from the Adagio. Elgar's 'tadpoles' and 'straddlebugs' are fun, but such keyboard figuration cannot disguise the threadbare music above them. The second tune is no improvement. The syncopations and perfunctory chromatics are merely tawdry, and their layout for the strings is hardly a success. Shaw hit the nail on the head: 'The jazz was much better when you were taking it along. It is extremely difficult to induce an English fiddler to dissociate vigor from dryness of tone'. The development begins with a neat idea: a wide-spanned motif on the piano involves the drop of a major seventh; the viola turns it upside down at once to wriggle up a minor ninth. The rest of the development is largely concerned with reminiscence of the first movement chant and the 'Spanish' tune, now in triple time. Shaw was dubious: 'I am not sure that the vitality of the finale is not too much for that little snatch of waltz when the leader mutes his fiddle. A vision of you offering a haporth of sweets to some dear old lady who didnt like classical music came into my irreverent head suddenly.' Recapitulation of the opening tune is subtly done, with variation of the tonal scheme and a nice continuity of texture. The coda presents both main ideas with panache, the 'jazz' now exultant in a grandiose A major.

Sometimes in a sketchbook Elgar would write 'cheap' above a thematic idea. Too many of the Quintet themes fall into that category, so as inevitably to mar what is obviously an ambitious work. Elgar's judgment is by no means impeccable, but usually some stroke of bold imagination will redeem a movement below his best. This he fails to achieve in the Quintet finale.

Violin music
Elgar's first surviving violin piece dates from March 1877, before his twentieth-birthday, when he was already teaching the violin but was also nursing ambitions for a virtuoso career. *Reminiscences* was dedicated to Oswin Grainger, a local grocer friend; it is a graceful

melodic piece exploiting the instrument's cantilena, pleasantly sequential in its main theme and middle section, but with no interest in technical display. Elgar's lessons with Adolphe Pollitzer from August 1877 were undertaken specifically to extend his range and facility as a player. The Birthplace Museum possesses an MS copy of 'A Daily Study' by Pollitzer; at the end is the encouraging inscription 'good luck to you'. This dates from the time Elgar was devising his own studies. A fair copy of his 'Exercise for the 3rd. finger' is dated 7 October 1878; when he copied it out for Heifetz in November 1920 and a facsimile appeared in the *Daily Telegraph* of 24 December, Elgar explained in an accompanying letter that Pollitzer 'was much amused by the studies and exercises of my invention'. He wrote also about the *Etudes caractéristiques* op. 24, published in 1892 by Chanot: 'Five of the studies (dedicated to Pollitzer), mainly for the "poise" of the bow, although the left hand is not neglected, were published long after their inception'. Multiple stopping is fiendishly exploited in them. An *Etude caprice* given to W. H. Reed comes from the same period, and a D minor study at the Birthplace is dated 19 October 1881. Elgar also wrote piano accompaniments to three studies by Kreutzer, nos. 2, 8 and 13.

Elgar's technical expertise is evident in the E minor *Romance*, probably written in 1878 and again dedicated to Grainger. Its publication as op. 1 by Schott in 1885 brought Elgar 'One Shilling & 20 Gratis copies'. The work is remarkable for its very romantic middle section building to a fine climax, and for the profusion of octaves and double-stops that crowd the end. Two Polonaises of March 1879, one in F dedicated to the Powick Asylum pianist and later transferred to *The Spanish Lady*, the other in D minor with hint of the future *King Olaf*, remained incomplete. The Scottish holiday of August 1884 produced *Une Idylle*, dedicated to 'E.E., Inverness' and published as op. 4 no. 1. The shapely tune inspired some harmonic piquancy, and the middle section, ardent and Schumannesque in its development, has a touch of mature Elgarian passion. The *Pastourelle* op. 4 no. 2 was dedicated to Hilda Fitton. The delightful lilt of the piece, fresh and engaging, keeps interest alive.

The Allegretto on the notes GEDGE of early 1885 is real duo music, with an integration of violin and piano parts that Elgar had not attempted before. There were seven sisters in the Gedge family; Elgar taught two of them the violin, and a third piano accompaniment. Elgar followed Schumann in basing his piece on musical letters, in the impetuous flair of the tunes, and in the prevalence of syncopation. His own, though, are the touches of pizzicato wit and the accomplishment of the writing. A Gavotte of August 1885 was dedicated to Charles

Buck, or rather 'Buché', as printed on the Schott edition. Elgar apologized in a letter of February 1886: 'I do not know what to say about the dedication. I hesitated, when I saw the mess they had made of it, between swearing and laughing; I chose the latter & hope you will.' He was modest about the Gavotte: 'The Violin Solo makes a good Show piece & 'tis intended to be nothing more.' The opening has old-world charm, but there is virtuosity in the flying staccato and some typical pauses in the flowing tune of the middle section. Elgar's first surviving letter on publishing matters, dated 23 March 1886, concerns an arrangement he had made for violin and piano of a keyboard *Berceuse* 'Petite reine' by G. Frank Blackbourne, who wrote under the name Victor Berard. Elgar made Blackbourne a gift of the new version: 'Please consider the arrangement of your Berceuse entirely your own property; I, of course, always intended that.' He also added a shrewd post-script: 'Of course if *you* have any interest in the PF solo you will stipulate that you retain it in the Violin & piano Edn if published.' It was brought out by Willcocks & Company.

November 1887 seemed to promise a work on an altogether more expansive scale. Elgar began a D minor violin sonata on the first of the month, but neither the Allegro nor the ensuing Adagio made much progress. The latter, however, provided an initial idea for *Sursum corda* op. 11. The inspiration for Elgar's next violin piece of September 1888 proved more sure. *Liebesgrüss* (with the superfluous umlaut) was written in anticipation of his engagement to Caroline Alice Roberts and published as *Salut d'amour* for a down payment of two guineas. Despite Schott's generously adding a royalty when the success of the work was assured, Elgar felt aggrieved that his bestseller brought him in so little. When negotiating with Novello about *Chanson de nuit*, Elgar made his position clear: 'I *wish* you could arrange terms for it which would leave me some interest in it: the last Violin piece I wrote, which unfortunately I sold some years ago for a nominal sum, now sells well – I understand 3000 copies were sold in the month of January alone'. The finely wrought piece was dedicated to Caroline Alice in a form the Elgars were to adopt for their only child, 'à Carice'. Perhaps the repeated notes leading to the drop of a seventh do not make Elgar's most distinguished thematic notion, and the central section, as often in Elgar's lighter music, is a cut above the opening; yet the material was instantly memorable and bears repetition more readily than many a piece with greater ambitions. The last pages draw out the sweetness of the music just long enough to stir a sigh of contentment, and the Elgars' engagement got off to a good start.

Two violin pieces of 1889 were both rejected by publishers, *Liebes-ahnung* by Schott, *Bizarrerie* by Simrock. They were eventually taken by Orsborn & Tuckwood for ten guineas as op. 13 nos. 1 and 2. The title of the former was changed to *Mot d'amour* in direct challenge to its predecessor, and likewise dedicated to 'Alice', but the ambiguity of its initial dissonances and its comparative reticence have slowed its progress. *Bizarrerie*, on the other hand, has the wayward brilliance and frank showiness to enhance a very seductive middle section. The last of the op. 4 pieces, *Virelai*, was probably written early in 1890, when Elgar was engaged with Froissart, his chronicles and poems. He dedicated the work to Frank Webb, who was puzzled by the title. Elgar explained it on 5 May 1890: 'Very sorry! "Virelai" is an old French poem – short &, like a Ballade, or a Rondel &c.&c., is of arbitrary construction: of course the music is not "constructed" like a poem.' Elgar ended playfully: 'Anyway it means a simple little "lay" & what am I if not simple? Now ARE you satisfied?' The piece begins with enough rhythmic ambivalence to intrigue and has a fluent charm. Elgar's last music of 1891 was *La capricieuse* op. 17. Alice Elgar's diary for Christmas Eve fixes the date: 'E. finished & wrote out *Capricieuse* Vn Solo.' At an earlier stage it was called 'Le Staccato'. This piece found a German publisher in Breitkopf & Härtel, but partly at Elgar's expense. It is light music of supreme skill, the sort of work Fritz Kreisler was to make his own, superbly written for the violin, with suave double-stopping in the middle section, and a final curtain skilfully brought down. The dedication went to Frank Ward, a Worcester pupil.

In May 1892 Elgar sent to Chanot the *Very Easy Melodious Exercises in the First Position for Violin* op. 22. Written for and dedicated to Elgar's niece, May Grafton, they were at the opposite extreme from the Pollitzer studies, but were the experience of many years' teaching grind. The *Offertoire* (Andante Religioso) was written at the end of 1893 but not published until 1903, when it appeared under the name of Gustav Franke as his op. 11, dedicated to Serge Derval of Antwerp. Elgar apparently told Troyte Griffith he had written the piece to encourage his brother Frank to pursue composition further. It makes a dignified piece with a climax almost too passionate for its context but not untypical of Elgar in religious mood.

The last two pieces of the century were *Chanson de nuit*, which Elgar had originally called 'Evensong', and *Chanson de matin*. Both were sketched in the autumn of 1897, but at first Elgar left only 'Evensong' with Novello. It was readily accepted; but the question of the title was long debated. Elgar wrote to Novello about it on 23 November 1897: 'As to the title of the little Violin Solo – do you think "Vesper" better than Evensong? I do; Chanson de Nuit was best but I dislike a french title.' Three days later Elgar wrote again: 'I forget if

I said that if the piece is called "Evensong" or "Vesper" people would play it in church at the many organ recitals with Violin solos interspersed now given: if it is called "Chanson de Nuit" they might think it profane.' The rich gravity of the piece is no more sacred than profane, and it has enough melodic strength to have survived the onslaughts of fashion. A faster middle section makes a beautiful transition to the original tune with its subtle keyboard embellishments. It was dedicated to Frank Ehrke, another local musician. Elgar did not submit *Chanson de matin* for publication till eighteen months later. He wrote to Novello about it on 6 March 1899, just after completing the Variations: 'Enclosed I send the M.S. of an easy Violin & pianoforte piece. I see from my sketch (which I found last week & have since completed) that this piece was intended to be a companion to the one you have already.' Elgar now suggested the obvious title himself. The opening melody begins as if in direct answer to *Salut d'amour* but develops a tender skittishness all its own. The central climax unwinds skilfully to a reprise adorned with new counterpoints. A rather conventional pedal point prepares for an end where imagination is again in full charge.

Piano music

Elgar's skill at keyboard improvisation, developed early in youth, stayed with him into old age. He was over seventy-two when he recorded five improvisations for the Gramophone Company at his own request. Dorabella had described his piano playing: 'I had never heard anything quite like this. He didn't play like a pianist, he almost seemed to play like a whole orchestra. It sounded full without being loud and he contrived to make you hear other instruments joining in.' Yet the recorded improvisations show a formidable piano technique, capable of the most delicate passagework and attempting considerable virtuoso flights with ease. Elgar claimed to 'know nothing about pianoforte music' and to 'hate the piano as an instrument'; the improvisations, however, reveal him playing idiomatically and *con amore*, devising piano music more adventurous than any he allowed to be published. Each of the pieces carries conviction and makes a rounded whole. There is much charm and delicacy, some lovely Elgarian phrase, power and caprice. As his closest friends knew, Elgar in his seventies was brimful of music.

Paradoxically, the bulk of Elgar's keyboard music is indeed 'orchestral'. When submitting a vocal score for publication, the keyboard part was his own, as near as mattered the working draft he had used as basis for the orchestration. Always the writing was competent and effective. He claimed never to have 'evolved his musical thoughts in a keyboard shape'; but ever practical, he could thus order his ideas with complete success. Elgar's keyboard version of the 'Enigma' Variations is the perfect example of this skill. But that the piano was not a favourite medium is clear from his slender output and its nature, miniatures for the most part. About the Concert Allegro, the one major work he attempted Elgar never resolved his doubts, leaving it unpublished despite a number of public performances.

If a song, *The Language of Flowers*, claims primacy among Elgar's completed compositions, the piano piece *Chantant* is a near competitor, written when he was about fifteen. It is Schumannesque in starting on dominant not tonic, in its impetuous drive, repetitiveness, and the gnomic simplicity of its central section. As piano music it is the most ambitious of his pieces till the Concert Allegro of almost thirty years later. The diminutive *Griffinesque*, again fanciful and Schumannesque, dates from 1884 but was reworked the following year and presented to Mrs C. W. Buck. The 'Enina' Waltz of December 1886 is more conventional; its origin may have been in the Elgar children's play, since 'Enina' was Elgar's original title for *Wand of Youth* suite no. 1. The Sonatina written in January 1889 for his niece May Grafton was revised in December 1930 and published the following year. The MS title page bears the signature of 'her affectionate uncle', but also suggests Elgar had at one time a three-movement work in mind. The central one was to have been an 'Andante'. The leisurely Allegretto, melodious and charming, with much simple two-part writing, was slowed to Andantino in the revision; the scampering Allegro was to be played 'as fast as you can!' by the niece. The revision involved many emendations and some recomposition. A G major Presto was written for Isabel Fitton's twenty-first birthday on 8 August 1889; its cheerful virtuosity was presumably to be interpreted by the mother. The Minuet published in 1897 was another child's piece, written for Paul Kilburn. It has a harmonic surprise or two in support of its attractive tunes.

The *May Song* survives in a number of versions. Alice Elgar's diary of 2 March 1901 suggests it was originally written for piano: 'finished May Song – & violin arrt.' The main theme, an airy creation of much charm, is shaped within a *ritmo ostinato*. The *Skizze* of the same year, dedicated to Julius Buths and played by Elgar to the renowned English pianist Leonard Borwick, is another miniature, this time concentrated and harmonically uneasy, so that much of the piece is at odds with its basic F major despite a lengthy tonic pedal at the end. It hardly rises above *pp* and also descends below *pppp*.

Elgar's most ambitious keyboard work, the Concert Allegro in C op. 41, also dates from 1901. It was written at the request of Fanny Davies, whose playing he was to commend in the Birmingham lectures. The MS title page has Elgar following Schumann and calling it a 'Concerto (without orchestra)'. It was quickly composed, then successfully performed on 2 December. *The Times* could detect little 'organic connection between one part and another'. The brilliance and power of the writing are undeniable, but the work betrays haste in its profusion of ideas, not all of which are followed through. The virtuosity is balanced by a broad second tune starting in E flat. The MS shows that Elgar took Fanny Davies's advice on keyboard layout in a number of places. Her suggestions were initialled 'Humbly F.D!' She played it again on two occasions in February 1906. Richter heard it in Manchester, where she repeated it as an unscheduled encore and reported him as saying: 'It is as though Bach and Liszt had married each other!!!' But Elgar was not satisfied with the work and wrote to Littleton on 23 October 1907: 'I do not think the P.F piece in its present form entirely satisfactory – I have the M.S. now & may re-cast it. Its *too* long!' Elgar wondered whether to turn it into a work for piano and orchestra, thus producing the 'Conzertstück' Fanny Davies had asked for originally. The MS has many references to 'orch', but Elgar's revisions were mainly concerned with tightening the structure of the piece. When John Ogdon gave the first modern performance of the Concert Allegro on 2 February 1969 (the MS had disappeared for many years), he played Elgar's original, uncut version. It was heard in its revised form when Malcolm Binns played it in 1976 and John McCabe recorded it the same year.

In Smyrna was the immediate musical result of Elgar's 1905 Mediterranean journey. Its delicate textures hardly represent the music heard in the 'Mosque of dancing dervishes'; indeed its rapt quality recalls initially the 'Canto popolare' from *In the South*. A move to the minor produces a motif more specifically 'eastern', later used by Elgar for Agra's song in *The Crown of India*. The middle section is quintessential Elgar, while the final cadenza contains a figure also impressed for the Coliseum masque and its 'Sacred Measure'. Elgar's last two piano pieces were sent to the publisher on 29 September 1932. The *Serenade* is light music, delicately wrought to Elgar's most fastidious standard. It was dedicated to 'Honest' John Austin, who had assisted Elgar's proof-reading as 'Friend and "Editor"' for forty years'. *Adieu* is a miniature in D major of comparable distinction, eloquent in its regret for earlier days. The last chord is of F sharp minor, and Elgar appends a note to his MS: 'I know this does not end in the key it begins in.'

Organ music

Elgar's organ-playing days were virtually over when he married in 1889; but at an earlier time the instrument had been a considerable stimulus. He remembered particularly the installation of the new Hill organ in the south transept of Worcester Cathedral, a gift of the Earl of Dudley in 1874. He explained to Rudolf de Cordova thirty years later that many distinguished organists were attracted by it: 'I went to hear them all. The services at the cathedral were over later than those at the Catholic church, and as soon as the voluntary was finished at the church I used to rush over to the cathedral to hear the concluding voluntary.' His regular duties at St George's, though, gave him little pleasure, and he expressed frustration to Charles Buck in January 1886. He remained, however, another three years.

The *Vesper Voluntaries* were the immediate result of the installation of an organ at Oaklands in October 1889. Though nothing is known of the instrument's specification, it was on this organ that Elgar gave final shape to the work. Orsborn & Tuckwood published the pieces as Book 26 in a series called 'The Vesper Voluntaries for the Organ, Harmonium, or American Organ'. A dedication to Mrs W. A. Raikes, the lady of Oaklands, was added at proof stage. The eight *Voluntaries* are framed by an Introduction and Coda, with a central Intermezzo, all thematically linked. The D minor start is arresting, an early example of Elgar's processional manner, and turns effectively into the major at the end of the work. There are many characteristic touches in the individual movements and much Schumannesque charm. No. 1 has an aspiring theme spanning an initial seventh and then larger intervals. In no. 2 there is a profusion of sequence that is not for a moment wearisome. No. 3 was originally sketched as a string quartet movement and has lovely touches of Schumannesque dissonance in the middle section. Melodic fluency typifies nos. 4 and 5. The short-breathed phrases of no. 6 make a more commonplace piece, amply compensated by the playful and again sequential no. 7, and the bell chimes of no. 8. It seems that Elgar planned a sequel to the *Voluntaries*, as one of the sketchbooks lists a suite of six movements with their keys. It too was to have an Introduction, Intermezzo and Coda. The only other work proposed before the op. 28 Sonata was a *Pastorale*, roughly sketched on the back of the MS organ part for *Sursum corda*.

The G major Organ Sonata no. 1 was requested by Hugh Blair for a recital to honour a Worcester visit by a group of American church musicians. Elgar began work on it immediately after finishing the 'Bavarians' on 9 April 1895. He wrote out the second movement under the title 'Intermezzo' and experimented with alternative schemes for the work. Systematic ordering of the Sonata had to wait another two months, and from 22 June Blair was in almost daily attendance at Forli. Elgar noted on his MS draft that copying of the sketches into their final sequence had been 'one week's work', from 9 p.m. on 28 June till the afternoon of 3 July. There was a plan to amalgamate the two Hill organs in Worcester Cathedral, but the task had not been completed, and the Sonata was to be played on the 1874 instrument the youthful Elgar so much admired. Rosa Burley commented unfavourably on Blair's performance (8 July): 'he had either not learned it or else had celebrated the event unwisely for he made a terrible mess of poor Elgar's work'. Novello was unwilling to publish the Sonata as a whole but suggested issuing the four movements separately. Thus the Sonata went to Breitkopf & Härtel, with dedication to Swinnerton Heap.

Whether Blair could play it or not, the Sonata is a virtuoso piece. A review of 11 September 1896 in the *Allgemeine Musik-Zeitung* described it as offering 'the performer a difficult task, but artistically thoroughly rewarding'. It was Elgar's only four-movement instrumental work before the symphonies, and the opening Allegro maestoso provides an instance of a development section on the same scale as the exposition. Here too Elgar used light double bars to subdivide the movements, not only for changes of time or key.

The start has Elgarian flair and boldness (Ex. 75). Accents are firmly on the first beat for a while, with the third bar lightened by a characteristic triplet. Then emphasis is shifted so that the whole of the first subject group, ending with fanfare chords, keeps rhythmic interest alert. The second subject in the dominant and 9/8 might initially have been planned for a 'Vesper Voluntary'; but before reaching the double bar that marks its continued presence in the codetta, the tune has shown a symphonic ability to spin new ideas from itself. Headed 'working out' in Elgar's sketches, the development is contrapuntally ingenious from the outset. The Sonata's opening intervals are treated in imitation and combined in a complex web with a transition theme from the exposition in the bass. There is much antiphonal use of the transition's first notes until in G minor a new expressive tune is evolved from the fanfare. The first subject is much abbreviated in the reprise, and the second group is in the orthodox G major. A lengthy coda makes as if to recapitulate the development, and for fifteen bars it essentially does so. Over a pedal A the fanfare is further extended until the first subject returns in splendour to close the movement.

The tripartite Allegretto begins and ends in G minor. The first section combines figuration on the choir manual with a cello-range tune below. When it returns to conclude the movement, Elgar shortens

Ex. 75

it considerably. The middle section doubles the speed and begins in C minor; but its heart is a broad C major tune on swell with soft reed that grows out of the previous bars and is accompanied on the choir by light figuration of dotted notes and triplets.

The Andante espressivo is based on a tune first noted in a sketchbook of 1887. There it was entitled 'Traumerie' [*sic*] as incipit for a suite movement. Two introductory bars modulate from the Allegretto's G minor to B flat. The tune itself (Ex. 76) is one of Elgar's grandest, self-generating for twenty-six bars, and spanning altogether two octaves and a fifth. The note-values are marvellously varied from bar to bar, and only at the tune's first climax, thirteen bars on, is the initial pattern repeated. At this moment the descending bass has reached F sharp. As the tune completes its course, the bass pattern repeats towards a pause. Elgar now takes the F sharp as his new key for a *tranquillo* second subject of delicate melodic embroidery. An *animato* takes the music down another third to D minor with further elaboration of the melody until a rising and falling fourth from the opening tune heralds a concentrated recapitulation of all the movement's material

Ex. 76

in the tonic B flat yet another third below. A brief coda is based on the opening of the first tune with Neapolitan leanings that remember the second chord of the movement.

The purposeful Presto of the finale opens in G minor with an idea that has more energy than character. The impertinence of the second tune in B flat (Ex. 77), a cheery pomp and circumstantial little march, makes a pleasant contrast. But snatches of the first theme soon infiltrate to take over the rest of the exposition with brilliant passagework and a full organ climax. The development recalls the start of the slow movement tune and intersperses it with the business of the main finale motif. The second tune sheds some of its impertinence, first by generating a stepwise tail in triplets and an arching countersubject, then by augmenting itself into B minor and managing the rest of the development from a succession of different keys. Recapitulation cuts down the opening tune by half but lets the little march, now in G major, run through all its previous capers. The full organ climax is delayed till the start of the coda, when the slow movement tune is again recalled, but in accents of the first movement. Semiquavers flash through the texture, and the brilliant end has a final Neapolitan pull.

The rest of the organ music published in Elgar's lifetime can be quickly summarized. Though printed by Novello in 1913, *Cantique* had its origin in the 'Shed' music of the late 1870s. The organ version

399

Ex. 77

was one of three Elgar made towards the end of 1912, the others being for small orchestra and piano. He dedicated it to Hugh Blair. The organ arrangement of the *Severn Suite* as Sonata no. 2 was made by Ivor Atkins in close cooperation with Elgar. A number of alterations were made to the music. There were additional bars at the end of the first movement. The Toccata was abbreviated overall, though some bars were expanded. The Minuet was omitted altogether. In the case of the new cadenza, Elgar carefully revised Atkins's work and made considerable adjustments. The fugue was originally composed for piano in June 1923. Two years later Atkins played it on the newly rebuilt Worcester Cathedral organ, and his C minor arrangement of it appeared separately.

There are also certain organ fragments that postdate the First Sonata. In 1904 Elgar wrote a cadenza for Charles Harford Lloyd's F minor Concerto for organ and orchestra. It was played at the Gloucester Festival by G. R. Sinclair with the composer conducting. Only the cadenza seems now to survive. Two years later Elgar's sister Helen Agnes ('Dot') requested a 'very simple & melodious tiny tune for the

Organ', as she wanted to learn. Elgar was at work on *The Kingdom* but responded with a minuscule piece mainly in minims and semibreves, 'For Dot's Nuns'. Elgar intended making a more ambitious organ piece out of the 'Memorial Chime' written for the opening of the Loughborough Carillon in July 1923. He held back the copyright with this in mind. Ideas were sketched in pencil, but no fair copy was made. An organ sonata fragment and other incipits for the instrument were eventually to find place in *The Spanish Lady*, and the sonata fragment was copied again for incorporation in the Third Symphony.

14

Musical characteristics

Elgar's starting-point in the process of composition is well known: 'My idea is that there is music in the air, music all around us'; all you had to do was 'take as much as you require!' Hence the outdoor jottings on envelope or map, information on a sketch about trout caught, and his statement to Troyte 'that he really composed the Apostles sitting in the porch of Queen Hill Church near Longdon'. These were his 'sketches & scraps for bicycle and fishing bags'. Elgar usually sketched in pencil, in keyboard format, and maybe no more than treble and bass. Throughout his life he might use figured bass to indicate harmonies. With growing certainty a sketch would be inked, but probably elaborated further and extended in pencil until it would trail away into uncertainty. A piano was useful for testing ideas, but Elgar scorned the keyboard composer. Often sketches would give hints about the eventual instrumentation; he claimed that a theme always came to him in its characteristic tone colour, and W. H. Reed indicated how it might be developed: 'Like Beethoven, he allowed an idea, which may have occurred to him as a short phrase, to germinate and transform and throw out branches'. When in the mood, Elgar worked at great speed, as he indicated to Fred Gaisberg and Harriet Cohen over tea on 17 August 1933: 'When I write music I am all of a tremble, as if I was in the hands of another person. My pencil flies over the paper – if a bit of grit retards it, away flies the pencil across the room and I grasp another. I can only write when the spirit moves me – I cannot write to order.' Elgar's handwriting confirms this account. As a young man he showed in his manuscripts the scrupulous penmanship of his legal training; later the hand is bold and commanding, with irresistible onward sweep.

When planning a complex movement or ensemble, Elgar sometimes wrote a verbal description of the procedure to be followed. Such a 'plan' exists, for instance, towards the 'Meditation' in *The Light of Life*, the two finales of *Gerontius*, the 'Beatitudes' section of *The Apostles* and the Adagio of the First Symphony. The scheme was not always followed, but a provisional listing of keys and thematic ideas helped channel inspiration. Elgar insisted that the sketchbooks were the foundation of his work. He annotated them, mainly late in life, indicating where themes had found their eventual home or labelling them as 'jolly good', even 'rather cheap'; and in his final burst of composition, when it seemed that both an opera and symphony might materialize, ideas conceived fifty years before were to prove serviceable. The sketchbooks contain also drawings and an infinite variety of comments. Two exploding cannons, a girl playing the violin, and some caricatures were delineated in five early sketchbooks of 1878–81, amid information about the Greek modes and some faltering attempts to transcribe their names into Greek characters. In the first of the eight sketchbooks supplied by Jaeger, Elgar explained another step in the composition process. When a sheet of manuscript had been copied towards the next stage of refinement, he would inscribe it with a large 'K', standing for the 'ridiculous word "Koppid"'.

When drafting a work, Elgar invariably laid it out for keyboard. His instinct was such that an acceptable version for piano would usually occur automatically. Hence it is difficult to determine primacy when a piece appeared at the same time in different 'arrangements'. In a sense the piano version is always the original. Even in a work as complex as the 'Enigma' Variations, when the first publication was said to be 'arranged for pianoforte solo by the composer', this was in no sense a reduction of the full score; it was rather its blueprint. Another consequence of this working method was that even for the largest choral works Elgar invariably produced the practical keyboard part that could go straight into the vocal score. When orchestrating, Elgar usually marked on the keyboard draft or proofs he used for the purpose the number of each full score page as he began it. With increasing mastery, Elgar was prepared to allow a miniature score to be printed in advance of performance. By the same token he would prepare his full score from draft pages that were in themselves hardly more than a rough sketch and seemed only an *aide-mémoire* towards the finished work. Elgar's orchestration was achieved quickly and surely; for him it was the process that required least thought. So it came about that the keyboard editions of the two symphonies were not by Elgar himself but by Sigfrid Karg-Elert, for the good reason that Elgar no longer needed a fully realized piano part to score from and so it did not exist.

Elgar's meticulous marking of his scores (he felt he overdid this with vocal works) has meant that performance of his music can seem almost foolproof, and has indeed often been so. Many of his indications are simply to ensure good and natural declamation within a very fluid idiom. Any exaggeration will distort his intention, as Bernard Shaw realized with some amusement after watching Landon Ronald during the recording by Elgar of *Falstaff*. A letter of Tovey's to Stewart Deas makes another crucial point in connection with the same work: 'It seems to be a psychological impossibility for composers to get their metronome marks less than a third too fast.' In Elgar's case this is simply not true. He revised his initial 'Nimrod' mark downwards, and a few of his own recordings are below the indicated speed. But for the most part metronome and tempo coincide, a fact that is responsible for the lithe tautness of an Elgarian performance when compared with so many others. It is not too much to say that the long dip in Elgar's posthumous reputation was to some extent due to conductors seduced by the sheer splendour of Elgar's sonorities into performances sadly lacking in the electric charge that leapt from the sometimes ungainly thrusts of Elgar's rapier baton. If the stiff, pompous and complacent Edwardian gentleman held centre stage for too long, his interpreters must take some blame.

Elgar's care with the layout of his scores went to great lengths: certain sections must begin a new page; some notes should be in smaller type; a third keyboard line might be needed in a choral work to make clear the interplay of motifs; on any page in the oratorios involving Jesus, he must always have the top stave; and Elgar gave precise instructions about the indentation he required for each line of the librettos he compiled himself. He had a particular request in connection with the First Symphony, as Littleton explained to his printing manager C. J. May on 10 August 1908: 'You will remember that Elgar wants the score to be got into as small a number of pages as can reasonably be done to avoid continual turning over.' An immediate result, of course, was to increase the total of bars per page; but equally important, Elgar's characteristic 'hairpins', those sudden upsurges of emotion, were contained within brief space. The visual effect suggested the aural effect, always so powerfully moving in Elgar's own recordings.

Dynamics, the intervals themselves, and details of scoring all give a vibrant intensity to Elgarian melodies. He took great risks with them, and often their success or failure depends on subtle matters of speed and rhythm. He knew the textbook rules for a good tune, and was happy to break them. The E flat lovers' theme at cue 5 in *Cockaigne* is a lawless tune that works splendidly. The *pp* dynamic helps, so that the initial octave is lightly taken; but more important is the placing of the minims, the points of repose to steady the wide range of the tune. The harmonic tension is low throughout. At the beginning of the Larghetto in the Serenade for Strings the steady upward movement culminating in the seventh leap is combined with a chord of considerable tension within the work's context. Elgar aims at maximum expressiveness and almost overdoes it. The start of *The Spirit of England* works less well. The close succession of rising sixths, in five out of six bars, is just too fast to avoid monotony.

Many Elgar themes explore their ground under the strict control of an ostinato rhythm. The first main tunes in the finale of both symphonies are obvious examples. That in the E flat Symphony is the more successful, if only because the rhythmic ingredients that make up the one-bar units are more varied. The *locus classicus* for such writing is the Moderato in the first movement of the Cello Concerto, where the 9/8 crotchet and quaver is repeated, with slight modification on one beat, over thirty-six bars. This might seem a recipe for disaster, but the ruminating tempo, the vast range of a melody that spans two octaves and a fifth in its first statement, the subtle harmonic changes and alternation between solo and orchestra, make for a paragraph of rare eloquence. This is a main Elgarian device for securing variety within unity. The opening of *The Music Makers* is comparatively jejune. It is one of those moments when Elgar's 'nobilmente' has more hope than conviction. The monotony of the rhythm is compounded by uninspired melodic sequences and a chromatic counterpoint that debilitates rather than stiffens. At half speed or less César Franck might have got away with it in a penitential organ piece.

The compound time that so beautifully serves the Cello Concerto was sometimes an Elgarian refuge when inspiration burnt low. An ambling 6/8, 9/8 or 12/8 was to become a hallmark of the English rural scene, and many of Elgar's weaker moments are pointers to a path his successors had better not have trod. The 9/8 theme in the 'Meditation' from *The Light of Life* already has some of the sequential and chromatic traits that were to mar the start of *The Music Makers*. It was a motif called by Herbert Thompson 'Jesus, the Healer and Consoler'; Mendelssohn or Gounod would have done much the same. The love duet of Thyri and Olaf or Eigen's apostrophe to the beauties of nature in Scene III of *Caractacus* are easygoing in like manner.

Yet Jaeger was right to see melody as an essential Elgarian strength. Perhaps most characteristic of him are the great march tunes, mystic, ceremonial, solemn, patriotic, sprightly and vulgar, that are scattered throughout his music. They are typical of Elgar as they are of Verdi. The very opening of *Gerontius*, the 'Judgment' motif that moves with 'unperturbèd pace', has the long-drawn, relentless tread of Elgar's slowest marches, to be found again in the *Grania* music and the Larghetto of the Second Symphony. More processional are the 'Committal' theme and the solemn farewell to this world in 'Proficiscere' and the final Part I ensemble. The 'motto' of the First Symphony is a tune of the same cast, diatonic, and with conscious nobility of gait. It is no distance to the sonorous incarnation of London's pride as demonstrated in the *Cockaigne* marches or the grand trio tunes of *Pomp and Circumstance* nos. 1, 4 and 5. Other marches are differently constructed. The 'New Faith' theme of *The Kingdom* ascends by solemn steps of one-bar sequence enclosed within a favourite Elgar rhythm. Its inversion, of course not exact, descending in similar guise, can be found in *The Music Makers* at cue 65, where the multitudes bring to pass 'the dream that was scorned yesterday'.

A 'great tune' is the *raison d'être* of Symphony no. 1; by contrast the opening of its successor is made of thematic fragments welded into an impetuous stream of melody with maximum intensity at the outset. Bold leaps of a sixth and seventh are apt to mark an Elgar tune, many of which have an early climax and lengthy dying fall. As complement to these high-arching shapes, Elgar's bass lines have an equally characteristic movement. Consider the start of *The Black Knight*, where the lowest part descends boldly and diatonically step by step until an upward octave leap allows the process to begin again. This firm foundation to the texture balances the wide-springing melodic line; the combination triumphantly passes the Brahmsian test of covering inner parts to try the strength of the outer ones. Such diatonic descents are ubiquitous. Obvious examples occur in the last pages of the 'Enigma' Variations, at 'Turn you to the Stronghold' in *The Apostles*, at the return of the 'Welsh' theme towards the end of the Introduction and Allegro or the beginning of the Second Symphony. Chromatic intervals are mingled with the descent in 'Softly and gently' at the end of *Gerontius*, as in the peroration of the 'Pride of London' theme in *Cockaigne* and Prince Hal's tune in *Falstaff*. A steadily chromatic descent such as typifies the beginning of the Eigen and Orbin duet in *Caractacus* is unusual in Elgar, whereas it is the norm in Delius. Diatonically rising basses occur notably in the 'Enigma' theme, at 'Go forth' in *Gerontius*, the start of Mary Magdalene's music in *The Apostles*, and in the 'Concord' motif of *The Kingdom*.

Elgar's harmonies are least successful where they attempt to be most novel. One of his outstanding gifts, due perhaps to a lifelong pleasure in the expert creation of lighter music, as also to England's happy insularity, was his ability to compose music as 'normal' as that of Brahms. This was rare among late-Romantic composers, all coming to maturity at a time of unprecedented musical turmoil. 'Progressive', certainly, as Strauss at once recognized in 1902; and Elgar was more than ready to emulate Strauss in such covert tone-poems as *Cockaigne*, *In the South* or *Falstaff*. But Elgar never attempted the harmonic audacities of a *Salome* or *Elektra*, to say nothing of the ironic asperities that characterize Mahler. The nearest Elgar got to portraying profound psychological disturbance is at the hammered climax of the Rondo in the Second Symphony. Yet the effect is achieved not so much by the intense harmonies and flashing counterpoints, bold though they are, as by the steadily mounting menace of the insistent percussion instruments. This was where Elgar had been thinking of Tennyson's *Maud*:

> And the hoofs of the horses beat, beat,
> The hoofs of the horses beat,
> Beat into my scalp and my brain ...

When Elgar consciously sets out to impress by harmonic means, as at the 'Roman' section of *In the South*, the effect is less convincing, and diminished by repetition. The same applies to a motif such as 'Christ the Man of Sorrows' in *The Apostles* and the sequences based on slithering chromatics in *The Music Makers* at 'Unearthly, impossible seeming', with their maudlin return near the end of the work at 'in spite of a dreamer who slumbers'.

More characteristic are the Elgarian ambiguities after the manner of Schumann, when a harmony will imply one thing only to lead else-where. Classical harmony as extended by recourse to Wagnerian added-notes and chromaticism is the staple of his art, so that 'Nimrod' for instance makes its effect with harmonies familiar to Beethoven; it is the building of the climax that he or indeed Wagner might have envied. Elgar's love of first inversion chords is as pronounced as Strauss's penchant for the second inversion, and he is at his happiest with the judicious placing of minor chords and avoidance of the leading note as in 'O gen'rous love' in Part II of *Gerontius*, or the 'Amen' that closes the first choral section in *The Kingdom*. The use of plainsong, familiar to Elgar from his Catholic upbringing, as essential thematic material in the two oratorios gives ready scope for Elgar's love of modal harmonies, and by the time of *The Kingdom* he has a fine-tuned flexibility of harmonic idiom, so that he can move almost imperceptibly and without in any way disturbing stylistic unity from traditional church usage to the comparative warmth of his normal processes.

Elgar's harmonic thinking was always criss-crossed with melody, though their independent strands never threaten to submerge the texture, as sometimes happens with Strauss. There was an essential spareness to Elgar's contrapuntal procedure in that he was usually happiest when working in three parts; indeed long stretches of the Introduction and Allegro or *Falstaff* are confined to the strenuous dialectic of only two parts. Yet he had also a ready knack in devising counterpoints bold of interval and lavish with accented passing-notes to endow a passage with unexpected tension. The 'Enigma' theme offers a good example. The restatement of the original bars generates a passionate countersubject on inner strings that greatly enriches the texture. The same skill is shown at the powerful climax of 'C.A.E.' and in many another passage of the work. The repetitions of the 'Committal' theme in the *Gerontius* prelude show comparable resource. Sometimes Elgar explores themes separately, and demonstrates their relationship only much later. This is by no means Wagner's device in the *Meistersinger* Prelude, where the combination of his three themes is essential for the dramatic point but is also musically improbable enough immediately to rivet attention. Elgar's purpose may be dramatic, theological or simply musical; it is invariably achieved with the art that conceals art, so that its full implications may be long latent. The most moving example occurs towards the end of *Gerontius* where the Souls in Purgatory sing their penitential psalm, and later join the orchestral 'Softly and gently' theme in a counterpoint as satisfying musically as it is apt theologically. An equivalent moment in *The Apostles* is the welding together at cue 221 in Scene VII of the 'Christ's Prayer' motif and the 'Apostles' Faith'. Both themes have made considerable impact independently, and it is impossible to say when or how Elgar first knew this was their ultimate destination, to support texts that again illustrate the subtlety of Elgar's thinking. Such combinations could be achieved because all the themes of a work had been created in the same 'oven', as Elgar described it. The effect is spontaneous, and the freedom of Elgar's attitude suggests Handel rather than Bach. Not a schoolman himself, he affected to despise the methods of the schools. Self-drilled in traditional musical learning, he yet delighted in mocking it. The traditional oratorio fugue was a moment of sublime celestial contentment or boredom for its audience. When Elgar wrote fugally there was usually devilment abroad, as in *The Light of Life* when affirming that 'The wisdom of their wise men shall perish', in the nihilistic mockery of the *Gerontius* demons, the 'devil of a fugue' in the Introduction and Allegro, the confusion of the speaking with 'tongues' in *The Kingdom*, the 'colossal mendacity' of Falstaff on the run after the Gadshill episode, the outrageous coruscations of the Bach transcription, and finally an imitative introduction for his operatic scoundrel, Meercraft, in *The Spanish Lady*.

Elgar's attitude to tonality was equally unorthodox. He early showed certain predilections. His fondness for G minor–major juxtaposition has often been remarked. It is important in *Sevillana*, *The Black Knight*, the Organ Sonata, *The Light of Life* and the 'Enigma' Variations, to name just a few examples, and persists at least as far as the Introduction and Allegro. But already in *King Olaf* Elgar was dividing the octave into a series of unusual key centres. The Ballad of no. 13, 'A little bird in the air', has a refrain delivered a major third apart on each of its repetitions, moving from G to B, D sharp (E flat) and finally G again. This, on a small scale, was Brahms's key scheme in the First Symphony (with C as starting point). Such a splitting of the octave into three was much favoured by Elgar. The Cello Concerto, on the other hand, shows a division by minor thirds into four, with E minor at the outset. A natural consequence of such thinking was to halve the octave. This was what Wagner had done in the opera Elgar knew best, *Die Meistersinger von Nürnberg*, where the G flat major of the Act 3 quintet lies between the two C majors of the mastersong's 'baptism' and the open-air festivities on the meadow. Elgar's most striking example is the polarization of D minor and A flat in the finale of the First Symphony.

Much needless criticism has been directed against Elgar's use of sequence in his larger structures. Occasionally, as in portions of *Cockaigne*, or the Second Symphony's Rondo, the device is overworked and Elgar has ignored at his peril Stanford's shrewd observation that three sequential steps are about enough. But for Elgar the sequence was not just what he called a 'musical waterwheel', one of those devices that 'enable composers to "carry on"' by repetition; it was an essential part of his allusive, modulating style. Here, too, Elgar's instinct led him in the same direction as his large-span tonal schemes, to make use of intervals a major or minor third apart. At its first appearance in the *Gerontius* prelude, the 'Despair' motif moves down-wards in three two-bar steps of a tone. When it resumes in modified form just before 'Committal', the steps are of a minor third, but on both occasions it is the restless shifting of the tonality that remains in the mind. At the first utterance of the word 'Praise' in Part II there is a one-bar sequence repeated three times, and on this occasion the steps are a major third apart so that they end where they began, with only awe and wonderment to fill the space. It was Parry who said that only those should criticize an Elgarian sequence who could themselves produce a more effective or beautiful one.

None the less, Elgar is at his happiest when waterwheeling is least needed, in those works where formally he is his own master. In the Variations, for instance, development is omnipresent, but it is the result of a fortunate combination of procedures instinctive to Elgar. Extemporization had taught him how to ring the change on ideas, how to make instant musical logic; the allusive mind that delighted in word-play and note-play could juggle a handful of sounds into an infinite number of patterns. The Introduction and Allegro was *sui generis*, with a gradual, almost hesitant presentation of data from which the 'brilliant string thing' should be evolved. The formal development intensified the brilliance, made oblique reference to earlier material, but was in no sense a discussion of it. It was a free fantasia in the old sense, so that recapitulation was the more exact, though seeming spontaneous in its swiftness. The Cello Concerto is equally successful, for the extemporary manner of the opening recitative that is indeed, as Elgar said, the beginning of a 'real large work', the laconic second tune of the 'scherzo', the continuous melody, searching and intense, of the Adagio, and the finale that tries in vain to escape the deep-seated pain of that melody.

Elgar's earliest reviews may cavil at his writing for chorus or the solo voice, but there was never any doubt about his orchestration. In this branch of his art he has few rivals. He achieves a greater brilliance than Wagner, avoids the excesses of Strauss and eschews the angularities of Mahler. When Fritz Steinbach gave the 'Enigma' Variations with the Meiningen orchestra in London, he expressed his enthusiasm to Edward Speyer: 'Here is an unexpected genius and pathfinder in the field of orchestration. Nowadays nearly every composer is content merely to adopt Wagner's innovations, but Elgar, as this work shows, is a real pioneer with a new technique in orchestration, combining entirely original effects with almost unique virtuosity.' What was it that so struck Steinbach? It is unnecessary to look further than the theme, where there is much to notice even in the first six bars for the strings alone. It is fascinating to see Elgar's careful use of *divisi* and unison in the second violin part, the *pianissimo* moment when the violas first rise above the seconds, the way the underparts eliminate the first rest in bar four and both rests two bars later, and above all the silence of the double basses. The central four bars of the theme are a miracle of subtlety. All have an ascending figure in thirds with climax and descent in the last two quavers; but the scoring of each bar differs widely. Only with the return of the opening section do the double basses enter; at the same time the harmony thins to Elgar's favourite three parts. The main event of these final bars is the new countersubject, which rises to *mf*, the dynamic high-point of the theme. The craftsmanship is impeccable, and it is such care for detail that makes the study of Elgar's methods infinitely rewarding. At the other extreme is Elgar's mastery of the orchestral tutti. In his 1920 assessment of Elgar, Bernard Shaw made special reference to *Gerontius*: 'what every genuine connoisseur in orchestration must have said at the first hearing (among other things) was "What a devil of a fortissimo!"'

The boy from Worcester continues to hold his countrymen in thrall. If we know in our heart of hearts that 'Land of Hope and Glory' has a less fine tune than Parry's *Jerusalem*, and certainly less fine words, yet still it can bring the larger lump to the throat. It helped the British Empire through two world wars, but in latter days it is the Cello Concerto that has come more to suit the national mood. Elgar had no illusions when he wrote it. His music deals always with a world that never was. Perhaps at one time he thought it might be called into existence, or at least pretended so. Like his Falstaff he had been prepared to salute 'rare words' and exult in a 'brave world'; with Gerontius he had rehearsed the ancient liturgy of his church; in the Variations he had celebrated the idea of friendship, and in the Violin Concerto perhaps a particular friend. But in the Cello Concerto he meditates in solitude on the human condition. Even Lady Elgar, who had watched over the years of his greatness, was soon to leave him. Perhaps we can now agree with him that 'sweetest songs are those that tell of saddest thought'.

Appendix A

Calendar

Year	Age	Life	Contemporary musicians and events
			Wagner 44 (completes draft of *Siegfried* Act 2 and begins *Tristan und Isolde*), S. S. Wesley 47. Indian Mutiny.
1858	1		Leoncavallo born 8 Mar, Puccini born 22 Jun, Reubke (24) dies 3 Jun, Ethel Smyth born 23 Apr. Wagner (45), *Wesendonck Lieder*. Lourdes visions of the Virgin.
1859	2	Family returns to Worcester, at 1 Edgar St. Frederick Joseph ('Jo', brother) born 28 Aug.	Spohr (75) dies 22 Oct. Berlioz (52), *Les Troyens*; Gounod (41), fp of *Faust*; Verdi (46), fp of *Un ballo in maschera*. Darwin's *Origin of Species*.
1860	3	Probable move to 2 College Precincts.	Albéniz born 29 May, Charpentier born 25 Jun, Mahler born 7 Jul, Paderewski born 6 Nov, Wolf born 13 Mar. Brahms (27) publishes with Joachim manifesto against 'New German' school and composes op. 18 Sextet. Garibaldi proclaims Victor Emmanuel king of Italy.
1861	4	Francis Thomas ('Frank', brother) born 1 Oct.	Arensky born 11 Aug, Chaminade born 8 Aug, MacDowell born 18 Dec, Marschner (66) dies 14 Dec. Liszt (50) leaves Weimar for Rome; Wagner (48), disastrous *Tannhäuser* perfs in Paris. Albert, the Prince Consort, dies 14 Dec, William I accedes to Prussian throne.
1862	5		Debussy born 22 Aug, Delius born 29 Jan, German born 17 Feb, Halévy (62) dies 17 Mar. Bismarck (47), Chief Minister of Prussia.
1863	6		Mascagni born 7 Dec, Somervell born 5 Jun. Bizet (25), *The Pearl Fishers*; Brahms (30), *Rinaldo*.

Elgar

Year	Age	Life	Contemporary musicians and events
1864	7	Attends Miss Walsh's Catholic School and begins to learn the piano. Helen Agnes ('Dot', sister) born 1 Jan, Henry John (15) dies of scarlet fever, 5 May.	d'Albert born 10 Apr, Meyerbeer (73) dies 2 May, Richard Strauss born 11 Jun. Bruckner (40), Mass in D minor; Wagner (51) rescued by Ludwig II, the new king of Bavaria.
1865	8		Dukas born 1 Oct, Glazunov born 10 Aug, Nielsen born 9 Jun, Sibelius born 8 Dec. Liszt (64), fp of *St Elisabeth*, *Missa choralis* written; Verdi (52), fp of rev. *Macbeth*; Wagner (52), fp of *Tristan und Isolde*.
1866	9	Writes the name Bach with one note and four clefs. Attends Three Choirs rehearsal of Beethoven Mass in C. Frederick Joseph (7) dies of consumption, 7 Sep.	Busoni born 1 Apr, Satie born 17 Mar. Brahms (33), op. 36 Sextet; Bruckner (41), Symphony no. 1, Mass in E minor; Smetana (41), fp of orig. version of *The Bartered Bride*. Austro-Prussian War and Treaty of Prague.
1867	10	Earliest known tune, used later in 'Fairies and Giants' (*Wand of Youth* 1, 1907). Schooling continued at Spetchley Park.	Granados born 27 Jul. Liszt (67), fp of *Hungarian Coronation Mass*; Verdi (54), fp of *Don Carlos*. Karl Marx publishes *Das Kapital* vol. 1.
1868	11	Attends Littleton House school.	Bantock born 7 Aug, Berwald (72) dies 3 Apr, Rossini (76) dies 13 Nov. Brahms (35), fp of *Ein deutsches Requiem*; Grieg (25), first version of Piano Concerto; Wagner (56), fp of *Die Meistersinger von Nürnberg*.
1869	12	Begins to study Anton Reicha's *Orchestral Primer* (Novello) and other technical books. A Three Choirs *Messiah* rehearsal inspires him to take up the violin. Possible date for a musical play supposed to have given ideas to the *Wand of Youth*	Berlioz (66) dies 8 Mar, Dargomïzhsky (56) dies 17 Jan, Walford Davies born 6 Sep, Pfitzner born 5 May, Roussel born 5 Apr. Bruckner (44), F minor Mass; Bruch (31) Violin Concerto in G minor; Verdi (56), fp of rev. *La forza del destino*; Wagner (56), fp of

Year	Age	Life	Contemporary musicians and events
		suites.	*Das Rheingold*. Suez Canal opened and *Rigoletto* inaugurates Cairo opera house. First Vatican Council.
1870	13	Plays violin at Crown Hotel Glee Club.	Balfe (62) dies 20 Oct, Lehár born 30 Apr, Lekeu born 20 Jan, Mercadante (75) dies 17 Dec, Novák born 5 Dec, Schmitt born 28 Sep. Musorgsky (31), *Boris Godunov*; Wagner (57), fp of *Die Walküre*. Lenin born 9 Apr. Franco-Prussian War and capitulation of Napoleon III. Papal Infallibility proclaimed. Rome becomes Italian capital. Schliemann discovers Troy.
1871	14	Alternative date for the musical play.	Auber (89) dies 12 May. Verdi (58), Cairo fp of *Aida*. German Empire under Wilhelm I proclaimed.
1872	15	Song, *The Language of Flowers* and piano piece, *Chantant*. Apprenticed to the solicitor, William Allen. First playing of organ for Mass.	Skryabin born 6 Jan, Vaughan Williams born 12 Oct. Bizet (34), *L'arlésienne*; Brahms (39), fp of *Triumphlied*; Bruckner (48), Symphony no. 2; Franck (50), *Les béatitudes*. Nietzsche (28), *The Birth of Tragedy*.
1873	16	Leaves Allen's office. Credo on themes from Beethoven symphonies.	Rakhmaninov born 20 Mar, Reger born 19 Mar. Bruckner (49), Symphony no. 3; Dvořák (32), Symphony no. 3.
1874	17		Cornelius (50) dies 26 Oct, Holst born 21 Sep, Ives born 20 Oct, Franz Schmidt born 22 Dec, Schoenberg born 13 Sep, Suk born 4 Jan. Bruckner (50), Symphony no. 4, first version; Musorgsky (35), fp of *Boris Godunov*; Johann Strauss (49), fp of *Die Fledermaus*; Verdi (61), *Requiem* in Milan; Wagner (61) completes the *Ring*. Pope institutes cult of

Year	Age	Life	Contemporary musicians and events
			the Sacred Heart. First Impressionist exhibition, Paris.
1875	18	Plays in Spohr's *The Last Judgment* and *Messiah*.	Sterndale Bennett (59) dies 1 Feb, Bizet (37) dies 3 Jun, Coleridge-Taylor born 15 Aug, Glière born 11 Jan, Reynaldo Hahn born 19 Aug, Ravel born 7 Mar, Roger-Ducasse born 18 Apr, Tovey born 17 Jul. Bizet (37), *Carmen*; Tchaikovsky (35), Piano Concerto no. 1. Jung born 26 Jul. Opening of Paris Opéra.
1876	19	*Tantum ergo* and *Salve regina* for St George's. Arranges *Der fliegende Holländer* overture for Glee Club ensemble, of which he is now accompanist. Begins teaching the violin.	Havergal Brian born 29 Jan, Falla born 23 Nov, Goetz (36) dies 3 Dec, S. S. Wesley (65) dies 19 Apr, Wolf-Ferrari born 12 Jan. Borodin (43), Symphony no. 2; Brahms (43), fp of Symphony no. 1; Delibes (42), fp of *Sylvia*; Ponchielli (42), fp of *La Gioconda*; Tchaikovsky (36), *Swan Lake*; Wagner (63), the *Ring* at First Bayreuth Festival. Queen Victoria Empress of India. Edison invents the phonograph.
1877	20	*Reminiscences* for violin and piano. Attends Worcester recital of August Wilhelmj. Violin lessons with Adolphe Pollitzer. Becomes leader of Worcester Amateur Instrumental Society. Plays bassoon and writes *Peckham March* for the Brothers Wind.	Dohnányi born 27 Jul, Dunhill born 1 Feb, Quilter born 1 Nov. Brahms (44), fp of Symphony no. 2; Bruckner (53), Symphony no. 5; Dvořák (36), Symphonic Variations; Saint-Saëns (42), fp of *Samson et Dalila*; Tchaikovsky (37), fp of *Eugene Onegin*; Wagner (64), Royal Albert Hall concerts reviewed by Bernard Shaw.
1878	21	Begins *Harmony Music* series and *Promenades* for wind quintet. More lessons with	Boughton born 23 Jan, Holbrooke born 6 Jul, Schreker born 23 Mar.

Year	Age	Life	Contemporary musicians and events
		Pollitzer bring introduction to August Manns and the Crystal Palace concerts. Plays in Three Choirs Festival. Begins symphony on model of Mozart's Symphony no. 40 in G minor and starts first sketchbooks.	Tchaikovsky (38), Violin Concerto and Symphony no. 4. Catholic hierarchy restored in Scotland.
1879	22	Appointed musical director of Worcester City and County Pauper Lunatic Asylum at Powick and writes dance music for the band. *Tantum ergo* and *Domine salvam fac* for St George's. Sister Pollie marries William Grafton, and Elgar moves to their house.	Frank Bridge born 26 Feb, Ireland born 13 Aug, Jensen (42) dies 23 Jan, Karg-Elert born 21 Nov, Respighi born 9 Jul, Cyril Scott born 27 Sep. Brahms (46), fp of Violin Concerto; Bruckner (55), String Quintet; Franck (57), Piano Quintet; George Grove (59), *Dictionary of Music and Musicians*. Einstein born 14 Mar, Stalin born 21 Dec.
1880	23	Credo in E minor. Summer holiday in Paris with Charles Pipe. Chamber music at Whinfield's Severn Grange and the Fittons' Fair Lea, where he meets the cello players Henry Bellasis and Edward Capel Cure.	Bloch born 24 Jul, Metner born 5 Jan, Offenbach (61) dies 5 Oct, Pizzetti born 20 Sep. Dvořák (39), Symphony no. 6; Mahler (20), *Das klagende Lied*; Offenbach (61), *Les contes d'Hoffmann* complete in VS; Parry (32), fp of Piano Concerto and *Scenes from Prometheus Unbound*; Rimsky-Korsakov (36), *May Night*. First Boer War begins.
1881	24	*Pas redoublé* marches and *Air de ballet*. Attends Richter concert and hears *Meistersinger* overture. Plays in Three Choirs Festival. Sister Lucy marries Charles Pipe.	Bartók born 25 Mar, Musorgsky (42) dies 28 Mar, Myaskovsky born 20 Apr, Rubinstein (45) dies 23 Mar. Brahms (48), fp of *Academic Festival Overture* and Piano Concerto no. 2; Bruckner (57), Symphony no. 6; Fauré (36), Ballade; Mackenzie (34), fp of *The Bride*; Stanford (29), fp in Hanover of *The Veiled Prophet of Khorassan*; Verdi (68), fp of

Year	Age	Life	Contemporary musicians and events
			rev. *Simon Boccanegra*. Tsar Alexander II assassinated.
1882	25	Meets Charles Buck at Worcester conference of British Medical Association and spends holiday with him at Settle, Yorkshire. Piano trio fragment results in the tune later to become *Rosemary* (1915). Appointed conductor of the Amateur Instrumental Society. Plays in Stockley's Concert Orchestra (Birmingham). Visit to Leipzig (31 Dec) and Helen Weaver.	Grainger born 8 Jul, Kodály born 16 Dec, Malipiero born 18 Mar, Raff (60) dies 24 Jun, Stravinsky born 17 Jun, Szymanowski born 6 Oct. Balakirev (45), *Tamara*; Liszt (71), *Von der Wiege bis zum Grabe*; Wagner (69), fp of *Parsifal*. Britain occupies Egypt and Sudan.
1883	26	Hears much Brahms, Rubinstein, Schumann, Wagner in Leipzig. Attends Wagner Memorial concert at Crystal Palace. Moves to home of Charles and Lucy Pipe. *Intermezzo moresque* performed in Worcester. Writes Fantasia Gavotte. Engaged to Helen Weaver. Plans overture after Lake District holiday with Charles Buck. Stockley performs *Intermezzo moresque*.	Bax born 8 Nov, Berners born 18 Sep, Casella born 25 Jul, Varèse born 22 Dec, Wagner (69) dies 13 Feb, Webern born 3 Dec. Brahms (50), fp of Symphony no. 3; Bruckner (59), Symphony no. 7; Mackenzie (34), fp of *Columba*; R. Strauss (19), Horn Concerto no. 1. Karl Marx (65) dies 14 Mar. Salvation Army founded.
1884	27	*Sevillana* performed in Worcester and at Crystal Palace. Engagement to Helen Weaver broken off. Scottish holiday and meeting with 'E.E.' *Idylle* for violin and piano. Dvořák conducts his *Stabat mater* and Symphony no. 6 at Three Choirs Festival with Elgar in the orchestra. Publication of *Romance* for violin and piano as op. 1. Resigns conductorship at Powick Asylum.	Smetana (60) dies 12 May. Bruckner (60), *Te Deum*; Debussy (22), *L'enfant prodigue*; Mackenzie (35), fp of *The Rose of Sharon*; Mahler (25), *Lieder eines fahrenden Gesellen*; Massenet (42), fp of *Manon*; Puccini (26), fp of *Le villi*, Verdi (71), fp of rev. *Don Carlos*.

Year	Age	Life	Contemporary musicians and events
1885	28	Proposed 'Scotish' overture. Allegretto on GEDGE for violin and piano. *Through the Long Days*. Becomes organist at St George's Church.	Benedict (81) dies 5 Jun, Berg born 7 Feb, Butterworth born 12 Jul, Hiller (73) dies 10 May, Wellesz born 21 Oct. Brahms (52), fp of Symphony no. 4; Dvořák (44), Symphony no. 7; Franck (63), *Variations symphoniques*; Liszt (73), *Bagatelle sans tonalité*; Wolf (25), *Penthesilea*. General Gordon (51) dies at Khartoum 26 Jan.
1886	29	Fragmentary piano trio for performance at Settle. Caroline Alice Roberts (born 9 Oct 1848) begins lessons in accompaniment. Song *Is she not Passing Fair?* Article on Brahms for the *Malvern Advertiser*.	Liszt (74) dies 31 Jul, Ponchielli (51) dies 17 Jan. Fauré (41), *Requiem*; Franck (64), Violin Sonata; Stanford (34), *The Revenge*. Ludwig II of Bavaria (40) dies 13 Jun. Nietzsche (42), *Jenseits von Gut und Böse*.
1887	30	*Pie Jesu* (later *Ave verum corpus* op. 2 no. 1) in memory of W. A. Allen. Plays in Verdi *Requiem* at Birmingham. Lute Song from Tennyson's *Queen Mary*. Starts ladies' orchestral class.	Borodin (53) dies 28 Feb, van Dieren born 27 Dec, Villa-Lobos born 8 Feb. Borodin (53) abandons *Prince Igor*; Brahms (54), fp of Double Concerto; Bruckner (63), Symphony no. 8; Delius (25), *Florida Suite*; Strauss (23), fp of *Aus Italien*; Verdi (74), fp of *Otello*.
1888	31	Suite in D performed at Birmingham, Suite for Strings at Worcester. *The Wind at Dawn* as first setting of words by Alice Roberts. *Salut d'amour*. Engaged to Alice Roberts 22 Sep. *Ecce sacerdos magnus*.	Alkan (74) dies 29 Mar, Heller (73) dies 14 Jan. Franck (66), Symphony in D minor; Parry (40), *Judith*; Satie (22), *Gymnopédies*; Tchaikovsky (48), Symphony no. 5. Wilhelm II becomes German Emperor.
1889	32	Piano Sonatina. Marriage to Alice Roberts at Brompton Oratory 8 May. Honeymoon in Isle of Wight. Move to Kensington. Summer in Malvern and outline for *The Black Knight*. At Oaklands,	Dvořák (48), Symphony no. 8; Franck (67), String Quartet; Mahler (29), Symphony no. 1; Strauss (25), fp of *Don Juan*. Adolf Hitler born 20 Apr.

Elgar

Year	Age	Life	Contemporary musicians and events
		Upper Norwood for the winter. *Vesper Voluntaries* op. 14. Partsongs *O Happy Eyes* and *My Love Dwelt in a Northern Land*. Worcester Three Choirs commission.	
1890	33	Move to Kensington. Carice Irene born 14 Aug. Première of Concert Overture *Froissart* 10 Sep. Resumes West Midlands violin teaching Nov.	Franck (67) dies 8 Nov, Gade (73) dies 21 Dec, Ibert born 15 Aug, Frank Martin born 15 Sep, Martinů born 8 Dec. Busoni (24), *Konzertstück*; Mascagni (26), fp of *Cavalleria rusticana*; Strauss (26), fp of *Burleske*, *Tod und Verklärung* and *Macbeth*; Wolf (30), *Spanisches Liederbuch*. Cardinal Newman (89) dies 11 Aug. Bismarck resigns as German Chancellor.
1891	34	Decision to leave London. Move to 'Forli' at Malvern. Rosa Burley of The Mount takes violin lessons and Elgar buys Gagliano violin. *La capricieuse* op. 17.	Bliss born 2 Aug, Delibes (55) dies 16 Jan, Prokofiev born 13 Apr. Brahms (58), Clarinet Trio and Quintet; Fauré (46), *La bonne chanson*; Rakhmaninov (18), Piano Concerto no. 1; Wolf (31), *Italienisches Liederbuch*.
1892	35	Serenade for Strings op. 20, *Spanish Serenade* op. 23, *The Black Knight* op. 25. Visit to Bayreuth for *Parsifal* (twice), *Tristan* and *Meistersinger*. In Worcester gives Beethoven violin sonata lecture–recitals.	Honegger born 10 Mar, Howells born 17 Oct, Kilpinen born 4 Feb, Lalo (69) dies 22 Apr, Milhaud born 4 Sep, Sorabji born 14 Aug. Dvořák (51), *Te Deum*; Nielsen (27), Symphony no. 1; Sibelius (27), *Kullervo* and *En Saga* orig. version.
1893	36	Takes up golf. Première of *The Black Knight* 18 Apr. Studies German before another Bavarian holiday, initially in Garmisch. The *Ring, Die Feen, Tannhäuser, Tristan* in Munich. Played violin in Three Choirs	Eugene Goossens born 26 May, Gounod (75) dies 18 Oct, Hába born 21 Jun, Tchaikovsky (53) dies 6 Nov, having completed Symphony no. 6. Dvořák (52), Symphony no. 9 'From the New World'; Humperdinck (38), fp under

Year	Age	Life	Contemporary musicians and events
		Festival for last time.	Strauss of *Hänsel und Gretel*; Verdi (80), fp of *Falstaff*. Pan-German League founded. Lenin forms Marxist circle in Samara.
1894	37	*Sursum corda* op. 11. Arranges *Parsifal* Good Friday Music for Worcester High School. Begins *King Olaf*. Bavarian holiday with *Götterdämmerung* and *Die Meistersinger* in Munich. Orchestrates Hugh Blair's *Advent Cantata*. Partsongs *The Snow* and *Fly, Singing Bird*, op. 26 nos. 1 and 2.	Bülow (63) dies 12 Feb, Chabrier (53) dies 13 Sep, Heseltine (Warlock) born 30 Oct, Lekeu (24) dies 21 Jan, Moeran born 31 Dec, Pijper born 8 Sep, Piston born 20 Jan, Rubinstein (64) dies 20 Nov. Brahms (61), Clarinet Sonatas; Debussy (32), fp of *Prélude à l'après-midi d'un faune*; Verdi (81), *Otello* ballet music. Tsar Alexander III dies, succeeded by Nicholas II.
1895	38	*Scenes from the Bavarian Highlands* op. 27. Première of Organ Sonata op. 28 (8 Jul). Bavarian holiday, with some work on Capel Cure's libretto for *The Light of Life*. *Der fliegende Holländer* in Munich. Work on *King Olaf*, commissioned for North Staffordshire Festival. Worcester Three Choirs Festival commission for short oratorio.	Castelnuovo-Tedesco born 3 Apr, Hindemith born 16 Nov, Orff born 10 Jul. Dvořák (54), Cello Concerto; Mahler (35), fp of Symphony no. 2; Rakhmaninov (22), Symphony no. 1; Satie (29), *Messe des pauvres*; Sibelius (30), *Lemminkäinen Legends*; Strauss (31), fp of *Till Eulenspiegel* and *Guntram*. Lenin arrested.
1896	39	Premières of *Scenes from the Bavarian Highlands* by Worcester Festival Choral Society (21 Apr), of *The Light of Life* at the Worcester Three Choirs Festival (8 Sep), and of *King Olaf* at the North Staffordshire Festival, Hanley (30 Oct). Commissions from Novello for *Imperial March* op. 32 and *The Banner of St George* op. 33.	Bruckner (72) dies 11 Oct, leaving Symphony no. 9 incomplete; Gerhard born 25 Sep, Sessions born 28 Dec, Thomas (85) dies 12 Feb, Virgil Thomson born 25 Nov. Brahms (63), *Vier ernste Gesänge*; Mahler (36), Symphony no. 3; Nielsen (31), *Hymnus amoris*; Puccini (38), fp of *La bohème*; Strauss (32), fp of *Also sprach Zarathustra*.
1897	40	Première of *Imperial March* at	Brahms (63) dies 3 Apr, Cowell

Year	Age	Life	Contemporary musicians and events
		the Crystal Palace (19 Apr) and perf. at Royal Garden Party to celebrate Diamond Jubilee of Queen Victoria. Premières of *The Banner of St George* by St Cuthbert's Hall Choral Society, London (18 May), and of the *Te Deum and Benedictus* op. 34 at the Hereford Three Choirs Festival (12 Sep). Begins correspondence with A. J. Jaeger of Novello ('Nimrod'). Bavarian holiday in Garmisch, and Munich for *Tristan* and *Don Giovanni*, both under Strauss. *Chanson de nuit.* Foundation of Worcestershire Philharmonic Society. Leeds commission for *Caractacus* op. 35.	born 11 Mar, Korngold born 29 May. Busoni (31), Violin Concerto; Parry (49), *Elegy for Brahms*; Schoenberg (23), String Quartet in D; Verdi (84) sends *Quattro pezzi sacri* for pubn. First Zionist Congress at Basle. Lenin exiled to Siberia.
1898	41	Composition of *Caractacus* and lease on Birchwood Lodge. First Worcestershire Philharmonic Society concert (7 May). Première of *Caractacus* at Leeds (5 Oct). Idea for 'Gordon' symphony. Beginning of 'Enigma' Variations op. 36 (21 Oct).	Gershwin born 26 Sep, Harris born 12 Feb. Strauss (34), fp of *Don Quixote. The Perfect Wagnerite* by Bernard Shaw. German naval expansion.
1899	42	Revision of Suite in D as *Three Characteristic Pieces* op. 10. Completed Variations sent to Hans Richter for consideration. Move to Craeg Lea, Malvern. *To her Beneath whose Steadfast Star* performed at Windsor on Queen Victoria's 80th birthday (24 May). Première of 'Enigma' Variations under Richter at St James's Hall (21 Jun). Finale extension completed (31 Jul). Revision	Chausson (44) dies 10 Jun, Poulenc born 7 Jan, Johann Strauss (73) dies 3 Jun. Sibelius (34), Symphony no. 1; Strauss (35), fp of *Ein Heldenleben*. Second Boer War.

Year	Age	Life	Contemporary musicians and events
		of *The Light of Life* at Worcester Three Choirs Festival (13 Sep). Première of *Sea Pictures* op. 37 at Norwich Festival (5 Oct). Indecision about Birmingham commission for October 1900.	
1900	43	Decision for *The Dream of Gerontius*. Death of Swinnerton Heap (11 Jun), chorus master for the Birmingham Festival. *Gerontius* full score completed (3 Aug). Inadequate première of *Gerontius* at Birmingham (5 Oct). Cambridge doctorate (22 Nov).	Copland born 14 Nov, Křenek born 23 Aug, Sullivan (58) dies 22 Nov, Weill born 2 Mar. Debussy (38), fp of *Nocturnes*; Fauré (55), fp of *Prométhée*.
1901	44	Première of *Cockaigne* op. 40 at Queen's Hall (20 Jun). Plans for *Coronation Ode*. Orchestrates *Emmaus* for Herbert Brewer. Welsh holiday at Rosa Burley's invitation. Meets the Edward Speyers at Leeds. Première of *Pomp and Circumstance Marches* nos. 1 and 2 in Liverpool (19 Oct) and *Grania and Diarmid* music at the Gaiety Theatre, Dublin (21 Oct). Première of *Concert Allegro* for piano op. 46 at St James's Hall (2 Dec). Birmingham commission for *The Apostles*. Düsseldorf perf. of *Gerontius* under Buths (19 Dec).	Egk born 17 May, Finzi born 14 Jul, Rheinberger (62) dies 25 Nov, Rubbra born 23 May, Stainer (60) dies 31 Mar, Verdi (87) dies 27 Jan. Delius (39), fp of *Paris*; Mahler (41), fp of Symphony no. 4; Rakhmaninov (28), fp of Piano Concerto no. 2; Strauss (37), fp of *Feuersnot*. Queen Victoria (81) dies 22 Jan, and Edward VII accedes.
1902	45	*Dream Children* op. 43. Second Düsseldorf *Gerontius* (20 May) and the Strauss toast to Elgar. Edward VII's illness and postponement of *Coronation Ode*. Begins gathering material for *The*	Walton born 29 Mar. Debussy (40), fp of *Pelléas et Mélisande*; Mahler (42); fp of Symphony no. 3; Schoenberg (28), fp of *Verklärte Nacht*; Sibelius (37), Symphony no. 2. *What is to be Done?* by Lenin.

Year	Age	Life	Contemporary musicians and events
		Apostles. Bayreuth holiday for *Der fliegende Holländer*, *Parsifal* and the *Ring* (except *Götterdämmerung*). Death of mother (1 Sep). Bowdlerized *Gerontius* at Worcester Three Choirs Festival (11 Sep). Première of *Coronation Ode* at Sheffield (2 Oct). Meeting with Stuart Wortleys. Begins composition of *The Apostles*.	
1903	46	Morecambe Competition Festival and meeting with Canon Gorton. Changes of plan over *The Apostles*. First London *Gerontius*, at Westminster Cathedral (6 Jun). *Coronation Ode* in presence of king and queen (25 Jun). *The Apostles* full score completed (17 Aug). Première of *The Apostles* at Birmingham (14 Oct). Plan for Elgar Festival at Covent Garden. Death of Rodewald (9 Nov). Departure for Italy (21 Nov), to Bordighera then Alassio. Decision to write *In the South* for the Elgar Festival.	Berkeley born 12 May, Blacher born 3 Jan, Khachaturian born 6 Jun, Wolf (42) dies 22 Feb. Ravel (28), String Quartet.
1904	47	Return to London for dinner at Marlborough House with King Edward and the Prince of Wales (3 Feb). *In the South* completed (21 Feb). Elgar Festival (14–16 March), with première of *In the South* (16 Mar). Knighthood announced (24 Jun). Move to Plas Gwyn, Hereford. Meets Samuel Sanford. Negotiations over professorship of music at University of Birmingham. Elgar accepts (26 Nov).	Dallapiccola born 3 Feb, Dvořák (63) dies 1 May, Kabalevsky born 30 Dec, Petrassi born 16 Jul, Skalkottas born 8 Mar. Delius (32), fp of Piano Concerto; Janáček (50), fp of *Jenůfa*; Mahler (44), fp of Symphony no. 5; Puccini (46), fp of *Madama Butterfly*; Stanford (52), *Songs of the Sea*. Entente Cordiale between Britain and France.

Year	Age	Life	Contemporary musicians and events
		Continental trip with Schuster to hear *In the South* and *The Apostles*.	
1905	48	Honorary doctorate at Oxford arranged by Parry (7 Feb). Premières of Introduction and Allegro op. 47 and *Pomp and Circumstance* 3 at Queen's Hall (8 Mar). Inaugural lecture at Birmingham University (16 Mar). Departure to USA (9 Jun). Honorary doctorate at Yale (28 Jun). Departure for England (11 Jul). Freedom of the City of Worcester (12 Sep) arranged through Hubert Leicester as mayor. Departure for Mediterranean cruise (15 Sep). Visits Istanbul (25 Sep) and Smyrna (30 Sep). Return to England (12 Oct). Begins work on *The Kingdom* amid further Birmingham lectures and conducting tour with the LSO.	Jolivet born 8 Aug, Lambert born 23 Aug, Rawsthorne born 2 May, Seiber born 4 May, Tippett born 2 Jan. Debussy (43), fp of *La mer*; Lehár (35), fp of *The Merry Widow*; Schoenberg (31), fp of *Pelleas und Melisande*; Strauss (41), fp of *Salome*. Bernard Shaw's *Man and Superman* performed. Battleship *Potemkin* mutiny and uprising of Moscow Soviet.
1906	49	Crisis over *The Kingdom*; decision to treat only the Church in Jerusalem. Completion of Scenes I–III (27 Mar). Departure for USA (6 Apr). Arrival at Cincinnati (17 Apr) for performances of *Gerontius*, *The Apostles*, *In the South*, Introduction and Allegro. Scoring of *The Kingdom* begun. Return journey started (18 May). Illness delays completion of *The Kingdom* till 31 August. Honorary doctorate at Aberdeen University arranged by Charles Sanford Terry (26	Arensky (44) dies 25 Feb, Frankel born 31 Jan, Lutyens born 9 Jul, Shostakovich born 25 Sep. Delius (44), fp of *Sea Drift*; Mahler (46), fp of Symphony no. 6. Britain launches the *Dreadnought*.

Year	Age	Life	Contemporary musicians and events
		Sep). Première of *The Kingdom* at Birmingham (3 Oct). More Birmingham lectures and ill-health. Departure for Naples (28 Dec).	
1907	50	Naples, Capri and Rome. Meets Perosi and Sgambati. Departure for England (23 Feb). Elgar leaves for USA (2 Mar) for concerts including *The Kingdom* in New York. Returns to Hereford (27 Apr). *Ave Maria* and *Ave maris stella* to complete op. 2. *Pomp and Circumstance* 4 first perf. (24 Aug). *Wand of Youth* completed. Begins string quartet. Departure for Rome (5 Nov). Continues string quartet and takes French lessons. Starts First Symphony (3 Dec), incorporating some of string quartet. Première of *Wand of Youth* 1 at Queen's Hall (14 Dec). *A Christmas Greeting, The Reveille,* and op. 53 partsongs.	Fortner born 12 Oct, Grieg (64) dies 4 Sep, Maconchy born 19 Mar. Parry (59), fp of *A Vision of Life*; Schoenberg (33), fp of String Quartet no. 1; Sibelius (42), fp of Symphony no. 3; Stravinsky (25), fp of Symphony in E flat; Vaughan Williams (35), fp of *Toward the Unknown Region*.
1908	51	Death of William Grafton (13 Jan). Departure from Rome (8 May). Elgar returns to Hereford (29 May). Resumption of Symphony. Attends Elgar concert in Ostend (14 Aug). Resigns Birmingham professorship (29 Aug). Première of *Wand of Youth* 2 at Worcester Three Choirs Festival (9 Sep). First Symphony completed (25 Sep). Manchester première of Symphony under Richter (3 Dec), and London première (7	Elliott Carter born 11 Dec, Ferguson born 21 Oct, MacDowell (46) dies 23 Jan, Messiaen born 10 Dec, Rimsky-Korsakov (64) dies 21 Jun. Mahler (48), fp of Symphony no. 7; Rakhmaninov (35), fp of Symphony no. 2; Schoenberg (34), fp of Second Quartet. Thomas Hardy completes *The Dynasts*. Kaiser Wilhelm II increases Anglo-German tension with article in the *Daily Telegraph*.

Year	Age	Life	Contemporary musicians and events
		Dec).	
1909	52	Ill-health. Arrival at Careggi, near Florence (22 Apr). Sketches for Violin Concerto and Symphony no. 2. *The Angelus*, and *Go, Song of Mine*. Visits to Venice and Richard Strauss at Garmisch. Return to Hereford (22 Jun). *Elegy, They are at Rest* and op. 59 Parker songs. Pietro d'Alba adaptations op. 60, *The Torch* and *The River*.	Albéniz (48) dies 18 May. Delius (47), *A Mass of Life* performed complete; Rakhmaninov (36), fp of Piano Concerto no. 3; Strauss (44), fp of *Elektra*; Vaughan Williams (37), fp of *The Wasps*.
1910	53	Work on Violin Concerto and *Romance* for bassoon. Première of Parker songs at Jaeger memorial concert (24 Jan). Alice Stuart Wortley becomes the 'Windflower'. Move to 58 Cavendish St (7 Mar). Motor tour with Frank Schuster to include the Stuart Wortleys at Tintagel. Deaths of Peter Rabbit (3 May) and Edward VII (7 May). W. H. Reed helps with the Violin Concerto (from 28 May). Return to Plas Gwyn (18 Jun). Orchestration of the Violin Concerto completed (5 Aug). Begins setting of Psalm 48. Première of the Violin Concerto with Kreisler (10 Nov). Concentrated work on Symphony no. 2.	Barber born 9 Mar, Balakirev (73) dies 29 May, Reinecke (85) dies 10 Mar, Schuman born 4 Aug. Bartók (29), fp of First Quartet; Mahler (50), fp of Symphony no. 8; Stravinsky (28), fp of *The Firebird*; Vaughan Williams (38), fp of *A Sea Symphony* and *Tallis Fantasia*. *Howards End* by E. M. Forster. George V succeeds Edward VII.
1911	54	Première of bassoon *Romance* in Hereford (16 Feb). Agrees to succeed Richter as conductor of LSO. Completes Second Symphony (28 Feb). Leaves for tour of Canada and the USA (25 Mar). Returns to Hereford (9	Mahler (50) dies 18 May, Menotti born 7 Jul. Debussy (49), fp of *Le martyre de Saint-Sébastien*; Delius (49), fp of *Songs of Sunset*; Mahler, posthumous fp of *Das Lied von der Erde*; Ravel (38), fp of *L'heure espagnole*; Sibelius

Year	Age	Life	Contemporary musicians and events
		May). Première of Second Symphony (23 May). Awarded the Order of Merit (20 Jun). *Coronation March* and *O Hearken Thou* for crowning of George V (22 Jun), which the Elgars do not attend. Edition of *Matthew Passion* by Elgar and Atkins at Worcester Three Choirs Festival (14 Sep).	(46), fp of Symphony no. 4; Strauss (47), fp of *Der Rosenkavalier*; Stravinsky (29), fp of *Petrushka*. *The White Peacock* by D. H. Lawrence. Rasputin's pilgrimage to the Holy Land. Transfer of Indian capital from Calcutta to Delhi.
1912	55	Move to Severn House, Hampstead (1 Jan). Première of *The Crown of India* (11 Mar), and of Psalm 48 setting at Westminster Abbey (16 Jul). Completes *The Music Makers* (20 Aug), which has its première in Birmingham (1 Oct).	Cage born 15 Sep, Coleridge-Taylor (37) dies 1 Sep, Françaix born 23 May, Massenet (70) dies 13 Aug. Mahler, posthumous fp of Symphony no. 9; Parry (64), fp of Symphony no. 5 and *Ode on the Nativity*; Ravel (37), fp of *Daphnis et Chloé*; Schoenberg (38), fp of *Pierrot lunaire*; Strauss (48), fp of *Ariadne auf Naxos*. Conference fails to halt Anglo-German naval race. War in Balkans.
1913	56	Departure for Naples (31 Jan). Return to Severn House (23 Feb). Begins work on *Falstaff* (22 Mar). Death of Julia Worthington (9 Jun). Chaliapine at Severn House (20 Jul) and talk of *King Lear* opera. *Falstaff* completed (5 Aug). Welsh holiday and writing of *Falstaff* analysis. Première of *Falstaff* at Leeds (1 Oct). Approached by Gramophone Company about recordings and writes *Carissima*. Sends piano concerto sketch to the Windflower.	Britten born 22 Nov, Lutosławski born 5 Jan. Fauré (68), production of *Pénélope*; Rakhmaninov (40), fp of *The Bells*; Schoenberg (39), fp of *Gurrelieder*; Stravinsky (31), fp of *The Rite of Spring*. *Chance* by Joseph Conrad. *Sons and Lovers* by D. H. Lawrence. *Pygmalion* by Bernard Shaw.
1914	57	Henry Vaughan partsongs op.	Lyadov (59) dies 28 Aug,

Year	Age	Life	Contemporary musicians and events
		71. *Death on the Hills* op. 72. Recording of *Carissima* (20 Jan). Partsongs from the Russian op. 73. Signs pledge against Irish Home Rule (2 Mar). Silver wedding (8 May). Scottish holiday (19 Jul). Outbreak of First World War (4 Aug). Return to Severn House (14 Aug). Volunteers as Special Constable (17 Aug). Visits his sister Pollie at Stoke Prior. Première of *Carillon* (7 Dec).	Sgambati (73) dies 14 Dec. Strauss (50), fp of *Josephslegende*; Stravinsky (32), fp of *The Nightingale*; Vaughan Williams (42), fp of *A London Symphony*. *Satires of Circumstance* by Thomas Hardy. *Common Sense about the War* by Bernard Shaw.
1915	58	Colvin's proposal for a setting of Binyon poems. Resigns from Special Constabulary and joins Hampstead Volunteer Reserve. Completes 'For the Fallen'. Première of *Polonia* (6 Jul). Completes *Une voix dans le désert*. Autumn break with the Stuart Wortleys near Ravenglass. Première of *The Starlight Express* (29 Dec).	Goldmark (84) dies 2 Jan, Skryabin (43) dies 27 Apr, Searle born 26 Aug, Taneyev (58) dies 19 Jun, Waldteufel (77) dies 16 Feb. Sibelius (50), fp of Symphony no. 5; Strauss (51), fp of *Eine Alpensinfonie*. *The Rainbow* by D. H. Lawrence. Dardanelles expedition.
1916	59	Première of *Une voix dans le désert* (29 Jan). Recording of *The Starlight Express* (18 Feb). Collapse on train journey to Stoke Prior (8 Apr). Première of 'To Women' and 'For the Fallen' (3 May). August holiday in the Lake District.	Babbitt born 10 May, Butterworth (31) dies 5 Aug, Granados (48) dies 24 Mar, Reger (43) dies 11 May, Hans Richter (73) dies 5 Dec. Bax (33), fp of *The Garden of Fand*; Holst (42), fp of *Sāvitri*; Parry (68), fp of *Jerusalem* and *Songs of Farewell*; Strauss (52), second version of *Ariadne auf Naxos*. Battles of the Somme and Jutland. Withdrawal from Dardanelles. Lloyd George succeeds Asquith as prime minister.
1917	60	Premières of *The Sanguine Fan* (20 Mar), *Le drapeau belge* (14 Apr), and *The*	Bax (34), *November Woods*; Debussy (55), fp of Violin Sonata; Falla (41), fp of *The*

Year	Age	Life	Contemporary musicians and events
		Fringes of the Fleet (11 Jun). First stay at Brinkwells (24 May). Touring with *The Fringes of the Fleet*. Première of complete *Spirit of England* (24 Nov). Much ill-health.	*Three-cornered Hat*; Pfitzner (48), fp of *Palestrina*; Puccini (59), fp of *La rondine*. Joseph Conrad, *The Shadow Line*. Virginia Woolf, *The Voyage Out*. Battle of Passchendaele. Russian Revolution and abdication of Nicholas II. Visions of the Virgin at Fátima.
1918	61	Operation for tonsils (15 Mar). First sketch of Cello Concerto, and start on String Quartet. Move to Brinkwells (2 May). *Big Steamers*. Arrival of piano (19 Aug). Start on Violin Sonata (20 Aug). Completion of Violin Sonata and start on Piano Quintet (26 Sep). String Quartet continued simultaneously (from 9 Oct). Operation on Lady Elgar for a wen (29 Oct). Armistice Day (11 Nov). Burglary at Severn House (16 Dec). String Quartet finished (24 Dec). Return to London (27 Dec).	Bernstein born 25 Aug, Boito (76) dies 10 Jun, Cui (83) dies 24 Mar, Debussy (55) dies 25 Mar, Parry (70) dies 7 Oct. Bartók (37), fp of *Duke Bluebeard's Castle*; Prokofiev (27), fp of *Classical Symphony*; Puccini (60), fp of *Il trittico*; Strauss (54), fp of *Der Bürger als Edelmann*. Kaiser Wilhelm II flees to Holland. Emperor Charles of Austria abdicates.
1919	62	Piano Quintet completed (9 Feb). Severn House run-through of the three chamber works in presence of Bliss and Shaw (7 Mar). Public première of the chamber works (21 May). Cello Concerto completed (8 Aug). Thoughts of continuing with a piano concerto. Première of Cello Concerto with Felix Salmond (27 Oct). Recording of Cello Concerto with Beatrice Harrison.	Leoncavallo (61) dies 9 Aug. Delius (57), fp of *Fennimore and Gerda* and the Violin Concerto; Holst (45), fp of *The Planets*; Strauss (55), fp of *Die Frau ohne Schatten*. Treaty of Versailles. League of Nations founded.
1920	63	Bernard Shaw article in *Music & Letters*. *With Proud Thanksgiving* made from 'For	Bruch (82) dies 2 Oct, Fricker born 5 Sep, Maderna born 21 Apr. Delius (58), fp of Double

Year	Age	Life	Contemporary musicians and events
		the Fallen'. Illness of Lady Elgar and her death (7 Apr). Funeral at St Wulstan's, Little Malvern (10 Apr). Loan of £500 from Embleton towards completion of the third oratorio. Heifetz at Severn House.	Concerto and *A Song of the High Hills*; Holst (46), fp of *Hymn of Jesus*; Ravel (45), fp of *La valse*; Stravinsky (38), fp of *Pulcinella*. *Women in Love* by D. H. Lawrence. Canonization of Joan of Arc. Hitler's Party becomes the National Socialist German Workers' Party.
1921	64	Carice Elgar engaged to Samuel Blake. Orchestration of Bach Organ Fugue completed (25 May). Severn House for sale and move to 37 St James's Place. Première of Bach Fugue (27 Oct).	Malcolm Arnold born 21 Oct, Humperdinck (67) dies 27 Sep, Saint-Saëns (86) dies 16 Dec. Delius (59), fp of Cello Concerto; Janáček (67), fp of *Kát'a Kabanová*; Stravinsky (39), fp of Symphonies of Wind Instruments. *Back to Methuselah* by Bernard Shaw.
1922	65	Marriage of Carice Elgar (16 Jan). Orchestrates the Bach Organ Fantasia. Première of Bach–Elgar Fantasia and Fugue at Gloucester Three Choirs Festival (7 Sep).	Lukas Foss born 15 Aug, Nikisch (66) dies 23 Jan, Xenakis born 29 May. Bliss (31), fp of *A Colour Symphony*; Vaughan Williams (50), fp of *Pastoral Symphony* and *The Shepherds of the Delectable Mountains*; Walton (20), fp of *Façade*. Broadcasts of music begin in England. *The Waste Land* by T. S. Eliot.
1923	66	Première of music for Binyon's *Arthur* (12 Mar). Move to Napleton Grange, Kempsey (31 Mar). Carillon piece for Loughborough. C minor fugue later in *Severn Suite*. Orchestration of overture to Handel's Second Chandos Anthem. Partsongs *The Wanderer* and *Zut! Zut! Zut!* Première of the Handel–Elgar Overture at the Worcester Three Choirs Festival (2 Sep). Departure for	Ligeti born 28 May. Bartók (42), fp of *Dance Suite*; Sibelius (58), fp of Symphony no. 6; Stravinsky (41), fp of *Les noces*. Unsuccessful Munich putsch by Hitler and Ludendorff.

Year	Age	Life	Contemporary musicians and events
		Amazon cruise (15 Nov). Return to England (30 Dec).	
1924	67	Master of the King's Musick (28 Apr). Première of *Empire March* and songs for *Pageant of Empire* (21 Jul).	Busoni (58) dies 27 Jul, Fauré (79) dies 4 Nov, Nono born 29 Jan, Puccini (65) dies 29 Nov, Stanford (71) dies 29 Mar. Schoenberg (50), fp of *Erwartung* and *Die glückliche Hand*; Sibelius (59), fp of Symphony no. 7; Strauss (60), fp of *Schlagobers* and *Intermezzo*; Vaughan Williams (52), fp of *Hugh the Drover*. *A Passage to India* by E. M. Forster. *St Joan* by Bernard Shaw. Hitler imprisoned and begins *Mein Kampf*.
1925	68	Resigns from the Athenaeum Club. Partsongs *The Herald* and *The Prince of Sleep*. Death of sister, Lucy Pipe (23 Oct).	Boulez born 25 Mar, Satie (59) dies 1 Jul. Berg (40), fp of *Wozzeck*; Holst (51), fp of Choral Symphony; Ravel (50), fp of *L'enfant et les sortilèges*; Vaughan Williams (53), fp of *Flos campi* and Violin Concerto. Locarno Pact guarantees current West European borders.
1926	69	Lord Stuart of Wortley dies (24 Apr)	Henze born 1 Jul. Bartók (45), fp of *The Miraculous Mandarin*; Hindemith (31), fp of *Cardillac*; Janáček (72), fp of *The Makropulos Affair*; Kodály (44), fp of *Háry János*; Puccini, posthumous fp of *Turandot*; Shostakovich (20), fp of Symphony no. 1; Sibelius (61), fp of *Tapiola*; Vaughan Williams (54), fp of *Sancta civitas*; Walton (24), fp of *Portsmouth Point*; Warlock (32), fp of *Capriol Suite*. General strike in Britain. Germany admitted to the

Year	Age	Life	Contemporary musicians and events
			League of Nations.
1927	70	*Gerontius* under Elgar at the Albert Hall, partly recorded (26 Feb). Conducts 70th birthday concert for BBC (2 Jun). Schuster gives concert of the chamber works (26 Jun). Première of *A Civic Fanfare* at Hereford Three Choirs Festival (4 Sep). Death of Schuster (27 Dec), who leaves Elgar £7000. At Battenhall Manor.	Berg (42), fp of Chamber Concerto; Busoni, posthumous fp of *Dr Faustus*; Rakhmaninov (54), fp of Piano Concerto no. 4; Schoenberg (53), fp of String Quartet no. 3; Stravinsky (45), fp of *Oedipus Rex*. *To the Lighthouse* by Virginia Woolf. Hindenburg repudiates 'War Guilt' clause of Versailles Treaty.
1928	71	Appointed KCVO. Move to Tiddington House, Stratford. Attends Shakespeare Festival with Shaw. Brother Frank dies (7 Jun). Premières of *Beau Brummell* music (5 Nov) and *I Sing the Birth* (10 Dec).	T. Baird born 26 Jul, Barraqué born 17 Jan, Janáček (74) dies 12 Aug, Musgrave born 27 May, Stockhausen born 28 Aug. Bliss (37), fp of *Pastoral*; Holst (54), fp of *Egdon Heath*; Ravel (53), fp of *Boléro*; Schoenberg (54), fp of Variations; Stravinsky (46), fp of *Apollo* and *The Fairy's Kiss*. *Lady Chatterley's Lover* by D. H. Lawrence. Britain, France, German, Italy, Japan, the USA sign the Kellogg–Briand Pact renouncing war to settle disputes.
1929	72	Speech at Malvern Festival at opening of Shaw exhibition (17 Aug). Takes Marl Bank for Worcester Three Choirs Festival. Records improvisations (5 Nov). Première of *Good Morrow* (9 Dec).	Diaghilev (57) dies 19 Aug. Delius (67), fp of *Cynara*; Hindemith (34), fp of *Neues vom Tage*; Prokofiev (38), fp of Symphony no. 3; Vaughan Williams (57), fp of *Sir John in Love*; Walton (27), fp of Viola Concerto; Webern (46), fp of Symphony. *The Apple Cart* by Bernard Shaw. Wall Street crash.
1930	73	*Severn Suite* completed (16 Apr) and dedicated to Bernard Shaw. Première of *Pomp and Circumstance 5* (18	Warlock (36) dies 17 Dec. Bliss (39), fp of *Morning Heroes*; Stravinsky (48), fp of Symphony of Psalms; Vaughan

Year	Age	Life	Contemporary musicians and events
		Sep) and of *Severn Suite* (27 Sep). Foreword for Hubert Leicester's *Forgotten Worcester*. Completes the *Nursery Suite*, revises the 1889 Piano Sonatina, and writes *It isnae me*.	Williams (58), concert fp of *Job*. *Ash Wednesday* by T. S. Eliot.
1931	74	Basil Maine approaches Elgar about a proposed book (May). Furore over Dent's article in the Adler *Handbuch der Musikgeschichte*. Becomes First Baronet of Broadheath (3 Jun). Trouble with 'sciatica'. Meets Vera Hockman (7 Nov). Sets three Mackay poems as unison songs for children.	d'Indy (80) dies 2 Dec, Nielsen (66) dies 3 Oct. Honegger (39), fp of First Symphony; Ravel (56), fp of Piano Concerto for the Left hand; Stravinsky (49), fp of Violin Concerto; Walton (29), fp of *Belshazzar's Feast*. *The Waves* by Virginia Woolf. Britain abandons the gold standard.
1932	75	Orchestration of funeral march from Chopin B flat minor Piano Sonata (Mar). *Severn Suite* scored for full orchestra. Première of *So Many True Princesses* (8 Jun). Discusses proposal for Third Symphony with Keith Prowse (early Jun). Recording of Violin Concerto with Menuhin (14 and 15 Jul). Approaches Barry Jackson for help over a libretto for the Ben Jonson opera he was planning, to be called *The Spanish Lady*. Composes *Serenade*, *Adieu* and *Mina*. Three BBC concerts to celebrate 75th birthday. Announcement that the BBC was commissioning the Third Symphony (14 Dec).	d'Albert (68) dies 3 Mar, A. Goehr born 10 Aug, Sousa (77) dies 6 Mar. Delius (70), fp of *Songs of Farewell*; Ravel (57), fp of Piano Concerto.
1933	76	Work on symphony and opera. Flies to Paris (28 May) for performance of the Violin Concerto with Menuhin and	Duparc (85) dies 13 Feb, Karg-Elert (55) dies 9 Apr, Penderecki born 23 Nov. Strauss (69), fp of *Arabella* and

Year	Age	Life	Contemporary musicians and events
		visit to Delius. Created KCVO (3 Jun). Viola version of Cello Concerto at Hereford Three Choirs Festival (6 Sep). Enters South Bank nursing home for exploratory operation. Inoperable cancer revealed. Correspondence with Delius. Shaw sends his latest play, *On the Rocks*.	working on *Die schweigsame Frau*; Vaughan Williams (61), fp of Piano Concerto. Hitler comes to power in Germany. Pius XI praises him for his stand against Communism. Concordat between Nazi Germany and the Holy See. Strauss becomes president of German Reichsmusikkammer.
1934	76	Return to Marl Bank (3 Jan). Listens to recording session of Triumphal March from *Caractacus* and asks for 'Woodland Interlude' (22 Jan). Criticizes *Mina* recording (15 Feb). Dies (23 Feb).	Birtwistle born 15 Jul, Maxwell Davies born 8 Sep, Delius (72) dies 10 Jun, Holst (59) dies 25 May, Schreker (56) dies 21 Mar. Malcolm Arnold 13, Auric 35, Babbitt 18, T. Baird 6, Bantock 66, Barber 24, Barraqué 6, Bartók 53, Bax 51, Berg 49, Berio 9, Berkeley 31, Berners 51, Bernstein 16, Blacher 31, Bliss 43, Bloch 54, Boughton 56, Boulez 9, Havergal Brian 58, Frank Bridge 55, Britten 21, Cage 22, Elliott Carter 24, Casella 51, Castelnuovo-Tedesco 39, Chaminade 77, Charpentier 74, Copland 34, Cowell 37, Cowen 82, Dallapiccola 30, Walford Davies 65, van Dieren 57, Dohnányi 57, Dukas 69, Dunhill 57, Egk 33, Falla 58, Ferguson 26, Finzi 33, Fortner 27, Lukas Foss 12, Françaix 22, Frankel 28, Fricker 14, Gerhard 38, German 72, Gershwin 36, Glière 59, Goehr 2, Goossens 41, Grainger 62, Hába 41, Reynaldo Hahn 59, Harris 36, Henze 8, Hindemith 39, Holbrooke 56, Honegger 42, Howells 42, Ibert 44, Ireland 55, Ives 60, Jolivet 29, Kabalevsky 30, Khachaturian

Year	Age	Life	Contemporary musicians and events

Contemporary musicians and
events
31, Kilpinen 42, Kodály 52,
Korngold 37, Křenek 34,
Lambert 29, Lehár 54, Ligeti
11, Lutosławski 21, Lutyens
28, McEwen 66, Mackenzie 87,
Maconchy 27, Maderna 14,
Malipiero 52, Frank Martin
44, Martinů 44, Mascagni 71,
Menotti 23, Messiaen 26,
Metner 54, Milhaud 42,
Moeran 40, Musgrave 6,
Myaskovsky 53, Nono 10,
Novák 64, Orff 39, Paderewski
74, Penderecki 1, Petrassi 30,
Pfitzner 65, Pijper 40, Piston
40, Pizzetti 54, Poulenc 35,
Prokofiev 43, Quilter 57,
Rakhmaninov 61, Ravel 59,
Rawsthorne 29, Respighi 55,
Rieti 36, Roussel 65, Rubbra
33, Schmidt 60, Florent
Schmitt 64, Schoenberg 60,
William Schuman 24, Cyril
Scott 55, Searle 19, Seiber 29,
Sessions 38, Shaporin 45,
Shostakovich 28, Sibelius 69,
Skalkottas 30, Ethel Smyth 75,
Somervell 71, Sorabji 42,
Stockhausen 6, Strauss 70,
Stravinsky 52, Suk 60,
Szymanowski 51, Virgil
Thomson 38, Tippett 29,
Tovey 59, Turina 52, Varèse
50, Vaughan Williams 62,
Villa-Lobos 47, Walton 32,
Webern 51, Weill 34, Wellesz
49, Wolf-Ferrari 58, Xenakis
12, Zandonai 51

Appendix B

List of works

The publication of Elgar's works did not always follow directly on their composition. The main date(s) given refer to composition; if the year of publication was much different, it has been given. Nearly all Elgar's completed works were published during his lifetime; those he left unpublished were designedly so. Since his death certain works have been completed and printed; they are listed below. The fifteen volumes of the Elgar Complete Edition (ECE) so far published have in many instances included relevant sketches, drafts, rejected passages and works left incomplete; the volume numbers are listed here. The present catalogue has taken note of the more important fragmentary pieces, but Elgar's habit of beginning a piece and abandoning it after only a few bars has meant that this aspect of the listing could not be complete. Further details can be found in *Edward Elgar: A Guide to Research* by Christopher Kent (Hamden, CT, 1993).

EARLY CHURCH MUSIC

? 1872	*O salutaris hostia*, unacc. chorus; inc., reconstructed by Timothy Hooke
1872	*Litanies* for various occasions, unacc. chorus
1873	Credo on themes from Beethoven Symphonies nos. 5, 7, 9 for chorus, org
1876	*Salve regina*, chorus, org
1876	*Tantum ergo*, chorus, org
1877	Credo in E minor, chorus, org
1878	Hymn tunes in C, G and F major, the last pubd as 'Drake Broughton', no. 151 in *Westminster Hymnal* (1898) and quoted in 'Aubade' of *Nursery Suite* (1931)
1879	*Brother, for thee He Died*, inc. Easter anthem, chorus, org

1879		*Tantum ergo*, chorus, org
1879		*Domine, salvam fac reginam*, chorus, org
1880		Gloria, chorus, org; adapted from the Allegro 2nd movt of Mozart's Violin Sonata in F, κ547
? 1880		*O salutaris hostia* in F, chorus, org
? 1880		*O salutaris hostia* in E flat, chorus, org
1882		*Benedictus sit Deus pater*, chorus, org, str; inc.
1882		*O salutaris hostia* in A, B solo; inc., ed. Percy Young
1886		*Four Litanies for the Blessed Virgin Mary*, unacc. chorus
1887	op. 2 no. 1	*Ave verum corpus*, chorus and org; originally set to the words 'Pie Jesu'
? 1887	op. 2 no. 2	*Ave Maria*, chorus, org
? 1887	op. 2 no. 3	*Ave maris stella*, chorus, org
1888		*Ecce sacerdos magnus*, chorus, org or orch (1893)

ORATORIOS AND OTHER RELIGIOUS WORKS

1895–6	op. 29	*The Light of Life* (E. Capel Cure, on biblical basis), short oratorio, S, C, T, B, SATB chorus, orch (ECE vol. 3)
1900	op. 38	*The Dream of Gerontius* (J. H. Newman), Mez, T, B, semi-chorus, SATB chorus, orch (ECE vol. 6)
1902–3	op. 49	*The Apostles* (Elgar, compiled from biblical texts), oratorio, S, C, T, 3 B, SATB chorus, orch (ECE vol. 8)
1903–6	op. 51	*The Kingdom* (Elgar, compiled from biblical texts and the *Didache*), oratorio, S, C, T, B, SATB chorus, orch (ECE vol. 9)
1906–		*The Last Judgement* (Elgar, to be compiled from biblical texts and perhaps *The City of God* by St Augustine), projected conclusion to the oratorio trilogy; libretto ideas and some musical sketches survive

SACRED CHORAL WORKS

1897	op. 34	*Te Deum and Benedictus*, chorus, org or orch
1902		*O Mightiest of the Mighty*, hymn, chorus, org
1909		*Lo! Christ the Lord is Born* (Wensley), carol, unacc. chorus; adapted from *Grete Malverne on a Rock*, sent as private Christmas card (1897)
1909		Two single chants for the *Venite*
1909		Two double chants for Psalms 68 and 75

1909	op. 56	*Angelus* (Tuscan dialect words translated), unacc. chorus
1910–12	op. 67	*Great is the Lord* (Psalm 48), anthem, SSAATB chorus (with B solo), org or orch (1913)
1911	op. 64	*O Hearken Thou* (from Psalm 5), chorus, org or orch
1914	op. 74	*Give unto the Lord* (Psalm 29), anthem, chorus, org or orch
1914		*Fear not, O Land* (from *Joel* ii), harvest anthem, chorus, org
1928		*I Sing the Birth* (Jonson), carol, unacc. chorus (with A, B, soli)
1929		*Goodmorrow* (G. Gascoigne), carol, unacc. chorus; based on an early hymn tune

SECULAR CHORAL WORKS

1889–92	op. 25	*The Black Knight* (Uhland, trans. Longfellow), symphony, chorus, orch
1895	op. 27	*Scenes from the Bavarian Highlands* (C. A. Elgar, after Bavarian folksongs), 6 choral songs with pf (1895) or orch (1896) acc.
1894–6	op. 30	*Scenes from the Saga of King Olaf* (Longfellow and H. A. Acworth), cantata, S, T, B, SATB chorus, orch
1896–7	op. 33	*The Banner of St George* (Wensley), ballad, chorus, orch
1898	op. 35	*Caractacus* (Acworth), cantata, S, T, Bar, B, chorus, orch; sketch of 1887 begins Scene III (ECE vol. 5)
1902	op. 44	*Coronation Ode* (A. C. Benson), S, C, T, B, chorus, orch; no. 7, 'Land of Hope and Glory', uses trio tune of *Pomp and Circumstance* no. 1 (1901)
1912	op. 69	*The Music Makers* (A. O'Shaughnessy), ode, C, chorus and orch; sketches from 1900 on and quotations from Elgar's earlier works incorporated (ECE vol. 10)
1915–17	op. 80	*The Spirit of England* (Binyon), T or S, chorus, orch; no. 1 quotes from the Demons' chorus in *The Dream of Gerontius* (1900) (ECE vol. 10)
1920–21		*With Proud Thanksgiving* (Binyon), chorus and military or brass band, or orch (1921); reworking of 'For the Fallen', no. 3 of *The Spirit of England* (ECE vol. 10)
1932		*So Many True Princesses* (Masefield), ode for chorus and military band

DRAMATIC MUSIC

1901	op. 42	*Grania and Diarmid* (play by Moore, Yeats); Incidental music, Funeral March, 'There are seven that pull the thread' (S song)
1902		'Rabelais' ballet music; abandoned, but sketches used elsewhere
1912	op. 66	*The Crown of India* (imperial masque by H. Hamilton); Mez (Agra), T (St George), chorus and orch; incorporating many earlier sketches and part of *In Smyrna*; 1a Introduction; 1b Sacred Measure; 2 Dance of Nautch Girls; 2a India greets her Cities; 3 Song (Agra): 'Hail, Immemorial Ind!'; 3a Entrance of Calcutta; 3b Entrance of Delhi; 4a Introduction; 4b March of the Moghul Emperors; 5 Entrance of John Company; 5a Entrance of St George; 6 Song (St George): 'The Rule of England'; 7 Interlude; 8a Introduction; 8b Warriors' Dance; 9 The Cities of Ind; 10 March: The Crown of India; 10a The Homage of Ind; 11 The Crowning of Delhi; 12 'Ave Imperator!'. Suite for orch consisting of nos. 1a, 1b, 2, 5, 8b, 7 4b
1914	op. 75	*Carillon* (Cammaerts), recitation with orch
1915	op. 77	*Une voix dans le désert* (E. Cammaerts), recitation and S Song, 'Quand nos bourgeons se rouvriront', with orch.
1915	op. 78	*The Starlight Express* (play by V. Pearn after A. Blackwood's *A Prisoner in Fairyland*); Incidental music and songs, S (Laugher), Bar (Organ-Grinder), orch; incorporating music from *The Wand of Youth* (1907); 'To the Children', 'The Blue-eyes Fairy', Curfew Song (Orion), 'Laugh a Little Ev'ry Day', 'I'm Everywhere', 'Night Winds', 'Oh Stars, Shine Brightly', 'We shall Meet the Morning Spiders', 'My Old Tunes', 'Dandelions, Daffodils', 'They're all Soft-shiny now', 'Oh, Think Beauty', 'Hearts Must be Soft-shiny Dressed' (duet); 3 Organ-Grinder songs pubd (1916)
1917	op. 81	*The Sanguine Fan* (scenario by I. Lowther), ballet based on a fan design by Charles Conder; unpubd
1917	op. 79	*Le drapeau belge* (Cammaerts), recitation with orch; unpubd
1917		*The Fringes of the Fleet* (Kipling), songs, 4 Bar, orch; 'The Lowestoft Boat', 'Fate's Discourtesy', 'Submarines', 'The Sweepers'; additional song (G. Parker) for 4 Bar, unacc., 'Inside the Bar'

1923		*Arthur* (play in 9 scenes by Binyon); Incidental music, small orch; Suite arr. by A. Barlow
1928		*Beau Brummell* (play in 4 acts by B. Matthews); incidental music; only Minuet pubd
1929–33	op. 89	*The Spanish Lady* (libretto in 2 acts by B. Jackson and Elgar after *The Devil is an Ass* by Jonson); unfinished opera incorporating music sketched over much of Elgar's career and pieces from both *Arthur* and *Beau Brummell*; 2 songs, 'Modest and Fair' and 'Still to be Neat' ed. Percy Young (1955); Suite for str ed. Percy Young (1956); whole material in ECE vol. 41

ACCOMPANIED PARTSONGS

1891	op. 23	*Spanish Serenade*, 'Stars of the Summer Night' (Longfellow), SATB, 2 vns, pf, or orch (1892)
1894	op. 26 no. 1	*The Snow* (C. A. Elgar), SATB, 2 vn, pf/orch (1903)
1894	op. 26 no. 2	*Fly, Singing Bird* (C. A. Elgar), SATB, 2 vns, pf, or orch (1903)
1907	op. 52	*A Christmas Greeting* (C. A. Elgar), 2 S, TB chorus *ad lib*, 2 vn, pf

UNACCOMPANIED PARTSONGS

For SATB unless indicated otherwise

1881		*Why so Pale and Wan*; lost
1889	op. 18 no. 1	*O Happy Eyes* (C. A. Elgar)
1889		*My Love Dwelt in a Northern Land* (A. Lang)
1899		*To her Beneath whose Steadfast Star* (F. W. H. Myers)
1902		*Weary Wind of the West* (T. E. Brown)
1902	op. 45	Five Partsongs from the Greek Anthology, TTBB; 1 *Yea, Cast me from the Heights* (anon., trans. A. Strettell), 2 *Whether I Find thee* (anon., trans. A. Lang), 3 *After many a Dusty Mile* (anon., trans. E. Gosse), 4 *It's oh! to be a Wild Wind* (anon., trans. W. M. Hardinge), 5 *Feasting I Watch* (Marcus Argentarius, trans. R. Garnett)
1905		*Evening Scene* (Patmore)
1907	op. 18 no. 2	*Love* (A. Maquarie)
1907		*How Calmly the Evening* (T. Lynch)
1907	op. 54	*The Reveille* (B. Harte), TTBB
1908	op. 53	Four Choral Songs; 1 *There is Sweet Music* (Tennyson), SSAATTBB, 2 *Deep in my Soul*

		(Byron), 3 *O Wild West Wind* (Shelley), 4 *Owls* (Elgar)
1909	op. 57	Chorus, SAATTB; *Go, Song of Mine* (Cavalcanti, trans. D. G. Rossetti)
1909		Elegy; *They are at Rest* (Newman)
1914	op. 71	Two Choral Songs; 1 *The Shower* (Vaughan), 2 *The Fountain* (Vaughan)
1914	op. 72	Choral Song; *Death on the Hills* (Maykov, trans. R. Newmarch)
1914	op. 73	Two Choral Songs; 1 *Love's Tempest* (Maykov, trans. Newmarch), 2 *Serenade* (Minsky, trans. Newmarch)
1923		*The Wanderer* (anon., adapted by Elgar from *Wit and Drollery*, 1661), TTBB
1923		*Zut! Zut! Zut!* (Richard Mardon, pseud. for Elgar), TTBB
1924		*A Song of Union* (A. Noyes), from the *Pageant of Empire*
1925		*The Herald* (A. Smith), TTBB
1925		*The Prince of Sleep* (de la Mare)

UNISON AND CHILDREN'S SONGS

1907	*Marching Song* (W. de Courcy Stretton) reissued as *Follow the Colours* (1914), male voices, TB chorus; also SATB
1914	*The Birthright* (G. A. Stocks), boys' chorus, bugles, drums; also SATB
? 1914	*The Merry-go-round* (F. C. Fox), unison chorus
? 1914	*The Brook* (E. Soule), 2-part choir
? 1914	*The Windlass* (W. Allingham), SATB
1918	*Big Steamers* (Kipling), unison chorus
1922	*The Ballad of Brave Hector* (E. Anderson), song with unison chorus; inc.
1922	*The Worcestershire Squire* (E. Anderson), song with unison chorus; inc.
1924	*The Bull (in May Week)* (F. Hamilton), male voice, optional chorus, pf
1924	*The Heart of Canada* (A. Noyes), from the *Pageant of Empire*; song with unison chorus
1932	*The Rapid Stream* (C. Mackay), unison children's chorus
1932	*The Woodland Stream* (Mackay), unison children's chorus
1932	*When Swallows Fly* (Mackay), unison children's chorus

SONGS WITH ORCHESTRA

1899	op. 37	*Sea Pictures*, C, orch; 1 'Sea Slumber Song' (R. Noel), 2 'In Haven (Capri)' (C. A. Elgar), 3 'Sabbath Morning at Sea' (E. B. Browning), 4 'Where Corals Lie' (R. Garnett), 5 'The Swimmer' (A. L. Gordon); no. 2 is a revision of *Love Alone Will Stay* (1897) and the music may be as early as 1889
1901	op. 42	'There are Seven that Pull the Thread' (Yeats), from *Grania and Diarmid*, S, small orch
1902		'Land of Hope and Glory' (Benson), from *Coronation Ode*, C, chorus and orch, with carillon *ad lib* (1927)
1908	op. 48	*Pleading* (A. L. Salmon)
1909–10	op. 59	Song Cycle (G. Parker); 1 *Oh, Soft was the Song*, 3 *Was it some Golden Star?*, 6 *Twilight*; Elgar also intended to set 'Proem', 'The Waking' and 'There is an Orchard' but proceeded no further than a few sketches
1909	op. 60 no. 1	*The Torch* (Elgar as 'Pietro d'Alba'); orchd 1912
1910	op. 60 no. 2	*The River* (Elgar as 'Pietro d'Alba'); orchd 1912; Elgar planned two further songs for op. 60, *The Shrine* and *The Bee*, but these were not composed

SONGS WITH PIANO

1872		*The Language of Flowers* (J. G. Percival); unpubd
1870s		*The Self-banished* (E. Waller); unpubd
1878		*If she Love me* ('R.C.G.'); inc. acc.; unpubd
1884		*A Soldier's Song* (C. F. Hayward); pubd 1890; reissued 1903 as *A War Song*
? 1885		*A Phylactery* (J. Hay); inc. but later considered for *The Spanish Lady*
1885	op. 16 no. 2	*Through the long Days* (J. Hay); pubd 1887
1886		*Is she not Passing Fair?* (Duc d'Orléans, trans. L. S. Costello); pubd 1908
? 1887		*A Song of Autumn* (A. L. Gordon); pubd 1892
1887		*As I Laye a-thynkynge* (R. H. Barham, as 'Thomas Ingoldsby'); pubd 1888
1887		*Roundel* (Swinburne); unpubd
1888		*The Wind at Dawn* (C. A. Roberts); pubd 1888; orchestrated 1912
1887		*Queen Mary's Song* (Tennyson); pubd 1889
1892		*Like to the Damask Rose* (S. Wastell); pubd 1893

443

1892		*The Poet's Life* (E. Burroughs); pubd 1907
1892	op. 16 no. 1	*The Shepherd's Song* (B. Pain); pubd 1895
1894	op. 16 no. 3	*Rondel* (Froissart, trans. Longfellow); pubd 1896
1895	op. 31 no. 1	*After* (P. B. Marston); pubd 1900
1895	op. 31 no. 2	*A Song of Flight* (C. Rossetti); pubd 1900
1897		Lute Song, *Love Alone will stay* (C. A. Elgar); pubd 1897; rev. as no. 2 of *Sea Pictures*
1899		*Dry those Fair, those Crystal Eyes* (H. King)
1900		*The Pipes of Pan* (A. Ross)
1901		*Come, Gentle Night* (C. Bingham)
1901		*Always and Everywhere* (Krasiński, trans. F. E. Fortey)
1902	op. 41 no. 1	*In the Dawn* (A. C. Benson)
1902	op. 41 no. 2	*Speak, Music* (Benson)
1903–4		*Speak, my Heart* (Benson)
1904		*In Moonlight* (Shelley); arr. of 'Canto popolare' from *In the South*
1908	op. 48	*Pleading* (A. L. Salmon); orchd 1908
1909		*A Child Asleep* (E. B. Browning)
1909		*The King's Way* (C. A. Elgar); adaptation of the trio tune from *Pomp and Circumstance* no. 4; alternative words later provided by A. Noyes and A. P. Herbert
1914		*Arabian Serenade* (M. Lawrence)
1914		*The Chariots of the Lord* (J. Brownlie)
1914		*Soldier's Song* (H. Begbie); unpubd and suppressed
1916		*Fight for Right* (W. Morris)
1917		*Ozymandias* (Shelley); inc. song for Mez, earlier version for B (?1905)
1924		Songs from *Pageant of Empire* (A. Noyes); 1 'Shakespeare's Kingdom', 2 'The Islands', 3 'The Blue Mountains', 4 'Sailing Westward', 5 'Merchant Adventurers', 6 'The Immortal Legions'; *see also* UNACCOMPANIED PARTSONGS and UNISON AND CHILDREN'S SONGS
1930		*It isnae me* (S. Holmes)

ORCHESTRAL WORKS

1883		*The Lakes*, overture; unfinished; lost
1885		*Scotish Overture*; unfinished; lost
1890	op. 19	*Froissart*, overture
1890		Violin Concerto; destroyed
1896–7	op. 32	*Imperial March*
1898–9	op. 36	Variations on an Original Theme ('Enigma') (ECE vol. 27)

1901	op. 39	*Pomp and Circumstance Marches*: no. 1 in D major (see also *Coronation Ode* and 'Land of Hope and Glory'); no. 2 in A minor
1901	op. 40	*Cockaigne (In London Town)*, concert overture
1901–		*Cockaigne* overture no. 2 ('City of Dreadful Night'); projected
1903–4	op. 50	*In the South (Alassio)*, concert overture
1904	op. 39	*Pomp and Circumstance March* no. 3 in C minor
1907	op. 39	*Pomp and Circumstance March* no. 4 in G major; see also *The King's Way*
1907–8	op. 55	Symphony no. 1 in A flat (ECE vol. 30)
1909–10	op. 61	Violin Concerto in B minor (ECE vol. 32)
1909–11	op. 63	Symphony no. 2 in E flat (ECE vol. 31)
1911	op. 65	*Coronation March*; incorporating sketches from the proposed 'Rabelais' ballet (1902)
1913	op. 68	*Falstaff*, symphonic study in C minor with 2 interludes in A minor; sketches from 1901 (ECE vol. 33)
1918–19	op. 85	Cello Concerto in E minor (ECE vol. 32)
1924		*Empire March*; see also *Pageant of Empire*
1930	op. 39	*Pomp and Circumstance March* no. 5 in C major
1932–3	op. 88	Symphony no. 3 in C minor; unfinished; some sketches pubd in Reed (1936) and Anderson (1990); material incorporated from *The Last Judgement*, *Callicles*, *Arden*, *Arthur*
1914–	op. 90	Piano Concerto; projected; sketches transferred to *The Spanish Lady*; Poco Andante completed, pf, str (1950)

SMALLER ORCHESTRAL

1879–84	Dances for Worcester City and County Pauper Lunatic Asylum; 3 sets of 5 quadrilles: *La brunette*, Die junge Kokette, *L'Assomoir* (1879); 5 quadrilles: *Paris* (1880); 5 lancers: *The Valentine*; 5 polkas: *Maud*, *Nellie*, *La blonde*, *Helcia*, *Blumine* (1880–84); no. 5 of *L'Assomoir* set used for 'Wild Bears' in *Wand of Youth* suite no. 2
1881	*Air de ballet*; unpubd
1881	*Pas redoublé*, Marches nos. 1 and 2; unpubd; no. 2 used as finale of Suite in D and considered later for *The Spanish Lady*
1882	*Air de ballet*; unpubd
1882–4	Suite in D; Mazurka, Intermezzo–*Sérénade mauresque*, Fantasia gavotte, March–*Pas redoublé*; nos.

		1–3 rev. for *Three Characteristic Pieces* op. 10 (1899)
1884	op. 7	*Sevillana*
1889	op. 12	*Salut d'amour*; arr. of vn piece (1889)
1894	op. 11	*Sursum corda*, str, brass, org and timp; incorporates sketch for vn sonata (1887)
1897	op. 21	Minuet; arr. of pf piece (1897)
1897		*Three Bavarian Dances*; arr. of nos. 1, 3 and 6 of *Scenes from the Bavarian Highlands* (1895)
1899	op. 10	*Three Characteristic Pieces*; 1 Mazurka, 2 *Sérénade mauresque*, 3 Contrasts: The Gavotte A.D. 1700 and 1900
1899	op. 15 no. 1	*Chanson de nuit*; arr. of vn and pf piece (1897)
1899	op. 15 no. 2	*Chanson de matin*; arr. of vn and pf piece (1899)
1900		*Sérénade lyrique*
1902	op. 43	*Dream Children*, 2 pieces after Lamb (ECE vol. 25)
1907	op. 1A	*Wand of Youth* suite no. 1; 1 Overture; 2 Serenade, 3 Minuet, 4 Sun Dance, 5 Fairy Pipers, 6 Slumber Scene, 7 Fairies and Giants; incorporates music written for a childhood play; the initial idea of no. 7 is based on 'Humoreske a tune from Broadheath 1867'; see also *The Starlight Express* (1915)
1907	op. 1B	*Wand of Youth* suite no. 2; 1 March, 2 The Little Bells, 3 Moths and Butterflies, 4 Fountain Dance, 5 The Tame Bear, 6 Wild Bears; source for some numbers as above and *L'Assomoir* quadrille for Powick Asylum; see also *The Starlight Express* (1915) (both suites ECE vol. 25)
1910	op. 62	*Romance* in D minor, bn and orch
1912	op. 66	Suite from *The Crown of India*; nos. 1a, 1b, 2, 5, 8b, 7, 4b of the Imperial Masque (1912)
1912	op. 3	*Cantique*; arr. of Andante arioso from 'Shed' 6 (1879)
1913		*Carissima* for small orch
1915		*Rosemary*; arr. of Trio from pf trio Menuetto (1882)
1915	op. 76	*Polonia*, symphonic prelude (ECE vol. 33)
1927		*Civic Fanfare*; pubd 1991
1928		*May Song*; arr. of pf piece (1901)
1928		Minuet from *Beau Brummell* music
1930	op. 87	*Severn Suite* for brass band (Elgar's scoring revd by H. Geehl; 1 Introduction (Worcester Castle), 2 Toccata (Tournament), 3 Fugue (Cathedral), 4 Minuet (Commandery), 5 Coda; titles added when scored by Elgar for full orch (1932); Fugue orig-

inally composed for pf (1923); Minuet adapted
from *Harmony Music* no. 5 (1879) and *Promenade*
no. 5 (1878); arr. as Organ Sonata no. 2 op. 87A
by I. Atkins

1930	*Nursery Suite*; 1 Aubade (including 'Drake's Broughton' hymn tune of 1878), 2 The Serious Doll, 3 Busy-ness, 4 The Sad Doll, 5 The Wagon passes, 6 The Merry Doll, 7 Dreaming – Envoy
1930	*Soliloquy*, ob; orchd by G. Jacob (1967)
1933	*Mina* for small orch

STRING ORCHESTRA

1888		3 pieces; unpubd, lost; possibly rev. for op. 20
1892	op. 20	Serenade in E minor
1904–5	op. 47	Introduction and Allegro, str qt and str orch; incorporates sketches from 1901
1909	op. 58	*Elegy*
1914	op. 70	*Sospiri*, str, harp, org

CHAMBER MUSIC

1877	*Peckham March*, wind qnt; unpubd
? 1877	2 variations on *Adeste fideles*, fl, str qt; unpubd
? 1877	Andante and Allegro, ob, str qt; inc.; unpubd
1878	String Quartet in B flat; inc. (ECE vol. 38)
1878	String Quartet in A minor; inc. (ECE vol. 38)
1878	String Quartet in D minor; inc.; opening proposed for *The Spanish Lady* Act 2 (ECE vols. 38 and 41)
1878	String Quartet in D major; inc. (ECE vol. 38)
1878	String Trio in C, 2 vn, vc; inc.; material incorporated in *Harmony Music* 4 (ECE vol. 38)
1878	*Harmony Music* nos. 1–4, wind qnt; pubd 1976
1878	*Promenades 1–6*, wind qnt; pubd 1976; no. 5 incorporated in Minuet of *Severn Suite* (1930)
1878	Andante con variazioni ('Evesham Andante'), wind qnt; pubd 1977
1878	Adagio cantabile ('Mrs Winslow's Soothing Syrup'), wind qnt; pubd 1977
? 1878	Andante and Allegro, ob, str qt; inc.; unpubd
? 1878	2 trios, 2 vn, pf; inc. (ECE vol. 38)
1879	String Quartet in G major; inc.; material incorporated in *Harmony Music* 7 (1881) (ECE vol. 38)
1879	Intermezzos 1–5, wind qnt; pubd 1977
1879	Four Dances, wind qnt; Menuetto, Gavotte ('The Alphonsa'), Sarabande, Giga; the last 3 movts were considered for *The Spanish Lady*; pubd 1977

1879		*Harmony Music* no. 5 ('The Mission'), wind qnt; pubd 1977
1879		*Harmony Music* no. 6, wind qnt; Andante arioso rev. for 1912 *Cantique* op. 3; unpubd
1880		String Quartet fragment, E minor (ECE vol. 38)
? 1880		String Quartet fragments, E minor, A minor (ECE vol. 38)
1881		*Harmony Music* no. 7, wind qnt; including music from String Quartet in G (1879); unpubd
1882		Menuetto and Trio, pf trio; Trio transcribed as *Douce pensée*, pf (1882) and scored for small orch as *Rosemary* (1915)
1883		Fugue in D minor, ob, vn; unpubd
1886		Piano Trio in D minor; inc. (ECE vol. 38)
1887	op. 8	String Quartet; destroyed
1887		Duet, trbn, db; pubd 1970
? 1888		String Quartet in D minor; inc.; Intermezzo 3rd movt completed for no. 3 of *Vesper Voluntaries* op. 14
? 1880s		2 fragments, str trio (ECE vol. 38)
1907		Andantino, vn, mandoline, gui; inc. (ECE vol. 38)
1907		String Quartet fragments; material incorporated in Symphony no. 1 and *The Music Makers* (ECE vol. 38)
1918	op. 83	String Quartet in E minor (ECE vol. 38)
1918–19	op. 84	Piano Quintet in A minor (ECE vol. 38)
1924		March, pf trio (arr. of *Empire March*); unpubd

VIOLIN MUSIC

1877		*Reminiscences*, vn, pf; unpubd
1877		Study for Strengthening the Third Finger; recopied for Jascha Heifetz (1920); facsimile in the *Daily Telegraph* of 24 Dec 1920
1878		Fantasia, vn, pf; inc.
1878		*Etude caprice*, unacc. vn; unpubd
1878	op. 1	*Romance*, vn, pf; pubd 1885
1878		Sonata in C, vn, pf; inc.
1879		Two Polonaises, vn, pf, in F major and D minor; inc.; the F major became a 'Bolero' for *The Spanish Lady* (ECE vol. 41)
1879		Second Study, unacc. vn; unpubd
1879		Fantasia on Irish Airs, vn, pf; inc.
1884	op. 4 no. 1	*Une Idylle*, vn, pf; pubd 1885
? 1884	op. 4 no. 2	*Pastourelle*, vn, pf; pubd ? 1887
1885		Gavotte, vn, pf; pubd 1886

1885		Allegretto on GEDGE, vn, pf; pubd 1889
1887	op. 9	Violin Sonata; destroyed; material incorporated in *Sursum corda* op. 11 (1894)
1888	op. 12	*Salut d'amour* (Liebesgrüss), vn, pf; also pf, small orch; pubd 1889
1889	op. 13 no. 1	*Mot d'amour* (Liebesahnung), vn, pf; pubd 1890
1889	op. 13 no. 2	*Bizarrerie*, vn, pf; pubd 1890
? 1880s	op. 24	*Etudes caractéristiques pour violon seul*; pubd 1892
1890	op. 4 no. 3	*Virelai*, vn, pf; pubd 1890
1891	op. 17	*La capricieuse*, vn, pf; pubd 1893
1892	op. 22	*Very Easy Melodious Exercises in the First Position*, vn, pf; pubd 1892
1893		*Offertoire* (Andante Religioso), vn, pf; pubd under name of 'Gustav Franke' in 1903
1897	op. 5 no. 1	*Chanson de nuit*, vn, pf; orchd 1899
1897–9	op. 15 no. 2	*Chanson de matin*, vn, pf; orchd 1899
1901		*May Song*, vn, pf; originally pf
1918	op. 82	Sonata in E minor, vn, pf

PIANO MUSIC

1872		*Chantant*; unpubd
1879		Hungarian (Melody); unpubd
1882		*Douce pensée*; transcription of pf trio movt (1882); orchd as *Rosemary* (1915); unpubd
1884		*Griffinesque*; pubd 1981
1886		'Enina' Waltz; unpubd
1889		Sonatina; rev. (1931) for publication (1932)
1889		Presto; pubd 1981
1897		Minuet; pubd 1897; orchd as op. 21 and pubd 1899
1901		*May Song*; also vn, pf; orchd 1928
1901		*Skizze*; pubd 1976
1901	op. 46	Concert Allegro; pubd 1973
1905		*In Smyrna*: pubd 1905
1917		Echo's Dance, from *The Sanguine Fan*; pubd 1917
1932		*Serenade*; pubd 1932
1932		*Adieu*; pubd 1932

ORGAN MUSIC

1870s		Fugue in G minor; inc.; pubd 1916 (ECE vol. 36)
1870s		Fugue in C minor; inc. (ECE vol. 36)
? 1879		Organ Concerto in D minor; inc. (ECE vol. 36)
? 1881		Fragment in F (ECE vol. 36)
1889	op. 14	*Vesper Voluntaries*; pubd 1891 (ECE vol. 36)

? 1894		*Pastorale*; inc. (ECE vol. 36)
1895	op. 28	Sonata no. 1 in G major; pubd 1896 (ECE vol. 36)
1904		Cadenza for C. H. Lloyd's Organ Concerto in F minor (ECE vol. 36)
1906		*For Dot's Nuns* (ECE vol. 36)
1912	op. 3 no. 1	*Cantique*; rev. of Andante arioso from *Harmony Music* 6 (1879); other versions for small orch and pf; pubd 1913 (ECE vol. 36)
1923		Loughborough Memorial Chime arr. for org; inc. (ECE vol. 36)
1923		Fugue in C minor; originally for pf; incorporated in *Severn Suite* (1930); pubd 1932 (ECE vol. 36)
? 1920s		Sonata and Toccata fragments; considered for *The Spanish Lady* and the sonata for Symphony no. 3 (ECE vols 36, 41)
1933	op. 87A	Sonata no. 2 in B flat; arr. Ivor Atkins from *Severn Suite*; pubd 1933 (ECE vol. 36)

CARILLON

| 1923 | *Memorial Chime*, Loughborough War Memorial Carillon; cyclostyled by Societas Campanariorum (USA) |
| 1927 | Obbligato for 'Land of Hope and Glory'; unpubd |

FULL ORCHESTRAL TRANSCRIPTIONS

1921–2	op. 86	Bach, Fantasia and Fugue in C minor BWV537
1923		Handel, Overture in D minor from Chandos Anthem no. 2
1933		Chopin, Funeral March from Piano Sonata in B flat minor

ORCHESTRATIONS OF VOCAL WORKS BY OTHER COMPOSERS
All for chorus and orchestra unless indicated otherwise

1901	A. H. Brewer, *Emmaus*
1902	*God Save the King*, S, chorus, orch
1922	Parry, *Jerusalem*
1923	Battishill, *O Lord, Look down from Heaven*
1923	S. S. Wesley, *Let us Lift up our Hearts*
1929	Purcell, *Jehova, quam multi sunt hostes mei*

ARRANGEMENTS

? 1880	Schumann, Scherzo from Overture, Scherzo and Finale op. 52, pf; unpubd
1883	Wagner, Entry of the Minstrels from *Tannhäuser* Act 2, pf; unpubd
1886	G. F. Blackbourne, *Berceuse*, under the pseudonym 'Victor Berard'
1890	*Clapham Town End*, folksong, 1 voice, pf
1894	Wagner, Good Friday Music from *Parsifal*, small orch; unpubd
1911	Bach, Two Chorales from the *St Matthew Passion*, brass; unpubd

EDITION

1911	Bach, *St Matthew Passion* VS in collaboration with I. Atkins

RECORDINGS CONDUCTED BY ELGAR
Acoustic recordings

1914	*Carissima; Pomp and Circumstance Marches* nos. 1 and 4; *Salut d'amour; Bavarian Dances* nos. 2 and 3
1915	*Carillon*
1916	*The Starlight Express* songs; Violin Concerto (much cut)
1917	*Bavarian Dance* no. 1; *Cockaigne* (abridged); *The Dream of Gerontius*: Prelude and Angel's Farewell; *Wand of Youth* suite no. 2: The Tame Bear, Wild Bears; *Fringes of the Fleet*
1919	*Polonia* (cut); *Chanson de nuit; Wand of Youth* suite no. 1: Overture, Serenade, Sun Dance, Fairy Pipers, Fairies and Giants; *Wand of Youth* suite no. 2: March, Little Bells, Moths and Butterflies
1919–20	Cello Concerto (cut)
1920	*The Sanguine Fan* selection
1920–21	'Enigma' Variations
1921	Bach–Elgar Fugue in C minor; *King Olaf*: 'A Little Bird in the Air', orch
1921–3	*In the South* (abridged)
1922–3	*Sea Pictures*
1923	Handel–Elgar Overture in D minor; Bach–Elgar Fantasia in C minor
1924–5	Symphony no. 2
1925	*The Light of Life*: 'Meditation'

451

Electrical recordings

1926	*Cockaigne; Pomp and Circumstance Marches* nos. 1 and 2; *Chanson de nuit;* 'Enigma' Variations; Bach–Elgar Fantasia and Fugue in C minor; *The Light of Life*: 'Meditation'
1927	*The Dream of Gerontius* (excerpts); Symphony no. 2, including Elgar speaking at rehearsal; *Pomp and Circumstance Marches* nos. 3 and 4; *Bavarian Dances* nos. 1 and 2; *Civic Fanfare; The Music Makers* (excerpts)
1928	*God Save the King* and *O God our Help in Ages Past* (arr. Elgar); *The Banner of St George*: 'It comes from the misty Ages'; 'Land of Hope and Glory'; Cello Concerto; *Wand of Youth* suites nos. 1 and 2; *Beau Brummell*: Minuet
1929	Five Improvisations by Elgar at the piano; *Sérénade lyrique; Rosemary; May Song; Carissima; Falstaff*: Two Interludes; Minuet op. 21; Mazurka from *Three Characteristic Pieces; Salut d'amour*
1930	*Crown of India* Suite; *In the South; Pomp and Circumstance March* no. 5; Symphony no. 1
1931	*Nursery Suite;* 'Land of Hope and Glory' introduced by Elgar and filmed for Pathé News
1931–2	*Falstaff*
1932	*Bavarian Dance* no. 3; *Severn Suite;* Violin Concerto; *Pomp and Circumstance Marches* nos. 1 and 2
1933	*Froissart;* Contrasts: Gavotte from *Three Characteristic Pieces; Cockaigne; Pomp and Circumstance March* no. 4; *The Kingdom*: Prelude; Serenade for Strings; *Elegy*

Supervised by Elgar from his deathbed

1934	*Caractacus*: Woodland Interlude, Triumphal March; *Dream Children; Mina*

WRITINGS

1898–1903	Programme notes for Worcestershire Philharmonic Society
1899	Notes for programme at fp of 'Enigma' Variations; repr. in Powell, *Memories of a Variation*, p. 121
1904	Preface to D. ffrangcon-Davies, *The Singing of the Future* (1906)
1905	Notes for programme at fp of the Introduction

	and Allegro; repr. in Powell, *Memories of a Variation*, p. 68
1908	Programme note for fp of *Wand of Youth* suite no. 2
1913	'Falstaff', *MT*, liv (1913), p. 575, analytical essay; repr. separately (1932)
1919	'A Poet as Critic', letter to the *Daily Telegraph* (12 April 1919)
1919	'Gray, Walpole, West and Ashton, the Quadruple Alliance', letter to *TLS* (4 September 1919); repr. in Young, *Letters of Edward Elgar*, p. 253
1920	Preface to H. E. Button, *System in Musical Notation* (1920); repr. as 'Musical Notation', *MT*, lxi (1920), p. 513
1920	Letter on Parry in reply to Shaw, *ML*, i (1920), p. 165, repr. in Redwood, *An Elgar Companion*, p. 250
1921	'Scott and Shakespeare', letter to *TLS* (21 July 1921); repr. in Young, *Letters of Edward Elgar*, p. 270.
1922	'Swift in Bury Street', letter to *TLS* (10 August 1922)
1923	'Poluphloisboisterous', letter to *TLS* (2 August 1923)
1924	'The Vernal Anemones: a beautiful native', communication to *The Times* (28 April 1924), partially repr. in J. N. Moore, *Edward Elgar: a Creative Life*, p. 569
1925	'A Frisk', letter to *TLS* (6 August 1925)
? 1927	*My Friends Pictured Within*, notes for pianola rolls of the 'Enigma' Variations
1929	*The Wand of Youth: a Note by the Composer* for gramophone records of the two suites in HMV Album 80, repr. from draft, with minor differences, in Moore, *Elgar on Record*, p. 93
1930	Foreword to H. A. Leicester, *Forgotten Worcester* (1930); repr. in Young, *Letters of Edward Elgar*, p. 303
1932	'A Christmas Fable' ('God made a Puppy'); repr. in Young, *Letters of Edward Elgar*, p. 313
1933	'A Visit to Delius', communication to the *Daily Telegraph* (1 July 1933)

Elgar

Lectures

1905–6   Birmingham University lectures delivered by Elgar
                                as professor of music, ed. Young, *A Future for
                                English Music and other Lectures* (1968)

Speeches

1921   Speech delivered at the opening of The Gramo-
                                phone Company's new premises at 363–7 Oxford
                                Street on 20 July 1921; repr. in Moore, *Elgar on
                                Record*, p. 38
1927   Speech at the Gramophone Company's reception
                                for demonstration of the Electrical Reproducer on
                                16 November 1927; repr. in Moore, *Elgar on
                                Record*, p. 77
1929   Speech at the opening of a Shaw exhibition at the
                                Malvern Festival on 17 August 1929, repr. in
                                Young, 'Elgar and the Irish Dramatists' in *Edward
                                Elgar: Music and Literature*, ed. Raymond Monk,
                                pp. 136–8

Appendix C
Personalia

Atkins, Ivor Algernon (1869–1953) was organist and master of the choristers at Worcester Cathedral 1897–1950. He first met Elgar at the première of *Froissart* in 1890 when assistant to G. R. Sinclair at Hereford Cathedral. As conductor of the Worcester Three Choirs Festivals from 1899, he was responsible for many Elgar performances, and the lively correspondence of the two men witnesses to his unfailing support. In 1905 Elgar compiled a libretto for his *Hymn of Faith*.

Baker, William Meath (1858–1935) was an energetic Alpine climber and squire of Hasfield, Gloucestershire. He came to know Elgar through Alice Roberts, and the Elgars were later frequent guests at Hasfield Court. 'W.M.B.' in the 'Enigma' Variations deals with an aspect of his hospitality. His three sons, William George Corbet (1885–1947), Francis Ralph (1886–1940) and Edward John (*b.* 1887), were responsible for Elgar's 'Nanty Ewart' persona.

Bantock, Granville (1868–1946), the composer, conductor and educator, became musical director at the Tower, New Brighton in 1897. An advocate for new English music, he performed much Elgar. Principal of the Birmingham and Midland Institute School of Music from 1900, he was largely instrumental in securing Elgar as the first Peyton Professor of Music in the University of Birmingham. Bantock succeeded to the post on Elgar's resignation in 1908.

Bennett, Joseph (1831–1911) was the main music critic of the *Daily Telegraph* from 1874. Strongly suspicious of Wagner, he was generous in his attitude to the emerging Elgar. A successful compiler of librettos for such works as Sullivan's *The Golden Legend*, Mackenzie's *The Dream of Jubal*, *Ruth* by Cowen and the *Emmaus* of Brewer, he was approached by Elgar on the subject of St Augustine. Nothing came of the request.

Benson, Arthur Christopher (1862–1925) was the second son of Edward Benson, Archbishop of Canterbury. An assistant master at Eton, later Fellow and Master of Magdalene College, Cambridge, he wrote biographies of his father and brother Hugh and edited Queen Victoria's correspondence. He collaborated with Elgar on the *Coronation Ode* and provided the words for three songs.

Binyon, Laurence (1869–1943) was an art historian in the Department of Prints and Drawings at the British Museum, where he began as assistant to Sidney Colvin. His special interests were English watercolourists and the art of the Far East. In *The Spirit of England* Elgar set three of his poems written at the outbreak of the First World War. He tried to interest Elgar in various opera subjects and eventually persuaded him to write incidental music for his tragedy, *Arthur*.

Blackwood, Algernon (1863–1947) was for a time a journalist in New York. Author of adventure and ghost stories, he wrote also the semi-mystical *A Prisoner in Fairyland*. This provided the basis of *The Starlight Express*, which led to a close friendship with the Elgars.

Blair, Hugh (1864–1932) was assistant organist at Worcester Cathedral 1886–95 and succeeded William Done as organist in 1895. He played a large part in bringing to performance Elgar's *The Black Knight*, *Sursum corda*, the op. 28 Organ Sonata and *The Light of Life*. He resigned his post in 1897 and became organist of Holy Trinity, Marylebone.

Blake, Carice Irene Elgar (1890–1970) was the only child of Edward and Alice Elgar. She was sent away early to boarding school so that Elgar should have the requisite calm at home. During the First World War she worked in the Censorship Department and after Lady Elgar's death remained as companion to her father until her marriage to the Surrey farmer Samuel Blake in 1921. She was largely responsible for the layout of the Birthplace Museum at Broadheath and for its early administration.

Bliss, Arthur (1891–1975) first visited Severn House during the First World War on leave from army service in France. Lady Elgar heard a string quartet of his and admired it. Elgar brought about a Three Choirs commission for 1922 that resulted in *A Colour Symphony*. Bliss's later music was alien to Elgar, but a period of estrangement came to an end when Bliss dedicated the 1928 *Pastoral* to him.

Boult, Adrian Cedric (1889–1983) became a well-established Elgar conductor. He had the advantage of being able to discuss with Elgar interpretation of his works, but his temperament had none of the composer's electricity. In 1930 Boult became director of music at the BBC and was closely involved in the broadcast concerts celebrating Elgar's seventy-fifth birthday.

Brewer, Alfred Herbert (1865–1928) was a chorister at Gloucester Cathedral and became organist there in 1896. As a Three Choirs conductor, he was prepared to programme many modern works. In 1901 Elgar came to his assistance by scoring his short oratorio *Emmaus*; in his turn Brewer made a number of arrangements for organ of Elgar works.

Buck, Charles William (1851–1932) met Elgar in 1882 at the Worcester meeting of the British Medical Association. A doctor in medical practice at Giggleswick, Yorkshire, Buck was a keen amateur musician and recognized Elgar's gifts at once. His home offered hospitality and chamber music in Elgar's bachelor days, and during the 1880s he became an important confidant by correspondence. Buck was at Elgar's wedding in 1889, and they exchanged letters again in the year of Buck's death.

Buckley, Robert J. was Elgar's first biographer (*Sir Edward Elgar*, 1904). A Birmingham critic, Buckley was an early Elgarian, writing generously about *The Black Knight* and preparing for the biography with a number of published interviews. At the time of the première he saw little future for *The Dream of Gerontius*.

Burley, Rosa Campbell (1866–1951) was headmistress of The Mount, Malvern, where Elgar taught the violin. She became a cycling companion of Elgar's and Carice attended her school. More than once she shared a holiday with the Elgars, and her memoir of the composer, published in 1972, has a certain tartness mixed with acute observation and undoubted shrewdness.

Buths, Julius (1851–1920) was a German conductor, composer and pianist who became musical director at Düsseldorf in 1890. The appointment involved responsibility for the Lower Rhine Music Festivals, at which he championed such composers as Mahler, Strauss, Delius and Debussy. After attending the first performance of *The Dream of Gerontius*, he translated it into German and performed it twice in Düsseldorf to considerable acclaim. He also translated *The Apostles* and *The Kingdom*.

Cammaerts, Emile (1878–1953), the Belgian poet and writer, settled in England at the age of thirty. He married Tita Brand, daughter of Marie Brema, the first Angel in *Gerontius*. He translated Ruskin and Chesterton into French, and during the First World War became the authentic voice for suffering Belgium. Elgar used three of his poems for the wartime recitations, *Carillon*, *Une voix dans le désert* and *Le drapeau belge*.

Capel Cure, Edward (1860–1949) was an amateur cellist and composer, who became friendly with the Fitton family in Malvern and married Hilda in 1919. A curate in Worcester, he was later vicar of Bradninch in Devon and Stour Provost in Dorset. He provided Elgar with the libretto of *The Light of Life* and was also consulted about the text for *The Apostles*.

Cohen, Harriet (1895–1967) first met Elgar when a young girl in Hampstead. Her specialities as a pianist were Bach and Arnold Bax, but she recorded the Elgar Quintet in 1933. He envisaged her as protagonist for the piano concerto he never completed, and she gave the first performance in 1956 of its slow movement as published by Percy Young.

Colvin, Frances (1839–1924) married Sidney Colvin, her second husband, in 1903. She was a close friend of Robert Louis Stevenson, who called her 'Madonna' in their correspondence. She was the first among Elgar's friends to hear that Pietro d'Alba had died. The Colvins received the dedication of the Cello Concerto.

Colvin, Sidney (1845–1927) was a Fellow of Trinity College, Cambridge, Director of the Fitzwilliam Museum and Keeper of Prints and Drawings at the British Museum 1884–1912. He published lives of W. S. Landor and Keats, edited the works of Stevenson and his letters. He hoped to engineer an operatic collaboration between Thomas Hardy and Elgar. As president of the Literary Society, he secured Elgar's election in 1920.

Davies, Henry Walford (1869–1941) was a pupil of both Parry and Stanford. Elgar influenced the choice of his work *The Temple* for the Worcester Three Choirs Festival of 1902. Organist of the Temple Church for twenty years, he became professor of music at the University of Wales, was well known as a successful broadcaster, and succeeded Elgar as Master of the King's Musick.

De Navarro, Antonio (1860–1932) first studied law, then music with Massenet. He married Mary Anderson in 1890, and they settled in Broadway, Worcestershire, where they entertained many musicians and literary figures. Elgar consulted de Navarro about the Spanish inscription for the Violin Concerto.

De Navarro, Mary Anderson (1859–1940) was born in California and had an early stage career in America and England. Tennyson expressed admiration for her, but she settled for married life in the Cotswolds. The construction of a fine music room with two pianos and organ provided a grand setting for the entertainment of musical guests such as Elgar. In her book, *A Few More Memories*, she wrote her impressions of Elgar.

Elgar, Ann Greening (1822–1902), the composer's mother, was the daughter of a Gloucestershire farm labourer who moved to Herefordshire. She married William Henry Elgar on 19 January 1848 and Elgar was her fourth child. A keen reader and of wide interests, she was an important influence on Elgar's early years. A convert to Roman Catholicism, she was perhaps partly responsible for this aspect of Elgar's alienation from the society in which he grew up.

Elgar, Caroline Alice Roberts (1848–1920) was born in India, daughter of a distinguished army officer, Major-General Sir Henry Gee Roberts, who retired to Hazeldine House, Redmarley d'Abitot. She developed literary, musical and geological interests, marrying Elgar in 1889 despite implacable family opposition. Elgar was a Catholic, his father was in trade, and his prospects as a musician seemed as poor as his health. Her support for Elgar was such that he produced his first major work, *Froissart* a year after his marriage and his final masterpiece, the Cello Concerto, not long before her death. Her diaries are a day-to-day record of the background to Elgar's creative achievement.

Elgar, Helen Agnes (1864–1939) was Elgar's youngest sister, known as Dot. Until her mother's death in 1903, she tended her parents. She then became a Dominican nun at the Convent of St Rose, Stroud, Gloucestershire. As Sister Mary Reginald, she was eventually to become Mother General of the English Dominicans. Elgar wrote a tiny organ piece, 'For Dot's Nuns', in 1906.

Elgar, William Henry (1821–1906), the composer's father, was born in Dover and moved to Worcester in 1841. He set up as a piano tuner and was in demand at many of the great houses in the neighbourhood. As a good violinist, pianist and organist, he played an important part in local music-making, to which he eventually introduced his fourth child. Though never a convinced Catholic, he was organist at St George's, Worcester for almost forty years, a post to which Elgar eventually succeeded. His shop at 10 High Street became the city's main music store and a source of embarrassment to the composer.

Embleton, Henry (1854–1930) was a mining engineer who derived a considerable fortune from colliers working out of Newcastle-upon-Tyne. For a time he was assistant organist at Leeds Parish Church, but as secretary and treasurer of the Leeds Choral Union he was in a position to demonstrate his admiration for Elgar's music, subsidizing performances in England, France and Germany. His efforts to secure completion of the third oratorio for Leeds were unavailing.

Ettling, Henry, a wine merchant from Mainz, was known to the Elgars as 'Uncle Klingsor' because of his conjuring ability. A great admirer of Hans Richter, he furthered Elgar's cause on the Continent with considerable energy, enlisting the support of such conductors as Steinbach and Weingartner. An amateur timpanist, he sometimes played in the Worcestershire Philharmonic concerts under Elgar.

Fitton, Isabel (1868–1936) was the third daughter of Harriet Fitton (a very able Malvern pianist and early chamber music companion of Elgar's). Isabel played violin and viola, taking lessons from Elgar. These are immortalized in 'Ysobel' of the 'Enigma' Variations. Elgar also wrote a keyboard Presto for her twenty-first birthday.

Gaisberg, Frederick (1873–1951) was an American recording expert who became largely responsible for the discs conducted by Elgar. Associated initially with the Phonograph Company, in England he became Recording Artists Manager for The Gramophone Company. Elgar found him a sympathetic colleague, and a warm friendship developed. The Paris trip of 1933 (including the visit to Delius) was made together, and Gaisberg was one of those to hear Elgar play the Third Symphony.

Gorton, Charles Vincent (1854–1912) founded the Morecambe Competition Festival for choirs and persuaded Elgar to act as an adjudicator in 1903. Rector of Poulton-le-Sands and a Canon of Manchester Cathedral, he was well-versed in biblical scholarship and Elgar turned to him for advice in compilation of the *Apostles* and *Kingdom* librettos. Ill-health made him leave Morecambe, and he retired to Hereford in 1909.

Grafton, Susannah Mary Elgar (1854–1936) was Elgar's favourite sister and married Martin William Grafton in 1879. Known as 'Pollie', she became the mother of May, Madge, Clare, Gerald and Vincent. Elgar lodged with the Graftons in Worcester after their marriage and was a frequent visitor to their home at Stoke Prior. Grafton died in 1908, and eventually Pollie moved to Bromsgrove. In wartime her house was a welcome refuge to Elgar. After Lady Elgar's death, the daughters undertook housekeeping tasks for Elgar.

Griffith, Arthur Troyte (1864–1942) was a Malvern architect with office in the Priory Gateway. His most important work was All Saints' Church, Malvern Wells, not far from Elgar's home, Craeg Lea. He was a sensitive watercolourist but also designed sets for Shaw's *The Devil's Disciple* at the Royal Court Theatre, London. His friendship with Elgar, based on many shared interests, dates from 1897. The 'Troyte' variation in op. 36 perhaps depicts a walk on the Malvern Hills interrupted by a thunderstorm.

Harrison, Beatrice (1892–1965) twice recorded the Cello Concerto under

Elgar. Delius wrote his Double Concerto for her and her sister May and dedicated to her other cello works. Beatrice later turned to nightingales, but during Elgar's lifetime the Harrison family bred dogs and supplied him with a number of Aberdeen terriers.

Heap, Charles Swinnerton (1847–1900) studied with Moscheles in Leipzig and sometimes deputized for Reinecke at Gewandhaus concerts on the organ. He became conductor of the Birmingham Philharmonic Union in 1870, directed Wolverhampton and North Staffordshire Festivals, and took on the Birmingham Festival Choral Society in 1895. His admiration for *The Black Knight* led to the commissioning of *King Olaf*, and Heap's untimely death was a factor in the initial failure of *The Dream of Gerontius*.

Hull, Percy Clarke (1878–1968) spent the whole of his career in the service of Hereford Cathedral. He was appointed assistant organist to G. R. Sinclair in 1896 and was interned in Germany during the First World War. Sinclair died in 1917, but on Elgar's recommendation the post was reserved for Hull until his release in 1918. He gave Elgar some driving lessons, and received the dedication of *Pomp and Circumstance* no. 5.

Jackson, Barry (1879–1961), a playwright and producer, founded the Birmingham Repertory Theatre, where he gave the first performance of Shaw's Metabiological Pentateuch, *Back to Methuselah*. His admiration for and co-operation with Shaw led to the foundation in 1929 of the Malvern Drama Festival, which Elgar attended. Jackson was instrumental in helping Elgar to make a practical libretto from Ben Jonson's *The Devil is an Ass* for the unfinished *Spanish Lady*.

Jaeger, August Johannes (1860–1909) was born in Düsseldorf and settled in England when eighteen. He joined the staff of Novello in 1890 and, though diffident about his musical abilities (he claimed he could not readily read a score), became a trusted adviser to the firm. He had an instinct for quality, and from 1896 was a forthright champion of Elgar, supporting him in all his moods. Their correspondence is testimony to a very creative friendship; 'Nimrod' was Elgar's tribute to his most discerning critic.

Kilburn, Nicholas (1843–1923) was an iron merchant by profession but sufficiently a musician to gain a Cambridge Mus.B and Durham Mus.D. He was an indefatigable conductor of choirs, and his home at Bishop Auckland became the centre for a wide range of musical activities. He first met Elgar at the Three Choirs Festival of 1897 and went on to conduct most of his major works. Elgar considered him for the 'Enigma' Variations; ultimately he became the dedicatee of *The Music Makers*.

Kreisler, Fritz (1875–1962) gave the first performance of Elgar's Violin Concerto in 1910 and received its dedication. The most distinguished violinist of his time, Kreisler made his English début in 1902 and became a Royal Philharmonic gold medallist two years later. He stated publicly that he considered Elgar the greatest of living composers and their co-operation over the concerto was exemplary.

Legge, Robin (1862–1933) was a music critic first on *The Times*, and then with the *Daily Telegraph*, where he succeeded Joseph Bennett in 1908. He was a great admirer of Elgar as man and artist, leaving a memorable account of early rehearsals with Kreisler of the Violin Concerto. It was he who first approached Elgar in connection with possible music for *The Starlight Express*.

Leicester, Hubert (1855–1939) was the son of a printer at 6 High St, Worcester, and so a close neighbour of the Elgars at no. 10. He was Elgar's constant boyhood companion and one of the flautists in the 'Brothers Wind' quintet. Leicester became choirmaster at St George's when Elgar was organist there and he never relinquished the position. A Worcester accountant, he became the city's first Catholic mayor in 1905, serving four more terms. He secured the Freedom of Worcester for Elgar, who wrote a preface to his *Forgotten Worcester* (1930).

Maine, Basil Stephen (1893–1972) wrote the most extensive book on Elgar to appear during the composer's lifetime. He was a welcome guest at Marl Bank while gathering material and recorded much of Elgar's casual conversation there. He too heard what existed of the Third Symphony. A writer for the *Daily Telegraph* and *Sunday Times*, he was the orator in the première of Bliss's *Morning Heroes* (1930) and later took orders in the Church of England.

Manns, August (1825–1907) came to England in 1854 with considerable experience of Prussian army bands behind him. The following year George Grove secured his appointment to the Crystal Palace, where Manns quickly developed the wind band into a full symphony orchestra with main platform at the Saturday Concerts. In 1884 he produced *Sevillana*, the first Elgar work to be heard publicly in London. He followed Elgar's career with interest, performing much of his music.

Menuhin, Yehudi (*b.* 1916) was an infant prodigy of astonishing gifts. A New York performance in 1927 of the Beethoven Violin Concerto launched his international fame, and in 1932, when it seemed clear that Kreisler would never record the Elgar Concerto, the Gramophone Company asked Menuhin to do so. The result, under the seventy-five year old composer, was a complete success and has since become a recording classic.

Moore, George (1852–1933) was a prolific Anglo-Irish novelist involved also in the foundation of the Irish National Theatre. He collaborated with W. B. Yeats on *Diarmuid and Grania* (1901), but the two men later quarrelled. Elgar's music for the play so impressed Moore that he urged him to develop it into an opera; nothing came of the idea.

Nevinson, Basil (1853–1908) was a competent cellist, as 'B.G.N.' makes clear in op. 36. At Oxford he was prominent in the recently founded University Musical Club, and continued his music-making when studying for the bar in London. For a time his home was Elgar's London base; but Nevinson was often in Malvern, where a brother was a partner in the architectural firm that employed Troyte Griffith and a cousin was the Elgars' solicitor.

Newman, Ernest (1868–1959) was born William Roberts, but changed his name when writing became more important than his career as a bank clerk. Elgar early appreciated his critical gifts, though Newman considered the oratorios a dead-end and pronounced some stern judgments in his *Elgar* of 1906. None the less, Elgar turned to him repeatedly for articles on newly completed works and showed his appreciation by dedicating to him the Piano Quintet.

Norbury, Florence (1858–1937) and Winifred (1861–1938) lived at Sherridge, a house in the close neighbourhood of Birchwood Lodge, where Elgar spent some of his Malvern summers. They were ardent tennis players, cyclists and musicians. 'W.N.' featured in the 'Enigma' Variations, though Elgar claimed their home was the real subject. W. N. helped Elgar with proofs, and later became one of the Worcestershire Philharmonic Society secretaries.

Parry, Charles Hubert Hastings (1848–1918) did much to improve standards in English musical life both by his compositions and his teaching. He was unstinting in his support for Elgar if suspicious of his frank emotionalism and apparent waywardness. As professor of music at Oxford, Parry secured for Elgar an honorary doctorate. For his part, Elgar thought little of Parry's orchestration but always revered his name and memory.

Penny, Dora (1874–1964) was the daughter of Rev Alfred Penny, Rector of Wolverhampton. She met Elgar in 1895, and it was not long before Alice Elgar employed her as keeper of the archives and encouraged the good influence of her youthful charm on Elgar, whether in cycle rides or the spontaneous dances she improvised to his music. Soon she became 'Dorabella' after Mozart's *Cosi fan tutte* and the subject of an 'Enigma' variation. Her *Edward Elgar: Memories of a Variation* is more enchanting than accurate.

Pipe, Charles (1853–1938) and Lucy Elgar (1852–1925) provided Elgar with his last bachelor home in 1883–9. Charles was Elgar's companion on the 1880 Paris excursion and he married Elgar's eldest sister Lucy the following year. Memoirs by Pipe were published in *Berrow's Worcester Journal* forty years after his death; they contain much of interest on Elgar. The Pipes were not well-off, and Elgar bought for them the small house in which they ended their days.

Reed, William Henry (1876–1942) was the violinist most closely connected with the genesis of Elgar's Concerto, much valued for his advice on technical matters. He was a founder member of the London Symphony Orchestra in 1904 and its leader from 1912. Friendship with Elgar ripened, and Reed was repeatedly summoned to try over works in the making. *Sospiri* was dedicated to him, and he wrote two books on Elgar.

Reeve, Francis (1825–1912) was headmaster of Littleton House, the Catholic boys' school Elgar attended 1868–72. He had been in the job only a year when Elgar became his pupil. Hubert Leicester also attended the school, and both of them became head boy. Elgar maintained that Reeve had provided the original inspiration for *The Apostles*; he renewed contact with him when the work was complete and wrote to him about the knighthood.

Richter, Hans (1843–1916) was closely associated with Wagner in preparation of *Die Meistersinger* and conducted the first complete *Ring* at Bayreuth in 1876. He gave also the first performances of Brahms Symphonies nos. 2

and 3 and Bruckner Symphonies nos. 1, 3, 4 and 8. His association with Elgar began with the 'Enigma' Variations in 1899, continued with *The Dream of Gerontius* (a disastrous performance) and reached its climax with the première of Symphony no. 1, the long awaited work that Elgar dedicated to him. Elgar succeeded him as conductor of the London Symphony Orchestra in 1911.

Rodewald, Alfred E. (1861–1903), a Liverpool cotton broker of German descent, was Richter's only conducting pupil. He founded and directed the Liverpool Orchestral Society, which gave the first performance of *Pomp and Circumstance* 1 and 2 under his baton. Elgar often stayed at his Liverpool home and in his North Wales country house. He was much upset by Rodewald's early death, memories of which coloured the slow movement of Symphony no. 2.

Sanford, Samuel Simons (1849–1910) was professor of Applied Music at Yale University. He was a gifted pupil of Rubinstein's but did not have the temperament for a concert career. He was invited to perform at the 1890 Three Choirs Festival, an offer he refused; but he came to Worcester in 1899, when the 'Enigma' Variations were first performed with the new finale. Admiration for Elgar led to an honorary degree at Yale, when Sanford proved a generous and congenial host to the Elgars. The Introduction and Allegro op. 47 was dedicated to him.

Schuster, Leo Francis Howard (1852–1927) was a man of means and generous patron of the arts. He gave much hospitality to the Elgars, both in his Westminster house and at The Hut, on the Thames near Maidenhead, where Elgar did much work on Symphony no. 1, the Violin Concerto and *Falstaff*. Schuster was the leading spirit in organization of the 1904 Elgar Festival at Covent Garden. *In the South*, first performed on that occasion, was dedicated to him. Schuster left Elgar a considerable sum in his will.

Shaw, George Bernard (1856–1950) was a notable inspiration to Elgar's last years. Having admired his music criticism, Elgar delighted more and more in the plays. Shaw's unquenchable high spirits proved a ready stimulus to the sometimes moody Elgar, and the succession of coruscating septuagenarian plays seemed to demand a creative response. Elgar's operatic plans were such, and Shaw almost succeeded in getting a Third Symphony from him. The *Severn Suite* was dedicated to him.

Sinclair, George Robertson (1863–1917) moved to Truro Cathedral after a year as assistant organist at Gloucester. He was appointed to Hereford Cathedral in 1889 and remained there for the rest of his life. In 1897 he commissioned the *Te Deum and Benedictus* from Elgar, and that was the year Elgar began 'The Moods of Dan, Illustrated' in his visitors' book. Themes for *Gerontius*, *In the South*, *The Crown of India* and 'For the Fallen' were originally conceived in honour of Sinclair's bulldog who, with his master, also features in op. 36.

Speyer, Edgar (1862–1932) was head of the Frankfurt banking firm domiciled in London. He married Leonora von Stosch, a violinist pupil of Ysaÿe, who played frequently at the 1900 Proms under Henry Wood, and was the first to try privately the Andante of the Elgar Violin Concerto. Speyer was head of the Queen's Hall syndicate and negotiated with Elgar for the first performance of the Second Symphony in 1911. He became a privy councillor but suffered harassment from anti-German feeling during the First World War and eventually emigrated to America.

Speyer, Edward (1837–1934) was a cousin of Edgar and grew up in Frankfurt, where his father was a wealthy amateur composer. Speyer could remember Rossini and Spohr; later he was friendly with Clara Schumann and Brahms. As his second wife he married in 1885 the noted Schumann and Brahms singer, Antonia Kufferath. Their house, 'Ridgehurst' in Hertfordshire, became a notable musical centre. The Elgars first went there in 1901, and the following year Speyer ensured that the 'Enigma' Variations should be played at the London concerts of the Meiningen orchestra.

Stanford, Charles Villiers (1852–1924) was equally distinguished as composer and teacher, doing much to revivify English church music and, from Cambridge and the Royal College of Music, spreading an invigorating influence to the next generation of composers. He performed Elgar, arranged his Cambridge doctorate and joined Parry in proposing him for membership of the Athenaeum Club. But relations between them deteriorated about the time of the Birmingham professorship, when some of Elgar's lectures caused Stanford considerable offence. The breach was never properly healed.

Steuart-Powell, Huw David (1851–19??) was pianist enough to be a duet partner for Parry when they were both at Exeter College, Oxford, and a contemporary review speaks well of his Chopin. It was as a pianist that he became friendly with Elgar, and it is as a pianist that he features in the 'Enigma' Variations. Elgar remained in touch with him, and he came to Severn House in early 1920, perhaps in connection with the Welwyn Garden City project, for the committee of which Elgar's name had gone forward.

Strauss, Richard (1864–1949) was considered by Elgar the greatest of his contemporaries. They first met in 1897, and Strauss conducted the first German performance of *Cockaigne*. His speech at the second Düsseldorf performance of *Gerontius* finally convinced Elgar's countrymen that there was a genius in their midst. After the wartime interruption, Elgar welcomed Strauss to London in 1922 with a lunch involving younger composers and Bernard Shaw. Ten years later both composers were working on a Ben Jonson opera, *The Spanish Lady* and *Die schweigsame Frau*; Elgar felt at the time he was producing fresher music than Strauss.

Stuart of Wortley, Lady (Alice Stuart Wortley, 1862–1936) was the third daughter of John Millais, the Pre-Raphaelite painter, and second wife of Charles Stuart Wortley, a member of parliament for Sheffield made a baron in 1916. Elgar met the Stuart Wortleys in 1902, and a more than thirty-year correspondence began between him and Alice. She was a considerable pianist, and about the time of the Violin Concerto became much involved with Elgar's composition process. She became his 'Windflower' and regularly received sketches of works in progress (now at the Birthplace Museum). It was with her playing in mind that Elgar planned a piano concerto.

Terry, Charles Sanford (1864–1936) was Professor of History at the University of Aberdeen, 1903–30. He founded a large choral society and orchestra in the city and was its conductor. In the musical world he became known as one of the foremost Bach scholars of his day. In 1906 he organized a doctorate for Elgar at Aberdeen, and a warm friendship developed. Elgar gave Terry full score proofs of the Violin Concerto (in the British Library) and sketches of the Second Symphony (at the Athenaeum Club) in gratitude for expert help with proof reading. Elgar dedicated the partsong, *Love's Tempest*, to him.

Townshend, Richard Baxter (1846–1923) was a great traveller in his early years, prospecting for gold and attaining to sympathetic understanding of the American Indians. A series of Tenderfoot books record his experiences. A teacher of classics at Bath College, R.B.T. married a sister of W.M.B. in 1881. They settled in Oxford to a life of authorship. His 'Enigma' variation gives only a partial impression of him.

Trefusis, Lady Mary (1869–1927) was the 'L.M.L.' or '***' of the 'Romanza' in op. 36. Born Lady Mary Lygon, she lived at Madresfield Court between Worcester and Malvern and founded the Madresfield Musical Competition in 1896. Herself a conductor and organizer of choirs, she often asked Elgar for help and advice. A Woman of the Bedchamber to the future Queen Alexandra, she married H. W. Hepburn-Stuart-Forbes-Trefusis in 1905. Elgar dedicated to her the *Three Characteristic Pieces* of 1899.

Webb, Frank (1866–1951) was a violin pupil of Elgar's, as were some of his sisters. The family had a furniture business in the Worcester High Street, and Webb often joined Elgar for chamber music. He was a member of the Worcester Amateur Instrumental Society. His son Alan was to become curator of the Elgar Birthplace Museum.

Whinfield, E. W. was the head of an organ-building firm who made his home, Severn Grange near Claines, a musical centre for the neighbourhood. The young Elgar was a leading light there till the time of his marriage. As a lover of books and pictures, Whinfield did much to foster Elgar's own interests, giving him various seminal volumes as well as print collections.

Wood, Henry Joseph (1869–1944) was conductor of the Queen's Hall orchestra and of the Promenade Concerts from their inception in 1895. The first Elgar he conducted was the 'Meditation' from *The Light of Life* in May 1899; he went on to give first performances of *Wand of Youth* suite no. 1, *Pomp and Circumstance* no. 4 and *Sospiri*. He considered Elgar's op. 61 'the loveliest concerto ever written for a violin'. Elgar dedicated the *Grania and Diarmid* music to him and spoke highly of him in his Birmingham lectures.

Appendix D

Bibliography

MANUSCRIPTS AND OTHER SOURCE MATERIALS

Anderson, Robert, *Elgar in Manuscript* (London, 1990)

Foreman, R. L. E., 'Elgar', *The British Musical Renaissance: a Guide to Research* (diss., Library Association Fellowship, London, 1972)

Grogan, Christopher, *Aspects of Elgar's Creative Process in The Apostles with Particular Reference to Scene II* (diss., University of London, 1989)

Kent, Christopher, *Edward Elgar, a Composer at Work: a Study of his Creative Process as Seen through his Sketches and Proof Corrections* (diss., University of London, 1978)

Knowles, John, *Elgar's Interpreters on Record: an Elgar Discography* (London, 1977, rev. 1986)

Moore, Jerrold Northrop, *Elgar: a Life in Photographs* (London, 1972)

Willetts, Pamela: 'The Elgar Sketch-books', *British Library Journal*, xi/1 (1985)

CORRESPONDENCE AND LECTURES

Atkins, E. Wulstan, *The Elgar-Atkins Friendship* (Newton Abbot, 1984)

Foreman, Lewis, *From Parry to Britten: British Music in Letters 1900–1945* (London, 1987)

Moore, Jerrold Northrop, *Elgar on Record: the Composer and the Gramophone* (London, 1974)

—— *Elgar and his Publishers: Letters of a Creative Life* (Oxford, 1987)

—— *Edward Elgar: The Windflower Letters* (Oxford, 1989)

—— *Edward Elgar: Letters of a Lifetime* (Oxford, 1990)

Young, Percy M., ed., *Letters of Edward Elgar and Other Writings* (London, 1956)

—— *Letters to Nimrod* (London, 1965)

—— *A Future for English Music and Other Lectures by Edward Elgar* (London, 1968)

LIFE AND WORKS

Anderson, William R., *Introduction to the Music of Elgar* (London, 1949)

Buckley, Robert J., *Sir Edward Elgar* (London, 1904; 2nd ed., 1912)

Burley, Rosa and Carruthers, Frank C., *Edward Elgar: the Record of a Friendship* (London, 1972)

De-la-Noy, Michael, *Elgar: the Man* (London, 1983)

Dunhill, Thomas, *Sir Edward Elgar* (London, 1938)

Hurd, Michael, *Elgar* (London, 1969)

Kennedy, Michael, *Portrait of Elgar* (London, 1968; 2nd ed., 1973; rev., 1983; 3rd ed., 1987)

McVeagh, Diana, *Edward Elgar: his life and Music* (London, 1955)

Maine, Basil, *Elgar, his Life and Works* (London, 1933; repr., 1973)

Moore, Jerrold Northrop, *Edward Elgar, a Creative Life* (Oxford, 1984)

—— *Spirit of England: Edward Elgar in his World* (London, 1984)

Mundy, Simon, *Elgar, his Life and Times* (Tunbridge Wells, 1980)

Newman, Ernest, *Elgar* (London, 1906; repr., 1977; 2nd ed., 1922)

Parrott, Ian, *Elgar* (London, 1971)

Porte, John F., *Sir Edward Elgar* (London, 1921)

—— *Elgar and his Music* (London, 1933)

Powell, Dora M., *Edward Elgar: Memories of a Variation* (London, 1937; rev. 3rd ed., 1949)

Reed, William H., *Elgar as I Knew him* (London, 1936; repr., 1973)

—— *Elgar* (London, 1939; rev. 3rd ed., 1949)

Sheldon, A. J., *Edward Elgar* (London, 1932)

Shera, Frank H., *Elgar: Instrumental Works* (London, 1931)

Young, Percy M., *Elgar O.M.: a Study of a Musician* (London, 1955; rev. 2nd ed., 1973)

BIOGRAPHICAL BACKGROUND

Anderson, Robert, 'Gertrude Walker: an Elgarian Friendship', *MT*, cxxv (1984), p. 698

Atkins, E. Wulstan, *1890–1990: The Centenary of the Birth of a Friendship: Edward Elgar and Ivor Atkins* (Worcester, 1990)

Bury, David, *Elgar and the Two Mezzos* (London, 1984)

Buttrey, John, 'Elgar and Lady Mary Lygon', *ML*, liv (1973), pp. 122, 382

Collett, Barry, *Elgar Country* (London, 1981)

Collett, Pauline, *Elgar Lived Here* (London, 1981)

—— *An Elgar Travelogue* (London, 1983)

Dibble, Jeremy C., 'Parry and Elgar: a New Perspective', *MT*, cxxv (1984), p. 639

Hamilton, Gervase, 'Elgar and the Baker Family', *MT*, cxx (1979), p. 121

Hodgkins, Geoffrey, *Providence and Art: a Study of Elgar's Religious Beliefs* (London, 1979)

Kennedy, Michael, 'Elgar and the Festivals', *Two Hundred and Fifty Years of the Three Choirs Festivals*, ed. B. Still (Gloucester, 1977)

McVeagh, Diana, 'Mrs Edward Elgar', *MT*, cxxv (1984), p. 76

Menuhin, Yehudi, *Sir Edward Elgar: my Musical Grandfather* (London, 1976)

Mitchell, William R., *Elgar in the Yorkshire Dales* (Settle, 1987)

Moore, Jerrold Northrop, and Kennedy, Michael, 'Edward Elgar and Ralph Vaughan Williams', *Heritage of Music*, vol. 4, ed. M. Raeburn and A. Kendall (Oxford, 1989)

Pirie, Peter, 'World's End: A Study of Edward Elgar', *MR*, xviii (1957), p. 89

—— 'The Personality of Elgar', *MM*, xxi (1972–3), p. 32

Reed, Nicholas, 'Elgar's Enigmatic Inamorata', *MT*, cxxv (1984), p. 430

Sams, Eric, 'Elgar's Cipher Letter to Dorabella', *MT*, cxi (1970), p. 151

Simmons, Kenneth E. L. and Marion, *The Elgars of Worcester* (London, 1984)

Weaver, Cora, *The Thirteenth Enigma?* (London, 1988)

ESSAY COLLECTIONS

Chambers, H. A., ed., *Edward Elgar Centenary Sketches* (London, 1957), J. Barbirolli, 'Forty Years with Elgar's Music'; C. Elgar Blake, 'A Family Retrospect'; A. C. Boult, 'Composer as Conductor'; H. A. Chambers, 'Publishing Office Memories'; B. Herrman, 'An American Voice'; A. J. Kirby, '*The Apostles* and *The Kingdom*'; Y. Menuhin, 'Impressions – Musical and Personal'; D. M. Powell, 'The Music Maker'; S. Robinson, 'Elgar's Light Music'; D. Willcocks, 'A Modern View'; P. M. Young, 'Elgar as a Man of Letters'

Monk, Raymond, ed., *Elgar Studies* (Aldershot, 1990), P. Dennison, 'Elgar's Musical Apprenticeship'; I. Parrott, 'Elgar's Harmonic Language'; M. Pope, '*King Olaf* and the English Choral Tradition'; P. M. Young, 'Friends Pictured Within'; M. Kennedy, 'Elgar the Edwardian'; R. D. Anderson, 'Elgar's Magus and Projector'; D. McVeagh, 'Elgar and *Falstaff*'; K. E. L. Simmons, 'Elgar and the Wonderful Stranger: Music for *The Starlight Express*'; R. Taylor, 'Shaw and Elgar'; M. Kennedy, 'Some Elgar Interpreters'; J. Knowles, 'A Select Elgar Discography'; J. N. Moore, 'Envoy'

—— *Edward Elgar: Music and Literature* (Aldershot, 1993), E. W. Atkins, 'Introduction'; D. McVeagh, 'A Man's Attitude to Life'; C. Grogan, '*The Apostles*: Some Thoughts on the Early Plans', I. Keys, '*The Apostles*: Elgar and Bach as Preachers'; R. Meikle, ' "The True Foundation." The Symphonies'; M. Kennedy, 'The Soul Enshrined: Elgar and his Violin Concerto'; C. Kent, '*Falstaff*: Elgar's Symphonic Study'; I. Keys, ' "Ghostly Stuff ": the Brinkwells Music'; P. M. Young, 'Elgar and the Irish Dramatists'; C. Grogan, 'Elgar, Streatfeild, and *The Pilgrim's Progress*'; R. D. Anderson, 'fyrst the noble Arthur'; B. Trowell, 'Elgar's Use of Literature'; R. Taylor, 'Music in the Air: Elgar and the BBC'.

Redwood, Christopher, ed., *An Elgar Companion* (Ashbourne, 1982):

I *The Early Years*: reviews of *The Black Knight* and *King Olaf*; E. A. Baughan, review of *Caractacus*; J. N. Moore, 'Young Elgar at the Festival'; F. G. Edwards, 'Edward Elgar' (from *MT*, xli (1900));

II *The 'Enigma'*: R. C. Powell (from *ML*, xv (1934)); A. H. Fox Strangways (from *ML*, xvi (1935)); J. A. Westrup (from *PRMA*, lxxxvi (1959–60)); R. Fiske (from *MT*, cx (1969)); I. Parrott, 'The Enigma – V';

III *The 'Gerontius' Débâcle*: E. A. Baughan, review from *The Musical Standard*; W. Bennett, 'A Memory from the Choir'; Mrs R. Powell, 'A Memory from the Auditorium' (from *MT*, c (1959)); G. H. Lewis, 'Hans Richter and *Gerontius*';

IV *Elgar at Home*: R. J. Buckley, 'Elgar at "Forli"': R. de Cordova, 'Elgar at "Craeg Lea"' (from *Strand Magazine* (May 1904)); G. Cumberland, 'Elgar at "Plas Gwyn"' (from *Set Down in Malice* (London, 1918)); unsigned, 'Elgar at "Severn House"' (from *The World* (Oct 1912)); P. Scholes, 'Elgar at "Severn House"' (from *The Music Student*, viii/12 (1916));

V *Memories of those who Knew him*: M. B. Alder, 'Memories of a Pupil'; R. R. Terry, 'Elgar as I Knew him' (from *The Radio Times* (Mar 1934)); E. Newman, 'Some Aspects of the Man in his Music' (from the *Sunday Times* (25 Feb 1934)); C. Mackenzie, 'Sir Edward Elgar'; M. Sargent, 'Elgar – as I Knew him' (from *MM* (Jun 1957)); C. Elgar Blake, 'Memories of my Father' (from *MM* (Jun 1957)); A. Webb, 'Some Personal Memories of Elgar';

VI *Elgar and other Composers*: W. J. Turner, 'Elgar and Handel'; V. Waite, 'Elgar, Parry and Stanford' (from *ESN* (Jan and May 1978)); C. Redwood, 'Elgar and Delius'; N. Cardus, 'Elgar and Mahler' (from *The Radio Times* (1 May 1931)); G. Sampson, 'Elgar and Strauss' (from *The Bookman* (March 1931)); A. E. Keeton, '*The Starlight Express*' (from *ML*, xxvi (1945));

VII *Elgar and the Theatre*: B. Jackson, '*The Spanish Lady*' (from *ML*, xxiv (1943)); A. E. Keeton, '*The Starlight Express*' (from *ML*, xxvi (1945));

VIII *Elgar's Art Examined*: F. A. Baughan, '*The Apostles* and Elgar's Future'; G. B. Shaw, 'Edward Elgar' (from *ML*, i (1920)); W. H. Reed, 'The Violin Concerto' (from *ML*, xvi (1935)); F. Howes, 'The Two Elgars (from *ML*, xvi (1935)); R. Vaughan Williams, 'What have we Learnt from Elgar?' (from *ML*, xvi (1935)); C. W. Orr, 'Elgar and the Public' (from *MT*, lxxii (1931)); H. Keller, 'The First of the New' (from *MM* (June 1957)); D. Mitchell, 'Some Thoughts on Elgar' (from *ML*, xxxviii (1957)); S. Lloyd, 'Elgar as Conductor'

Music and Letters, xvi (Jan 1935), D. F. Tovey, 'Elgar, Master of Music'; H. J. Foss, 'Elgar and his Age'; R. Vaughan Williams, 'What have we Learnt from Elgar?'; A. E. Brent Smith, 'The Humour of Elgar'; F. Howes, 'The Two Elgars'; W. H. Reed, 'The Violin Concerto'

The Music Student, viii (Aug 1916), P. Scholes, 'Sir Edward Elgar'; T. F. Dunhill, 'Choral Music'; P. Scholes, 'Sir Edward Elgar at Home'; E. C. Bairstow, 'Songs'; W. Wells-Harrison, 'Symphonies and Shorter Orchestral Works'; P. Scholes, 'Elgar and the War'; N. Kilburn, 'A Personal Note'; G. S. Talbot, 'Church Anthems'; W. W. Cobbett, 'Violin Concerto', 'Shorter Violin Works'; E. J. Bellerby, 'Organ Sonata'

The Musical Times, lxxv (Apr 1934), obituary by H. Grace and W. McNaught; 'Memorial Service in Worcester Cathedral'; 'Life and Career'; list of *MT* articles on Elgar; 'Some of Elgar's Friends'; tributes from I. Atkins, Bax, H. Coward, W. Davies, E. German, H. Harty, C. Lambert, B. Maine, Y. Menuhin, Paderewski, H. Rabaud, M. Sargent, Sibelius,

Stravinsky, Strauss, R. R. Terry, H. Wood; 'Three Critics on Elgar' (E. Evans, Fox-Strangways, E. Newman); I. Atkins, 'Elgar's "Enigma" Variations'

—— xcviii (Jun 1957), 'The Elgar Centenary'; 'Elgar Today' (contributions from Vaughan Williams, Ireland, J. Harrison, Bliss, Howells, G. Jacob, Rubbra, P. Hadley, Westrup, Steuart Wilson, H. Sumsion, E. Blom, F. Howes, G. Dyson, T. Armstrong, E. Bullock, Greenhouse Allt, E. Cundell, R. F. J. Howgill, M. Johnstone, E. Wass); A. Robertson, review of 'Centenary Sketches'; D. McVeagh, 'Elgar's Birthplace'; H. Rutland, 'Elgarian Notes and Comments'

MUSICAL BACKGROUND

Cardus, Neville, *Ten Composers* (London, 1945; repr. as *A Composer's Eleven*, 1958)

Dann, Mary G., 'Elgar's Use of the Sequence', *ML*, xix (1938), p. 255

Dennison, Peter, 'Elgar and Wagner', *ML*, lxvii (1985), p. 93

Dent, Edward J., 'Modern English Music', in G. Adler, *Handbuch der Musikgeschichte* (Frankfurt am Main, 1924; 2nd ed., 1930; repr. 1961)

Gray, Cecil, *A Survey of Contemporary Music* (Oxford, 1924)

Howes, Frank, 'Edward Elgar', *The Heritage of Music*, iii, ed. H. J. Foss (London, 1951)

Keller, Hans, 'Elgar the Progressive', *MR*, xviii (1957), p. 294

Mellers, Wilfrid, 'Elgar and Vaughan Williams', in *Romanticism and the 20th Century* (London, 1957)

Mitchell, W. R., *The Giggleswick Scores of Edward Elgar* (Settle, n.d.)

Shaw, George Bernard, 'Sir Edward Elgar', *ML*, i (1920), p. 7

Temperley, Nicholas, ed., *The Romantic Age, 1800–1914, Athlone History of Music in Britain*, v (London, 1981)

Tovey, Donald F., 'Elgar, Master of Music', *ML*, xvi (1935), p. 1

—— *Essays in Musical Analysis* (Oxford, 1935–9)

Trowell, Brian, 'Elgar's Marginalia', *MT*, cxxv (1984), p. 139

Whittall, Arnold, 'Elgar's *Last Judgement*', *MR*, xxvi (1965), p. 23

CHORAL AND DRAMATIC WORKS

Anderson, Robert, 'Elgar and some Apostolic Problems', *MT*, cxxv (1984), p. 13

Bennett, Joseph, *Scenes from the Saga of King Olaf: Book of Words, with Analytical Notes* (London, 1899)

—— *Coronation Ode: Analytical Notes* (London, 1902)

Burton, Nigel, 'Oratorios and Cantatas', in *The Romantic Age, 1800–1914*, ed. N. Temperley, *Athlone History of Music in Britain*, v (London, 1981)

Gorton, C. V., *The Apostles: an Interpretation of the Libretto* (London, 1903)

—— 'Dr. Elgar's oratorio *The Apostles*', *MT*, xliv (1903), p. 656

—— *The Kingdom: an Interpretation of the Libretto* (London, 1907)

Grogan, Christopher, 'Elgar's Rejected Apostle', *MT*, cxxix (1988), p. 70

—— '"My dear Analyst": Some Observations on Elgar's Correspondence with A. J. Jaeger regarding the "Apostles" Project', *ML*, lxxii (1991), p. 48

Jackson, Barry, 'Elgar's *Spanish Lady*', *ML*, xxiv (1943), p. 1

Jaeger, August J., *The Dream of Gerontius: Book of Words, with Analytical Notes* (London, 1901; 2nd ed., 1974)

—— *The Apostles: Book of Words, with Analytical and Descriptive Notes* (London, 1903)

—— *The Kingdom: Book of Words, with Analytical and Descriptive Notes* (London, 1906)

—— 'Elgar's new Choral Works', opp. 53 and 54, *MT*, xlix (1908), p. 453

Kent, Christopher, 'Elgar's Music for St George's Church, Worcester', *Annual Report* (Church Music Society), no. 77 (London, 1983), p. 12

Newman, Ernest, '*The Music Makers* by Edward Elgar', *MT*, liii (1912), p. 566

—— *The Spirit of England*: Edward Elgar's New Choral Work', *MT*, lvii (1916), p. 235

—— 'Elgar's "Fourth of August"', *MT*, lviii (1917), p. 295

Powell, Mrs R. [Dora M.], 'The Words of *The Apostles* and *The Kingdom*', *MT*, lxxxix (1948), p. 201; xc (1949), p. 21

—— 'The First Performances of *The Apostles* and *The Kingdom*, *MT*, ci (1960), p. 21

Temperley, Nicholas, 'Elgar's Church Music', in *The Romantic Age, 1800–1914*, *Athlone History of Music in Britain*, v (London, 1981)

Thompson, Herbert, *Caractacus: Book of Words, with Analytical Notes* (London, 1900)

Young, Percy M., 'Elgar and *The Spanish Lady*', *MT*, cxxvii (1986), p. 272

SOLO SONGS

Bush, Geoffrey, 'Elgar's Songs', *The Romantic Age 1800–1914*, ed. N. Temperley, *Athlone History of Music in Britain*, v (London, 1981)

Jacobs, Arthur, 'Elgar's Solo Songs', *MT*, xc (1949), p. 158

ORCHESTRAL, CHAMBER AND INSTRUMENTAL WORKS

Anderson, Robert, and Moore, Jerrold Northrop, Foreword to study score of Symphony no. 2 (London, 1984)

Atkins, Ivor, 'Elgar's *Enigma* Variations', *MT*, lxxv (1934), pp. 328 and 411

Barber, Cecil, 'Enigma Variations – the Original Finale', *ML*, xvi (1935), p. 137

Bonavia, Ferruccio, 'Edward Elgar', *The Symphony*, ed. R. Hill (London, 1949; 2nd ed. 1956), p. 313

Brand, Geoffrey, 'The *Severn Suite*: Whose Scoring?', *British Bandsman* (4 Oct 1980), p. 16

Burton, Humphrey, 'Elgar and the BBC with Particular Reference to the Unfinished Third Symphony', *Journal of the Royal Society of Arts*, cxxvii (1979), p. 224

Byard, Herbert, 'Edward Elgar', *The Concerto*, ed. R. Hill (London, 1952), p. 252

Colles, H. C., 'Sir Edward Elgar's Symphony', *MT*, xlix (1908), p. 778

—— 'Elgar's Violoncello Concerto', *MT*, lxi (1920), p. 84

—— 'Elgar's Quintet for Pianoforte and Strings (Op. 84)', *MT*, lx (1919), p. 596

Cox, David, 'Edward Elgar', *The Symphony*, ii, ed. R. Simpson (Harmondsworth, 1967), p. 15

Fanselau, Rainer, *Die Orgel im Werk Edward Elgars* (Göttingen, 1974)

Fiske, Roger, 'The Enigma: a Solution', *MT*, cx (1969), p. 1124

—— 'Shakespeare in the Concert Hall', *Shakespeare in Music*, ed. Phyllis Hartnoll (London, 1964), p. 218

Gairdner, William H. T., 'On Elgar's Second Symphony', *W.H.T.G. to his Friends* (London, 1930), p. 157

Grace, Harvey, 'The Bach–Elgar Fugue', *MT*, lxiii (1922), p. 21

Hudson, Derek, 'Elgar's Enigma, the Trail of Evidence', *MT*, cxxv (1984), p. 636

Jones, Vernon, 'Helen Weaver, the "Soul" of Elgar's Violin Concerto', *Royal Academy of Music Magazine*, no. 237 (1985), p. 328

Kennedy, Michael, *Elgar Orchestral Music* (London, 1970)

Kent, Christopher, 'A View of Elgar's Methods of Composition through the Sketches of the Symphony no. 2 in E flat (op. 63)', *PRMA*, ciii (1976–7)

—— 'Elgar's Third Symphony: the Sketches Reconsidered', *MT*, cxxvii (1979), p. 224

McVeagh, Diana, 'Elgar's Concert Allegro', *MT*, cx (1969), p. 135

—— Prefaces to study scores of Symphonies 1 and 2 (London, 1985)

—— ' "Moriah" and the "Introduction and Allegro" ', *ESJ*, iv/4 (1986), p. 23

Maine, Basil, 'Elgar's Sketches in Relation to Musicology' [on Symphony 3], *Basil Maine on Music* (London, 1945), p. 31

Moore, Jerrold Northrop, 'An Approach to Elgar's Enigma', *MR*, xx (1959), p. 38

Newman, Ernest, 'Elgar's Violin Concerto', *MT*, li (1910), p. 631

—— 'Elgar's Second Symphony', *MT*, lii (1911), p. 295

—— 'Elgar's Third Symphony', *Sunday Times* (22 Sep, 20 and 27 Oct 1935)

—— 'Elgar and his Enigma', *Sunday Times* (16, 23, 30 Apr, 7 May 1939)

Newmarch, Rosa, *The Concert-goer's Library of Descriptive Notes*, articles on the Symphonies, Violin Concerto, *Cockaigne*, *Pomp and Circumstance* nos. 1–4, *Coronation* and *Mogul Emperors* marches, *Wand of Youth*, *Bavarian Dances*, vols. 1–4 (Oxford, 1928–31)

Parrott, Ian, 'Elgar's Two-fold Enigma: a Religious Sequel', *ML*, liv (1973), p. 57

Parry, John, 'Elgar's piano music', *The Romantic Age 1800–1914*, ed. N.

Temperley, *The Athlone History of Music in Britain*, v (London, 1981), p. 430

Pitt, Percy, and Kalisch, Alfred, *In the South: Analytical and Descriptive Notes* (London, 1904)

Pope, Michael, Foreword to miniature score of the Piano Quintet (London, 1971)

Powell, Richard, 'Elgar's "Enigma"', *ML*, xv (1934), p. 203; reply by A. H. Fox Strangways, *ML*, xvi (1935), p. 37

Reed, William H., 'Elgar's Violin Concerto', *ML*, xvi (1935), p. 32

—— 'Elgar's Third Symphony', *The Listener* (28 Aug 1935)

—— 'Elgar', *Cobbett's Cyclopaedic Survey of Chamber Music* (Oxford, 1929; rev. 2nd ed. 1963 by Colin Mason), p. 372

Sams, Eric, 'Variations on an Original Theme (Enigma)', *MT*, cxi (1970), p. 258

—— 'Elgar's Enigmas: a Past Script and a Postscript', *MT*, cxi (1970), p. 692

Shore, Bernard, 'Elgar's Second Symphony', *Sixteen Symphonies* (London, 1949), p. 263

van Houten, Theodore, ' "You of All People": Elgar's Enigma', *MR*, xxxvii (1976), p. 130

Westrup, J. A., 'Elgar's Enigma', *PRMA*, lxxxvi (1959–60), p. 79

PERIODICAL

The Elgar Society Newsletter (1973–9), renamed as *The Elgar Society Journal* (1979–)

RELATED LITERATURE

Bliss, Arthur, *As I Remember* (London, 1970)

Boult, Adrian C., *My Own Trumpet* (London, 1973)

—— *Boult on Music* (London, 1984)

Brewer, A. Herbert, *Memories of Choirs and Cloisters* (London, 1931)

Cohen, Harriet, *A Bundle of Time* (London, 1969)

Cumberland, Gerald, *Set Down in Malice* (London, 1919)

De Navarro, Mary Anderson, *A Few More Memories* (London, 1936)

Gaisberg, Frederick W., *Music on Record* (London, 1946)

Goossens, Eugene, *Overture and Beginners* (London, 1951)

Graves, Charles L., *Hubert Parry: His Life and Works* (London, 1926)

Greene, Harry Plunkett, *Charles Villiers Stanford* (London, 1935)

Howes, Frank, *The English Musical Renaissance* (London, 1966)

Leicester, Hubert, *Forgotten Worcester* (Worcester, 1930)

MacDonald, Malcolm, ed., *Havergal Brian on Music* (London, 1986)

Mackenzie, Alexander, *A Musician's Narrative* (London, 1927)

Moore, Jerrold Northrop, *Music and Friends: Seven Decades of Letters to Adrian Boult* (London, 1979)

Mottram, R. H., *Portrait of an Unknown Victorian* (London, 1936)

Elgar

Ponsonby, Sir Frederick, *Recollections of Three Reigns* (New York, 1952)

Sassoon, Siegfried, *Diaries 1920–1922* and *1923–1925* (London, 1981, 1985)

Sitwell, Osbert, *Laughter in the Next Room* (London, 1950)

Speyer, Edward, *My Life and Friends* (London, 1937)

Stockley, William C., *Fifty Years of Music in Birmingham 1850–1900* (Birmingham, 1900)

Vandervelde, Lalla, *Monarchs and Millionaires* (London, 1925)

Walker, Ernest, *A History of Music in England* (Oxford, 1907; rev. 2nd ed., 1924; rev., enlarged 3rd ed. by J. A. Westrup, 1952)

Wood, Henry J., *My Life of Music* (London, 1946)

Young, Percy M., *Alice Elgar: Enigma of a Victorian Lady* (London, 1978)

Index